A Companion to African American History

D0861739

BLACKWELL COMPANIONS TO AMERICAN HISTORY

This series provides essential and authoritative overviews of the scholarship that has shaped our present understanding of the American past. Edited by eminent historians, each volume tackles one of the major periods or themes of American history, with individual topics authored by key scholars who have spent considerable time in research on the questions and controversies that have sparked debate in their field of interest. The volumes are accessible for the non-specialist, while also engaging scholars seeking a reference to the historiography or future concerns.

Published

In preparation

A COMPANION TO AFRICAN AMERICAN HISTORY

Edited by

Alton Hornsby, Jr

Delores P. Aldridge
Editorial Associate

Angela M. Hornsby
Editorial Assistant

© 2005, 2008 by Blackwell Publishing Ltd
except for editorial material and organization © 2005, 2008 by Alton Hornsby, Jr

BLACKWELL PUBLISHING
350 Main Street, Malden, MA 02148-5020, USA
9600 Garsington Road, Oxford OX4 2DQ, UK
550 Swanston Street, Carlton, Victoria 3053, Australia

The right of Alton Hornsby, Jr to be identified as the Author of the Editorial Material in this Work
has been asserted in accordance with the UK Copyright, Designs, and Patents Act 1988.

First published 2005
First published in paperback 2008 by Blackwell Publishing Ltd

1   2008

Library of Congress Cataloging-in-Publication Data

A companion to African American history / edited by Alton Hornsby.
p. cm. — (Blackwell companions to American history)
Includes bibliographical references and index.
ISBN 978–0–631–23066–3 (hardback : alk. paper) — ISBN 978–1–4051–7993–5 (pbk : alk. paper)
1. African Americans—History.   2. African Americans—Historiography.   I. Hornsby, Alton.
II. Series.

E185.C66 2005
973′.0496073—dc22

2004011680

A catalogue record for this title is available from the British Library.

Set in 10/12pt Galliard
by Graphicraft Ltd, Hong Kong
Printed and bound in Singapore
by C.O.S. Printers Pte Ltd

The publisher's policy is to use permanent paper from mills that operate a sustainable forestry policy,
and which has been manufactured from pulp processed using acid-free and elementary chlorine-free
practices. Furthermore, the publisher ensures that the text paper and cover board used have met
acceptable environmental accreditation standards.

For further information on
Blackwell Publishing, visit our website:
www.blackwellpublishing.com

A Companion to African American History

Board of Advisors

Contents

Notes on the Contributors

Delores P. Aldridge is Grace Towns Professor of Sociology and African American Studies at Emory University. She is the author of *Focusing: Black Male-Female Relationships* (1995) and co-editor, with Carlene Young, of *Out of the Revolution: The Development of Africana Studies* (2000).

James D. Anderson is Professor of Educational Policy and Professor of History as well as Head of the Department of Educational Policy Studies at the University of Illinois, Urbana-Champaign. His book, *The Education of Blacks in the South, 1850–1935* won the Outstanding Book Award from the American Education Research Association in 1990.

Jeffrey Elton Anderson is an Assistant Professor of History at Middle Georgia College. His forthcoming work is tentatively titled *Conjure in African American Society*.

Abel A. Bartley is Associate Professor of African American and Urban History, and Director of the Pan-African Center for Community Studies at the University of Akron. He is the author of *Keeping the Faith: Race Politics and Social Development in Jacksonville, Florida 1940–1970* (2000). Another book on the history of blacks in Akron, Ohio is forthcoming in 2005.

Marcellus C. Barksdale is Professor of History and Director of the African American Studies Program at Morehouse College. His articles and essays have appeared in the *Journal of Social and Behavioral Sciences* and the *Journal of Negro History*.

Juan J. Battle is Professor of Sociology at the Graduate Center of the City University of New York. His several publications highlight the intersection of race, gender, and class on a variety of social phenomena. He is presently directing a study of social justice and philanthropy.

Natalie D. A. Bennett is Assistant Professor of Women and Gender Studies at DePaul University, Chicago, Illinois. She has been a Research Fellow at the Five Colleges Women's Studies Research Center and a Visiting Scholar at the Center for the Study of Women in Society at the Graduate Center of the City University of New York. She is preparing a study of Caribbean immigrant women and work in the United States.

Hayward "Woody" Farrar is Associate Professor of History at Virginia Polytechnic Institute and State University. He is the author of *The Baltimore Afro-American 1892–1950* (1998) and the forthcoming works *The Hampton Estate, 1690–1890* and *African Americans in the New Age: Baltimore's Black Community, 1945–2000*.

Debra Foster Greene is Assistant Professor of History at Lincoln University, Missouri. Her works have appeared in the *Dictionary of Missouri Biography*.

Stanley Harrold is Professor of History at South Carolina State University. His most recent publication is *The Rise of Aggressive Abolitionism: Addresses to the Slaves* (2004).

Antonio F. Holland is Professor of History and Chairman of the Division of Social and Behavioral Sciences at Lincoln University, Missouri. He is co-author, with Lorenzo Greene and Gary Kremer of *Missouri's Black Heritage*.

Alton Hornsby, Jr is Fuller E. Callaway Professor of History at Morehouse College. He is the former editor of the *Journal of Negro History*. His latest work is *A Short History of Black Atlanta, 1847–1990*. One of his forthcoming works is *Southerners Too: Essays on the Black South, 1733–1990* (2005).

Angela M. Hornsby is Assistant Professor of History at the University of Mississippi. Her articles and essays have appeared in *Southern Cultures*, the *Journal of Negro History* and *Notable American Black Women*.

Anne R. Hornsby is Associate Professor of Economics and Chair of the Department of Economics at Spelman College. Her articles and essays have appeared in the *Journal of Negro History* and in Juliet E. K. Walker, *Encyclopedia of African American Business History* (1999).

Mark Andrew Huddle is Assistant Professor of History at St. Bonaventure University. His book, *The Paradox of Color: Mixed Race Americans and the Burden of History* is forthcoming in 2005.

David H. Jackson, Jr is Professor of History at Florida A&M University. His most recent work is *A Chief Lieutenant of the Tuskegee Machine: Charles Banks of Mississippi* (2002).

Hasan Kwame Jeffries is Assistant Professor of History at the Kirwan Institute for the Study of Race and Ethnicity at the Ohio State University. He is writing a history of the black freedom struggle in Lowndes County, Alabama.

Rhonda Jones is a research associate for the "Behind the Veil" Project at the Center for Documentary Studies at Duke University.

Maghan Keita is Associate Professor of History and Director of Africana Studies and Interim Director of the Center for Arab and Islamic Studies at Villanova University. His most recent work is the edited volume, *Conceptualizing/Reconceptualizing Africa: the Construction of African Historical Identity* (2002).

Frederick C. Knight is Assistant Professor of History at Colorado State University.

Augustine Konneh is Professor of History and Chair of the Department of History at Morehouse College. His *History of Liberia* is forthcoming in 2005.

Barbara Krauthamer is Assistant Professor of History at New York University. She is currently preparing a book entitled *Native Country: African American Slavery, Freedom and Citizenship in the Creek, Choctaw and Chickasaw Indian Nations*.

Samuel T. Livingston is Assistant Professor of History at Morehouse College. He is currently writing a book on the Nation of Islam and Hip-Hop Culture, 1970–2004.

Charles W. McKinney, Jr is a Research Associate, Program Coordinator, and Director of Undergraduate Studies for the African Americans Studies Program at Duke University. He is currently studying black nationalism and social change and African American working class political formation in the American South.

Tiya Miles is Assistant Professor in the program in American Culture, Center for Afro-American and African Studies and Native American Studies at the University of Michigan, Ann Arbor. Her book *Ties that Bind: The Story of an Afro-Cherokee Family in Slavery and Freedom* will be published in 2005.

Frederick D. Opie is Associate Professor of History and Director of the African Diaspora Program at Marist College, New York. He is currently writing books entitled *The Guatemalan Atlantic World* and *The Origins of Soul Food in the Atlantic World*.

Walter C. Rucker is Assistant Professor of African and African American Studies at the Ohio State University. His forthcoming book treats the role of African culture in resistance movements in North America.

Christopher M. Span is Assistant Professor in the Department of Educational Policies at the University of Illinois Urbana-Champaign. His articles and essays have appeared in the *Journal of Negro Education* and *Urban Education*. He is currently preparing a book on African American education in Mississippi 1862–75.

Julius E. Thompson is Professor of History and Director of the Black Studies Program at the University of Missouri, Columbia. His latest works include *Black Life in Mississippi: Essays on Political, Social and Cultural Studies in a Deep South State* (2001) and *Pan African Nationalism in the Americas: The Life and Times of John Henrik Clarke* (2004).

Shirley E. Thompson is Assistant Professor of American Studies at the University of Texas at Austin. Her forthcoming book is entitled *The Passing of a People: Creoles of Color in Mid-Nineteenth Century New Orleans*.

Akinyele Umoja is Associate Professor of African American Studies at Georgia State University. He has contributed to Charles Jones (ed.), *Liberation, Imagination and the Black Panther Party* and is currently writing a book entitled *Eye for an Eye: The Role of Armed Resistance in the Mississippi Freedom Movement*.

Oscar R. Williams III is Assistant Professor of History in the Department of Africana Studies at the State University of New York at Albany. He has published several articles and essays on George S. Schuyler and is currently writing a biography of Schuyler.

Jason R. Young is Assistant Professor of History at the State University of New York at Buffalo. He is currently preparing a book on the role of religion and spirituality in the resistance against the slave trade and slavery in West-central Africa and in the Lowcountry region of Georgia and South Carolina.

Acknowledgments

The production of a work of this magnitude and scope has been compared to the birthing of a child – a long period of gestation, followed by an often painful delivery, but ending with happiness and a sense of profound accomplishment. In this process, I have been immeasurably aided by several persons and I wish here to express my deep appreciation.

Susan Rabinowitz and her colleagues at Blackwell Publishing conceived the project and offered guidance in its earliest stages. The distinguished board of advisors assisted in the development of the project, including possible topics and authors. Delores P. Aldridge and Angela M. Hornsby provided invaluable editorial assistance as did E. Delores Stephens. Ken Provencher, senior editor at Blackwell Publishing, proved to be meticulous as well as helpful and patient throughout the project. I am also grateful to other editors at Blackwell Publishing, Gerard M-F Hill and Sue Hadden. Finally, the success of the project benefited greatly by the work of my student assistants, Robert A. Bennett III and Hassan Alhassan, together with Bettye Spicer, who did much of the final typing of the manuscript.

Alton Hornsby, Jr
August 2004

Introduction

ALTON HORNSBY, JR

Although free northern blacks, even in antebellum times, had written popular historical works detailing the contributions of Africans – in their homelands and in the Diaspora – to world civilization, prominent Euro-American scholars continued early into the twentieth century to paint the African race as innately inferior and as a beneficiary of, rather than a contributor to, the development of civilization in the West and in the World. Prominent among the historians who took this view were Albert Bushnell Hart and U. B. Phillips.

Racist historiography persisted even after trained black historians like George Washington Williams, William Wells Brown, W. E. B. Du Bois and Carter G. Woodson emerged to provide scientific studies of African and African American achievements. With the exception of Du Bois, who provided an early Marxian interpretation of Black Reconstruction, all of the black scholars continued in the Contributionist mode of the early popular African American historians. By 1920, Woodson, as a founder of the Association for the Study of Negro Life and History and founder and editor of the *Journal of Negro History*, had taken the lead in writing and publishing scholarly works on black life and history.

By the time of the Second World War, a few white scholars, primarily Jewish and Leftist ones, had begun to contribute major works on African and African American history. Since, however, most of these were denied access to the major publishing houses and the major scholarly journals, they wrote in such publications as the *Journal of Negro History* and were read principally by black and Leftist or liberal whites. Foremost among these were such scholars as Herbert Aptheker, Melville Herskovits, and August Meier and Elliott Rudwick.

As the ranks of white scholars interested in the Black Experience continued to grow in the post-war period, they tended to concentrate on the periods of slavery and Reconstruction and continued to see blacks largely as inferiors and as victims. But, by the late 1950s and the approach of "the Civil Rights Revolution," some Euro-American scholars began to see African American assertiveness, even when they were in bondage.

The Civil Rights Era not only revolutionized race relations in the United States, but it forced scholars to look at African American life and history through new lenses. Much of the impetus for the new historiography stemmed from the demands of black activists. However, the wider opening of the best graduate schools in the country to the post-war generation of African American students also led to new studies and new views. African American Contributionism took on new forms in African American agency.

Although some scholars, especially Euro-American ones, thought that some of the "New Black History" overstated the contributions of ancient Africans as well as Africans in the Diaspora, they endorsed the views of many of the new black historians – some of whom they had trained. It should not be implied that the new black scholars were all of one mind or one perspective in retelling the African American story. Indeed, some of them challenged the views of their fellow black historians concerning the predominance of race as the major paradigm in the African American Experience. Several saw class and gender as looming larger as theoretical and practical constructs. They also parted with some of their colleagues in positing assimilationist and integrationist views, as opposed to insular and separatist or nationalist approaches. The latter group, including such scholars as Vincent Harding and Sterling Stuckey, also called for a radical reexamination of the American Creed. In the manner of Carter G. Woodson, the journalist-historian Lerone Bennett took these views to a popular audience in his column in *Ebony Magazine* as well as in several monographs.

Once the Feminist Movement and the anti-Vietnam War Movement, which many contended were spawned by the Civil Rights Movement, emerged and fostered their own new histories – generally characterized as "the New Social History" – some scholars raised questions anew about the "objectivity question" in the American historical profession. They asserted that American historiography had gone from "everyman his own historian" to every ethnic group and gender their group's own historians.

Nevertheless, by the post-Civil Rights era, the American historical profession as well as many scholars in other parts of the world had embraced the viability and significance of researching and assessing the African American Experience. They then raised and answered new questions that turned conventional, and often racist, views of the Black Past, on their heads and heels.

Finally, as historians worldwide began to reinterpret the roles of various nationalities, ethnic groups, and genders in the origins and development of civilizations, they also saw links in the Human Experience that transcended these boundaries. Thus, the African and African American experiences were also subjected to new international or global inspections, introspections, and fresh analyses. Globalism also, significantly, raised new questions about transculturation, even suggesting the demise of any lingering uniquenesses in African American culture. Interestingly enough, these questions and approaches appeared at the same time that some suggested that a new, distinct variation of African and African American culture had emerged – Hip-Hop.

The Black Experience in the United States and its backgrounds in Africa and the African Diaspora are the subject of the essays in this volume, written by historians, sociologists, economists, and Africana scholars. They provide the latest examinations and assessments of the changing vicissitudes of African American historiography during the last two centuries.

PART I

African and Other Roots

CHAPTER ONE

Life and Work in West Africa

AUGUSTINE KONNEH

This chapter depicts the everyday lives of various inhabitants of this region. It describes and interprets the social, economic, cultural, and religious activities in which Africans were engaged as they searched for self-fulfillment as individuals and as members of communities and groups. This is not ethnography, but rather a historical and historiographical essay on the period from ancient times to the era of the African Slave Trade.

West African Institutions

Family

One outstanding feature of the communal structure of West African societies was the importance of the family and the ever-present consciousness of ties of kinship. When one speaks of the family in an African context, one is referring not to the nuclear family – husband, wife, and children – but to kin, the extended family, which comprises a large number of blood relatives who trace their descent from a common ancestor. The family was held together by a sense of obligation one to the other. Early African family values included solidarity, mutual helpfulness, interdependence, and concern for the well-being of every individual member of a society – the highest and most spontaneous expression. Indeed, as Gyekye (1996) has indicated, the African extended family system was held as a fundamental value, both social and moral. Thus, each member of the family was brought up to think of himself or herself always and primarily in relationship to the group as a cohesive unit. Each family member was required to seek to bring honor to the group. The children had obligations to their parents and parents had obligations to their children. Both the children and parents also had obligations to the members of extended families – brothers, sisters, in-laws, cousins, uncles, aunts, nephews, nieces, and so on.

These were the elements of strong family ties that people of African descent brought with them to the Americas. Scholars, such as Blassingame (1972), Herskovits

(1941), and Gutman (1976), have observed the strength of the family in the survival of Africans in the Americas. Unlike E. Franklin Frazier (1939), who in his work *The Negro Family* postulated that Africans in the Americas brought no elements of the family with them, Gutman and Herskovits argue that African family resilience was transmitted to the Americas and, thus, assisted in Africans' survival both during slavery and freedom. In fact, historically, West African family or lineage constituted a clan whose members might reside in the same area and share a number of common activities and interests. These lineages performed diverse functions including economic, educational, religious, social, and cultural. The lineages often acted as authoritative bodies for enforcing roles of behavior and, in the case of interlineage strife, for resolving such conflict through mediation or arbitration by a council of elders (McCall 1995).

John McCall discusses the formation of West African lineages in pre-slavery times through such principles as matrilineality, patrilineality, matrilocal residence and patrilocal residence (1995). These were principles that governed inheritance and citizenship in a community. All relationships were subsumed under the concept of kinship network. In West Africa, as elsewhere, some kin were adopted – what is sometimes called a feticious principle of kinship. Status, legal rights, and identity emanating from kinship are still clearly to be observed in modern West Africa, where the continued significance of kinship is expressed in ethnic politics.

The lineage in West Africa was the custodian of wealth and all economic assets. Production assets, such as land and labor, were in the hands of the family. McCall asserts, for example, that in many parts of West Africa land used for farming or the houses and land where people lived were not considered to "belong" to the people who utilized them. Instead, this property was held by a community, which claimed descent from a common ancestor. In some societies this descent was reckoned through the male line. This was the case in the establishment of a business that relied on the support of the family in terms of putting up the resources and providing the required labor. The male head of the family or lineage administered property in the interests of all family members, particularly males, because of the patrilineal nature of descent in many West African societies (Vaughan 1986).

The family was responsible for the upbringing of children in West Africa. Their proper nurturing was essential for the continuity of the family, lineage, and clan. Children, therefore, were not considered primarily as individuals but, instead, belonged to the family and the community. Everyone was expected to be a keeper of one's neighbor's child (Azevedo 1998). Thus, the popular saying, "It takes a village to bring up a child," was a way of life in West Africa. As Azevedo (1998) reports, because of the continuity of lineage through children, many people in West Africa desired to have many children and to do what they could to assist them to become successful and wealthy, because these children were their legacy. The children would care for them in their old age, give them a glorious burial when they died, and keep their memory alive long after they had passed on. Some obvious benefits of this practice in child rearing included the prevention of vagrancy and crime. Thus, it was not surprising that incidences of rape, child abuse, and molestation were rare. Although changes have occurred because of Western influence, the family remains a highly valued cornerstone of society.

Marriage

Many marriages in traditional West Africa were inextricably related to kinship. Marriage was governed by a variety of rules. Some of these rules were exogamous (marriage outside the family line) in their basis, and others were endogamous (marriage inside the family line). McCall advances the idea that marriage between persons who in English would be classified as cousins was practiced in some West African societies. Marriages between cross-cousins (children of the marriages of a brother and sister) were the more preferred arrangements, whereas a marriage between parallel cousins (children of the marriages of two brothers or two sisters) would be forbidden as incestuous. Those marriages based on exogamous practice were designed to create alliances between two lineages (McCall 1995).

Marriages in West Africa were arranged relatively early in the life of adults. Sometimes future partners were earmarked in childhood for the purpose of solidifying social relationships. As Adepoju noted (1992 and 1997), marriage in the African sense was the traditionally recognized point of entry into family formation. It was, indeed, a complex affair. For example, identification of a bride (or groom), consolidation of the search through payment of bride price, formation of the rites of marriage, consummation of marriage – all of these components of the process were arranged by families who also had an enduring responsibility to ensure the stability of the union through a variety of controls and a mutual support network (Adepoju 1992). Thus, the overall good of the families was considered to be more important than the desires of the two individuals involved. McCall notes that the practice of arranged marriages reflects the fact that marriage in West Africa was not concerned only with building a family, it was concerned also with the construction and maintenance of a larger network of relationships within the community as a whole (McCall 1995). To West Africans, marriage by no means involved just two individuals. Rather, it was an alliance between two extended families of the bride and groom. Therefore, even the choice of a fiancé(e) required careful consultation with relatives and close friends. If the father or mother in either family was against his or her child's selection, the chances for the young people getting married were rather slim (Azevedo 1998).

The existence of different cultural values, customs, and taboos among various ethnic groups required a careful examination of any inter-ethnic marriages. The backgrounds – social and sentimental histories of the prospective wife or husband – were closely scrutinized. For instance, among the Akan of Ghana, a literal investigation was discreetly carried out to check for "skeletons in the closet." Within this context, it is easy to understand how appalled West Africans still are to hear that Americans may decide to marry people from totally strange origins, sometimes without even knowing much of their fiancé(e)'s family background.

Once the choice of a mate had been approved, the marriage procedure could begin. The traditional version of the wedding took place before the modern one. It involved a meeting of the bride and groom, a number of relatives – parents did not attend this ceremony – and maybe a couple of brothers or sisters of the groom. The ritual was performed in the bride's family's house. A few weeks before the gathering, the future husband's relatives offered several expensive items. Those usually included some traditional fabrics and vintage alcoholic beverages. During the actual ceremony, the elders on the bride's side would pour some of the beverages on the ground, uttering prayers to the ancestors' spirits. In these prayers, they wished for a peaceful marriage, many children, and harmonious relations between the two families. At this stage, the couple was actually considered married (McCall 1995).

Once the traditional ceremony was completed, the couple could start a new life, confident that they had all of the familial framework to support the marriage in times of difficulties. This was actually the main reason why, according to Robertson (1995), young West Africans would rather not get married against their parents' advice. For example, a spiritual curse implied a very unhappy relationship, since the marriage was not blessed by the family. Then, in case of crisis, parents could not be called upon to provide their expertise at conjugal trials. Among the Akan people of Ghana, when husband and wife proved unable to resolve their differences, they resorted to older brothers or sisters, marriage witnesses, or very close friends. If all those options failed, the last resort for mediation lay with the parents or elders.

For instance, a husband might have found no satisfactory compromise in discussing his wife's cousins' or brothers' extended stays in his home. A meeting would have to be called eventually to settle the protracted dispute. Parents, brothers, sisters, marriage witnesses, and/or any person aware of the couple's problems would be present to discuss various alternatives with the spouses. For such a conference to be summoned, the taboo word of "divorce" had probably been uttered by one of the parties. The couple would be urged to speak out frankly and expose any hidden element that might give some insight into the causes for tension. A decision had to be reached by the end of the session. At times, the meeting would last several hours, until the family had determined who was responsible for the trouble and had devised a way of avoiding its recurrence. The wronged party would finally be asked to forgive his or her spouse and to promise that such a crisis would never occur again. If the council was proven wrong, the spouse had to inform the members, who would call for another, more dramatic meeting. A large number of relatives would participate in the discussion because it would be seen as imperative that the situation be solved through family channels and not in court.

The preceding example demonstrates why it was vital for a married West African literally to "pamper" the in-laws in difficult times, as they would play a crucial and moderating role in, perhaps, saving a marriage. To some married West Africans, however, having to take into account their own extended family's opinions, plus those of their in-laws, was viewed as an immense nuisance, on top of the complication of the traditional relationship where the husband was custodian to the wife. Yet, in the final analysis, the concept of marriage as a concern of all the blood relatives could save a couple the cost and trauma of having to seek professional help with counselors or therapists. The extended familial network, in effect, was designed to provide all the psychological and material support needed in times of crisis.

Indigenous African Religion

The awareness of the existence of some ultimate, Supreme Being who is the origin and sustainer of this universe – and the establishment of constant ties with this being – influenced, in a comprehensive way, the thoughts and actions of the West African people (Gyekye 1996). The West African heritage was intensely religious.

The African world into which European Christian missionaries entered in the late seventeenth century was a religious world in which the idea of God as the Supreme Being was already known and held by the West African people. In a study of African Religions and Philosophy, Professor Mbiti (1975) noted that "Africans are notoriously religious, and each people has its religious system with a set of beliefs and practices." This implies that religion permeated into all the aspects of African life so fully that it was not easy or possible always to isolate it. Thus, in African religion, there was no formal distinction between the sacred and the secular, between the religious and the non-religious, between the spiritual and the material areas of life. Wherever the African was, there was his/her religion; the early Africans carried their religions with them, wherever they would find themselves. It is also important to note that there were no sacred scriptures in African religions. Religion in West African societies was written not on paper but in people's hearts, minds, oral history, rituals, and religious personages like the priests, rainmakers, officiating elders, and even kings. Everyone was a potential carrier of religion. African religions had neither founders nor reformers. These religions did, however, incorporate national heroes, heroines, leaders, rulers, and other famous men and women into their body of beliefs and mythology. Belief in the continuation of life after death was found in all African societies.

Certainly up to the period of the major European incursions into West Africa, the vast majority of the African people engaged in religious practices that were indigenous to the continent. These practices were only outward manifestations of certain religious beliefs and, like symbols in other religions, they did not indicate the specific character of the religion. The religion of early West Africans can most accurately be described as ancestor worship. West Africans believed that the spirits of their ancestors had unlimited power over their lives. In this, as in almost every aspect of West African life, the kinship group was important. It was devoutly believed that the spirit that dwelled in a relative was deified upon death and that it continued to live and take an active interest in the family. The spirits of early ancestors had been free to wield an influence for such a long time that they were much more powerful than the spirits of the more recently deceased; hence, the devout worship and the complete deification of early ancestors. Not only were the spirits of deceased members of the family worshiped, but also a similar high regard was held for the spirits that dwelt on the family land, in the trees and rocks in the community of the kinship group, and in the sky above the community.

Because of the family character of African religions, the priests of the religions were the patriarchs of the families. They were the oldest living descendants of the initial ancestor and had therefore inherited the earthly prerogatives of their predecessors. Thus, they had dominion over the family grounds, water, and atmosphere. It was the family patriarch who entered into communication with the souls of his ancestors and natural forces in his immediate vicinity. Consequently, he was authorized to conduct ceremonies of worship. The temples of worship could be any structures set aside for that purpose. They contained holy objects, such as bones of the dead, consecrated pieces of wood, rock, or metal, and statuettes representing objects to be worshiped. Bells or rattles were used to invoke the spirits and the worshipers. The blood of victims – chickens, sheep, goats, or human beings – was offered as a sacrifice to appease the gods. The practice of sacrificing human beings in

Africa was never a universal one, but, in some areas, prisoners and captives were sacrificed during the worship of various deities. Libations of palm wine, beer, or other fermented drinks were offered in various forms of worship. Prayers and songs were expressions of adoration.

It was only natural that in a society such as that found in West Africa there would be considerable reliance on the magical power of amulets, talismans, and the like. Anything that helped to explain and answer the imponderables was a welcome addition to tribal practices. Magic was, therefore, practiced on a grand scale. By resorting to ill-defined powers, known only to him, the magician invented techniques and created rites designed to secure for individuals the specific ends they desired. Where religion was a collective attempt to secure satisfaction for the kinship groups, magic was an individual attempt to achieve certain satisfactions on the part of a particular person. Even in areas where animistic worship prevailed, belief in magic was widespread. Many Africans had great confidence in the efficacy of magical practices, and it may be that the reliance on the divination of sorcerers was responsible in part for the course that the civilization of West Africa took.

The elaborateness of funeral rites all over the continent attests to the regard that Africans had for the idea that the spirits of the dead played an important part in the life of the kinship groups. The funeral was the climax of life; costly and extensive rituals were held as sacred obligations of the survivors. The dead were generally buried in the ground either beneath the huts in which they lived or in cemeteries. Burial often took place within a few days after death, but at times the family delayed interment for several weeks or longer. The grave was not completely closed until every member of the family had an opportunity to present offerings and to participate in some rite pertinent to interment. Nothing more clearly demonstrates the cohesiveness of the African family than the ceremonies and customs practiced on the occasion of the death and burial of a member.

Franklin (2000) suggests that in all probability the early influence of Islam on the African way of life has been greatly exaggerated. This is certainly true during the period before the fourteenth century. Muslims crossed from Arabia over into Egypt in the seventh century. In the following century, they swept across North Africa where they met with notable success, but religious conversion was slow south of the Sahara. Africanists such as Basil Davidson (1994), Kevin Shillington (1995), and Robert July (1992) agree that the kingdoms of Ghana, Mali, and the Songhay accepted Islamic faith quite reluctantly, while other groups rejected it altogether. Some African kings accepted Islam, along with their subjects, for what appear now to be economic and political reasons. However, they frequently and tenaciously held to their tribal religious practices. Muslims were never able, for example, to win over the people of Mali, Hausaland, and Yorubaland. The commercial opportunities offered by the Muslims were especially attractive. It must also be added that the followers of the Prophet accepted Africans as social equals and gave them the opportunity to enjoy the advantages of education and cultural advancement, which the religion offered. Even as a slave, the black Muslim was considered a brother. To many black Africans these features were doubtless as important as the purely ritualistic aspects of the new religion. Even so, large numbers of Africans resoundingly rejected Islam in favor of a preference for the cults and rituals that were historically a part of their way of life.

Christianity, in contrast, was entrenched in North Africa early. It was when Islam made its appearance in the seventh century that the two great faiths engaged in a life-and-death struggle for the control of the area. In West Africa, where the population was especially dense and from which the great bulk of slaves was secured, Christianity was practically unknown until the Portuguese began to establish missions in the area in the sixteenth century. It was a strange religion, this Christianity, that taught equality and brotherhood and at the same time introduced on a large scale the practice of tearing people from their homes and transporting them to a distant land to become slaves. If the Africans south of the Sahara were slow to accept Christianity, it was not only because they were attached to their particular forms of tribal worship but also because they did not have the superhuman capacity to reconcile in their own minds the contradictory character of the new religion.

Diviners and Other Supernatural Powers

Divination in West African religion was vital because it told priests, patients, and the entire community what ritual they must perform. Successful diviners were highly intelligent and often high-strung men or (occasionally) women. They were often also physically handicapped. Divination was one of the specialties most likely to attract the person with an intellectual bent. Diviners had to possess an excellent intuitive knowledge of the societies in which they lived – and often the knowledge was not merely intuitive but could be made explicit. They also had to be men and women of courage. The diviners were the ones who were putting their fingers on, and brought into the open, the inadequacies and the sore spots in day-to-day living. Unless they were strong and forceful, they could be cowed. Many diviners who completed their training never practiced, specifically because they could "not stand the heat in the kitchen" (Stewart 1984).

Most indigenous African religions believed that, were it not for the workings of the forces of evil, human beings would live forever in health and happiness. Therefore, when disease and misery struck, the source had to be rooted out. That source contained two elements. There was, on the one hand, the cause of the difficulty. Africans, within their knowledge, were as sensible about cause as anyone else, and most of them knew that some diseases were communicable and that droughts appeared in recurring cycles. Cause in this sense, however, left certain questions unanswered – all of the "why" questions. Therefore, misfortune had not only a cause but it had a source of motivation as well.

The very fact that misfortune struck was an indication that all was not well in the world and in the cosmos. The cause and motivation of the misfortune had to be discovered. Contrary to westerners, who were not trained to ask questions about misfortune, Africans did seek answers in such situations. In arriving at answers, they linked social problems to divine action. In so doing, they exposed and often solved the social problems in the course of seeking to counter the divine manifestations.

The first thing a person had to do when misfortune struck was to go to a diviner to discover the device which was used to bring it about and, perhaps, also to discern the author of the misfortune. That author might have been a spirit to whom insufficient attention had been paid or an ancestor who was punishing a descendant for immorality, or spiritual shortcomings in the group of his descendants. Or it may have been a "witch" who was a human author of evil, venting his or her anger, envy, or selfishness (Stewart 1984).

African diviners used many modes of carrying out their task of obtaining an answer to the misfortune. For example, they threw palm nuts and read answers to their queries in the juxtaposition of the fallen kernels. They tossed chains of snake bones. They rubbed carved oracle boards together. They also became possessed, and received their answers through a spiritual intermediary. These methods were means of seeking results in solving problems, which were not understood by outsiders.

In contemporary scholarship, it is important to note several issues as they relate to the in-depth investigation and study of African traditional religions as an academic discipline. These issues primarily center on the debate over the reference to African traditional religion in the singular or plural, methodology, and interpretation. African scholars who adhere to the philosophies of E. B. Idowu consistently contend that scholars and critics should refer to the "religion" under the rubric of *One African Traditional Religion*. J. S. Mbiti, on the other hand, insists that there is an insufficient and unstable foundation for such a premise. He does accept the commonly held belief of the existence of a single, basic religious philosophy for Africa, yet he is insistent in his assertion of the existence of [as many] religions in the sub-Saharan African background in tandem with the number of ethno-language groups. Mbiti contends, "We speak of African religions in the plural because there are about one thousand African peoples (tribes), and each has its own religious system" (Mbiti 1969: 1–2). Further, as it relates to the issue of nomenclature, Mbiti asserts that Christianity and Islam should – in contemporary scholastic study – be viewed as indigenous and traditional religions of Africa due to the longevity of their historical existence in the continent (Mbiti 1975: 223).

While scholars remain divided on the views emanating from Mbiti and Idowu, recent scholarship pervasively embraces the use of African Traditional Religion in the singular. These scholars contend that the common world-view within these religions, as well as the similarity in rituals, belief-systems, value formulations, and institutional formation across the vast African continent, provide a basic and firm foundation for maintaining the reference to a singular form in referring to African traditional religions even while accepting and acknowledging (contemporaneously) the existence of a burgeoning number of denominations.

In the systematic, contemporary approach to the study of African traditional religion, it is important to note that the religion is based in orality. It is a religion and movement that maintains its authenticity and accuracy largely through a reliance on the transmission and interpretation through socio-cultural networks of verbal communication. For the most part, the tenets of African traditional religion are not to be found in sacred books but in the substance and continuity of historically-transmitted daily behaviors and more stylized ritualized practices. It is, therefore, quite clear that African traditional religion is one based in local, folk-based formulations. The African peoples embraced and assimilated the religion of their ancestors in a worship-based tradition that pervasively refers back to the local shrines and oracles.

The orality and folk-based foundations of African religion contribute to the complexity in the interpretation of the materials of the study of the religion. Scholars of various backgrounds – historically and in the twentieth and twenty-first centuries

– have contributed and continue to contribute their various perspectives to the study of African traditional religion. This creates a complex situation due to the training and backgrounds of many of the most prominent scholars in the field. The scholars' backgrounds and training are diverse, with some emerging as evolutionists, diffusionists, ethnographers, social anthropologists, and Christian scholars. Contemporary students and scholars face a critical challenge in deciding how these various scholars' backgrounds may have both negatively and positively contributed to what currently exists as the scholarship on traditional African religious expression and experience. Several critics of the current scholarly formulations, such as Newell S. Booth, Jr, R. Horton, and Okot p'Bitek, keenly question the validity and stability of some historical and critical materials. Booth, for example, asserts, "Many Western students of Africa – historians of religions, anthropologists, and others – exploit Africa for their own academic or ideological purposes" (Booth 1977: 4). Okot p'Bitek goes further to label some African scholars as "intellectual smugglers" (p'Bitek 1971: 107) who portray African deities "as mercenaries in foreign battles, none of which was in the interest of African peoples" (p'Bitek 1971: 102).

What emerges as most important in the debate, methodology, and interpretation of African traditional religion is the acknowledgement of the continuity of the religion. How can the student, scholar, and critic move to a more lucid and accurate description of African traditional religion? Wilfred Cantell Smith offers sound advice: "anyone who writes about a religion other than his own today does so, in effect, in the presence of those about whom he is speaking . . . no statement about a religion is valid unless it can be acknowledged by that religion's believers" (quoted in Booth 1977: 4).

Islam and Christianity

Islam has had a history of about a thousand years in West Africa. It was carried into the region and the continent through trade in the eighth century by Arab traders from North Africa. Today, in the northern part of West Africa from Senegal to Nigeria, nearly 90 percent of the population is Muslim. The northern parts of Sierra Leone, Liberia, Cote d'Ivoire, and Ghana also have substantial adherents to the Islamic faith. The spread of Islam is credited to the traders, who were often accompanied by clerics who set up Islamic schools and embarked upon the conversion of non-Muslims. Most of the Muslims in West Africa are Sunni (Konneh 1996).

Christianity has operated in West Africa for centuries. Many countries in the region – such as Cote D'Ivoire, Liberia, Ghana, and Sierra Leone – have traditionally had great Christian influence. In the nineteenth century, missionary movements (Methodist, Presbyterian, Episcopal, and Lutheran) spread into the region and many inhabitants were attracted to Christianity. These missionaries set up Western schools and clinics and attracted the locals to them. The result was conversion to the religion because of what it offered socially as well as spiritually (Keim 1995).

West Africans, however, made their own adaptations of Christianity and Islam – introducing elements from their own traditions, such as approaches to healing, veneration of the dead, Africanized rituals, and music. In some cases this led to conflict with the established leaders of church and state. Another expression of religion in West African cities was the evolution of indigenous Christian churches.

A compelling example is the Aladura religious movement among the Yoruba in Nigeria. Aladura, which literally means "owner of prayer," is the generic name for a group of Christians whose origin goes back to the late nineteenth century, and whose religious doctrine centered on the healing power of prayer. The physical assurance of this doctrine, if one is ever needed, is provided by the water which, when blessed, is believed to be endowed with divine power (Jegede 1995).

In cities, religious syncretism was a major force. Some West Africans differed substantially in their mode of worship, some only marginally so, but all worshiped the same God according to West African people. Many people who professed Christianity or Islam, nominally at least, broke down religious boundaries by participating at will in the observance of some aspects of traditional religion. In urban society, where people came in contact with new ideas and values, syncretism became relevant. It allowed a degree of tolerance and mutuality. For example, Christians and Muslims alike could participate in rites, rituals, festivals, and other observances inherited from their ancestors. These practices continue [today] in spite of the imposing presence of religious edifices (Mazrui 1986).

In several cities in West Africa, annual religious festivals brought together "sons of the soil," to use the local parlance, who were drawn from far and near by the excitement of the occasion. Christian and Muslim alike delighted in joining the traditionalists in reenacting the pact of their religion, respecting the sacred shrine of the goddesses who would, in return, protect the city and ensure its prosperity.

Education and Power Associations

The Power Associations (secret societies) were responsible for the education of the young in traditional West Africa. They served to integrate the people of a community into a harmonious entity. They also provided the framework for teaching the youth how to live in relation with themselves and with everyone in the community. Konneh (1996) observed that in Liberia, to this day, most Mel- and Mande-speaking groups feature the Poro society for males and the Sande society for females. One of the principal purposes of the societies was that they defined interests and activities in terms of community instead of exclusively along lineage or clan lines. The roles the Poro, Sande, and other societies played may be summarized by noting that they provided social and vocational education, operated various social services, which ranged from medical treatment to recreation, and oversaw economic and political activities. All youths had to be initiated into their respective association before they could be considered adults and, consequently, contributing members of the community. The initiation schools, which the officials of the societies conducted for the youth to prepare them for membership in the associations, were located in an area physically remote from the village, and the sessions could take up to three or four years. Now, they usually take only a few weeks (Konneh 1996).

Kenneth Little (1951) has assessed the significance of the rite of passage that was associated with the associations in cultivating the minds and behaviors of young people in West African societies. He argues that the rite of passage provided the intellect, continuation of the group, and training that was practical in solving societies' problems. Thus, for Little, the rite of passage served as a public institution.

The power associations were the principal institutions that upheld traditional beliefs and practices. They served as binding forces – the core of community life. Their basic belief was that some extraordinary force allowed association members to speak with "one voice," which provided a systematic means for everyone to share a set of behaviors and moral codes that contributed to the continuity of society. Each Poro or Sande lodge was built near a sacred shrine, which included the graves of the town's founding elders and the past leaders of the associations. Membership in the power associations was compulsory and passage through them was an important prerequisite for persons to be considered as adult participants in society. Initiates of both associations were accountable to God through the ancestral and the cultic spirits. Cultural guidelines were also taught during instruction of initiates. Violators were tried by the Poro society, which also carried out the prescribed punishment (Konneh 1996).

Because they were veiled in secrecy, much that has been said and written about the power associations has been either fanciful or speculative. For example, Alice Walker – in her novel *Possessing the Secret of Joy* – condemned the Sande practice of a rite of passage that involved cutting of the clitoris of girls. She believed this practice to be inhuman, cruel, and hazardous to the health of young girls. Even in light of such questionable practices, the importance of the Poro and Sande cannot be underestimated. The Poro assumed a higher authoritative role than the Sande and wielded executive, judicial, and legislative authority in indigenous society. It maintained law, order, and decorum in communities; capital punishment was in the hands of its leaders. The association also mobilized men and women for labor and supervised market operations. Men also solidified and maintained their dominance over women by removing boys from their mothers and initiating them in the manner prescribed by Poro's god.

The chief and other leaders in the Poro hierarchy controlled large farms. As a part of the initiation process, boys worked on these farms to support themselves, to cultivate crops, and to "laid" (work on) the farms of others in an effort to help the chief generate revenues to meet the public's needs. Similar activities were engaged in by the Sande initiates, in that girls performed such tasks on the farms as weeding and harvesting the crops (Ray 1976).

The Poro and the Sande combined the powers of both the ancestors and the nature divinities. It was through the interaction of various spirit components and the power manifested through the power associations that order was maintained and balanced, and well-being for humans was preserved. The Poro and Sande provided different intermediary relationships with their respective authoritative entities in the spirit world. The origins of the spirit guardians were embedded in the power associations' myth and lore. For instance, in the Sande a male ancestral water spirit was impersonated by a masked dancer. However, in the Poro, the key spirit was the "bush spirit"; it was not impersonated by a masked dancer. Although they both have natural divinity, the "bush spirit" of the Poro was considered more powerful than the ancestral spirit impersonated by the Sande masked dancer. When asked where the Sande masked dancer came from, many Africans responded that they found it near the river or that it came from the water. This belief was shared by all of the female respondents, some of whom were quoted as saying that they pledged more respect to the masked impersonator than to their real-life husbands. The bearer of the mask of the ancestral water spirit was always a high-ranking Sande member. Other Sande masks, however, had no spiritual significance and were borne by low-ranking members. Those masks were used more for socialization and entertainment (Ray 1976).

The power associations were often characterized by members as important factors in an elaborate life drama. It was the power associations that first combined men and women into corporate units and allied them with the forces in the spirit world. In their roles as guardians of sacred and social values, they represented the central core of a society's world view, which was dramatically played out in Poro and Sande rituals and ceremonies. These rituals and ceremonies operated in cycle of life dramas whose themes centered on gender rivalry and the shifting power of their tutelary nature-spirit guardians.

Both the Poro and the Sande played central roles in the funeral rites of their members. Among the power associations' members were those who possessed specialized skills as morticians, doctors, and grave-diggers for the purpose of funeral functions. The collective consciousness of the associations was brought to bear in the funerary ceremonies, especially those of chiefs and high-ranking power association officials. The corpses of such officials were not seen by non-members, not even by relatives. The specialists of the associations were in charge until the final burial.

The authority and respect wielded by chiefs and other leaders was supplemented by their ritual authority, which they held as highly-placed members of the power associations. As religious practices comprised a major part of political leaders' sanctions and powers, rulers often participated in traditional religious activities, such as leading the celebrations at the time of a funeral or pouring libations to ensure a bountiful harvest.

To a large extent the power associations excluded outsiders; only in a few instances were they allowed to join. These power associations particularly resented the encroachment of Islamic and Christian religious practices, especially the use of magical charms and medicine, on their spiritual territory. Also, there well may have been a reluctance by Muslims to join the associations because of their belief that to associate anything with God contravenes the concept of *shirk* (the Muslim belief that God is one) while the associations were adherents of African traditional religions which encompass a belief in a pantheon of gods.

West African Economic Activities

Occupations in the Forest

The forest regions of southern West Africa – Guinea, Liberia, Sierra Leone, Cote d'Ivoire, Ghana and Nigeria – run along the coast and stretch about 200 miles inland. Most of the West African forests were not technically rain forests because they did not receive enough rainfall. Rainforests need approximately 70 inches of rainfall a year with no completely dry season. Most of the West African forest region had at least one dry season. The people in the rural areas earned their living in many different ways. The major occupations in traditional West Africa were trade, agriculture, fishing, blacksmithing, herding (pastoralism), and hunting. These occupations served as the major economies for peoples in the rainforest and savanna regions of West Africa.

People used peanuts, fruits, and palm products directly from the forests. However, in most areas, farmers cut the trees to grow crops. In traditional farming, some of the larger trees were left because they were too difficult to cut down and because they provided shade. Most of the smaller trees were cut and the areas were burned. The ash from the burned trees increased the fertility of the soil. The farmer then planted cassava or cocoyams, but after a few years, the soil lost its fertility. Bananas could be planted on the less fertile land. However, eventually the land was abandoned and was allowed to regain its fertility. The new forest would grow back in forty to fifty years. While it looked like the original forest, it usually had fewer species. Almost all of the forests in West Africa were cut at least once. Palm trees also may have been planted instead of allowing the traditional forest to regrow (McNulty 1995).

Most farms in the forest region had several crops, which reached maturity at different times. Farmers planted cocoa trees that took from five to seven years to mature and bear fruit, but they continued to yield for several years. Swamp rice, peanuts, rubber palms, coffee, and oil palms were also grown as cash crops in the forest region. Farmers grew yams, plantains, bananas, cocoyams, cassava, corn, rice, peppers, okra, onions, tomatoes, and various fruits, such as oranges and pineapples, to eat themselves.

Agriculture was the keystone of West Africa's prosperous economies of the forest region. A large percentage of the rural population was engaged in crop growing, which was used for subsistence as well as for export. By the end of the nineteenth century many West African farmers in the forest area took advantage of relatively favorable market opportunities to open up extensive areas for cultivation and to accumulate productive capital in the form of coffee, cocoa, and rubber trees. As their incomes from the sale of export crops increased, so did their expenditures on a variety of domestically produced goods, ranging from foodstuffs to furniture, which in turn created new opportunities for expanded production and commerce with the region. Tree crop farmers also invested part of their earnings in other forms of capital, including trade, transport, and housing, and in such public facilities as schools, clinics, and market stalls. They also often paid school fees for their children and other young relatives, thus contributing to the growth of an educated labor force.

Throughout the forest zone the tsetse fly prevented people from keeping cattle. Most villages, however, had sheep, goats, and poultry. The forest regions, of course, provided plenty of wood for building materials and for making furniture and household implements. Large, elaborately carved homes could be found in some of the forest regions. Wood carving was a major art form for some of the people of this region.

While agriculture and wood carving were central occupations, the use of iron was also a central aspect of economic activity in West Africa. Kathy Schick (1995) pointed out that several West African kingdoms benefited significantly from their trade in iron, beginning in the ninth century. After Arab traders began to reach West Africa by the ninth and tenth centuries, the developing and expanding trade networks begun to evolve into iron-age societies, which enhanced the development of large urban communities and the centralization of political power in the West African kingdoms that regulated the trade. John Hope Franklin (2000) contends that West Africans were involved in the iron trade long before the Europeans. He argues that Africans exported for many years, with evidence emanating from the large numbers of blacksmiths and other iron workers in the region.

Blacksmithing was indispensable to the forest region. Smiths forged implements from scrap metal over a charcoal fire, using hand-worked hide bellows. In the nineteenth century, they kept the techniques of the profession secret from others. Only blacksmiths were allowed to work iron, wood, or clay. The Mandinka people of West Africa were and still are excellent blacksmiths – highly skilled and respected artisans who have been plying their ancient and fundamental craft for generations, forging the same vital products and employing the same technology. Mandinka blacksmiths smelted ores when necessary, but preferred to use imported iron when it was available (Konneh 1996).

Blacksmiths manufactured guns for hunting and made drums for chiefs. They were particularly significant for agricultural tools such as hoes, knives, and cutlasses. The farmers depended on blacksmiths for these supplies, which were cheaper than those manufactured in Europe. In addition to farm implements, blacksmiths produced domestic utensils and weapons using a few raw materials and tools such as fire, charcoal, a rooted iron anvil, tongs, skin bellows, and a variety of hammers (McNaughton 1988).

The craft of blacksmithing was basically hereditary in that sons inherited the occupation directly, mainly patrilineally. At the same time, the profession was open to newcomers. Unrelated youths, perhaps the son of a neighbor or affinal relative, were sometimes taken on by smiths as apprentices and taught the difficult skills of the craft. The profession of blacksmithing was more an honorable, than a money-making, endeavor. Despite the men's special skills, few artists earned a living at their trade in blacksmithing and nearly all were part-time specialists, who were also agri-culturists like those found in other regions. The products produced by blacksmiths served the basic needs of the community, and, for the most part, practical needs were simply met.

Savanna

Tall grass and trees make up the plants of the savanna region in West Africa. Savanna regions are found from Senegal southward to Sierra Leone, and eastward to central Nigeria. In the rainy season, savanna looks like a park with green grass and widely spaced trees. The grasses are tall and include elephant grass, which burns easily in the dry season. Rivers are usually lined with trees. In some savanna areas, particularly in Ghana, vegetation is often clumped around termite mounds. Many crops such as millet, guinea corn, and yams grow. As the savanna fades into the desert and rainfall goes below 15 inches a year, vegetation changes. Grasses and bushes become sparse and succulents become common. Some botanists believe that the savanna was once forest, which was changed to grassland by humans and fire. Some of Africa's grasslands are the result of man's burning forests or using them for cultivation and animal grazing.

In the savanna there are rainy seasons in the period from the end of April to September and dry seasons from October to March. During the dry season, trees lose their leaves, and grass turns brown. By the end of the dry season, grasses have usually become fibrous and coarse, so burning them clears the way for fresh, new growth. If the land is not burned over, scrub and thorn trees spread rapidly. When the rainy season comes, new grass grows and may become six feet tall or more.

Early farmers in the savanna area grew yams, corn, rice, peanuts, cassava, tomatoes, shea butter, guinea corn, tobacco, and millet. Agriculture in the savanna could be precarious because rainfall varied from year to year. Cattle raising was one of the main occupations in the region. Cattle manure was often used to fertilize crops. Sheep, goats, chickens, and guinea foul were also raised. Housing in the savanna ranged from elaborate buildings of sun-dried bricks to simple, portable homes for people who traveled with their cattle.

Desert

The Sahara desert, in the north of West Africa, received 10 inches of rainfall a year or less. Sometimes there was no rain for years. When rain did come, it was usually in a storm, which ran off without penetrating the soil. Temperatures could be extreme – climbing as high as 130 degrees Fahrenheit – and July temperatures averaged 95 degrees Fahrenheit. In the middle of the night, there could be freezing temperatures in the northern Sahara. Early Africans lived wherever there was adequate water from wells. Small groups of people learned to make a living from the very limited plant and animal resources available in the desert. Trade routes across the Sahara were a major source of livelihood before ship and air trade routes were well developed in the last century.

Kathy Schick (1995) argues that the Sahara desert has not always been dry. She contends that about 10,000 years ago a period of higher rainfall lasted in the region for some time, making the area an important center for food production. During the early period the Sahara supported substantial populations in settlements around lakes, ponds, and rivers interspersed throughout plains that, although sparsely vegetated, had a Mediterranean climate and were considerably better watered than today.

Trade in West Africa

Trade was the principal stimulant for the interaction of West African societies and an important catalyst for state building. Long before the slave trade era, West Africans along the coast initiated direct contact with other parts of the world. George Brooks (1986) contends that West Africans established trade routes that linked them to markets in the Middle East, the Red Sea, and the Far East. Traders, artisans, envoys, and pilgrims were among the travelers who used these routes.

West Africa had a most highly developed trading system: coastal riverine and caravan networks, notably those developed by Mande- and Hausa-speaking groups, expedited the exchange of products from the Sahel, savannas, rain forests, deserts, and coastlands. Exchange between ecological zones and the other parts of the world involved a wide range of commodities, including iron, iron utensils, cloth, gold, grains, livestock, pots, baskets, beads, leather goods, captives, kola nuts, salt, dried fish and mollusks, and numerous other foodstuffs, condiments, and medicinal substances. Some of these commodities, notably gold and captives, were transported across the Sahara to pay for salt mined in the Sahara, horses, prestige cloth, and other luxury goods.

The trade in West Africa was facilitated by landlord–stranger reciprocities. Hosts accorded strangers safety and security for their possessions in return for acknowledgment of their prerogatives as landlords, including the rights to levy taxes, to act as middlemen in trade, and to allocate land use. For example, where Mande blacksmiths and traders settled, they formed lodges of the "power associations." These acquired great influence among landlord groups, so much so that they were able to gain control over local rulers, mediate conflict between groups, protect trade routes from warfare and brigandage, and otherwise promote the interests of Mande traders and settlers, their families, and affiliated groups. Thus, Joseph Harris (1998) observes that long before Europeans arrived, West African societies were linked by extensive and growing trading patterns that connected areas from the Atlantic to Lake Chad and from the Gulf of Guinea to the Sahara. These trade networks testify to the viability of the social and political institutions that ensured the safe movement of travelers and merchandise.

West Africa was and still is a major region that has made significant contributions to the development of the entire continent. From the rural areas to the cities, these contributions can be directly and indirectly attributed to key aspects of West African society. Such aspects include West African institutions in which the extended family (lineage and clans) was a cornerstone for individual and communal success and survival. Another key institution was religion, which served as the foundation for all life both temporal (earthly) and eternal. The West African belief in One God, the creator of all life, was extremely prevalent. Yet there was also the belief in many lesser gods, as well as in ancestral spirits. Respect for all life, particularly animals, was also interwoven into the fabric of West African life. Early West African society also tended to embrace two major world religions – Islam and Christianity. The practices of these religions also played a significant role in educational and economic life. While Muslims established many of the early schools in West Africa, missionaries used the offering of more advanced educational opportunities and better schools as a means of converting West Africans to Christianity.

Education and power, in many instances, were inextricable in early West African society. The acquisition of knowledge was strongly encouraged, highly valued, and closely coveted. As such, it was not left up to chance but, rather, was often placed in the hands of the Poro and Sande – power associations that were dedicated to upholding traditional beliefs and practices many of which centered on the search for knowledge. Membership in the associations was highly prized and served as the key to much of a West African's life destiny.

The economics of West Africans were varied. In some regions, people changed the areas in which they worked in order to survive. As a result, the occupations of the people were mixed and changed depending on the situation. Such occupations included agriculture, fishing, blacksmithing, hunting, and horticulture. The forest and the savanna served as two primary locations for work. Even the desert was "cultivated" to produce a living from its limited plant and animal life.

To understand West Africa requires a willingness to take an in-depth look at the multiple factors that comprise life in this part of the continent. Only when examined as individual components and as parts of a larger whole can these factors combine toward more lucid and accurate historical understandings of the region. While the historiography on West Africa is rich and growing, areas that still beckon for further study include traditional medicine and healing, women's role in West African politics, kinship network, the role of art in West Africa, and women's role in traditional religions.

BIBLIOGRAPHY

Works Cited

Adepoju, A. (1992) "The African family and the survival strategy," Keynote address delivered at the Pan-African Anthropological Association Conference on the African family (Yaounde), August 24.
—— (1997) *Family, Population and Development in Africa*. London: Zed Books.
Azevedo, M. (1998) *African Studies: A Survey of Africa and The African Diaspora*, 2nd edn. Durham, NC: Carolina Academic Press.
Bitek, O. p' (1971) *African Religions in Western Scholarship*. Nairobi: Kenyan Literature Bureau.
Blassingame, John (1972) *The Slave Community*. London: Oxford University Press.
Bohannan, P. and Curtin, Philips (1995) *Africa and Africans*, 4th edn. Prospect Height, IL: Waveland Press.
Booth, N. S., Jr (1977) "An approach to African religions" in N. S. Booth (ed.), *African Religions: A Symposium*, 1–11. New York.
Brooks, G. E. (1986) "African 'landlords' and European 'strangers': African–European relations to 1870" in Phyllis Martin and Patrick O'Meara (eds.) *Africa*, 2nd edn. Bloomington: Indiana University Press.
Davidson, B. (1994) *The Lost Cities of Africa*. Boston: Little Brown.
Dunbar-Nelson, Alice (1916) "People of color in Louisiana," *Journal of Negro History* 1 (October).
—— (1917) "People of color in Louisiana," *Journal of Negro History* 2 (January).
Fitchett, E. Horace (1941) "The origin and growth of the free Negro population in Charleston, South Carolina," *Journal of Negro History* 26 (October).
Foner, Laura (1970) "The free people of color in Louisiana and St. Dominique: A comparative portrait of two three-caste slave societies," *Journal of Social History* 3: 406–30.
Frazier, E. Franklin (1939) *The Negro Family in the United States*. Chicago: Chicago University Press.
Franklin, John H. (2000) *From Slavery to Freedom*, 8th edn. New York: McGraw-Hill.
Gutman, H. G. (1976) *The Black Family in Slavery and Freedom 1750–1925*. New York: Vintage.
Gyekye, K. (1996) *African Cultural Values*. Philadelphia: Sankofa Publishing.
Harris, J. E. (1998) *Africans and Their History*. New York: Meridian.
Hastings, A. (1979) *A History of African Christianity, 1950–1975*. New York: Cambridge University Press.
Herskovits, Melville (1941) *The Myth of the Negro Past*. New York: Harper & Bros.
Idowu, Bolaji E. (1973) *African Traditional Religion: A Definition*. London: SCM Press.
Imes, William L. (1919) "The legal status of free Negroes and slaves in Tennessee," *Journal of Negro History* 4 (July).
Jegede, D. (1995) "Popular culture in urban Africa" in Phyllis Martin and Patrick O'Meara (eds.) *Africa*, 3rd edn, 273–94. Bloomington: Indiana University Press.
July, R. (1992) *History of the African People*, 4th edn. Prospect Height, IL: Waveland Press.

Keim, C. A. (1995) "Africa and Europe before 1900" in Phyllis Martin and Patrick O'Meara (eds.) *Africa*, 3rd edn. Bloomington: Indiana University Press.

Kimmel, Ross M. (1976) "Free blacks in seventeenth century Maryland," *Maryland Historical Magazine* 71: 19–25.

Konneh, A. (1996) *Religion, Commerce and the Integration of the Mandingo in Liberia.* Lanham, MD: University Press of America.

Little, Kenneth L. (1951) *The Mende of Sierra Leone.* London: Routledge & Kegan Paul.

McCall, John C. (1995) "Social organization in Africa" in Phyllis Martin and Patrick O'Meara (eds.) *Africa*, 3rd edn. Bloomington: Indiana University Press.

McNaughton, P. R. (1988) *The Mande Blacksmiths.* Bloomington: Indiana University Press.

McNulty, M. L. (1995) "The contemporary map of Africa" in Phyllis Martin and Patrick O'Meara (eds.) *Africa*, 3rd edn. Bloomington: Indiana University Press.

Mazrui, A. (1986) *The Africans: A Triple Heritage.* Boston: Little, Brown.

Mbiti, J. S. (1969) *African Philosophies and Religions.* New York: Praeger.

—— (1975) *An Introduction to African Religion.* London: Heinemann.

Ray, B. (1976) *African Religions: Symbol, Ritual, and Community.* Englewood Cliffs, NJ: Prentice-Hall.

Robertson, C. (1995) "Social change in contemporary Africa" in Phyllis Martin and Patrick O'Meara (eds.) *Africa*, 3rd edn. Bloomington: Indiana University Press.

Schick, Kathy D. (1995) "Prehistoric Africa" in Phyllis Martin and Patrick O'Meara (eds.) *Africa*, 3rd edn. Bloomington: Indiana University Press.

Shillington, K. (1995) *History of Africa*, 2nd edn. New York: St. Martin's Press.

Stewart, C. C. (1984) *Religions in Africa.* Urbana-Champagne: Illinois University Press.

Vaughan, J. H. (1986) "Population and social organization" in Phyllis Martin and Patrick O'Meara (eds.) *Africa*, 2nd edn. Bloomington: Indiana University Press, 159–80.

Suggestions for Further Reading

Ajayi, J. F. (1976) *History of West Africa.* New York: Columbia University Press.

Bennett, N. R. (1975) *Africa and Europe from Roman Times to the Present.* New York: African Publishing.

Boahen, A. (1986) *Topics in West Africa.* London: Longman.

Davidson, Basil (1972) *Africa: History of a Continent.* New York: Macmillan.

Hopkins, A. G. (1975) *An Economic History of West Africa*, rev. edn. London: Longman.

Oliver, Roland, and Atmore, Anthony (eds.) (1972) *Africa since 1800*, 2nd edn. London: Cambridge University Press.

CHAPTER TWO

Africans in Europe Prior to the Atlantic Slave Trade

MAGHAN KEITA

Madam, there were no black people in England before 1945. (Gerzina 1997)

In his innocence of the stories of Biblical or Greek and Roman antiquity, Raphael, Leonardo, Michelangelo, Rembrandt, and all the others can say nothing to him. All he sees are colors and forms – modern art. In short, like almost everything else in his spiritual life, the paintings and statues are abstract. No matter what modern wisdom asserts, these artists counted on immediate recognition of their subjects and, what is more, on their having a powerful meaning for their viewers. The works were the fulfillment of those meanings, giving them a sensuous reality and hence completing them. Without these meanings, and without their being something essential to the viewer as a moral, political, and religious being, the works lose their essence. It is not merely the tradition that is lost when the voice of civilization elaborated over millennia has been stilled. It is being itself that vanishes beyond the dissolving horizon. (Bloom 1987: 63)

Africa is no vast island, separated by an immense ocean from other portions of the globe, and cut off through the ages from the men who have made and influenced the destinies of mankind. She has been closely connected, both as source and nourisher, with some of the most potent influences which have affected for the good the history of the world. (Blyden 1880, quoted in Davidson 1991: frontispiece)

This chapter is a historiographic critique. It is a critique of the conventional historiographies of modernity and their histories; historiographies and histories constructed on a foundation of racialized epistemologies. Epistemologies within which the dominant body of knowledge diminishes, eschews, even attempts to erase constructions not so privileged. The methodology employed in this chapter moves the reader by "steps backward" from our acknowledged and conventional representations – or the lack thereof – of Africans in pre-Columbian Europe to analysis of their historical and cultural constructions and discovery of their possible historical foundations.

Race has become a way of knowing. Some have argued that it is the dominant way of knowing. Within such a context, it is possible to construct an argument that focuses on race and the writing of history (Keita 2000a; 2002), and that argument might be illustrated by interrogating historical sources, and implicitly the histories constructed around them, in relation to the question of Africans in Europe through the opening of the "Columbian" Age. Both Allison Blakely and Gretchen Gerzina have spoken of the difficulties of such a task (Blakely 1986, 1993; 1997: 1: 11–13; Gerzina 1995; 1997: 15–17; Miller 1985). Even in that light, neither has equated "difficulty" with "impossibility." In fact, in some ways, it seems that the task is much more straightforward than suspected. It involves an engagement with primary, literary, iconographic, and historical sources in relation to what has been ignored or passed by. In this case, an ignorance and passing very much related to race.

Here, Bloom's "voice of civilization elaborated over millennia has been stilled" through the attempts to ignore or even erase it. Of course, Bloom is at odds with the analysis presented here, but his observation still holds sway. In an analysis of Africans in pre-Columbian Europe and their relation to the construction of its civilization, the acts of ignoring Africans (ignorance) and the attempts at their erasure from the historical and cultural records are both historiographic and episte-mological. William Leo Hansberry interpreted this as histories of denial (Hansberry 1960: 376–7). The resulting histories and historiographies, and the epistemologies that constitute their foundations, are racialized. These are the racialized epistemologies that Houston Steward Chamberlain argued were responsible for the histories of modern times by those solely capable of constructing them: Europeans – Western Europeans – those of Anglo-Teutonic stock; in particular, Anglo-Saxons.

> Scarcely any one will doubt . . . that the inhabitants of Northern Europe have become the makers of the world's history. (Chamberlain [1914] 1993: 49)

These were histories, as Cecil Rhodes would inform us, of and by the "best race the world could offer." Extrapolating from George Frederickson's seminal work on the foundations of race, racialized thought, and racism in the United States, the "best race" – the "whitest of the white" – was fundamentally a phenomenon institutionalized in the late eighteenth through mid-nineteenth centuries, whose focus became the "purity" of Western Civilization. It appears that Europeans were very much in lock-step with this conceptualization (Frederickson 1971; Bernal 1987). Of course, Du Bois was pointed in his 1939 recollection of racialized histories and the bodies of knowledge that informed them. Du Bois acknowledged Africa, its study, and its relation to the construction of a modern world dominated by Europe and its descendants by referencing one of its earliest and most iconographic states:

> One must remember that Egyptology, starting in 1821, grew up during the African slave trade, the Sugar Empire and Cotton Kingdom. Few scholars during the period dared to associate the Negro race with humanity, much less civilization. (Du Bois [1939] 1975: 25)

Historical constructions – histories themselves – pose problems for the "purists" in that history records interaction, and that in itself precludes the kind of actual and theoretical "purity" that underlies racially constructed historiography and its his-tories. These constructions lead to the kind of commonplace assumptions that Blakely and Gerzina record: questions that are not asked because the historical agents are presumed not to exist in a certain time and space. Racialized epistemologies and historiographies, and their histories, are a hallmark of what Du Bois critiqued as the "pseudo-scientific" construction of race. Both the constructions of knowledge and history have had at their cores the implicit – sometimes explicit – notions that there are certain biologically determined, essentialized characteristics that define various human populations and determine their historical agency and the quality and dynamism of their historical interactions.

The result of this type of thinking has been modern histories of exclusivity where no populations overlap. Nowhere is this more evident than the modern histories of pre-modern Europe and their strident absenting and ignorance of the Africans in their midst. This is a point Gerzina's essay makes in its opening; it is also one of the underlying themes of Paul Gilroy's *Black Atlantic* (Du Bois 1939, 1946; Roper 1970; Gilroy 1993; Gerzina 1997: 15). However, the recognition of such biologically and racially constructed histories should not cause us to overlook the dramatic and decisive intersection of the pseudo-scientific with very real political economic concerns and structures.

Historiographically, Blakely, Gerzina, Gilroy, and others point to a need for the intellectual interrogation of the historical players they present – the "Afro-European" – in the pre-modern eras. This is not simply the interrogation of a physical presence, but a conceptual and intellectual one as well.

The "Whitest of the White": Elizabethan England

So here we might open with the question of how Africa has shaped the European conceptual landscape. From that consideration we might unearth some tangible elements that allow for the concrete historical construction of Africans in European space before the voyages of Columbus.

In the modern age, we are tentatively clear that Europe – as Chamberlain argued – is the "shaper" of history (Miller 1985; Said 1993; Mudimbe 1988, 1994; Hammond and Jablow 1992). Yet even in the face of such surety there is still the question of the degree to which Africa has shaped Europe's notions of Africa. Again the issues of ignorance and absence are central to this conceptualization. In fact, this is the dominant trope in the "knowing" of Africa – its "unknow-ability." The summaries in the historical and literary texts that make Africa known are Africa the "*terra incognita*" *cum* "the Dark Continent," – "the Heart of Darkness," for the undiscerning and uncritical reader. These very "readings" are the reason for the assumption that there were "no Africans in [Europe] before 1945."

However, discerned and critical readings of the texts that become the basis for such an assumption – the texts that precede the modern, and some that might be constituted as modern themselves – on re-reading make it an Africa as "known" as any other area of the globe for the times in question. There are a series of critiques of peoples of African descent in modern space that compel an examination of the construction of "Europe" and the "European" for the eras that precede their inquiries (Fishkin 1995; Morrison 1992; Gilroy 1993; duCille 1996). The resulting analysis is an interrogation of pre-Columbian Europe as simply "white" space, and England as the "whitest" of those white spaces. The fundamental recognition gained by such an analytical approach is seen in an inquiry into the construction of Anglo-Saxon identity and its relation to subsequent Acts of Union that would constitute the "United Kingdom." These are "racialized" cultural projects that both propelled and became the consequence of the construction of modern English identity.

The illustration is seen in the conventional assumptions that surround some of the most astute critiques of a work like Shakespeare's *Othello*. Those assumptions are dominated by the ideas that *Othello* must – in large part – be a drama about race, because its main character is assumed to be an anomaly – not only in the conceptual and geographic space of Elizabethan England, but in Europe at large. Shakespeare and Othello need to be read "backwards" from the point of inception and then forward from the historical and mythistorical foundations that buttress them and give meaning to contemporary Elizabethan audiences. This is Bloom's admonition and observation: Othello is "known." The question is how?

Shakespeare and *Othello* become important to this argument because they, along with the Elizabethan Age, become the putative and unconscious markers for the commencement of English "whiteness" and the histories of England, Europe, and the world that would proceed from such a cultural construction. This culture and its histories become a culture and histories of whiteness that are reiterated, reified, and refined by Victorian tendencies.

Yet, even before this refinement, Spenser underscored what his and Shakespeare's audiences already knew. In his political treatment of Ireland he reveals the English prototype for "Othering." It is Catholic, and then Irish. The Catholic is reiterated in *The Faerie Queene* and his transformation of the enemy of the English state – Catholic Spain – into Muslims, "Saracens," and "Moors." Spenser literally de-humanizes the enemies of the state. They become "*Sans Loie*," "*Sans Foie*," and "*Sans Joie*." However, it is here that the critical reading becomes most important. Both Shakespeare and Spenser are extremely nuanced, and their analytical treatment can been constructed in terms of a certain epistemological, historiographic, and historical complementarity that speaks to the foundations of their cultural and political economic constructions.

As Elizabethan standards, Shakespeare and Spenser are remarkable in their retention of one of the most pivotal figures of Arthuriana – an Arthur that Elizabeth's father sought to co-opt. Spenser's central figure, "Sir Courtesie," also known as "Sir Caledor," is a figure of five centuries of literary refinement prior to his resurrection and metamorphosis in Spenser, and it seems, more than a millennium of mythical and historical treatment. Spenser's Sir Courtesie/Caledor – certainly one of the possible models for Shakespeare's Othello – is part of Celtic mythic and literary production. In the prose *Romance of Tristan* he is Sir Palamedes – Rene Curtis dubs him the "black knight" (Curtis 1994: 47).

The image of Sir Palamedes, "the Saracen," as the "best knight ever" (*Curtis* 1994: 47; Malory [1485] 1994: 249) is lost neither on Shakespeare nor Spenser. A century before, what would become the most popular introduction to the Arthurian tradition emerged. Sir Thomas Malory's 1485 *Morte d'Arthur* must have had considerable impact in reinforcing the "once and future" England among both literary figures and polemicists. The "Saracen" *cum* "Moor" found its standard equivalent in the term "Negro" if the etymologies of the *Oxford English Dictionary* have any credence. The etymological evolution is logical in light of what Snowden tells us of the prevalent meaning of the Latin "*maure*" as the universalized equivalent for the term "African," writ large, at the opening of the first millennium of the Common Era (Snowden 1970: 1–33; 1983: 1–17; *Oxford English Dictionary* 1981: 1,846, 2,639).

If we measure conventional assumptions against our notions of "whiteness," Europe, and "Europeans," then the construction of England, "the English," and their interplay with the rest of Europe, becomes an epistemological lever in the interrogation of Africans in pre-Columbian Europe. Now for considerations of how we get there.

Towards Britain/England

My father was a decurion of Constantina [Cirta], my grandfather a soldier; he had served in the *comitatus* for our family is of *Moorish* origin. (Jones 1964: 53)

In many ways, some Celtic myths of British origin lend themselves to paradigms of a greater Europe and Africa's role in it. Take the founding myths of "Britain" and "Scotland." The sagas of the Trojan prince Brut and the Egyptian Princess Scotia as the mythic founders of Britain and Scotland respectively are prime examples (Geoffrey of Monmouth circa 1135–7; Nennius circa 700; Wace circa 1190; Jones 1996: viii). In the cultural space that Bloom envisions – a space juxtaposed to the modern – for pre-modern audiences, Brut and Scotia must have conjured up Aeneas and Dido. They must have conjured up Troy, Greece, and of course Africa; the Trojan War and its aftermath, and Africa again. Here are Trojans, Danaans, and Ethiopians, let alone, Scotia's Egypt and Dido's Carthage. At the very root of these Celtic origins are Africa and Europe's foundations intertwined (in Homer, *The Iliad*, trans. A. Lang, W. Leaf, and E. Meyers, New York: Modern Library, 1950: 13; Homer, *The Odyssey*, trans. W. H. D. Rouse, New York: Mentor, 1970: 11; Quintus Smyrnaeus, *The Fall of Troy*, trans. A. S. Way, London: Heinemann/New York: The Macmillan Co., 1913: 77; Vergil, *The Aeneid*, trans. P. Dickinson, New York and Scarborough, Ontario: New American Library, 1961; Pliny, *Natural History*, trans. H. Rackham, Cambridge, MA: Harvard University Press, 1958, vol. II: 321, vol. XXII: 295; Herodotus 1983: 143, 149–50, 167; Diodorus Siculus, *The Antiquities of Egypt*, trans. E. Murphy, New Brunswick, NJ: Transaction, 1989: 162–3; Du Bois 1915, 1939, 1946; Snowden 1970; Keita 1994: 149, 159; 2000a: 15–26, 41–151).

The mythic *and* historical interactions of this period are well-documented and still hotly contested. They simmer in the aftermath of Bernal's *Black Athena* and the contention of "Afro-asiatic roots" for Classical European civilization (Keita 2000a; 2000b). The mythistorical and historical collude in their depictions of Africans in "European" space. So much so, that as one moves from what might be articulated as "myth," the questions posed by the historical become that much more problematic in light of conventional historiography and epistemology.

We can try to illustrate this by attempting to dismiss two, of what have become, "controversial" sources in the debate that fuses early Eurasia and Africa: Homer and Herodotus. *The Iliad* and *The Odyssey* contain pointed references to Africa, which coincide with ancient conceptualizations of Africa's impact on the constructions of pre-Mycenaean and Mycenaean Greece, and the Eastern Mediterranean basin. Bernal opens his treatment by referring to Homer's proclivity for naming the Greeks either as "Achaeans" or "Danaans" – the latter, a most specific reference to an African origin associated with Danaus, king of Libya, brother to Aigyptos, king of Egypt. Frank Snowden had made the same observations years earlier in his analysis of Aeschylus and other Greek playwrights. In *The Suppliants*, Aeschylus provides the genealogy that underscores and grounds the cultural context out of which Homer's work emerges. *The Suppliants*, according to Snowden, is only one work in a body of ancient Greek texts that makes the same assertion of an African foundation for the formation of Mycenaean Greece (Snowden 1970, 1983; Bernal 1987; Keita 1994, 2000a).

The paradigms presented by the mythic treatment are taken up historically by Herodotus and then reiterated by those who follow him. The archetype for sound and virtuous governance and a life of heroic and even reverent proportions comes "out of Africa." Perseus, son of Danae, granddaughter of Danaus, becomes the model for the hero/king; as Herodotus puts it:

> The common Greek tradition is that the Dorian kings as far back as Perseus, the son of Danae . . . are as they stand in the accepted Greek lists and are rightly considered as of Greek nationality . . . If . . . we trace the ancestry of Danae, the daughter Acrisius, we find that the Dorian chieftains are genuine Egyptians. This is the accepted Greek version of the Spartan royal house. (Herodotus)

Snowden and Hansberry emphasize an essential point concerning this interaction. It is, in their minds, indisputably African (Hansberry 1974, 1981; Snowden 1970, 1983; Keita 2000a). They dismiss the dispute over the "African-ness" or blackness of Egypt, and therefore Africa's influence on Greece, the Eastern Mediterranean basin, and greater Europe, to favor Ethiopia as the font of it all. They begin again with Homer and march through Herodotus and his successors. What they articulate is an Africa that is the seat of everything the Greeks and, it appears through Homer, the Trojans held dear. The civilizing influence of their world is Ethiopia, and Egypt is its grandest product. The Egypt that Herodotus gloried was the result of an Ethiopian-directed renaissance three centuries earlier. Generically put, Africa is the center and source of their universe.

> Now, the Ethiopians [i.e. the black peoples], as historians relate, were the first of all men . . . they . . . were the first to be taught to honor the gods . . . in consequence their piety has been published abroad among all men . . . They say also that the Egyptians are colonists sent out by the Ethiopians [i.e., the black peoples], Osiris having been the leader of the colony. (Diodorus Siculus)

Within this context, a conceptual framework is laid. From there the historical and cultural parameters of the argument concerning a tangible African presence in Classical Europe are presented by scholars like Woodson, Du Bois, Hansberry, and Snowden.

The material evidence for these historical conclusions – Africans in Classical European space – is solidly interdisciplinary. There are literary and cultural devices. There is the iconographic and archaeological. And there is the historical, whose range moves from primary sources to their analysis and synthesis (Woodson 1936;

Hansberry 1974, 1981; Snowden; Bugner 1976). Within all this is the odd coalescence of competing historiographies. A coalescence hardly recognized among the contending parties (Lefkowits and Rogers 1996; Levine 1992; Bernal 1987; Davidson 1991; Bourgeois 1971; Mudimbe 1988, 1994; Keita 2000a, 2000b).

From Herodotus' descriptions of the "types" of Ethiopians, to the African contingents in the Persian army (Herodotus: 486; Snowden 1970: 2, 123–4), the dynamics are laid for African and European (and Asian) interaction, and an African presence in what is about to become "Europe." Possibly the most curious of the analyses for the period, however, are those that center on Carthage. After Egypt, Carthage becomes the epitome of African imperial space for the European Classical Age, rivaled only by Rome. Yet, it is hardly spoken of as such.

The work of the Picards becomes the prime example here. Among the leading experts on the construction of the Carthaginian state, their interpretation of its demographics and its socio-political organization is rigidly isolationist and racially conventional in relation to the possibilities of describing Carthage as an African state. Here, they are historical "purists" who deny the interaction that must surely have constituted Carthaginian state formation.

Indeed, the work of the Picards "turns" on itself, in their inability to explain some of the contradictions in their own writings. Take, for instance, their "analysis" of a richly appointed sarcophagus, which when opened revealed only the bones of an "aged negress." No curiosity is expressed as to how an "aged negress" might come to have such lavish accommodations in death, let alone the implication for what her entombment might say of the "racial" demographics of the Carthaginian hierarchy. For the Picards, and many who follow them, Carthage remains "Asian," one of the earliest of the "Oriental" states – it is the place and time, according to them, where *imperial* Phoenicia is retained – incorruptible. In this rendering of Carthage there is still a tendency to overlook another melding of "Afroasiatic" construction that critically and decisively impacts the construction and development of what will become Europe, from the English Channel through the Aegean Sea (Smith 1908: 19; Du Bois 1915; 1939: 6, 39; 1946: 136, 141–2; Warmington 1960: 16, 32; Picard 1961, 1969; Diop 1974: 70, 118–19, 122; Bourgeois 1971: 14–19; Snowden 1970: 2, 124–5; Mudimbe 1988, 1994; Keita 1994).

There are, conceivably, no "Africans" in this African space (Picard 1961, 1969; Keita 1994: 153–6). Forget the marriages to the princesses of this space. Forget the peasants who till its soil, who rise in revolt over imperial policy. Forget the class of "Libyphoenicians" who provide notions of ethnic mélange here and the expansion of empire. Forget the men at arms, and their great beasts who spark both the imagination and terror of their adversaries, from contention with the Greeks over Syracuse to the Roman declaration of "*Carthago delenda est.*" In convention, Carthage is simply, the "Orient" in Africa – African time and space "asianized." Time and space "asianized," and therefore, contested.

Epistemologically and historiographically, this is the Hamitic thesis that Edith Sanders so ably critiques. It is the dual attempt to separate Africa from interactions with Asia, and then to constitute the "Asian" as "white" (Sanders 1969). And, of course, the concluding statement of this thesis is that Africans had no role in the earliest constructions of European space and its civilization. In regard to Carthage, this is an argument that even an overwhelming majority of Africanists accept. They are among the vast numbers for whom 15 years of invasion and occupation of the Italian countryside and an imperial domain that included present-day Spain and Portugal seem of no consequence in the scheme of things African. For them the notion of Rome as the client state of an African empire has no resonance (Du Bois 1915, 1939, 1946; Snowden 1970; Keita 1994).

The shift in this client/patron relationship and the emergence of "Roman Africa" open another line of inquiry. In the empire and civilization that come to epitomize the European notion of itself, and whose iconographic and emulative powers are with us still, if one cannot speak of "African Rome," one can certainly find "Africanized" Rome and Romans, and Roman Africans. In fact, their presence – the presence of Romanized Africans, the Africans of the Roman Empire – becomes the segue way from the ancient to the medieval. Both Rome's political economy and its culture are affected by a long and intense contact with Africa (Beardsley 1929; Snowden 1970, 1983; Thompson 1989).

Rome's encounter with Africa seems the chief prerequisite for its ascension to empire. The activities of Carthage placed Africans on European soil in the heart of Rome's empire. Africans were a significant part of Carthaginian forces in actions against both the Greeks and the Romans. Subsequent struggles with African polities showed Rome the prowess and skill of African military personnel. Hence, the incorporation of various African states and peoples into the empire meant that Africans were placed throughout Roman institutional structures, and in particular in the military (Livy, *The War with Hannibal*, trans. A. de Selincourt, Harmonsworth, Middx: Penguin, 1965; Sallust, *The Jugurthine War*, trans. S. A. Handforth, Harmondsworth, Middx: Penguin, 1967; Snowden 1970: 125, 131; Keita 1994: 32–42). With the Roman occupation of Britain there followed at least three centuries of what Roy Blount would call "Africo-Celtic" interaction of the most intense and intimate kind.

Here, we return to the paradigm that opened this segment: the attempt to argue that Anglo-Saxon hegemony, and from that the notions of Europe and what it means to be "European" historically, are racially constituted. It is a paradigm that compels us to try to make sense of the declaration made to Gerzina: "Madam, there were no black people in England before 1945." Consider the nature of the Roman Empire. In spite of the grandeur of Rome itself and its major cities, the empire was a garrison state. The "garrison" mandated a certain interaction that fundamentally characterized the nature of the military in the expansion and maintenance of the state.

Again, the question of Britain *cum* England. The conditions of Roman military service mandated interactions. After the invasion of Britain in 43 CE, the length of service in the Roman army was regularized. Military personnel were awarded citizenship and the right to marry after 25 years of service. The rights of citizenship were extended to male children who were expected to seek military careers as well; in fact, these children were privileged over others in terms of their access into military service and the possibilities of their upward mobility in the military ranks and imperial Roman society in general.

However, it was quite clear that prior to the further liberalization of these policies in the second century, soldiers had taken wives among the indigenous populations of the provinces and had established families and households without the sanction of Roman law. Soldiers had done this *de facto* because of the length of service prior to its standardization. Roman authorities recognized and sanctioned the settlement of military populations because they were key to the security of Roman frontiers. In fact, G. R. Watson has argued that the lifting of the ban on intermarriage in 197 CE "encouraged the growth of considerable communities" on Rome's frontiers (Cheesman [1914] 1975: 31–4; Watson 1969: 14, 140, 153; 160; Holder 1982: 53).

Watson goes on to state that it was the occupation of Britain which necessitated such changes in Roman military service, in particular, the length of service. These changes, along with the relatively high number of troops quartered in Britain, had important demographic implications (Watson 1969: 14). The strength of Roman occupation in Britain by the second century has been placed at between 42,000 and 47,000 troops. These would include three regular legions and a contingent of roughly 25,000 to 30,000 *auxilii* (Cheesman [1914] 1975: 52; Collingwood 1923: 21). Cheesman offers the possibility that by the second century Roman auxiliary strength was approximately 280,000 men, of which there were 21 African regiments with 44 provincial postings. Of these 21, Mauretania alone provided two regiments which totaled 15,000 men. Extrapolating from these figures, it can be speculated that Africans made up 10–25 percent of Rome's military auxiliary forces at any given time of the Empire (Cheesman [1914] 1975: 52–6; Collingwood 1923: 21).

The weight of all this becomes apparent when it is coupled with Collingwood's observations on the demography of the Roman empire in general, and Britain in particular. Collingwood argues that Rome gave the Briton and Britain a "spiritual" and "physical" "kinship with everyone from the Tyne to the Euphrates and from the Sahara to the Rhine." He goes on to state that "The British frontier was garrisoned by all kinds . . . even Orientals . . . men who took wives and lived in villages outside the fort." For these people, our contemporary "barriers of colour and race and language . . . were absolutely unknown in the Roman world" (Collingwood 1923: 13–16, 20–1).

The cultural and physical interaction that defined the Roman world, and a cosmo-politan Roman identity, rested in large part on the Roman military and its *auxilii.* "Maures" ("Moors"), "Numidians," "Ethiopians," "Blemmyes," "Troglodytes," "Egyptians," "Libyans," "Nobadae," "Africans," and so on, served Roman interests in Britain for three centuries or more (Jones 1964: 611; Edwards 1990: 2). Africans served in every possible capacity from auxiliary infantrymen to commissioned naval and cavalry officers. It is the cavalry that commands our attention here. It opens the door to the culture that would create and support an iconographic chivalric notion, which pervades the historical imaginations of medieval and Renaissance England and Europe to this day. This is the "space" in which Arthur and his knights were created. As Webster puts it, "medium and heavy cavalry . . . were a very important arm of the late [Roman] Army . . . it could almost be said that here was to be found the precursor of the medieval knight" (Webster 1998: 152–3).

According to Cheesman, the military of the late imperial period offered unpre-cedented opportunities for social advancement. Promotion from the ranks to com-missioned officer was high among the "attractions of the profession" (Cheesman 1914: 45; Holder 1982: 52). The cavalry seemed to hold more possibilities: "this is another reason for the popularity of the cavalry and the desire of cohorts to become *equitata.*"

For Africans, *per se*, it is speculated that the rise of Septimus Severus accelerated their recruitment and admission into imperial service:

> Africa in particular sent praefecti from its many flourishing towns to almost every frontier during the latter half of the second century, and the accession of the African Septimius Severus at its close possibly gave his fellow countrymen specially favored position in the succeeding period. (Cheesman 1914: 70, 86–96; cf. Collingwood 1923: 13; Webster 1998: 89)

For Britain, the possibilities for Africans are witnessed in the broadest sense in the service of auxiliary units, two of which included the Moorish *numerus* stationed at Burgh by Sands, and a Thracian cohort raised in Africa, which also served in Britain (Webster 1998: 150; Edwards 1990: 2). The rise of the knightly class – the *equites* – continued with the establishment of the *Equites Singulares Imperatoris*. These were modeled on and recruited from auxiliary cavalry units. As an elite corps, their functions evolved from serving as the personal escort of prefects into "part of the imperial guard." Extrapolation from first-century tombstones indicates that at least 5 percent of the *Equites Singulares Imperatoris* were of African descent (Cheesman 1914: 41, 80–1).

By the third century, there was a significant "change in social standing for commanders of auxiliary units" who were apparently drawn from their own ranks (Cheesman 1914: 24; Holder 1982: 64). Men of substance and authority appear, and here the case for the "African knight" – the "Black Knight" – in European space can be made. This is certainly one of the implications that can be drawn from the remarks of young, Moorish Victor quoted in the epigraph that opens this section (Jones 1964: 53). His declaration recognizes and emphasizes the African presence in late Roman imperial service at the very beginning of the medieval period. It articulates African integration and ascension in Roman society, specifically in the military, and particularly the provinces. They, too, were constructing Europe.

Victor is emphatic in his defense: his grandfather, a Moor, was a member of the *comitatus*. The *comitatus* was a highly "mobile force" dating at least from the time of Diocletian. In many ways the historical presence of the *comitatus* represents one stage in the evolution and refinement of the Roman cavalry. Again, as Jones indicates, "cavalry regiments styled *Comites* ranked high in the field armies of the *Notitia*." And again, the "African" – the "Moor" – is seen as an integral element of the cavalry unit – "presumably the *Equites Mauri* of the *Notitia* were well known as belonging to the *comitatus*" (Jones 1964: 52–3).

It is clear from the names of military units, from the documentation concerning their personnel and activities, from the civil records, from the chronicles of where soldiers served, lived their remaining lives, and were laid to rest, that the "Moor" as a type was well known. The Moor was simply part of the broader physical type that the ancients termed "Ethiopian" (Snowden 1970: 11–14, 143). As Rome dealt with various allies as "federations," a policy which provided some level of autonomy and decentralization and yet maintained the necessary levels of recruitment, we are told that under the Emperor Justinian federation troops included the "Moors from the Sahara" (Jones 1964: 611–63; Keppie 1984: 78, 186–7).

Interestingly enough, within the context of the Empire, these Africans were assumed to be more cosmopolitan and culturally sophisticated than the Briton. One could imagine that among the upwardly mobile of the British ruling class these dark men were a welcome addition and augmentation to early medieval British life because of their culture, their status, and the trappings of power. As Collingwood noted, "the civilization of Britain, high as it was, did not attain the same height as that of Gaul or Spain or Africa" (Collingwood 1923: 87). Yet, these various Africans came to Britain replete with cultural retentions, which were not totally Roman. Many were, as Watson puts it, "less romanized," keeping many of their "native styles . . . weapons . . . [and] tongues" (Watson 1969: 16). It is not difficult to imagine Sir Palamedes and the other "Saracens"/"Moors" of the Round Table sporting their locks in the "twists" or "dreds" that were "their characteristic African hairstyle" as depicted on Trajan's Column (Webster 1998: 143).

Medieval Space: Arthur and His Africans – European Icons

[T]he black knight had already done wonders. (Curtis (trans.) *Romance of Tristan*: 47)

"Ah!" exclaimed Tristan, "he's the best knight I ever encountered." (Curtis (trans.) *Romance of Tristan*: 116)

[A]ll manner of knights were adread of Sir Palomides and many called him the knight with the black shield. (Malory 1485: 249)

With the decline of Empire, "Afro-Romano-Britons" must have emerged in significant numbers – numbers significant enough to be seen as members of communities, which imparted cultural legacies that became embedded in British lore. Their interaction, intermarriage, and building of communities are witnessed in their incorporation into British life, and in their very deaths (Edwards 1990: 2).

The British Roman experience offers numerous illustrations and opportunities that contribute to our understanding of how identities are crafted. The reality presented here is that there were Africans of rank and bearing who seized the imaginations and inspired their fellow countrymen in the land of their adoption. Medieval British chroniclers, in structuring a "usable past," relied on all the inventions of the classical age – including the Roman Empire – to satisfy their project. In their reliance they understood, in much the same way that Bloom postulated, the nuances of classical history, literature, and mythology. In fact, the uses of "mythistory" within this context must carry with them an implicit understanding that eludes most modern critiques.

Geoffrey of Monmouth begins a much criticized section of his *History of the Kings of Britain* by referring to Britain's mythical founder, Brute, as a Trojan prince who flees Troy in the company of Aeneas. The implications here are simply too rich in terms of marking what Morrison would call the "africanist" structures. We ask the following questions: Did Geoffrey know that the princes of Troy were related to one Memnon, Prince of Ethiopia? Would he know that Dido, queen of Carthage, princess of Tyre and daughter of Belus – sometimes reputed king of both Tyre and

Egypt – was also the mythological sister of Aegyptos and Danaus, kings of Egypt and Libya respectively? (Tripp 1974: 21–4, 135, 200–1, 371). Geoffrey obviously had reasons for having Brute and his crew ply the coast of Africa and ravage Mauretania, though they may be lost to some of us. There is even a cryptic reference to the "Barclenses" who were "banished out of Spain" to Ireland (Geoffrey of Monmouth 1848: 131–2). Is this the famous noble Carthaginian house whose African retinue left its mark on Rome as well? Is Geoffrey dating a Carthaginian/African presence in the British Isles as early as the close of the Second Punic War?

By the same token, why is a chronicler of fifth-century Britain so taken with Africa? There are numerous allusions to Africa. One in particular clearly indicates how Geoffrey defines the "Moor"/"Saracen" of his time. Geoffrey writes that the rise of Arthur will strike fear into the "Moor"/"Saracen": "The Arab and the African shall be adread of him, for even into furthest Spain shall sweep the swiftness of his career" (Geoffrey of Monmouth 1848: 143). By his allusion to Spain, Geoffrey has indicated the Arab and African characteristics of the Moors; though, like many who follow him, his reference is implicitly one to Islam, an Islam that does not exist for a fifth-century Arthur.

Arthur's quest for empire is met with the resistance of empire. The Roman force arrayed against him in Europe includes the "Kings of the Orient": "Mustensar, King of the Africans; . . . Sertorius of Libya; . . . Pandrasus, King of Egypt" (Geoffrey of Monmouth 1848: 210, 225–6). Geoffrey has set the stage for the literary treatments that follow him, yet even in his mythic elements there is some historical truth.

The most mysterious passage of Geoffrey's is long after Arthur's demise and the subsequent disarray which wracks Britain. Britain is ruled by Careticus,

> hateful unto God and unto the Britons. The Saxons having had experience with his shiftiness, went unto Gormund, King of the Africans, in Ireland, wherein, adventuring thither with a vast fleet, he had conquered the folk of the country. Thereupon, by the treachery of the Saxons, he sailed across with a hundred and sixty thousand Africans into Britain . . . with his countless thousands of Africans, the more part thereof which was called England did he make over unto the Saxons through whose treachery he had come into the land. (Geoffrey of Monmouth 1848: 240–1)

Several pages later, Geoffrey has the Prince Edwin seek out the future king Cadwallo. In their exchange, Edwin laments the fate of Britain from Arthur's betrayal by Modred to those

> belying their fealty unto King Careticus they brought in upon him Gormund, King of the Africans, by whose invasion hath the country been reft from the people and the King himself driven forth with shame. (Geoffrey of Monmouth 1848: 247)

Geoffrey not only utilized mythistory in the construction of his "desired past," he also made crucial portions of that dependent on what Morrison has termed the "shadow of the African." What is clear about Geoffrey's exposition is that his work is an attempt to establish a British cultural identity and with that a national identity and history. And within the framework of his Arthuriana the African is there (Geoffrey of Monmouth, ed. Giles 1848: xii; Summers 1987: 20).

So, no incredible leap of historical or literary faith is necessary in making the presumption that Sir Palamedes et al. were intimately known to the popular sources which contributed to the original forms of Arthuriana. It was from those forms that Malory, Spenser, and subsequent Arthurists drew their inspiration and material. As Collingwood put it, closing his work *Roman Britain*, "the Arthurian legend may, like the 'departure of the Romans,' be taken to stand as fact." So too, might our Sir Palamedes (Collingwood 1923: 99).

If Celtic folklore and the early attempts at the construction of British history provide any guidance, then the popular case for the Saracen, Moor, or *blamanna* may give some credence to how such figures might emerge within the context of medieval Britain and not damage the works' credibility with medieval audiences. An example of this is seen in Paul Edwards' work. Edwards lists a number of historical incidents and folkloric and literary instances, posited in the popular culture of the age.

Citing material from the ninth through the thirteenth centuries, Edwards provides evidence of engagements with Africans and the various other peoples who came to settle the British Isles. His sources for the ninth-century Scandinavian settlements in Dublin and Orkney speak of the presence of black captives taken from raids in Moorish Spain and North Africa. It seems that the frequency of these raids was such that it precipitated an ambassadorial exchange from one of the Moorish states to the Danish court. There is also some confirmation of this in Arabic sources as well. And while the assertion that "blue men were 'long in Erin'" has yet to be substantiated, their presence is acknowledged in some Irish folklore. Edwards concludes that "no doubt like the Roman soldiers, 'the blue men' were assimilated into the local population" (Edwards 1990: 2–5). Edwards, in a reading of a thirteenth-century saga of twelfth-century daring, inadvertently supports the Saracen/Moor association. The text he cites states that

the people of the *dromond* being Saracens [O. Icelandic *Saraceni*], whom we call the infidels of Mohammed, among them being a good many black men [O. Icelandic, *mart blamanna*, literally "blue men"], who put up strong resistance . . . (Edwards 1990: 4–5; cf. Africanus 1600; Jones 1964: 22; Debrunner 1979: 22)

One of Edwards' most interesting examples is a warning not to take British names, and the crests that honor them, literally. Yet, Edwards' historical treatment of "McLelland of Bombie" in 1460 is enticingly close to Malory's lines on Tristan's father, Sir Boudwin's defeat of a Saracen invasion of Cornwall. Is Malory making art of history? (Malory 1485: 415; Edwards 1990: 8). To pose this question of Malory by way of Edwards is to interrogate the entire body of work that might be called Arthuriana and its interpretations, from their inception to the present. Such an interrogation leads to a recognition of racialized epistemologies and historiographies and the purposes they serve. Taking this, and the African presence in pre-Columbian Europe into the modern age, we might reference Sir Walter Scott.

Scott's work encompasses several genres and serves an assortment of political purposes. Scott informs his public that he is an historian turned novelist – the inventor of the historical novel – and a preserver of Scottish folklore. Scott was also loyal to the English Crown, a covert champion of the Act[s] of Union, and a key architect in the construction of English identity. Proud of his credentials as an historian – many of his novels were footnoted and carried extended rationales concerning the choices of characters and context – Scott sought to meld twelfth-century Anglo-Norman hegemony with a pre-existent, yet conquered, Saxon nobility.

The scope and depth of Scott's impact on the development of the historical novel has been termed one of the most profound "intellectual developments of the last two hundred years" and the initiator of a " 'modern historical' consciousness." However, that is not the subject of this chapter (Shaw 1983: 9). What is most important here is his use of the African as an historical actor in his literary and cultural production about medieval England and in the construction of English identity. And here, he goes to lengths to justify the African presence in what have become seminal works: *Ivanhoe* and *The Talisman*.

P. J. C. Field contends that Malory's work presented itself as history; Scott's admirers emphasize that Scott was an historian. While opinions of Scott's historical skills varied, some have argued that history was Scott's "ultimate concern" (Shaw 1983: 11; Lascelles 1980: 1; Anderson 1981: 1–2). In any case, Scott regarded himself as an historian and commented openly on historiography and methodology (Anderson 1981: 8). Mary Lascelles alludes to Scott's work as "fresh historical activity" within the context of Sir Richard Southern's 1972 inaugural address as President of the Royal Historical Society. This was praise for historical activity that "was not confined to historians" but was the product of "non-historians" too (Lascelles 1980: x). Scott, from this rationale, emerges as the first in a long line of "popular historians." Why mention that here? Because it is within the context of such historical production that the African gains recognition and carries weight and has presence in the world of pre-Columbian Europe. Yet, it is an historical weight and presence that has been fundamentally ignored and unexamined in the conventional epistemologies and historiographies of the modern world. The analyses of Scott's novels as history reflect a certain "convenience" and, within that, inquiry into Africans in medieval England has been historically inconvenient.

Scott's construction of English identity is tied to the emergence of a horse-culture in Europe – chivalry – which he attaches, historically, to Rome. For Scott, the essence of chivalric order was found in the rise of the mounted warrior within the Roman military: the "*Domitor equi*... a character of superior gallantry." His source for this is none other than Tacitus (Scott [1834] 1972: 3, 6, 24; Debrunner 1979: 29–30). What is interesting about Scott's use of Tacitus is that a more analytical reading of his works and their implications might have revealed at least a direction which would have made Roman horsemen less ubiquitously "white" than Scott and his nineteenth- and twentieth-century audiences wished. Then again, the possibilities of such a realization by way of Tacitus et al. may, in fact, be the exact reason that so many nineteenth-century scholars chose the Germanic *cum* Aryan root for chivalric pretensions.

Yet, not even the Teutonic pedigree could emerge unblemished in the Age of Chivalry. In the story of Parzival, knight of Arthur's Round Table, we learn that his father, the king, Gamuret falls in love with the African Queen, Belacane. Belacane bears a child for Gamuret whose name is Feirefez Anschevin (of Anjou, the House of Plantagenet). Feirefez is known by his coloration: he is striped "like a magpie," black and white. Parzival and Feirefez meet, unknown to one another that they are brothers. They battle and being unable to overcome the other, they reveal their identities and recognize each other as brothers. Feirefez becomes king of many African lands, meets King Arthur, and sees the Holy Grail. He then marries Repanse, the lady of the Grail and to them is born "Johan – later known as Prester John." In his elevation of the Teutonic horseman over all others in his construction of chivalry, Scott does make an off-hand reference to the "Moor." In a chivalric tradition instigated by northern Europeans (the very image that Houston Stewart Chamberlain reprises), Scott tells us that "even the Moors of Spain caught the emulation, and had their orders of knighthood as well as the Christians" (Scott 1834: 107).

However, there are certainly those who disagree with Scott on this account. W. A. Clouton, writing in 1887, argued that

> it is certain . . . that European chivalry owed much to the Arabs; and that many scenes and incidents from "Antar" and other Arabian romances were appropriated by early Spanish authors of similar works, which they had derived from their Moorish conquerors; and we may fairly consider "Antar" as the prototype of European romances of chivalry. (quoted in Mitchell 1987: 32)

An interesting aside to all this is that the "Antar" in question, the famous poet-warrior, was of African descent.

The issue here, from Geoffrey of Monmouth and Nennius through Malory and then on to Shakespeare and Spenser, and the historical literary production of those like Scott, is that the African presence is almost ubiquitous. The question that might have been posed at some earlier juncture would have questioned its material historical validity. In many ways, that recedes into an historical horizon. What is witnessed here, even if one is skeptical of the material data, is the way in which the image and concept of the African become critical features in medieval and Renaissance Europe's construction of itself.

And, it needs to be reiterated here, this is an analysis of Africans in pre-Columbian Europe. Britain *cum* England is simply a metaphor. Even late imperial/imperialist works such as Scott's, still reference Europe – a Europe where the African is iconographic.

Islamic Africans in Europe: Redux

We need to be reminded. When the historical Arthur emerged at the close of the Roman Empire in the fifth century, neither he nor his compatriots knew of Islam or Muslims. They simply did not exist. However, it seems safe to speculate that Arthur and the other Romano-British lords who surrounded him were quite aware of, had done battle with, and were quite possibly allied to men whom they would call variously "Saracen," "Moor," "Arab," and even "African." There is an historical and conceptual relation that becomes conflated here in which fifth-century "Saracens," "Moors," "Arabs," and "Africans" become Muslims. There is the assumption that they had *always* been. Yet just as intriguing are the ambiguities of their existence in Europe in an age dominated by Islam.

By the eighth century there is such a thing as Islamic Europe and the Islamic Mediterranean. It is this Islamic world that becomes a driving force in the construction of the modern European identity. It still maintains the cultural sophistication and superiority that were attributed to the "Orient" at the close of the Empire, as Collingwood has written. This is the power displayed in a work like Geoffrey of Monmouth's and the assumptions it places on its audiences in light of who and what twelfth-century Africans were. This is certainly borne out and reiterated in the texts and the iconography that precede and then supersede Geoffrey right through Shakespeare and Spenser. And alongside power is opulence.

The medievalists Robert Lopez and Irving W. Raymond, in a very important source book, *Medieval Trade in the Mediterranean World*, provide hundreds of fascinating documents, which uncover issues of trade and politics, public- and private-sector relationships, and the friendships and intimacies of trading partners, that cross cultural and religious boundaries. They also comment, almost inadvertently, on the development and evolution of cultures and cities during the period. They write that by the tenth century CE, in Islamicized space, the city surpassed anything that Europeans might have imagined. As they put it, Islamic culture and economy, represented by its urban centers, was a "full cycle" ahead of its European counterparts. Possibly, we need to be reminded that Africa had been, and increasingly was being, incorporated into this space (Lopez and Raymond 1955: 51, 53, 71; Lopez 1971: 24). Of course, Africans were present at Islam's inception (al-Jahiz 1969: 198; Ali 2003: 24) and critical to its expansion. Through the close of the Renaissance, the economies of Western Europe were dependent on African gold. All this, we should understand, by way of the *Notitia*, Geoffrey, and Lopez and Raymond, deeply affected European imagination and reality.

Again, if we interrogate the literature and the iconography of the period, the African presence is there. Historically, it is rejuvenated and underscored in the northern Mediterranean through the cultural and political economic construction of al-Andalus. In the account of the twelfth-century Almoravid ruler Ali b. Yusuf b. Tashfin, the *Al-Hulal* indicates that his pedigree was in part Sudani as was the army with which he invaded al-Andalus. Norman Daniel's analysis of *chansons de geste* also illustrates this point for us. By looking at the tenth through the fifteenth centuries and commenting on the etymological evolution of the Latin term *maurus* to the French *more*, he provides the correct sequencing. It is his time-frame that is too short. He has missed the *longue durée*:

> extending use of the word *maurus, more* in French, suggests a widespread realisation of invasion from North Africa; the *chansons* speak of "Africa" rather than of Moors, and this seems to mean Tunisia rather than Morocco. (*Al-Hulal al-mawshiyya fi dikhr al-akhbar al Marrakushiyya* [c.1300] 1981: 310–14, quoted in Daniel 1984: 14)

The irony of this pronouncement is that the reference to "Africa" could be to both Morocco and Tunisia *and* to the African Sudan as well.

The thirteenth-century recollection of the eighth-century encounter at Roncesvalles, recounted in *Chanson de Roland*, is also instructive as to what might be said of African lords and the men who followed them. There were the "beautiful" Africans, of whom Malquaint was one, and then there were the "ugly" ones – the hordes who win the day. The mythistoric and literary proportions extend themselves through some of the most famous authors of medieval *chansons* and romances. Both Chaucer and Chretien de Troyes have their African allusions, and a significant element of the genre that contextualizes them is much more pointed. Here, in an Islamic space in which Africans are foregrounded and impressive, four texts illustrate the literary and historical resonance of the African in pre-Columbian Europe. They also pose the historiographic questions: why have *these* authors chosen to include *these* figures – both men and women; and why have their audiences responded to them with a warmth and an intimacy that defy conventional modern analyses? The prose *Romance of Tristan* and the epoch-ending *Morte d'Arthur* have already been cited. Their central African character, Sir Palamedes, has been identified as Muslim – a fact that greatly concerns Tristan. Around Palamedes is a retinue of Africans whose religious affiliations fluctuate, and in their fluctuation they put to rest the questions of the African as Christian and Muslim, *and* Moor/Saracen, before the Columbian era. A fourteenth-century entreaty from Rome to "the dear black Christians of Nubia and the other countries of Upper Egypt" reinforces this African existence; this, along with Axumite emissaries, whose presence at Vatican councils was warranted as indispensable (Debrunner 1979: 24).

Between the "bookends" of the prose *Tristan* and *Morte d'Arthur* are the German *Parzival* and the Dutch Arthurian variant *Morien*. Both provide a rich representation of a Europe populated by Africans who are both Muslim *and* Christian, *and* beautifully and self-assuredly black (von Eschenbach [c.1300] 1991; *Morien* [c.1300] 1901). They are the entrée to the sense of Spenser's Sir Courtesie/Caledor against an anti-Islamic subterfuge that services the very real and growing anti-Catholicism of its age. They suggest that the historical, literary, and iconographic depictions of Africans in this pre-Columbian space are far more complex and nuanced than the notion that they "did not exist."

African iconography for medieval and Renaissance Europe is simply too extensive to do analytical justice within the scope of this chapter. However, from Magdeburg to Brinsop, we should be astounded by the existence of Africans in graphic and plastic productions, our ignorance of the meanings of it, and our reluctance to interrogate that ignorance:

> As it happens, there is an unnoticed English footnote . . . in Brinsop you will find a superb East Window in which the stained glass of the Middles Ages has wonderfully outlived the assaults of time. And in the center of this thirteenth-century Brinsop splendor you will see the portrait figure of a knight in armour. About that, in itself, there is nothing to be surprised – except that the face of the knight is . . . black. (Davidson 1987: 13–14; cf. Debrunner 1979; Mark 1988)

Closing the Circle: Modern Slavery and the Racialization of the European Past

I should be indulged one last time in referencing Du Bois. However, he phrases the historiographic conundrum so succinctly. What is the relation between modern, racialized slavery and a modern historiography of pre-Columbian Europe? The relationship is exactly as Du Bois put it, and as Davidson would later reinforce: given cotton, sugar, and tobacco, who would dare "to associate the Negro race with humanity, much less civilization" (Du Bois 1946: 25). The racialization of the European past can be conceived of as the "moral justification – the necessary justification – for doing to black people what the church and state no longer thought it permissible to do to white people" (Davidson 1991: 3).

Even here, however, the records of an African presence and impact are ambiguous: ambiguous in terms of our interpretation of them, or the lack thereof. In many ways, we can understand and accept the ways in which the institutions of modern, racialized slavery attempted to expunge them; yet, what has greater resonance is the way in which Africans in Europe keep reoccurring to haunt us historically. To haunt us at the very moment they are to be historically exorcised. This might be calculated as the very moment in 1599 that Elizabeth issues her edict expelling all "blackamoors and Negars" from London and the political events that framed it and their cultural repercussions (Jones 1971: 13). Think of this as both backdrop and "black-drop" for the cultural, literary, and propagandistic productions that close this century – productions that define "England," English identity, and the right to empire.

Still, within it all is huge ambiguity. The ambiguity of heroes: Sir Courtesie/ Caledor (Sir Palamedes by any other name) and Othello; and the ambiguity of the presence of Africans in common pursuits from the Renaissance through the Enlightenment, some of them slaves – and former slaves – whose presence has only been conventionally interpreted. Their representations are iconographic and literary, polemic and historical. Their presence is as textural and tangible, as ubiquitous and mundane, as the carpets on the floors, the tapestries at the windows, or the salt-cellars on the tables of great halls in European manors (Mark 1988; Bassani and Fagg 1988).

Look at the late fifteenth-century masterpieces of Carpaccio, query the works of Rembrandt or Velázquez (Honour 1989); or take in Hogarth's raucous eighteenth-century London street scenes (Hogarth c.1800). Reference Jan Capitein (Debrunner 1979: 78, 80–2) or ask of the most celebrated of the number – Equiano – how one moves from slave to slaveholder, to abolitionist and all with the appearance of landed gentry replete with English wife and the genuine credentials of a European literatus?

Here, a digression on Equiano is necessary. If we refer to the Gretchen Gerzina epigraph that frames the opening of this piece, the importance of a figure like Equiano is magnified to the extent of altering the most immediate histories, historiographies, and epistemologies of the modern era. Here, in the eighteenth century, Equiano explodes all of the assumptions regarding the African presence in Europe from its westernmost to easternmost reaches. He speaks not only to an African presence, but also to issues of African mobility, not only across and throughout Europe, but globally as well. We can speculate that the presence and mobility of the Equianos of this era are the inspiration for historiographic and post-modernist interpretations like those of Gilroy (1993) and Bolster (1997). This, in fact, is an implication of Debrunner's work. Blakely has replicated it in her *Russia and the Negro* (1986) and in *Blacks in the Dutch World* (1993).

That Equiano has "associates" in this space also belies the notion of the singular and "exceptional black." Equiano is exceptional, and he is black; but in neither is he singular. He is not the only black to occupy this place. He shared ideas and space with the likes of Ottobah Cugoano and Ignatio Sanchez. Theirs was a path earlier trod, if only for a short period, by Phillis Wheatley, among others (Hill 1998: 93,

116–19). The ensuing discourses on slavery, its abolition, and the personal and concrete manifestations of black intellectuality, underscore the dynamic linkages of a far-flung, yet focused African diaspora – well before 1945.

In considering African numbers in Europe during the period of the transatlantic slave trade, we also need to keep in mind the role of Africans in the quests of individual European states for empire, and their subsequent repatriations. "Repatriations" because many of them ended up not only in Africa in newly created states, but in Europe as well, as subjects of the nations they had served. Equiano's service in the Seven Years' War is a testimony to this.

Finally, Equiano becomes illustrative of African presence *and* impact on Europe and a larger world. That *The Interesting Narrative* should be "one of the eighteenth century's best works" is a real distinction, yet it, too, is not a singular one within the context of African intellectual production and social and political economic protest for the period. As importantly, the works of Equiano and his colleagues mark the emergence of African critiques of "whiteness" and Europe. These critiques are sometimes rendered obliquely, yet in many instances they are overwhelmingly incisive. And, as the editors of *Call and Response* note, these works carry "significant implications for people of African descent even at the end of the twentieth century" (Hill 1998: 119).

* * *

The lives of Equiano and his counterparts emphasize the degree to which the era of racialized slavery is conditioned by the dictates of Africa upon Europe. Without regard for the nature of the new slavery, it was trade with Africa that mattered most. That trade, in human cargo or not, meant a series of sustained relationships between Africa, Europe, and the new European dominions that would present peoples of African descent as an altogether different anomaly when juxtaposed with conventional racialized analysis. In the era of racialized slavery, *free* black women and men walked the streets of Europe and its dependencies. Black women and men struggled against the institution of modern racialized slavery in Europe and its dominions. And Europeans and Euro-Americans, on continents north and south, still vied among themselves for the favors of Africans well after the close of the transatlantic slave trade.

Portuguese terminology of the late fifteenth and early sixteenth centuries epitomized the presence and impact of Africans on European consciousness and space at this time: *signares* – "the ladies." The Ladies' roles were extensive in the construction of this new Atlantic world. Their African influences extended from the Senegal River in the north to Sierra Leone in the south. Their European political economic, cultural, and linguistic sway encompassed Portuguese, French, English, and even later, American drives for commercial hegemony in West Africa. Their daughters and sons would be pursued by the most influential houses of Marseilles and Bordeaux – and New Orleans. The Ladies, it might be argued, were the chief architects of French colonial policy in West Africa, the African women who held the life-blood of European empire – particularly that of the French – in their "elegant hands." (Brooks 2003; Charles 1977; Crowder 1972; Cruise O'Brien 1972; Marcroft 1995: 14–15, 24, 27–8; Hall 1992)

This power takes full form in the primary sources of the period. Mungo Park both records and alludes to the powers of these women within the Senegambian context (Park [1799] 1954: 19). The Abbé Boilat, a son of *signares*; a product of French education; a high aspirant of the French Catholic church in both Senegambia and France – a Francophile, in some regards – provides an extremely intimate and insightful view of the powers of these women and their impact on the fortunes of French empire (Boilat 1984: 40; Debrunner 1979: 185–6). However, it is the notes, diaries, and letters of the Comte and Comtesse de Bouffleur – he being the last royal governor of the tenuous French claims in Senegambia and she being the object of much gossip at the court of Louis XVI (Debrunner 1979: 99–100).

From the gossip and letters of pre-Revolutionary France emerges one of the most intriguing and poignant stories of the African presence in Europe, and the modern constructions of racial and gendered identity. *Ourika* by Claire de Duras (1823) is the fictive account of a young, African child brought to France by the Comte de Bouffleurs, and raised in an aristocratic French household.

Without laying out the narrative, the implications of *Ourika* are voluminous. Based on a real person, the novel is the first piece of French literature to present an African woman as its protagonist. It goes to great lengths to justify not only her presence, but the actions of those who surround her – French aristocracy – and their relation to modern slavery, the constructions of race, and their own humanity. It also establishes a trope – *the* trope – that seems existentially and historically imposs-ible; the trope of Gerzina's clerk: that Ourika is the only black person in France.

Ourika herself becomes a trope: the initiation of stereotype whose uses register the impact of the African presence in Europe on European conceptualization. Ourika, the slave child rescued – purchased – by the Comte de Bouffleur, raised as French aristocracy, only to become – through Duras' novel – the symbol of a newly racialized world. Again, like Othello in Venice, and Equiano in London, we are led to believe that she is the only black in France. Again, if only for the immediate period in question, Debrunner informs us that Bouffleur – though resistant to the slave trade – had taken up the vocation of collecting *des souvenirs vivants* for French aristocrats. Among these living curios were a number of Senegambian children (Debrunner 1979).

The lives of the Abbé Boilat and, by implication, the members of his convocation – a growing *métisse* consanguinity – give lie to this idea that there were no Africans in Europe: as must have the considerable number of sons – and probably daughters – of Haitian, and other French Caribbean descent (Duras [1823] 1994; Boilat 1984). This is also the implication of the men who represented the *quatre communes* of Senegal through the early twentieth century. Many of them were, from roughly 1848 on, Africans of *métisse* background, who, I would argue, were committed to their mothers' vision of Senegal rather than that of their fathers (Crowder 1972: 2–11, 21–3, 32; Cruise O'Brien 1972: 33). They become icons.

Again, the presence and impact of African women is an historical "re-visitation" of their presence and impact in France – Europe – centuries earlier. Debrunner relates the story of Salam Cassais, the daughter of a noble family of Songhai – possibly Senegambian – who married the "noble Toulousian trader," Anselme d'Ysaguier. On their return to France the couple brought with them Cassais' personal attendant, "Aben Ali, . . . a skilled physician who healed in 1419 the French Crown Prince Charles" (Debrunner 1979: 23). These are presences that are recorded. They also have a rich iconographic representation. That representation deserves the implicative analysis that works like those of David Summers and Stuart Hall underscore (Summers 1987; Honour 1989; Hall 1992).

The historical possibilities – all recognized within Jewsiewicki's notion of a "speculative philosophy of history" – are seen in Simi Bedford's precocious, 6-year-old protagonist. Remi sits on her grandfather's knee, and the sharp, insistent – and what must seem to the grandfather – incessant inquiry begins. Grandfather reveals that it was his grandfather who was a slave who fought for the British during the American Revolution. With that there is the rejuvenation of an African Britain that is hardly entertained. If *Yoruba Girl Dancing* is too fictive, too imaginative, we need only be reminded of Lord Dunsmore and his 1775 appeal (Bedford 1994). From that, there is the re-dispersion of Africans throughout the northern regions of North America, Britain, and finally to Africa itself. Equiano was solicited to aid in their repatriation. And many, like Equiano, chose to remain in England.

* * *

The dynamics of the "Columbian Age" and the construction of a new Atlantic World and its new European polities were firmly grounded in an African presence. The immediacy of that presence has been the defining factor of the modern age. The irony is that the "foundations" of such a presence have hardly been examined, and in that light their insights remain obscured. The America and the Europe that we have come to know are part of the constitution of a *new* Atlantic World whose earliest incarnation was its pre-Columbian link.

That link, in the very least, underwrote the economies of Western Europe and provided it with its symbols of piety, heroism, decorum, and wealth. In the modern age, that wealth and its symbols were physically manifested in black bodies; black bodies whose only assumed proportions were slavery and subservience. Slavery and subservience became the conceptual and symbolic representation of the African in the conventional mind.

Beyond symbolism, however, was the actual African physical presence in which symbol was embodied. That the "meaning" of symbol might change is neither strange nor inconsequential. However, what might be considered "strange" for scholars in the late modern or postmodern is our reluctance and/or inability to analyze and measure that change; to view it in relation to what the sources indicate existed before our times; to contemplate how *that* existence has shaped who and what we are; and then to employ such an analysis as the impetus to speculate on who we might become – a contemplation on the possibilities of "our better selves."

Africa is no vast island.

BIBLIOGRAPHY

Works Cited

Africanus, Leo (1969 [1600]) *A Geographical Historie of Africa*. Amsterdam: Theatrum Orbis Terrarum; New York: Da Capo Press.

Ali, Tariq (2003) *The Clash of Fundamentalisms: Crusades, Jihads and Modernity*. London and New York: Verso.

Anderson, James (1981) *Sir Walter Scott and History, with Other Papers*. Edinburgh: Edinburgh University Press.

Bassani, Ezio and Fagg, William B. (eds.) (1988) *Africa and Renaissance Art in Ivory*. New York: Center for African Art and Prestl-Verlag.

Beardsley, Grace H. ([1929] 1967) *The Negro in Greek and Roman Civilization*. [Baltimore and London] New York: Russell and Russell.

Bedford, Simi (1994) *Yoruba Girl Dancing*. New York: Penguin.

Bernal, Martin (1987) *Black Athena: The Afroasiatic Roots of Classical Civilization*, vol. I. New Brunswick, NJ: Rutgers University Press.

Blakely, Allison (1986) *Russia and the Negro: Blacks in Russian History and Thought*. Washington, DC: Howard University Press.

—— (1993) *Blacks in the Dutch World: the Evolution of Racial Imagery in a Modern Society*. Bloomington: Indiana University Press.

—— (1997) "Problems in studying the role of blacks in Europe," *Perspectives*, 35, 5 (May/June).

Bloom, Allan (1987) *The Closing of the American Mind*. New York: Simon & Schuster.

Blyden, Edward Wilmot ([1880] 1887) *Christianity, Islam and the Negro*. London: W. B. Whittingham.

Boilat, Abbé David (1984) *Equisses Senegalaises*. Paris: Karthala.

Bolster, Jeffrey W. (1997) *African American Seamen in the Age of Sail*. Cambridge, MA: Harvard University Press.

Bourgeois, Alain (1971) *La Grèce antique devant la négritude*. Paris: Présence Africain.

Brooks, George E. (2003) *Eurafricans in Western Africa: Commerce, Social Status, Gender, and Religious Observance from the Sixteenth to the Eighteenth Century*. Athens: Ohio University Press.

Bugner, Ladislas, general ed. (1976) *The Image of the Black in Western Art, Volume I*. Houston: The Menil Foundation, distributed by Harvard University Press.

Chamberlain, Houston Stewart ([1914] 1993) in F. and C. Carrier (eds.), *Ideas that Shaped the West and the Modern World*. Dubuque, IA: Kendall/Hunt.

Charles, Eunice (1977) *Precolonial Senegal: The Jolof Kingdom 1800 to 1890*, African Research Studies, XII. Boston: African Studies Center.

Cheesman, G. L. ([1914] 1975) *The Auxilia of the Roman Imperial Army*. Chicago: Ares.

Collingwood, Robin (1923) *Roman Britain*. London: Oxford University Press.

Crowder, Michael (1972) *Senegal: A Study of French Assimilation Policy*. London: Methuen.

Cruise O'Brien, Rita (1972) *White Society in Black Africa: the French of Senegal*. Evanston, OH: Northwestern University Press.

Curtis, R. L. (trans.) (1994) *The Romance of Tristan*. Oxford and New York: Oxford University Press.

Daniel, Norman (1984) *Heroes and Saracens: An Interpretation of Chansons de Geste*. Edinburgh: Edinburgh University Press.

Davidson, Basil (1987) "The Ancient world and Africa: whose roots?" *Race and Class* 29 (2).

—— (ed.) (1991) *African Civilization Revisited*. Trenton, NJ: Africa World Press.

Debrunner, Hans (1979) *Power and Prestige: Africans in Europe*. Basel: Basler Afrika Bibliographien.

Diop, Cheikh Anta (1974) *The African Origin of Civilization: Myth or Reality* [selections from *Antériorité des civilisations nègres*]. New York: L. Hill.

Du Bois, William Edward Burghardt ([1915] 1970) *The Negro*. London and New York: Oxford University Press.

—— ([1939] 1975) *Black Folk Then and Now*. Millwood, NY: Kraus-Thomson.

—— ([1946] 1965) *The World and Africa*, revd and enlarged edn. New York: International Publishers.

duCille, Ann (1996) *Skin Trade*. Cambridge, MA: Harvard University Press.

Duras, Claire de ([1823] 1994) *Ourika*. New York: Modern Language Association of America.

Edwards, Paul (1990) "The early African presence in the British Isles," occasional papers. Edinburgh: Centre for African Studies, Edinburgh University.

Eschenbach, Wolfram von ([c.1300] 1991) *Parzival*, Andre Lefevere (ed.). New York: Continuum.

Fishkin, Shelley Fisher (1995) "Interrogating 'whiteness,' complicating 'blackness': remapping American culture," *American Quarterly*, 47, 3 (September).

Frederickson, George M. (1971) *The Black Image in the White Mind: The Debate on Afro-American Character and Destiny, 1817–1914*. Middletown, CT: Wesleyan University Press.

Geoffrey of Monmouth (1848) *Historia Regum Britannie*, in J. A. Giles (ed.), *Six Old English Chronicles*. London: H. G. Bohn.

Gerzina, Gretchen Holbrook (1995) *Black London: Life before Emancipation*. New Brunswick, NJ: Rutgers University Press.

—— (1997) "The black presence in British cultural history," *Perspectives*, 35, 5 (May/June).

—— (2003) *Black Victorians/Black Victoriana*. New Brunswick, NJ: Rutgers University Press.

Gilroy, Paul (1993) *The Black Atlantic: Modernity and Double Consciousness*. Cambridge, MA: Harvard University Press.

Hall, Gwendolyn Midlo (1992) *Africans in Colonial Louisiana: The Development of Afro-Creole Culture in the Eighteenth Century*. Baton Rouge: Louisiana State University Press.

Hammond, Dorothy and Jablow, Alta (1992) *The Africa that Never Was: Four Centuries of British Writing about Africa*. New York: Waveland Press.

Hansberry, William Leo (1960) "Ancient Kush, Old Aethiopia and the Balad *[sic]* es Sudan," *Journal of Human Relations* 8.

—— (1974) *Pillars in Ethiopian History: The William Leo Hansberry Notebook, Vol. 1*, Joseph E. Harris (ed.). Washington, DC: Howard University Press.

—— (1981) *Africa and Africans as Seen by Classical Writers: The William Leo Hansberry Notebook, Vol. 2*, Joseph E. Harris (ed.). Washington, DC: Howard University Press.

Herodotus ([1910] 1983) *The Histories*, trans. G. Rawlinson. London: Dent.

Hill, Patricia Liggins, general ed. (1998) *Call and Response*. Boston and New York: Houghton Mifflin.

Hogarth, William (n.d.) *Works of Hogarth with Sixty-eight Engravings*. New York: Hurst.

—— (c.1800) *Works of Hogarth with Sixty-two Illustrations*. London: J. Dicks.

Holder, P. A. (1982) *The Roman Army in Britain*. New York: St. Martin's Press.

Honour, Hugh (1989) *The Image of the Black in Western Art*. Cambridge, MA: Harvard University Press.

al-Jahiz (1969) "The superiority of blacks to whites" in *The Life and Works of Jahiz*, Charles Pella (ed.). Berkeley: University of California Press.

Jobson, Richard ([1623] 1968) *The Golden Trade*. Amsterdam: Da Capo Press.

Jones, A. H. M. (1964) *The Later Roman Empire*. Oxford: Basil Blackwell.

Jones, Eldred (1971) *Othello's Countrymen: The African in English Renaissance Drama*. Charlottesville: Folger Shakespeare Library, University of Virginia Press.

—— (1996) *Othello's Countrymen*. London: Oxford University Press.

Keita, Maghan (1990) "Scholarship as a global commodity: intellectual communities in Renaissance and Medieval Africa," *Proceedings of the PMR Conference*, Summer.

—— (1993) "Deconstruction and reconstruction: Africa and Medieval and Renaissance history," *Medieval Feminist Newsletter*, 16, Fall.

—— (1994) "Deconstructing the classical age: Africa and the unity of the Mediterranean world," *Journal of Negro History*, 74, 2 (Spring).

—— (2000a) *Race and the Writing of History: Riddling the Sphinx*. Oxford and New York: Oxford University Press.

—— (2000b) "The politics of criticism: *Not Out of Africa* and *Black Athena Revisited*," Review Essay, *Journal of World History* II, 2.

—— (2002) "Africa and the construction of a grand narrative in world history" in E. Fuchs and B. Stuchtey (eds.), *Across Cultural Borders: Historiography in Global Perspective*. Lanham, MD, Boulder, CO, New York and Oxford: Rowman & Littlefield.

Keppie, Lawrence (1984) *The Making of the Roman Army: From Republic to Empire*. London: B. T. Batsford.

Lascelles, Mary (1980) *The Storyteller Retrieves the Past: Historical Fiction and Fictitious History in the Art of Scott, Stevenson, Kipling and Others*. Oxford: Clarendon Press.

Lefkowits, Mary R. and Rogers, Guy Maclean (1996) *Black Athena Revisited*. Chapel Hill: University of North Carolina Press.

Levine, Molly (1992) "The use and abuse of *Black Athena*," *American Historical Review*, 97, 2 (April).

Lopez, Robert (1971) *The Commercial Revolution in the Middle Ages*. Englewood Cliffs, NJ: Prentice-Hall.

Lopez, Roberto and Raymond, Irving W. (1955) *Medieval Trade in the Mediterranean World*. London: Oxford University Press.

Malory, Thomas ([1485] 1994) *Morte d'Arthur*. New York: Random House.

Marcroft, Andrew Douglas (1995) "The signares of Senegambia," unpublished master's thesis, Villanova University.

Mark, Peter (1988) "European perceptions of black Africans in the Renaissance" in E. Bassani and W. B. Fagg (eds.), *Africa and Renaissance Art in Ivory*. New York: Center for African Art/Prestel-Verlag.

Miller, Christopher L. (1985) *Blank Darkness: Africanist Discourse in French*. Chicago and London: University of Chicago Press.

Morien ([c.1300] 1901) *Morien: Arthurian Romance unrepresented in Malory's "Morte d'Arthur"*, no. IV, Jessie L. Weston (trans.). Bournemouth, Hants: Nutt.

Morrison, Toni (1992) *Playing in the Dark: Whiteness and the Literary Imagination*. Cambridge, MA: Harvard University Press.

Mudimbe, V. Y. (1988) *The Invention of Africa*. Bloomington: University of Indiana Press; London: James Curry.

—— (1994) *The Idea of Africa*. Bloomington: University of Indiana Press; London: James Curry.

Nennius (1848) *Historia Britonum*, in J. A. Giles (ed.), *Six Old English Chronicles*. London: H. G. Bohn.

Park, Mungo ([1799] 1954) *Travels into the Interior of Africa*. London: Eland Books.

Picard, Gilbert Charles- (1961) *Daily Life in Carthage*, A. E. Foster (trans.). New York: Macmillan.

—— (1969) *Life and Death in Carthage*, D. Collon (trans.). New York: Taplinger.

Roper, Hugh Trevor- (1970) *The Rise of Christian Europe*. London: Thames & Hudson.

Said, Edward (1993) *Culture and Imperialism*. New York: Knopf.

Sanders, Edith (1969) "The Hamitic hypothesis: its origins and functions in time perspective," *Journal of African History* X (5).

Scott, Walter ([1834] 1972) *Essays on Chivalry, Romance and Drama*. Freeport, NY: Books for Libraries Press.

Shaw, Harry (1983) *The Forms of Historical Fiction: Walter Scott and His Successors*. Ithaca, NY and London: Cornell University Press.

Smith, Reginald Bosworth (1908) *Carthage and the Carthaginians.* New York: Longmans, Green.

Snowden, Frank M. (1970) *Blacks in Antiquity: Ethiopians in the Greco-Roman Experience.* Cambridge, MA: Belknap Press of Harvard University Press.

—— (1983) *Before Color Prejudice: The Ancient View of Blacks.* Cambridge, MA: Harvard University Press.

Summers, David (1987) "The development of King Arthur as a cultural icon from early British tradition to *The Faerie Queene*," unpublished doctoral dissertation. Spokane: University of Washington.

Thompson, Lloyd A. (1989) *Romans and Blacks.* Norman: University of Oklahoma Press.

Tripp, Edwin (1974) *The Meridian Handbook of Classical Mythology.* New York: New American Library.

Wace (1996) *Roman de Brut,* in Eugene Mason, trans., *Arthurian Chronicles.* Toronto: University of Toronto Press.

Warmington, Brian Herbert (1960) *Carthage.* London: Robert Hale.

Watson, G. R. (1969) *The Roman Soldier.* Ithaca, NY: Cornell University Press.

Webster, Graham (1998) *The Roman Imperial Army of the First and Second Centuries AD.* Norman: University of Oklahoma Press.

Woodson, Carter G. ([1936] 1968) *The African Background Outlined.* Washington, DC: Association for the Study of Negro Life and History; reprint, New York: Negro Universities Press.

CHAPTER THREE

The African and European Slave Trades

WALTER C. RUCKER

The dynamic set of processes by which millions of Africans were captured, sold, and transported to Western Hemisphere plantation societies was one of the most tragic chapters in human history. The opening-up of Atlantic World commerce, spearheaded by the Portuguese in the early fifteenth century, spawned a set of sizable migrations – both voluntary and forced – from the Old World to the Americas. Most of this movement was centered in West and West-central Africa, which accounted for roughly 75 percent of all transoceanic migration before the American Revolution. Ironically, less is known about the details of this massive movement of people than the much smaller migration of Europeans. Even so, this trade in black flesh and the rise of racialized slavery throughout the Americas has been keenly studied by historians for the past few decades (Eltis 2000; Mann 2001).

An impressive array of research centers, academic journals, professional organizations and university press book series have developed in the field of Atlantic World slavery, greatly enhancing scholarly understandings of this subject. Endeavors such as the Nigerian Hinterland Project based at York University – which focuses on enslaved African exports from the Bights of Biafra and Benin – have sought to trace the various "Diasporas" which originated in the Niger River Delta as a result of the transoceanic and trans-Saharan slave trades. Project organizers Paul Lovejoy, Robin Law, David Trotman, and Elisée Soumonni hope to trace a variety of slave routes, which included such destinations as North Africa, Arabia, and the Americas, greatly expanding prior understandings of the scale and extent of the African Diaspora. In addition, two projects sponsored by UNESCO – the Slave Trade Archives Project and the Slave Route Project – will help bring to light additional sources and further details regarding the African role in the creation of the Atlantic World (Mann 2001; Heywood 2002).

In recent years, the most impressive work on the slave trade has been performed by scholars at the W. E. B. Du Bois Institute for Afro-American Research at Harvard University. Named after a true pioneer in the field, this institute sponsored a project that sought to provide more reliable estimates on the volume and nature of the Atlantic slave trade. Co-edited by David Eltis, Stephen Behrendt, David Richardson, and Herbert Klein, this meticulous effort has produced the most thorough and reliable dataset, cataloguing approximately 70 percent of all Atlantic slave voyages. The resulting CD-ROM has breathed greatly needed new life into this important topic. Not only do scholars have a good idea about the volume of the slave trade, but now the Du Bois Institute CD-ROM allows for precise estimates of mortality rates and gender ratios on slave ships, the ethnic origins of enslaved Africans, the regional patterns of the trade in Africa and the Americas, and the frequency and results of shipboard revolts. What is clear is that, for decades to come, this dataset will continue to be the key basis for a steady stream of scholarly assessments and reassessments of the slave trade (Gates 2001; Davis and Forbes 2001; Eltis, Behrendt, Richardson, and Klein 1999; Eltis and Richardson 1997).

The historiography of the field begins with the pioneering 1896 PhD dissertation, "The suppression of the African slave trade to the United States, 1638–1870" by W. E. B. Du Bois. Appearing as the first volume in the Harvard Historical Studies book series, this work became one of the first serious inquiries into the nature, structure, and scope of the Atlantic slave trade and the various attempts to abolish this form of commerce. The publication of Carter G. Woodson's *Journal of Negro History* two decades later further advanced the field. As practically the only outlet for scholarship pertaining to the black experience in the western hemisphere, this journal – under Woodson's editorship until 1950 – provided an active platform for works by scholars researching the various dimensions of the African Diaspora (Heywood 2002; Wesley 1965; Goggin 1983). Between 1917 and 1956, for example, the *Journal of Negro History* published eight articles on various aspects of the Atlantic slave trade and, almost single-handedly, kept alive interest in the topic for decades (Dowd 1917; Adams 1925; Riddell 1927; Wesley 1942; Williams 1942; Nelson 1942; Merrill 1945; Staudenraus 1956). More recently, journals like *Slavery and Abolition*, the *William and Mary Quarterly*, and *Contours* have continued the tradition established by the *Journal of Negro History* in advancing understandings of the trade in enslaved Africans.

Since perhaps the early 1960s, a decisive shift in scholarly views regarding Africa's place in both the Atlantic world and the Atlantic slave trade occurred. Moving away from the Eurocentric interpretation, which contended that Europeans were the principal source of dynamism in Atlantic commerce, individuals such as Basil Davidson (1961), James Duffy (1962), and Walter Rodney (1974) began to construct a revisionist model to reorient scholarly attention. They recognized that African contacts with Europeans were generally negative experiences and concluded that the Atlantic trade was unequal, unbalanced, and detrimental to Atlantic African societies. For some, especially Walter Rodney (1974), these factors serve as the precursor to the export syndrome that Africa continues to suffer from in contemporary times. This argument is standard fare for modern dependency theorists; essentially it is that the demands of the world capitalist economy, rather than internal and local factors, which determined change within Atlantic Africa (Cardoso and Faletto 1979 [1971]). In making these types of claims, the revisionists join the Eurocentric school in emphasizing European actions and processes in the formation of the Atlantic World.

The first comprehensive revisionist study of the Atlantic slave trade was Basil Davidson's *Black Mother* (1961), re-issued a year later in paperback as *The African Slave Trade: Precolonial History, 1450–1850*. Davidson – primarily known for his work on ancient to early modern African history – sought to answer three vital questions in this important study: "What kind of contact was [there between] Europe and America? How did the experience affect Africa? Why did it end in colonial invasion and conquest?" (Davidson (1980 [1961]: xi) His important work concludes that Europeans arrived at the Atlantic coast of Africa after the fifteenth century and encountered a series of powerful African kingdoms and states more than willing to engage in mutually beneficial commercial enterprises. Initially, this trade was characterized by commercial agreements between willing and equal partners. Over time, however, this relationship shifted in favor of European interests: "Europe dominated the connection, shaped and promoted the slave trade, and continually turned it to European advantage and to African loss" (Davidson (1980 [1961]: 24). In his estimation, this shift in the balance of power led to the removal of 15 million Africans to the Americas (not including the estimated 35 million that died during the trade) and the decline in economic and political power of Atlantic African polities, and it opened the door for European imperial domination three centuries after the Atlantic slave trade began (Curtin 1969; Davidson 1980 [1961]).

In 1969, Philip Curtin offered a corrective to some of the assertions made by Davidson and others. Curtin's *The Atlantic Slave Trade: A Census* was a landmark study on many levels. Drawing upon mostly published sources, this work offered the first reliable estimates of the volume of the slave trade (11.8 million exported from Africa and 9.4 million imported into the Americas), mortality figures (roughly 2.4 million died during the Middle Passage), places of embarkation and disembarkation, as well as provenance zones and the ethnic composition of the overall trade. Though Curtin's work represented an important watershed, he was followed – almost immediately – by dozens of economic historians, demographers, and other cliometricians who sought to tease out more details regarding the scope and scale of the slave trade (Curtin 1969; Heywood 2002; Eltis and Richardson 1997). The resulting works, according to Linda Heywood (2002: 4–5) "stressed the economic organization of the trade, investment patterns and profitability, slave demography, mortality, and the economic impact of the trade in Africa, Europe, and the Americas."

The demography of the slave trade became the primary concern of scholars studying the topic during the 1970s and 1980s (Heywood 2002; Curtin 1975; Klein 1978; Inikori and Engerman 1981; Lovejoy 1982; Lovejoy 1983; Henige 1986; Miller 1988; Richardson 1989). Of course, the crowning achievement in the field was the collaborative work, beginning in 1992, which sought the creation of a definitive dataset for the Atlantic slave trade. As the culmination of close to a decade of laborious research, the Du Bois Institute CD-ROM will be entering its second edition by early 2005 and will include as many as 80 percent of all slave trading voyages. This database offers adjustments to Curtin's estimates for the volume of the slave trade (11 million exported from Africa and 9.5 million imported into the Americas), mortality figures (about 1.5 million died during the Middle Passage), as well as reliable estimates regarding places of embarkation and disembarkation (Eltis and Richardson 1997; Solow 2001; Eltis 2000; Eltis, Behrendt, Richardson, and Klein 1999).

The various research endeavors regarding the Atlantic slave trade have not come without significant areas of controversy. In some ways, one of the sources of the modern dispute about the nature and composition of the slave trade comes from a work of historical fiction published a generation ago – Alex Haley's *Roots* (1976) and the 1977 television mini-series based on the book. In perhaps the most dramatic scene in the television version, protagonist Kunta Kinte – an adolescent from the Gambian town of Jufferee – is captured in 1767 by a group of African mercenaries led by a European factor. Later, this adventurous factor sells Kinte and a number of others to the reluctant captain of the slave ship *Lord Ligonier* (Haley 2002 [1977]). For millions of Americans, this sequence of visual images became their first and only entrée into the historical details of the Atlantic slave trade. Between 80 and 100 million people in the US watched each of the hour-long episodes of the television mini-series. Approximately 85 percent of all television homes saw all or part of the mini-series, which explains why it was such a shaping influence on non-academic perceptions on the slave trade and slavery.

In part because the *Roots* mini-series received so much popular acclaim, a number of myths and misconceptions regarding the slave trade became ubiquitous in the US. In *Roots*, Europeans were depicted as the prime movers, the principal agents and the guiding intelligence of the entire slave trading venture (Haley 2002 [1977]). For many, this only served to confirm what was reflected in the world around them – European and Euro-American nations command a disproportionate amount of power in current world affairs. As a product of more modern processes and historical phenomena, this unique power relationship is often projected back into time and has the unintended result of distorting the historical record. This notion, which is almost ubiquitous in the non-academic world, has many parallels in scholarly discourse as well. Basil Davidson (1980 [1961]) began this tradition when he asserted that Europeans eventually created an unbalanced relationship with Atlantic African polities in a process which eventually facilitated imperial domination.

Another concrete example of this tradition in the scholarly realm would be the white hands seen choking the African continent on the cover of Walter Rodney's revisionist work, *How Europe Underdeveloped Africa* (1974). Borrowing from dependency theory developed largely by Latin Americanists, Rodney (1974) concluded that the uneven relationship created between Africans and Europeans during the slave trade era was the point of origin of colonial and neo-colonial economic domination in modern times. Thus, as early as the first European contacts with Atlantic Africans in the fifteenth century, Africans were no longer actors and agents in the historical processes that affected them and Europeans would dominate them for more than four centuries.

While it is quite true that European imperial domination of the continent indeed contorted its features and disrupted its outlines, down-streaming that specifically modern reality back to the sixteenth, seventeenth, or eighteenth centuries might be to project too much European power and control back through time. The slave trade, as a number of scholars contend, was a much more dynamic process and interaction than the image of a European factor deep in the Senegambian interior – as depicted in *Roots* (1976) – would imply. Although they offered scathing critiques of Eurocentric historians and anthropologists, the revisionist school continued to view Europeans as the primary actors and agents of historical change throughout the era of the Atlantic slave trade. In essence these scholars tend to view the fifteenth century as a watershed, which marked the beginning of a long period of economic, political, and social decline in Africa. Chancellor Williams embodies this notion best by stating: "it was this very transforming external influence that played a decisive role in first destroying the best in African civilization while at the same time giving worldwide publicity to all remaining elements of barbarism that could be found" (Williams 1987 [1976]: 249).

The most recent interpretation of the slave trade, what can be rightly called the neo-revisionist school, further critiqued the Eurocentric approaches by offering a major re-orientation within the debates surrounding the slave trade and the creation of the Atlantic World. Instead of ascribing complete agency to Europeans, over the past few decades these scholars began to view Africans as actors on a number of historical stages. Africa and Africans moved from the margin to the center of analyses and, thus, new insights were reached. Neo-revisionists such as Elliott Skinner (1964), David Eltis (1989), John Thornton (1992) and George Brooks (1993) contend that Africans were a key source of dynamism, action, and change in Atlantic World commerce. Africans interacted with Europeans on an equal basis and only in the period after the 1870s, when Europeans began to engage in empire building in Africa, can one perceive a decided shift away from prior trade equality, balance, and partnership.

John Thornton provides a prime example of this neo-revisionist interpretation. African agency is at the center of his analysis and is even explicit in the title of his work, *Africa and Africans in the Making of the Atlantic World, 1400–1800* (Thornton 1998a [1992]). In this book, Thornton makes a series of interconnected conclusions: Africans participated in the Atlantic trade as equal partners; Africa was on a similar level of technological and commercial development as Europe; African production, technology, and trade can be seen as strong and productive rather than weak and subordinate; and Africans generally controlled the nature of their interactions with Europeans. Thus, Africans were the primary agents in the shaping of their reality and, he claims, "Europeans possessed no means, either economic or military, to compel African leaders to sell slaves" (Thornton 1998a [1992]: 125). This approach, however, tends to be problematic in that Thornton seemingly underplays Europe as a locus of power and may overestimate the amount of balance and equality in the trade relationship between Europeans and Africans. Like other neo-revisionists however, Thornton is challenging the conventional wisdom that Europeans were an indomitable force in the making of the early modern world.

African Slavery and Slave Trading

In the fifteenth century, Europeans – beginning with the Portuguese – engaged in trade relations with Africans along the Atlantic coast. In search of commercial opportunities and allies against the Islamic conquest of Iberia, Portuguese navigators encountered a series of kingdoms and smaller polities in West and West-central Africa. This contact with Atlantic Africans, beginning in the period after 1444, culminated in the erection of Elmina Castle by the Portuguese on the aptly named Gold Coast. Given the name the Portuguese chose for their castle and for the region they established it in, it should be no surprise that gold and gold-mining became the central elements of commercial activity for the first century after contact. Even before this historical moment, a number of economic and political forces converged to explain the eventual rise of the Atlantic slave trade. First, the Portuguese and the Spanish colonized a number of Atlantic islands, beginning in the fourteenth century. Second, sugar and sugar-cultivation techniques were rapidly spreading eastward from West Asia and Arabia. Third, since at least the twelfth century AD, the trade in enslaved West African women to serve primarily as domestic servants in North Africa and Arabia produced a lucrative stream of commerce. It was this convergence of Iberian colonization from the north, Asian sugar from the east, and African slavery from the south that allowed for the enormous trade in enslaved Africans and their transportation across the Atlantic for more than three centuries (Thornton 1998a [1992]; Duncan 1972; Klein 1986; Manning 1990; Conniff and Davis 1994; Schwartz 1985).

It is important to note, however, that though slavery existed in Africa before European contact, it could often be quite different from chattel bondage in the Americas. While it is always difficult to evaluate whether a system of slavery was "benign" or "mild," quite a few qualitative differences are evident: slaves in Atlantic Africa were often manumitted; slavery did not transcend generation, it was not an inheritable status and, thus, race or nativity were never employed as signifiers of caste; slaves could, at times, achieve high social rank, status, and wealth; and the relationships between slaves and their African owners were not always mediated by the use or threat of force. With this said, it is also quite true that a continuum of slave experiences existed in Atlantic Africa from brutal chattel slavery to relatively milder forms of clientage and debt servitude. Perhaps the most important difference between African and European/American variants of slavery was that women were the most significant group of enslaved Africans in Atlantic Africa and, in the Atlantic slave trade, men were strongly preferred by European slave buyers (Robertson 1996; Thornton 1998a [1992]; Handler 2002).

Qualitative differences between African and European/American variants of slavery were given voice in a number of ex-slave narratives. Perhaps the most written about and analyzed ex-slave memoir would be Olaudah Equiano's *Interesting Narrative* (Potkay and Burr 1995; Handler 2002). In many ways, his life opens an instructive window into the internal workings of the slave trade as well as the critiques and fears of European traders as voiced by enslaved Africans. Though Vincent Carretta (1999) has recently raised doubts about the veracity of Equiano's account, this narrative includes verifiable information and perhaps epitomizes an "authentic" Igbo account of enslavement and the Middle Passage. Kidnapped in 1756 from the Igbo village of Essaka – a minor eastern tributary of the Kingdom of Benin – Equiano was held as a slave by various African merchants for six months before finally arriving at the coast of Calabar. He apparently embarked on a ship in the Bight of Biafra with other Igbo-speakers, for it was among some of his "own nation" that young Equiano found some degree of comfort (Potkay and Burr 1995).

The "brutal cruelty" and "savage manner" of the European crew and the "intolerably loathsome" conditions on this ship confirmed his belief that he had indeed been handed over to evil spirits and demons who intended to eat his flesh. This apparently was a ubiquitous belief among captives from the Bight of Biafra who witnessed the various horrors and inhumane abuses made famous by the European traffickers of enslaved Africans. It was in this horrid context that two of his countrymen committed suicide by jumping into the ocean. Equiano himself noted an intense interest in following the path of his comrades. At least according to this particular account, the alleged Igbo propensity for suicide was directly related to the savage treatment they received at the hands of European shippers. In this particular regard then, enslaved Africans voiced their collective opposition to abuse at the hands of Europeans through the most drastic means. This perhaps solidifies the point that Africans perceived qualitative differences in their status as slaves once they were handed over to Europeans (Potkay and Burr 1995; Chambers 1997; Gomez 1998; Austen 2001; Curtin 1967).

Slavery, in its variety of forms, was widespread in Atlantic Africa primarily because enslaved Africans were the principal form of private, income-producing property throughout the region. In an area with an over-abundance of land, gaining access to – and control over – additional labor became a primary motivator for Atlantic African kingdoms and city-states. In this regard, the concept of private land owner-ship never fully developed in Atlantic Africa and, when kingdoms or city-states expanded militarily, the goal was typically to gain control over more people by capturing smaller polities or villages and forcing them to pay tribute. In sum, the Atlantic African ruling classes keenly understood the "labor theory of value," which contends that human effort is the principal means to derive value or revenue from natural resources and raw goods (Thornton 1998a [1992]; Robertson 1996; Brooks 1993; Eltis 2000). Indeed, as John Thornton notes, "Owning land in the end never amounts to more than owning dirt, and it is ownership of the product of the land that really matters" (Thornton 1998a [1992]: 75). So the thrust of military conquest in Atlantic Africa focused on acquiring additional tributaries and labor, not land.

Slavery, pawnship, clientage, indentured and debt servitude, and other forms of forced labor were means to guarantee agricultural surplus and steady flows of revenues for powerful states in Atlantic Africa (Thornton 1998a [1992]). This pri-vate ownership or control over labor does not mean that forced labor was central to Atlantic African economies, as Paul Lovejoy (1983) contends in *Transformations in Slavery*. It does mean that the idea of humans becoming commodities predated the arrival of Europeans in Atlantic Africa and set the stage for the Atlantic slave trade. The pre-existence of slavery and other forms of forced labor was augmented by a long-standing trans-Saharan slave trade, which was the first step in the formation of an Atlantic African Diaspora. The trans-Saharan slave trade, beginning sometime near the twelfth century, was utilized by the Portuguese after 1448, decades before they established castles and fortresses along the Atlantic African coast. With Euro-pean interests in acquiring slaves increasing exponentially after the establishment of colonies in the Atlantic Islands and the Western Hemisphere, the former trans-Saharan slave trade shifted from North Africa to the Atlantic coast by the late 1490s to early 1500s. Thus, the indigenous African forms of slavery and slave trading facilitated the role that Europeans would begin to play in Atlantic World affairs (Thornton 1998a [1992]).

In addition to the existence of indigenous forms of slavery and slave trading in Africa, several key factors contributed to the decisions made by Europeans to rely so heavily on enslaved African labor in the western hemisphere. Due to their exposure to a tropical disease ecology, Atlantic Africans had developed natural resistances to malaria – a disease that wiped out large numbers of Native Americans and Euro-peans. Thus, the rice swamps of the Carolinas or the tobacco fields of the Chesapeake were not as deadly for enslaved Africans, making them an ideal labor pool. Another important determinant was the fact that the vast majority of enslaved Africans came from agricultural surplus-producing societies. This meant that Atlantic Africa was densely populated and thus a prime location to use as a foundation for a substantial labor force. It also meant that, unlike the subsistence to small surplus-producing Native Americans encountered in the Caribbean, coastal Brazil or North America, enslaved Africans were more likely to be used to the intensive labor required for cash crop cultivation. This was especially true in the case of rice cultivation in the Carolinas and Georgia. In both colonies, enslaved Africans from Sierra Leone and Senegambia had a particularly useful expertise in rice cultivation, which generated enormous profits in the southern colonies. In this regard, both African brawn and brains made them an attractive group of dependent laborers for European plantations through-out the Americas (Benjamin, Hall, and Rutherford 2001; Thornton 1998a [1992]; Schwartz 1985; Wax 1973; Littlefield 1981).

Finally, because men and women tended crops in Atlantic Africa, both groups could be enslaved by Europeans, insuring a self-reproducing labor force. This cir-cumstance proved advantageous to European planters on a number of different levels. First, early attempts to enslave Algonkians in the Chesapeake had utterly failed, mainly because of the unique gender division of labor among this native group. In most Algonkian societies, women tended crops and men hunted. Thus, when British colonists attempted to enslave the men for tobacco cultivation, this enterprise was doomed to failure. While all European powers tended to concentrate on importing enslaved African men, even if they managed to bring over large numbers of enslaved women, both groups were fully equipped and socialized to engage in agricultural labor. Second, by importing men and women together, the natural outcome would be enslaved children and a new generation of labor. This was deemed advantageous over using white indentured servants, in the Chesapeake especially. Not only did the service of indentured workers terminate after a set number of years, but their children were always legally free and owed no labor obligation to their parents' master. By enslaving the womb of African women, planters throughout the Americas could guarantee a steady supply of labor that transcended generations (Benjamin, Hall, and Rutherford 2001; Thornton 1998a [1992]; Schwartz 1985; Wax 1973).

Europeans, Transoceanic Trade and the Birth of the Atlantic World

When the Portuguese first arrived on the Atlantic coast of Africa in the fifteenth century, they witnessed commerce on a scale Europeans had not seen since Roman times. West Africa, far from being the backwater many scholars have envisioned it as, was one of the key centers of trade in the early modern world. Linked to East and North Africa via the trans-Saharan trade and, as a result, indirectly connected to Arabia, India, and Indonesia, goods were flowing into Atlantic Africa that ori-ginated thousands of miles away. Ultimately, the Portuguese search for the mythical Prester John – combined with their commercial interests – led to the establish-ment of trading posts, factories, and fortresses along the West and East African coasts beginning in the early to mid-sixteenth century. By effectively replacing East African Swahili merchants in the Indian Ocean trade network, the Portuguese positioned themselves as a global power with economic interests in Africa, Arabia, India, and Indonesia (Hogendorn and Johnson 1986; Klein 1986; Thornton 1998a [1992]).

In the birth of the Atlantic World, one of the most important events that led to the Atlantic slave trade was the colonization of the numerous inhabited and uninhabited Atlantic islands by Iberians. By the 1450s, the Portuguese had colonized the previously uninhabited Azores, Madeira, the Cape Verde Islands, and São Tomé and, within a few decades, had transformed each territory into a profitable sugar plantation colony. This pattern was repeated by the Spanish in the Canary Islands with one slight difference – the Canaries were already inhabited by the Guanches. This group, of likely Native American origin, became a slave labor force throughout the Atlantic islands, and both Spain and Portugal quickly became experts in acquiring additional dependent labor. By the early 1500s, all of the Atlantic islands were utilizing a mixture of Guanche, Moor, and Atlantic African slave labor, establishing a pattern that would be replicated on a much a larger scale in the Americas (Klein 1986; Thornton 1998a [1992]; Duncan 1972).

Beginning with Christopher Columbus' 1492 expedition through the establishment of Hispaniola and Brazil as sites of Iberian colonization in the Americas, the patterns that began in the Atlantic islands became a foundation for a variety of activities engaged in by the Spanish and Portuguese. The depopulation of the Taino in the Spanish Caribbean and the Tupi-Guarani in Portuguese Brazil created a massive demand for labor in these burgeoning sugar plantation colonies. The solution to this demand for labor was offered first by Bartolomé de Las Casas, a Spanish friar who supported the mass importation of African slaves as a means to protect Native Americans living in the Caribbean and elsewhere. The flood gates were opened soon after, beginning with the massive importation of enslaved Africans into Portuguese Brazil. In the early 1570s, Portugal conquered Angola and established peaceful commercial relations with the nearby Kongo Kingdom. West-central Africa therefore would be an early source of labor for the Portuguese colony of Brazil and the rest of the Americas, accounting for about 45 percent of all enslaved Africans brought to the western hemisphere between 1519 and 1867 (Davies 1970; Thornton 1998a [1992]; Klein 1986; Heywood 2002).

Entering the fray by the late 1580s were the English, who began to establish a series of settlements in North America. The first permanent English colony, Jamestown, was founded in 1607. Though they struggled mightily for the first four years, by 1611 the colonists of Jamestown had discovered a means to create enormous profits – tobacco cultivation. After a brief and failed experiment with Native American slavery, the tobacco planters of the region began to rely heavily on white indentured servants. This solution was only a stop-gap and became completely unfeasible after 1640. Indentured servants, including the 300 Africans imported into the Chesapeake between 1619 and 1640, represented a significant set of problems to tobacco planters: they only worked a set number of years before they were freed; once freed, they received "freedom dues" including seed, land, farming tools, and guns; as land-owning tobacco farmers, ex-servants represented a source of competition for the tobacco-planting elite; and the increased production of tobacco caused by the ever increasing number of tobacco planters drove down the price of the once lucrative crop (Conniff and Davis 1994; Benjamin, Hall, and Rutherford 2001; Eltis 2000; Wood 2003 [1996]; Morgan 1975).

The problems inherent in the indentured servant system were magnified in the 1640s when, for no clear reason, a higher percentage of white servants survived their terms of indenture to accept their freedom dues. This required immediate reaction by the Tidewater elite who moved to eliminate land as a portion of the freedom dues, purchased most of the arable land, and extended the term of indenture with the hope that more servants would die before becoming free. While they successfully stunted the creation of more competition, the Tidewater planting elite also managed to destroy their most reliable source of labor. While the notion of land ownership had appealed to the English poor, compelling many thousands to come to the Chesapeake to labor in the tobacco fields, this incentive was gone and other North American colonies offered better economic opportunities and higher living standards. Beginning in 1640, a slow but decided shift towards racialized slavery occurred in the Chesapeake colonies, which culminated in the legalization of slavery by the late 1660s and the increasing importation of enslaved Africans (Eltis 2000; Wood 2003 [1996]; Morgan 1975). As Peter Wood states, this "terrible transformation" of enslavement based on race in North America "would shape the lives of all those who followed them, generation after generation" (Wood 2003 [1996]: 23).

The intense rivalry between several European powers – Spain, Portugal, the Netherlands, France, and England – convulsed both sides of the Atlantic in a series of imperial conflicts. A number of colonies changed hands in the Americas and a number of trading posts and fortresses were captured and re-captured by a long line of European interests. Between the 1590s and the 1670s, Portugal was integrated into the Spanish Crown; northern European pirates were attacking Iberian possessions throughout the Atlantic; the Dutch waged long-standing wars against the Spanish, the Portuguese, and the English; the French gained a sizable foothold in the Americas with their colonization of the western half of Santo Domingo; and the English founded several North American and Caribbean colonies in direct opposition to Spanish territorial claims. In the decade between 1637 and 1647 alone, the Dutch West India Company claimed the Portuguese possessions of Elmina, Príncipe, Angola and São Tomé through military conquest. Even though the Dutch could manage to control Angola only from 1641 to 1648, they had effectively replaced the Portuguese as the dominant European power in Africa by the mid-1640s. This complex web of inter-connections within the Atlantic World, fostered by trade, international rivalry, and war, became an essential component in the development of a number of Euro-American societies (Thornton 1998a [1992]); Davies 1970; Klein 1986; Boxer 1965).

While European nations were vying for power in the Atlantic, a number of expansionist kingdoms emerged in Atlantic Africa during the fifteenth and sixteenth centuries, which played fundamental roles in the slave trade. While the "inter-tribal" warfare model was once the dominant theory in explaining the rapid expansion of slave trading activities in Atlantic Africa, there was perhaps more conflict between European powers than between African kingdoms and city-states. Nevertheless, the very nature of military expansion and the tributary system in Atlantic Africa meant the creation of a large number of slaves for purchase by European buyers. Principally, the kingdoms of Asante, Dahomey, Benin, Kongo, Loango, and Futa Jallon

– among others – expanded significantly, creating political and social ripples that displaced hundreds of thousands of people. At the same time, European traders were importing guns and horses, which further contributed to military expansion and displacement (Thornton 1998a [1992]; Brooks 1993; Curtin 1975; Heywood 2002; Lovejoy 1983; Miller 1988; Richards 1980; Kea 1971).

At least during the early years of this trade relationship between European merchants and African traders, there existed a partnership based on equality and balance. European slave raiding undoubtedly occurred, but it was not the primary way by which enslaved Africans were acquired. Instead, Europeans typically followed African protocol and obeyed African laws, paid rent for their use of coastal slave fortresses, and even paid tribute to coastal kingdoms. In certain cases, European merchants had their goods confiscated and lost trade privileges if they violated protocols established by coastal polities (Conniff and Davis 1994; Eltis 2000; Thornton 1998a [1992]). In other cases, Europeans lost their lives in retaliation for raiding for African slaves. In this regard, as John Thornton (1998a [1992]) notes, one of the many loci of power of the slave trade resided in Atlantic Africa among African kingdoms. Thus, they played a much larger role in the creation of the Atlantic World and the formation of the Atlantic slave trade than previously understood.

One pattern that shaped African–European relations was the significant amount of resistance to the continuation of the slave trade mounted by certain Atlantic African polities and even enslaved Africans themselves. This is one level of agency that is often understated or ignored by scholars of the Atlantic slave trade. Resistance to the slave trade occurred on a number of different levels: the 400 or more instances of shipboard revolts; the thousands of suicides during the Middle Passage; the formation of escaped slave communities in Atlantic Africa; the numerous mass revolts organized by slaves or peasants; the involvement of a handful of religious opposition movements, inspired by Islam, Christianity or traditional religion; and active attempts by states – principally Djola and Balanta – or their leaders to suppress the trade. Indeed, it may even be possible to discuss the African roots of abolitionism given the fact that, as early as 1614, an Islamic scholar named Ahmad Baba al-Timbucti wrote a detailed legal treatise that critiqued and undermined the various justifications for enslavement (Austen 2001; Curtin 1967; Gomez 1998; Eltis and Richardson 1997; Thornton 1998a [1992]; Thornton 1998b; Taylor 1996; Richardson 2001; Blier 1995; McGowan 1990; Harrak 1997).

This evidence runs counter to the claim by Ralph Austen that "In contrast to European abolitionism, African moral stigmatization of the slave trade is not associated with much evidence of political opposition to such commerce during the era of its operation" (Austen 2001: 239). Africans both supported and resisted enslavement and the slave trade. They were active agents in the shaping of the Atlantic World and this should not be meant to absolve or mitigate European responsibility. The modern scholarship of the slave trade should ideally find a way to wed the moral memory of the descendants of enslaved Africans with the "objective" empirical assessments of professional historians. While precision has typically been the goal of scholars like Philip Curtin, David Eltis, and Paul Lovejoy, historians should never forget the lasting scars left by the slave trade and the emotional connection that millions of people have to this tragic event (Austen 2001).

BIBLIOGRAPHY

Works Cited

Adams, Jane Elizabeth (1925) "The abolition of the Brazilian slave trade," *Journal of Negro History* 10: 607–37.

Austen, Ralph (2001) "The slave trade as history and memory: confrontations of slaving voyage documents and communal traditions," *William and Mary Quarterly*, 3rd ser. 58: 229–51.

Benjamin, Thomas, Hall, Timothy, and Rutherford, David (eds.) (2001) *The Atlantic World in the Age of Empire*. Boston: Houghton Mifflin.

Blier, Suzanne Preston (1995) *African Vodun: Art, Psychology, and Power*. Chicago: University of Chicago Press.

Boxer, Charles R. (1965) *The Dutch Seaborne Empire, 1600–1800*. New York: Oxford University Press.

Brooks, George (1993) *Landlords and Strangers: Ecology, Society, and Trade in Western Africa, 1000–1630*. Boulder, CO: Westview Press.

Cardoso, Fernando Henrique and Faletto, Enzo ([1971] 1979) *Dependency and Development in Latin America*. Berkeley: University of California Press.

Carretta, Vincent (1999) "Olaudah Equiano or Gustavus Vassa? New light on an eighteenth-century question of identity," *Slavery and Abolition* 20: 96–105.

Chambers, Douglas (1997) "'My own nation': Igbo exiles in the Diaspora," *Slavery and Abolition* 18: 72–97.

Conniff, Michael L. and Davis, Thomas J. (1994) *Africans in the Americas: A History of the Black Diaspora*. New York: St. Martin's Press.

Curtin, Philip D. (1967) *Africa Remembered: Narratives by West Africans from the Era of the Slave Trade*. Madison: University of Wisconsin Press.

—— (1969) *The Atlantic Slave Trade: A Census*. Madison: University of Wisconsin Press.

—— (1975) *Economic Change in Pre-Colonial Africa: Senegambia in the Era of the Slave Trade*. Madison: University of Wisconsin Press.

Davidson, Basil ([1961] 1980) *The African Slave Trade: Precolonial History, 1450–1850*. Boston: Little, Brown.

Davies, K. G. (1970) *The Royal African Company*. London: Longmans Green.

Davis, David Brion and Forbes, Robert P. (2001) "Foreword," *William and Mary Quarterly* 3rd ser., 58: 7–8.

Dowd, Jerome (1917) "Slavery and the slave trade in Africa," *Journal of Negro History* 1: 1–20.

Duffy, James (1962) *Portugal in Africa*. Cambridge, MA: Harvard University Press.

Duncan, T. Bentley (1972) *Atlantic Islands: Madeira, the Azores and the Cape Verdes in Seventeenth-Century Commerce and Navigation*. Chicago: University of Chicago Press.

Eltis, David (1989) "Trade between Western African and the Atlantic world before 1870: estimates of trends in value, composition and direction," *Research in Economic History* 12: 197–239.

—— (2000) *The Rise of African Slavery in the Americas*. Cambridge: Cambridge University Press.

Eltis, David and Richardson, David (eds.) (1997) *Routes to Slavery: Direction, Ethnicity, and Mortality in the Transatlantic Slave Trade*. London: Frank Cass.

Eltis, David, Behrendt, Stephen, Richardson, David, and Klein, Herbert (eds.) (1999) *The Trans-Atlantic Slave Trade: A Database on CD-ROM*. Cambridge: Cambridge University Press.

Gates, Henry Louis (2001) "Preface," *William and Mary Quarterly* 3rd ser., 58: 3–5.

Goggin, Jacqueline (1983) "Countering white racist scholarship: Carter G. Woodson and *The Journal of Negro History*," *Journal of Negro History* 68: 355–75.

Gomez, Michael (1998) *Exchanging Our Country Marks: The Transformation of African Identities in the Colonial and Antebellum South*. Chapel Hill: University of North Carolina Press.

Haley, Alex (1976) *Roots: The Saga of an American Family*. New York: Doubleday.

—— ([1977] 2002) *Roots*. Directed by Marvin Chomsky. 570 min., Warner Studios (videocassette).

Handler, Jerome S. (2002) "Survivors of the Middle Passage: life histories of enslaved Africans in British America," *Slavery and Abolition* 23: 25–56.

Harrak, Fatima (1997) "Ahmad Baba of Timbuktu and the discourse of slavery," unpublished conference paper presented at Northwestern University, Program of African Studies: Seminar on Islamic Discourse in Africa, May.

Henige, David (1986) "Measuring the immeasurable: the Atlantic slave trade, West African population and the Pyrrhonian critic," *Journal of African History* 27: 295–313.

Heywood, Linda M. (ed.) (2002) *Central Africans and Cultural Transformations in the American Diaspora*. Cambridge: Cambridge University Press.

Hogendorn, Jan and Johnson, Marion (1986) *The Shell Money of the Slave Trade*. Cambridge: Cambridge University Press.

Inikori, Joseph and Engerman, Stanley (eds.) (1981) *Forced Migration: The Impact of the Export Slave Trade on African Societies*. London: Hutchinson.

Kea, Ray (1971) "Firearms and warfare on the Gold and Slave Coasts from the sixteenth to the nineteenth centuries," *Journal of African History* 12: 185–213.

Klein, Herbert S. (1978) *The Middle Passage: Comparative Studies in the Atlantic Slave Trade*. Princeton, NJ: Princeton University Press.

—— (1986) *African Slavery in Latin America and the Caribbean*. Oxford: Oxford University Press.

Littlefield, Daniel (1981) *Rice and Slaves: Ethnicity and the Slave Trade in Colonial South Carolina*. Baton Rouge: Louisiana State University.

Lovejoy, Paul E. (1982) "The volume of the Atlantic slave trade: a synthesis," *Journal of African History* 23: 473–501.

—— (1983) *Transformations in Slavery: A History of Slavery in Africa*. Cambridge: Cambridge University Press.

McGowan, Winston (1990) "African resistance to the Atlantic slave trade in West Africa," *Slavery and Abolition* 11: 6–29.

Mann, Kristin (2001) "Shifting paradigms in the study of the African Diaspora and of Atlantic history and culture," *Slavery and Abolition* 22: 3–21.

Manning, Patrick (1990) *Slavery and African Life: Occidental, Oriental and African Slave Trades*. Cambridge: Cambridge University Press.

Mendez, Ivan (1975) "Resistance to slavery in West Africa during the eighteenth and nineteenth centuries with specific emphasis on the Upper Guinea coast," unpublished paper presented at the School of Oriental and African Studies, Institute of Commonwealth Studies, African History Seminar, June.

Merrill, Louis Taylor (1945) "The English campaign for abolition of the slave trade," *Journal of Negro History* 30: 382–99.

Miller, Joseph C. (1988) *Way of Death: Merchant Capitalism and the Angolan Slave Trade, 1730–1830*. Madison: University of Wisconsin Press.

Morgan, Edmund S. (1975) *American Slavery, American Freedom: The Ordeal of Colonial Virginia*. New York: W. W. Norton.

Nelson, Bernard H. (1942) "The slave trade as a factor in British foreign policy, 1815–1862," *Journal of Negro History* 27: 192–209.

Potkay, Adam and Burr, Sandra (eds.) (1995) *Black Atlantic Writers of the 18th Century*. New York: St. Martin's Press.

Richards, W. A. (1980) "The import of firearms into West Africa in the eighteenth century," *Journal of African History* 21: 43–59.

Richardson, David (1989) "Slave exports from West and West-central Africa, 1700–1810: new estimates of volume and distribution," *Journal of African History* 15: 1–22.

—— (2001) "Shipboard revolts, African authority, and the Atlantic slave trade," *William and Mary Quarterly* 3rd ser., 58: 69–91.

Riddell, William Renwick (1927) "Encouragement of the slave-trade," *Journal of Negro History* 12: 22–32.

Robertson, Claire (1996) "African into the Americas? Slavery and women, the family, and the gender division of labor" in David Barry Gaspar and Darlene Clarke Hine (eds.), *More than Chattel: Black Women and Slavery in the Americas*, 3–40. Bloomington: Indiana University Press.

Rodney, Walter (1974) *How Europe Underdeveloped Africa*. Washington, DC: Howard University Press.

Schwartz, Stuart B. (1985) *Sugar Plantations in the Formation of Brazilian Society*. Cambridge: Cambridge University Press.

Skinner, Elliott (1964) "West African economic systems" in Melville Herskovits and Mitchell Harwitz (eds.), *Economic Transition in Africa*, 77–97. Evanston: Northwestern University Press.

Solow, Barbara L. (2001) "The transatlantic slave trade: a new census," *William and Mary Quarterly* 3rd ser., 58: 9–17.

Staudenraus, P. J. (1956) "Victims of the African slave trade, a document," *Journal of Negro History* 41: 148–51.

Taylor, Eric (1996) "Resistance on the deadly Atlantic: a history of slave insurrection during the Middle Passage," MA thesis, UCLA.

Thornton, John (1998a) *Africa and Africans in the Making of the Atlantic World, 1400–1800*. New York: Cambridge University Press.

—— (1998b) *The Kongolese Saint Anthony: Dona Beatriz Kimpa Vita and the Antonian Movement, 1684–1706*. New York: Cambridge University Press.

Wax, Darold (1973) "Preferences for slaves in colonial America," *Journal of Negro History* 58: 371–401.

Wesley, Charles H. (1942) "Manifests of slave shipments along the waterways, 1808–1864," *Journal of Negro History* 27: 155–74.

—— (1965) "W. E. B. Du Bois – the historian," *Journal of Negro History* 50: 147–62.

Williams, Chancellor (1987) *The Destruction of Black Civilization: Great Issues of a Race from 4500 B.C. to 2000 A.D.* Chicago: Third World Press.

Williams, Eric (1942) "The British West Indian slave trade after its abolition in 1807," *Journal of Negro History* 27: 175–91.

Wood, Peter H. ([1996] 2003) *Strange New Land: Africans in Colonial America*. New York: Oxford University Press.

Suggestions for Further Reading

Anstey, Roger T. (1975) *The Atlantic Slave Trade and British Abolition, 1760–1810*. London: Macmillan.

Austen, Ralph (1979) "The trans-Saharan slave trade: a tentative census" in Henry Gemery and Jan Hogendorn (eds.), *The Uncommon Market: Essays in the Economic History of the Transatlantic Slave Trade*. New York: Academic Press.

Austin, Allan D. (1997) *African Muslims in Antebellum America: Transatlantic Stories and Spiritual Struggles.* New York: Routledge.

Barker, Anthony J. (1978) *The African Link: British Attitudes to the Negro in the Era of the Atlantic Slave Trade, 1550–1807.* London: Frank Cass.

Barry, Boubacar (1998) *Senegambia and the Atlantic Slave Trade.* Cambridge: Cambridge University Press.

Baum, Robert M. (1999) *Shrines of the Slave Trade: Diola Religion and Society in Precolonial Senegambia.* New York: Oxford University Press.

Behrendt, Stephen D. (2001) "Markets, transaction cycles, and profits: merchant decision making in the British slave trade," *William and Mary Quarterly* 3rd ser., 58: 171–204.

Berlin, Ira (1981) "The slave trade and the development of Afro-American society in English mainland North America, 1619–1775," *Southern Studies* 20: 122–36.

—— (1998) *Many Thousands Gone: The First Two Centuries of Slavery in North America.* Cambridge, MA: Harvard University Press.

Birmingham, David (1966) *Trade and Conflict in Angola: The Mbundu and Their Neighbours under the Influence of the Portuguese, 1483–1790.* Oxford: Clarendon Press.

Boxer, Charles R. (1969) *The Portuguese Seaborne Empire, 1415–1825.* New York: Knopf.

Burnard, Trevor, and Morgan, Kenneth (2001) "The dynamics of the slave market and slave purchasing patterns in Jamaica, 1655–1788," *William and Mary Quarterly* 3rd ser., 58: 205–28.

Burnside, Madeleine and Robotham, Rosemarie (eds.) (1997) *Spirits of the Passage: The Transatlantic Slave Trade in the Seventeenth Century.* New York: Simon & Schuster.

Carretta, Vincent (ed.) (1996) *Unchained Voices: An Anthology of Black Authors in the English-Speaking World of the Eighteenth Century.* Lexington: University Press of Kentucky.

Chambers, Douglas (2001) "Ethnicity in the diaspora: the slave-trade and the creation of African 'nations' in the Americas," *Slavery and Abolition* 22: 25–39.

Coughtry, Jay (1981) *The Notorious Triangle: Rhode Island and the African Slave Trade, 1700–1807.* Philadelphia: Temple University Press.

Curtin, Philip D. and Lovejoy, Paul E. (eds.) (1986) *Africans in Bondage: Studies in Slavery and the Slave Trade.* Madison: University of Wisconsin Press.

Curtin, Philip D. and Vansina, Jan (1964) "Sources of the nineteenth century Atlantic slave trade," *Journal of African History* 5: 185–208.

Daaku, Kwame Yeboa (1970) *Trade and Politics on the Gold Coast, 1600–1720: A Study of the African Reaction to European Trade.* Oxford: Clarendon Press.

DeCorse, Christopher (1992) "Culture contact, continuity and change on the Gold Coast, A.D. 1400–1900," *African Archaeological Review* 10: 163–96.

—— (2001) *An Archaeology of Elmina: Africans and Europeans on the Gold Coast, 1400–1900.* Washington, DC: Smithsonian Institution Press.

Diouf, Sylviane (1998) *Servants of Allah: African Muslims Enslaved in the Americas.* New York: New York University Press.

Donnan, Elizabeth (1927) "The slave trade into South Carolina before the revolution," *American Historical Review* 33: 804–28.

Drescher, Seymour (1999) *From Slavery to Freedom: Comparative Studies in the Rise and Fall of Atlantic Slavery.* New York: New York University Press.

Eltis, David (1983) "Free and coerced transatlantic migrations: some comparisons," *American Historical Review* 88: 251–80.

—— (1987) *Economic Growth and the Ending of the Transatlantic Slave Trade.* New York: Oxford University Press.

—— (1990) "The volume, age/sex ratios, and African impact of the slave trade: some refinements of Paul Lovejoy's review of the literature," *Journal of African History* 31: 485–92.

—— (1993) "Europeans and the rise and fall of African slavery in the Americas: an interpretation," *American Historical Review* 98, 1399–1423.

—— (2001) "The volume and structure of the transatlantic slave trade: a reassessment," *William and Mary Quarterly* 3rd ser., 58: 17–46.

Eltis, David and Engerman, Stanley L. (1992) "Was the slave trade dominated by men?" *Journal of Interdisciplinary History* 23: 237–57.

—— (1993) "Fluctuations in sex and age ratios in the transatlantic slave trade, 1664–1864," *Journal of Economic History* 46: 308–23.

Eltis, David and Walvin, James (eds.) (1981) *The Abolition of the Atlantic Slave Trade: Origins and Effects in Europe, Africa, and the Americas.* Madison: University of Wisconsin Press.

Engerman, Stanley L., Haines, Robin, Klein, Herbert S., and Shlomowitz, Ralph (2001) "Transoceanic mortality: the slave trade in comparative perspective," *William and Mary Quarterly* 3rd ser., 58: 93–117.

Frey, Sylvia R. and Wood, Betty (1999) *From Slavery to Emancipation in the Atlantic World.* London: Frank Cass.

Geggus, David (1989) "Sex ratio, age, and ethnicity in the Atlantic slave trade: data from French shipping and plantation records," *Journal of African History* 30: 23–44.

Gray, Richard and Birmingham, David (eds.) (1970) *Pre-Colonial African Trade.* London: Oxford University Press.

Hall, Gwendolyn Midlo (1992) *Africans in Colonial Louisiana: The Development of Afro-Creole Culture in the Eighteenth Century.* Baton Rouge: Louisiana State University Press.

Harms, Robert W. (1981) *River of Wealth, River of Sorrow: The Central Zaire Basin in the Era of the Slave and Ivory Trade, 1500–1891.* New Haven, CT: Yale University Press.

Hawthorne, Walter (2001) "Nourishing a stateless society during the slave trade: the rise of Balanta paddy-rice production in Guinea-Bissau," *Journal of African History* 42: 1–24.

Higgins, W. Robert (1971) "The geographical origins of Negro slaves in colonial South Carolina," *South Atlantic Quarterly* 70: 34–47.

Hine, Darlene Clark and McLeod, Jaqueline (eds.) (1999) *Crossing Boundaries: Comparative History of Black People in Diaspora.* Bloomington: Indiana University Press.

Hogendorn, Jan (1984) "The economics of the African slave trade," *Journal of American History* 70: 854–61.

Ingersoll, Thomas (1996) "The slave trade and the ethnic diversity of Louisiana's slave community," *Louisiana History* 37: 133–61.

Inikori, Joseph E. (1992) "Export versus domestic demand: the determinants of sex ratios in the transatlantic slave trade," *Research in Economic History* 14: 117–66.

Inikori, Joseph E. and Engerman, Stanley L. (eds.) (1992) *The Atlantic Slave Trade: Effects on Economies, Societies, and Peoples in Africa, the Americas, and Europe.* Durham, NC: Duke University Press.

Janzen, John (1982) *Lemba, 1650–1930: A Drum of Affliction in Africa and the New World.* New York: Garland.

Johnson, Marion (1966) "The ounce in eighteenth-century West African trade," *Journal of African History* 7: 197–214.

Kea, Ray (1982) *Settlements, Trade, and Polities in the Seventeenth-Century Gold Coast.* Baltimore: Johns Hopkins University Press.

Klein, Herbert S. (1972) "The Portuguese slave trade from Angola in the eighteenth century," *Journal of Economic History* 33: 894–918.

—— (1975) "Slaves and shipping in eighteenth-century Virginia," *Journal of Interdisciplinary History* 5: 383–412.

—— (1999) *The Atlantic Slave Trade.* New York: Cambridge University Press.

Klein, Martin A. (2001) "The slave trade and decentralized societies," *Journal of African History* 42: 40–65.

Law, Robin (1991) *The Slave Coast of West Africa, 1550–1750: The Impact of the Atlantic Slave Trade on an African Society.* Cambridge: Cambridge University Press.

Law, Robin, and Mann, Kristin (1999) "West Africa in the Atlantic community: the case of the Slave Coast," *William and Mary Quarterly* 3rd ser., 56: 307–34.

Lewis, Bernard (1990) *Race and Slavery in the Middle East: An Historical Enquiry.* New York: Oxford University Press.

Lovejoy, Paul E. (1989) "The impact of the Atlantic slave trade on Africa: a review of the literature," *Journal of African History* 30: 365–94.

Lovejoy, Paul E. and Richardson, David (1999) "Trust, pawnship, and Atlantic history: the institutional foundations of the Old Calabar slave trade," *American Historical Review* 104: 333–55.

Lydon, James (1978) "New York and the slave trade, 1700–1774," *William and Mary Quarterly* 3rd ser., 35: 375–94.

McGowan, Winston (1990) "African resistance to the Atlantic slave trade in West Africa," *Slavery and Abolition* 11: 5–29.

Manning, Patrick (1981) "The enslavement of Africans: a demographic model," *Canadian Journal of African Studies* 15: 499–526.

Mannix, Daniel and Cowley, Malcolm (1962) *Black Cargoes: A History of the Atlantic Slave Trade, 1518–1865.* New York: Viking Press.

Martin, Phyllis (1972) *The External Trade of the Loango Coast, 1576–1870: The Effects of Changing Commercial Relations on the Vili Kingdom of Loango.* Oxford: Clarendon Press.

Meillassoux, Claude (1991) *The Anthropology of Slavery: The Womb of Iron and Gold.* Chicago: University of Chicago Press.

Menard, Russell R., and Schwartz, Stuart B. (1993) "Why African slavery? Labor force transitions in Brazil, Mexico, and the Carolina lowcountry" in Wolfgang Binder (ed.), *Slavery in the Americas*, 89–114. Würzburg: Konigshausen & Neumann.

Miers, Suzanne and Kopytoff, Igor (eds.) (1977) *Slavery in Africa: Historical and Anthropological Perspectives.* Madison: University of Wisconsin Press.

Miller, Joseph C. (1984) "Capitalism and slaving: the financial and commercial organization of the Angolan slave trade, according to the accounts of António Coelho Guerreiro (1684–1692)," *International Journal of African Historical Studies* 17: 1–56.

—— (ed.) (1999) *Slavery and Slaving in World History: A Bibliography, 1900–1996*, 2 vols. Armonk, NY: M. E. Sharpe.

Minkema, Kenneth P. (1997) "Jonathan Edwards on slavery and the slave trade," *William and Mary Quarterly* 3rd ser., 54: 823–34.

Morgan, Jennifer L. (1997) " 'Some could suckle over their shoulder': male travelers, female bodies, and the gendering of racial ideology, 1500–1770," *William and Mary Quarterly* 3rd ser., 54: 167–92.

Morgan, Philip D. (1991) "British encounters with Africans and African-Americans, circa 1600–1780" in Bernard Bailyn and Philip D. Morgan (eds.), *Strangers within the Realm: Cultural Margins of the First British Empire*, 157–219. Chapel Hill: University of North Carolina Press.

Northrup, David (1978) *Trade Without Rulers: Pre-Colonial Economic Development in South-Eastern Nigeria.* Oxford: Clarendon Press.

Nwokeji, G. Ugo (2001) "African conceptions of gender and the slave traffic," *William and Mary Quarterly* 3rd ser., 58: 47–67.

Patterson, Orlando (1969) *The Sociology of Slavery: An Analysis of the Origins, Development, and Structure of Negro Slave Society in Jamaica.* Rutherford, NJ: Farleigh Dickinson University Press.

Phillips, William D., Jr (1985) *Slavery from Roman Times to the Early Transatlantic Trade.* Minneapolis: University of Minnesota Press.

Piersen, William D. (1977) "White cannibals, black martyrs: fear, depression, and religious faith as causes of suicide among new slaves," *Journal of Negro History* 62: 147–50.

Postma, Johannes (1972) "The dimension of the Dutch slave trade from Western Africa," *Journal of African History* 13: 237–48.

—— (1990) *The Dutch in the Atlantic Slave Trade, 1600–1815.* Cambridge: Cambridge University Press.

Pritchett, Jonathan B. (2001) "Quantitative estimates of the United States interregional slave trade, 1820–1860," *Journal of Economic History* 61: 467–75.

Rawley, James (1981) *The Transatlantic Slave Trade: A History.* New York: Norton.

Richardson, David (2001) "Shipboard revolts, African authority, and the Atlantic slave trade," *William and Mary Quarterly* 3rd ser., 58: 69–92.

Roberts, Richard (1987) *Warriors, Merchants, and Slaves.* Stanford, CA: Stanford University Press.

Robertson, Claire and Klein, Martin (eds.) (1983) *Women and Slavery in Africa.* Madison: University of Wisconsin Press.

Rodney, Walter (1966) "African slavery and other forms of social oppression on the Upper Guinea Coast in the context of the Atlantic slave trade," *Journal of African History* 7: 431–43.

—— (1969a) "Gold and slaves on the Gold Coast," *Transactions of the Historical Society of Ghana* 10: 13–28.

—— (1969b) "Upper Guinea and the significance of the origins of Africans enslaved in the New World," *Journal of Negro History* 54: 327–45.

—— (1970) *A History of the Upper Guinea Coast, 1545–1800.* Oxford: Clarendon Press.

Searing, James (1993) *West African Slavery and Atlantic Commerce: The Senegal River Valley, 1700–1860.* Cambridge: Cambridge University Press.

Sheridan, Richard B. (1972) "Africa and the Caribbean in the Atlantic slave trade," *American Historical Review* 88: 19–26.

Solow, Barbara L. (ed.) (1991) *Slavery and the Rise of the Atlantic System.* New York: Cambridge University Press.

Stein, Robert (1979) *The French Slave Trade in the Eighteenth Century: An Old Regime Business.* Madison: University of Wisconsin Press.

Sundiata, Ibrahim K. (1996) *From Slaving to Neoslavery: the Bight of Biafra and Fernando Po in the Era of Abolition, 1827–1930.* Madison: University of Wisconsin Press.

Thomas, Hugh (1997) *The Slave Trade: the Story of the Atlantic Slave Trade, 1440–1870.* New York: Simon & Schuster.

Thornton, John (1980) "The slave trade in eighteenth-century Angola: effects on demographic structures," *Canadian Journal of African Studies* 14: 417–27.

—— (1998) "The African experience of the '20 and odd Negroes' arriving in Virginia in 1619," *William and Mary Quarterly* 3rd ser., 55: 421–34.

—— (1998) "The Coromantees: an African cultural group in colonial North America and the Caribbean," *Journal of Caribbean History* 32: 161–78.

Vaughan, Alden T. (1995) *Roots of American Racism: Essays on the Colonial Experience.* New York: Oxford University Press.

Walsh, Lorena S. (2001) "The Chesapeake slave trade: regional patterns, African origins, and some implications," *William and Mary Quarterly* 3rd ser., 58: 139–69.

Walvin, James (1999) *Making the Black Atlantic: Britain and the African Diaspora.* New York: Continuum International.

Wax, Darold (1978) "Black immigrants: the slave trade in colonial Maryland," *Maryland Historical Magazine* 73: 30–45.

—— (1984) "'New negroes are always in demand': the slave trade in eighteenth-century Georgia," *Georgia Historical Quarterly* 68: 193–220.

Wood, Betty and Frey, Sylvia (eds.) (1999) *From Slavery to Emancipation in the Atlantic World*. London: Frank Cass.

Wood, Peter H. (1996) *Strange New Land: African Americans, 1617–1776*. New York: Oxford University Press.

Wright, Donald (1990) *African Americans in the Colonial Era: From African Origins through the American Revolution*. Arlington Heights, IL: Harlan Davidson.

CHAPTER FOUR

Africans in the Caribbean and Latin America: The Post-Emancipation Diaspora

FREDERICK D. OPIE

Diaspora studies represent a conceptual framework borrowed from Judaism and employed in the study of other communities. Typically they share several historical characteristics: migration and geo-social displacement, social oppression, relationships of domination and subordination, resistance and struggle, and cultural and political action. Scholars using diasporic frameworks tend to argue that social and cultural change occurs as a collective, continually negotiated process between the various people and cultures involved. They maintain that change is not a product of the imposed, hegemonic influence of elites but a struggle between various interest groups. Moreover, classic diasporic studies like those by W. E. B. Du Bois (essays), C. L. R. James (*Black Jacobins*), and Eric Williams (*Capitalism and Slavery*) illustrate that common experiences and interest create social bonds that are often as important as kinship bonds. In short, diasporic studies are a methodology used to study the spread, flow, and mixture of peoples and cultures (Greene 1999: 332–3; Whitten and Torres 1998: 15; Kelley 1999; Holt 1999: 35, 41).

Many but not all the most recent historiographical contributions to Afro-Latin American studies have utilized the diasporic framework. This chapter will review some of these contributions. Specifically, the chapter will center on historiographical debates related to immigration laws, how people of African descent were viewed, and black consciousness and mobilization in Afro-Latin American diasporas. The penetration of US and European capital into Latin America in the late nineteenth century created an immense, interrelated Atlantic world in which people, cultures, institutions, and ideas traveled back and forth between different parts of the Americas. As foreign companies built their export enclaves, they increased the size of Latin America's African diaspora. They did this with the large-scale importation of black workers, largely as unskilled laborers (Gilroy 1993: 17, 19, 37; Clifford 1994: 302–38, 320, 321; Greene 1999: 329; Schoonover 1991; Petras 1988: 101).

Until recently the historiography of Latin America provided no in-depth study of Afro-Latin American communities. Like other fields of history, historians of Latin America for many years focused on powerful elite groups and ignored people of

African descent in their work. With the exception of work on Brazil, which this chapter does not address in detail, most discussions of Afro-Latin Americans in the literature done before the 1980s have generally been in one way or another "directly related to slavery or its end." Magnus Mörner argued that historians of Latin America "seem to lose all interest" in Afro-Latin Americans "as soon as abolition is accomplished" (Wright 1990: 2–4; Wright 1974: 331–2; Fontaine 1994: 191; Mörner 1970: 214–15).

For example, historian Winthorp Wright argues that since the 1860s national historians in Venezuela have generally overlooked the presence of Afro-Venezuelans as a separate ethnic group. When they did start discussing Afro-Latin Americans in their work they did so in the context of colonial slavery, soldiers in the wars of independence, or marginal contributors to colonial society (Wright 1990: 2–4; Wright 1974: 331–2). Similarly, Aviva Chomsky has argued that orthodox Costa Rican historiography "has virtually ignored the presence of blacks in the country, perpetuating the myth of Costa Rican racial homogeneity and social peace." Ronald N. Harpelle, who also worked on Costa Rica, came to similar conclusions. He holds that the "real Costa Rica," in his words, "is much larger and more diverse than is evident in the current historiography. Regional and ethnic differences are treated as anomalies, when they should be the starting point of any discussion of Costa Rican's development." He adds, "The desire to perpetuate the perception of a homogenous identity among Costa Ricans also explains why Limón [an Atlantic coast province and a center of the African diaspora] continues to be one of the poorest provinces in the country despite extensive agricultural development and why people of African descent continue to be discriminated against because of the colour of their skin" (Chomsky 1996: 147–8; Harpelle 2001: 189–90). Until the 1980s, anthropologists and sociologists shaped our knowledge of twentieth-century Afro-Latin American diasporas.

Scholars such as Nina S. de Friedemann, Jaime Arocha, Peter Wade, and Norman E. Whitten, Jr, P. Rafael Savoia, Giulio Girardi, and Susan Faludi have made important contributions to our understanding of blacks in Colombia and Ecuador. Much of the anthropological research, however, revolves around the development of black culture (particularly music and religion) within a system of *mestizaje*, or miscegenation. Discussions of national ideologies and of the myth of a racial democracy in Latin America have dominated the field. George Reid Andrews writes: "Latin American sociologists have proven reluctant to contest their societies' self-image as 'racial democracies' . . . the belief that people of African ancestry have been satisfactorily integrated into their national societies has tended to remove them as objects of study for local anthropologists" (Andrews 1994: 363–4; see Andrews 1994 for anthropological studies). In short, racist hegemony argues that non-whites in Latin America never experienced the same type of Jim Crow and segregationist public policies that plagued the United States between about the 1880s and 1980s. Moreover, the obstacles to social mobility that existed, the myth goes, were primarily class- and not race-based. Revisionist works argue that Latin American societies were never free of racism: they just manifested it in different ways than did the United States. It is now clear that Afro-Latin Americans were systemically rejected as a group because of the myth of racial democracy. Sociologists Mauricio Solaún and Sidney Kronus have coined the phrase "nonviolent discrimination" for this phenomena (Hanchard 1994; Wright 1990: 2).

In such an environment, Afro-Latin Americans have had less opportunity to develop an expressively Pan-African political consciousness. Most have not politicized their struggles nor had a civil rights struggle because of lack of institutional space to organize one. As Octavio Ianni argues, most often they operate within religious, artistic, and political institutions that whites, Indians, and mestizos created and controlled. Most anthropologists and sociologists tend to overlook the period between the abolition of slavery and the 1930s in Latin America. This is a fascinating period because of the enormous transformation that occurred at the turn of the century. What follows is an explanation of why black migrants filled so much of the demands for labor in Latin America at the turn of the century. The question of why so many workers were available for emigration from the West Indies and the southern United States directs our discussion of the historiography (Ianni 1977: 74–5).

Researchers have used Panama Canal administration files, interviews, newspapers, foreign ministry/state department records, and travel accounts to study the African diaspora in Latin America. Some government records make no specific mention of people of African descent in the second half of the nineteenth century. In Venezuela for example, blacks disappeared officially, making archival research extremely difficult. Robert Hill, the editor, and the other editors of the Marcus Garvey Papers project started their Latin American volumes in the late 1990s. The collection will go a long way in aiding historians of Latin America. (The Marcus Garvey and Universal Negro Improvement Association Papers Project is located at the University of California at Los Angeles.)

Modernization Schemes

During the late nineteenth century, Latin American regimes commonly granted railroad concessions to state, foreign, and local ventures to build railroads, but nationalized them when construction was complete. This was because Latin American governments lacked capital to build their countries' infrastructure but did not lack the will to control it. Because most Latin American peasants existed in well-established subsistence economies, Latin American nationals showed no serious interest in serving as the labor pool for railroad contractors throughout the region. In particular, Ladinos refused to work on the malaria-infested coastal regions (Solien Gonzalez 1969; Meléndez, Savaranga, and Garinagu 1997: 15–20).

Even the early African communities – the Garifuna – were unviable for wage labor. The Garifuna were a community of runaway slaves and other fugitives, who created autonomous communities of escaped slaves called maroons. They relocated to Central America from the British colony of Saint Vincent in the West Indies in the late eighteenth century. Until the beginning of the twentieth century, Garifuna throughout Central America operated subsistence economies, showing little to no interest in railroad wage labor until after the 1920s, when foreign capitalist encroachment eventually led to increasing proletarianization of their isolated communities in Guatemala, Belize, and Honduras. Therefore labor recruiting outside of Latin America became a necessity (ibid.).

First, beginning in 1867, British colonial authorities passed several laws that called for the confiscation of lands with unpaid taxes. This effectively led to the dislocation of small Jamaican farmers and squatters, many of whom became the tenants of the government or of the people who purchased the foreclosed land. Many of the dislocated in Jamaica opted for job opportunities in Central America. Second, the failure of small Jamaican farmers and the break-up of small peasant freeholds increasingly caused rural Jamaicans to turn to proletarianization. Third, during the 1880s the European beet sugar industry, with government encouragement and subsidies, substantially increased its output. As a result, the world price for sugar decreased sharply between 1881 and 1896. Over time, European beet-sugar producers displaced Caribbean cane-sugar exporters in the European market. Ultimately the shift in the world sugar market devastated Jamaican sugar estates, interrelated businesses, and the workers they employed. Finally, as less profitable Jamaican sugar estates went out of business, demand decreased for artisans and craftsmen who made products used in the sugar industry. Many of these unemployed Jamaicans abandoned the agricultural sector and moved into towns, where they joined the growing ranks of the island's urban floating-labor reserve. They were forced to remain mobile in order to respond to unstable market conditions (Petras 1988: 49–52, 71, 96; Haskin 1914: 156–7).

As wages and opportunities declined in the West Indies, workers grew increasingly responsive to the offers of labor recruiters in urban centers like Kingston, Jamaica, or elsewhere. The erosion of the Jamaican sugar industry made the Jamaican worker "geographically mobile." These workers began to ignore state-constructed impediments to their mobility and negotiate the sale of their labor in the country of their choice. Railroad contractors early on relied on newspaper notices and informal information networks to advertise competitive wages, food and lodging, and medical care in Central America. Many Jamaicans migrated to Latin America without the assistance of labor recruiters. In his investigation into the matter, Frederic J. Haskin learned that less than two years after the start of the Panamá canal zone project, little labor recruiting in the West Indies was needed: "Every ship that went back to Barbados or to Jamaica carried with it some who had made what they considered a sufficient fortune." Returnees came "with savings enough to set them up for life. This fired dozens from each of those same communities with the desire to go and do likewise. The result was that the canal employment lists were kept full by those who came on their own initiative." From Panamá, many of these West Indian workers made their way to other parts of Latin America. Again, sometimes companies sent labor recruiters to Panamá to pay for their passage and other times workers came at their own expense and initiative (Haskin 1914: 156–7).

Similar to their West Indian colleagues during this period, both white and black North Americans migrated to various parts of Latin America in search of opportunities to improve their status. Most often they departed the United States from the docks of New Orleans, Mobile, Alabama, or Galveston, Texas, in the late nineteenth and early twentieth century. Between the 1880s and early 1900s the populations of southern cities skyrocketed as increasing numbers of both black and whites abandoned the plantations of the Black Belt for the greater opportunities available in the South's developing towns and cities. As a result, employers in New Orleans often dispatched labor agents to southern port cities such as Mobile and Savannah, and other parts of the South, to acquire large numbers of replacement workers to defeat striking employees. Southern blacks also freely pursued construction and track-crew jobs in spite of the severity of the work and the sporadic compulsion labor recruiters used. They viewed wage labor in the railroad industry as far more attractive than gang labor, sharecropping, or plantation work. Railroads paid them higher cash wages than anything they might earn performing agricultural work. In New Orleans, railroad officials depended on a large reserve army of out-of-town tramp laborers who journeyed to the Crescent City during the winter months in search of work. The number of destitute in New Orleans became so large that officials there reestablished their workhouse facilities and restored the chain gang for the unemployed and homeless (Opie, forthcoming: ch. 1).

Starting in the 1890s, southern state and local legislatures passed a flood of segregation laws that restricted opportunities for African Americans. Mob violence enforced the authority of white men, intimidated blacks, inhibited black behavior, restrained open black resistance against racial injustice, and restricted black economic competition. Southern blacks increasingly looked outside their home regions for hope of a better life. Some migrated to Latin America (Ibid.). Many of these black immigrants arrived in different parts of Latin America after a stint working on the failed French canal project in Panamá between the 1850s and 1880s or the Isthmian Canal Commission under United States control between 1904 and 1914. Workers migrated to Panamá from various regions of the Americas, Europe, Africa, and Asia. However, the West Indies represented the most important source of labor.

In the year 1882 alone, more than a thousand Jamaicans per month migrated to Latin America. Many of these Jamaican laborers were part of a pattern of recurring migrations within the Caribbean basin that started in the mid-nineteenth century. Other scholars have shown that thousands of workers migrated to Panamá, and then from Panamá to railroad construction projects throughout Latin America. Then at the start of the twentieth century many of the railroaders transitioned to jobs in the sugar and banana industries in the Caribbean basin. In addition, foreign companies like the United Fruit Company of Boston (UFCO) imported additional black workers, using them in various capacities in their holdings throughout Latin America (Mack 1944: 338–9; Petras 1988: 101; Kepner 1936; Knight 1985: 104–9).

Anti-Black Immigration Policies

Recruiting foreign workers at the turn of the century was a complex process, involving government officials from the host country among others. Debates relating to immigration restrictions and prohibition on non-white foreign workers divide into three interpretive frameworks: economic/class, race, and nationalism/nativism.

The orthodox interpretations view immigration policies in class terms. They see these policies as the attempts of Latin American elites to insure the entrance into their countries of economic contributors instead of economic burdens. Thus anthropologist Angelina Pollak-Eltz argues that during the nineteenth century Venezuelan officials promoted immigration from Europe to bolster the ranks of the professional sector and not just to whiten the population. After the Second World War, Venezuelan officials wanted the immigration of skilled laborers and professionals, and most of the West Indians, she argues, "had no skills to offer." But Elizabeth McLean Petras' study of Jamaican migrants contradicts Pollak-Eltz's claims. Petras' work shows that poor labor-market conditions in Jamaica resulted in the emigration of the better-skilled craftsmen and artisans to Latin America: "Those who left first were the displaced artisans, craftsmen, and the skilled workers" (Pollak-Eltz 1994: 98; Petras 1988: 47, 68–9).

The view, which has dominated the historiography, interprets Latin American immigration policy as a form of elite genetic engineering. Starting in the mid- to late nineteenth century, Latin American government officials began making public policy with the help of the racist, positivist theories of French philosopher and sociologist Auguste Comte (1798–1857) and British philosopher and sociologist Herbert Spencer (1820–1903). The work of Mexican philosopher Zea Leopoldo has argued that positivism dominated the ideology of governments at the turn of the century. Latin American technocrats used positivism, and related European racist theories, to argue that race mixing during the European conquest of the Americas and the African slave trade caused the contemporary political and economic problems of their respective countries (Leopoldo 1963).

My research on Guatemala shows that government officials as early as the 1860s started offering aid and privileges exclusively to white immigrants willing to settle and cultivate undeveloped regions. Often these settlements were in lowland, malaria-infested areas. Guatemalan officials passed the first of several twentieth-century anti-non-white immigration policies in 1914. This followed a bloody 1914 race riot involving Guatemalan and Jamaican workers on a UFCO banana plantation in the Atlantic coast department of Izabal. Historian Steven Scott Gillick maintains that the goals of Guatemalan immigration laws had been to "stem the influx of African laborers and to prevent permanent African settlement." He adds that the "government had long sought to entice immigrants to the country, [but clearly] national leaders wanted fair-skinned settlers, not Africans, to populate and develop the country" (Opie, forthcoming: ch. 2; Gillick 1995: 177–9).

Lara Putnam's work shows that an 1862 decree prohibited African or Chinese colonization schemes in Costa Rica. By the end of the 1920s, insists Putnam, "race-based immigration restrictions at Central American ports and informal restrictions on black movement within Costa Rica were truncating West Indian travel in unprecedented ways." Michael L. Conniff shows that Panamanian officials also passed laws that blocked the immigration of non-Spanish-speaking blacks in the 1920s. Officials there also required that 75 percent of the employees of any business be Panamanian (Putnam 2002: 39, 74; Conniff 1985: 65). In Venezuela, Winthorp Wright found government commitments to whitening in Venezuela at the beginning of the century led to prohibitions against the entrance of Chinese, Middle Easterners, and almost all West Indians. Officials there also advocated European colonization schemes to "save the country." In Brazil, as Teresa Meade and Gregory Alonso Pirio show, officials prevented essentially bourgeois Afro-North American colonists from settling in the 1920s (Wright 1990: 76–8; Holloway 1980; Meade and Pirio 1988). However in contrast to the above countries, Mexican President Álvaro Obregón welcomed Afro-North American settlers because he saw them as excellent farmers and small-scale foreign investors who could make valuable contributions to Mexico's civil war-torn economy during the time of the revolution, 1910–23 (Opie 1995: 13).

In general, between the 1860s and 1920s Latin American politicians put anti-black immigration laws on their books both to whiten their countries and, in the words of Ronald Harpelle, to curb what was seen as "Africanisation." However, until the start of the great depression and the Second World War, Latin American governments sparingly enforced racist immigration policies. For example, Wright argues that foreign-owned petroleum companies exploited loopholes in the immigration and colonization code of 1918 to import large numbers of black laborers (Harpelle 2000: 317; Wright 1990: 77–8).

Foreign companies like United Fruit continued to import black workers, despite the passage of anti-black immigration laws, because their operations in countries like Mexico, Guatemala, Belize, Honduras, Nicaragua, Costa Rica, Panamá, Cuba, Venezuela, Colombia, Ecuador, and Brazil were dependent on their labor. In most of the region, the majority of dockworkers, railroad and bridge construction labor, miners, and coastal agricultural workers came from the West Indies and the southern United States. As a result, thousands of black immigrants arrived annually to become dockworkers and plantation workers. Even more came seasonally to provide agricultural labor for the private estates of Latin American oligarchs. Wright argues that, for example, the majority of Venezuela's domestic servants and petroleum workforce came from the West Indies (Rosenthal 1990: 31, 49–50; Bak 1998; Fisher 2000: 118–19; Wright 1990: 77–8).

Putnam and others see the end of the 1920s as a period of change in Caribbean basin immigration policy. It was a period when Latin American officials became more vigilant in enforcing race-based immigration restrictions at Latin American ports. New enforcement efforts within national borders greatly restricted travel by blacks (Putnam 2002: 74–5; Harpelle 2000: 319–20). Venezuelan politicians, like others in Latin America, used immigration policies to garner support from working-class citizens. In addition, immigration policy reflected elite preferences for white over black, Indian, or mestizo citizens. According to Putnam, the politics of race and nation changed across the region during the economic crisis of the 1930s and 1940s. During this period nation states "made whiteness a prerequisite for full citizenship" (Wright 1974: 336–7; Putnam 2002: 74–5; Harpelle 2000: 319–20).

How People of African Descent Were Viewed

During the initial years of investment in Latin America, says historian Philippe Bourgeois, foreign firms experimented with different ethnic groups to find what they considered acceptable workers. Attitudes about African Americans in Latin America are documented over hundreds of years; the process by which they evolved was extended and complicated. George Reid Andrews indicates that scholars doing research on race relations in Latin America have tended to provide a race-based interpretation of black–white relations. This interpretation argues that, dating back to the colonial period, Latin Americans associated whiteness with intelligence and progress, among other positive characteristics. In contrast, they associated blackness with the less intelligent, lazy, and criminal "other" (Bourgeois 1989: 46–8; Andrews 1994: 372–3). Recent scholarship by historians Christopher H. Lutz, Paul Thomas Lokken, and Catherine Komisaruk has moved beyond the race-first interpretation to add culture as an additional interpretive framework.

For example, work on Guatemala's Afro-Latin American diaspora suggests that during the colonial period acculturated Africans, mulatto slaves, and free wageworkers enjoyed more privileges and opportunities than people of African descent who did not have an understanding of Spanish Catholicism and other elements of Iberian culture. The most recent studies indicate that during the colonial period people of African descent possessed greater status than Indians. This is because economically they served as important middlemen between Spanish bosses and their indigenous subordinates. But, despite their status, both Spaniards and Indians most often treated blacks as outsiders and foreigners in Guatemala (Opie, forthcoming, ch. 2).

Michael Conniff's work shows that cultural differences also affected relationships between recent and not-so-recent black immigrants. Native blacks in the parts of Colombia that later became Panama gained their freedom after independence in 1819. In the 1870s several Liberal Colombian military caudillos extended the suffrage to the lower classes and thereby managed to win control of the cities. Poor black voters from neighborhoods in and around cities, including Colon, Panama, formed what some scholars have called the Negro Liberal party. Afro-Colombians monopolized civil service jobs and held considerable sway over city politics, "even after the Conservatives returned to power in Bogotá, [Colombia]." In Panama, Conniff writes, liberal oligarchs made peace with the black liberals for several decades, "giving them public jobs and other favors in exchange for electoral and military support."

Conniff holds that black liberals viewed West Indian newcomers to Panama with "suspicion, due to cultural differences and economic competition." The larger Panamanian community, insists Conniff, accepted the West Indian immigrants "as a necessary condition of getting a canal built." But they resented the fact that Canal Zone blacks showed no signs of assimilating into Panamanian society. After 1914, Panamanians developed a "love–hate" attitude toward the 40,000–50,000 West Indians in the country. They loved them as consumers but "resented their presence." Specifically they resented the fact that their presence drove housing, food, and prices for other necessities drastically upward. For example, rent prices increased 25 percent to 50 percent in and around the Canal Zone enclave (Conniff 1985: 19, 22, 46, 64–5). Tomás Fernández Robaina also provides a similar and economic interpretation to views of blacks in his study of the internal dynamics of Cuba's African diaspora.

Covering the same period as Conniff, Fernández Robaina maintains that whereas white Cubans feared that West Indian laborers would blacken the island, Afro-Cubans viewed them with hostility because they undercut their wages. Conniff and Fernández Robaina thus apply Earl Lewis's suggestion that scholars "pay close attention to the encounters between diverse groups of immigrants" from the United States, West Indies, and Latin America "whose meetings created a trans-geographical America." Historians of the Americas, in the words of Lewis, "must be cognizant of understanding the diversity and overlapping diasporas that are a part of black community life" (Robaina 1998: 122; Lewis 1999: 21–2).

Economic interpretations of race relations in early twentieth-century Latin America dominate the historiography. For example, several studies show that hostility towards black immigrants coincided with the boom and bust of the banana, sugar, and mining industries. In addition, the completion of the Panama Canal and the recruiting of thousands of black workers to other parts of Latin America served to increase the fear of an Africanization and black takeover in some nations. Thus working-class Latin American nationals gave black newcomers hostile treatment in

Costa Rica, Cuba, and Guatemala (Bourgeois 1998: 126; Harpelle 2001: 39–40). In the late 1920s, economic nationalism demanded racial separation in Latin America. In the 1930s and 1940s the view of black immigrants as an alien element within Latin America – "whose earnings were sent abroad and who had no allegiance" to their host countries – became common among Latin American workers, planters, and intellectuals. At times lawmakers passed apartheid-like laws restricting the movement and job opportunities of black workers (Putnam 2002: 73; Chomsky 1996: 328). As Hispanics entered these jobs they claimed a position equal to white North Americans in the semiformal racial hierarchy of UFCO banana enclaves across the Caribbean basin.

Putnam holds that during the 1930s and 1940s Costa Rican government officials introduced racial segregation in public spaces like swimming pools and cinemas. She writes, "Skin color became the measure of health and worth in a way it had never before." Cultural anthropologist Judith Ewell shows that in 1929 Venezuelan President Juan Vicente Gómez (1908–1935) issued a decree that both prohibited the immigration of West Indians and required those already in the oilfield to register with government authorities and carry identification cards. Guatemalan authorities required a similar registration of black foreigners in the late 1920s, apparently also to track their whereabouts (Putnam 2002: 167; Ewell 1984: 64).

For some scholars, external forces help explain hegemonic views of people of African descent in late nineteenth- and twentieth-century Latin America. Particularly, scholars point to importation of North American and British views of blacks in the business enclaves they controlled throughout the region. My work on Guatemala shows that contractors and middle-level managers from Canada, different parts of Europe and the United States institutionalized Jim Crow racism and segregation. For example, the Jim Crow color line that the International Railroad of Central America (IRCA) and UFCO managers enforced influenced how Guatemalan nationals viewed and treated black immigrants. Thus the argument here that external forces (the penetration of both foreign capital and racist hegemony) exacerbated Latin American views of blacks that dated back to the colonial period. Edmund T. Gordon's work on the British – and later US – enclave in Bluefields, Nicaragua shows a similar phenomenon.

Bluefields was once an area that indigenous groups, enslaved Africans, and a British planter class populated. Nicaraguans called the descendants of relationships between the three ethnic groups "Mosquito Indians." Mosquitos lived under several governments at different times in Central American history – British, Spanish, and finally Nicaraguan after the end of Spanish colonialism about 1825. The British whites that remained in Nicaragua after the start of the national period viewed blacks as "inferior – ignorant, tending to the savage, and incapable of regulating their own affairs." Moravian missionaries from the United States also held similar racist views of blacks. They saw blacks as morally depraved and lazy. Gordon insists that for Atlantic coast whites, people of African descent "no matter how Anglo-cultured, were inferior because they were, at least partially, racially identified as African." Likewise Hispanic Nicaraguans' perceptions of people of African descent consisted of stereotypes that saw blacks as racially inferior foreigners.

In 1894 the government of Nicaragua established control over the Atlantic coast region. Starting at the turn of the century and later during the boom in the banana industry (1910s–1930s), US investors introduced both foreign capital and Jim Crow policies to the Atlantic coast of Nicaragua. In the process they also lured thousands of southern blacks and West Indians, who came to work as dockworkers, sailors, banana producers, and railroad laborers in US-controlled enterprises. Between 1899 and 1925, Nicaragua's African-Diaspora population doubled in size. Company officials, many of them from the southern United States, established Jim Crow policies in company-supported towns, social clubs, and churches. As in the US South, people of African descent and European descent received different treatment from police officials and in judicial courts. "As elsewhere where patriarchy is articulated with racial supremacy," writes Gordon, "white males took advantage of their power and status to initiate exploitative relationships with Creole [black] women" (Gordon 1998: 67–8, 47–8).

Not all racists were North American. Nicaraguan mestizos saw themselves as the rightful heirs of Hispanic civilization and superior to people of African descent. Banana industry jobs attracted them to the coast and when they arrived they resented competition from black workers. In 1912 conflicts erupted on US-owned banana plantations between black and mestizo laborers. When the fighting stopped, mestizos had slain several of their co-workers. Gordon found that in the 1920s race riots occurred again in Puerto Cabezas, an Atlantic coast port in Nicaragua. Mestizos again killed several blacks, promising more fatalities if foreign black workers remained on the Atlantic coast. After that coast was reincorporated in Nicaragua in 1894, Hispanic Nicaraguans systematically marginalized Afro-Nicaraguans in government employment and in the private sector as business professionals (ibid: 68–9). Historian Charles Bergquist shows a similar picture in the early twentieth-century US-operated petroleum enclaves on Venezuela's Atlantic coast. White North American bosses in Venezuela – set on maintaining white supremacy – underpaid, disrespected, and segregated black workers. According to Wright, some black immigrants prospered in the petroleum enclaves despite the Jim Crow economy, while others "suffered the vagaries of the hard eastern life and its mercurial economy" (Bergquist 1986: 223; Wright 1990: 78).

Conniff is the only scholar who deviates from the "external forces" interpretation. He acknowledges that North American businesses in Central America "adopted a southern-style division of labor where whites supervised and blacks did the heavy, dirty, disagreeable, yet increasingly skilled work." North American unions in the Canal Zone ran Jim Crow shops that prohibited black members and therefore restricted black mobility. Conniff states that the Republican administrations of Presidents Roosevelt and Taft acted to institute Jim Crow policies in the Canal Zone, and the Democratic Wilson administration did nothing to end them. Yet Conniff insists: "The oft-repeated view that the Canal Zone was racist due to southern influence is simply a myth." He adds, "many arrived without racist ideas or experience with blacks, but when confronted with the need to supervise British colonial subjects, they adopted bigoted behavior." Conniff's central argument is that US imperialism did not introduce racism; it simply reinforced it. Jim Crow in the Canal Zone continued into the 1940s and thereafter, and Conniff maintains "it compared unfavorably with race relations in Louisiana and Mississippi" (Conniff 1985: 26, 34–5, 51). The literature discussed in this section indicates that people of African descent in Latin America faced a host of racist challenges coming from different influences, some native and some foreign. However, they did not passively accept racist treatment.

Black Consciousness in Latin America

This final section looks at the myriads of ways black people in Latin America struggled collectively against racism, and how scholars have interpreted the causes and failure of this black consciousness and group mobilization, in a chronicle framework. Two question arise here. First, how do scholars explain the enthusiasm among Afro-Latin American newcomers (West Indian and North American immigrants) for Black Nationalism and black institution-building like Marcus Garvey's United Negro Improvement Association (UNIA)? Second, why have native-born Afro-Latin Americans been seemingly so slow to embrace, if not remain completely averse to, Black Nationalism and black institution-building?

Several scholars provide interpretations for the first question. Similar to African American culture during the US antebellum period, the banana trade and the constant revitalization of Pan-African cultural traditions with the arrival of newcomers and segregated housing patterns on large plantations constituted the two most salient factors in black cultural survivals in Latin America. A pattern of segregated company housing isolated black employees from other cultural influences. Black Nationalism in Latin America in the early twentieth century had international origins, but few Hispanic influences. Black immigrants from different parts of the Americas lived and worked side by side. In Latin America they exchanged world views on the struggles of people of African descent in the United States and the West Indies. This exchange led to the development of various black institutions and radicalism in some Latin American UNIA chapters (Genovese 1976; Stuckey 1987).

Aviva Chomsky argues that black churches on UFCO banana plantations in Costa Rica provided the infrastructure on which immigrants developed other black-controlled institutions. Black infrastructures at these plantations contained newspapers, mutual-aid societies, lodges, and labor unions. Chomsky insists that these Atlantic coast institutions helped black immigrants maintain an alternative Pan-African society in the "shadow of the plantations" (Chomsky 1996: 153, 187–9). Similar developments most likely occurred across the border on UFCO plantations in Panama. We know from historian Michael Conniff that they occurred in the Canal Zone. Segregated housing patterns, segregated schools, the English language, English-language newspapers, businesses, churches, and mutual aid societies collectively acted as important sources of black immigrant solidarity. Newspapers by and for West Indians held together the diverse and expanding black community in Panama of the 1920s. Conniff holds that the *Panama Tribune*, for example, "featured columns by local writers and picked up material from the Negro wire services in the United States" (Conniff 1985: 18, 72). Gordon shows that black Creoles and immigrants also established black newspapers in Bluefields, Nicaragua, as early as 1890. However, his interpretation of Black Nationalism in Bluefields centers on the re-creation of African and African-influenced cultural traditions among large numbers of African diaspora residents.

Examples of these traditions include the Creole language, religious practices, food, music, dances, and the recording of oral history. Gordon argues that together

African traditions worked to maintain a separate Pan-African cultural tradition among the masses within the African diaspora of Nicaragua's Atlantic coast region. This was a cultural tradition they often employed in struggles against white supremacy in Nicaragua. Black coastal residents established about five branches of the UNIA. White church officials in Bluefields, Nicaragua, called the Garvey movement extremely popular. Church officials also claimed that the movement championed Black Nationalist teachings. Gordon argues that, in Bluefields, UNIA leaders generally increased the racial consciousness and organizational experience of local residents. The Garvey movement, according to Gordon, equipped Afro-Nicaraguans for the important role they were to play in race-based political upheavals that shook the coast in the 1920s and 1930s (Gordon 1998: 48–9, 58–60, 75–6).

Jamaican-born Black Nationalist Marcus Garvey published the *Negro World*, the Black Nationalist organ of the UNIA that black immigrants in Latin America avidly read. Garvey himself traveled to the Atlantic coast of Costa Rica at age 21 in 1910. In Costa Rica he lived with his maternal uncle who worked for UFCO. His uncle found a job for Garvey as a timekeeper on a banana plantation. Later he worked as a stevedore at Puerto Limon, Costa Rica. Garvey started the newspaper *La Nación* to reach Costa Ricans with Black Nationalist views. The theme of the paper led Costa Rican and British Authorities to label him as a troublemaker. UFCO officials did not view Garvey's activism favorably either. Garvey next traveled to Guatemala, Nicaragua, Panamá, Ecuador, Chile, and Peru. During his travels Garvey once again published a newspaper, this time called *La Prensa*. He eventually returned to Jamaica and soon thereafter founded several Black Nationalist organizations (Martin 1986 [1976]: 16). In 1916 Garvey moved the headquarters of the Universal (later changed to) United Negro Improvement Association (UNIA) from Jamaica to Harlem in New York City's upper West Side (ibid.).

Cuba had the largest number of UNIA chapters outside the United States, 52 branches. Some 22,000 Jamaicans migrated to Cuba between 1911 and 1921. Large numbers of Haitians also traveled there during the same period. Only the United States had a larger West Indian diaspora. In Cuba, West Indians established UNIA branches near black urban communities and in rural communities near sugar plantations where black immigrants lived and worked. The UNIA in Cuba served as the immigrant's government, civic association, social club, political action committee, and place of worship (ibid: 15–16, 69–70; Martin 1983a: 82–3).

"The greater Caribbean area (including Central and northern South America)," according to Garvey specialist Tony Martin, "was undoubtedly the biggest Garveyite stronghold outside of the United States." West Indian immigrants established 46 branches of the UNIA in the Panamá Canal Zone, third in size to the United States and Cuba. The UNIA "played an important role" uniting the diverse black population of Panamá and other parts of Central America that came from very different national and cultural backgrounds. Because it emphasized the mutual reality of race and second-class treatment, the UNIA significantly reduced resentment and competition between people of African descent within the Afro-Latin American diaspora (Martin 1983a). In Costa Rica, Teofilo Horace Fowler founded the first Limón UNIA chapter eight years after Garvey left Costa Rica in 1919. Eventually West Indians established 23 branches of the UNIA in Costa Rica. Scholars disagree on what the Costa Rican UNIA chapters did. For example, Chomsky argues that in contrast to UNIA chapters in Guatemala and Panamá, there is no record that Limón chapters ever supported labor organizing in UFCO's Costa Rican Division. She insists that, despite the fears of authorities in the 1920s, in Costa Rica the UNIA served a social and religious function rather than a radical labor organizing one (Chomsky 1996: 203–5).

Historian Judith Stein provides an economic interpretation of UNIA conservatism in Latin America. According to Stein, "Garvey's immediate interest in the Caribbean and in Central America, as well as everywhere else, was building up the Black Star Shipping Line, which conflicted with the creation of a strike fund." Garvey instructed his followers to view white employers as their best friend until they achieved economic freedom. Garvey started the Negro Factories Corporation and the Black Star Line to demonstrate the power of economic independence from white employers and owners (Stein 1986: 143). The Black Star Line also provided a needed alternative for black travelers, who suffered insults on white-owned ships that practiced segregated Jim Crow policies. Personal experience with such indignities helps to explain why so many itinerant black workers in Latin America became supporters and shareholders of the Black Star Line (Cronon 1969 [1955]: 195–6, 222; Martin 1983a: 55–6; Martin 1986 [1976]: 31, 182; Stein 1986: 143). In general, Garvey stood between white radical movements and the black masses. He refused to have anything to do with socialism or communism because he saw them as white-controlled movements and therefore inherently prejudiced against black workers. At the same time he found no problem collaborating with "certain types of radicals," usually those involved in "anti-colonial, anti-imperialist or antiracist struggles" (Martin 1986 [1976]: 31).

In contrast to Chomsky's and Stein's conservative view of the UNIA, historian Ronald Harpelle argues that some of the Costa Rican chapters took radical stands against racist UFCO managers. Harpelle found that the Universal African Legions (UAL), the paramilitary wing of the UNIA, prepared for a race war in the plantation region of the Costa Rican and Panamanian border on the Caribbean coast. UNIA chapters in this region focused their efforts on addressing anti-worker company policies and preparing to use arms to obtain greater autonomy (Martin 1983a: 82; Harpelle 2001: 61–2). Similarly, historian Winston James argues that in the Central American country of British Honduras the UNIA "figured prominently" in a 1919 working-class conflict involving black immigrants. Ex-sergeant Samuel Haynes served as one of the principal leaders of a large race-conscious labor revolt and protest movement in the capital city of British Honduras. Haynes also held the position of secretary of the UNIA in Belize. According to one scholar, the movement "shook the colonial structure to its very foundation." High merchant prices for subsistence goods and depressed wages at the start of the First World War stood at the core of working-class grievances. When British officials in Belize banned the distribution of Garvey's *Negro World*, UNIA members in nearby Mexico and Guatemala smuggled in even larger amounts of the periodical than were previously available (James 1998: 51, 64–6; Martin 1983a: 59, 77–8; and, on the Pan-African Connection, Martin 1983b: 54–6).

My work on Guatemala also supports a radical Black Nationalist interpretation of local UNIA chapters in Latin America. Barbadian Clifford Bourne organized the first UNIA branch on the Atlantic coast of Guatemala in February, 1920. In its first

year the Guatemalan branch of the UNIA in Puerto Barrios established and supported a union for UFCO workers. These workers promptly went on strike for
increased wages. Tony Martin points out that, although Garvey never embraced
communism, some members of his staff did (Hill 1983: 514–15; Martin 1983a:
60). For example, in 1919 the editor of *Negro World* – W. A. Domingo, a socialist
and later a member of the African Blood Brotherhood (ABB), a black communist
organization – used his post on the paper to publish Bolshevik propaganda that
circulated to local UNIA chapters in Latin America. Garvey quickly fired Domingo
when he learned about his radical political views. UNIA member Cyril Briggs was
also a member of ABB and later of the Communist Party USA. Ottoman Hall
belonged to both the UNIA in Chicago and the radical labor organization, the
Industrial Workers of the World (IWW). He served as a member of the UNIA's
Universal African Legions and later joined the ABB and the Communist Party USA
(Martin 1983a: 54; Martin 1986: 236–7).

The argument here is that black workers rallied around the UNIA in Latin America
because the UNIA and its auxiliaries provided black-controlled institutional space
where immigrants developed and encouraged a black political consciousness.

Scholars like Harpelle still call the UNIA the "single most influential vehicle" of
its time in aiding black immigrants in their fight against Latin American forms of
racism and discrimination. Harpelle believes that even though "Garvey based his
financial schemes for independence on capitalist enterprise, the fundamental underpinnings of the UNIA were based on communal efforts for communal gain" (Harpelle
2000: 188–9). In sum, scholars disagree on the conservative *versus* the radical component of the UNIA. However, there is a consensus that during the 1920s UNIA
chapters on UFCO plantations provided an important institutional infrastructure for
black immigrants. This infrastructure gave them renewed confidence in confronting
sometimes-hostile state and company officials and Hispanic workers who wanted
their jobs.

Jim Crow in American-operated enclaves created spaces for the development of
independent black institutions. Simultaneously, the strict security and policing in
and around them inhibited exchanges between black immigrants and native-born
Afro-Latin Americans. Several studies provide interpretations of Afro-Latin American political apathy in the early part of the twentieth century. The debates can be
grouped into scholarly camps stressing (variously) elite hegemony, integration,
clientelism or class. Historians Aline Helg, George Reid Andrews and others show
that Latin American elites discouraged and even made it illegal to organize exclusively black political parties and/or black Nationalist movements. This was the case in
Cuba, Brazil, Guatemala, Venezuela, and Colombia (Helg 1995; Andrews 1991;
Opie forthcoming, ch. 5; Wright 1990: 13–14). Similarly, political institutions controlled by fair-skinned Hispanics offered networks of clientelism and patronage to
Afro-Latin Americans, and this systemically stifled black mobilization. At the same
time, these networks increased conflict and division within Afro-Latin American
diasporic communities over political favors from political bosses (Andrews 1994:
374).

Another interpretation of political apathy among Afro-Latin Americans examines
the effects of integration. Angelina Pollak-Eltz argues that racial integration and
the absence of racial consciousness among Afro-Venezuelans has suppressed racial

conflicts. In Panama, many of the Latin American blacks migrated to the isthmus from Cartagena, Colombia. Conniff holds that they avoided immigrant blacks and their institutions because they disliked the different cultural patterns of the new immigrants. Another interpretation argues that Afro-Latin Americans have historically viewed identifying with the black masses or joining their black institutions as jeopardizing their social gains. Integration had provided gains that could be lost if Afro-Latin Americans realigned themselves with a black community (Pollak-Eltz 1994: 99–101; Wright 1990: 113–14; Conniff 1985: 19). Studies of the descendants of black immigrants reveal similar findings. Harpelle insists that integration and emigration from isolated plantation regions to the capital city (for secondary and university schooling and/or jobs) caused significant changes. Those who left black communities decreased the importance they once placed on an alternative black identity and belonging to a black organization. In the 1940s, the National Progressive Association of the Youths of Colour of the Atlantic Zone, which later changed its name to the National Association for the Advancement of Young Coloured People, the Afro-Costarrican Youth Uplift Association, the National Association of the Progress of Coloured Costa Ricans, and National Association for the Progress of Coloured Costa Ricans, represented the last wave all-black organizations in Costa Rica. Afro-Costarricans would organize similar movements in the 1970s and thereafter (Harpelle 2000: 324, 328, 341).

Class interpretation of Afro-Latin American political apathy states that middle-class blacks see themselves as having less in common with the poor masses of blacks than they do with the largely white and mestizo middle class that they go to university with and later work and live alongside. As a result, (outside recent-immigrant enclaves) Afro-Latin Americans had almost no black organizations that articulated their political objectives until the 1960s. There were of course isolated uprisings, but nothing one could call a sustained mobilization effort. For example, after the passage of an Ecuadorian Agrarian Reform Law in 1964, small black farmers in the Chota-Mira Valley region "shed the status of rural share croppers" and in the words of Norman E. Whitten, Jr and Arlene Torres, "entered a system of covert and overt conflict with the power wielders of the region" (Whitten and Torres 1998: 81). Peter Wade describes another incident in Medellín, Colombia. Afro-Colombian migrants from rural provinces founded the Association of Chocoanos Residents in 1963. Black residents in Medellín organized to stop racist attacks on female Afro-Colombian domestic servants. Wade holds that because discrimination against blacks seemed to be class-oriented or "individualistic, unsystematic, and non generalized," it was difficult to mobilize people (Wade 1998: 401, 408).

Until the 1970s, native-born acculturated black people in Colombia and other parts of Latin America traditionally turned to white-controlled institutions like the international Catholic Church for support in their struggle against systems of oppression. However, independent black movements developed in some parts of Latin America in the 1970s and 1980s. Experiences with prejudice and discrimination in job competition during this period mobilized some black middle-class Afro-Latin Americans. Many claimed that they gained the inspiration to organize from following the US civil rights and black power movements along with African Liberation movements. These movements were important in raising the political consciousness of many Afro-Latin Americans (Andrews 1994: 374). In Nicaragua, Edmund Gordon argues, in the 1970s, black Sandinistas (members of the Frente Sandinista de Liberación Nacional – Sandinista National Liberation Front) placed their struggle in Nicaragua in an "international and African diasporic perspective by citing Kwame Nkrumah of Ghana and the struggle for African independence." It is important to point out that no similar developments happened in Venezuela where middle-class Afro-Venezuelans did not address racism in depth for survival reasons (Gordon 1998: 177–8; Wright 1990: 113).

In 1977, Afro-Latin Americans organized the First Congress of Black Culture in the Americas. It was held in Cali, Colombia. This represented the first Pan-African institution in the region since the Garvey movement of the 1920s. The difference here is that Garvey's UNIA failed to reach native Afro-Latin Americans in any substantial way. Delegates at the 1977 gathering called for redefining the language of black culture to associate it with positive, progressive attributes. In 1980 the Panamanian government hosted the Second Congress of Black Culture. Most recently, independent Afro-Latin American and indigenous movements have been developing alliances. For example, in Colombia's department of Chocó and Ecuador's provinces of Esmeralda and Carchi, black and indigenous movements are discussing ways to network their resources and organizations to more effectively confront racist Latin American customs and traditions that have historically overlooked their group interest (Conniff 1985: 169; Whitten and Torres 1998: 4, 26–7, 36).

BIBLIOGRAPHY

Works Cited

Andrews, George Reid (1991) *Blacks & Whites in São Paulo, Brazil, 1888–1988*. Madison, Wisconsin: University of Wisconsin Press.
—— (1994) "Afro-Latin America: the late 1900s," *Journal of Social History* 28 (2, Winter): 363–4, 372–3.
Bak, Joan L. (1998) "Labor, community, and the making of a cross-class alliance in Brazil: The 1917 railroad strikes in Rio Grande do Sul," *Hispanic American Historical Review* 78 (2, May): 179–227.
Bergquist, Charles (1986) *Labor in Latin America: Comparative Essays on Chile, Argentina, Venezuela, and Colombia*. Stanford, CA: Stanford University Press.
Bourgeois, Phillipe I. (1989) *Ethnicity at Work: Divided Labor on a Central American Banana Plantation*. Baltimore: Johns Hopkins University Press.
—— (1998) "The black Diaspora in Costa Rica: upward mobility and ethnic discrimination" in Norman E. Whitten, Jr and Arlene Torres (eds.), *Blackness in Latin America and the Caribbean: Social Dynamics and Cultural Transformations*, vol. 1, *Central America and Northern and Western South America*, 119–32. Bloomington: Indiana University Press.
Chomsky, Aviva (1996) *West Indian Workers and the United Fruit Company in Costa Rica 1870–1940*. Baton Rouge and London: Louisiana State University Press.
Clifford, James (1994) "Diaspora," *Cultural Anthropology* 9 (3): 302–38, 320, 321.
Conniff, Michael (1985) *Black Labor on a White Canal: Panama, 1904–1981*. Pittsburgh: University of Pittsburgh Press.
Cronon, E. David ([1955] 1969) *Black Moses: The Story of Marcus Garvey and the United Improvement Association*. Madison: University of Wisconsin Press.
Domínguez, Jorge I. (ed.) (1994) *Race and Ethnicity in Latin America*. New York and London: Garland.

Ewell, Judith (1984) *Venezuela: A Century of Change*. Stanford, CA: Stanford University Press.

Fisher, Geoffrey (2000) "Conflict in the Pailón: the British experience in Esmeralda Province, Ecuador, 1860–1914" in Oliver Marshall (ed.), *English-Speaking Communities in Latin America*, 118–19. London: Macmillan.

Fontaine, Pierre-Michel (1994) "Research in the political economy of Afro-Latin America" in Jorge I. Domínguez (ed.), *Race and Ethnicity in Latin America*. New York and London: Garland.

Genovese, Eugene D. (1976) *Roll, Jordan, Roll: The World the Slaves Made*. New York: Vintage Books.

Gillick, Steven Scott (1995) "Life and labor in a banana enclave: bananeros, the United Fruit Company and the limits of trade unionism in Guatemala, 1906–1931," PhD dissertation, Tulane.

Gilroy, Paul (1993) *The Black Atlantic: Double Consciousness, and Modernity*. Cambridge, MA: Harvard University Press.

Gordon, Edmund T. (1998) *Disparate Diasporas: Identity and Politics in an African Nicaraguan Community*. Austin: University of Texas Press.

Greene, Jack P. (1999) "Beyond power: paradigm subversion and reformulation and the re-creation of the early modern Atlantic world" in Darlene Clark Hine and Jacqueline McLeod (eds.), *Crossing Boundaries: Comparative History of Black People in Diaspora*, 329, 332–3. Bloomington: Indiana University Press.

Hanchard, Michael George (1994) *Orpheus and Power: The Movimento Negro of Rio de Janeiro and São Paulo, Brazil, 1945–1988*. Princeton, NJ: Princeton University Press.

Harpelle, Ronald N. (2000) "Identity in transition: from West Indian immigration to Afro-Costarricense" in Oliver Marshall (ed.), *English-Speaking Communities in Latin America*. London: Macmillan.

—— (2001) *The West Indians of Costa Rica: Race, Class, and the Integration of an Ethnic Minority*. Montreal and Kingston, London and Ithaca, NY: McGill-Queen's University Press.

Haskin, Frederick J. (1914) *The Panama Canal*. New York: Doubleday, Page.

Helg, Aline (1995) *Our Rightful Share: The Afro-Cuban Struggle for Equality, 1886–1912*. Chapel Hill and London: University of North Carolina Press.

Hill, Robert A. (ed.) (1983) *The Marcus Garvey and Universal Negro Improvement Association Papers*, vol. II: 514–15. Berkeley: University of California Press.

Holloway, Thomas H. (1980) *Immigrants on the Land: Coffee and Society in São Paulo, 1886–1934*. Chapel Hill: University of North Carolina Press.

Holt, Thomas C. (1999) "Slavery and freedom in the atlantic world: reflections on the diasporan framework" in Darlene Clark Hine and Jacqueline McLeod (eds.), *Crossing Boundaries: Comparative History of Black People in Diaspora*. Bloomington: Indiana University Press.

Ianni, Octavio (1977) "Organización social y alienación" in Manuel Moreno Fraginals (ed.), *África in América Latina*, 74–5. Mexico City: siglo veintiuno editors.

James, C. L. R. (1963) *Black Jacobins: Toussaint L'Ouverture and the San Domingo Revolution*. New York: Vintage Books.

James, Winston (1998) *Holding Aloft the Banner of Ethiopia: Caribbean Radicalism in Early Twentieth-Century America*. London and New York: Verso.

Kelley, Robin D. G. (1999) "'But a local phase of a world problem': black history's global vision, 1883–1950," *Journal of American History* 86 (3): 1055–8.

Kepner, Charles David, Jr (1936) *Social Aspects of the Banana Industry*, 6. New York: Columbia University Press.

Knight, Franklin W. (1985) "Jamaican migrants and the Cuban sugar industry, 1900–1934" in Manuel Moreno Fraginals, Frank Moya Pons, and Stanley L. Engerman (eds.), *Between Slavery and Free Labor: The Spanish-Speaking Caribbean in the Nineteenth Century*. Baltimore and London: Johns Hopkins University Press.

Kronus, Sidney and Solaún, Mauricio (1973) *Discrimination without Violence: Miscegenation and Racial Conflict in Latin America*. New York: Wiley.

Leopoldo, Zea (1963) *The Latin American Mind*, trans. James H. Abbott and Lowell Dunham. Norman, OK: University of Oklahoma Press.

Lewis, Earl (1999) "To turn as on a pivot: writing African Americans into a history of overlapping diasporas" in Darlene Clark Hine and Jacqueline McLeod (eds.), *Crossing Boundaries: Comparative History of Black People in Diaspora*, 21–2. Bloomington: Indiana University Press.

Mack, Gerstle (1944) *The Land Divided, A History of the Panama Canal and Other Isthmian Canal Projects*, 338–9. New York: Alfred A. Knopf.

Martin, Tony (1983a) *Marcus Garvey, Hero: A First Biography*, 59–60, 77–8, 82–3. Dover, MA: Majority Press.

—— (1983b) *The Pan-African Connection: From Slavery to Garvey and Beyond*, 54–6. Dover, MA: Majority Press.

—— ([1976] 1986) *Race First: The Ideological and Organizational Struggles of Marcus Garvey and the Universal Negro Improvement Association*, 16, 236–7. Dover, MA: Majority Press.

Meade, Teresa and Pirio, Gregory Alonso (1988) "In search of the Afro-American 'Eldorado': attempts by North American blacks to enter Brazil in the 1920s," *Luso-Brazilian Review* 25 (1): 85–110.

Mélendez, Armando Crisanto, Savaranga, Uayujuru, and Garinagu, Adeija Sisira Gererun Aguburigu (1997) *El Enojo de Las Sonajas; Palabras Del Ancestro*, 15–20. Tegucigalpa, Honduras: Graficentro Editores.

Mörner, Magnus (1970) "Historical research on race relations in Latin America during the National Period" in *Race and Class in Latin America*. New York: Columbia University Press.

Opie, Frederick D. (1995) "Afro-North American migration to Latin America, 1880–1932," paper presented to the Latin American Studies Association Conference, Guadalajara, Mexico (April 17–19): 13.

—— (forthcoming) *The Guatemalan Atlantic World: Race and Working Class Culture in the Caribbean, 1880s–1920s*.

Petras, Elizabeth McLean (1988) *Jamaican Labor Migration: White Capital and Black Labor, 1850–1930*, 68–9, 89, 101. Boulder, CO: Westview Press.

Pollak-Eltz, Angelina (1994) *Black Culture and Society in Venezuela*, 98–101. Caracas, Venezuela: Lagoven.

Putnam, Lara (2002) *The Company They Kept: Migrants and the Politics of Gender in Caribbean Costa Rica, 1870–1960*, 39, 73–5, 167. Chapel Hill and London: University of North Carolina Press.

Robaina, Tomás Fernández (1998) "Marcus Garvey in Cuba: Urrutia, Cubans, and black nationalism" in Lisa Brock and Digna Castañeda Fuertes (eds.), *Between Race and Empire: African-Americans and Cubans before the Cuban Revolution*. Philadelphia: Temple University Press.

Rosenthal, Anton Benjamin (1990) "Controlling the line: worker strategies and transport capital on the railroads of Ecuador, Zambia and Zimbabwe, 1916–1950," PhD thesis, University of Minnesota.

Schoonover, Thomas D. (1991) *The United States in Central America, 1860–1911: Episodes of Social Imperialism and Imperial Rivalry in the World System*. Durham, NC and London: Duke University Press.

Solien Gonzalez, Nancie L. (1969) *Black Carib Household Structure: A Study of Migration and Modernization*. Seattle: University of Washington Press.

Stein, Judith (1986) *The World of Marcus Garvey: Race and Class in Modern Society*, 143. Baton Rouge and London: Louisiana State University Press.

Stuckey, Sterling (1987) *Slave Culture: Nationalist Theory and the Foundations of Black America*. New York: Oxford University Press.

Wade, Peter (1998) "Migrants in Medellín" in N. E. Whitten, Jr and A. Torres (eds.), *Blackness in Latin America and the Caribbean: Social Dynamics and Cultural Transformations*, vol. 1, Central America and Northern and Western South America, 401, 408. Bloomington: Indiana University Press.

Whitten, Norman E., Jr and Torres, Arlene (eds.) (1998) *Blackness in Latin America and the Caribbean: Social Dynamics and Cultural Transformations*, vol. 1, Central America and Northern and Western South America, 15, 81. Bloomington: Indiana University Press.

Williams, Eric Eustace (1944) *Capitalism and Slavery*. London: André Deutsch.

Wright, Winthrop R. (1974) "Elite attitudes toward race in twentieth-century Venezuela" in Robert Brent Toplin (ed.), *Slavery and Race Relations in Latin America*, 325–47. Westport, CT: Greenwood Press.

—— (1990) *Café Con Leche: Race, Class, and National Image in Venezuela*, 2–4, 13–14, 76–8. Austin: University of Texas Press.

PART II

Africans in Early North America

CHAPTER FIVE

Ethnicity, Nationality, and Race in Colonial America

JEFFREY ELTON ANDERSON

Some of the finest books and articles of the past fifty years have dealt with the history of race. Traditionally, however, the most persistent goal of the historical profession has been the production of narratives detailing the rise, maturation, and, if applicable, fall of nations. Books tracing the historical development of the United States, Great Britain, and other Western countries have been popular for hundreds, and in some cases thousands, of years. Following the upheavals of the French Revolution of the late eighteenth century, scholars began to produce an increasing number of works telling the story of ethnicities, often for the purpose of mobilizing particular populations in the cause of nationalism. Only during the last two hundred years have substantial numbers of works examined the histories of particular races. This trend has grown in popularity in the United States following the success of the Civil Rights Movement during the 1950s, 1960s, and 1970s. Today, courses in African American history and minority studies are common fare on most college campuses. Clearly race has come to rival the nation as a focus of group identity.

One of the most profound changes of the second half of the twentieth century was the realization that identity, whether national, ethnic, racial, or otherwise, is a social construct. This fact has had little impact on the world outside of academia thus far. Laypersons continue to view nationality, ethnicity, and race as fixed categories. For intellectuals, however, the question of constructed identities is a thorny issue that complicates any attempt to write the history of particular peoples, however defined. In response, historians have expended vast amounts of energy scrutinizing the processes through which collections of individuals produce group identities. In no area of American historiography has this development been more profound than in the study of the development of racial identities that trump both national and ethnic identifications. Of particular importance to scholars is the colonial period, an era during which Europeans, Africans, and Native Americans interacted closely for the first time. It was in this unstable period that the first steps toward the polarized white-*versus*-black society of nineteenth- and early twentieth-century America were made. Among the chief issues under consideration have been the question of whether slavery or race came first, and, if the latter, when and why it surpassed ethnicity and nationality as the supreme form of otherness. Other studies examine the interplay of other social constructions and race, the definition of non-black races, and most recently, the importance of racial self-definition.

Toward Race as a Construct

Scholarly debate over the roots of race is a recent phenomenon, but its background stretches back to early anthropologists and sociologists. Before historians could argue about the origins of race, they first had to accept that African Americans were not inherently inferior to Western Europeans. The first step in this direction was anthropologist Franz Boas' 1911 book, *The Mind of Primitive Man*, which redefined anthropological inquiry by rejecting race as a determinant of culture, intelligence, or temperament. He went on to argue that other races and cultures cannot be ranked in a progressive hierarchy. Later sociologists and anthropologists, most notably Margaret Mead (1928), built on his assertions, articulating a concept of "cultural relativism," the idea that one must judge other cultures by their own criteria and not those of the observer's society. For many years, this departure from traditional anthropological (and historical) tradition went unnoticed, but today it is clear that the work of Boas and his successors helped undermine scholars' established biases against "inferior peoples."

Social scientists contributed more than just the theory of cultural relativity, however. They were also driven by the more practical aim of eliminating the racial, ethnic, and cultural prejudices common to Western society during the first decades of the twentieth century. Boas' own experiences with the prejudice he experienced because of his Jewish heritage helped inspire him to break free from tradition. Mead, too, worked out of more than scholarly concern. For instance, her most famous work, *Coming of Age in Samoa: A Psychological Study of Primitive Youth for Western Civilisation* (1928), was partly an attempt to "reform" American sexual practices by adopting "superior" Samoan ones (Gossett 1963: 417–24; Newman 1996). The same reformist impulse that drove the early social scientists was later to inspire many of the seminal works to address the history of race.

By the 1940s, some anthropologists had gone on to reject race as well as racism. Ashley Montagu presented such an argument in *Man's Most Dangerous Myth: The Fallacy of Race* (1942). He acknowledged that common physical traits could distinguish different populations of humans. He denied, however, that physical characteristics provided adequate grounds to separate humankind into rigidly delineated racial categories. Although many historians embraced the concept of cultural relativism, most initially saw the rejection of race as a valid categorization of humankind as throwing "out the baby of race with the bathwater of racism" (Jordan 1968: 609).

Debate on the origin of slavery was a more recent ancestor of the history of race. Nineteenth-century historians assumed that British North American slavery began in 1619 when the first Africans arrived in Virginia. Shortly after the turn of the century, however, James C. Ballagh (Vaughan 1995: 137–40; Ballagh 1902) reevaluated the evidence and concluded that colonists had treated the first African Americans as indentured servants. As such, they would eventually regain their freedom. Ballagh argued that slavery did not begin until the 1660s and 1670s, when legislation condemned blacks to lives of permanent servitude. A few other prominent historians accepted Ballagh's argument, most notably Ulrich B. Phillips (1918).

Over the years, the origin of slavery would gradually develop into a prominent topic in the historiography of colonial America (see Chapter Eight). Such works had little to say about race as a concept, however. Nevertheless, by subjecting the traditional explanation for the origins of slavery to questioning, historians separated race from an institution with which it had been strongly tied. In the past, most scholars had uncritically assumed that both race and slavery had existed from the first contact of white Virginians and unwilling African immigrants. With the latter assumption subjected to reevaluation, it became possible for the former to be questioned as well.

Colonial Americans and Other Races

The categories of race, ethnicity, and nationality were competing and unstable concepts in colonial America. To be sure, the English had drawn notable distinctions between Africans and other non-English populations, such as competing European nations or Native Americans. For instance, though both Africans and Indians possessed notable physical differences from the English, white settlers responded to them in very different ways. As historian Kathleen Brown put it, "Enslaved Africans in British North America were viewed as culturally malleable compared to Indians but less easily physically transformed . . . by unions with the English" (Brown 1999: 95). In fact, the Europeans initially thought of Indians as physically identical to themselves, explaining obvious dissimilarities in terms of exposure to the elements and distinctive dress. They judged Africans, however, as inherently different, though more open to English efforts to "civilize" them than the Indians living beyond the bounds of colonial rule. Colonists eventually came to admire Indians as "noble savages" outside the bonds and benefits of European civilization, but also to loath them as potentially threatening others. Observers frequently recorded the supposed barbarism of Africans and African American slaves, but they rarely found noble qualities to praise.

Much less did British colonists acknowledge any African American right to an independent national identity in the New World. As historian Alden T. Vaughan has noted, Europeans rarely identified African arrivals in the colonies with terms denoting either nation or ethnicity (Vaughan 1995: 172–3). Pale-skinned colonists might be English, Irish, Dutch, or the like. Even Indians might be Iroquois, Catawba, or Cherokee. Africans, meanwhile, were rarely Yorubas, Kongolese, Igbo, or the like. They were simply "Negroes," a term referring to skin color.

Although the British colonists had certainly adopted a form of slavery based on otherness by the late seventeenth century, slave status had by no means been confined to a particular "race." The English had few qualms about consigning their fellow countrymen and countrywomen to temporary slavery in the form of indentured servitude. More important, hostile Native American peoples provided a vast reservoir of potential laborers. The historical record provides many instances of Indian enslavement. For example, between 1704 and 1710, historians estimate that

English slave raids into Spanish Florida captured as many as 12,000 Native American prisoners. Likewise, by 1708, nearly one-third of the Carolinas' slaves were Native Americans (Nash 2000: 99–102, 119–20).

In the same vein, racial concepts developed differently among the various colonial peoples, such as the French and English. The English early showed a preoccupation with purity of blood. As early as the late seventeenth century, laws designed to preserve white racial purity by forbidding interracial sexual liaisons were common in the colonies. By the nineteenth century, possessing a single drop of African blood defined a person as black in the eyes of the American descendants of the English. The French took a different course. They understood race as a hierarchy of blackness and whiteness based on the proportion of black or white forebears one possessed. Mulattoes, with one white and one black parent, were of a higher status than full-blooded Africans. Quadroons and octoroons, of one quarter and one eighth black ancestry respectively, filled a higher niche in the social hierarchy. As the prevalence of so many categories in the French colonies suggests, racial classification there was not the all-or-nothing proposition that it was in the English territories – which may mean the French were far less concerned with purity than the English, or that they were more sensitive to fine distinctions. By the late colonial period, wealthy white youths even attended "quadroon balls," during which they danced with mixed-race women. In many cases, these balls were a time for white men to choose a concubine. The Spanish, the other major colonial power in the area, adopted a similarly hierarchical view of race. With such alternatives available, historians are faced with the question of why the English and their descendants adopted a strict black–white dichotomy to define race.

At the same time, though most surviving sources refer to all Africans as "Negroes," international slave traders and their customers certainly recognized national and ethnic designations in their choice of slaves. For example, South Carolinian planters shunned purchasing Igbo captives, whom they characterized as small, weak, lazy, and given to suicide. They were much more willing to purchase peoples from the areas of Senegal, Gambia, and the Gold Coast (Gomez 1998: 114–17). At the same time, historians now recognize that such ethnicities were often white inventions, used to impose order on scattered villages with little concept of any ethnic and/or national identity. On the contrary, many African societies stressed kinship networks on a village level far more than any abstract concept of a more widespread group unity (Northrup 2000).

As historians approached the middle of a century – the twentieth – that would see a profound shift in racial attitudes, they had begun to question whether the long history of racial discord that had defined so much of American history could have been avoided. Clearly, the fact that an opposition of black and white would come to define the meaning of both race and slavery was uncertain during the colonial period. The great questions exposed by the social scientists and historians studying the question of slavery were quite broad. First, assuming that Europeans' enslavement of Africans had taken place gradually, decades after the arrival of the first blacks in 1619, did race and racism play a role in the process? If not, did slavery help to create race? Second, if race truly was a construct, why did it develop into a category of difference that trumped such other major classifications as ethnicity and nationality?

Early Historical Debates about Race

Historians failed to realize the possibilities suggested by the slavery debate for several years. By 1940, however, they had begun to study race explicitly in the context of the origins of racism. One of the first examples of this type of work is *Race: Science and Politics*, by Ruth Benedict ([1940] 1945: 97–164). European nationalist racism, particularly that of Hitler's Third Reich, provided much of its inspiration. As a result, the book broadly focused on racism throughout Europe and the Americas. According to Benedict, true racism was based on the idea that certain races are biologically inferior. It did not develop until the post-Darwin era, she averred, but an earlier form of in-group/out-group prejudice had existed from prehistoric times. A type of *de facto* race prejudice, without the ideological backing of biological racism, originated during the early period of European expansion into the New World. As applied to blacks, this early prejudice became an excuse for colonial slavery.

As Benedict explained, almost all of the blacks were non-Christians, allowing Europeans to enslave them as enemies of Christ. As increasing numbers of African Americans converted to the Christian faith, their owners had to turn to other grounds to justify slavery. Skin color proved to be the most obvious difference between the races, so colonists adopted it as the factor that would separate the slaves from the free. In time, class differences and nationalist ethnocentrism broadened the gap between slaveholders and their chattels. Benedict departed sharply from previous historical works by stating that slavery played a part in transforming in-group/out-group prejudice into racism and followed her social scientist predecessors by using her scholarly work to attack prejudice. Although later historians debated (and continue to debate) what part slavery played in creating racism, the struggle to overcome prejudice has remained constant as an implicit and sometimes explicit motivation for their work.

With Frank Tannenbaum's *Slave and Citizen* (1947), two new features entered the study of racism's origins. First, unlike Benedict's *Race*, Tannenbaum's work was a response to America's own racial inequities. It was specifically geared to facing the fact that the freedom-loving United States continued to define African Americans as second-class citizens and to erect strict barriers between whites and blacks. Second, Tannenbaum followed a commonly held but later debunked assumption that Latin America was free of racism, comparing the British and Spanish slave systems in an effort to determine the origins of North American racism. Tannenbaum concluded that Latin American slavery differed from that of the English because Spain's ancient Roman and Catholic-influenced legal codes accorded slaves moral equality with their masters. In Britain, however, slavery and early laws governing it had faded away by the period of European expansionism. Therefore, when other nations introduced black slavery to the British colonies, white settlers came to equate Africans with slaves. In the absence of laws or customs that defined slaves as in any way equal to their masters, the English quickly came to see blacks as an inferior race fit only for slavery.

To be sure, not everyone accepted Benedict and Tannenbaum's conclusions. Most, in fact, paid them little attention. Others criticized their conclusion. One of the chief to do so was Wesley Frank Craven (1949), who attacked the idea that racism was a result of slavery. He maintained that whites had been prejudiced against Negroes from the outset. Craven's assault, however, did little to weaken the Benedict–Tannenbaum hypothesis. After all, both Benedict and Tannenbaum's conclusions about the origin of racism had little immediate impact on the scholarly world. Naturally, Craven's critique went largely unnoticed.

The Origins Debate

By the late 1940s, those scholars who had studied deeply in the literature of slavery understood the possible distinctions between racism and the peculiar institution. By the 1950s, the times were ripe for studies of race to enter the arena of scholarly debate. In 1947, Jackie Robinson became the first African American to be integrated into a white major-league baseball team. The following year, Harry Truman banned racial discrimination in the hiring of federal employees and ended military segregation. In 1950, the Supreme Court took the first tentative step toward desegregation in education by ruling that a separate black law school in Texas could not measure up to white ones because its students were unable to interact with white lawyers, who composed the majority of the legal profession.

Within this progressive milieu, husband-and-wife team Oscar and Mary F. Handlin provided the vehicle that catapulted race to the center of historical debate. In a profoundly influential article entitled "Origins of the southern labor system" (1950), they introduced a new version of the racism-from-slavery argument. According to the Handlins, laws against runaways, interclass marriage, and the like gradually came to be more strictly applied to black servants/slaves than to white servants. Thereby, slavery became tied to color, locking blacks into colonial North America's lowest socioeconomic class. As slave populations increased in the late-seventeenth century, further legislation widened the gap between the races. By 1700, African Americans had ceased to be people and had become property.

The Handlins' analysis reflected the optimism of their time. By concluding that racism had not been a constant feature of American society, they provided hope that it could also be stamped out. Events seemed to prove them right. The 1950s saw monumental events in the history of the struggle for racial equality, including the Supreme Court's *Brown versus Board of Education of Topeka, Kansas*, a decision that effectively paved the way for the desegregation of all public schools, and the successful Montgomery Bus Boycott. In light of such changes, the Handlins' thesis proved attractive to scholars. For the next nine years, their conclusions went virtually unchallenged. Intellectuals agreed that racism was not a given in American society.

Carl Degler forever shattered the consensus. In "Slavery and the genesis of American race prejudice" (1959), he vociferously attacked the Handlins. Degler argued that racism was present from the time that blacks arrived in America and that it played a role in enslaving blacks. To back up his contention, Degler cited documentary evidence, which demonstrated that colonists treated their black servants worse than white ones. He also pointed out that prejudice existed in colonial New England, where slavery played only a minor role, and that colonists held racist attitudes toward Native Americans before Negroes first arrived in Virginia. "Slavery and the genesis of American race prejudice" sparked a response from the Handlins, and an often passionate and sometimes bitter argument erupted between the two parties.

It continued for the next three years and set the intellectual tone for what would follow.

For the six years following 1962, debate died down. The cause for this was Winthrop D. Jordan's essay published that year, "Modern tensions and the origins of American slavery." Jordan took a different path from either the Handlins or Degler. Jordan suggested that racism and slavery originated at approximately the same time and that each strengthened the other. Assigning an identical chronological origin to both the institution and the mindset mollified both sides of the debate for the moment. After all, it removed the chief focus of debate by providing an alternative that specifically attacked neither the Handlins nor Degler. Jordan's interpretation quickly gained wide acceptance among scholars and temporarily decided the issue for many.

Although the dispute abated from 1962 to 1968, it did not disappear. In 1963, Thomas F. Gossett produced *Race: The History of an Idea in America*. Gossett's work combined elements from both the Handlin and Degler positions, though he ultimately fell within the Handlin camp. He argued that race prejudice had existed before the English ever colonized North America. Gossett claimed that it had originated in English Protestants' exclusivity toward non-Christian blacks. Moreover, since English men typically brought their families with them when they settled in America, they were less likely to bridge the widening racial gap by intermarriage. Nevertheless, he argued, race prejudice remained unimportant until slavery grew in prominence during the eighteenth century. By that time, whites had observed the degraded condition of their slaves and concluded that blacks must have had different biological origins from whites. At the heart of Gossett's conclusion was a narrow definition of "race" that relied on biological concepts. The prejudice against blacks that had existed from earlier days had lacked the scientific aspect, rendering it different from true racism. This new level of nuance was to mark much of what followed.

Ironically, Winthrop D. Jordan, the man who had gone far toward resolving the origins debate, was to reopen it by backing away from the conclusions he presented in "Modern tensions." He did so with *White over Black: American Attitudes Toward the Negro, 1550–1812* (1968). In some ways, his work was an in-depth elaboration of the Degler thesis, but he went further than any previous historian (and many since, for that matter) by detailing the rise of racism among the English. According to Jordan, the road toward prejudice began with the first contact between the Elizabethan English and sub-Saharan Africans. As a first impression, the British described Africans as "black," a term loaded with negative connotations at the time, "heathens," "savages," and "lewd." Through these "observations," English Protestants projected their own subconscious fears and fixations upon blacks. Since Africans were lewd, heathens, and savage potential enemies, they qualified for slavery, which the English modeled on Spanish and Portuguese predecessors. As blacks gradually became similar to the English in religion, morals, and civilization, the British unthinkingly made skin color the rationale for enslavement. During the eighteenth century, race-consciousness increased as slave populations grew and as whites applied philosophical and scientific concepts of classification to blacks. The American Revolution, by proclaiming equality among men, forced whites to explain the presence of inequality in their midst. They produced the first true ideology of black racial inferiority. In the face of a rejuvenated slave economy, fading libertarian-ism, a weak antislavery movement, and growing numbers of free blacks, nineteenth-century conservatives hardened concepts of racial inferiority into a rigid form of biological racism.

It is difficult to understate the importance of Jordan's work. In one sense, it presented a Gossett-like argument, stressing a gradual development of racism. Unlike Gossett, however, Jordan stressed the pre-slavery origins of what would later develop into racism. At the same time, by examining the changing face of racial prejudice in greater detail than ever before, Jordan had produced the first in-depth history of race. Historians were impressed. *White Over Black* remains staple fare for graduate students to this day and frequently appears in professors' lectures to undergraduate students. Despite its influence, however, historians had a difficult time coming to grips with the implications of Jordan's new approach to race (Vaughan 1995: 144–5; Campbell and Oakes 1993: 172–83).

The most immediate impact of Jordan's work was that it forced subsequent studies to take on a new level of complexity. Nevertheless, scholars generally slipped back into the origins debate. The fourth edition of Lerone Bennett, Jr's *Before the Mayflower: A History of Black America* (1969) appeared shortly after *White over Black*. It was one of the first books to deal in depth with white class differences and their effect upon race prejudice. According to Bennett, white elites had created racism as a strategy to keep black slaves, Indians, and poor whites from forming a unified lower class. The threat of lower-class unity had been proven in such notable upheavals as Nathaniel Bacon's revolt against Virginia's colonial authorities in 1676.

Though not a scholarly work and lacking footnotes that would have supported its conclusions, *Before the Mayflower* strongly influenced later historians. During the first half of the 1970s, several scholars adopted its conclusions about elites' role in creating racism. One of the most important authors to do so was Edmund S. Morgan, who examined the role that slaveowning elites had played in creating race prejudice (Morgan 1972–3: 5–29; Morgan 1975: 316–37). On the basis of evi-dence suggesting that increased importation of African slaves followed the white-led Bacon's Rebellion, he concluded that racism had been a class strategy to break up the laboring class. Theodore Allen's " 'They would have destroyed me': slavery and the origins of racism" (1975) laid even greater blame than did Morgan's studies on class conflict. Focusing on the latter half of the seventeenth century, Allen depicted planters as becoming ever more fearful that the combined black and white prole-tariat would overthrow their rule. Following the class-based rebellion, planters placed stronger restrictions on their slaves and co-opted lower-class whites, as a "superior race," to control the growing black population.

The early 1970s also saw the production of a number of more orthodox versions of the Handlin and Degler theses. One of the most important was George M. Fredrickson's "Toward a social interpretation of the development of American racism" (1971), which reinterpreted the Handlin thesis primarily by differentiating between implicit and explicit racism. The former variety, he posited, evolved out of early colonists' aversion to African Americans' foreign culture and black skin. It was essentially the same as the chauvinism that the English directed toward any outsider. This antipathy amounted to little more than mild prejudice until the late 1600s. By the end of the seventeenth century and the beginning of the eighteenth, however, colonists' fear of the growing number of blacks, whites' pursuit of privilege, and their greed for profit created an implicitly racist hierarchy. Nevertheless, it was not until the antebellum period that explicit racism, based on the openly argued principle that blacks were biologically inferior to whites, was adopted. On the other hand, Alden T. Vaughan entered the debate by offering a new interpretation of documentary evidence in support of Degler's thesis. Vaughan's 1972 essay "Blacks in Virginia: a note on the first decade" convincingly demonstrated that prejudice toward African Americans was a powerful force in colonial Virginia from the outset.

From 1974 to 1990, most of the dispute on racism's origins centered around variations on the Handlin thesis. For instance, Theodore Breen and Stephen Innes produced a local study demonstrating that Morgan and Allen's stress on the effects of Bacon's Rebellion – and the consequent increased slave importation as the turning point in creating modern racism – was accurate, at least for Virginia's Eastern Shore. Before the insurrection, economic status had determined both whites' and blacks' place in society. Within a few years after the rebellion, the upward mobility allowed by economic status had disappeared for African Americans (Breen and Innes 1980: 3–6). Three years later, John B. Boles followed Ruth Benedict and George Fredrickson by dividing race prejudice into categories. Like some of his predecessors' works, *Black Southerners, 1619–1869* suggested that a vague form of implicit racism characterized the seventeenth century and that a legally precise and rigid societal racism replaced it in the 1700s (Boles 1983: 7–24). As with the earlier authors, Boles emphasized that biologically-based explicit/ideological racism was a product of nineteenth-century thought.

Other authors were pushing the origins of racism forward chronologically. Duncan J. Macleod, in his *Slavery, Race, and the American Revolution*, argued that racism was a product of the American Revolution (Macleod 1974: 80). Its stress on liberty required the slaveholding elites who formed the backbone of the movement to explain why their concepts of freedom did not extend to black slaves. In 1990, Barbara Jeanne Fields likewise focused on the Revolution as the focal point around which racism developed (Fields 1990: 95–117). Both works echoed Winthrop Jordan, who had claimed that racism arose out of whites' attempt to justify black slavery in a time of libertarian ideology.

The 1980s were the high point for the Handlin thesis. Though the racism-from-slavery interpretation remained popular, a new wave of Deglerites forced their opponents to adopt a defensive posture by the end of the decade. In 1989, Alden T. Vaughan produced an article tracing the history of the origins debate. Although the essay was primarily meant as a historiographical work, he took the opportunity to present his own conclusions on the beginnings of racism. He argued that its source could be found outside of British North America, in Britain itself. Vaughan also carried his interpretations well beyond many of his predecessors by explaining exactly why race became such an important category of identity. According to him, the English understood Africans from the standpoint of the Biblical "curse of Ham." Genesis 9: 20–27 states that Noah had cursed Ham's son, Canaan, to a life of perpetual servitude to his brothers, Shem and Japheth. The English identified Ham as the ancestor of black Africans and themselves as descendants of Japheth. Along with their observations of Africans' unusual color and "lewd" sexual practices, this belief was enough to create a definite ideological racism, albeit not based on biological concepts, that predated slavery and even most Englishmen's first encounters with Africans.

After Vaughan, scholars gradually pushed the origins of racism further and further into the Old World past. Bernard Lewis, author of *Race and Slavery in the Middle East* (1990), helped the process by his examination of the construction of race outside of a Western context. Writing to refute the traditional interpretation of Islamic slavery that describes it as quite benign and free of racial connections, Bernard concluded that medieval and early modern Muslims defined their dark-skinned slaves in ways remarkably similar to what would later develop in the British colonies. According to him, they considered black slaves unintelligent, vicious, dishonest, smelly, dirty, ugly, overly sexual, and the like. Unlike slaves of other nationalities, they rarely rose to positions of authority, and they were also more often made eunuchs than other peoples. Moreover, in the case of black Africans, Muslims frequently overlooked Koranic proscriptions banning the enslavement of co-religionists. As early as the 1500s, black jurists found it necessary to refute Arab claims that the Curse of Ham authorized the capture and sale of black Muslims. In 1997, James Sweet linked Lewis' conclusions to New World racism by pointing out the long-standing cultural interaction between Muslims and Christians in the Iberian Peninsula. According to him, Islamic racial concepts easily made the crossover to their Spanish and Portuguese foes, who were to later provide the model for English racial thought.

One of the most original recent contributions to the origins debate was Ivan Hannaford's *Race: The History of an Idea in the West* (1996). Like Sweet, he found the roots of modern racism outside of Western Europe. On the other hand, however, he argued that the most important source for modern racial thought was the medieval Jewish Cabbalah. Cabbalah made the concept of races possible by dividing humans into groups through its "Doctrine of Countenances." This doctrine, wrote Hannaford, was the first to argue that a population's physical characteristics were outside indications of the interior character of the people. By the nineteenth century, a wide array of other influences, including hemetic philosophy, stress on the folk, and scientific systems of classification, acted to transform this "pre-idea" into true racism. Hannaford's originality was striking and suggested an origin for racism that no one had investigated before. By the time *Race* appeared in print, Hannaford was dead. His contribution was to be one of the last major works of the origins debate.

Escaping the Origins Debate

The origins question had defined the historiography of race throughout most of its history, but by the mid-1990s historians had begun to discover a wide range of previously unexplored aspects of race. Probably the most important work of this period was not a book, but a special 1997 issue of the *William and Mary Quarterly* devoted entirely to the construction of race. Many of the articles that filled its pages fit snugly into the Handlin–Degler dichotomy. At the same time, it included examples of some of the new directions that scholars were taking, in their studies of race. As was the case with the Handlins, who had provided the foundation for the historical study of race, this new wave of scholarship was a response to the issues of the day, most notably feminism, environmentalism, and animal rights, the reasons for the persistence of racism, and African American agency.

Feminist scholarship had made it possible for historians to treat gender as a construct, much as early social scientists had made debates on the origin of race possible. One of the most original of the *William and Mary* articles examined the interplay of these two constructs. In " 'Some could suckle over their shoulder': male travelers, female bodies, and the gendering of racial ideology, 1500–1770", Jennifer Morgan argued that European males focused on female Africans and Native Americans in their efforts to define race. For instance, travelers and colonists contrasted African women's quick return to labor after childbirth, supposed sexual deviance, and "distorted" bodies sporting distended breasts with their ideal of European women's reputation for weakness after childbirth, chaste lives, and attractive bodies. Blacks' obvious shortfalls in European concepts of femininity supposedly proved their inferiority to whites.

A year earlier, Kathleen Brown had produced a similar but much more detailed study of specifically American attitudes to race entitled *Good Wives, Nasty Wenches, and Anxious Patriarchs: Gender, Race, and Power in Colonial Virginia* (1996). In it, she examined the interplay of race, gender, and to a lesser degree, class. Before American colonization began, the English had well-defined images of sex roles, placing women in the home as "good wives" while their husbands performed productive labor. They carried these gender images with them to the New World. In contrast, race was ill-defined before the massive influx of slaves to the colonies during the mid-seventeenth century. During the course of the 1600s, gender defined all groups of society. For example, in the wake of Bacon's Rebellion, laws removed blacks' right to own a gun, a crucial feature of colonial manhood. By deliberately ascribing feminine characteristics to African Americans, white colonists not only broke the ties binding white and black producers together but also defined blackness as feminine, and thus subordinate.

Not all historians accepted the gender theory of racial construction. Others preferred a similar theory that stressed colonial descriptions of slaves in terms usually reserved for animals. Winthrop Jordan had identified such comparisons as early as 1968, but recent scholars have examined them in greater depth. According to scholars like Karl Jacoby (1994), slavery blurred the distinction between human chattels and animals. Colonists throughout the New World usually recognized the humanity of slaves but described their bondspersons' lives as resembling those of animals. Comparisons between slaves and hogs, horses, cattle, and the like were common in colonial documents. By explicitly drawing such comparisons, colonists constructed race in such a way that it placed Africans and other non-white peoples in a hierarchy somewhere between animal and human, thereby permanently defining them as inferior.

Jacoby and his successors were responding to environmentalists and animal rights activists who argued that the environment and domestic animals were the unwilling slaves of the human race. To be sure, Jacoby did not advocate animal liberation. In fact, he had dismissed most such arguments by pointing out a fact that most such radicals forget, that domestic animals and humans are dependent on each other for survival. At the same time, he did apply radical environmentalists' descriptions of human tyranny over the natural world to explain why whites were willing to similarly extend their lordship over peoples physically different from themselves.

During the 1960s, Winthrop Jordan and most other historians had rejected the social science assertion that races did not exist. While racism might be a construct, race was not. Over the succeeding three decades, most had changed their minds. By the 1990s, many had come to wonder whether the popular separation of humankind into races was not itself a cause of racism and the reason for its survival despite more than four decades of government attempts to end it. In consequence, scholars found it necessary to determine how races other than that of blacks came into being. This development was reflected in the pages of the *William and Mary Quarterly* special issue. Two of the articles (Kupperman 1997: 193–228; Chaplin 1997: 229–52) specifically addressed the question of how Europeans defined Native Americans as a race. The colonists did this by gradually moving away from a belief that Indian physical differences were a result of cultural and environmental factors. The authors differ on the reasons for the change, but stress that an idea of an Indian race was clearly developing by the late colonial era.

Indians were not the only race to receive new attention. Historians also came to the conclusion that whiteness was just as much a social construction as was blackness. A few prominent books on the topic have appeared in recent years. One early example was Theodore Allen's *The Invention of the White Race* (2 vols: 1994, 1997). As he had in his earlier works, Allen maintained that racism was a form of social control begun by elite whites. On the other hand, he also stressed that the construction of a superior white race was a vital ingredient of the racist program. Other works have stressed the exclusivity of the white race, conclusively demonstrating that it has not always embraced everyone with a pale skin. At times, the English and their American descendants identified Anglo-Saxons as the only true whites. Frequently excluded were Celts, Jews, Germans, and virtually any other nationality or ethnicity (Ignatiev 1996; Jacobson 1998).

One recent development that was not represented in the *William and Mary* special issue was the search for black agency in the creation of race. African American agency had been increasingly important in studies of slavery and slave life since the publication of Eugene Genovese's *Roll, Jordan, Roll: The World the Slaves Made* (1974). Genovese had argued that slaves, far from being victims completely at the mercy of an unjust system, had worked to resist oppression and create their own society. Over the next two decades, historians were slow to apply his conclusions to the concept of race because their arguments usually centered on the rise of racism, not race *per se*. Thus, it was both unpersuasive and impolitic to argue that African Americans had taken part in creating a belief in black racial inferiority. Once scholars began to break free from an idea of race defined solely by racism, uncovering black agency became possible.

One of the boldest proponents of African American agency has been James Sidbury. In *Ploughshares into Swords: Race, Rebellion, and Identity in Gabriel's Virginia, 1730–1810*, he argued that black slaves were already developing an "incipient racial identity" by the end of the colonial period (Sidbury 1997: 12). Expanding settlement sparked the process, which accelerated following the American Revolution and early nineteenth-century evangelical revivals. Together, these events led to a new group identity that transcended religion, ancestral African ethnicity, and local community.

James Sidbury was not alone in seeing African American agency at work in constructing race. One year later, Michael Gomez presented a similar argument in *Exchanging Our Country Marks: The Transformation of African Identities in the Colonial and Antebellum South* (1998). Gomez accepted that the idea of race was an invention of Europeans, which they later foisted upon blacks as part of their sordid history of oppression. Nevertheless, African Americans early began to adopt a racial identity in place of older ethnic identifications. Gomez added a new dimension to his argument by emphasizing lower-class blacks' role in formulating race. While many earlier historians had argued that elite whites were the driving force in creating race, he maintained that elite blacks had worked against it by fighting to be included in the freedoms of American life and by rejecting distinctive African elements of their culture. Many lower-class blacks, in contrast, turned to spirituality in the form of Christianity and Afro-European hoodoo as a means to achieve equality. In practice, religion had a unifying effect, leading blacks to embrace a common racial identity by the early antebellum era. In short, according to Sidbury and Gomez, while blacks did not create the white–black dichotomy of slavery, they worked to reshape it by emphasizing a strong self-identification that valued those qualities of blackness scorned by whites. For the first time, historians had recognized the role African Americans had played in shaping their racial identity.

The history of race has come a long way from the days of Degler and the Handlins. Today, scholars agree on many features of race. Most concede that some form of prejudice existed before slavery appeared on the scene. At the same time, they are in general agreement that racial categories grew more rigid over time. On the other hand, many disputes remain unresolved. For one, few agree on just what constitutes racism, much less race. For many, racism and race can only exist once societies accept a biological basis for difference and the supposed inferiority of outsiders. Others, however, see the results of prejudice as more important than their ideological underpinnings. In addition, scholars have only begun to evaluate the impact of other categories of group identity on race, most notably nationality, ethnicity, and gender. Likewise, historians have yet to fully examine the extent of African American agency in choosing to create or accept racial categories over national and ethnic identities. Finally, the definition of race for non-blacks also remains severely understudied. The existence of disagreements and tentative steps in new directions, however, guarantee that the topic will remain a fertile field for scholars, who will continue to shed new light on the history of race for years to come.

BIBLIOGRAPHY

Works Cited

Allen, Theodore W. (1994, 1997) *The Invention of the White Race*, 2 vols., Haymarket Series. London and New York: Verso.
—— (1975) " 'They would have destroyed me': slavery and the origins of racism," *Radical America* 9 (May–June): 40–63.
Ballagh, James Curtis (1902) *A History of Slavery in Virginia*. Baltimore: Johns Hopkins Press.
Barker, Anthony J. (1978) *The African Link: British Attitudes to the Negro in the Era of the Atlantic Slave Trade, 1550–1807*. London: Frank Cass.

Benedict, Ruth ([1940] 1945) *Race: Science and Politics*, revised edn., with *The Races of Mankind* by Gene Weltfish. New York: Viking Press.

Bennett, Lerone, Jr (1969) *Before the Mayflower: A History of Black America*, 4th edn. Chicago: Johnson Publishing.

Boas, Franz (1911) *The Mind of Primitive Man*. New York: Macmillan.

Boles, John B. (1983) *Black Southerners, 1619–1869*. Lexington: University Press of Kentucky.

Breen, Theodore H. and Innes, Stephen (1980) *"Myne Owne Ground:" Race and Freedom on Virginia's Eastern Shore, 1640–1676*. New York and Oxford: Oxford University Press.

Brown, Kathleen (1996) *Good Wives, Nasty Wenches, and Anxious Patriarchs: Gender, Race and Power in Colonial Virginia*. Chapel Hill: University of North Carolina Press.

—— (1999) "Native Americans and early modern concepts of race" in Martin Daunton and Rick Halpern (eds.) *Empire and Others: British Encounters with Indigenous Peoples, 1600–1850*, 79–100. London: UCL Press.

Campbell, James and Oakes, James (1993) "The invention of blacks: rereading White over Black," *Reviews in American History* 21: 172–83.

Chaplin, Joyce E. (1997) "Natural philosophy and an early racial idiom in North America: comparing English and Indian bodies," *William and Mary Quarterly* 3rd ser., 54: 229–52.

Craven, Wesley Frank (1949) *The Southern Colonies in the Seventeenth Century, 1607–1689*, vol. 1 of Wendell H. Stephenson and E. Merton Coulter (eds.), *A History of the South*. Baton Rouge: Louisiana State University.

Degler, Carl N. (1959) "Slavery and the genesis of American race prejudice," *Comparative Studies in Society and History* 2: 49–66.

Fields, Barbara Jeanne (1990) "Slavery, race and ideology in the United States of America," *New Left Review* no. 181 (May/June): 95–117.

Fredrickson, George M. (1971) "Toward a social interpretation of the development of American racism" in Nathan I. Huggins, Martin Kilson, and Daniel M. Fox (eds.), *Key Issues in the Afro-American Experience*, vol. 1: 240–54. 2 vols. New York: Harcourt Brace Jovanovich.

Genovese, Eugene (1974) *Roll, Jordan, Roll: The World the Slaves Made*. New York: Pantheon.

Gomez, Michael (1998) *Exchanging Our Country Marks: The Transformation of African Identities in the Colonial and Antebellum South*. Chapel Hill and London: University of North Carolina Press.

Gossett, Thomas F. (1963) *Race: The History of an Idea in America*. Dallas: Southern Methodist University.

Handlin, Oscar and Mary F. (1950) "Origins of the southern labor system," *William and Mary Quarterly* 3rd ser., 7: 199–222.

Hannaford, Ivan (1996) *Race: The History of an Idea in the West*. Washington, DC and Baltimore, MD: Woodrow Wilson Center and Johns Hopkins University Press.

Ignatiev, Noel (1996) *How the Irish Became White*. New York: Routledge.

Jacobson, Matthew Frye (1998) *Whiteness of a Different Color: European Immigration and the Alchemy of Race*. Cambridge, MA and London: Harvard University Press.

Jacoby, Karl (1994) "Slaves by nature? Domestic animals and human slaves," *Slavery and Abolition*, 15: 89–99.

Jordan, Winthrop D. ([1962] 1968) "Modern tensions and the origins of American slavery," with omissions, in Allen Weinstein and Frank Otto Gatell (eds.), *American Negro Slavery: A Modern Reader*, 13–24. New York and Oxford: Oxford University Press.

—— (1968) *White over Black: American Attitudes toward the Negro, 1550–1812*. Chapel Hill: University of North Carolina Press.

Kupperman, Karen Ordahl (1997) "Presentment of civility: English reading of American self-presentation in the early years of colonization," *William and Mary Quarterly* 3rd ser., 54: 193–228.

Lewis, Bernard (1990) *Race and Slavery in the Middle East*. New York and Oxford: Oxford University Press.

Macleod, Duncan J. (1974) *Slavery, Race, and the American Revolution*. London and New York: Cambridge University Press.

Mead, Margaret (1928) *Coming of Age in Samoa: A Psychological Study of Primitive Youth for Western Civilisation*. New York: W. Morrow.

Montagu, Ashley (1942) *Man's Most Dangerous Myth: The Fallacy of Race*, 4th edn. Cleveland, OH and New York: World Publishing.

Morgan, Edmund S. (1972–3) "Slavery and freedom: the American paradox," *Journal of American History* 59: 5–29.

—— (1975) *American Slavery, American Freedom: The Ordeal of Colonial Virginia*. New York: Norton.

Morgan, Jennifer L. (1997) "'Some could suckle over their shoulder': male travelers, female bodies, and the gendering of racial ideology, 1500–1770," *William and Mary Quarterly* 3rd ser., 54: 167–92.

Nash, Gary B. (2000) *Red, White and Black: The Peoples of Early North America*, 4th edn. Upper Saddle River, NJ: Prentice-Hall.

Newman, Louise M. (1996) "Coming of Age, but not in Samoa: reflections on Margaret Mead's legacy for Western liberal feminism," *American Quarterly* 48: 233–72.

Northrup, David (2000) "Igbo and myth Igbo: culture and ethnicity in the Atlantic world, 1600–1850," *Slavery and Abolition* 21: 1–20.

Phillips, Ulrich Bonnell (1918) *American Negro Slavery: A Survey of the Supply, Employment and Control of Negro Labor*. New York and London: D. Appleton.

Sidbury, James (1997) *Ploughshares into Swords: Race, Rebellion, and Identity in Gabriel's Virginia, 1730–1810*. Cambridge: Cambridge University Press.

Sweet, James (1997) "The Iberian roots of American racist thought," *William and Mary Quarterly* 3rd ser., 54: 143–66.

Tannenbaum, Frank (1947) *Slave and Citizen: The Negro in the Americas*. New York: Vintage Books.

Vaughan, Alden T. (1972) "Blacks in Virginia: a note on the first decade," *William and Mary Quarterly* 3rd ser., 29: 469–78.

—— (1989) "The origins debate: slavery and racism in seventeenth-century Virginia," *Virginia Magazine of History and Biography* 97: 311–54.

—— (1995) *Roots of American Racism: Essays on the Colonial Experience*. New York and Oxford: Oxford University Press.

Suggestions for Further Reading

Barker, Anthony J. (1978) *The African Link: British Attitudes to the Negro in the Era of the Atlantic Slave Trade, 1550–1807*. London: Frank Cass.

Bartels, Emily C. (1997) "Othello and Africa: postcolonialism reconsidered," *William and Mary Quarterly* 3rd ser., 54: 45–64.

Berlin, Ira (1998) *Many Thousands Gone: The First Two Centuries of Slavery in North America*. Cambridge, MA and London: Belknap Press of Harvard University Press.

Blackburn, Robin (1997) "The Old World background to European colonial slavery," *William and Mary Quarterly* 3rd ser., 54: 65–102.

Braude, Benjamin (1997) "The sons of Noah and the construction of ethnic and geographical identities in the medieval and early modern periods," *William and Mary Quarterly* 3rd ser., 54: 103–42.

Carretta, Vincent (1999) "Olaudah Equiano or Gustavus Vassa? New light on an eighteenth-century question of identity," *Slavery and Abolition* 20: 96–105.

Clinton, Catherine and Gillespie, Michele (eds.) (1997) *The Devil's Lane: Sex and Race in the Early South*. New York and London: Oxford University Press.

Elkins, Stanley M. (1959) *Slavery: A Problem in American Institutional and Intellectual Life*. Chicago: University of Chicago Press.

Hall, Kim F. (1995) *Things of Darkness: Economies of Race and Gender in Early Modern England*. Ithaca, NY and London: Cornell University Press.

Hodes, Martha (ed.) (1999) *Sex, Love, Race: Crossing Boundaries in North American History*. New York: New York University Press.

Hudson, Nicholas (1996) "From 'nation' to 'race': the origin of racial classification in eighteenth-century thought," *Eighteenth-Century Studies* 29: 247–64.

Malcolmson, Scott L. (2000) *One Drop of Blood: The American Misadventure of Race*. New York: Farrar, Straus, & Giroux.

Montagu, Ashley (1965) *The Idea of Race*. Lincoln: University of Nebraska Press.

Morgan, Philip D. (1995) "Slaves and livestock in eighteenth-century Jamaica: Vineyard Pen, 1750–1751," *William and Mary Quarterly* 3rd ser., 52: 47–76.

Noel, Donald (1972) *The Origins of American Slavery and Racism*. Columbus, OH: Merrill.

Pierson, William D. (1988) *Black Yankees: The Development of an Afro-American Subculture in Eighteenth-century New England*. Amherst: University of Massachusetts Press.

Rael, Patrick (2002) *Black Identity and Black Protest in the Antebellum North*. Chapel Hill: University of North Carolina Press.

Roediger, David R. (1994) *Towards the Abolition of Whiteness: Essays on Race, Politics, and Working Class History*. London and New York: Verso.

Taylor, Quintart (1998) *In Search of the Racial Frontier: African Americans in the American West, 1528–1990*. New York: W. W. Norton.

Vaughan, Alden T. and Vaughan, Virginia Mason (1997) "Before Othello: Elizabethan representations of sub-Saharan Africans," *William and Mary Quarterly* 3rd ser., 54: 19–44.

Wheeler, Roxann (2000) *The Complexion of Race: Categories of Difference in Eighteenth-century British Culture*. Philadelphia: University of Pennsylvania Press.

Williams, Eric E. (1944) *Capitalism and Slavery*. Chapel Hill: University of North Carolina Press.

CHAPTER SIX

Not Chattel, Not Free: Quasi-Free Blacks in the Colonial Era

ANTONIO F. HOLLAND AND DEBRA FOSTER GREENE

The study of African American history has grown phenomenally over the last three decades. Studies on slavery are voluminous and, with the new emphasis on Africans in the Diaspora, the potential for recovering additional knowledge seems limitless. The historiography of the free black population in North America continually builds on earlier works such as William Cooper Nell's *The Colored Patriot of the American Revolution* (1855) and George Washington Williams' *History of the Negro Race in America from 1619 to 1880* (1883). Unlike some aspects of African American history, where earlier works are discredited, the studies of the free black community extend a dialogue that began more than a century ago.

The history of the free black people in the slaveholding and slave societies of North America has been examined by such scholars as Lorenzo J. Greene, *The Negro in Colonial New England* (1943), John Hope Franklin, *The Free Negro in North Carolina, 1790–1860* (1943), Leon Litwack, *North of Slavery: The Negro in the Free States* (1961), Ira Berlin, *Slaves without Masters: The Free Negro in the Antebellum South* (1974), A. Leon Higginbotham, *In the Matter of Color: Race and the American Legal Process* (1978) and Gary B. Nash, *Forging Freedom: The Formation of Philadelphia's Black Community, 1720–1840* (1988). More recent studies of the free black population build on these earlier works.

The Earlier Twentieth Century

The purpose of this chapter is to provide an overview of historical works that examine the lives of the free black population in North America during the colonial era. In recent studies, historians have articulated regional, racial, and economic distinctions in the free black communities of this period. Modern scholarly interest in the free African American population began in the early twentieth century in the African American intellectual community. During what John Hope Franklin termed the second generation of African American scholarship, Carter G. Woodson founded the Association for the Study of Negro Life and History and provided a publishing outlet through the *Journal of Negro History* and the Associated Publishers for scholars interested in African Americans.

Alice Dunbar-Nelson was among the first scholars to have a monograph on free people of color published in the *Journal of Negro History*. Her article "People of color in Louisiana" – published in October 1916 and January 1917 – recounted the story of African importation to the colony of Louisiana and the growth of the *gens de color libres*. Dunbar-Nelson found that free people of color suffered certain restrictions, such as paying a capitation (head) tax, that the free white population did not. Moreover, the free people of color in Louisiana were subject to the laws of the *Code Noir*, published in 1724, which also applied to the enslaved population. Under the *Code*, "freed or free-born Negroes" who harbored fugitive slaves had to pay 30 livres for each day the fugitive was under their protection. White persons who were guilty of the same crime, however, were fined only 10 livres a day. If the free person of color was unable to pay the fine, they risked being sold into slavery. As a social restriction, under the *Code Noir* "neither free-born blacks nor slaves were allowed to receive gifts from whites" (Dunbar-Nelson 1916, 1917). Dunbar-Nelson's article presaged a number of later works that dealt with the difficulties free African Americans had in maintaining their freedom and interacting with others in the population, both black and white.

Dunbar-Nelson's article in the *Journal of Negro History* was followed by William L. Imes' "The legal status of free Negroes and slaves in Tennessee" in July 1919. Imes recovered several essential elements of the free African American population that resonated through colonial African American historiography. On the eve of the national period in American history, the free black population was relatively small; and, once free, their status was relatively precarious. The available avenues to freedom included manumission by will or deed and acts of emancipation by colonial governments. Throughout the colonial era, various colonial governments set restrictions on slaveholders' right to manumit their slaves. In addition most colonies required the emancipated person to be transported from the colony or risk being re-enslaved. As the doors to freedom closed on Africans and their American offspring, they sought alternative ways to gain freedom; among them was conversion to Christianity.

Works that examined the community during the nineteenth century, when the population was large and more visible, have dominated the historiography of free African Americans. Many studies took 1790 as their starting point because the first United States census provided evidence of a free African American population. In his article, "The origin and growth of the free Negro population of Charleston, South Carolina," published in 1941, E. Horace Fitchett indicated that his paper was "designed to throw some light on the genesis of the free Negro in Charleston's community." Fitchett found what other historians of the lower South and Gulf states area came to realize – that people of mixed racial origin dominated the free black population of those regions. Like many scholars of his era, he could not determine how early the free black population developed in the area he studied.

Lorenzo J. Greene and John Hope Franklin, writing about New England and North Carolina respectively, also indicated that the genesis of the free African American population was unknown. One of the difficulties Greene encountered in his study was that in New England at least, and possibly elsewhere, enslaved people were referred to as "servants" rather than "slaves," making it difficult to distinguish the free population who might also work as servants. Greene found that blacks were freed as early as 1646 and manumissions increased during the revolutionary era. As Fitchett found, Africans and African Americans faced a number of restrictions on their liberty, and their status was defined within the slave codes, which also included Indians. Greene concluded that the condition of free African Americans in New England was no better than anywhere else in colonial America and their freedom was restricted politically, economically, and socially.

In his work on North Carolina, John Hope Franklin found that there were more free African Americans in North Carolina than in any of the states south of it. The North Carolina free black population was essentially a rural and agricultural group, unlike free blacks in other states who were urban people. A factor that contributed to the black North Carolinian's desire to live in the countryside was that free blacks were required to pay ten shillings to town officials for the use of their towns. This regulation was not applied to free blacks living in the country. Franklin believed that free African Americans probably existed in the North Carolina colony from the beginning (Greene 1942; Franklin 1943).

Antebellum Studies in the 1960s and 1970s

There was a long gap until Leon F. Litwack wrote *North of Slavery: The Negro in the Free States, 1790–1860*, published in 1961. Although the work focused on the nineteenth century and highlighted the many restrictions that northern states placed on the liberties of free African Americans, Litwack made a very important observation about the black population of the United States. He argued that northern free blacks, because of their freedom, could use the tools of free people – the ability to organize, petition the government, and publish the facts of their situation – to improve their position in society. In the middle of the civil rights era, this was an important reminder that the struggle was not new but a legacy from ancestors who had worked hard to attain, preserve, and advance their free status in the nation. That same year, Benjamin Quarles (1961) reinforced the argument that African Americans were active participants in their own freedom and that of the nation. In *The Negro in the American Revolution*, Quarles focused on the black population in general, rather than specific individuals, and argued that black men actively and consciously offered their service to "the side which made him the quickest and best offers in terms of unalienable rights."

While historians of colonial British American history were having difficulty tracking free African Americans, historians of colonial Louisiana had extensive records from which to draw a portrait of the free people of color in the New Orleans colony. Donald E. Everett, writing in the middle of the 1960s, found that the French government was concerned about the governing of black people, not because they were slaves, but because they were believed to think differently from white people. This was why the *Code Noir* was issued in 1724, though only two provisions in the *Code* applied to free people of color. The distinctions between slave and free, and white and black, were also clouded by terms of service. Everett found that free people of color in New Orleans often indentured themselves as servants for a specific term. This practice occurred in the British American colonies as well. Everett also found that free men of color were routinely accepted in the Louisiana militia during French and Spanish rule and were viewed as an asset to the government. For people of color, military service was another avenue to freedom. Over time, service in the militia gave elevated social status among the free black population (Everette 1966).

Beginning in the 1970s, however, more historians began researching the genesis of the nineteenth-century free African American communities. Laura Foner found that, while British colonial governments were legislating manumission, Louisiana left the preference to the slaveholder as long as he was over the age of 25. Although "good and faithful service" could be used to manumit slaves who had provided important service to the government, Foner discovered that this standard was most often used when a concubine or blood relative was to be manumitted. More importantly, Foner found that during the early colonial period under French rule the free black population was African-born, while after the Spanish took control in 1769 a free colored society dominated by mulattoes began to emerge. The Spanish continued liberal policies of the French toward manumission and provided a number of additional ways for slaves to gain their freedom, most notably self-purchase. Foner's primary argument was that free people of color wanted no distinctions between themselves and the white population. Lacking that, however, they established themselves as a distinctive and important element of Louisiana society. H. E. Sterkx, also writing about Louisiana, argued that although the free black population enjoyed considerable advantages, their freedom did not give them equal status to whites, a position they did not challenge as a matter of survival (Sterkx 1972).

Letitia Woods Brown's *Free Negroes in the District of Columbia, 1790–1846* (1972) provided a narrative of the growth of the free black community in the nation's capital. By the end of the eighteenth century, one-fourth of the African American population in the District was free. Brown argued that several factors encouraged the growth of the free black population, including geographic location and the ideological climate of the District during its formative years. Brown further posited that the growth of the city was congenial to the growth of a free African American population and that men with ideas sympathetic to freedom were in positions to implement their ideas.

Adding to this body of work was Ira Berlin's *Slaves Without Masters: The Free Negro in the Antebellum South* (1974). Berlin believed he was doing for the South what Litwack had done for the North. In so doing he helped illustrate the fact that, for African Americans, being responsible for one's own liberty was not an easy job. African American freedom was restricted during the antebellum period so as to be an almost undesirable state. The saving grace, Berlin argued, was that freedom – no matter how restricted – was not slavery. Free African Americans could benefit personally from their own labor and were able to worship, entertain, educate, and protect themselves within the political and social framework they had to inhabit.

While Berlin argued African American agency, A. Leon Higginbotham dealt specifically with legal limitations on the African American population during the colonial era. In his *In the Matter of Color: Race and the American Legal Process, the Colonial Period* (1978), Higginbotham provided a colony-by-colony analysis of laws and legal cases that distinguished free blacks from whites in the society. He found that early in the colonial period, even before laws regarding slavery had hardened, slaveholders were emancipating slaves; and that legislatively controlled manumission followed a period of unrestricted personally controlled manumission. As laws were written to limit manumission, requirements such as removal from the colony of origin and surety bonds were added. Higginbotham found that despite efforts to limit access to freedom, African Americans sought various other ways to freedom when one avenue was closed to them. For example in 1644, Virginia allowed baptized mulatto servants to be treated as other Christian servants. But when Elizabeth Key, ten years later, successfully sued for her freedom on the grounds that her baptism freed her, the Virginia Assembly declared that baptism did not alter one's bondage.

The legal status of blacks in seventeenth-century Maryland was the subject of a 1976 article by Ross M. Kimmel. After examining colonial court records, Kimmel concluded that there was "little legislative proscription on the free black person's personal rights and liberties" and free black men seem to have been treated the same as free white Englishmen before the courts. Kimmel cautioned, however, that the absence of explicit proscription on the rights of free blacks did not guarantee to protect any rights they might have had. Kimmel also found that the majority of the free black population was concentrated on the eastern shore, where some had migrated from Virginia after Bacon's Rebellion. Among the migrants was the Anthony Johnson family. In *"Myne Owne Ground:" Race and Freedom on Virginia's Eastern Shore, 1640–1676* (1980), T. H. Breen and Stephen Innes discovered that in the mid-seventeenth century quite a few blacks who had bought their freedom went on to become substantial landowners. Moreover, Breen and Innes found that in Northampton County, Virginia between 1664 and 1677, ten out of fifty-three free householders were African American males. They owned land and farmed, raised livestock, traded and raised families like their white counterparts. In the middle of the seventeenth century the free African American population was relatively small: about 300 in a population of 13,000.

James O. Horton and Lois E. Horton closed the 1970s with the publication of *Black Bostonians: Family Life and Community Struggle in the Antebellum North*. Although the focus of the study is the nineteenth century, the Hortons made two observations that could be applied not only to colonial Boston but also to the larger free African American population. They argued that free African Americans tended to move to urban centers because labor opportunities were greater. Boston's seaport status added even more opportunity for African American employment. Secondly, the Hortons found that, during the revolutionary era, black Bostonians were involved in every aspect of Boston's political and military life. They argued that African Americans had responded to the revolutionary rhetoric of freedom and natural rights not only by offering themselves for military service but also by petitioning the legislature to abolish slavery.

Regional and Local Studies

During the 1980s the study of the free African American population expanded to include more regional and local studies. Appropriately, the decade opened with an article by Ira Berlin, who believed that scholars of slavery had not respected the fact that changes and differences existed over time and from place to place. The same could be argued for the study of the free black community. In response to this urge to respect time and space, scholars such as William D. Pierson, Gary B. Nash, and Shane White sought to provide a clear understanding of the people who made up the free African American population before the nineteenth century. In his *Black Yankees: The Development of an Afro-American Subculture in Eighteenth Century New England* (1988), William Pierson argued that New England's black population maintained African values and approaches to life, and that the creation of a subculture was done purposely in order that they could maintain a positive self-image. According to Pierson, this double identity – descendants of Africans and citizens of British New England – was created to preserve cultural ties to Africa.

He found that black New Englanders developed an Afro-American folk culture by clustering together in cities and by the constant infusion of African culture because of the importation of Africans until the revolutionary era. Pierson believed that this folk culture probably allowed black Yankees to withstand the harsh realities of freedom. Unlike the lower South and the Mississippi valley, where free African Americans could often depend on continued patronage and protection from former owners, free blacks in New England usually left the site of their bondage in search of jobs, thereby leaving behind any possibility of protection from their former owner. Finally, Pierson found that for free black New Englanders, their material comforts and success got worse, not better, with freedom. Free blacks that were forced to leave towns and cities found themselves living on the edge of communities in the most primitive housing conditions, including root cellars, shacks and caves. Those that stayed in the urban centers for better economic and social opportunities were often forced to live in very poor and unhealthy housing conditions, and some ended up in the poorhouse. Many New England communities feared that new free black migrants would become financial burdens to the town so the town's selectmen frequently urged the migrants to leave town.

African Americans in Philadelphia fared better than Pierson's New Englanders. Gary B. Nash, in *Forging Freedom: The Formation of Philadelphia's Black Community, 1720–1840* (1988), found a more assertive community that stemmed from its larger and more concentrated population. Nash claimed that Philadelphia was the largest and most important center of free black life in the United States. Despite that distinction, black Philadelphians created a community for themselves in the midst of anti-black sentiment. Nash also found that at the end of the colonial era, black Philadelphians had formed family and friendship networks, begun educating themselves, and adopted Christianity. By the end of the Revolutionary War, there were twice as many free African Americans as there were slaves in the city. The black community attracted and nourished such leaders as Absalom Jones and Richard Allen. Nash argued that these men and others understood that their community's success depended on their activities within organizations of their own making. He argued that the independent black church movement led by Jones and Allen represented a growing African American self-confidence and determination, as well as a realization that freedom and equality for the African American population could come only through independent black action.

A number of articles were published on specific cities during the decade. Among them was Jean Soderlund's "Black women in colonial Pennsylvania" (1983). She found that Pennsylvania's use of European labor and its abolitionist sentiment affected the lives of free people in the colony. Although black women's work varied little over time and place, black women in the city of Philadelphia had unique life situations. Many of them because of their work did not live with their husbands and children. Because they lived in the city, they had access to a large supportive black community and were able to read, write, and train for occupations. Some owned property in the form of houses or lots. Finally, Soderlund noted that in 1720, when a certain slave owner approached his female slave about the possibility of freeing her, she turned down the offer. By 1776, however, the political climate and slave attitudes had changed enough to encourage one woman to boldly demand her liberty rather than wait to be offered it. Soderlund concluded that the revolutionary rhetoric and a large supportive black community spurred this request.

In a study of free blacks in the Virginia Southside before 1820, Michael L. Nicholls found that the trends in the free black population reflected those in the rest of the state, but on a smaller scale. Most importantly, Nicholls found that most of the Southside free blacks in 1790 owed their freedom to free blacks who lived there during the colonial period, not to emancipation by slave owners. The eight counties that made up the Southside included the cities of Richmond and Petersburg. The restrictions on manumission enacted in the seventeenth and eighteenth centuries created several major conditions for the free black population before the revolutionary period. First, the free black population was largely the offspring of white mothers and black fathers, and their descendants. Second, because marriages between blacks and whites were not recognized, the children of these unions were considered illegitimate and by law were tied to an indenture for a major portion of their young lives. Finally, free blacks and mulattoes were not safe from enslavement, since a migrating master could take the indentured person away from the place where their freedom could be proven. Nicholls argued that an understanding of the history of free blacks in the Virginia Southside during the colonial period would lead to a better understanding of free black population patterns in the early nineteenth century (Nicholls 1984).

In a study of Old Somerset County, Maryland, Thomas E. Davidson found that although the free black population obtained their freedom through the usual avenues – private manumission and free white mothers – during the mid-eighteenth century the free black population mainly consisted of persons who had been free from birth. "Free mulattoes outnumbered free blacks in Maryland prior to the American Revolution." Davidson concluded that manumissions seemed to have had little impact on the growth of the mulatto segment of the free black population, while dark-skinned, free blacks were most often manumitted slaves. But the occurrence of manumission was so rare that blacks made up only a small part of the county's total free black population, whereas the mulattoes had a multi-generational tradition of freedom (Davidson 1985).

In the same region, Richard Dunn – in "Black society in the Chesapeake" (1993) – stated that before the American Revolution free blacks made up only 4 percent of Maryland's black population, but there was a great increase in that population during and after the revolution. By the end of the first decade of the nineteenth century free African Americans made up 20 percent of Maryland's total black population. Free blacks in Virginia, however, accounted for only 7 percent of the state's black population at the same time. After the revolution, both Maryland and Virginia loosened their manumission laws. This, along with black military service and runaways, increased the free black population tremendously. According to Christopher Phillips, in *Freedom's Port: The African American Community of Baltimore, 1790–1860* (1997),

Baltimore had the largest free black population in the region. In Virginia, free blacks were attracted to the urban centers of Richmond, Norfolk, and Petersburg. African Americans living in Maryland had greater opportunities for freedom than those living in Virginia, thus accounting for Ross Kimmel's discovery of black migration from Virginia to Maryland beginning in the seventeenth century.

In 1988, Shane White presented his initial study of free blacks in New York City. He indicated that during the colonial period there were never more than 100 free blacks in the city. After the American Revolution, however, the number grew to more than 7,000. The small number of free blacks prior to the revolutionary period was probably due to the fact that a 1712 manumission law required New York slaveholders to post a £200 bond to guarantee that the emancipated person would be self-supporting. White attributed the large increase in the free black population to migration into the city in search of jobs. Like Soderlund, White found that free black persons remained in white households even after they received their liberty. They usually lodged in attic rooms and cellars and did work similar to that done by slaves. For those free blacks who were heads of households, White found that they were more apt to be skilled workers. White expanded his article on New York City in the book, *Somewhat More Independent: The End of Slavery in New York City* (1991). In the larger work, White indicated that New York City had been second only to Charleston, South Carolina in the number of slaves during the eighteenth century, but by 1810 the percentage of blacks in New York City was just 10 percent; and only 16 percent of those were still slaves. Most free blacks did manual or artisan labor. As African Americans became householders, they also began to build cultural institutions.

Specialized Studies since 1990

The volume of studies on the free African American population expanded tremendously during the 1990s and the early twenty-first century. Studies covered all aspects of the continental United States, including the French and Spanish territories of the old southeast and the Louisiana territory. Scholars concerned themselves not with the limitations placed upon the free African American population but with the black communities' activities and efforts to carve a niche for themselves despite legal limitations and hostile social climates. At the beginning of the decade, Loren Schweninger did a study of the most prosperous blacks in the South. In his article, "Prosperous blacks in the South, 1790–1880" (1990), published in the *American Historical Review*, Schweninger reported that the most prosperous group of African Americans traced their origins to the late eighteenth and early nineteenth centuries when black women or their mulatto children were bequeathed land and slaves by their white men and fathers. These types of families were predominant along the Atlantic seaboard, the Gulf coast and in Louisiana where French and Spanish customs prevailed.

Gary Nash and Jean Soderlund teamed up to reexamine access to freedom in Pennsylvania in their work, *Freedom by Degrees: Emancipation in Pennsylvania and Its Aftermath* (1991). In his earlier work, Nash had documented the growth and activism of Philadelphia's African American community. In this work, Nash and Soderlund found the struggle for black freedom depended greatly on white Pennsylvanians finding no conflict between ideological commitments to African American freedom and their personal economic interests. The authors also confirmed in Philadelphia what Shane White had discovered in his study of New York – urban life was difficult for free African Americans. Many African Americans who received their freedom remained in the households of their former owners after their freedom, because they could not afford an independent household of their own. Finally, Nash and Soderlund argued that the idea of black liberty was amenable to white Pennsylvanians because they could take advantage of black labor and the increasing number of white laborers who were also available after the Revolutionary War. For those reasons, Nash and Soderlund argued that white Pennsylvanians were not pushed by antislavery sentiment to free slaves but by favorable economic consequences.

Carol Wilson broke new ground with her study of kidnapping, *Freedom at Risk: The Kidnapping of Free Blacks in America* (1994), among the free African American population. Wilson argued that the entire black community feared the possibility of being kidnapped and sold into slavery. Although all free blacks were vulnerable, Wilson found that the residents of the states bordering the Mason-Dixon Line were more likely to fall victims to kidnapping. In addition to geography, age was an element of vulnerability as well, making children a favorite target. Poverty was a third factor. Poor adults could also be deceived by offers of work. Wilson argued that the profits from kidnapping were great and the risk minimal, because the white community tolerated it as a way of enslaving free blacks without admitting they were doing so. Whites and African Americans were guilty of kidnapping (Wilson 1994).

In his 1996 work, *From Africa to America*, William D. Pierson posited that the job of the historians was to rethink the key issues rather than replace old evidence. Working from that philosophy, Pierson approached the study of colonial African American history with the view that blacks were builders of the nation rather than victims of it. Pierson's major argument was that colonial history could not be understood or appreciated without an awareness of the importance of Africans and their culture in the formation of the American nation. Pierson wrote that, during the American Revolution, African Americans fully understood the incongruity between the theory of natural rights and the reality of their racial bondage and responded with a "double-faced" political strategy – overt expressions of African American nationalism and self-help through ethnically based institutions. Pierson argued that the use of the word "African" in the names of cultural institutions was an assertion of cultural pride; and that African Americans adopted a "three-pronged reaction to American culture which included the special theology and practice of the Black Church, the satiric style in African American music and a jeremianic tradition among African American intellectuals of being intensely critical of the meaning of America. Leading the emerging Afro-American consciousness was the small free black urban community" (Pierson 1996: 145).

James Horton and Lois E. Horton, *In Hope of Liberty: Culture, Community and Protest Among Northern Free Blacks* (1997), argued that in the period between 1700 and 1860 African American culture became more American while American culture became more African. As free people, African Americans were never isolated, never passive, and never a monolithic group. They affected – and were affected by

– political, social, and economic changes in the country. In response to these influences, by the end of the first decade of the nineteenth century African Americans
in Philadelphia and Boston had formed many organizations, which New Yorkers
organized slightly later, as African Americans emerged from slavery. As more black
communities developed and grew, members created institutions, which differed from
region to region and city to city but which addressed the same basic issues – poverty,
and social and political disadvantages. In a later article, Lois E. Horton found that,
in colonial America and in the early republic, working-class alliances had offered
African Americans opportunities for political expression and some promise of occupational advancement. These opportunities faded in the nineteenth century when
social, political, and economic changes made race an important determinant of political and economic prospects (Horton 1999).

During the late 1990s several studies were done of cities previously not examined.
Whittington B. Johnson and Betty Wood looked at Savannah; Tommy Bogger
studied Norfolk. Johnson offered what he called a holistic interpretation of African
Americans in Savannah because, as he observed, blacks in Savannah did not respect
the legal distinctions between slaves and free blacks. Johnson's study therefore
concentrated on independent black community-building rather than legal status, by
examining the creation of an independent church, black efforts to establish an
economic niche and the formation of black families. Johnson anchored his study at
the founding of the independent Black Church in 1788 and the abolition of slavery
in 1864. The free black population of Savannah was smaller than any other major
southern city but Savannah had the largest independent black church in the South.
Although Savannah differed significantly in many areas from sister cities such as
Charleston and New Orleans, the fact that free black women were a majority of the
free population and were the largest property owners within the free black community made the city similar. The uniqueness of Savannah was further emphasized
by Betty Wood's study of gender in the Georgia Lowcountry. Woods found a
diverse free black community in Savannah in terms of ethnicity, religion, and socioeconomic differences (Johnson 1996; Wood 2000).

In his study of free blacks in Norfolk, Tommy Bogger found that the majority of
manumissions in Norfolk between 1790 and 1820 occurred because blacks paid for
their freedom. He also found that economic fluctuations did not affect the rate of
self-purchase. Bogger argued that free blacks in Norfolk were different from free
blacks further south primarily because of the absence of rigid color lines between
mulattoes and other free blacks, although color consciousness existed in social
relations. The issue of complexion may also have been negligible because mulattoes
made up only 36 percent of the free African American population (Bogger 1997).

Although Charleston had been a much-studied city, by examining the miscellaneous records of the colony and state of South Carolina, Robert Olwell found evidence of a free black population during South Carolina's colonial era. In his article,
"Becoming free: manumission and the genesis of a free black community in South
Carolina, 1740–1790" (1996), Olwell posited that the most likely groups to be
freed were mulattoes, females, and children. The least likely to be freed were adult
black men. The American Revolution had little effect on this. Olwell's work was new
ground for Charleston since most studies of its free black community dated the
community from 1790 with the first federal census and the establishment of the

Brown Fellowship Society. The status of free blacks in South Carolina was so ambiguous that they rarely came into the public record, not even tax records.

New Orleans received new treatment in the 1990s as well. Kimberly Hanger expanded the knowledge of colonial Louisiana. Hanger has written extensively on the free black society of colonial New Orleans, with special emphasis on free black women. Her article "Patronage, property, and persistence" (1996) highlighted the emergence of the free black elite after the Spanish took over the Louisiana territory. According to Hanger the free black community made its greatest advances in terms of demographics, privileges, responsibilities, and social standing. Hanger argued that the Spanish supported their growth because they needed allies. The Spanish need for allies allowed free blacks to play important roles in the New Orleans economy and in the territory's defense. One major advantage for free blacks was Spanish support of the practice of *coartacion*, the right of slaves to purchase their freedom for an amount agreed upon by master and slave or arbitrated in the courts. Hanger concluded that the success or failure of a free black person depended on their skills, their relationship or reputation in the white community, kinship and patronage of white people and being born free or having free relatives.

In her article "Coping in a complex world: free black women in colonial New Orleans" (1997), Hanger argued that free black women used the advantages available to them to combat the limitations they faced because of race, gender, and public perception of their sexuality. Hanger posited that free black women were able to exercise more control than slave women over their choices of a husband or a consort. She also found that many free black women were heads of households, although it was necessary that they work. In her book, *Bounded Lives, Bounded Places: Free Black Society in Colonial New Orleans, 1769–1803* (1997), Hanger focused on Spanish New Orleans. She found that free blacks played an important role in New Orleans society during the era of Spanish rule, that they had more rights, opportunities and better treatment then, and that Spanish law and family money helped many to receive their freedom. Like other scholars of New Orleans, Hanger discovered that among free people of color in Louisiana there were more free women than men, and women held more personal property than free men. Service in the militia was an important aspect of free black life in New Orleans. Hanger argued that it was an important instrument of political expression, an avenue for social advancement, and a means through which to gain honor, prestige and recognition. She counted the militia first as an important community institution that encouraged group cohesiveness and identity among the free black population in colonial New Orleans. For Hanger, it was the Spanish period, 1769–1803, that enabled the *gens de color libres* to dominate colonial New Orleans history.

In a later article, Hanger discussed the plight of free black women in New Orleans. In "Desiring total tranquility and not getting it" (1998), she argued that free black women did more to extend equality beyond the confines of gender than any other group because they faced and fought oppression daily. Their assertiveness, she argued, stemmed from three things: their desire to be recognized for their true selves, not as stereotypes of loose women; their striving for freedom for themselves and others; and their desire to have stable, long-lasting marriages that produced children and established kinship networks. Equally important was the need to be seen and respected as hardworking, religious members of society.

Thomas N. Ingersoll in "Free blacks in a slave society: New Orleans, 1718–1812" (1991) posited that, though free blacks became more numerous under Spanish law, their status did not change because white planters maintained racial distinctions. When Louisiana was transferred to the United States, the American government with the help of local planters brought Louisiana in line with slave laws in the southern states. The planters outlawed self-purchase as a way to freedom. Legislation was enacted to halt the growth of the free black community by limiting the influx of free blacks from outside Louisiana, outlawing marriages between free blacks of any color and slaves, and continuing the prohibition of interracial marriage. The New Orleans city council required all free blacks to be able to prove their status at any time. But while free persons of black complexions had to prove their status, mulattoes were presumed to be free. The council also tried to exclude free blacks from positions in which they were required to bear arms. Ingersoll argued that several characteristics of the free black population in Louisiana prevented it from mounting a resistance. The population was too small and dispersed and even in New Orleans there was no black neighborhood. The population was overwhelmingly female and therefore had little leverage in a male-dominated society. The population was stratified and divided by color. Lastly, many free blacks lived in white households as servants and their livelihood depended on not offending their employers. Ingersoll concluded that the point of the government's campaign against the free black population was to exclude it from all institutions of power and freedom.

In the 1990s, Jane Landers added to her study of colonial Florida and its free African presence. The work in Florida and Louisiana has long been connected to the study of the Americas. Recently scholars such as Landers have looked at Florida's black community and culture and exposed its connection to the British colonies. In an earlier article, "Sanctuary: fugitives in Florida, 1687–1790" (1984), Landers documented changes in the Florida territory as a sanctuary for runaway slaves. Landers found that during the first Spanish period (1565–1763) runaway slaves had benefited from the international rivalry between Spain and England and had been given refuge from a common enemy. By 1784, however, the fugitives were seen as a source of trouble because their presence invited attacks from American planters attempting to retrieve their property. In addition the planters had the support of the American government. In her article "Black community and culture in the southeastern borderlands" (1998), Landers looked at the interaction between blacks, British slaveholders and the Spanish government in Florida during the second Spanish period, 1784–1821.

Landers found that a free black population grew after slaves ran away during the British evacuations of Florida in 1784. Spain's seventeenth-century sanctuary policy for escaped slaves seeking Catholic conversion was still in effect and more than 250 African Americans formerly owned by British slaveholders were registered and freed by the Spanish governor. Landers argued that the governor realized that the escaped slaves were not driven by desire for religious conversion, but the freedmen were valuable sources of skilled labor and military reserves for the Spanish community. The free black community remained small and the exact number has not been determined because the free people lived outside the city. One significant black settlement in Spanish Florida was Gracia Real de Santa Teresa de Mose, two miles north of St. Augustine. At the end of the first Spanish period, when Spain lost

Florida to Britain in 1763, black and Spanish citizens fled. Those free black people who stayed behind experienced a sharp curtailment of freedom and were eventually forced to wear silver armbands engraved with the word "free." These acts and other policies of white supremacy forced black property-holding Floridians to sell their property cheaply and migrate to Cuba and Mexico.

* * *

The American Revolution played a pivotal role in the growth of the free African American population in the United States. But since the 1970s, historians of the colonial era have been looking for the genesis of the free black community in the two hundred years before 1790. What they have found is a people, small in number, seeking to make and remake lives in a land that was both foreign and familiar. They have found a spirit of self-confidence and determination. They have found the progenitors of the nineteenth-century free African American population. As we enter a second century of rigorous study of African American life in the Western Hemisphere, there are many opportunities for fascinating and significant study of the free African American population before the nineteenth century. Despite our efforts to categorize in terms of gender, race, class, and culture, the evidence will determine the issues. Continued study of the population in the areas of the Upper and Lower South, the middle Atlantic coast and the Mississippi valley are still needed. Studies on Gulf port cities such as Mobile could provide an excellent comparison to New Orleans. Examinations of Natchez, St Louis, and other Mississippi River port cities should expose some interesting detail of free black economies, culture and agency. The studies of Landers, Ingersoll, Hanger, and others point to the intricate connection between the British colonies and the French and Spanish territories of North America. Finally, particular attention should be given to studies of rural communities, such as the population Franklin found in North Carolina. More than twenty years ago, Berlin cautioned historians to respect time and space. As more work is done, special attention should be paid to regional, gender, class, and cultural differences over time and space.

BIBLIOGRAPHY

Works Cited

Alexander, Adele Logan (1991) *Ambiguous Lives: Free Women of Color in Rural Georgia, 1789–1879.* Fayetteville: University of Arkansas Press.
Berlin, Ira (1974) *Slaves without Masters: The Free Negro in the Antebellum South.* New York: Pantheon.
—— (1980) "Time, space and the evolution of Afro-American society on British mainland North America," *American Historical Review* 85: 44–78.
—— (1996) "Free blacks, 1619–1860" in Jack Salzman, David Lionel Smith, and Cornell West (eds.), *Encyclopedia of African American Culture and History*, vol. 2: 1059–62. New York: Simon & Schuster, Macmillan.
—— (1998) *Many Thousands Gone: The First Two Centuries of Slavery in North America.* Cambridge, MA: Belknap Press of Harvard University Press.

Bogger, Tommy L. (1997) *Free Blacks in Norfolk, Virginia, 1760–1860: The Darker Side of Freedom*. Charlottesville: University Press of Virginia.

Bolster, W. Jeffrey (1997) *Black Jacks: African American Seamen in the Age of Sail*. Cambridge, MA: Harvard University Press.

Breen, T. H. and Innes, Stephen (1980) *"Myne Owne Ground:" Race and Freedom on Virginia's Eastern Shore, 1640–1676*. New York: Oxford University Press.

Brewer, James H. (1955) "Negro property holders in seventeenth-century Virginia," *William and Mary Quarterly* 12: 575–80.

Brown, Letitia Woods (1972) *Free Negroes in the District of Columbia, 1790–1846*. New York: Oxford University Press.

Davidson, Thomas E. (1985) "Free blacks in Old Somerset County, 1745–1755," *Maryland Historical Magazine* 80: 151–6.

Dunbar-Nelson, Alice (1916) "People of color in Louisiana," *Journal of Negro History* 1 (October).

—— (1917) "People of color in Louisiana," *Journal of Negro History* 2 (January).

Dunn, Richard S. (1993) "Black society in the Chesapeake" in Ira Berlin and Ronald Hoffman (eds.), *Slavery and Freedom in the Age of Revolution*. Charlottesville: University of Virginia Press.

Everette, Donald (1966) "Free persons of color in colonial Louisiana," *Louisiana History* 7: 21–50.

Fields, Barbara J. (1985) *Slavery and Freedom on the Middle Ground: Maryland during the Nineteenth Century*. New Haven, CT: Yale University Press.

Fitchett, E. Horace (1941) "The origin and growth of the free Negro population of Charleston, South Carolina," *Journal of Negro History* 26 (October).

Fogel, Robert W. and Engerman, Stanley L. (1974) "Philanthropy at bargain prices: notes on the economics of gradual emancipation," *Journal of Legal Studies* 13.

Foner, Laura (1970) "The free people of color in Louisiana and St. Dominique: a comparative portrait of two three-caste slave societies," *Journal of Social History* 3: 406–30.

Foner, Philip S. (1975) *History of Black Americans: From African to the Emergence of the Cotton Kingdom*. Westport, CT: Greenwood Press.

Franklin, John Hope ([1943] 1971) *The Free Negro in North Carolina, 1790–1860*. New York: W. W. Norton.

Greene, Lorenzo J. ([1942] 1971) *The Negro in Colonial New England*. New York: Atheneum.

Hall, Gwendolyn Midlo (1992) *Africans in Colonial Louisiana: The Development of Afro-Creole Culture in the Eighteenth Century*. Baton Rouge: Louisiana State University Press.

Hanger, Kimberly S. (1996) "Patronage, property and persistence: The emergence of a free black elite in Spanish New Orleans" in Jane Landers (ed.), *Against the Odds: Free Blacks in the Slave Societies of the Americas*. Portland, OR: Frank Cass.

—— (1997a) *Bounded Lives, Bounded Places: Free Black Society in Colonial New Orleans, 1769–1803*. Durham, NC: Duke University Press.

—— (1997b) "Coping in a complex world: free black women in colonial New Orleans" in Catherine Clinton and Michele Gillespie (eds.), *The Devil's Lane: Sex and Race in the Early South*. New York: Oxford University Press.

—— (1998) "Desiring total tranquility and not getting it: conflict involving free black women in Spanish New Orleans," *The Americas* 54 (4): 541–56.

Harris, Sheldon H. (1972) *Paul Cuffe: Black America and the African Return*. New York: Simon & Schuster.

Higginbotham, A. Leon (1978) *In the Matter of Color: Race and the American Legal Process, the Colonial Period*. New York: Oxford University Press.

Horton, James O. (1993) *Free People of Color: Inside the African American Community.* Washington, DC: Smithsonian Institute Press.

Horton, James O. and Horton, Lois E. ([1979] 1999) *Black Bostonians: Family Life and Community Struggle in the Antebellum North.* New York: Holmes & Meir.

—— (1997) *In Hope of Liberty: Culture, Community, and Protest among Northern Free Blacks, 1700–1860.* New York: Oxford University Press.

Horton, Lois E. (1999) "From class to race in early America: northern post-emancipation racial reconstruction," *Journal of the Early Republic* 19 (Winter): 629–49.

Imes, William L. (1919) "The legal status of free Negroes and slaves in Tennessee," *Journal of Negro History,* 4 (July).

Ingersoll, Thomas N. (1991) "Free blacks in a slave society: New Orleans, 1718–1812," *William and Mary Quarterly* 48: 173–200.

Johnson, Whittington B. (1996) *Black Savannah, 1788–1864.* Fayetteville: University of Arkansas Press.

Jordan, Winthrop D. (1968) *White over Black: American Attitudes toward the Negro, 1550–1812.* Chapel Hill: University of North Carolina Press.

Kaplan, Sidney and Kaplan, Emma N. (1989) *The Black Presence in the Era of the American Revolution.* Amherst: University of Massachusetts Press.

Kimmel, Ross M. (1976) "Free blacks in seventeenth-century Maryland," *Maryland Historical Magazine* 71: 19–25.

Kirsh, Leo H., Jr (1931) "The Negro and New York, 1783–1865," *Journal of Negro History* 16: 382–473.

Landers, Jane (1984) "Sanctuary: fugitives in Florida, 1687–1790," *Florida Historical Quarterly* 62: 296–313.

—— (1996) "Acquisition and loss on a Spanish frontier: The free black homesteaders of Florida, 1784–1821" in Jane Landers (ed.), *Against the Odds: Free Blacks in the Slave Societies of the Americas.* Portland, OR: Frank Cass.

—— (1998) "Black community and culture in the southeastern borderlands," *Journal of the Early Republic* 18 (1): 117–34.

Lebsock, Suzanne (1984) *The Free Women of Petersburg: Status and Culture in a Southern Town, 1784–1860.* New York: Norton.

Litwack, Leon (1961) *North of Slavery: The Negro in the Free States, 1790–1860.* Chicago: University of Chicago Press.

Melish, Joanne Pope (1998) *Disowning Slavery: Gradual Emancipation and Race in New England, 1780–1860.* Ithaca, NY: Cornell University Press.

Morgan, Philip D. (1998) *Slave Counterpoint.* Chapel Hill, NC: North Carolina Press.

Moss, Simeon F. (1950) "The persistence of slavery and involuntary servitude in a free state, 1685–1866," *Journal of Negro History* 35.

Nash, Gary B. (1973) "Slaves and slaveowners in colonial Philadelphia," *William and Mary Quarterly* 30: 223–56.

—— (1983) "Forging freedom" in Ira Berlin and Ronald Hoffman (eds.), *Slavery and Freedom in the Age of Revolution.* Charlottesville: University of Virginia Press.

—— (1986) "To arise out of the dust: Absolom Jones and the African Church of Philadelphia, 1785–1795" in Gary B. Nash (ed.), *Race, Class, and Politics: Essays on American Colonial and Revolutionary Society,* 323–55. Urbana: University of Illinois Press.

—— (1988) *Forging Freedom: The Formation of Philadelphia's Black Community, 1720–1840.* Cambridge, MA: Harvard University Press.

—— (1989) "New light on Richard Allen: the early years of freedom," *William and Mary Quarterly* 46: 332–40.

—— (1990) *Race and Revolution.* Madison: Madison House.

Nash, Gary B. and Soderland, Jean R. (1991) *Freedom by Degrees: Emancipation in Pennsylvania and Its Aftermath*. New York: Oxford University Press.

Nell, William Cooper (1855) *The Colored Patriots of the Amercian Revolution*. Boston: R. F. Wallcut.

Nicholls, Michael L. (1984) "'Passing through this troublesome world': free blacks in the early Southside," *Virginia Magazine of History and Biography* 92.

Nieman, Donald G. (1991) "Promises to keep" in *African Americans and the Constitutional Order, 1776 to the Present*. New York: Oxford University Press.

Olwell, Robert (1996) "Becoming free: manumission and the genesis of a free black community in South Carolina, 1740–1790" in Jane Landers (ed.), *Against the Odds: Free Blacks in the Slave Societies of the Americas*. Portland, OR: Frank Cass.

Phillips, Christopher (1997) *Freedom's Port: The African American Community of Baltimore, 1790–1860*. Chicago: University of Illinois.

Pierson, William D. (1996) *From Africa to America: African American History from the Colonial Era to the Early Republic, 1526–1790*. New York: Twayne.

—— (1988) *Black Yankees: The Development of an Afro-American Subculture in Eighteenth Century New England*. Amherst: University of Massachusetts Press.

Quarles, Benjamin (1961) *The Negro in the American Revolution*. Chapel Hill: University of North Carolina Press.

Schilling, Peter (1996) "Free African society" in Jack Salzman, David Lionel Smith, and Cornell West (eds.), *Encyclopedia of African American Culture and History*, vol. 2: 1036. New York: Simon & Schuster.

Schwarz, Phillip J. (1987) "Emancipators, protestors, and anomalies: free black slaveowners in Virginia," *Virginia Magazine of History and Biography* 95 (3): 317–38.

Schweninger, Loren (1990) "Prosperous blacks in the South, 1790–1880," *American Historical Review* 95: 31–56.

Smith, Betty G. and Wojrowicz, Richard (1989) "The precarious freedom of blacks in the mid-atlantic region: excerpts from the *Pennsylvania Gazette*, 1728–1776," *Pennsylvania Magazine of History and Biography* 113.

Soderlund, Jean R. (1983) "Black women in colonial Pennsylvania," *Pennsylvania Magazine of History and Biography* 107: 49–68.

Sterkx, H. E. (1972) *The Free Negro in Antebellum Louisiana*. Rutherford, NJ: Fairleigh Dickinson University Press.

White, Shane (1988) "We dwell in safety and pursue our honest callings: free blacks in New York City, 1783–1810," *Journal of American History* 75: 445–70.

—— (1991) *Somewhat More Independent: The End of Slavery in New York City, 1770–1810*. Athens: University of Georgia Press.

Williams, George Washington (1883) *History of the Negro Race in America from 1619 to 1880*. New York: G. P. Putnam's Son.

Wilson, Carol (1994) *Freedom at Risk: The Kidnapping of Free Blacks in America*. Lexington: University of Kentucky Press.

Winch, Julie (1988) *Philadelphia's Black Elite: Activism, Accommodation, and the Struggle for Autonomy, 1787–1848*. Philadelphia: Temple University Press.

Wood, Betty (2000) *Gender, Race and Rank in a Revolutionary Age: The Georgia Lowcountry, 1750–1820*. Athens: University of Georgia Press.

Wright, Donald (1990) *African Americans in the Colonial Era*. Arlington Heights, IL: Harlan Davidson.

—— (1998) *African Americans in the Early Republic, 1789–1831*. Arlington Heights, IL: Harlan Davidson.

CHAPTER SEVEN

Africans and Native Americans

TIYA MILES AND BARBARA KRAUTHAMER

The earliest meetings between peoples of indigenous African and indigenous American descent have not been sufficiently documented. However, scholars of African Diaspora Studies and Native American Studies such as Ivan Van Sertima and Jack Forbes have argued that the first meetings between Africans and American Indians likely occurred before the arrival of Europeans in the Americas (Van Sertima 1976; Forbes 1993: 6–25). They base this supposition on analyses of African and Native American ship-making techniques, ocean currents, written and oral accounts of oceanic travel, crops transplanted between Africa and America, and cultural artifacts such as textiles that appear to be bi-culturally influenced. These examples, which have been contested by other scholars, suggest – but cannot conclusively prove – transatlantic travel and cross-cultural encounters prior to European exploration of the African and American continents (Thornton 1992: 16).

Whether or not blacks and Indians met each other independently on the shores of Africa and the Americas before Columbus's voyage, by the late eighteenth century these two populations were joined together metaphorically and ideologically in the minds of Europeans. During the latter part of the eighteenth century, Euro-Americans shifted from thinking about race as the product of climate, culture, and geography and as something that could mutate through time and space, and increasingly thought about race as a biological phenomenon. This was a period, therefore, during which European Americans' racial thinking cohered in a set of ideas and beliefs that posited race as an inherent bodily condition, visible in the individual's physical characteristics as well as moral and intellectual capacities. In his magisterial work, *White Over Black: American Attitudes Toward the Negro, 1550–1812*, Winthrop Jordan follows the development of European and American ideas about African people's complexion, and details the associations Europeans made between color, culture, and status. In their early descriptions of Africans' and Native Americans' appearance and physique, Europeans asserted their own cultural, moral, and intellectual superiority. During the eighteenth century the idea that differences in appearance dictated cultural, moral, and intellectual hierarchies took hold and developed into the racial, and racist, thinking of the late eighteenth and nineteenth centuries.

In a primary example, English visitors to – and settlers in – the Virginia colony fashioned elaborate interpretations of Native Americans' culture, labor patterns, land use, and gender roles that served to distinguish between Europeans and Indians. Native American religions were deemed inferior to Christianity and thus were considered a marker of Indian peoples' inferiority. Native land-use patterns, specifically their seasonal hunting and herding economies, contrasted sharply in English eyes with Europeans' systems of permanent towns and farms cultivated all the year. Travelers and settlers regularly maintained that Indians lacked organized labor routines and believed that Indians had failed to harness the land's potential to yield resources and riches. European observers did not understand the complex and well-established patterns of hunting, herding, and seasonal migration that structured Native Americans' production of food and other resources for consumption and trade (Axtell 1981; Cronon 1983).

Increasingly, scholars interested in the intersections between race and gender ideologies have sought to explore the ways in which Euro-Americans' ideas about Native American and African difference were gendered in their formulation and expression. Indian men, for example, were considered insufficiently masculine because they did not engage in European modes of agriculture (Morgan 1997). Because indigenous women had the primary responsibility for cultivating crops, Euro-Americans deemed them unfeminine, and their labor underscored Indian men's weaknesses. In this manner, Indian men were judged as racially inferior and their condition was evidenced, in the eyes of European observers, by their land use and labor patterns. Native American and African women's bodies and their productive and reproductive labor were subjected to similar kinds of scrutiny.

English writers, for example, contended that Indian women did not experience much, if any, pain during childbirth. This judgment contrasted sharply with the prevailing European Judeo-Christian belief that women endured great pain during labor and delivery to pay for Eve's sins. In this opposition, European and Euro-American women were held to be civilized by virtue of their Christianity and femininity, while Indian women were cast as animalistic and closer to nature. Similar ideas informed European perceptions of African women. Historian Jennifer Morgan has shown that this degradation of African women served to justify their enslavement and exploitation as laborers and as reproducers of subsequent generations of enslaved people. African women who were enslaved in the English colonies during the seventeenth and early eighteenth centuries did not give birth to high numbers of children, but Europeans nonetheless described these women as exceptionally fecund and well suited for manual labor. Such erroneous assertions, however, served to create a vast gulf between Euro-American and African women and to reassure colonists and investors that African women's manual labor and their reproduction would generate profit (Morgan 1997).

As Euro-Americans interacted with Indians and Africans, these negative racial and gender notions about both groups were enacted in everyday life and codified in colonial custom and law. Detailed studies by Kathleen Brown and Kirsten Fischer investigate the connections between race and gender ideologies in the southern colonies and focus on the social and legal categories developed to differentiate African and Native American women's reproductive and productive labor from that of Euro-American women. As Kathleen Brown explains in her book, *Good Wives,*

Nasty Wenches & Angry Patriarchs, colonial legislators viewed African women as drudges able to undertake heavy physical labor, in contrast to European women whose domestic labor was considered appropriate female household activity. Consequently, the earliest laws establishing slavery in colonial Virginia imposed taxes on African but not European women, effectively equating African women with other household property owned by English men (Brown 1996: ch. 4, esp. 108–20). Kirsten Fischer follows similar events in her study of colonial North Carolina, where laws imposed taxes on the children born to Indian-European as well as Indian-African couples and also taxed any man or woman who married a person born to these couples. As both scholars demonstrate, these colonial laws worked to create racial categories by equating color and ancestry with legal status and by rendering instances of sexual union or marriage between Native Americans, Europeans, and Africans invisible with stark racial labels and categories (Fischer 2002: ch. 2, esp. 85–6).

The system of racial classification and hierarchy took shape as Europeans and Euro-Americans sought to subordinate and exploit Native Americans' and Africans' land, bodies, and labor. As racial categories gained meaning in colonial North America, both Africans and Native Americans paid careful attention to the boundaries and meanings of racial labels and formulated their own patterns of identifying themselves and others. In his work, *Exchanging Our Country Marks*, Michael Gomez looks to the diverse worldviews, histories, and cultures of the African peoples enslaved in North America to understand the ways in which they identified themselves and others. He illustrates the regional, cultural, linguistic, and religious diversity among the African men and women who were enslaved in North America and describes the ways in which enslaved Africans understood themselves as having particular ethnic, religious, cultural, or linguistic identities before developing a shared African American culture and identity that allowed them to impart meaning and dignity to the racial categories and hierarchies imposed upon them by Euro-Americans (Gomez 1998).

During the early colonial period, most Indians had little interest in skin color and the concept of physically distinct races. Native Americans identified themselves and others by kinship networks, culture, and language. From this vantage, Africans were more like Europeans to the extent that both were outsiders whose presence in North America heralded dramatic demographic, political, and economic changes in the southeast. The work of historian Nancy Shoemaker examines the circumstances that informed the ways Indians thought about race. Shoemaker suggests that Indians may have embraced a color – red – to identify themselves as a group in response to the color terminology – white and black – employed by Euro-Americans. She goes on to discuss the internal structure of Indian societies that would have bolstered Native peoples' self-identification as red people.

Southeastern Indian societies embraced a dualistic perspective in which red and white symbols represented war and peace respectively, taking the "white path," for example, meant pursuing peaceful relations between Indian towns and nations. Indians in the southeast, according to Shoemaker, would have understood the label red as "the logical rejoinder to 'white'." The English, however, "probably understood the Indian phrase 'red people' to be only a reference to complexion" (Shoemaker 1997: 632). It is important to note that Shoemaker concludes her article with an important reminder to scholars. Indians likely identified themselves as red people, but Euro-American ideas about racial hierarchy construed the term and category as derogatory and debased.

Indians in the southeast may not have initially shared Euro-Americans' interest in racial classification and hierarchy, but the growing colonial population in the southeast – along with the continual expansion of slavery – precipitated changes in Native Americans' ideas about race and slavery. Native Americans in each of the five principal southeastern nations held African Americans as slaves, yet slaveholding practices varied between and even within these nations. Scholarship by Theda Perdue on the subject of slavery in the Cherokee nation endures as pioneering work in the field. In more recent years, scholars have followed Perdue's lead and examined the development of racial slavery in southeastern Indian nations but have also moved towards greater theoretical analysis of the dynamics of race and status within Indian societies (Perdue 1979). There are very few studies that detail the emergence of black slavery in the Choctaw and Chickasaw nations, though works by Clara Sue Kidwell and James Taylor Carson briefly touch on the subject (Kidwell 1995; Carson 1999).

Among the Creek Indians, who occupied much of present-day Georgia, Alabama, and northern Florida, there was great concern over the rise of plantation slavery in the British colonies. During the late eighteenth century, Creeks found the extreme distinctions of status between free and enslaved people troubling and were even more distressed by the brutal treatment endured by the enslaved. The Creeks, like other southeastern Indian peoples, organized their society through kinship, networks of families joined together by reciprocity, loyalty, and obligation. Through their carefully maintained family and social ties, Creeks ensured a balance of power in their society. From their vantage, the extreme inequality between masters and slaves in the colonies was unthinkable, and it became threatening as the colonial populations of Europeans and Africans expanded (Saunt 1999).

Creeks were not entirely unfamiliar with slavery and subordination, but their patterns of slaveholding contrasted sharply with the Euro-American model. According to Kathryn Braund's work on the Creeks, their slaves had been enemy warriors and non-combatant women and children captured during wars between the Creeks and other Indians. Male captives were usually executed but women and children were held as subordinates, or slaves, within particular kinship groups, or clans. Captive women worked alongside Creek women, growing food for the family's consumption and tending to other household labors. The status distinction between captive women and their hosts was signaled by the slaves' lack of kinship ties to the host family and clan. Such ties, however, could be established over time through rituals of adoption and inclusion. Evidence suggests that some Africans ran away from their Euro-American masters and sought refuge among the Creeks. These fugitives were most likely incorporated into Creek clans through this pattern of subordination and adoption. By the late eighteenth century, however, Creeks increasingly encountered Africans and African Americans who were owned by the European traders conducting business in the Creek nation.

Both Kathryn Braund and Claudio Saunt have written studies of the Creek nation that discuss the emergence of black bondage in the Creek nation. Braund, for example, notes that during the Revolution many Creeks raided nearby plantations, seizing black slaves and retaining them as war booty that could be used for barter and trade with white people on either side of the conflict. Braund also points out that some British traders settled among the Creeks, sometimes marrying Creek women, and often bringing their own black slaves into Creek communities. The children born to Euro-American traders and their Creek wives inherited this human property, making them some of the largest slaveholders in the Creek nation (Braund 1991: 618–19). Many Creek slaveholders, however, did not seek to replicate the brutality of bondage as it existed in the United States, but instead regarded the new pattern of enslaving black people as an extension of older slaveholding practices. Few Creek slaveholders engaged in large-scale, commercial agriculture but instead operated subsistence farms, perhaps producing small quantities of surplus goods for sale and trade. Consequently, many who were enslaved in the Creek nation lived with their own families and labored alongside the members of their owners' families. Evidence suggests, furthermore, that Creeks and enslaved blacks occasionally inter-married, making strict racial or status boundaries difficult to locate or maintain (Saunt 1999: 120).

The most notable divergence from the patterns discussed above occurred among the Seminoles in Florida. The subject of slavery and relations between African Americans and Seminoles has been of great interest to scholars studying black and Indian contacts. Kevin Mulroy's book, *Freedom on the Border*, stands out as a recent study tracing the early contact between African Americans and Seminoles, and following this history into the middle of the twentieth century (Mulroy 1993). The Seminoles coalesced as a group formed from various small bands of southeastern Indians. Like other southeastern indigenous peoples, their early patterns of slaveholding entailed the subordination and eventual adoption of war captives. Among the Seminoles, captives owed their hosts an annual tribute of food or livestock and loyalty in battle. European observers noted that Indians enslaved by the Seminoles dressed as elaborately as their captors and enjoyed the same privileges and freedoms as Seminoles. In the eighteenth century, Seminoles encountered Africans and African Americans when the latter fled their Euro-American masters and headed further south to Florida. The region was a Spanish territory and royal edicts dating back to the 1680s extended freedom to slaves who fled to Spanish soil. Spaniards relied on both these fugitive slaves and Seminoles to assist in their military campaigns to defend Florida against British forces. This early contact between African Americans and Seminoles included, of course, intermarriage, making distinctions between blacks and Indians difficult and arbitrary. Consequently, many people today choose to use the term Black Seminoles – or, like Mulroy, the term Seminole Maroons – to describe the runaway slaves who settled among the Seminole.

The presence of an established community of African Americans and Indians so close to the burgeoning plantations of the Deep South must have given some hope of escape to those who were enslaved by Euro-Americans in the surrounding region. The Seminoles' proximity to the southern states and their willingness to give refuge to fugitive slaves, however, caused great consternation among southern slaveholders. Consequently, the United States first sought to relocate the Seminoles to more southern reaches of Florida and later engaged in a protracted military campaign to remove the Seminoles entirely from the South. The latter wars, known as the Seminole Wars, occurred during the 1830s and 1840s and were protracted affairs due to African Americans' and Seminoles' fierce resistance against removal.

Although African Americans' participation in the war has been covered in detail by Kenneth W. Porter in his 1971 work, *The Negro on the American Frontier*, this history remains virtually absent from studies of slavery and resistance in the American South. Mulroy credits the fugitive slaves with "fostering and strengthening Seminole opposition to removal" (Mulroy 1993: 28–9). Indeed, when General Thomas S. Jesup assumed command of the US forces in Florida in the winter of 1836, he remarked, "This, you may be assured is a negro and not an Indian war; and if it be not speedily put down, the south will feel the effects of it before the end of next season" (quoted in Mulroy 1993: 29). Ultimately, however, the Seminole nation, both Indians and fugitive slaves, were removed west to the Indian Territory (present-day Oklahoma), where they joined the other Indian nations – Cherokee, Creek, Choctaw, and Chickasaw – that had already been forcibly removed and relocated.

It is worth noting that not all of the Black Seminoles were removed to the west. Anthropologist Rosalyn Howard has written a book entitled *Black Seminoles in the Bahamas* about the early nineteenth-century flight of some Black Seminoles from Florida to the Bahamas, where they hoped to find safety and refuge from American raids. In the first chapters of her work, Howard traces the Black Seminoles' early history in Florida and their escape to the Bahamas. The bulk of the study is then devoted to the present-day community of Bahamian Black Seminole descendants, most of whom live in Red Bays on Andros Island (Howard 2002).

Despite the wealth of evidence pointing to the relative freedoms enjoyed by the African Americans who were enslaved by Indians, episodes of resistance remind us that slavery necessarily entailed some form of degradation. Although African Americans enslaved in Native American nations often lived and labored on their own and were not subject to the dehumanization and brutality that characterized slavery in the southern states, their efforts to flee their Indian masters point to their determination to exert control over their lives. In 1842, for example, over one hundred African Americans enslaved in the Cherokee nation ran away from their masters and attempted to cross Texas with the hope of reaching freedom in Mexico. Their plan ultimately failed, and they were captured and returned to their masters. Another well-known episode occurred in 1849, when slaves under the leadership of a free Black Seminole made a successful escape to Mexico (Littlefield and Underhill 1977; McLoughlin 1974).

During the Civil War, enslaved people in the Indian Territory, like their counterparts in the southern states, seized opportunities to liberate themselves. Each of the Five Tribes, with the exception of the Seminole, split into Union and Confederate factions. One of the Creek Union leaders promised freedom to enslaved men who joined with him to fight against Confederate forces. In other instances, enslaved men and women gathered their families and fled, much like their counterparts in the southern states, to nearby camps of Union soldiers. Again, these actions make clear that enslaved African Americans were determined to acquire freedom from bondage. Works by Kenneth Porter and Edwin C. Bearss should be consulted for detailed descriptions of Indians' and African Americans' participation in the Civil War in the Indian Territory. Those who are interested in the Confederacy's and Union's efforts to secure Indians' allegiance during the Civil War should consult the documentary histories of Annie Heloise Abel (Porter 1967; Bearss 1972; Abel 1919, 1925).

Slaves in the Native American nations were emancipated after the Civil War, in 1866, when the Cherokee, Creek Choctaw, Chickasaw, and Seminole each signed new treaties with the United States. The treaties contained numerous provisions. They laid the groundwork for the dissolution of tribal sovereignty and they set out the criteria and procedures for freed slaves to obtain Indian citizenship; in general, freedpeople had a specific window of time to request citizenship and they had to present oral and written testimony documenting their lives in the Indian nations. From the outset, the issue of freedpeople's status in the Indian nations was framed by US–Indian political relations and by competing conceptions of race and status. Congress viewed these African Americans as "former slaves" needing the rights of free people, but also as a group that seemed more "Indian" than "black," and should, therefore, remain among Indians.

Scholars of Native American legal history have not yet fully studied these 1866 treaties. There are, however, many important studies of US Indian policy and federal efforts to eradicate Indian sovereignty and land title after the Civil War. Works by Frederick Hoxie, John Wunder, M. Thomas Bailey, David Wilkins, and K. Tsianina Lomawaima all address issues of federal policy and Indian sovereignty that are critical for a thorough understanding of the 1866 treaties (Hoxie 1984; Wunder 1994; Bailey 1972; Wilkins and Lomawaima 2001). One cannot study this history without consulting the collected works of Daniel F. Littlefield, Jr. as he offers a comprehensive picture of emancipation and freedpeople's lives in the five nations.

Drawing on Littlefield's studies, historians and anthropologists are now going on to analyze the definitions and dynamics of race that came to inform relations in the Indian nations after the Civil War. From 1866 until 1907, when the Indian Territory became the state of Oklahoma, Native American nations struggled to maintain their sovereignty against the political and physical incursions of Congress and illegal white squatters. In their efforts to shore up their cultural and territorial boundaries, the nations altered their definitions of Indian identity and citizenship, thus ensuring the exclusion of not only their former slaves and unscrupulous white men seeking Indian wives and access to Indian lands. Murray R. Wickett's book, *Contested Territory: Whites, Native Americans, and African Americans in Oklahoma, 1865–1907*, offers a thorough overview of the tripartite race relations in the Indian Territory and Oklahoma. Indian leaders drew increasingly rigid distinctions between "Indians" and non-Indians by using restrictive classifications of race and racial difference (Wickett 2000). In her sophisticated study of the Cherokee nation, anthropologist Circe Sturm writes about the ways in which Cherokees defined themselves in racial and political terms, both to consolidate their resistance against the United States and to exclude African Americans from legal and cultural identities as citizens of the Cherokee nation (Sturm 2002).

Many black people in the Indian Territory understood themselves as having an identity that encompassed both African American and Native American history and culture, and they desired a legal identity as Indian citizens. In the 1930s, the Works Progress Administration (WPA) employed individuals to travel through the southern states and interview former slaves. The collection of former slaves' narratives offers an extraordinary window onto African Americans' experiences and understandings of bondage and freedom. In Oklahoma, there were a number of former slaves who had been owned by Native Americans, and their narratives tell of their distinctive experiences. Historian Celia Naylor-Ojurongbe has read and interpreted these narratives to reveal the many ways in which African Americans had deeply rooted historical and cultural ties to the Indians among whom they had lived and labored. Her work, like that of other scholars currently writing in this field, also devotes considerable attention to African Americans with Native American ancestry, and thus illuminates the complex and shifting boundaries and meanings of racial identity in the late nineteenth century and beyond (Naylor-Ojurongbe 2002; Miles 2002; Lovett 2002).

In an oft quoted phrase from a 1920 *Journal of Negro History* article, a founding father of African American history observed: "One of the longest unwritten chapters of the history of the United States is that treating of the relations of the Negroes and Indians" (Woodson 1920: 45). Beginning in the 1920s and continuing into the early twenty-first century, a cadre of scholars has taken up Carter G. Woodson's challenge to draft the unscripted chapter on blacks and Indians, seeking to fill out the contours, meanings, and legacies of African American and Native American historical relationships. In doing so, these historians are extending our collective knowledge of black life in America beyond the customary geographical locales of the rural South and urban North and beyond the limited framework of a long prevailing black–white racial binary. By closely considering dynamics internal to African diasporic communities as well as between communities of color in the United States, students of Afro–Native relations are participating in a broader conversation about the effects of historical displacement and the processes of belonging, meaning-making, cultural production, and identity formation across the landscape of what Earl Lewis has called "overlapping diasporas" (Lewis 1999: 5).

For decades, the intersectional and comparative study of African Americans and Native Americans has been the specialized interest of a small group of scholars in the fields of African American history, Native American history, and Ethnohistory. However, the sheer duration of black and American Indian contacts, the large numbers of African Americans who have closely engaged with Native peoples over an extended period of time, and the growing numbers of black Americans who are self-identifying with the biracial-bicultural term "Black Indians," are calling greater attention to this salient but under-studied facet of African American life. In the 1990s and early 2000s, a surge in scholarly attention in this area of study, likely encouraged by a public interest in multiraciality and personal genealogy, has led to "Black Indian" symposia, conferences, and museum exhibitions across the nation, the development of college-level courses on the subject, and the publication of essay collections and monographs by both university and popular presses.

In classic and newly emerging scholarship on black and Indian intersections, locations commonly recognized as Indian spaces, especially Native communities of the Atlantic seaboard, the northeast, and the southeast, the Indian Territory of present-day eastern Oklahoma, and the Indian lands and reservations of the west, are proving to be important sites of African American and Afro-Native historical experience, cultural production, and political organizing. (Likewise, research on black urban centers of the northeast, middle west, and south, including early twentieth-century Harlem, are unveiling little known aspects of American Indian historical experience.) This scholarship has revealed, and continues to uncover with greater depth and specificity, that Africans and the indigenous peoples of the Americas have been in contact since at least the mid-1500s, and that the numbers of persons engaged in these cross-cultural encounters grew exponentially with the development of the transatlantic slave trade and the systemization of slavery in the Caribbean, the North American colonies, and later, the United States.

Thousands of African slaves in the West Indies and the US crossed paths with thousands of Indians from the Caribbean and North America, who, in their own diaspora, were also sold across land routes and water routes to be held as slaves of Europeans and indentured as servants in the 1600s and early 1700s. Many of these captive Africans and Indians lived and worked in shared slave communities on large plantations. In the seventeenth, eighteenth, and nineteenth centuries, hundreds of enslaved blacks fled English colonies in the Carolinas and Georgia to seek refuge among Creek migrants and other interlinked Native groups, who became jointly known as the Seminole Indians of Florida. These runaway slaves, often referred to as Black Seminoles, waged war against the United States with their Seminole allies in the First and Second Seminole Wars of 1817 and 1835. In contrast, in the nineteenth century, approximately 5,000 black slaves were possessed by slave-owning Indians of the "Five Civilized Tribes" (the Cherokees, Creeks, Choctaws, Chickasaws, and Seminoles), and lived out their lives in these Native communities of the South and present-day Oklahoma (Doran 1978: 346–7). Thousands more black people descended from these Indian-owned slaves lived in Oklahoma at the turn of the twentieth century and saw their communities enlarged by an influx of southern-born African Americans who emigrated west to Kansas, Nebraska, and Indian Territory to escape the racial violence and economic exploitation of the post-Reconstruction era.

Though precise population numbers are difficult to determine, many thousands of African Americans directly interacted with Native peoples and negotiated their lives in Native communities and nations over the four hundred years of US colonial and national history. Given the volume of these approximate numbers, it is impossible to make general claims about the nature of encounters between African Americans and American Indians or the resulting cross-cultural assessments, affinities, or antipathies that resulted from these interactions. Rather than being consistent and predictable, African American relations with American Indians have been diverse and varied, depending upon the context, region, time period, and interpersonal dynamics of contact.

Scholarship on African American and Native American historical crossings has therefore been varied as well, most often taking the form of:

1 Tribal histories that include attention to the African American presence;
2 Slavery and emancipation studies that examine joint Indian and African enslavement, American Indian participation in the larger US southern slave economy, black experience as slaves of Indians, or post-bellum shifts in Afro–Native relationships;
3 Histories of the American west, especially the state of Oklahoma, that explore black settlement, black cowboy, and "frontiersman" culture, and African American men's participation in US military actions; and
4 Micro-histories of local institutions and families in which intimate contact between blacks and Indians took place.

Major themes of scholarly enquiry have ranged from a focus on documenting cohabitation and intermarriage, to pursuing questions of alliance *versus* antagonism in black and Indian interactions, to comparing the nature of white slave-ownership and Native slave-ownership, to more recent work that explores the complexities and contingencies of black and Indian intersecting lives, identities, political movements, cultural ways, and gender dynamics.

As the quotation by Carter G. Woodson shows, the current awareness among scholars that historical Native America is significant to our understanding of African America is far from novel. Research in the area of African American and Native American relations appears in the *Journal of Negro History* as early as the 1920s and 1930s. Editor Woodson wrote the first article to appear in the *Journal* on the topic, entitled "The relations of Negroes and Indians in Massachusetts." Woodson's major argument in this piece is that black and Indian intermarriage occurred to such a great degree in Massachusetts, that Native communities there should be defined as "melting pots" (Woodson 1920: 45). In addition, Woodson concludes that a number of escaping African American slaves found safety in Indian communities in the antebellum period and that many blacks are therefore able to trace their ancestry back to Indian tribes.

In 1929, James Hugo Johnston published "Documentary evidence of the relations of Negroes and Indians" in the *Journal of Negro History*. In this brief essay Johnston argues that the relationship between blacks and Indians in the colonial through antebellum periods was influenced by their shared oppression in a white-dominated society. He writes: "Neither the law nor social barriers forbade the intermixture of these two races; both shared the antipathies of the white man, and when held as slaves their treatment differed in no degree" (Johnston 1929: 25–6). Johnston argues, finally, that a sensibility of "unity" developed between blacks and Indians, and that Indian people were absorbed into the "black race" through the processes of sexual intimacy and intermarriage (Johnston 1929: 26).

In 1932 and 1933, Kenneth Wiggins Porter published two richly researched articles in the *Journal*, entitled "Relations between Negroes and Indians within the present limits of the United States," and "Notes supplementary to 'Relations between Negroes and Indians.'" Porter explores and documents in great detail the "intimate and extensive" relations between blacks and Native Americans in various regions of what became the USA, from the early 1500s through the late 1800s, pointing out that his work is a corrective to the narrow paradigm of Euro–Indian relations that has been privileged in historical accounts (Porter 1932: 287). Porter indicates in the first article of this set that his interest in the topic was motivated by the work of anthropologist Melville Herskovits of Howard University (aided by research assistant Zora Neale Hurston), who found in studies conducted between 1926 and 1928 that 33 percent of the African American population claimed Native ancestry.

In order to test this finding, Porter raises and addresses the question: "When, where, and under what circumstances did this intermixture take place?" (Porter 1932: 288). Porter concludes that there exists significant evidence of black and Native intermarriage as well as economic and political relationship across the span of US history. He argues, similarly to Woodson and Johnston, that as a result of this contact there occurred an "Africanizing of . . . Indian tribes" and "the infusing into the blood of the American Negro of a perceptible and significant Indian element"

(Porter 1932: 367). At the same time, though, Porter's analysis differs from Johnston's in that Porter argues against the notion of a natural or prevailing affinity between African Americans and Native Americans, asserting instead that there is little evidence of a "mystical bond" or "'consciousness of kind'" at work, but rather, that black and Indian interactions shifted in type and degree (Porter 1932: 298).

In 1933, the same year that Porter published his "Notes supplementary," research on black and Indian relations also appeared in the *Chronicles of Oklahoma* in an article titled "Slavery in the Cherokee Nation." It had a different slant from the articles in the *Journal of Negro History*. The author, J. B. Davis, approached the subject through a focus on adversarial rather than cooperative relationships. Davis argues that, although slavery was nonexistent among Cherokees before white contact, "the Indians were quick to perceive their value as servants and were soon buying and selling Negro slaves" (Davis 1933: 1057). Davis traces Cherokee slaveholding over time, paying particular attention to the development of laws regulating and restricting slave activity. The phenomenon of Native Americans owning black slaves has proven to be a compelling topic to many historians who published after Davis, and continues to be the subject of the majority of published books and articles that examine black and Native relationships.

In the 1960s and 1970s, when historians began to respond to urgent questions posed by race-conscious movements for social change, the rapidly growing field of black history inspired further inquiries into overlapping aspects of the African American and American Indian pasts. In a 1963 issue of the *Journal of Negro History*, William Willis, in "Divide and rule: red, white and black in the southeast," proposed not only that blacks and Native Americans had formed relationships, but also that whites had a political interest in keeping the two groups apart. He indicated that European colonists feared coalition-building between blacks and Indians and explicitly sought to separate them through ideology and policy.

Just over a decade later in 1974, William McLoughlin, a leading scholar of Cherokee history, published an article in the *American Quarterly* titled "Red Indians, black slavery and white racism: America's slaveholding Indians." In this piece McLoughlin undertook the tasks of summarizing the historical findings on blacks and Indians to date and raising new questions for future study. McLoughlin explains that historians disagree about how to assess black–Indian relations and how to make sense of Indian slaveholding. He posits that these scholarly differences are due not to politics or ideology, but rather to a lack of "evidence upon which to draw any general conclusions" (McLoughlin 1974: 368). In reference to William Willis's argument that colonial powers purposely divided black and Native people, McLoughlin implies that historians should differentiate between Native treatment of blacks in British territory *versus* that in Spanish territory. In addition, McLoughlin considers the effects of white supremacist ideologies on Native views of blacks by looking at what he describes as the Cherokee assumption of racial hierarchies. McLoughlin concludes his essay with a call to scholars to consider the "multiracial aspects" of Native American history (McLoughlin 1974: 383).

The late 1970s and early 1980s saw a burgeoning of scholarship on black and Indian historical ties. Daniel F. Littlefield, Jr, a Native Studies scholar and prolific researcher working in the area of conjoined Native American and African American studies, began publishing histories of blacks among the five primary slaveholding tribes (previously referred to in this essay as the "Five civilized tribes") in 1976. Littlefield's major works – which include, among others, *Africans and Seminoles* (1977), *The Cherokee Freedmen* (1978), and *Africans and Creeks* (1979) – chart the key events and figures that influenced the direction of black–Indian history in the southeast and Indian Territory. In these books Littlefield chronicles the struggles that African Americans faced, as well as the roles they played in Indian communities: from slaves, to judges, to interpreters, to rebels. His research demonstrates the variety of Afro–Native relations, even as it gives form and substance to a past that has received little attention in traditional historiography. In the 1976 article, "The Beams family: free blacks in Indian Territory," co-authored by Mary Ann Littlefield, the Littlefields foreground a family drama to encapsulate and explain the chaos and insecurity of black life in the west, especially with the passage of the Fugitive Slave Act of 1850.

In "Slave 'revolt' in the Cherokee Nation," Daniel F. Littlefield and co-author Lonnie E. Underhill recount a failed mass escape among slaves of the Indian Territory. And in his recent book, *Seminole Burning, A Story of Racial Vengeance*, Daniel F. Littlefield extends the theoretical scope of his previous scholarship and explores connections between racialization and mob violence perpetrated against black men and American Indian men (Littlefield 1996). Here he links the lynching of a Seminole accused of the rape and murder of a white woman to the ritualized violence perpetrated against black people in the South, and sees the discriminatory treatment of Seminoles in Oklahoma as a partial result of the "Negroization" of Seminoles in the view of whites.

Theda Perdue, a prominent Cherokee history scholar whose work is also foundational to the current study of black–Indian relations, examined Cherokee slaveholding in her 1979 book, *Slavery and the Evolution of Cherokee Society*, concluding that the cultural changes that elite Cherokees adopted to survive white encroachment led to plantation slavery, which in turn furthered culture change among Cherokees. Perdue probed this subject further in a number of articles, including: "Cherokee planters, black slaves, and African colonization" in which she explored the tendency of Cherokee planters to support the return of freed slaves to Africa (Perdue 1982). In later studies on Cherokee women and on "mixed-bloods" in Native nations, Perdue again attends to the presence and impact of African Americans and mixed-race Afro-Native peoples in Cherokee and other southern Native societies. Rudi Halliburton, Jr also reconstructed the history of Cherokee slavery in his 1974 article "Origins of black slavery among the Cherokees" and his 1977 book *Red Over Black: Black Slavery among the Cherokee Indians*. Whereas Theda Perdue sees change over time in Cherokee attitudes toward blacks and notes exceptions to anti-black prejudice in the mid- to late nineteenth century, Halliburton argues in both these works that Cherokee slavery replicated white southern slavery. He challenges the argument that Native people were kinder, gentler masters who allowed their slaves more freedom than white slave owners.

In 1982, the same year that Perdue's essay on Cherokee planters appeared, Monroe Billington presented a statistical accounting of the treatment of Indian-owned slaves by using the Works Progress Administration (WPA) ex-slave narratives as his major source. His article "Black slavery in Indian Territory: the ex-slave narratives" notes numbers of slaves living on farms *versus* those on plantations, types of food eaten by slaves, and degrees of physical punishment. Billington concludes with the assertion that Native American slaveholders were nearly equivalent to whites in their treatment of slaves.

In the mid-1980s through the 1990s, scholars studying Afro–Native historical relations became less interested in the issues that had dominated the literature in previous decades – the catalyst and character of American Indian slave systems and the comparison of Indian slaveholding with white southern slaveholding – and more interested in the nuances of temporal and localized black–Indian interactions in national (tribal and United States) and institutional domains. In his 1984 essay "The racial education of the Catawba Indians," colonial historian James Merrell stressed the crucial point that had been previously made by Kenneth Porter, that Native–black relations (in this case, Catawba–black relations) were dynamic and erratic, rather than static and consistent. Merrell argues that the Catawbas of the Carolinas accepted or rejected persons of African descent on an individual basis until circa 1800, when Catawbas developed a fairly widespread prejudice against blacks based on a combination of factors.

Donald Grinde and Quintard Taylor assessed the effects of the Civil War on black–Indian relationships in their 1984 article: "Red vs black: conflict and accommodation in the post Civil War Indian territory, 1865–1907," tracing a decline in relations that stemmed in part from Indian support of the Confederacy. In that same year, William Katz's popular book, *Black Indians: A Hidden Heritage*, charted a history of mixed-race black Indian people, demonstrating intermarriage and cooperation in a variety of regions in the nineteenth and twentieth centuries, and highlighting well-known historical figures, such as Langston Hughes, who had both black and Native ancestry (Katz 1986). Katz's publication, though intended for young adult readers, introduced the term "black Indian" to a broad adult audience and inspired widespread interest in the subject matter.

Cultural critic bell hooks inserted a political urgency into the study of African American and American Indian relations by approaching this work with a post-colonial sensibility that claimed emotion as a legitimate impetus for research. In her essay "Revolutionary 'renegades': Native Americans, African Americans, and black Indians," hooks insists that ignoring or denying the interconnected pasts of black and Native people contributes to "white supremacist constructions of history," which "have effectively erased from public collective memory the recognition of solidarity and communion among Native Americans, Africans, and African Americans" (hooks 1992: 181). For hooks, recalling shared black and Native history is an act of resistance to colonialism and a necessity for "political solidarity" (hooks 1992: 190). Her essay in effect reprised the debate about natural affinity between blacks and Indians that James Hugo Johnston and Kenneth Porter launched in the 1920s and 1930s. Though hooks's argument seems at times to valorize Afro–Native relations and to gloss over more complicated realities in a way that other scholars would dispute, her post-colonialist reading was a unique contribution to the field that acknowledged an inherent political aspect of this research.

In his important contribution, *Africans and Native Americans: The Language of Race and the Evolution of Red-Black Peoples*, Jack Forbes (1993) traces intercultural contact prior to and during the transatlantic slave trade, looking not only at anthropological and historical evidence, but also at the meanings, uses, and transformations of racialized language. Forbes's work reveals connection and friction between blacks and Native Americans, showing how enslavement of Natives in South America and Africans in the Caribbean led to a shared experience of oppression but not necessarily to an automatic alliance. In his analysis of language, Forbes reveals among other things that as white American elites developed a race-based sorting system, they often lumped blacks and Native Americans together, using the term "mulatto" to signify the children of Indian and white as well as black and white parents, and jointly categorizing black slaves, Afro-Native slaves, and even Native American slaves as "Negro."

Donal Lindsey's (1995) study *Indians at Hampton Institute, 1877–1923* analyzes the dynamics of race relations at a school intended for African American freedpeople that experimented in accepting a limited number of Native American students. Lindsey asserts that it is impossible to arrive at a full understanding of Hampton's history without looking at both black and Native students' experiences and how those experiences intersected with racial ideologies and policies at both the institutional and national levels. He alludes to connections between black–Indian relations and the history of US imperialism with his biographical account of Hampton's founder, Samuel Chapman Armstrong, who grew up in Hawaii as the son of a missionary. Underpinning Lindsey's well-interpreted account is his assertion of an unstable character of black–Indian relations, which he describes as the shifting formations of "friction and fraternity" (Lindsey 1995: 156).

In *African Americans and Native Americans in the Creek and Cherokee Nations, 1830s to 1920s*, Ethnic Studies scholar Katja May (1996) collects intriguing evidence and makes creative claims that complicate previous findings about black slaves and freedpeople of the Five Tribes. May describes interracial alliances, such as the Green Peach Rebellion among Creek freedmen and Creek traditionalists, as well as failed possibilities for coalition. She observes that booster sheets urging African Americans to relocate to Indian Territory after Reconstruction described the Indian Territory as a potential black homeland akin to Africa. Further, she offers a tentative theory about the role of gender in the Cherokee and Creek adoption of black slavery. May challenges the accepted notion that "whites 'taught' Native people that African American men and women were useful as fieldworkers" (May 1996: 40). Instead, she suggests that internal factors, such as gender norms, also made the enslavement of black outsiders feasible.

Over the course of nearly 75 years, historians have constructed a rich body of work on the subject of African American and Native American interactions. This scholarship, which focuses mainly on those Native communities of the southeast, northeast, and Indian Territory to which black people migrated or were forcibly transported, leaves no doubt about the frequent occurrence of African American and Native American encounters, both cooperative and adversarial, nor about the fact of intimate relationships that led to an innumerable population of mixed-race Afro-Native people.

New Research and Future Directions

At the start of the twenty-first century, emerging scholarship on African American and Native American interrelated histories has moved beyond the previously necessary task of demonstrating the very fact of these relationships. Building on the foundation of important previous work, contemporary research and writing in this growing sub-field seeks to engage and enliven the subject on theoretical as well as evidentiary grounds, by incorporating fresh or rejuvenated analytical and interpretive frameworks such as diaspora, nationalism, racial formation, and racial identity, with overlooked or differently interpreted bodies of evidence, such as papers of black civic organizations in Indian Territory, African American slave narratives and autobiographies, Spanish colonial records of the lower South, and tribal and missionary records read for revelations of black experience.

To date, historian James Brooks has compiled the most diverse and intriguing publication on the topic of Native and black historical relations. In a special issue of the *American Indian Quarterly* (1998), later augmented and published as an essay collection entitled *Confounding the Color Line: The Indian-Black Experience in North America* (2002), editor Brooks challenges his contributors and readers "to engage carefully with the ambiguities of cultural hybridity" (Brooks 1998: 128–9). The essays in this volume emerge out of an ethnohistorical tradition that combines historical and anthropological modes of enquiry, and therefore engages questions of culture and identity in addition to change over time. Brooks's own essay in the collection takes up the challenging task of representing the complex identity of Euterpe Cloud Taylor, a woman of Ute and black ancestry. Brooks concludes that Taylor engages in a shifting process of self-representation, which leads her to sometimes claim an essentialized black racial identity and at other times to emphasize a Ute cultural identity. Other scholars in the collection explore issues as wide-ranging as race relations in colonial New Mexico, slavery among the southeastern tribes, mixed-race communities, legalized racial segregation, and contemporary tribal justice.

In addition to James Brooks's volume, edited collections focusing on Afro-Native literary traditions, black and Native historical encounters, and Afro-Native overlapping experience as an aspect of African Diaspora, have recently been released or are currently in press, attesting to the vibrancy of this subject. Key areas of future research on African American and Native American historical intersections are readily apparent in conference papers, dissertations, and works-in-progress that are probing, among other themes and questions: definitions of citizenship and the nation, freedmen and freedwomen's political organizing, Afro-Native women's experience, intimacies, and sexualities, "Indianization" as well as African cultural retentions among Native-owned slaves, African American and Native American cross-cultural borrowing and syncretism, definitions of "blackness" and "Indianness" in US courts, and, finally, contemporary Afro-Native identity formation, political struggles, and cultural production. Even more significant, perhaps, than the proliferation of new works that focus in the main on a shared black and American Indian past, is the way questions now being posed in the broad field of African American history recognize the significance of Native America in African American life, history, and culture.

BIBLIOGRAPHY

Works Cited

Abel, Annie Heloise ([1919] 1992): *The American Indian as Slaveholder and Secessionist*. [Cleveland, OH: Arthur H. Clark]; reprint, with introduction by Theda Perdue and Michael D. Green. Lincoln: University of Nebraska Press.

—— ([1925] 1993) *The American Indian and the End of the Confederacy, 1863–1866.* [Cleveland, OH: Arthur H. Clark]; reprint, with introduction by Theda Perdue and Michael D. Green. Lincoln: University of Nebraska Press.

Axtell, James (1981) *The European and the Indian: Essays in the Ethnohistory of Colonial North America.* New York: Oxford University Press.

Bailey, M. Thomas (1972) *Reconstruction in Indian Territory: A Story of Avarice, Discrimination, and Opportunism.* Port Washington, NY: Kennikat Press.

Bearss, Edwin C. (1972) "The Civil War comes to Indian territory, 1861: the flight of Opothleyoholo," *Journal of the West* 11: 9–42.

Billington, Monroe (1982) "Black slavery in the Indian territory: the ex-slave narratives," *Chronicles of Oklahoma* 61: 56–65.

Braund, Kathryn E. Holland (1991) "The Creek Indians, blacks, and slavery," *Journal of Southern History* 57 (November): 601–36.

Brooks, James F. (ed.) (1998) "Confounding the color line: Indian–black relations in historical and anthropological perspective," special issue, *American Indian Quarterly* 22 (Winter/Spring): 125–258.

—— (2002) *Confounding the Color Line: The Indian–Black Experience in North America.* Lincoln: University of Nebraska Press.

Brown, Kathleen (1996) *Good Wives, Nasty Wenches & Angry Patriarchs: Gender, Race, and Power in Colonial Virginia.* Chapel Hill: University of North Carolina Press.

Carson, James Taylor (1999) *Searching for the Bright Path: The Mississippi Choctaws from Prehistory to Removal.* Lincoln: University of Nebraska Press.

Cronon, William (1983) *Changes in the Land: Indians, Colonists, and the Ecology of New England.* New York: Hill and Wang.

Davis, J. B. (1933) "Slavery in the Cherokee Nation," *Chronicles of Oklahoma* 11 (December): 1056–72.

Doran, Michael F. (1978) "Negro slaves of the five civilized tribes," *Annals of the Association of American Geographers* 68 (September): 335–50.

Fischer, Kirsten (2002) *Suspect Relations: Sex, Race, and Resistance in Colonial North Carolina.* Ithaca, NY: Cornell University Press.

Forbes, Jack D. (1993) *Africans and Native Americans: The Language of Race and the Evolution of Red-Black Peoples.* Urbana: University of Illinois Press.

Gomez, Michael (1998) *Exchanging Our Country Marks: The Transformation of African Identities in the Colonial and Antebellum South.* Chapel Hill: University of North Carolina Press.

Grinde, Donald and Taylor, Quintard (1984) "Red vs. black: conflict and accommodation in the post Civil War Indian territory, 1865–1907," *American Indian Quarterly* 8 (Summer): 211–29.

Halliburton, Rudi, Jr (1974) "Origins of black slavery among the Cherokees," *Chronicles of Oklahoma* 52 (Winter): 483–96.

—— (1977) *Red over Black: Black Slavery among the Cherokee Indians.* Westport, CT: Greenwood Press.

hooks, bell (1992) "Revolutionary 'renegades': Native Americans, African Americans, and black Indians," *Black Looks: Race and Representation.* London: Turnaround Press.

Howard, Rosalyn (2002) *Black Seminoles in the Bahamas.* Gainesville: University of Florida Press.

Hoxie, Frederick E. (1984) *A Final Promise: The Campaign to Assimilate the Indians, 1880–1920.* Lincoln: University of Nebraska Press.

Johnston, James Hugo (1929) "Documentary evidence of the relations of Negroes and Indians," *Journal of Negro History* 14 (January): 21–43.

Jordan, Winthrop (1968) *White over Black: American Attitudes toward the Negro, 1550–1812.* Chapel Hill: University of North Carolina Press.

Katz, William Loren (1986) *Black Indians: A Hidden Heritage*. New York: Atheneum.

Kidwell, Clara Sue (1995) *Choctaws and Missionaries in Mississippi, 1818–1918*. Norman: University of Oklahoma Press.

Lewis, Earl (1999) "To turn as on a pivot: writing African Americans into a history of over-lapping diasporas" in Darlene Clark Hine and Jacqueline McLeod (eds.), *Crossing Boundaries: Comparative History of Black People in Diaspora*. Bloomington: Indiana University Press.

Lindsey, Donal F. (1995) *Indians at Hampton Institute, 1877–1923*. Urbana: University of Illinois Press.

Littlefield, Daniel F., Jr (1977) *Africans and Seminoles: from Removal to Emancipation*. Westport, CT: Greenwood Press.

—— (1978) *The Cherokee Freedmen: from Emancipation to American Citizenship*. Westport, CT: Greenwood Press.

—— (1979) *Africans and Creeks: from the Colonial Period to the Civil War*. Westport, CT: Greenwood Press.

—— (1980) *The Chickasaw Freedmen: A People without a Country*. Westport, CT: Green-wood Press.

—— (1996) *Seminole Burning: A Story of Racial Vengeance*. Jackson: University Press of Mississippi.

Littlefield, Daniel F., Jr and Littlefield, Mary Ann (1976) "The Beams family: free blacks in Indian territory," *Journal of Negro History* 61 (January): 16–35.

Littlefield, Daniel F., Jr and Underhill, Lonnie E. (1977) "Slave 'revolt' in the Cherokee Nation, 1842," *American Indian Quarterly* 3 (Summer): 121–9.

Lovett, Laura (2002) "'African and Cherokee by choice': race and resistance under legalized segregation" in James F. Brooks (ed.), *Confounding the Color Line: The Indian–Black Experience in North America*. Lincoln: University of Nebraska Press.

McLoughlin, William G. (1974) "Red Indians, black slavery and white racism: America's slaveholding Indians," *American Quarterly* 26: 367–85.

May, Katja (1996) *African Americans and Native Americans in the Creek and Cherokee Nations, 1830s to 1920s: Collision and Collusion*. New York: Garland.

Merrell, James (1984) "The racial education of the Catawba Indians," *Journal of Southern History* 50: 363–84.

Miles, Tiya (2002) "Uncle Tom was an Indian: tracing the red in black slavery" in James F. Brooks (ed.), *Confounding the Color Line: The Indian–Black Experience in North America*, 137–60. Lincoln: University of Nebraska Press.

Morgan, Jennifer (1997) "'Some could suckle over their shoulder': male travelers, female bodies, and the gendering of racial ideology, 1500–1770," *William and Mary Quarterly* 54 (January): 167–92.

Mulroy, Kevin (1993) *Freedom on the Border: The Seminole Maroons in Florida, The Indian Territory, Coahila, and Texas*. Lubbock, TX: Texas Tech University Press.

Naylor-Ojurongbe, Celia (2002) "'Born and raised among these people, I don't want to know any other': slaves' acculturation in nineteenth-century Indian territory" in James F. Brooks (ed.), *Confounding the Color Line: The Indian–Black Experience in North America*. Lincoln: University of Nebraska Press.

Perdue, Theda (1979) *Slavery and the Evolution of Cherokee Society, 1540–1866*. Knoxville: University of Tennessee Press.

—— (1982) "Cherokee planters, black slaves, and African colonization," *Chronicles of Oklahoma* 60: 322–31.

—— (2003) *"Mixed-Blood" Indians: Racial Construction in the Early South*. Athens: University of Georgia Press.

Porter, Kenneth Wiggins (1932) "Relations between Negroes and Indians within the present limits of the United States," *Journal of Negro History* 17 (July): 287–367.

—— (1933) "Notes supplementary to 'Relations between Negroes and Indians,'" *Journal of Negro History* 18 (July): 282–8.

—— (1967) "Billy Bowlegs (Holata Micco) in the Civil War," *Florida Historical Quarterly* 45 (April): 391–401.

—— (1971) *The Negro on the American Frontier*, preface by William Loren Katz. New York: Arno Press.

—— (1996) *The Black Seminoles: History of a Freedom-Seeking People*, revised by Alcione Amos and Thomas Senter (eds.). Gainesville: University Press of Florida.

—— (1998) *Cherokee Women: Gender and Culture Change, 1700–1835*. Lincoln: University of Nebraska Press.

Saunt, Claudio (1999) *A New Order of Things: Property, Power, and the Transformation of the Creek Indians, 1733–1816*. New York: Cambridge University Press.

Shoemaker, Nancy (1997) "How Indians got to be red," *American Historical Review* 102 (June): 625–44.

Sturm, Circe (2002) *Blood Politics: Race, Culture and Identity in the Cherokee Nation of Oklahoma*. Berkeley: University of California Press.

Thornton, John (1992) *Africa and Africans in the Making of the Atlantic World, 1400–1800*, 2nd edn. Cambridge: Cambridge University Press.

Van Sertima, Ivan (1976) *They Came Before Columbus: The African Presence in America*. New York: Random House.

Wickett, Murray R. (2000) *Contested Territory: Whites, Native Americans, and African Americans in Oklahoma, 1865–1907*. Baton Rouge: Louisiana State University Press.

Wilkins, David E. and Lomawaima, K. Tsianina (2001) *Uneven Ground: American Indian Sovereignty and Federal Law*. Norman: University of Oklahoma Press.

Willis, William S. (1963) "Divide and rule: red, white and black in the southeast," *Journal of Negro History* 48 (July): 157–76.

Woodson, Carter G. (1920) "The relations of Negroes and Indians in Massachusetts," *Journal of Negro History* 5 (January): 45–62.

Wunder, John R. (1994) "Retained by the People": A History of American Indians and the Bill of Rights. New York: Oxford University Press.

Suggestions for Further Reading

Alexander, Adele Logan (1991) *Ambiguous Lives: Free Women of Color in Rural Georgia, 1789–1879*. Fayetteville: University of Arkansas Press.

Brennan, Jonathan (ed.) (2003) *When Brer Rabbit Meets Coyote: African-Native American Literature*. Urbana: University of Illinois Press.

Burton, Art (1991) *Black, Red, and Deadly: Black and Indian Gunfighters of the Indian Territories*. Austin, TX: Eakin Press.

Chang, David A. Y. O. (forthcoming) "Where will the nation be at home? Race, nationalisms and emigration movements in the Creek nation" in Tiya Miles and Sharon Holland (eds.), *Crossing Waters, Crossing Worlds: The African Diaspora in Indian Country*. Durham, NC: Duke University Press.

Debo, Angie (1940) *And Still the Waters Run*. Princeton, NJ: Princeton University Press.

Hart, William (1998) "Black 'go-betweens' and the mutability of 'race,' status, and identity on New York's pre-revolutionary frontier" in Andrew Cayton and Fredrika Teute (eds.), *Contact Points: American Frontiers from the Mohawk Valley to the Mississippi, 1750–1830*. Chapel Hill: University of North Carolina Press.

Johnston, James Hugo (1970) *Race Relations in Virginia and Miscegenation in the South, 1776–1860*. Amherst: University of Massachusetts Press.

Krauthamer, Barbara (forthcoming) "In their 'native country': freedpeople's understandings of culture and citizenship in the Choctaw and Chickasaw nations" in T. Miles and S. Holland (eds.), *Crossing Waters, Crossing Worlds: The African Diaspora in Indian Country*. Durham, NC: Duke University Press.

McLoughlin, William (1986) *Cherokee Renascence in the New Republic*. Princeton, NJ: Princeton University Press.

Malcomson, Scott. L. (2000) *One Drop of Blood: The American Misadventure of Race*. New York: Farrar, Straus, & Giroux.

Merrell, James (1989) *The Indians' New World: Catawbas and Their Neighbors from European Contact through the Era of Removal*. New York: W. W. Norton.

Miles, Tiya and Holland, Sharon (eds.) (forthcoming) *Crossing Waters, Crossing Worlds: The African Diaspora in Indian Country*. Durham, NC: Duke University Press.

Porter, Kenneth Wiggins (1956) "Negroes and Indians on the Texas Frontier, 1831–1876," *Journal of Negro History* 41 (October): 285–310.

Taylor, Quintard (1998) *In Search of the Racial Frontier: African Americans in the American West, 1528–1990*. New York: W. W. Norton.

Twyman, Bruce Edward (1999) *The Black Seminole Legacy and North American Politics, 1693–1845*. Washington DC: Howard University Press.

Wright, J. Leitch (1981) *The Only Land They Knew: The Tragic Story of the American Indians in the Old South*. New York: Free Press.

Young, Mary (1989) "Racism in red and black: Indians and other free people of color in Georgia law, politics, and removal policy," *Georgia Historical Quarterly* 73 (Fall): 492–518.

PART III

In the House of Bondage

CHAPTER EIGHT

Origins and Institutionalization of American Slavery

JASON R. YOUNG

Were there more evidence, historians might have come to definitive conclusions decades ago regarding the origins of American slavery. The opposite holds equally true: that had less of the relevant documentary evidence survived the seventeenth century, scholars might have resolved the matter sooner, basing their conclusions on the scraps and fragments that the past provides. Instead, the debate regarding the ultimate origins of American slavery has spanned a century and continues to intrigue and confound us. This chapter traces some of the key historiographical moments in this debate, focusing – as have many of the historians in the discussion – on colonial Virginia during the seventeenth century.

The general contours of the debate are fairly well established. By 1660, slavery had emerged in several colonies as a legal institution. Between 1640 and 1660, some evidence – though rather scant, ambiguous, and at times even contradictory – suggests a debasement of African labor and, in some cases, black labor in perpetuity. The period between 1619 and 1640 is most difficult to assess. Not only is the condition of the first Africans who arrived in British North America during this period open to debate, but also the general condition of Africans over the course of the subsequent twenty years is hotly contested. To be sure, shreds of fragmentary evidence exist for the period 1619–40, but the scarcity of such evidence makes conclusions tentative.

The debate has typically divided historians into two broad camps. Some scholars argue that economic factors – in particular, the rise of plantation slavery – led to institutionalized slavery and racism. Others maintain that a general antipathy towards and discrimination against Africans preceded the large enslavement of blacks in British North America. Still others focus on the complex interplay between these factors. Given the trajectory of American history from the seventeenth century to the present, some might question the lasting relevance of these inquiries. For, whatever the status of those "20 Odd Negroes" who were landed in Virginia in August 1619, the lion's share of American history is marked in its hatred and violence, in its slavery and racism.[1]

What importance, then, are we to ascribe to those formative decades of ambiguity and angst when colonists struggled to develop social and economic institutions that might ensure the prosperity of the region? The answer to this question lies not only in the centrality of slavery and racism to any understanding of American history, but also, and perhaps more importantly, in the need of each successive generation to define and orient itself in light of that formative period. As such, this chapter points out the critical relationship that pertained between pressing social concerns and their subsequent reflection in historical revisions of America's past in slavery. Our understanding of slavery continues to be crucial to our notions of contemporary black as well as white working-class life, and to our understanding of the relationship between racial politics and class strife.

Though historical discussion of the origins of slavery and racism extends as far back as the mid-nineteenth century, little debate – and perhaps even less interest – was afforded the subject by most historians of the American past (Ballagh 1902; Russell 1913; Ames 1940; Craven 1949). Not until the mid-twentieth century did the debate fully enter the mainstream of American historical debate. Oscar and Mary Handlin's "Origins of the Southern labor system" sparked a debate that would continue for the duration of the century when they argued that slavery emerged in British North America as an adjustment to American conditions of previous forms of forced labor already prevalent in the mother country. Coerced labor was not a new institution for the English who settled in the New World and indeed, British authorities had devised several mechanisms for the extraction of labor, including conviction for villeinage, vagrancy, debt, and vagabondage. Moreover, miscreants were subject to servitude as a form of punishment, while children and wives could be sold into forced labor by the head of a household. In this sense, the British "antithesis of 'free' was not 'slave' but unfree; and within the condition of unfreedom, law and practice recognized several gradations" (Handlin 1948: 7; Handlin and Handlin 1950: 200).

The status of the first blacks in the New World, they contend, "must be viewed within the perspective of these conceptions and realities of servitude (Handlin and Handlin 1950: 202). For much of the seventeenth century, black labor was not marked as especially different from other forms of labor. Like other servants, some blacks worked for the duration of their term, to be freed upon its completion. That the colonial record occasionally referred to black laborers as slaves should not, the Handlins maintain, be read as any indication that they were indeed enslaved. Without any legal precedent in England, slavery implied a general debasement of labor that might be applied variously to European laborers as easily as it was applied to blacks.

In this view, slavery developed incidentally in colonial America as economic circumstances – namely the scarcity of cheap labor, the abundance of land, and the helplessness of Africans – resulted in the institution of African slavery. Planters originally preferred white workers, who would typically sign indentures with a term of five to seven years, during which they would work as required in return for board, lodging, and clothing. If the servant came from Europe, the employer would also pay their travel costs. At the end of the term, the servant was entitled to "freedom dues," usually in the form of a modest plot of land along with grain, livestock, and implements. New England planters actively sought to encourage European immigration by reducing the term of indenture and improving the general condition of white labor. But as conditions for whites improved, the situation for blacks – who were "farthest removed from the English" – deteriorated more and more:

> It is not necessary to resort to racialist assumptions to account for such measures; these were simply the reactions of immigrants lost to the stability and security of home . . . Like the millions who would follow, these immigrants longed in the strangeness for the company of familiar men and singled out to be welcomed those who were most like themselves. (Handlin and Handlin 1950: 208–11)

Colonists soon "became aware of the differences between themselves and the African immigrants" and "color emerged as the token of the slave status; the trace of color became the trace of slavery" (ibid: 208, 216). As the expansion of large-scale plantations continued, the number of Africans brought to the New World as laborers also increased tremendously.

The mark of chattel was impressed indelibly on the African in 1661, when Virginia legally instituted the condition of slavery on Africans. Other colonies followed suit and slavery eventually flourished in colonial America on a grand scale. For the Handlins, slavery grew out of the peculiar marriage of Old World labor in a New World setting and eventually gave birth to the institution of racism. Some historians have subsequently noted that the Handlins' argument reflected the American optimism prevalent during the post-war period and the hope, articulated only a few years before the tremendous disruptions of the Civil Rights era, that "if whites and Negroes could share the same status of half freedom for forty years in the seventeenth century, why could they not share full freedom in the twentieth?" (Jordan 1962: 20).

On its most central points: that early African laborers enjoyed rights much on a par with their white counterparts, that economic conditions led eventually to slavery and that racism was a consequence rather than a cause of the enslavement of Africans, the Handlins' view correlates with several preceding theories (Ballagh 1902; Russell 1913). Of particular note is the argument of Eric Williams, famed Trinidadian historian who – hoping to "undermine imperial legitimacy and discredit the historical support system that sustained contemporary race prejudice" – argued that slavery was born simply of economic necessity and racism was invented by Europeans as the faulty and flimsy support for subsequent imperial designs (Green 1988: 27; Williams 1944: 19). Indeed, Williams argued, "white servitude was the historic base upon which Negro slavery was constructed . . . [slavery] had to do not with the color of the laborer, but the cheapness of the labor" (Williams 1944: 19). Williams hoped that if slavery could be so roundly castigated and discarded in an increasingly modern and capitalistic world, then certainly its terrible brainchild, racism, should meet some similar and immediate doom.

The Handlins' argument, though convincing on several points, fails to address several matters of consequence. The Handlins failed to fully explain why color – or a notion of race, even if only vaguely articulated – became the most important marker of difference in a colony rife with other, presumably equally significant, differences of language, religion, class, culture, and custom. If colonists were looking to find common cause with those "who were most like themselves," then they could very well have done so without highlighting racial distinctions. Indeed, some whites and blacks had been successful enough in minimizing these differences when they absconded together; and colonial laws prohibiting interracial marriage and fornication suggest that the racial divide was not broad enough to preclude intimate relations between white and black servants. Indeed, race, or at least some notion of racial difference, must have operated prior to the general degradation of black labor, a matter addressed at length by subsequent scholars.

Writing in 1959, Carl Degler responded to the Handlins in "Slavery and the genesis of race prejudice," an article which, much like the Handlins' study, revived older work in the field (Ames 1940; Craven 1949). Unlike the Handlins, Degler asserted that the condition of white servants during the middle of the seventeenth century was not improving; so the mistreatment of Africans did not begin with ameliorating the condition of whites. Indeed, legislation of the period suggests that colonial governments were discriminating against Africans long before the introduction of large-scale agricultural production. Africans in Virginia, for example, were prevented from carrying arms by a 1640 statute; and when Maryland in 1639, and Virginia in 1643, "enacted laws fixing limits to the terms for servants who entered without written contracts, Negroes were never included in such protective provisions" (Degler 1959: 57). Africans had always been treated differently in the colonies and African labor in perpetuity existed as early as 1630. Even when there is no direct evidence, the fact that it was considerably more expensive to buy bonded black labor from Africa than indentured white labor from Europe – despite the planters' original preference for white labor – suggests that the Africans' term of service was longer, and probably perpetual.

It is worthy of note that where Degler read 'perpetual' to mean 'eternal or without end,' the Handlins read the same to mean "that which had no set time expressly allotted for its continuance, or indeterminate" (Handlin and Handlin 1950: 210). To the Handlins' contention that slavery, lacking an Old World legal precedent, was created out of the peculiar conditions in British North America, Degler argued that the colonists on the mainland had "ample opportunity before 1660 to learn of a different status for black men from that for Englishmen, whether servant or free," through the various examples of racial discrimination being practiced in the slave societies of the West Indies. In the end, Degler maintained that "the status of the Negro in the English colonies was worked out within a framework of discrimination; that from the outset . . . the Negro was treated as an inferior to the white man, servant or free" (Degler 1959: 52–3, 56–7, 59).

The Handlins connected the rise of American slavery and subsequent racism to the desire of white colonists to ameliorate the working conditions of European immigrants. Only as the number of African immigrants increased dramatically, and their labor became associated with a generally degraded position, did colonists begin to discern and exploit the differences they perceived between themselves and the Africans made to work in the colony. The mark of chattel and the stain of race, then, gradually followed from the debasement of black labor. This implies that, had there never been a large body of African laborers who eventually became associated with perpetual terms of service and poor working conditions, chattel slavery, and racism might never have emerged. Degler responded to this issue by asserting that while it was unquestionably a demand for labor that prompted colonists to enslave Africans, "the status which he acquired here cannot be explained by reference to that economic motive." Long before African workers became as economically important as their white counterparts, "the Negro had been consigned to a special discriminatory status" (Degler 1959: 62). He referred to evidence from New England where, despite the relatively small number of African laborers, vitriolic discrimination marked the lives of black residents (ibid: 62–5).

Degler addressed the critically important mass of counter-evidence in the issue, which included the experience of those blacks who, though initially serving as bondsmen, eventually became free. The life of Anthony Johnson is perhaps most notable here. In 1621, Johnson was brought to Virginia, where he was initially defined as a servant. He married, had four children and, after earning his freedom, became a successful planter in his own right. He owned servants, cattle, and significant landholdings. Even more than this, he filed suit against fellow whites in his community in order to secure, protect, and recover property and enjoyed some significant success in this regard. Degler responded to the experiences of Anthony Johnson and to other counter-evidence by asserting that the presence of blacks rising out of servitude does not invalidate the claim that most others were sinking steadily toward slavery: "it merely underscores the unsteady evolution of a slave status" (Degler 1959: 60). The experiences of Johnson's family may bear this assessment out. As the windows of opportunity and success became increasingly closed and the strictures placed on Africans more strident, Anthony Johnson left Virginia at mid-century to build a life in Maryland. In 1670, some months after his death, Virginia courts failed to restore to his family lands that Johnson had owned on grounds that Johnson was "a negro and by consequence an alien," thus highlighting the changing face of race and racism in the colonial period (Berlin 1998: 90; Johnson 1998: 44).

Though the Handlins' responses to Degler's claims were vituperative – contending that his argument was, at times, inept and obtuse and suggesting that its author was "handicapped . . . by the inability to use his terms properly" – they did acknowledge that the English had an ethnocentric preference, an assessment that falls somewhat short of Degler's stronger claim of racial discrimination (Handlin and Handlin 1959: 488–90).

Further support for the economic justifications of slavery came with the 1959 publication of Stanley Elkins' *Slavery*. For Elkins, American slavery was created wholly in America. Like Handlin, Elkins stressed the general improvement of the status and condition of white laborers and the subsequent deterioration of the condition of African laborers. As the seventeenth century progressed, the gulf between white and black labor increased dramatically, deepening the significance of color and depressing the African closer and closer to perpetual slavery (Elkins [1959] 1976: 38). The seemingly unending supply of land in the colonies and the increasing demand for tobacco encouraged planters to seek out cheap labor, for which the large-scale trade in Africans commenced and steadily increased throughout the seventeenth century. Elkins suggested that the emerging planter class was able to institute slavery on a large scale because there was simply no formidable opposition to the trade: "with the full development of the plantation there was nothing . . . to prevent unmitigated capitalism from becoming unmitigated slavery" (ibid: 49).

In the midst of this country's own struggles with discrimination, citizenship, and racial violence, Winthrop Jordan entered the debate in 1962. Jordan's awareness of the timeliness of his argument was reflected in the article's title, "Modern tensions and the origins of American slavery." Jordan claimed that the first fragmentary evidence relating to slavery dated back to 1640, when some Africans were serving for life in Maryland and Virginia. That other blacks were merely serving their regular indenture complicates the question (Jordan 1962: 22–4). Even if outright slavery did not exist between 1640 and 1660, Jordan maintained that discrimination against Africans had clearly been established during the twenty-year span, because they were forbidden to carry arms and because restrictions on sexual unions between the races became codified into law (ibid: 27–8). As the number of Africans imported into the region rose and large-scale plantation systems increasingly characterized the colonies, the terms African, Negro, and slave became increasingly synonymous. Writing some years later in *White Over Black*, Jordan made clear that slavery, as an "unthinking decision," was "neither borrowed from foreigners, nor extracted from books, nor invented out of whole cloth, nor extrapolated from servitude, nor generated from the English reaction to the Negroes as such, nor necessitated by the exigencies of the New World. Not any one of these made the Negro a slave, but all" (Jordan 1968: 72).

Jordan charted much the same territory as that earlier tread by Degler when he assessed the role and importance of race prejudice and slavery in New England. Writing in 1961, he inquired not only into the relatively weak nature of slavery in New England, but also into the reasons why slavery existed there at all. Given the very small numbers of blacks who lived in New England – approximately 3 percent of the total population in the eighteenth century – Jordan maintains that "no economic exigency required the establishment of a distinct status for such a small population of the labor force" (Jordan 1961: 245). Even absent the economic necessity of African slavery, New England colonists looked to their West Indian counterparts, with whom they maintained regular commercial contact (including the trade in West Indian slaves), as a model and guide for the treatment of black servants. New England slavery, then, like its Chesapeake or West Indian counterpart, "depended on a perception of the Negro as a peculiar kind of social being . . . fitting and proper to enslave for life" (ibid: 250). The prevalence of racial antipathies and discrimination in New England complicates the causal relationship that the Handlins and others drew between the increase of African immigration, the rise of plantation societies, and the development of American racism.

Perhaps most importantly, Jordan traced the history of white attitudes *vis-à-vis* blacks prior to English colonization. Through an extensive analysis of an impressive body of European sources, he noted the great depth of European enmity to blacks in the years prior to European exploration and colonization. At the center of these comparisons were British notions of race or, more accurately, color. Blackness, an idea loaded with meaning in sixteenth-century England was perceived as foul, wicked, and sinister – the handmaid and symbol of evil. Not surprisingly, the most arresting characteristic of the African was his skin color. From the outset, the African was seen as the dark savage: some odd mélange of man and ape (Jordan 1968: 4, 7). Jordan's argument may be read alongside anti-colonial literature of the same period where Frantz Fanon – writing somewhat earlier, in *Black Skins, White Masks* – noted that, "when European civilization came in contact with the black world, with those savage people, everyone agreed that the Negroes were the principle of evil symbolizing the lower emotions, the baser inclinations, the dark side of the soul" (Fanon [1952] 1967: 190–1).

Africans were also set apart from Europeans due to their religion. Whites perceived of heathenism as a fundamental defect, which forever set the African apart. In fact, Africans were set apart from Europeans in a number of ways such that clothing, housing, farming, warfare, and language all worked to separate the African from their European counterparts (Jordan 1968: 20, 24–8). As such, Europeans tended to set the African apart as a foil, conceiving of themselves as the perfect epitome of civility, Christianity, and morality, as they posited the African as barbaric, heathen, and lascivious. Africans became the manifestation of everything that the European did not want to be. To define Africans as ugly was to affirm Europeans' beauty; to define the African as libidinous was to suggest European sexual restraint; and to define the African as savage was to emphasize European civility. Moreover, Englishmen were inclined to identify Africans with apes and monkeys, so as to emphasize their supposed animalistic tendencies (ibid: 3–43).

Writing in 1987, St. Clair Drake agreed with Jordan, maintaining that prejudice and discrimination based upon skin color existed for several centuries before the beginning of European overseas expansion. Drake conceded that racism as we know it had not yet been institutionalized, but that, long before whites utilized racist ideologies to systematically defend the interests of those who profited from slavery and colonial imperialism, black people were being stereotyped such that the African became the embodiment of the savage within everyone that must be restrained, controlled, and civilized (Drake 1987: 32–40). By contrasting themselves with Africans, British colonists were better able to convince themselves of their role as God's chosen people destined to carry their culture to all corners of the earth.

Returning now to Jordan, one notes that though his evidence and analysis are quite striking and thoroughly convincing, he vitiated some of his claims by maintaining a stance that he had earlier taken in 1961: namely, that the slow descent to slavery and racism were mutually generative. Or, more precisely, that slavery and prejudice "may have been equally cause and effect, continuously reacting upon each other, dynamically joining hands to hustle the Negro down the road to complete degradation" (Jordan 1968: 80). This matter is explored further by A. T. Vaughan who, writing in "Blacks in Virginia: a note on the first decade," responds to Jordan's claim that the data for the years prior to 1640 were too sketchy to be conclusive. Vaughan argues that the African men and women brought to Virginia in the period 1619–29 "held from the outset a singularly debased status in the eyes of white Virginians" (Vaughan 1972: 469). Regarding census data from the early period, Vaughan notes the absence of crucial data including the age and date of arrival for black servants, matters of importance for determining the term of indenture. Moreover, the names of black servants whose names appear on the census rarely include last names, while others include no name at all. Without drawing any sweeping conclusions based on these data, Vaughan does argue that "Negroes as a group received by far the scantiest and most impersonal entries in the census" (ibid: 472).

A new interpretation surfaced when Edmund Morgan asserted in *American Slavery, American Freedom* – as had the Handlins – that, prior to 1660, planters preferred white labor. During this time, planters were careful not to rely too heavily on slave labor because the disease environment of the colony discouraged heavy investment in slave labor. By the mid-1660s, however, the situation changed drastically when the utilization of Africans as slaves became more advantageous to the planters as the incidents of disease dramatically decreased. In these formative years, there was little difference between white and black labor. In fact, as has been noted earlier, whites and blacks often ran away together and, as many seventeenth-century slaves were imported from Barbados, they were already proficient in the English language and were able to communicate with their white counterparts (Morgan 1975: 327).

As such, planters perceived the community of white and black labor as a threat to the established order in the colonies: "If freeman, with disappointed hopes should make common cause with the slaves, the results might be disastrous" (Morgan 1975: 328). Therefore, racism was constructed to separate dangerous free whites from equally dangerous black slaves. In order to effect a change in the general perception of blacks, planters attributed any number of negative stereotypes to Africans, many of which had been ascribed formerly to the white English poor. Thus, blacks were described as shiftless, lazy, irresponsible, drunk, dishonest, and ungrateful. These stereotypes were accompanied by legislation securing the total sexual separation of blacks and whites. Morgan concedes that a degree of racial prejudice existed, but contends that the unfamiliar appearance of the African may well have struck the white laborer as only skin-deep. Morgan writes equivocally, "[whether] or not race was a necessary ingredient in slavery, it was an ingredient" (ibid: 315, 328). But this assessment leaves several questions unanswered. If Morgan fails to document the operation of a unified social consciousness among planters, necessary for the construction and dissemination of the racial attitudes that he ascribes to them, then he is even less convincing regarding the reasons why lower-class whites accepted race prejudice when, by his own account, differences in color may have been perceived by whites and blacks alike as only skin-deep.

Joseph Boskin turned the debate away from early colonial laws, to the realm of education, where he found a significant – though somewhat haphazard – attempt on the part of English colonists to educate Native Americans in seventeenth-century colonial Virginia and Massachusetts. By mobilizing "finances, directives, and institutions to 'civilize' and Christianize" Native Americans, the English presumed them to be educable and worthy of the efforts therein directed (Boskin 1976: 23–5). Boskin asserts that British colonists did not seriously entertain the idea of formally educating the African because, from a relatively early point, white colonists presumed that Africans occupied a lesser position in the hierarchy of human ability and capacity. While many scholars presume that notions of race and slavery developed out of the interaction between black and white immigrants in colonial America, Boskin does well to illustrate the degree to which notions of black, white, and Indian identity were all forged of the same social and ideological crucible.

Writing in *Myne Owne Ground*, T. H. Breen and Stephen Innes sought to change the very terms of the historiographical debate regarding the origins of American slavery and racism. Instead of searching for ultimate origins, Breen and Innes "inquired into the ways the free blacks dealt with the local gentry; with middling white people; with slaves; and with other free blacks" (Breen and Innes 1980: 32). Rather than searching for the early signs of black debasement, the authors sought to chart the complex social relationships within which free black planters found themselves. For, as the authors maintain, anyone "with a sharp eye can . . . ferret out signs of racial discrimination long before the appearance of the first statutory references to slavery in the 1660s" (ibid: 22).

The free blacks that populate the pages of *Myne Owne Ground* bought and sold land, brought suit to local courts, married, had children, and lived otherwise full and satisfying lives. Still, the social position of free blacks was closely connected and indebted to patron–client networks that blacks were made to maintain with wealthy whites who, in many cases, were their former owners (Breen and Innes 1980: 22, 97). To take but one example, Francis Payne – one of the free blacks that figure largely in the study – feared, after gaining his freedom, that other planters would try to re-enslave him and so negotiated with his former masters to post a bond, which testified to his free status and prevented other planters from laying a claim on him. Even after blacks had earned their freedom, these patron–client relationships continued, though they were not governed by "the color of a man's skin, but by his economic status" (ibid: 110). If this is so, then one would like to know if any whites, newly released from their indentures, felt the same fears that Payne suffered and whether they sought to protect their new status through the law, a matter that Breen and Innes do not address.

Not until after Bacon's Rebellion do Breen and Innes find that the status of free blacks deteriorated, though they hesitate to place a specific date on the change, noting rightly that Bacon's Rebellion was not the single cause of the gradual debasement of free blacks. Several factors – including a demographic shift – occurred, whereby increasing numbers of Africans were introduced to the colony, increasing the general antipathy that whites felt toward blacks. Responding to scholars who perceive much earlier evidence of racial antipathy toward blacks, Breen and Innes maintain that free blacks did not operate at much of a disadvantage with regard to non-gentry whites, "regardless of what Virginia Statute may have decreed." Indeed, if the "county clerk had not from time to time inserted the word 'Negro' next to their names, it would have been impossible to distinguish" many of the free blacks from their white counterparts (Breen and Innes 1980: 107–9, 111).

Making a much broader claim, the authors hold that neither Anthony Johnson nor Francis Payne thought of themselves as living in a racist society; nor, for that matter, did it occur to them that their white neighbors were making an "unthinking decision" that would reduce all black people to the lowest levels of society simply because they were black. In the end, economic opportunity and prosperity served as the primary distinctions between men; and as the growth of the plantation system gradually undermined the position of free blacks, they eventually found their status eroded. Competing against the great planters became difficult, as the wealthy monopolized larger tracts of land and directed the labor of many (Breen and Innes 1980: 112–14).

Breen and Innes are right to shift the terms of this debate to matters of historical context. Race relations were, as the authors suggest, neither monolithic not inevitable. The degree to which some free blacks enjoyed social mobility is instructive as we investigate the material at hand. Still, that observation should not obscure other matters of critical importance. While it is true that, had the county clerk mentioned above not attached the term Negro to certain residents, then we might not have been able to distinguish them from other whites. But the clerk did make the distinction and if it was important enough to the clerk to mark the differences between the white and black residents, then it is equally valid for historians to investigate the importance of those differences.

While the authors make compelling, even if not fully convincing, arguments regarding colonial law early in the study, they simply abandon that approach when they suggest that whites and blacks operated on fairly equal terms, regardless of colonial law. If blacks and whites did interact on equal terms, and there is compelling evidence that they did on many occasions, then this would have happened not regardless of colonial law, but in spite of it. The willingness of whites to live and work and resist alongside blacks makes their later assumption of racist sentiment, ostensibly at the behest of wealthy planters, all the more baffling. On a related point, it may be true, as the authors suggest, that there is no evidence that some of the more racially discriminatory legislation in the colony [particularly those laws that discouraged interracial escape] effectively deterred efforts to abscond, but it is also true that the legislation nevertheless existed, a point that the authors fail to address (Breen and Innes 1980: 22–7, 30–2).

While both blacks and whites would have felt some financial pressure being exerted on their lives by the rise of wealthy planters, Breen and Innes are not correct to suggest that this pressure was merely a matter of economics – that blacks "lost the possibility to acquire property, the basis of genuine freedom in this society." Indeed, the true shift was that free blacks were not only losing property, but that blacks were gradually becoming property, a transition that was intimately implicated in race (Breen and Innes 1980: 113–14).

Returning to the subject years later in *Many Thousands Gone*, Ira Berlin maintains that "New World slavery did not have its origins in a conspiracy to dishonor, shame, brutalize, or reduce slaves on some perverse scale of humanity – although it did all of those at one time or another" (Berlin 1998: 5). Without minimizing the role that race prejudice played in the construction of American slavery, Berlin does highlight the ambiguity of the source material and the vast debate that preceded him, finally concluding that the first black immigrants in colonial America were slaves inasmuch as they were sold by international slave traders and bought by men familiar with black slavery throughout the Atlantic. Still, they were treated much like other servants and won their freedom in many instances. Berlin acknowledges that his presumptions do not "resolve the debate over the origins of racism, the chronology of slavery's codification, or the changing nature of bondage – whether slavery or servitude – in early America" (ibid: 386). Instead, he contends, if slavery made race, its larger purpose was to make class, "and the fact that the two were made simultaneously by the same process has mystified both" (ibid: 5).

Writing similarly, Betty Wood argues that, in establishing race-based slavery in British North America, colonists "acted in a pragmatic, economically rational manner. Economic necessity and a quest for profits drove them to enslave West Africans" (Wood 1997: 7). Not content with this explanation, however, Wood goes on to suggest that economic considerations alone "do not satisfactorily explain why slavery became a status reserved principally for people of West African ancestry" (ibid: 7). Instead, pre-existing English racial attitudes may have justified, though they did not dictate, African slavery.

The 30- to 40-year period between the first evidence of racial discrimination in the colonies and the eventual legal recognition of slavery in the 1660s has proved particularly vexing to scholars who presume that racial prejudice instigated, if not caused outright, the establishment of slavery. If, indeed, racial prejudice led to the institutionalization of slavery then one would expect the system to have been codified into law much earlier. Betty Wood addresses this problem by noting other impediments to an earlier establishment of slavery. She holds that during the 1620s and 1630s, and indeed well into the 1680s, Virginia planters relied heavily on Dutch traders to supply their labor needs. For their part, Dutch traders found little financial incentive to trade heavily in the Chesapeake region whose market was less secure, less stable, and certainly less lucrative than the West Indian or South American trade where high African mortality rates ensured more profitable markets (Wood 1997: 80). Perhaps because the African population remained so small in colonial Virginia, the status of these laborers retained some degree of ambiguity.

Like Morgan, Wood argues that – after tobacco became an established and profitable crop – colonists imported African labor at an alarming rate, preferring it to previous forms of indenture. In the process, planters enlisted the support of non-elite whites in an attempt to nullify the common bonds formerly forged between poor whites and blacks. Though without sufficient explanation, Wood argues that poor whites subscribed to this novel racial antipathy even against their own better economic interests (Wood 1997: 90–1). That is, the importation of greater numbers of Africans allowed wealthy planters to extend their landholdings and to augment the social and economic distance between themselves and non-elite whites. Meanwhile, the opportunities for poorer whites to become landowners themselves were diminishing as large planters continued to secure their hegemony. Many poorer whites were forced to work as tenant farmers or as hired hands.

In a wonderfully incisive argument, even if not fully convincing, Barbara J. Fields sought to change, not only the direction of the debate, but also the very terms and presumptions upon which the discussion rested. Writing in "Slavery, race, and ideology in the United States of America," Fields challenged the notion of race as a category and questioned its use as a valid unit of analysis: "belief in the biological reality of race outranks even astrology, the superstition closest to it in the competition for dupes among the ostensibly educated" (Fields 1990: 96). Of particular concern to Fields is the fallacy of using 'race' to explain historical phenomena – specifically to suppose "that it explains why people of African descent have been set apart for treatment different from that accorded others" (ibid: 96). Given that race has neither a genetic basis, nor a trans-historical essence, Fields contends that one must treat race in its historical context as a continually constructed and reconstructed ideology which, as regards American notions of race, originated historically in the Revolutionary era. In this period, anti-slavery proponents and their opponents both attached to race a significance that was used variously to both challenge and justify the enslavement of men and women of African descent.

Regarding the early importation of Africans and Europeans in seventeenth-century Virginia, Fields maintains that race had not been sufficiently developed as an ideology to have effected a differential treatment between European and African servants based on color. Instead, European servants were regularly mistreated and brutalized, for which their race offered little or no protection. For Fields, perpetual inherited enslavement constituted the only degradation that white servants avoided, a fate that eventually befell African laborers. While some argue that the brutality waged against European servants was mitigated by race (or whiteness), she contends that these scholars "only believe such folklore when they are floating in the twilight world of racial ideology . . . Once restored to honest daylight, they know better" (Fields 1990: 102). Rather than viewing race as a mitigating factor in the relations between landlords and white servants, Fields proposes that the very real capabilities of white servants to resist (they were, in fact, well armed), explains the reluctance of landed whites to consign their European servants to the final degradation of outright slavery.

Africans, on the other hand, were not in a position to mount an effective resistance to enslavement. While news of slavery among white indentured servants could be disseminated back to the mother country, thereby resulting in a decreased willingness of white workers to emigrate to the colony, no such situation obtained for Africans, whose brutal mistreatment would never threaten the importation of ever more laborers. Responding to Jordan, and others, who argue that people are more readily oppressed when first generally degraded, Fields suggests that the opposite is also true; that "people are more readily perceived as inferior by nature when they are already seen as oppressed." Referring to that Virginia colonial legislation generally perceived to have criminalized miscegenation, Fields maintains that the law, in prohibiting unions between "Freeborne English women" and Negro slaves did not concern race; that the statute addressed not white women, but English women, thus vitiating its ostensible connections to race.

Race as a coherent ideology did not immediately accompany slavery but developed historically such that "slavery got along for a hundred years after its establishment without race as its ideological rationale" (Fields 1990: 106, 114). Fields argued that race emerged when it did because it explained why some people could be rightly denied rights normally afforded others. But if this is true of the Revolutionary Age, then it could also have been true of the seventeenth century to explain why some people served regularly longer terms (sometimes lifelong) terms of service, while others did not; why some people were denied the right to carry arms, while others were not; why marriage to some sectors of the population was disgraceful and damaging, while the unions of other sectors presumably were not.

Moreover, the choice to enslave Africans, though certainly instigated by economic motives, must have been accompanied by the same species of justifications later used during the Revolutionary Age; namely, an ideology that pointed to racial inferiority. While Fields notes that seventeenth-century law suggests a society "in the act of inventing race," she does not acknowledge that American society during the Revolutionary period was itself still inventing it; that is, the ideology of race in America, evident in the seventeenth century, was still in the process of becoming more than a century later. If, as Fields argues, the latter appears more coherent than the former, this may only be a testament to our greater familiarity (not to mention historical proximity) with eighteenth-century notions of race.

To these questions, A. T. Vaughan posed others, arguing that Fields, while correct in noting the brutalities suffered by white servants, "overstates both the severity of treatment and the existence of lifetime bondage for whites" (Vaughan 1995: 168). Meanwhile, Vaughan argues, Fields understates the extent of the debasement and violence suffered by African workers. To Fields' contention that colonial laws that ostensibly criminalized miscegenation actually had nothing to do with race,

Vaughan suggests that Fields has misread the evidence: that "numerous examples from contemporaneous statutes and other documents demonstrate that 'English Nation,' 'Christians,' and 'whites' were virtually synonymous, as were . . . 'negroes,' 'blacks,' and 'Africans'" (Vaughan 1995: 170). For Vaughan, these statutes do not reveal a society in the act of inventing race, but rather they reveal a society developing a "vocabulary to express its racial ideology" (ibid: 171). Indeed, Fields argued earlier that the "rise of slavery itself . . . was not in essence a racial phenomenon" (Fields 1982: 161).

Even more than this, Fields' comments regarding race and ideology constitute a wonderfully formulated challenge to historians even as they invite some critical attention. Fields argues throughout that race constitutes an ideology, defined as "the descriptive vocabulary of day-to-day existence through which people make rough sense of the social reality that they live and create from day to day." Ideologies have no material basis; they are not things to be passed from person to person or generation to generation. Nor are ideologies likened unto some "collection of disassociated beliefs" or attitudes. Fields anticipates a day when "the reification of conduct and demeanour in 'attitudes' will seem as quaint and archaic as their reification in bodily 'humours' – phlegmatic, choleric, melancholic, sanguine – does now" (Fields 1990: 110).

Fields explored this matter fully in an earlier article when she questioned an academic commonplace: the attempt to decide whether race or class played a more significant role in a given social moment. For Fields, the question itself is misbegotten because "class and race are concepts of a different order" (Fields 1982: 150). Class, though accompanied by ideology, refers in fact to a material circumstance. Race, on the other hand, is purely ideological, having no basis in material fact. As such, Fields is much more comfortable addressing the manner in which class antagonisms explains historical phenomena. I agree with Fields that queries pitting class against race are false but not, as she suggests, because class and race do not "occupy the same analytical and thus cannot constitute explanatory alternatives to each other" (ibid: 150). To the contrary, race and class – not to mention gender – in American life are ideologically defined in tandem and in relation to each other. Moreover, I am less convinced than Fields that the material basis of class – "the inequality of human beings from the standpoint of social power" – may be separated from the ideology of class.

Importantly, ideologies are not delusions but are "as real as the social relations for which they stand" (Fields 1990: 110). In effect, Fields admonishes historians who use ideology (race, in this instance) to explain historical phenomena rather than addressing and analyzing the social relations that operate below ideology. I am less convinced that social relations are such quantities as might be discretely excised from their attendant ideologies. That is to say, there is no social relation in the absence of ideology, be it an ideology of race, class, language, gender, or the like. When scholars refer to the causatory role that race might play in this or that historical moment, they are not referring to some presumed biological essence, but rather to the very complex social relations that accompany historical thought and action.

If academic language, as regards race, has typically been rather "loose" on this point, then Fields' work should be welcomed as a necessary corrective and encouragement towards clearer writing, and perhaps clearer thinking as well. But by 1619, the historical evidence suggests that well before the introduction of large-scale slavery in colonial America, even before the introduction of Africans into the New World, the English had already developed a fairly intricate conception of the African as other – as lesser, and as savage. These notions had undergone significant development and only later emerged as full-fledged racism. The choice to enslave the African was a result of this pervading sense of superiority coupled with equally compelling economic motives.

NOTE

1. Though long held to be the first Africans imported into British North America, evidence now suggests that blacks had been in the colony since at least April of the same year. See Wood 1997: 77; Thornton 1998: 421.

BIBLIOGRAPHY

Works Cited

Ames, Susan (1940) *Studies of the Virginia Eastern Shore in the Seventeenth Century*. Richmond, VA: Dietz Press.
Ballagh, James (1902) *A History of Slavery in Virginia*. Baltimore: Johns Hopkins University Press.
Berlin, Ira (1998) *Many Thousands Gone: The First Two Centuries of Slavery in North America*. Cambridge, MA: Belknap Press of Harvard University Press.
Boskin, Joseph (1976) *Into Slavery: Racial Decisions in the Virginia Colony*. Philadelphia: J. B. Lippincott.
Breen, T. H. and Innes, Stephen (1980) *"Myne Owne Ground:" Race and Freedom on Virginia's Eastern Shore, 1640–1676*. New York: Oxford University Press.
Craven, Wesley Frank (1949) *The Southern Colonies in the Seventeenth Century, 1607–1689*, vol. 1 of Wendell H. Stephenson and E. Merton Coulter (eds.), *A History of the South*. Baton Rouge: Louisiana State University Press.
Degler, Carl (1959) "Slavery and the genesis of race prejudice," *Comparative Studies in Society and History* 2 (1, October): 49–66.
Drake, St. Clair (1987) *Black Folk Here and There*. Los Angeles: University of California.
Elkins, Stanley ([1959] 1976) *Slavery: A Problem in American Institutional and Intellectual Life*, 3rd revised edn. Chicago: University of Chicago Press.
Fanon, Frantz ([1952] 1967) *Black Skins, White Masks*. New York: Grove Press.
Fields, Barbara (1982) "Ideology and race in American history" in J. Morgan Kousser and James M. McPherson (eds.), *Region, Race, and Reconstruction: Essays in Honor of C. Vann Woodward*, 143–77. New York: Oxford University Press.
—— (1990) "Slavery, race, and ideology in the United States of America," *New Left Review* 181 (May/June): 95–118.
Georgia Writers' Project (1940) *Drums and Shadows: Survival Studies among the Georgia Coastal Islands*. Athens: University of Georgia Press.
Green, William (1988) "Race and slavery: considerations on the Williams thesis" in Barbara Solow and Stanley Engerman (eds.), *British Capitalism and Caribbean Slavery: The Legacy of Eric Williams*. Cambridge: Cambridge University Press.

Handlin, Oscar ([1948] 1957) *Race and Nationality in American Life*. Boston: Little, Brown.

Handlin, Oscar and Handlin, Mary (1950) "Origins of the southern labor system," *William and Mary Quarterly* 3rd ser., 7 (April): 199–222.

—— (1959) "Letters to the editor," *Comparative Studies in Society and History* 2 (1, October): 488–90.

Johnson, Charles (ed.) (1998) *Africans in America*. New York: Harcourt, Brace.

Jordan, Winthrop (1961) "The influence of the West Indies on the origins of New England slavery," *William and Mary Quarterly* 18 (2, April): 243–50.

—— (1962) "Modern tensions and the origins of American slavery," *Journal of Southern History*, 28 (1, February): 18–30.

—— (1968) *White over Black: American Attitudes toward the Negro, 1550–1812*. Chapel Hill: University of North Carolina Press.

Morgan, Edmund (1975) *American Slavery, American Freedom: The Ordeal of Colonial Virginia*. New York: W. W. Norton.

Russell, John (1913) *The Free Negro in Virginia*. Baltimore: Johns Hopkins University Press.

Starr, Raymond and Detweiler, Robert (eds.) (1975) *Race, Prejudice and the Origins of Slavery in America*. Cambridge, MA: Schenkman.

Thornton, John (1998) "The African experience of the '20 and odd Negroes' arriving in Virginia in 1619," *William and Mary Quarterly* 3rd ser., 55 (3, July): 421–34.

Vaughan, Alden T. (1972) "Blacks in Virginia: a note on the first decade," *William and Mary Quarterly* 3rd ser., 29 (3, July): 469–78.

—— (1995) *Roots of American Racism: Essays on the Colonial Experience*. New York: Oxford University Press.

Williams, Eric ([1944] 1994) *Capitalism and Slavery*. Chapel Hill: University of North Carolina Press.

Wood, Betty (1997) *The Origins of American Slavery: Freedom and Bondage in the English Colonies*. New York: Hill & Wang.

Suggestions for Further Reading

Allen, Theodore (1975) "'. . . They would have destroyed me': slavery and the origins of racism," *Radical America* 9 (May–June): 40–63.

Billings, Warren (1973) "Blacks in seventeenth-century Virginia," *William and Mary Quarterly* 3rd ser., 20 (3, July): 467–74.

Countryman, Edward (1999) *How Did American Slavery Begin?* Boston: Bedford/St. Martin's Press.

Craven, Wesley Frank (1971) "Twenty Negroes to Jamestown in 1619?," *Virginia Quarterly Review* 47: 416–20.

—— (1971) *White, Red and Black: The Seventeenth Century Virginian*. Charlottesville: University Press of Virginia.

Davis, Brion David (1966) *The Problem of Slavery in Western Culture*. Ithaca, NY: Cornell University Press.

—— (1976) *The Problem of Slavery in the Age of Revolution*. Ithaca, NY: Cornell University Press.

—— (1984) *Slavery and Human Progress*. New York: Oxford University Press.

Frederickson, George M. (1971) "Toward a social interpretation of the development of American racism" in Nathan Huggins et al. (eds.), *Key Issues in the Afro-American Experience*. New York: International Thomson.

Jordan, Winthrop (1974) *The White Man's Burden: Historical Origins of Racism in the United States*. New York: Oxford University Press.

Noel, Donald (ed.) (1972) *The Origins of American Slavery and Racism.* Columbus, OH: Charles E. Merrill.

Starr, Raymond (1973–4) "Historians and the origins of British North American slavery," *The Historian* 36: 1–18.

Thornton, John (1998) "The African experience of the '20 and odd Negroes' arriving in Virginia in 1619," *William and Mary Quarterly* 3rd ser., 55 (3, July): 421–34.

CHAPTER NINE

Labor in the Slave Community, 1700–1860

FREDERICK C. KNIGHT

"I sho' has had a ha'd life," recalled Sarah Grudger about her years as a slave in antebellum North Carolina. "Jes work, an' work, an' work" (Berlin 1998b: 73). Grudger's testimony, though taken in the twentieth century, gave voice to the experience of millions of slaves, who spent the majority of their waking hours toiling in the fields, workshops, ports, and households of the Americas. Slaves irrigated coastal swamps, razed forests, ditched canals, produced clothing, and crafted pottery. They raised the houses of slaveholders and helped build the United States Capitol. Their agricultural labor developed small farms and large plantations and it also supplied goods to people throughout the mainland and across the seas. On the impact of antebellum slaves, W. E. B. Du Bois ([1935] 1976: 84) aptly remarked that they raised "a fiber that clothed the masses of a ragged world."

So important to the early United States and southern economies were cotton plantations that they overshadow the larger history of slavery in North America. In the popular imagination, the "typical" slave toiled on an antebellum cotton plantation. However, a growing literature on slave labor has revealed that slaves had different experiences over time and across space (Berlin 1980). During the colonial era, most slaves worked on tobacco, indigo, or rice plantations, while the generation of slaves after the American Revolution worked primarily on sugar, cotton, wheat, or corn estates. Slave labor took different forms in the countryside and the cities; on plantations and in industries; and in the Chesapeake, the South Carolina and Georgia Low Country, the Deep South, and the North (Berlin 1980; Berlin 2003; Berlin and Morgan 1993). Furthermore, enslaved men and women at times worked side-by-side, yet in other cases they performed different kinds of work (White 1999; Jones 1985).

In recent years, a number of scholars, influenced by the "New Labor History," have placed slave work at the center of their research on the history of slavery. For instance, Ira Berlin asserts, "Since labor defined the slaves' existence, when, where, and especially how slaves worked determined in large measure the course of their lives" (Berlin 1998a: 5). And to tell the story of slave workers, who left few written records behind, scholars have employed methods and materials from a range of disciplines in the social sciences and humanities. For example, slave labor has been investigated not only by historians but also by geographers and archaeologists (Carney 2001; Yentsch 1994). Economic historians have employed quantitative and qualitative methods to measure the financial impact of slave labor on the development of the modern world (Bailey 1990; Blackburn 1997; Inikori 2002). By crossing disciplines, scholars have shown the deep impact of slave labor on North America, from the colonial era into the Civil War. This body of scholarship has revealed that the history of slavery in North America was shaped by a number of factors, including ecological constraints, shifts in global markets, political crises, the source of the labor force, ideas about race and gender, and other factors. Yet, within these larger structures, slaves exerted historical agency through which they shaped their own lives and the world around them.

Slave Labor in the Colonial Era

In recent decades, historians have viewed the history of slavery on the colonial North American mainland within a larger context, that of the Atlantic World, underscoring the historical linkages between the American mainland, the Caribbean, and West Africa. For instance, Peter Wood termed early South Carolina "a colony of a colony" because of its historical ties to Barbados (Wood [1974] 1975: 133–34). A growing community of scholars has also argued that Africans brought across the Atlantic valuable labor skills that shaped American plantation development. The frontier settlements and rice and indigo fields of the South Carolina Low Country, Virginia tobacco plantations, and northern farms depended on slave labor, which generated substantial fortunes for American colonists.

The first wave of African workers in South Carolina migrated to the colony from the Caribbean. Their colonial masters, unable to compete in the capital-intensive sugar industry of the Caribbean, developed other economic strategies as a result. British colonists sought to raise staple crops such as cotton and indigo, envisioned raising livestock, and, like their counterparts in the Caribbean, deployed slave labor. Many of the early Carolina slaves, though brought from the Caribbean, were born in Africa and had experience with the work demanded of them in the Carolina frontier. As Wood suggests, Africans contributed to Carolina's livestock industry their skills in cattle-raising, which was particularly widespread in the West African Sahel and savanna (Wood [1974] 1975: 28–34). Within the fluid context of early Carolina, slaves experienced a degree of independence on the cattle ranges. In contrast to the highly regimented lives of slaves on large Caribbean sugar plantations, slave herders worked in smaller numbers, became familiar with a wider territory, and experienced more personal autonomy (Berlin 1998a: 67–8). While tending cattle or working on the Carolina frontier's lumber camps, slaves also produced food supplies for themselves. They used skills acquired in Africa to catch fish with traps, lines, and poisons, and learned from Native Americans how to tap Carolina's rivers (Wood [1974] 1975: 122). And more importantly, slaves cultivated rice, which became the colony's leading export early in the eighteenth century, a moment marked by a change in its demography.

The rise of South Carolina rice culture paralleled a demographic shift in the colony. Whereas whites outnumbered blacks in its opening years, the colony's direct importation of people from Africa shifted the balance so that by 1710 Carolina's

African population surpassed the number of whites. This transformation prompted a contemporary to state that the colony "looks more like a negro country than like a country settled by white people" (Wood [1974] 1975: 131–2). Africans made a critical impact on the colony's economic development; in particular, a substantial number of them brought rice production skills to the colony, a fact not lost upon some colonial elites. For example, a colonist in nearby Virginia noted that "we perceive the ground and Climate is very proper for it [rice cultivation] as our *Negroes* affirme, which in their Country is most of their food, and very healthful for our bodies" (Wood [1974] 1975: 35–62; quote from Littlefield [1981] 1991: 100). Furthermore, a South Carolina newspaper advertised the sale of slaves "from the Windward and Rice Coast, valued for their knowledge of rice culture" (Carney 2001: 90).

African women played a leading role in American rice production, contributing specialized knowledge of rice cultivation and processing techniques to the development of the Lowcountry coastal marshes. The historical geographer Judith Carney notes that, in West Africa, women were central to rice production, cultivated the crop in different micro-environments, pounded the rice with mortars and pestles, and "fanned" the seeds in hand-woven baskets to separate the grain from the husk. Black women in the South Carolina and Georgia Lowcountry maintained these practices *en masse* until the introduction of rice mills in the 1770s, after which they continued the practice on a small scale into the twentieth century (Carney 2001). Based upon the contributions of African labor, South Carolina planters exported approximately 60 million lbs of rice per year at the time of the American Revolution, and the crop eventually reached markets ranging from the Caribbean to Northern Europe (McCusker and Menard 1985: 179; Shepherd and Walton 1972: 133; Carney 2001: 107–41). Referring to South Carolina's slave labor force, one contemporary observer stated, "There is no raising rice without them" (West 1955: 118).

Although – or perhaps because – rice dominated the economy of colonial South Carolina, finding a secondary export became particularly important to the colony. Local elites experienced a major financial setback when war erupted between Britain and France and Spain in 1739, which disrupted the colony's access to its rice markets and forced planters to consider alternatives. They eventually found it in indigo, a crop with which many of Carolina's African workers had experience. In the Sea Islands of South Carolina and Georgia, slaves transformed the land into indigo fields, and transmuted the leaves into a valuable blue textile dye. To produce the final product, indigo workers engaged in different kinds of work and embodied a wide range of skills. Some cultivated the labor-intensive crop while others built and managed indigo vats, a highly skilled task reserved for male slaves. By the time of the Revolution, the colony exported approximately one million pounds of indigo per year (Knight 2000: 68–84). African Workers in the colony's indigo and rice fields made Carolina one of the wealthiest colonies on the British North American mainland, with the value of its exports being second only to Virginia, which likewise depended upon slave labor.

Historians of North American slavery have recently stressed that the experience of slaves varied according to the crop they cultivated. North of the rice and indigo fields of South Carolina, Virginia planters made their fortunes off tobacco exports and slave labor. Throughout most of the seventeenth century, local elites depended primarily upon British indentured servants for their labor force. However, Bacon's

Rebellion in 1676 prompted a fundamental shift in the colony's social, political, and labor dynamics. After this uprising, during which disenchanted elites, poor whites, and blacks challenged the sovereignty of the old colonial elite, the colony granted whites greater freedom and imposed heavy restrictions on both free and unfree blacks (Morgan 1975). The indentured servant population dwindled, and Chesapeake planters replaced them with slave labor imported directly from Africa.

In contrast to the more wealthy planters in the Caribbean who bought primarily male slaves, worked them to death in three to five years, and replaced them through the Atlantic slave trade, slaveholders on the North American mainland could not afford to manage their labor force through these means. As a result, by the middle of the eighteenth century, the slave labor force began to be reproduced through childbirth rather than importation from Africa and the North American slave population achieved gender balance much earlier than most of the Caribbean islands. However, Africans continued to play an important role in colonial Virginia. As with enslaved workers in Carolina's rice and indigo fields, it was not unusual for Africans to have experience with tobacco production. Indeed, merchants on the West African coast made note of local tobacco production. "Tobacco is planted about every mans house," noted the English merchant William Finch concerning Sierra Leone in August 1607, notably just months after the settlement of Jamestown in colonial Virginia (Purchas 1625: 415). Speaking of his homeland in what is now southeastern Nigeria, abolitionist Olauduh Equiano stated, "Our land is uncommonly rich and fruitful, and produces all kinds of vegetables in great abundance. We have plenty of Indian corn, and vast quantities of cotton and tobacco" (Equiano [1789] 1967: 7).

Africans in the colonial Chesapeake used their experience to clear the land, employ slash-and-burn methods to fertilize the soil with ashes, cultivate and transplant seedling plants, and top and succour the mature crops. With many of them carrying knowledge of tobacco production to the colonial Chesapeake, West Africans sustained and sped-up the development of the labor-intensive crop (Herndon 1969: 107–13; Walsh 1997: 61–80). Through their research of colonial indigo, rice, and tobacco plantations, historians have thus shown that Africans shaped the landscape of the Americas. As Michael Gomez affirms, "Although Africans may have left Africa, Africa never left them" (Gomez 1998: 185).

Researchers have also focused on the ways that the southern colonies depended upon slaves for more than their field labor. Slaves performed a wide range of subsidiary labor that kept large-scale staple production afloat. On tobacco plantations, they constructed curing barns in which they hung the leaves to dry. Also, plantation carpenters and coopers made barrels for the dried tobacco and manufactured sheds to store the hogsheads before shipping them off (Breen 1985: 50–3). Furthermore, by the middle of the eighteenth century, Chesapeake plantations increasingly mobilized slaves to produce other commodities for domestic consumption and export. For example, on planter–merchant Edward Lloyd IV's estate on Maryland's eastern shore, scores of slaves cultivated wheat, maize, and barley, raised livestock, or worked as smiths and coopers (Russo 1992). These practices continued into the nineteenth century, recalled Frederick Douglass ([1855] 1969: 69–70), who was born on the Lloyd estate. He remembered, "Horse-shoeing, cart-mending, plow-repairing, coopering, grinding, and weaving, all for the neighboring farms, were performed here, and slaves were employed in all these branches." Slave artisans helped keep the wheels of the plantations in motion.

Slaves also transported staple crops to nearby rivers or more distant coasts for markets in the larger Atlantic economy. Chesapeake slaves rolled hogsheads of tobacco over land or mounted horseback to pull cartloads of produce from the countryside to nearby rivers. Slaves, singing work songs to accompany their labor, lifted barrels onto boats docked on the waterways, ferried them down to Atlantic ships, and manned seagoing craft that crossed the ocean. Ironically, the dependence of planters on slaves for land and marine transportation exposed them to a wider world than the one experienced by people who were confined to agricultural labor. Their work culture particularly entailed a degree of independence at work, which in turn fueled their desire for complete freedom from their masters (Morgan 1998: 55–7; 236–9; Bolster 1997).

While the vast majority of slaves lived and worked in the countryside, slaves also shaped colonial southern cities. Scholars have demonstrated how slaves in urban settings accessed a range of opportunities that were not available to their rural counterparts. As South Carolina's main port for importing slaves and exporting rice and indigo, Charles Town developed into one of colonial North America's largest cities, and urban slaves played a central role in its evolution. At the time of the American Revolution, more than 6,000 blacks lived in Charles Town, constituting nearly half of the city's population (Berlin 1998a: 155). Masters often hired out their slaves, a practice which both allowed slave owners to make substantial profits and gave slaves an opportunity to have a degree of independence. For the Charles Town labor market, slaveholders hired slaves out generally in one of two ways – either they agreed to send their slaves off to the hirer for a set time and fee, or they expected their slaves to find their own work. In the second arrangement, slaves procured their own food, clothing, and shelter and also paid their owners a "wage." Though some authorities complained that this provided slaves with too much independence and the Carolina legislature banned the practice, hiring out continued throughout the colonial era. And while slaves always remained vulnerable and understood that they were still subject to their owners, the town's dependence on slave labor and the hiring-out system enabled some rural artisans to flee to the city, hire themselves out, and attain a degree of greater measure of personal autonomy than they experienced on plantations (Olwell 1998: 158–66).

Slaves took advantage of the commercial nature of Charles Town, where the boundaries of slavery and freedom at times blurred. Urban slaves with hard currency and rural slaves coming from the countryside to sell produce they grew in their provision grounds swapped goods in the town's marketplace. Enslaved women set up stalls and played a critical role in the town's local market, not unlike the part women played in local West African markets. Taking advantage of the opportunities created by their urban setting, Charles Town market women established trading relationships with urban slaves. As one contemporary noted: "women have such a connection with and influence on, the country negroes who come to the market, that they generally find means to obtain whatever they may chuse." Indeed, the influence of enslaved women in the market place set off considerable anxiety among local whites, who routinely labeled them as "insolent" "riotous" or "disorderly" (Olwell 1998: 166–80).

While some enslaved women worked in the urban marketplace, most others worked in the households of the well-to-do, attending to their owners, doing the drudgery of laundry and cleaning, and cooking the household's meals. In contrast, male slaves worked as stevedores, hauling loads of rice and indigo to waiting ships, interacting on the docks with black sailing crews and perhaps conversing about events in the larger Atlantic World. Slaves worked as carpenters, coopers, and shoemakers, in workshops and around town, and their dominance of these trades prompted the colonial government, as they did in northern towns, to place restrictions on slave artisanship (Berlin 1998a: 155).

Scholars have also highlighted the differences between the North and South. Slavery in colonial North America was not confined to the South but also took root in the North. At the time of the American Revolution, slaves constituted over 10 percent of the population of New York, with a large number of them concentrated in New York City (Horton and Horton 1997: 7–8). Of Pennsylvania's slave population, a substantial percentage lived in Philadelphia. They worked in the city's households, workshops, and ports, constituting perhaps as many as 20 percent of the working male population in the 1760s (Nash 1988: 9). While their percentage in the overall of New England population was small, slaves tended to live clustered together in towns and surrounding communities. Hence, though they generally constituted a smaller percentage of the overall population of the Northern colonies, slaves lived together, forged social networks, experienced a dynamic cultural life, and performed a wide range of work, including highly-skilled tasks (Piersen 1988).

In the rural North, slaves – often alongside white labor – worked on small farms and in industry. Most of them engaged in agricultural labor, clearing fields, cultivating the soil, and raising livestock on small farms. And, by the middle of the eighteenth century, growing numbers of enslaved women worked as domestic servants in northern households. Northern ironworks, mines, and tanneries employed slave labor (Berlin 1998a: 55–6, 182). Some slaves engaged in semi-independent labor, which enabled them to eventually obtain their freedom by "hiring out." For example, Venture Smith hired himself out, which enabled him to emancipate himself and later redeem his family from slavery. Born in Africa, captured at the age six, and eventually landed in Rhode Island and later Connecticut, Smith raised money by doing a variety of tasks, including raising food, shining shoes, hunting, and fishing. Determined to purchase his freedom, he convinced one of his owners to allow him to hire himself out during the winter. After several betrayals during which he lost his savings, he eventually acquired his freedom and then liberated his wife and two sons (Smith [1798] 1996).

Smith lived into his sixties and conducted a number of business enterprises, yet he proved to be an exception. Most other northern slaves were not able to achieve the independence or longevity of Smith and fared much worse. While some slaves worked as domestics and in urban craft workshops, others served as stevedores in the city's bustling port. This work took a tremendous toll on them, as their skeletal remains indicate. Archaeological research on New York's African burial ground, which holds the remains of as many as 20,000 enslaved people, reveals the harsh working conditions that they endured. The stress of heavy lifting, combined with poor nutrition, caused both slave men and women to suffer a rash of injuries, including torn muscles and ligaments. Furthermore, many experienced injuries in their upper spines and on the crown of their skulls, a result of both poor nutrition and being forced to carry excessive loads on their heads (Blakey 2001: 228–9).

From the temperate northern colonies to the semi-tropical environment of the Lowcountry, slaves played a variety of roles in the colonial economy, and the research of economic historians indicates that slaves made a considerable impact on the British American mainland's economy. On the eve of the American Revolution, slaves produced the bulk of North America's exports. Between 1768 and 1772, the slave-based Upper South colonies of Maryland and Virginia and Lower South colonies of North and South Carolina and Georgia exported an average of nearly 1.8 million pounds sterling of goods per year, nearly twice the exports of the New England and Middle colonies (Shepherd and Walton 1972: 133). Furthermore, slave-produced exports generated substantial personal fortunes, so that people in the Upper and Lower South controlled half of the wealth of the British North American mainland, and that did not include the value of their slaves. In addition, the nine richest people on the British mainland at this time were South Carolinians (Chaplin 1993: 8). Ironically, the labor of Africans and their descendants, though slaves, set the groundwork for American freedom.

The Transformation of Slavery During and After the American Revolution

The American Revolution ushered in a number of changes on the mainland, transformations which had important implications for the enslaved. Pushed by the petitions of slaves, protests by anti-slavery activists, and the demands of free white labor, the North began a process of emancipation, with some states mandating the immediate end of slavery while most others opted for a gradual approach. Although the new southern states never considered abolishing slavery, the institution underwent significant change during the Revolutionary era. In particular, before the Revolution, figures such as Thomas Jefferson and George Washington financed their opulent lifestyles off slave labor. Ironically, "It was Virginia slaves," colonial historian Edmund Morgan avows, "who grew most of the tobacco that helped to buy American independence" (Morgan 1975: 5–6).

If slave-grown tobacco bought American freedom, slave-produced cotton secured it. Throughout the Euro-American colonies, African workers had produced cotton as a commercial crop in the Caribbean and in small quantities for domestic consumption on the mainland. Most mainland slaveholders supplied their labor force with imported textiles for their blankets and clothing. However, their supply shrank during the colonial struggle against the mother country, which disrupted trade between the two and forced local planters to substitute imported goods with domestic manufactures (Chaplin 1993: 209; Knight 2000: 85–114). In colonies ranging from Maryland to South Carolina, planters turned to their slave labor force to produce textiles.

Many of the workers, particularly women, drew upon their experience in cotton textile production, which they had brought from Africa. During his travels in West Africa, the Scottish explorer Mungo Park observed a number of women at work spinning cotton. In one village, he noted at the door of a dwelling a woman spinning cotton. Later in his travels, Park fell into distress and, after he was fed by another woman, she "called to the female part of her family, who had stood gazing at [Park] all the while in fixed astonishment, to resume their task of spinning cotton; in which they continued to employ themselves a great part of the night" (Park [1799] 2000: 185, 195). Hence, African women were particularly equipped to produce textiles for the slave community. During the last quarter of the eighteenth century, slaves grew cotton on larger scales than they had previously and also produced their own tools to process the crop. For instance, archaeological research in South Carolina indicates that slaves used African spindle-whorls to transform the cotton into thread (Chaplin 1993: 208–20; Groover 1994: 52–4). Over the following decades, slave-based cotton production, combined with the transformation of cotton-ginning technology, fueled the westward expansion of the peculiar institution.

Economic historians have shown that, just as rice, tobacco, and indigo were central to the colonial economy, cotton exports became central to early United States economic development. As Douglass North explains, the early United States economy was characterized by regional specialization, linked through domestic trade, and driven by exports. In the northeastern and mid-Atlantic states, businesses focused on manufacturing cotton textiles, shipbuilding, and trading, and providing financial services such as banking, insurance, and accounting, which linked them to other sectors of the United States economy. Western states such as Ohio, Indiana, and Illinois focused primarily on the production of foodstuffs, which they shipped east and south. And the South concentrated on cotton, which they shipped to British and American manufacturers.

Although subject to fluctuations in price, slave-produced cotton was the country's leading export from the 1790s to the 1830s, and the robust trade allowed America to import goods from abroad and develop its commercial and industrial infrastructure (North [1961] 1966; Ransom 1989: 56). Feeding a seemingly insatiable demand for cotton, the South fostered the nation's material well-being while simultaneously it fell behind in its development. The small, extremely wealthy planter class – which dominated southern life – failed to invest in internal development, so the region generally lagged behind the country in urbanization, literacy among whites, commercial infrastructure such as railways and canals, and the development of local industry and markets (North [1961] 1966: 128–34).

Cotton production expanded in the South as eastern planters hoped to replicate the success with cotton in the Lowcountry and Sea Islands and snapped up land in the deep South states of Alabama, Mississippi, and Louisiana. The cotton boom had tragic consequences, as a planter-dominated political and economic machine displaced Native Americans to feed its seemingly insatiable hunger for the fertile cotton-yielding land in the piedmont of the Deep South. Furthermore, the plantocracy uprooted thousands of slaves, who endured what Berlin terms the "Second Middle Passage," which was "the central event in the lives of African-American people between the American Revolution and slavery's final demise in December 1865" (Berlin 2003: 161). It was not central only to African Americans, for as historian Walter Johnson states bluntly, "The history of the antebellum South is the history of two million slave sales" (Johnson 1999: 17).

With substantial profits to be made by selling slaves "down South," speculators tramped through the older slave states, buying slaves for sale in the major slave markets in Richmond, Charleston, Memphis, and New Orleans. Even some slaves in the North, who were due to be liberated under emancipation laws, were sold South through the domestic slave trade. Between 1820 and 1860, these merchants trafficked in nearly two million people, with one-third of them being taken across state lines and the domestic slave trade permeating almost every aspect of antebellum southern life. Bankers extended credit to slave traders, and planters not only tapped into this market for its labor supply but also used sale or the threat of sale to get rid of or threaten "unruly" slaves, an effective mechanism to control slaves who feared separation from their families (Jones 1990; Tadman 1989; Johnson 1999).

The domestic slave trade left bitter memories among African Americans, and the southern landscape remained dotted with painful reminders of the experience of the Second Middle Passage well into the twentieth century. For example, Thaddeus Goodson, born in South Carolina in 1869, pointed to a slave pen: "Here, right here, is de spot/ De yoke of de ox/ Was wored by de humans –/ Mens an' womens alike –/ Chained to de walls/ in Misery an' pain;/ Sold in de daytime/ Wid laughter an' joke/ like hogs in a pen" (Adams 1987: 282–3). Slaves survived and worked under the shadow of the auction block, and with emancipation they raised the song, "No more auction block for me, many thousands gone" (Brown [1941] 1969: 441). Through the slave trade and the increase in the slave population through childbirth, thousands of antebellum slaveholders were able to acquire substantial slaveholdings.

As with their research on regional variations of slavery during the colonial period, historians of the antebellum South have stressed that the lives of slaves differed, because plantations varied in size and raised different crops. While during the antebellum era most slaveholders owned fewer than twenty slaves, which meant that they had more personal contact with their labor force, most of the enslaved lived on plantations with twenty or more bondspersons (Stampp 1956: 30–1). Slaves also worked within different kinds of labor management systems. Lowcountry planters often lived away from their estates, so slaves worked under the task system, which required them to cultivate a quarter of an acre of rice per day, after which they could engage in semi-independent production. In contrast, slaves in the Chesapeake and Deep South were generally forced to work "from sun up to sun down" in a much more regimented gang system (Morgan 1998: 179–94; Stampp 1956: 54–6). Plantation overseers rang the bell or blew the conch shell to awaken the slave community, who trudged to the fields *en masse*.

Slaves on cotton plantations experienced different work routines depending upon the season, yet work was unremitting. The burden of food as well as cotton production fell on the shoulders of slaves, who from March to August ploughed the fields, opened "drills" to receive cotton and corn seeds, weeded the soil, cultivated the plants, and performed other tasks around the plantation. From September to December, they harvested and shucked the corn, picked, ginned, packed, and transported the cotton, repaired ditches and fences, and opened new fields. And from January to March, they slaughtered and cured livestock, fertilized the soil, worked on plantation buildings, and prepared fields for the following year of cultivation (Stampp 1956: 45–6).

Paralleling the expansion of cotton production after the American Revolution, sugar production grew in the early Republic and antebellum period as well.

Although sugar is generally associated with slavery in the Caribbean and Brazil, several historians have shown the place of Louisiana in satisfying Europe's sweet tooth. At the start of the nineteenth century, planters in the Lower Mississippi valley, who had for generations concentrated on indigo, tobacco, and rice production, shifted their plantations toward sugar production. This conversion was aided by *émigrés* who had left Saint Domingue during the Revolution and sought to style the French territory on the North American mainland after their Caribbean sugar islands (Berlin 1998a: 342–3). Tapping into the booming slave market in New Orleans, sugar planters preferred male slaves, who generally came to outnumber women of lower Louisiana. Planters drove their slaves at a feverish pace: the slaves ditched and drained fields, dug holes for the cane plants, manured the soil, and cut wood to fire the sugar-boiling vats. Work was particularly severe during the harvest season. As one contemporary noted, "when cutting cane begins, the slaves are taxed beyond their strength, and are goaded to labour until nature absolutely sinks under the effort." The taxing labor and the relatively low proportion of women led to both low birth and fertility rates in Louisiana sugar regions (Tadman 2000: 1542–55).

Concurrent with the cotton boom in the Deep South, the continued cultivation of rice in the Lowcountry, and sugar production in Louisiana, plantations in the Upper South raised staple food crops, which had a distinct impact on slave life and labor in the region. After the Revolution, planters in Maryland and Virginia decided to shift from tobacco to wheat and corn production. Whereas tobacco was a labor-intensive crop, wheat and corn required less attention and, as a result, slaves performed different kinds of work. For example, while slaves on tobacco plantations cultivated the fields mainly with hoes, it was not unusual to find slaves on staple food plantations behind the plow. Slaves tilled the fields, built the wagons to transport the produce to market, and labored in the workshops to make or repair farm tools. Furthermore, planters increasingly hired out their slaves, sending them to other plantations or the cities to find work (Berlin 1998a: 262–8). Like slavery in the colonial era, antebellum slavery was marked by regional variation. Furthermore, plantations maintained important gender and generational divisions of labor.

The Labor of Slave Women

Some of the most insightful research on slave labor has focused on the intersection between race and gender, and the impact of slave women on southern plantations. For instance, Jennifer Morgan (1997) has argued that European ideas about race and gender shaped the development of slave labor in the Americas. She posits that European travelers and merchants on the West African coast claimed that African women, unlike Christian women, bore children and labored in the fields without pain. During their early contact and trade on the West African coast, Englishmen saw African women as grotesque and monstrous, a belief that enabled planters to rationalize enslavement and to expect the same labor out of slave women as men (Morgan 1997). This gender and racial ideology shaped the history of slave labor from the colonial era to the antebellum period.

Interviews of former slaves and other aural sources reveal the impact of African American women on southern plantations. Anne Clark, born in Mississippi about

1825, recalled that "I ploughed, hoed, split rails. I done the hardest work ever a man ever did." And George Fleming remembered about slavery in South Carolina that "Women worked in de field same as de men. Some of dem plowed jes' like de men and boys. Couldn't tell 'em apart in de field, as dey wore pantalets or breeches" (Berlin 1998b: 90, 78). Furthermore, slaves gave voice to their experiences through songs that planters could not or simply refused to hear:

> Missus in the big house,
>> Mammy in the yard,
> Missus holdin' her white hands,
>> Mammy workin' hard, (× 3)
> Missus holdin' her white hands,
>> Mammy workin' hard.

> Old Marse ridin' all the time
>> Niggers workin' round,
> Marse sleepin' day time,
>> Niggers diggin' in the ground, (× 3)
> Marse sleepin' day time,
>> Niggers diggin' in the ground. (Courlander 1963: 117)

They clearly understood the dependence of slaveholders on their labor.

Scholars have reconsidered the lives of slave women as domestic workers, asserting that they neither experienced clear privilege nor failed to resist. Few antebellum estates with more than twenty slaves went without full-time house servants, who divided their lives between the slave quarters and plantation household. Planters attempted to groom slave girls for domestic work, assigning them chores such as nursing children and cleaning. They demanded that slave girls sleep at the foot of their beds, to be at their beck and call through the night. Over time, they learned how to manage the household affairs, which included spinning, weaving, and sewing, laundering, cleaning, and cooking. They worked under the constant surveillance of plantation mistresses, who often vented their rage at enslaved women, and they were subject to demands for sex or, at worst, sexual assault by masters (Fox-Genovese 1988: 152–3, 165).

For instance, Harriet Jacobs, a domestic slave before escaping to the North, recalled that her mistress ordered her to take off her shoes because they made too much noise, and then sent her "on a long distance, on an errand." Jacobs recalled, "As I went through the snow, my bare feet tingled. That night I was very hoarse; and I went to bed thinking the next day would find me sick, perhaps dead" (Jacobs [1861] 1987: 19, 27). When she turned 15, her master used a variety of tactics, from suggestion to threat of sale, to coerce Jacobs into being his concubine. In response, people like Jacobs fled; women like Ellen resorted to poisoning their masters, while most others found solace in the community of women in the slave quarters (Franklin and Schweninger 1999: 6).

While the early literature on slave labor often treated the male slave experience as "typical," recent scholarship has paid particular attention to the experiences of slave women. They experienced intense pressure to bear children and employed different strategies in response to the offers of reward and threats of punishment. Planters often reduced the workloads of pregnant women and in other cases put women incapable of bearing children on the auction block. Though planters attempted to impose their own measures to control the bodies of slave women, they developed their own reproductive strategies. Many young women followed the guidance of elders within the slave community and delayed bearing children for as long as possible, which frustrated and confounded plantation managers (Jones 1985: 11–43; White 1999: 100–5).

Children born into slavery faced perpetual bondage and a life of work, and endured what Wilma King (1995) termed a "stolen childhood." After surviving their initial years, enslaved children gradually entered plantation work regiments. They worked in and around plantation households, doing a wide range of chores including keeping flies away from bed-ridden planters, assisting cooks and laundresses to complete their tasks, fetching water, gathering firewood, sweeping the yard, spinning thread, feeding poultry, and milking cows (King 1995: 27–30). Mary Island, who was enslaved in Union Parish, Louisiana, recalled that she started work when she was 4 years old. "While the other hands was in the fields," she remembered: "I carried water. We had to cook out in the yard on an old skillet and lid, so you see I had to tote brush and bark and roll up little logs such as I could to keep the fire from one time of cooking to the other" (Berlin 1998b: 95).

Children provided similar support to agricultural workers, who relied upon them to tote drinking water into the fields and chase birds away from the growing plants. They also engaged in agricultural labor, which took different forms depending upon the kind of crop under cultivation. For instance, on the extremely labor-intensive tobacco estates, enslaved children "wormed" the tobacco leaves, removing the pests from the plants by hand. On antebellum cotton plantations, planters sent children to the fields during the late summer and fall to pick cotton, demanding that the young workers meet daily quotas. Children in the rice country of coastal Georgia and South Carolina helped clear, irrigate, and weed the fields, and in some cases, they pounded the harvested rice with mortar and pestle to remove the grain from the hull. Sugar production regimes also mobilized slave children, who hauled harvested cane stalks to carts and carried firewood to the sugar mills (King 1995: 31–5). Going out to the fields at an early age, young slaves could expect a lifetime of work. Most worked in agricultural production, yet others would ply crafts, or live and work in southern cities and industry.

Urban and Industrial Slavery

A wide literature bears witness to the high level of skills that slaves possessed, for slave workers toiled in the agricultural fields and also worked in antebellum workshops and industries. Many plantations achieved self-sufficiency, and slaves produced their own household goods. The African American F. J. Jackson of coastal Georgia recalled:

> Lots u . . . tings we make our ownsef . . . All du fishin cawd made out uh deah hide, and we make mos uh duh house needs sech as cheahs an tables, baskets an buckets an stools, an sometime spoons an beds and cubbuds. (Georgia Writers' Project 1940: 101)

When agricultural laborers worked in the fields, they could hear the sounds of the slave artisans at work, especially the ring of the blacksmith's hammer pounding iron (Berlin 1998b: 85–6). Enslaved women spun raw cotton into thread, weavers wove it into cloth, and seamstresses made clothing for the enslaved (Morgan 1952: 53–4; Vlach 1978). Slave labor placed its imprint throughout the South, notes historian Michel Sobel, who remarks about eighteenth-century Virginia, "All the Great Houses were built by slaves and needed slaves to run them" (Sobel 1987: 134).

Slave artisans and industrial workers, historians have argued, had access to power unavailable to agricultural workers. For example, slave artisans passed down their skills through the family line to young apprentices. Not unlike Camara Laye of Guinea who learned about the mysteries of goldsmithing from his father (Laye 1954: 31–41), young people on southern plantations sat at the feet of master artisans. In particular, skilled workers trained their male children in their crafts, knowledge that provided them with a greater measure of control over their labor and respect while ironically shifting the more arduous duties of agricultural labor onto enslaved women (Berlin 1998a: 269–71). And, as the research of Charles Dew – on Buffalo Forge in Rockbridge County, Virginia – illustrates, slaves received wages for producing more iron than their weekly quota demanded (Dew 1994: 108–21).

Scholars have shown that the use of slave labor in southern industry created a complicated, triangular relationship between slaves, slaveholders, and free white labor. During the colonial era, industrialists opened coal mines and iron forges in the Chesapeake region, taking advantage of the area's mineral wealth and relatively inexpensive transportation on the rivers leading into the bay. In the coal mines near the James River in Virginia, slaves opened and worked in the underground maze of tunnels, facing a number of hazards, especially suffocation. Slaves not only worked in coal mines, they also played a vital role in the large-scale iron furnaces that dotted the Upper South states of Virginia and Maryland. For instance, shortly after the American Revolution, the Baltimore Iron Works owned more than two hundred slaves who labored in the company's furnace and forges. By the time of the Civil War, the most important southern forge was Richmond's Tredegar Iron Works. Founded in 1836, Tredegar used a combination of slave and free labor, which set off resistance from highly skilled white artisans. Fearing that slave labor would replace them, white craftsmen went on strike rather than train slave apprentices. The protest ultimately failed, and slaves soon replaced free labor as the principal labor force at the forge (Lewis 1979: 31–2, 45–74).

The research of architectural historians reveals that the construction of the symbols of the new nation itself relied upon slaves in southern industries and crafts. After the American Revolution and with slavery permitted under the Constitution, the commissioners of the nation's new capital in Washington, DC, tapped into the local slave labor pool. Slave lumberjacks worked in Virginia's White Oak swamp, which supplied the capital with wood, and slave sawyers cut the wood into joists for the White House. Slave and free black labor operated brick-making kilns on the White House grounds, and they worked forges to produce nails for the capital in local workshops. Furthermore, slaves worked long hours in rock quarries in Stafford County, Virginia, cutting limestone for the capital's construction. The capital architects and commissioners hired highly-skilled slaves, who along with free black and white labor performed masonry and carpentry work on the White House. Ironically, slaves dug the foundations, hauled and unloaded building supplies, and cleared the streets of the capital (Allen 1995: 10–11; Kapsch 1995: 8–15).

In the first half of the nineteenth century, slaves continued to play an important role in southern cities, where their lives contrasted sharply with those of rural slaves. Historians have produced specialized studies of slavery in particular cities to complement the earlier research of urban slavery by Richard Wade (Wade 1964; Phillips 1997; Takagi 1999). As in the countryside, work dominated the lives of urban slaves. In most southern cities, the majority of slaves worked as domestic servants. In this occupation – as well as in the urban slave population as a whole – women generally outnumbered men, whom slaveholders preferred to sell in the lucrative slave market.

Most urban slaves lived behind their masters' homes, in small quarters enclosed by a high brick wall. Although slaveholders attempted to use these housing compounds as a way to control their slaves and restrict them to their households, workshops, and factories, the enslaved countered with different strategies to develop an active social life outside of the workplace. Urban slaves mingled with free blacks and poor whites in the grog shops, on the street corners, at dances, and in each other's households. Furthermore, slaves took advantage of opportunities in urban centers to obtain literacy and flocked on Sundays to black churches, which thrived in antebellum cities. Ironically, they lived in the shadows of the auction block, yet they routinely crossed the boundaries between slavery and freedom. As a result, the proportion of slaves declined from 22 percent of the total population of the urban South to 10 percent in 1860 (Wade 1964). At the time of the Civil War, urban slavery appeared to be a dying practice.

Prospects

Research on slave labor has produced reams of scholarship, adding to our knowledge of the subject while also providing opportunities for further research. Scholarship on the colonial period might continue to explore the ties between slavery on the mainland and the histories of the Caribbean and Africa. The early years of cotton production in the Deep South require further study. Also, even though urban slavery has been well researched, many antebellum cities have not been studied in depth. Research on slavery in particular southern cities has the potential to yield insight into a variety of issues: the interactions between free black workers and slaves, relationships between slaves and free white workers, and gender dynamics in the urban South. Furthermore, one of the strengths of research over the past three decades on slave labor has been its integration of fields and disciplines. Future research on slave labor will continue to cross disciplinary boundaries by drawing upon written documentation, oral history, folklore, archaeological findings, and other evidence.

For over two centuries, slaves worked on small farms and large plantations, in cities and industry, and in the households of North America. Slave labor on northern farms, Upper South tobacco and wheat plantations, and Lowcountry rice and indigo estates enriched the colonies. Louisiana sugar plantations and Deep South cotton estates fostered the development of the New Republic. Building on its colonial foundations, slavery embedded itself into the foundations of the United

States, and by the time of the Civil War, the South held nearly four million people as slaves. And while the war abolished the peculiar institution and the nation embarked upon an era of Reconstruction, it failed to address the inequalities created through generations of unfree labor, a legacy that still haunts America.

BIBLIOGRAPHY

Works Cited

Adams, Edward C. L. (1987) *Tales of the Congaree*, Robert G. O'Meally (ed.). Chapel Hill: University of North Carolina Press.

Allen, William C. (1995) "Capitol construction," *American Visions: The Magazine for Afro-American Culture* 10 (February/March): 10–11.

Bailey, Ronald (1990) "The slave(ry) trade and the development of capitalism in the United States: the textile industry in New England," *Social Science History* 14: 373–414.

Berlin, Ira (1980) "Time, space, and the evolution of Afro-American society on British mainland North America," *American Historical Review* 85: 44–78.

—— (1998a) *Many Thousands Gone: The First Two Centuries of Slavery in North America.* Cambridge, MA: Harvard University Press.

—— (1998b) *Remembering Slavery: African Americans Talk About their Personal Experiences of Slavery and Emancipation.* New York: New Press.

—— (2003) *Generations of Captivity: A History of African American Slaves.* Cambridge, MA: Harvard University Press.

Berlin, Ira and Morgan, Philip (eds.) (1993) *Cultivation and Culture: Labor and the Shaping of Slave Life in the Americas.* Charlottesville: University Press of Virginia.

Blackburn, Robin (1997) *The Rise of New World Slavery: From the Baroque to the Modern, 1492–1800.* New York: Verso Press.

Blakey, Michael (2001) "The study of New York's African burial ground: biocultural and engaged" in Sheila Walker (ed.), *African Roots/American Cultures: Africa in the Creation of the Americas,* 222–31. New York: Rowman & Littlefield.

Bolster, Jeffrey (1997) *Black Jacks: African American Seamen in the Age of Sail.* Cambridge, MA: Harvard University Press.

Breen, T. H. (1985) *Tobacco Culture: The Mentality of Tobacco Planters on the Eve of the American Revolution.* Princeton, NJ: Princeton University Press.

Brown, Sterling A., Davis, Arthur P., and Lee, Ulysses (eds.) ([1941] 1969) *The Negro Caravan.* Salem, NH: Ayer.

Carney, Judith (2001) *Black Rice: The African Origin of Rice Cultivation in the Americas.* Cambridge, MA: Harvard University Press.

Chaplin, Joyce E. (1993) *An Anxious Pursuit: Agricultural Innovation and Modernity in the Lower South, 1730–1815.* Chapel Hill: University of North Carolina Press.

Courlander, Harold (1963) *Negro Folk Music, U.S.A.* New York: Columbia University Press.

Dew, Charles (1994) *Bond of Iron: Master and Slave at Buffalo Forge.* New York: W. W. Norton.

Douglass, Frederick ([1855] 1969) *My Bondage and My Freedom.* [New York] New York: Dover.

—— ([1881] 1993) *Life and Times of Frederick Douglass.* [Hartford, CT] New York: Gramercy Books.

Du Bois, W. E. B. ([1935] 1976) *Black Reconstruction.* [New York] Millwood, NY: Kraus-Thomson.

Equiano, Olaudah ([1789] 1967) *Equiano's Travels: His Autobiography. The Interesting Narrative of the Life of Olaudah Equiano or Gustavas Vassa the African*. Portsmouth, NH: Heinemann.

Fox-Genovese, Elizabeth (1988) *Within the Plantation Household: Black and White Women in the Old South*. Chapel Hill: University of North Carolina Press.

Franklin, John Hope and Schweninger, Loren (1999) *Runaway Slaves: Rebels on the Plantation*. New York: Oxford University Press.

Georgia Writers' Project, Savannah Unit, Work Projects Administration ([1940] 1986) *Drums and Shadows: Survival Studies among the Georgia Coastal Negroes*. [Athens, GA] Athens: University of Georgia Press.

Gomez, Michael (1998) *Exchanging Our Country Marks: The Transformation of African Identities in the Colonial and Antebellum South*. Chapel Hill: University of North Carolina Press.

Groover, Mark D. (1994) "Evidence of folkways and cultural exchange in the 18th-century South Carolina backcountry," *Historical Archeology* 28: 41–64.

Herndon, George Melvin (1969) *William Tatham and the Culture of Tobacco*. Coral Gables, FL: University of Miami Press.

Horton, James Oliver and Horton, Lois E. (1997) *In Hope of Liberty: Culture, Community, and Protest among Northern Free Blacks, 1700–1860*. New York: Oxford University Press.

Inikori, Joseph E. (2002) *Africans and the Industrial Revolution in England: A Study in International Trade and Development*. New York: Cambridge University Press.

Jacobs, Harriet ([1861] 1987) *Incidents in the Life of a Slave Girl, Written by Herself*, Jean Fagan Yellin (ed.). [Boston] Cambridge, MA: Harvard University Press.

Johnson, Walter (1999) *Soul by Soul: Life inside the Antebellum Slave Market*. Cambridge, MA: Harvard University Press.

Jones, Jacqueline (1985) *Labor of Love, Labor of Sorrow: Black Women, Work, and the Family from Slavery to the Present*. New York: Basic Books.

Jones, Noreece T. (1990) *Born a Child of Freedom, Yet a Slave: Mechanisms of Control and Strategies of Resistance in Antebellum South Carolina*. Hanover, NH: Wesleyan University Press.

Kapsch, Robert (1995) "Building liberty's capital," *American Visions: The Magazine of Afro-American Culture* 10 (February/March): 8–15.

King, Wilma (1995) *Stolen Childhood: Slave Youth in Nineteenth-Century America*. Bloomington: Indiana University Press.

Knight, Frederick C. (2000) "Seeds of change: West African workers and the making of the British Americas, 1650–1850," PhD dissertation, University of California, Riverside.

Laye, Camara (1954) *The Dark Child*. New York: Farrar, Straus, & Giroux.

Lewis, Ronald L. (1979) *Coal, Iron, and Slaves: Industrial Slavery in Maryland and Virginia, 1715–1865*. Westport, CT: Greenwood Press.

Littlefield, Daniel ([1981] 1991) *Rice and Slaves: Ethnicity and the Slave Trade in Colonial South Carolina*. [Baton Rouge, LA] Urbana: University of Illinois Press.

McCusker, John J. and Menard, Russell R. (1985) *The Economy of British America, 1607–1789*. Chapel Hill: University of North Carolina Press.

Morgan, Edmund (1952) *Virginians at Home: Family Life in the Eighteenth Century*. Williamsburg, VA: Colonial Williamsburg.

—— (1975) *American Slavery, American Freedom: The Ordeal of Colonial Virginia*. New York: W. W. Norton.

Morgan, Jennifer L. (1997) "'Some could suckle over their shoulder'": male travelers, female bodies, and the gendering of racial ideology, 1500–1770," *William and Mary Quarterly* 3rd ser., 54: 167–92.

Morgan, Philip (1998) *Slave Counterpoint: Black Culture in the Eighteenth Century Chesapeake and Lowcountry*. Chapel Hill: University of North Carolina Press.

Nash, Gary (1988) *Forging Freedom: The Formation of Philadelphia's Black Community, 1720–1840*. Cambridge, MA: Harvard University Press.

North, Douglass C. ([1961] 1966) *The Economic Growth of the United States, 1790–1860*. [Englewood Cliffs, NJ] New York: W. W. Norton.

Olwell, Robert (1998) *Masters, Slaves, and Subjects: The Culture of Power in the South Carolina Low Country, 1740–1790*. Ithaca, NY: Cornell University Press.

Park, Mungo ([1799] 2000) *Travels in the Interior Districts of Africa*. [London] Durham, NC: Duke University Press.

Phillips, Christopher (1997) *Freedom's Port: The African American Community of Baltimore, 1790–1860*. Urbana: University of Illinois Press.

Phillips, U. B. (1929) *Life and Labor in the Old South*. New York: Grosset & Dunlap.

Piersen, William D. (1988) *Black Yankees: The Development of an Afro-American Subculture in Eighteenth Century New England*. Amherst: University of Massachusetts Press.

Purchas, Samuel (1625) *Purchas, His Pilgrimes in Five Books*, vol. 1. London.

Ransom, Roger L. (1989) *Conflict and Compromise: The Political Economy of Slavery, Emancipation, and the American Civil War*. New York: Cambridge University Press.

Russo, Jean B. (1992) "A model planter: Edward Lloyd IV of Maryland, 1770–1796," *William and Mary Quarterly* 3rd ser., 49: 62–88.

Shepherd, James F. and Walton, Gary M. (1972) "Trade, distribution, and economic growth in colonial America," *Journal of Economic History* 32: 128–45.

Smith, Venture ([1798] 1996) *A Narrative of the Life and Adventures of Venture, A Native of Africa*, in Vincent Caretta (ed.), *Unchained Voices: An Anthology of Black Authors in the English-Speaking World of the Eighteenth Century*, 369–87. [New London, CT] Lexington: University of Kentucky Press.

Sobel, Michael (1987) *The World They Made Together: Black and White Values in Eighteenth-Century Virginia*. Princeton, NJ: Princeton University Press.

Stampp, Kenneth (1956) *The Peculiar Institution: Slavery in the Antebellum South*. New York: Vintage Books.

Stuckey, Sterling (1987) *Slave Culture: Nationalist Theory and the Foundations of Black America*. New York: Oxford University Press.

Tadman, Michael (1989) *Speculators and Slaves: Masters, Traders, and Slaves in the Old South*. Madison: University of Wisconsin Press.

—— (2000) "The demographic cost of sugar: debates on slave societies and natural increase in the Americas," *American Historical Review* 105: 1534–75.

Takagi, Midori (1999) *Rearing Wolves to Our Own Destruction: Slavery in Richmond, Virginia, 1782–1865*. Charlottesville: University Press of Virginia.

Vlach, John Michael (1978) *The Afro-American Tradition in Decorative Arts*. Cleveland, OH: Cleveland Museum of Art.

Wade, Richard (1964) *Slavery in the Cities: The South, 1820–1860*. New York: Oxford University Press.

Walsh, Lorena (1997) *From Calabar to Carter's Grove: The History of a Virginia Slave Community*. Charlottesville: University Press of Virginia.

West, Frances (1955) "John Bartram and slavery," *South Carolina Historical Magazine* 56: 115–19.

White, Deborah Gray (1999) *Ar'n't I a Woman? Female Slaves in the Plantation South*, revised edn. New York: W. W. Norton.

Wood, Peter ([1974] 1975) *Black Majority: Negroes in Colonial South Carolina from 1670 through the Stono Rebellion*. [New York] New York: W. W. Norton.

Yentsch, Anne E. (1994) *A Chesapeake Family and Their Slaves: A Study in Historical Archaeology*. New York: Cambridge University Press.

CHAPTER TEN

Spirituality and Socialization in the Slave Community

JASON R. YOUNG

Slave Conversion

Serious contradictions attended British colonial efforts to proselytize slaves in North America. Defenders of slavery justified the institution on the grounds that the physical suffering and degradation inherent in the system would be rewarded by an impending eternity of grace in the presence of the Lord. Such was the argument espoused by Gomes de Azurara, fifteenth-century chronicler of the Portuguese slave trade, who maintained that the enslaved African profited more than the Portuguese merchant from the trade in men and women: "for though their bodies were now brought into some subjection, that was a small matter in comparison of their souls, which would now possess true freedom for evermore" (quoted in Raboteau 1978: 96).

Despite the promise of eternal salvation, planters expressed great concern regarding the conversion of slaves in line with the notion, only vaguely articulated in British law, that Christians could not legally hold other Christians in bondage. As a result, many planters feared that proselytizing bondspersons might legally confer freedom upon them (Hair 1992: 552). Southern supporters of slavery found themselves enmeshed in a conundrum, for the very notion that made Africans theoretically subject to enslavement – that is, their being non-Christian – also mandated their conversion, even if that conversion threatened their slave status.

As the seventeenth century drew to a close, colonial legislatures responded to this contradiction with a series of laws that maintained the legal status of slaves, whether they were converted or not. The measure passed by the Virginia Assembly in 1667 resembles laws adopted in other colonies:

> Whereas some doubts have risen whether children that are slaves by birth, . . . should by vertue of their baptisme be made free; It is enacted . . . that the conferring of baptisme doth not alter the condition of the person as to his bondage or freedome. (Wright 2001: 6)

The Virginia Assembly saw this measure as an act of kindness and piety with which colonists might "more carefully endeavor the propagation of Christianity by permitting children, though slaves . . . to be admitted to the sacrament" (ibid: 6).

The passage of this and similar measures marked a turning point in the legal, political, and religious development of the British North American colonies. The legal principle that Christians could not enslave other Christians had extended into most areas of British public and social life. As a result, in the late seventeenth century, when the transatlantic slave trade was starting to become established, British common law (ideally at least) was disposed *in favorem libertatis*, in favor of liberty (Jordan 1968: 50). But where British law and custom presumed the legal incongruity of a Christian slave, American colonists constructed a discrete legal category that preserved enslavement, regardless of Christian status. This Christianization of slavery required biblical and moral validation, a task to which missionaries devoted themselves fully, mining the Bible in search of scriptural justifications of enslavement.

In order to be allowed sufficient access to slaves, missionaries had first to convince slaveholders that the conversion of slaves in no way threatened the plantation system, a matter to which at least one missionary, the well-known Francis Le Jau, made explicit reference in 1709. Before administering baptism to slaves in South Carolina, Le Jau required would-be converts to affirm the following:

> You declare in the presence of God and before this congregation that you do not ask for the holy baptism out of any design to ffree [*sic*] yourself from the duty and obedience you owe to your Master while you live, but merely for the good of your soul and to partake of the graces and blessings promised to the members of the church of Jesus Christ. (Sernett 1999: 26)

Missionaries assured slaveholders that conversion would create a more docile, sober, and productive slave. To this end, they attacked aspects of slave culture that they felt ran contrary to the productive interests of the plantation. As a way of coercing slaves away from the feasts and dances that had previously marked their one day of rest, Le Jau mandated that in order to be baptized, slaves must "promise they'l spend no more the Lord's day in idleness, and if they do I'l cut them off from Comunion." Le Jau assured planters that, after being converted, slaves "do better for their Master's profit than formerly" (ibid: 26, 29).

The conflicts between western European Protestants and Catholics were played out in the colonial arena as missionaries draped themselves in doctrinal armor in a pitched battle for the soul of the "native." As colonial officials vied for land, capital, and labor in the western hemisphere, missionaries hoped to mine the plantations for souls. Le Jau and other Protestant missionaries expressed significant concern that greater numbers of so-called heathen souls were being converted by Catholics throughout Central and South America. Moreover, they consistently expressed disappointment at the laxity of American colonists in this regard. At least one observer at the time was clearly concerned:

> how far most protestant planters and other inhabitants of European colonies in America are from [proselytizing the slaves], every person that has conversed among them can tell. There, provided that the slaves can multiply, and work hard for the benefit of the masters, most men are well satisfied, without the least thoughts of using their authority and endeavors to promote the good of the souls of those poor wretches. In this particular . . . the Roman Catholicks of the American plantations are much more commendable. (Hair 1992: 552)

Despite legal sanctions to the contrary and missionaries' varied assurances and encouragements, many slaveholders – not to mention many slaves – held fast to the notion that conversion conferred freedom.

Juridical matters notwithstanding, planters expressed other apprehensions regarding the conversion of slaves; namely that slave conversion threatened to obscure the social and cultural distinctions between enslaved Africans and slaveholding planters. At a time when notions of race and racial difference were still developing in the country, religion remained a critical marker of status. The introduction of slaves into the eternal fold of Christianity threatened the special status that British colonists felt as Christians. Indeed, the oft-quoted concern of planters that, once converted, enslaved men and women became "saucy" might be read as evidence that pious bondsmen considered themselves on an equal (spiritual) footing with their enslavers. Albert Raboteau mentions several instances when planters complained of untoward haughty behavior, rebelliousness, and idleness in newly baptized slaves. Some planters argued that slaves were "ten times worse when a Xn, than in . . . [the] state of Paganism" (Raboteau 1978: 102, 119).

As a result, southern whites showed little interest in proselytizing among the slave community, leaving that task instead to various missionary societies and governmental agencies. As early as 1660, the king of England sent instructions to the Council for Foreign Plantations regarding the mandate of conversion: "And you are to consider how such of the natives or such as are purchased by you from other parts to be servants or slaves may be best invited to the Christian faith, and be made capable of being baptized . . ." (quoted in Jernegan 1916: 508).

By 1701, the Society for the Propagation of the Gospel in Foreign Parts (SPG) began work promoting the gospel through missionaries and religious tracts. In order to assuage planters' concerns that conversion engendered rebelliousness in the servile class, missionaries adopted a theology focused on social control. Missionaries expounded the benefits of a humble and obedient servile class and relied heavily on carefully selected passages from the Bible, including Ephesians 6: 5: "Servants, be obedient to them that are your masters according to the flesh, with fear and trembling, in singleness of your heart, as unto Christ." This verse, along with similar scriptural references, rang like a mantra throughout the slaveholding South. Even still, the work of the SPG was often retarded by planters adamant in their refusal to aid in the effort. Some SPG officials, frustrated by planter indifference, expressed themselves in no uncertain terms, acknowledging that it was not "so much their [the slaves'] fault as their unhappiness in falling into the hands of such ill Masters who not only neglect to instruct them but scoff at those that attempt it, and give them likewise strange ideas of Christianity from the scandalous lives they lead" (quoted in Mullin 1976: 53).

In 1724 the Bishop of London polled colonial ministers for information regarding their relative successes and failures in administering the sacraments, especially baptism, among slaves. The responses revealed that, after more than a century of North American slavery, the actual numbers of Christian slaves were, for the missionaries, embarrassingly low. These failures were attributed to the "planters' reluctance and outright resistance, by the great size of the parishes, by the scarcity of the clergy, by linguistic and cultural difficulties with African-born slaves, by the absence of legal support, and by the sheer size of the task" (Raboteau 1978: 107). Moreover, many slaveholders were themselves unconverted. "It can hardly be expected," one missionary wrote, "that those should promote the spiritual welfare of this meanest branch of their families who think but little (if at all) of their own eternal salvation" (quoted in Jernegan 1916: 526). Indeed, only a small minority of southern whites were church members, equaling no more than 5 percent of the total population at the beginning of the eighteenth century (Jackson 1931: 169).

The Great Awakening and the Revolution

Not until the Great Awakening did slaves enter the Christian fold to any significant degree. John Marrant, a black musician and carpenter, came face to face with the mandate of conversion in 1769. While on his way to play for a company of white men in Charleston, South Carolina, Marrant noticed a sizable crowd entering a large meeting house. He entered the building on a dare and immediately met the gaze of George Whitefield admonishing the congregants to "Prepare to thy GOD O Israel." And so he did:

> The Lord accompanied the Word with such power, that I was struck to the ground, and lay both speechless and senseless for near half an hour. When I was come a little too [sic], I found two men attending me, and a woman throwing water in my face, and holding a smelling-bottle to my nose; and when something more recovered, every word I heard from the minister was like a parcel of swords thrust in to me. (Potkay and Burr 1995: 78)

Marrant remained thus disposed until Whitefield approached him after the sermon to deliver a prophetic message: "JESUS CHRIST has got thee at last" (ibid: 78).

Whitefield arrived in Carolina in 1738 and became an early opponent of the slaveholding class. In an open letter to the inhabitants of Maryland, the Carolinas, and Virginia, written in 1740, he condemned the violence of the slave trade, the brutality of the master class and the cruelty that they exhibited to slaves. Whitefield admonished slaveholders for not being more forthright in converting slaves and threatened that a Heavenly retribution awaited slaveholders: "the blood of them spilt for these many years in your respective provinces, will ascend to heaven against you" (quoted in Boles 1988: 25). Many planters retorted harshly to Whitefield's claims, maintaining that his opinions promised to foment rebellion among slaves.

In the end, Whitefield's opposition to the planter class dissipated. Just five years after attacking the slaveholding class of the South, he became one of their number, acquiring a slave plantation in the mid-1740s. Still convinced that Africans were wrongly captured, Whitefield disapproved of the slave trade even as he owned slaves, arguing, "[the slave trade] will be carried on whether we will [it] or not; I should think myself highly favored if I could purchase a good number of them." Whitefield distinguished himself from the planters that he had earlier castigated by professing his duties "to make their lives more comfortable and lay a foundation for breeding up their posterity in the nurture and admonition of the Lord." Consistent with other missionaries of the day, Whitefield maintained that because they were brought up under the influence of Christianity, his slaves were more productive, generating more in one year, and with a quarter of the expense, than had been produced elsewhere in years. Ultimately, planters' fears that the evangelical movement threatened a social and racial upheaval proved unfounded, as missionaries abandoned demands for the immediate end of slavery in favor of a more gradual amelioration of the conditions under which slaves lived (Boles 1988: 33).

Despite these developments, significant numbers of slaves still desired conversion during the Great Awakening. Several reasons account for the attraction felt by some blacks to the missionary movement. Many slaves hoped for freedom in line with a trend in the late eighteenth century whereby slaveholders, under the influence of revivalist teachings, began manumitting slaves in significant numbers. In the late eighteenth century, slaveholders in Virginia manumitted their charges in numbers significant enough to cause concern among some whites. In 1787–8, Methodists emancipated upwards of one hundred slaves at a single session of the Sussex County Court in Virginia (Jackson 1931: 177–9). The promise of spiritual equality espoused by missionaries implied a concomitant social leveling. Throughout the Great Awakening, blacks and whites worshipped in racially mixed communities, though blacks often were relegated to separate pews. Blacks were allowed to act as exhorters of the faith, often preaching the benefits of Christianity to whites as well as blacks, an experience that proved essential to the later development of independent black churches. In addition, the revival movement allowed blacks and whites to engage in an expressive religious worship that may have more closely resembled African ritual patterns.

Although the revivalists espoused the equality of souls in the hereafter, they typically assented to the will of the planters in the here and now, adopting a theology that deferred the slave's body to the vagaries and brutalities of the harvesters of wealth while claiming her spirit for the balms and blessings of the Harvester of souls. The only major denomination to oppose slavery, the Society of Friends, formally denounced the system during its 1758 national meeting. Despite the efforts of some missionaries and even in light of the conversion of some slaves, the general landscape of Christian conversion during the eighteenth century remained only sparsely populated by blacks.

Upon the eve of the Revolutionary War, several factors – both political and religious – promised a new day for African Americans. The rhetoric of natural rights upon which the revolution was based raised a central hypocrisy of the American Revolution, namely, that a war of independence was waged in a land that regularly denied to slaves the very rights that it demanded from England. After the war, most northern states adopted some form of gradual emancipation and evangelical denominations became increasingly vociferous in their opposition to slavery.

In 1784 a Methodist conference in Baltimore took up the issue of slavery and established the Emancipation Laws, asserting that slavery was "contrary to the laws of God, man, and nature – hurtful to society; contrary to the dictates of conscience and pure religion" (Frey 1991: 246). Moreover, the emancipation laws called on all members to emancipate their slaves (Frey 1991: 245; Raboteau 1978: 143). Five years later the General Committee of Virginia Baptists followed suit, condemning slavery as a "violent deprivation of the rights of nature" (Frey 1991: 246). So swift and severe were the reactions of southern planters, not to mention the southern branches of these denominations, that the Methodists suspended their emancipation laws less than six months after their adoption. Within a few short years, the Baptists followed suit, also distancing themselves from earlier anti-slavery positions.

Perhaps due in part to the inability of the evangelicals to adopt a firm anti-slavery stance, independent black churches took shape throughout the South and in the urban areas of the North as the eighteenth century drew to a close. In 1790, Andrew Bryan, a former slave who had converted during the Great Awakening, established the First African Baptist Church of Savannah, Georgia, the oldest independent black church in the country. Richard Allen, the first black man to be ordained by the Methodist Church, recounts the event that finally led to the development of the African Methodist Episcopal Church. In the fall of 1792, while attending a service at St George's Methodist church, black churchgoers mistakenly occupied an area not designated for black worshipers. Once informed of this, the congregants, presently knelt down in prayer, asked church officials to "wait until prayer is over." Yet unyielding, church officials forcibly removed the transgressors as their heads remained bowed in prayer. Allen and his followers waited patiently for the prayer to be concluded, at which time, Allen recalls: ". . . we all went out of the church in a body, and they were no longer plagued by us" (Wesley 1935: 53).

Antebellum Period

On the eve of the Antebellum period, only a small minority of slaves were Christian. In the 1840s, C. C. Jones, a prominent missionary and proponent of the religious instruction of slaves, lamented, "[a] systematic religious instruction [of the slaves] has never received in the churches, at any time, that general attention and effort which it demanded; and a people have consequently been left, in great numbers, in moral darkness, and destitution of the means of grace" (Jones 1842: 100). Planters demanded that slaves "be exhorted in a safe and salutary manner, '*qui ne leur donnnerait point d'idees*'" (Kemble 1863: 125). James Andrew, a Methodist missionary and slaveholder from Georgia, acknowledged as much in 1831 before an audience of the South Carolina Agricultural Society:

> any attempt on the part of [missionaries], to pay anything like marked attention to the religious instruction of the slaves was met on the part of the owners [particularly those of the lowcountry] by a decided refusal . . . Not only did [the religious instruction of the slaves] hold out no inducements of honor or ease, but, in addition to its hardships and privations, it required so much prudence and delicacy of management, that most were afraid to enter upon it. (Andrew 1831: 314)

Much like their eighteenth- and seventeenth-century predecessors, planters in the antebellum period opposed the religious instruction of slaves on the grounds that it might be used to foment rebellion. On one South Carolina plantation, the religious instruction of the slaves was "done [only] in the daytime and confined to that part of the Bible which shows the duties of servants and masters" (Jackson 1930: 84). Missionaries responded to planter demands for a theology of obedience and deference, as evidenced by the 1852 publication of William Capers' *Catechism for the Use of the Methodist Missions*, which emphasized the obligations of the dutiful servant:

Let as many servants as are under your yoke count their own masters worthy of all honor . . . and they that have believing masters, let them not despise them because they are brethren, but rather do them service because they are faithful and beloved. (Capers 1852: 19)

Writing in *Twelve Years a Slave*, Solomon Northup recounts the manner of religious instruction adopted by slaveholder Peter Tanner, who expounded upon Luke 12: 47 – "And that *servant*, which knew his *lord*'s will, and prepared not himself, neither did according to his will, shall be beaten with many *stripes*" –

D'ye hear that? demanded Peter . . . Stripes, he repeated . . . That nigger that don't care – that don't obey his lord – that's his master – d'ye see? – that *'ere* nigger shall be beaten with many stripes. Now "many" signifies a *great* many – forty – a hundred, a hundred and fifty lashes. That's Scripter. (Northup 1970: 128)

Writing in *Slave Missions and the Black Church in the Antebellum South,* Janet Duitsman Cornelius asserts that white missionaries had great difficulty in fashioning a theology that both encouraged literacy and catechetical instruction among slaves, but also responded to planters' interest in social control. Against the recalcitrance expressed by slaveholders like Peter Tanner and others, some missionaries gave up hopes for a converted slave class among the plantations of antebellum America and instead extended the scope of their missionary activities to foreign colonization in Liberia and elsewhere (Cornelius 1999).

While slaveholders had many concerns regarding the religious instruction of slaves, many abolitionists vehemently opposed the missionaries' emphasis on slave obedience. David Walker highlighted the hypocrisy of many missionaries:

I have known pretended preachers of the gospel of my master, who not only held us as their natural inheritance, but treated us . . . as though they were intent only on taking our blood and groans to glorify the Lord . . . and told us that slaves must be obedient to their masters or be whipped. They chain us . . . and go into the house of God of justice to return him thanks for having aided them in their infernal cruelties. (Walker 1830: 58)

Echoing these sentiments, Frederick Douglass maintained that of all masters, religious masters were the most cruel and brutal. With an unflinching resolve, Douglass proclaimed:

The religion of the south is a mere covering for the most horrid crimes, – a justifier of the most appalling barbarity, – a sanctifier of the most hateful frauds, and a dark shelter under which the darkest, foulest, grossest and most infernal deeds of the slaveholders find the strongest protection. (Douglass 1845: 117)

Of particular concern to Douglass and others were the significant moral dilemmas that faced slaves who chose to convert to Christianity, especially as regards the sacrament of marriage. Slaveholders tolerated matrimony among slaves insofar as the unions accorded with the necessities of maintaining a permanent servile class.

Without any legal existence, slave marriages were ever subject to the whim of the master class and, when economic necessity called for the separation of enslaved spouses, slaves could do very little to preserve their holy union. Moreover, planters seriously discouraged the marriage of slaves from different plantations for fear that significant visitation to neighboring plantations might decrease the labor capacity of a slave while increasing his mobility. In these cases, slaveholders might be persuaded to buy the spouse from a neighboring plantation. More often, slaveholders encouraged marriage within the plantation itself.

Anti-slavery pressure increased throughout the antebellum period and throughout 1836 and 1837 abolitionists regularly made petitions to Congress calling for the end of slavery while they dispersed literature widely throughout the slave South. Under these conditions, slaveholders watched with suspicion any movement – as in religious instruction – that looked to the improvement of the slave.

Despite the strictures of southern planters, South Carolina Methodists established in 1831 a special department designed specifically to minister to the slave population. The task was daunting indeed: by 1830 only a very small percentage of slaves in the region attended church regularly or even heard a sermon (Washington [Creel] 1988: 131). Andrew Bryan admitted as much in 1831 when he wrote: "that the various denominations of Christians have done *something* we thankfully admit. But alas! *Much, very much* yet remains to be done . . . The Negro, through whose sweat and labour we have derived this substance, has too often been suffered to languish in ignorance the most imbruted" (Andrew 1831: 320).

After 15 years of missionary work in the region, a symposium on the religious instruction of the slaves was held at Charleston in 1845, attended by ministers and planters from South Carolina and surrounding states. While the published proceedings of the meeting proposed the utility of religious instruction to the slaves as a catalyst for slave obedience and deference, the report made clear the persistent and imposing barriers to the religious instruction of the slaves. The prevailing image of slave conversion based on the 1845 meeting at Charleston highlights the efforts made by some missionaries to instruct slaves, but illustrates a lack of widespread conversion of slaves to any of the main evangelical denominations (*Proceedings* 1845). Participants at the meeting noted the distance of many plantations from churches and the insufficiency of accommodation, were it practical to attend, the lack of missionaries devoted to the service, the inability of slaves generally being able to understand the gospel, the exorbitant costs involved, and the poor state of religious devotion on the part of the planters themselves, all matters that had been expressed over a century earlier by eighteenth-century missionaries (ibid: 7).

No less an authority than Charles Jones observed that the "numbers of professors of religion, in proportion to the whole, is not large, that can present a correct view of the plan of salvation . . . *True religion* they are inclined to place in *profession . . . and in excited states of feeling. And true conversion, in dreams, visions, trances, voices*" (Jones 1842: 125). This state of affairs caused many missionaries to question the ultimate utility of their work among slaves. One missionary, Thomas Turpin, regretfully acknowledged that he had added very few to the Church (Turpin 1834). Some scholars suggest that Turpin was far from alone; for, as Morgan recently noted, "the vast majority of eighteenth-century Anglo-American slaves lived and died strangers to Christianity" (Morgan 1998: 420).

Slave Religion

Slave religion constitutes one of the most hotly debated issues in African American historiography. Writing in 1918, U. B. Phillips maintains that slaves' engagements with Christianity were primarily imitative, that "the Negroes merely followed and enlarged upon the example of some of the whites" (Phillips 1918: 314). Phillips suggests that while the emotionalism of the evangelical churches was effective among white converts, it constituted a "perfect contagion" among blacks. Of those slaves who defied the mandate to convert by refusing to join the Christian fellowship, Phillips concludes that inevitably some "hard-headed Negro would resist the hypnotic suggestion of his preacher, and even repudiate glorification" (Phillips 1918: 314).

The notion that slaves simply parroted the religion of the master class enjoyed a long life in American slave historiography. Writing in *The Peculiar Institution*, Kenneth Stampp maintains that most so-called africanisms were "lost within a generation" because of the general decay of Black culture in the Americas. Of those aspects of slave spirituality that ran counter to evangelical Christianity, Stampp assures the reader, "there is no need to trace back to Africa the slave's . . . dread of witches, ghosts, and hobgoblins, his confidence in good-luck charms, his alarm at evil omens, his belief in dreams, and his reluctance to visit burying grounds after dark. These superstitions were all firmly rooted in Anglo-Saxon folklore" (Stampp 1956: 375). In effect, Stampp concludes that the religion of the slave was, "in essence, strikingly similar to that of the poor, illiterate white men of the antebellum south" (ibid: 375).

Departing from this trend and offering an early corrective to this view, W. E. B. Du Bois, writing in *The Souls of Black Folk*, chronicled a genealogy of the Black church that extended not back to Europe but rather to the African past (Du Bois [1903] 1989: 159). In contradistinction to those who roundly derided the religious traditions of Africa as senseless degradation, Du Bois acknowledged the black spiritual tradition as a "philosophy of life" (Du Bois 1915: 124). Rather than merely aping the religion of whites, blacks had early developed a particular form of religious expression which, in the dance of spirit possession, the cadence of the black preacher, and the melancholy of the slave spiritual, revealed a distinct theology both wed to yet divorced from evangelical American faiths (Du Bois [1903] 1989: 159).

As early as 1968, Sterling Stuckey articulated the notion that slaves created their own religion as a way of helping them manage not only the mandate of conversion, but also the strictures of plantation labor (Stuckey 1968). The main premise of that work was explored further in full monographs by John Blassingame, Lawrence Levine, and others (Blassingame 1972; Levine 1977). These scholars investigated the degree to which slaves adopted and developed their own mechanisms for interpreting and, in many instances, rejecting the mandate of conversion, noting that many slaves, "repelled by the brand of religion their masters taught, the racial inequalities in the white churches, and the limitations of the bondsmen's autonomy, formulated new ideas and practices in the quarters" (Blassingame 1972: 131). Albert Raboteau suggests that this rejection of white norms often took two different forms. On the one hand, blacks established their own independent churches, both in the South as well as in the North. These "visible institutions" worked alongside and simultaneously with the more "invisible institutions" of slave folk religion. The latter represented new creations whereby enslaved men and women drew from the religious and expressive cultures of the African past, along with elements from the evangelical denominations, to create an oft-times subversive religious practice (Raboteau 1978).

In an effort to resolve the two-ness of black religious expression as both within and without other American ritual forms, Eugene Genovese suggests that the contours of slave religious expression were worked out through compromise and conciliation (Genovese 1972). Genovese argued that the religious tradition of slaves inspired docility and submission, that it "softened the slaves by drawing the hatred from their souls, and without hatred there could be no revolt" (ibid: 163–4). Writing similarly in *Slavery and Social Death*, Orlando Patterson argued that while "it would be simplistic to interpret the role of religion in the slave South solely in terms of an opiate for the masses, a device used by the master class as an agent of social control," in the final analysis it was indeed just that (Patterson 1984: 73–4). Moreover, Patterson contends that the religion of the slave was the same as that of the master class "in all its essential doctrinal and cultic aspects . . . while the spirituals they sang may have had a double meaning with secular implications, it is grossly distorting of the historical facts to claim that they were covertly revolutionary in their intent" (Patterson 1982: 74).

Notwithstanding this interpretation, Frederick Douglass and others certainly perceived differences not only between the faith of the slave and that of the slaveholder, but also between the Christianity of the United States and the "Christianity of Christ"; a difference so wide in fact that "to receive the one as good, pure and holy, is of necessity to reject the other as bad, corrupt, and wicked." In announcing his adherence to a faith of peace and impartiality, Douglass declared a disdain for "the corrupt, slaveholding, women-whipping, cradle-plundering, partial and hypocritical Christianity of this land . . . The [slave] dealer gives his blood-stained gold to support the pulpit, and the pulpit, in return, covers his infernal business with the garb of Christianity. Here we have religion and robbery the allies of each other – devils dressed in angels' robes, and hell presenting the semblance of paradise (quoted in Gates 1996: 97–100).

In the last quarter century, much of the historiography on slave religion has continued to grapple with a litany of complex and subtle issues, including the relationship between slave religion, Africanity, the faith of the master class, and resistance among others. Much of this work explores what Du Bois revealed to us a century ago; namely that "the Negro is a sort of seventh son . . . an American, a Negro; two souls, two thoughts, two unreconciled strivings" (Du Bois [1903] 1989: 5). For her part, Margaret Washington Creel reveals the complications attending the interplay of (religious) cultures, especially evinced in the example of the praise-house (Washington [Creel] 1988).

First built in the slave South during the antebellum years as a mechanism of social control, planters erected these modest structures to deprive slaves from different plantations of the opportunity of gathering and worshiping together. In theory, the proscription of slave mobility ensured a docile slave population, more easily monitored and controlled. Despite the slight stature and humble constitution of praise-houses, and their early establishment as mechanisms for social control, planters soon came to understand the rebellious potentials of community gathering spaces outside the direct purview of the master class. After Nat Turner's slave rebellion in 1831, for example, many slaveholders in Virginia forbade worship in the praise-house, opting instead to appropriate the nether reaches of their own church balconies and galleries for slaves' use. Linda Brent, a runaway slave from Virginia recalled that "slaves begged the privilege of again meeting at their little church in the woods, with their burying ground around it. It was built by the colored people, and they had no higher happiness than to meet there . . . and pour out their hearts in spontaneous prayer. Their request was denied, and the church was demolished" (Brent 1973: 69).

The praise-house became the center of the slaves' religious life, the locus of ritual practice and ecstasy. Slaves assembled at the praise-house on several nights through-out the week and on Sunday afternoon to worship. Prayer was accompanied by song and sacred dance as the faithful formed a circle, performing the ring shout. The manner of worship in the praise-house often struck deep emotional chords in the hearts of observers. So Charlotte Forten offers a portrait of slave ritual practice rendered in shadow and light:

> The large, gloomy room, with its blackened walls, – the wild, whirling dance of the shouters, – the crowd of dark, eager faces gathered around, – the figure of the old blind man, whose excitement could hardly be controlled, and whose attitude and gestures while singing were very fine, – and over all, the red glare of burning pine-knot, which shed a circle of light around it, but only seemed to deepen and darken the shadows in the other parts of the room, – these all formed a wild, strange, and deeply impressive picture, not soon to be forgotten. (Forten 1864: 672)

Sterling Stuckey argues compellingly that the ring shout operated as the primary vehicle through which enslaved Africans "achieved oneness in America" (Stuckey 1987: 13). Moreover, the ring shout – even when performed in an ostensibly Christian setting – revealed the deep connections that slaves maintained to African ritual expression. From a multitude of African ritual traditions that featured coun-terclockwise dance, slaves created the ring shout in North America (Stuckey 1987: 12). The ring shout, beginning with slow and solemn steps, was marked out on the dusty floor by an ever-revolving circle of dancers. Their dragging feet never left the ground, but the steps of the dance built up in layer upon layer, gradually rising in pace and excitement until they reached a final, spinning crescendo. The ring shout represented a particular inscription of spiritual practice, the very tracks of the adherents marking off an inner circle of sanctity:

> The faithful begin first walking and by-and-by shuffling round, one after the other, in a ring. The foot is hardly taken from the floor, and the progression is mainly due to a jerking, hitching motion, which agitates the entire shouter, and soon brings out streams of perspiration . . . song and dance are alike energetic, and often, when the shout lasts into the middle of the night, the monotonous thud, thud, thud of the feet prevents sleep within half a mile of the praisehouse. (Allen 1867: xii–xiv)

Even when slaves were constrained to attend regular church services under the watchful eye of the master class, they continued to attach their primary loyalties to the praise-house congregation. While whites went to church (or stayed at home), slaves laid their primary religious loyalties with the praise-house – so much so that the slave faithful had first to obtain permission from the praise-house congregation before they could petition the master and the local church for official membership of a national denomination, such as the Methodists or the Baptists.

Though unadorned, the praise-house cloaked within its walls the heart of slave spiritual and religious practice. So Frederick Law Olmstead noted:

> The owner of the house told me that having furnished the prayer-house with seats having a back-rail, his Negroes petitioned him to remove it, because it did not leave them *room enough to pray* . . . it was their custom, in social worship, to work themselves up to a great pitch of excitement, in which they yell and cry aloud, and, finally shriek and leap up, clapping their hands and dancing, as it is done in heathen festivals. The back rail they found to seriously impede this exercise. (Olmstead 1996: 449)

Of particular note here are the demands that slaves made regarding the construction and constitution of the praise-house. For them, the very architecture of the cabins had to be made amenable to their particular form of worship. In this, the praise-house afforded a manner of worship that emphasized a particular liberality of movement: a point of no small importance for a people whose bodies were constrained under the threat of the lash. The location of the praise-house in wooded areas ensured yet another type of freedom; that is, the freedom from the purview of whites.

The record of the master class as it relates to praise-house worship is quite mixed. While some perceived it as a mechanism for social control, others saw in its communal expression the very real possibility of rebellion. For their part, Christian missionaries were largely appalled by praise-house worship. One observer wrote: "we cannot determine whether it has a religious character or not . . . but it is probable that they are the barbarous expression of religion handed down to them from their African ancestors" (Forten 1864: 593–4). Others linked the religious experience of slaves to lascivious frolic, savagery, and "idol worship." In such cases, slaves participated in the rituals without the knowledge of the master class, spiriting themselves away in secrecy.

The praise-house maintained an ambivalent relationship with Christianity. On the one hand, the praise-house was the primary institution through which slaves experienced the essential rites of Christian conversion, namely church membership and baptism. Many slaves met at the praise-house to hear sermons offered by black exhorters or white missionaries and the praise-house was the crucible in which the musical tradition of slaves was forged, the incubator of slave spirituals. On the other hand, the praise-house was the basis for the ring shout which, as earlier noted, operated as a mechanism through which many slaves adapted spiritual understandings connected with African culture.

Where the master class attempted to mobilize Christianity as a mechanism of social control, especially in the later antebellum period, slaves looked to alternative sources of ritual power as they conceptualized their religious worldview. Conjure lay at the heart of these negotiations, as a philosophy of belief and practice that enabled slaves access to the otherworld, and the spiritual power abiding therein. At the heart of slave belief in conjure lay the presumption of the intimate connections between the sacred world and the secular. Related to this, slave religion blurred the boundaries that separate the presumably discrete lands of the living and the dead. As a result, much of slave religion, whether in the realm of Christian practice or in the sphere of conjure, was devoted to maintaining effective and propitious communication between the two realms.

Conjure then operated as a theory of ritual practice and belief encompassing the use of poison, folk medicine, and rituals of birth and death. And though they were often perceived as strictly oppositional, the practice of conjure often stood alongside Christian worship. Michael Gomez suggests as much when he argues that "in conjunction with the practice of Christianity, the ways of the ancestors continued to reverberate" throughout slave society (Gomez 1998: 283). Conjure, then, was not a ritual practice hermetically sealed from other aspects of slave ritual and rite. Instead, it was one part of a much larger religious practice that slaves integrated into their lives.

W. E. B. Du Bois suggested the complexity and multiplicity of this ritual network when he described the conjure doctor as "the healer of the sick, the interpreter of the unknown, the comforter of the sorrowing, the supernatural avenger of wrong, and the one who rudely but picturesquely expressed the longing, disappointment, and resentment of a stolen and oppressed people" (Du Bois [1903] 1989: 159, 161). The centrality of slave conjure in antebellum America created a figure of considerable influence in the person of the conjure doctor, known variously as a two-head or a root worker. So important was the root doctor to the slave community that many of them enjoyed "even more importance than a preacher" (Bruce 1970: 115). This tremendous influence assumed a rather mystical character as illustrated in the following description:

> The consulting room is smoky, airless, and reeking with a queer pungent odor. The shades are drawn down tightly and the door is shut securely against intrusion. The furniture is scant, consisting of a lamp on a plain table, a couch for the visitor, and placed directly across the room a wooden armchair in which sits the dealer in magic. The most remarkable object in the room is a spirit picture, showing the head of one of the creatures of the shadow world. The eyes are closed, the face bears a rapt, exalted expression, and the picture fades off into a dim mist of clouds. (Georgia Writers' Project 1940: 38–9)

Some slaves saw little more than a hoax in the claims made by some conjure doctors. So Mary Jones, a former slave of Mississippi, claimed "no indeed, hoodoo ain't no count . . . won't nothing help but prayer and money, and I got plenty prayer" (quoted in Gomez 1998: 287). Indeed, some self-proclaimed root doctors were little more than charlatans. Charles Singleton, a former slave and resident of the Sea Islands region of Georgia, recalled his encounter with a traveling salesman who sold wings, at 25 dollars a pair, assuring residents that the wings were all one needed to fly. The salesman carefully took the measurements of local residents and requested a five-dollar deposit of all those interested, promising to return soon to collect the balance and distribute the coveted product. Singleton recalls "lots uh people gib deah awduh fuh wings, cuz all deah libes dey been heahin bout folks wut could fly. Duh man jis go roun takin awduhs an collectin five dolluhs. Das duh las any ub us ebuh heah uh duh man aw duh wings" (Georgia Writers' Project 1940: 42). This case, notwithstanding, the conjurer played a critically important role in the slave South and held tremendous influence over fellow slaves (see Blassingame 1972: 109–14).

Members of the master class often derided conjure, and the root doctor in particular, inasmuch as he challenged the ultimate authority of slaveholders. The Tennessee state legislature expressed concern over the possibility of rebellion and feared that a slave, "under the pretence of practicing medicine, might convey intelligence from one plantation to another, of a complicated movement; and thus enable the slaves to act in concert to a considerable extent, and perpetrate the most shocking massacres" (quoted in Catteral 1968: 2.521). These fears were not at all unfounded and the root worker might serve the slave well as a protector against the physical abuses of slavery. Frederick Douglass, writing in *Life and Times*, described Sandy, the root doctor. "A genuine African," Douglass maintained that Sandy "had inherited some of the so-called magical powers said to be possessed by the eastern nations." Sandy offered to prepare a root for Douglass, which, if kept always in his possession, would prevent any white man from striking him. Although Douglass was initially reticent about the professed power of the root doctor, he finally acquiesced: "I at first rejected the idea that the simple carrying of a root on my right side could possess any such magic power. I had a positive aversion to all pretenders to '*divination*'." But Douglass did relent since, "if it did me no good it could do me no harm, and it would cost me nothing anyway" (Douglass 1845: 111).

This is consistent with the widespread practice of carrying protective conjure bags described by C. C. Jones: "they have been made to believe that while they carried about their persons some charm with which they had been furnished, they were invulnerable" (Jones 1842: 128). In this connection, the root doctor played a critically important role in the slave community, not only as protector against the machinations of the master class but also as a revolutionary leader. Writing in *Denmark Vesey: The Slave Conspiracy of 1822*, Robert Starobin notes the presence and importance of Gullah Jack, a root worker and "conjurer who kept African religious traditions alive" by providing the rebels with African religious symbols that promised not only sure victory but also invincibility (Starobin 1970: 3, 5). The power of the root doctor to protect the slaves from the pains and oppression of plantation life rendered in some an obstinate defiance of members of the master class. In one case, the very lash of the overseer upon the back of the slave produced neither welt nor scar, but rather elicited laughter on the slave being thus punished (Boyle 1972: 201).

Islam

The varied engagements, rejections, and accommodations that many slaves made with Christianity have constituted the lion's share of the historiography on slave religion, but in recent years, several scholars have added refreshingly to both the depth and substance of slave religious historiography with their studies of antebellum Islam. The practice of Islam among antebellum slaves is among the most understudied, yet intriguing, aspects of slave religion and spiritual life, all the while encouraging a new dialogue between Africanists and African-Americanists. Michael Gomez, Sylviane Diouf, and others trained as Africanists, have extended their expertise of the social and religious landscape of pre-colonial West Africa to explicating the presence and maintenance of African religious expression in the Americas.

Although as many as 50 percent of the slaves exported to North America were captured from areas in West Africa where Islam was at least a religion of the minority, the experience of Muslim slaves has only begun to win the scholarly attention it deserves (Gomez 1994: 682, 684). This is all the more curious when one considers that some early indications suggest that some of the more prominent figures in African American history, including Frederick Douglass, Harriet Tubman, Martin Delaney, and others may have been descendants of enslaved Muslims (Diouf 1998: 199; Gomez 1994: 682). Moreover, several nineteenth-century observers mentioned the practice of Islam among the enslaved population, noting that enslaved Muslims simply conflated Christianity and Islam: "the Mohammedan Africans remaining of the old stock of importations, although accustomed to hear the Gospel preached, have been known to accommodate Christianity to Mohammedanism. 'God,' say they, 'is Allah, and Jesus Christ is Mohammed – the religion is the same, but different countries have different names'" (Jones 1842: 125).

The most comprehensive treatment of Muslim slaves began two decades ago with Allan Austin's *African Muslims in Antebellum America*, a rather expansive text that was greatly modified and condensed in 1997. The more recent publication gathers a wealth of source material regarding the lives and experiences of 75 African-born Muslims brought to North America between 1730 and 1860. Austin maintains that references to Muslims in America, though sparse, are provocative and he draws readers to references to African Muslims in the work of Melville, Twain, and others (Austin 1997: 14). Although he is not trained as an Islamicist or an historian, Austin's work is provocative in the sheer extent of the references that he has culled from extant sources, bringing to light the experiences of a significant community of slaves who had been largely ignored in scholarly writing.

In more recent years, historians have begun to lay out more precisely the historical contours of the lives of Muslim slaves. Michael Gomez, using a wide array of source material, including runaway slave advertisements, chronicles the presence of Muslim slaves in antebellum America. Importantly, Gomez maintains that the Muslim presence in North America "antedates the arrival of English colonists" (Gomez 1994: 683). In Spanish Florida and among the French in Louisiana the Muslim population was significant and in other regions, particularly the Sea Islands region of South Carolina and Georgia, Gomez maintains that "the Muslim presence . . . was active, healthy and compelling" (ibid: 699). Noting the difficulty and dearth of sources regarding Muslims in antebellum America, Gomez makes the crucial observation that "many Muslims may have continued to practice Islam, even if under the protective covering of Christian ritual expression" (ibid: 693). Moreover, given the ignorance of most observers, some Muslims may have practiced the religion in full view of whites and others without their ever having been detected (ibid: 683, 699). Sylviane Diouf, writing in *Servants of Allah*, attempts a reconstruction of antebellum Muslim communities not only in the antebellum United States but throughout the African Diaspora. Diouf argues that not only were Muslims present in significant numbers in the antebellum South but that they forged a life consistent with their faith and beliefs. To the extent that they could, African Muslims upheld the five pillars of Islam while maintaining religious dietary restrictions and forging community bonds with fellow Muslims (Diouf 1998).

The folk tradition of antebellum slaves is one of the most compelling sources for the persistence that some slaves showed in the expression of their religious faith. *Drums and Shadows*, a sourcebook of oral testimonies collected for the WPA, is rich with provocative illustrations of the role that Islam played in the antebellum South:

> Friday wuz duh day she call huh prayuh day . . . I membuh wen I wuz a chile seein muh gran Ryna pray. Ebry mawnin at sun-up she kneel on duh flo in uh room an bow obuh an tech uh head tuh duh flo tree time. (Georgia Writers' Project 1940: 144)

Because some Muslims were literate, they sought to preserve their culture by recording selected sections of the Qur'an, some portions of which still remain. For example Ibrahim Abd ar-Rahman, a Muslim enslaved in Mississippi, wrote copies of al-Fatiha, the opening chapter of the Qur'an, and passed it off to whites as an Arabic translation of the Lord's prayer (Austin 1997: 73). Diouf laments the fact that the presence and significance of enslaved Muslims in antebellum America has received so scant attention, noting that despite the lack of a continuously active Muslim community in the post-emancipation Americas, Islam still played a significant role in the lives, cultures, and religions of blacks throughout the Americas in the decades following enslavement.

Socialization

African culture is inscribed indelibly on the black cultures of the Americas in material culture, language, art, and – as demonstrated above – religion. At the same time, the black cultures of the Americas are not mere replicas of a presumed African prototype and are, moreover, inflected with the experiences, histories, and cultures specific to the American landscape, including Native American and European contributions. Scholars have, for decades, advanced theories to explain the process by which the cultures of West and West-central Africa, Western Europe, and the Americas interacted, referring variously to African survivals, syncretism, acculturation, assimilation, and, in more recent years, hybridity and creolization (see, for example, Herskovits 1941; Blassingame 1972; Price and Price 1999; Stuckey 1987). Following Edward Braithwaite, who defined creolization as "a cultural action – material, psychological and spiritual – based on the stimulus/response of individuals within the society to their environment and – as white/black, culturally discrete groups – to each other," many scholars have examined the process by which two or more cultures come together to create new cultural forms (Braithwaite 1971: 306). For Braithwaite, creolization provided "a way of seeing the society, not in terms of black and white, master and slave, in separate units, but as contributory parts of a whole" (ibid: 307). Charles Joyner applied "creolization" to his study of slave culture in South Carolina as a way of understanding the rise and development of particular linguistic, religious, and social formations among slaves and their progeny in All Saints' Parish, South Carolina (Joyner 1984).

Though creolization and several corollary terms have achieved significant currency in recent years, the theory is not without its detractors. Sterling Stuckey has argued that much of the work done in this regard has "masqueraded as being related to the historical process when serving, usually, to mask that process" (Stuckey 2000: 3). Of particular concern to Stuckey, studies of creole cultures "rarely demonstrate which culture, African or European, when interacting, brought with it the most artistic or spiritual energy" (ibid: 3). Added to this, many studies of creolization presume a critical hierarchy, as evidenced in Braithwaite's understanding of creole culture as "a 'new' construct, made up of newcomers to the landscape and cultural strangers each to the other; one group dominant, the other legally and subordinately slaves" (Braithwaite 1971: 296). From this hierarchical arrangement, many scholars have presumed that the "inferior" culture adjusts to its "superior" counterpart.

Likewise, evidences of European influences on slave cultures seemed, for some, much more obvious than the adjustments that members of the master class made to the cultures of slaves. This tendency resuscitates older conclusions including Stampp's contentions that "there is no need to trace back to Africa the slave's . . . [ritual beliefs]. These superstitions were all firmly rooted in Anglo-Saxon folklore" (Stampp 1956: 375). To his credit – and much more in line with historical evidence – Braithwaite rejected any notion of creolization as unidirectional. So Frederick Douglass agreed, in a discussion of language among antebellum whites, "even 'Mas' Daniel,' by his association with his father's slaves, had measurably adopted their dialect and their ideas" (quoted in Gates 1996: 169).

Not only in the realm of religion, language, and culture, but also as regards the most basic human institutions, were enslaved Africans and their progeny made to adjust to the conditions of slavery, the slave family constituting one of the most important realms of adjustment and change. Of utmost concern to bondsmen was the incredible vulnerability of the slave family. Black women – unlike their white counterparts – could expect neither the protection, nor the provision promised the "Victorian Lady," for whom marriage represented a critical and significant rite of passage. Instead, Linda Brent, writing in *Incidents in the Life of a Slave Girl*, begs the pardon of northern white women who might judge her morally lax:

> Pity me, and pardon me, O virtuous reader! You never knew what it is to be a slave; to be entirely unprotected by law or custom . . . you never shuddered at the sound of his footsteps, and trembled within hearing of his voice . . . I feel that the slave woman ought not to be judged by the same standard as others. (Brent 1861: 56)

Former slave Henry Bibb expressed similar sentiments when he noted that "a poor slave's wife can never be . . . true to her husband contrary to the will of her master. She can neither be pure nor virtuous, contrary to the will of her master. She dare not refuse to be reduced to a state of adultery at the will of her master" (quoted in Blassingame 1972: 173). Indeed, most sexual encounters between black women and white men were "exploitative and unspeakably cruel – nothing more than rapes by white men of black women – a testament to the ugliness of human relations when people are treated as objects" (Morgan 1998: 411).

In addition, the specter of family separation loomed large over the lives of slaves, especially on the first day of January when slaves were typically hired out and sold away. Linda Brent implored northern white women to contrast their New Year's day with that of an enslaved woman:

> with you it is a pleasant season, and the light of day is blessed . . . But to the slave mother, New Year's day comes laden with peculiar sorrows. She sits on her cold cabin floor, watching the children who may all be torn from her the next morning; and often does she wish that she and they might die before the day dawns. (Brent 1861: 14)

Brent had seen one mother lead all seven of her children to the auction block one New Year's day; by nightfall "her children were all far away," having been sold *en masse* to a slave trader (ibid: 14). Writing similarly in *My Bondage and My Freedom*, Frederick Douglass maintained:

> the practice of separating children from their mothers . . . is a marked feature of the cruelty and barbarity of the slave system. But it is in harmony with the grand aim of slavery, which . . . is to reduce man to the level with the brute. It is a successful method of obliterating from the mind and heart of the slave, all just ideas of the sacredness of *the family* as an institution. (quoted in Gates 1996: 142)

For decades after the end of slavery, common wisdom, both popular and scholarly, held that because slave families were subject to sale and separation, and slave women vulnerable to the sexual exploitation of white men, the slave family as a unit was so weak as to be virtually nonexistent. In 1965 Daniel Patrick Moynihan concluded that the "pathology" of black urban life, evidenced in drug addiction, criminal behavior, juvenile delinquency, and underperformance in school could be traced back to "the incredible mistreatment to which it has been subjected over the past three centuries," whereby "slavery vitiated family life . . ." (quoted in Rainwater and Yancey 1967: 75).

As a corrective to these conclusions, Herbert Gutman, writing in *The Black Family in Slavery and Freedom, 1750–1925*, maintained – based on a study of birth registers on the Good Hope plantation in South Carolina – that many slaves lived in long-standing, long-term unions, and that many slave children lived in two-parent family units. Moreover, a study of slave names revealed the persistence of particular family names spanning generations, as grandchildren were often named after their grandparents. For Gutman, the true source of black urban stress rested in the vitriolic racism and discrimination so prevalent in the country.

Even when slave families were not especially stable, slaves went to great lengths to establish fictive kin networks to help assuage the more deleterious effects of familial separation. Frederick Douglass asserted that, according to the etiquette of the plantation, younger slaves regularly addressed older slaves with the familial moniker "Uncle," as a way of showing respect and deference. Indeed, "there is not to be found, among any people, a more rigid enforcement of the law of respect to elders, than [slaves] maintain . . . A young slave must approach the company of the older with hat in hand, and woe betide him, if he fails to acknowledge a favor, of any sort, with the accustomed 'tank'ee' &c." (quoted in Gates 1996: 164).

With the existence and operation of the slave family more firmly established, historians sought to delve even deeper into the subject, focusing monograph-length studies on the various roles of enslaved men, women, and children in the family. Deborah Gray White's *Ar'n't I a Woman?* focused on the plight of slave women in the antebellum South who, being "black in a white society, slave in a free society, women in a society ruled by men" (White 1985: 15), had the least formal power in the country, making them the most vulnerable to its varied abuses of power. For black women, societal constraints and abuse were triangular, revolving around the separate axes of sexism, racism, and slavery. This matter was later taken up by other scholars, who emphasized the violence that attended the lives of black women in the slave South. Philip Morgan, writing in *Slave Counterpoint*, notes the ubiquity of slave women who did field labor while their male counterparts made up the vast majority of skilled positions. As manservants, boatmen, craftsmen, and drivers, skilled male slaves were granted greater mobility and, in some cases, better provisions than were commonly afforded most women (Morgan 1998: 253–4; see also Jones, Jacqueline, *Labor of Love, Labor of Sorrow*).

In more recent years, scholars have devoted increasing attention to the plight of enslaved children. Before the age of 9 or 10 years old, some enslaved children were spared the most taxing demands of plantation labor. They were commonly given as gifts to the children of planters as pets and playmates; such was the case for Harriet Jacobs who was, as a young woman, bequeathed to a 5-year-old. In her early years, a slave might move and play rather freely about the plantation with other children, both black and white, though never on a plane of true equality. Indeed, many slave children were afforded only the scantiest clothing, while others might "go about in the summer just as they left their mother's womb" (Morgan 1998: 133). Likewise, Frederick Douglass recalls the perpetual battle against hunger that he waged as a youngster due to a lack of adequate provisions. Still, Douglass remarked that he had been "out of the way of the bloody scenes that often occurred on the plantation" (quoted in Gates 1996: 19–20). That is, until Douglass witnessed, for the first time, a slave being whipped, which became emblematic of the relations between master and slave: "the blood-stained gate . . . through which [he] was about to pass" (quoted in ibid: 18).

Every child enslaved in the antebellum South experienced some similar epiphany. By the age of 9 or 10, the rather lax bonds of childhood were tightened as they were sent to the fields to work alongside other men and women or trained in the "Big House" for a life of domestic service. From age 9 to 15 or 16, children were considered a "half-share" and performed various duties, including hoeing crops, carrying water, fetching miscellaneous items, carding cotton, and the like, and in so doing passed through "the blood-stained gate" as Douglass called it, "the entrance to the hell of slavery" (quoted in Gates 1996: 18).

Much of the recent research on American slavery reveals the very real necessity for students of slavery to become conversant with African history in its specificity. The manner in which scholars of slavery have become increasingly willing to extend their research questions, discussions, and even teaching across the Atlantic is encouraging. Moreover, the detailed information that is now available regarding the transatlantic slave trade promises to shed new light on the socio-religious landscapes from which Africans were captured, and the spiritual worlds that they brought with them to the Americas.

BIBLIOGRAPHY

Works Cited

Allen, W. F. ([1867] 1951) *Slave Songs of the United States*. New York: Peter Smith.

Andrew, James (1831) "The southern slave plantation," *Methodist Magazine and Quarterly Review* 13: 312–22.

Austin, Allan (1997) *African Muslims in Antebellum America: Transatlantic Stories and Spiritual Struggles*. New York: Routledge.

Blassingame, John (1972) *The Slave Community: Plantation Life in the Antebellum South*. New York: Oxford University Press.

Boles, John (ed.) (1988) *Masters and Slaves in the House of the Lord: Race and Religion in the American South, 1740–1870*. Lexington: University Press of Kentucky.

Boyle, Virginia (1972) *Devil Tales*. Freeport, NY: Books for Libraries Press.

Braithwaite, Edward (1971) *The Development of Creole Society in Jamaica, 1770–1820*. Oxford: Clarendon Press.

Brent, Linda ([1861] 1973) *Incidents in the Life of a Slave Girl*, Maria Child (ed.). New York: Harvest Books.

Bruce, Philip A. (1970) *The Plantation Negro as a Freeman*. Williamstown: Corner House.

Capers, William (1852) *Catechism for the Use of the Methodist Missions*. Charleston: John Early.

Catterall, Helen (1968) *Judicial Cases concerning American Slavery and the Negro*. New York: Octagon Books.

Cornelius, Janet Duitsman (1999) *Slave Missions and the Black Church in the Antebellum South*. Columbia: University of South Carolina Press.

Creel *see* Washington [Creel]

Diouf, Sylviane (1998) *Servants of Allah: African Muslims Enslaved in the Americas*. New York: New York University Press.

Douglass, Frederick ([1845] 1987) *Narrative of the Life of Frederick Douglass*. New York: Penguin.

Du Bois, W. E. B. (1903) *The Negro Church*. Atlanta: Atlanta University Press.

—— ([1903] 1989) *The Souls of Black Folk*. New York: Penguin.

—— ([1915] 1975) *The Negro*. [Millwood, NY] New York: Kraus-Thomson.

Forten, Charlotte (1864) "Life on the sea islands," parts I–II, *Atlantic Monthly* (May): 587–96, 666–76.

Frey, Sylvia (1991) *Water From the Rock: Black Resistance in a Revolutionary Age*. Princeton, NJ: Princeton University Press.

Gates, Henry Louis (1996) *Douglass: Autobiographies*. New York: Library of America.

Genovese, Eugene (1972) *Roll, Jordan, Roll: The World the Slaves Made*. New York: Vintage Books.

Georgia Writers' Project (1940) *Drums and Shadows: Survival Studies among the Georgia Coastal Islands*. Athens: University of Georgia Press.

Gomez, Michael (1994) "Muslims in early America," *Journal of Southern History* 60 (4, November): 671–710.

—— (1998) *Exchanging Our Country Marks: The Transformation of African Identities in the Colonial and Antebellum South*. Chapel Hill: University of North Carolina Press.

Hair, P. E. H., Jones, Adam and Law, Robin (eds.) (1992) *Barbot on Guinea: The Writings of Jean Barbot on West Africa, 1678–1712*. London: Hakluyt Society.

Hall, Gwendolyn Midlo (1992) *Africans in Colonial Louisiana: The Development of Afro-Creole Culture in the Eighteenth Century*. Baton Rouge: Louisiana State University Press.

Herskovits, Melville (1941) *The Myth of the Negro Past*. Boston: Beacon Press.

Jackson, Luther (1930) "Religious instruction of Negroes, 1830–1860, with special reference to South Carolina," *Journal of Negro History* 15: 72–114.

—— (1931) "Religious development of the Negro in Virginia from 1760–1860," *Journal of Negro History* 16: 168–239.

Jernegan, Marcus W. (1916) "Slavery and Conversion in the American Colonies," *American Historical Review* 21: 504–27.

Jones, C. C. ([1842] 1969) *Religious Instruction of the Negroes in the United States*. New York: Kraus Reprint.

Jones, Jacqueline (1985) *Labor of Love, Labour of Sorrow: Black Women, Work, and the Family from Slavery to the Present*. New York: Basic Books.

Jordan, Winthrop (1968) *White over Black: American Attitudes toward the Negro, 1550–1812*. Chapel Hill: University of North Carolina Press.

Joyner, Charles (1984) *Down by the Riverside: A South Carolina Slave Community*. Urbana: University of Illinois Press.

Kemble, Fanny Ann ([1863] 1961) *Journal of a Residence on a Georgian Plantation in 1838–1839*. Athens: University of Georgia Press.

Levine, Lawrence (1977) *Black Culture and Black Consciousness: Afro-American Folk Thought from Slavery to Freedom*. New York: Oxford University Press.

McKitrick, Eric (1963) *Slavery Defended: The Views of the Old South*. Englewood Cliffs, NJ: Prentice-Hall.

Morgan, Philip (1998) *Slave Counterpoint: Black Culture in the Eighteenth-Century Chesapeake and Lowcountry*. Chapel Hill: University of North Carolina Press.

Mullin, Michael (1976) *American Negro Slavery: A Documentary History*. Columbia: University of South Carolina Press.

Northup, Solomon ([1853] 1970) *Twelve Years a Slave*. Mineola, NY: Dover.

Olmstead, Frederick Law (1996) *The Cotton Kingdom: A Traveler's Observations on Cotton and Slavery in the American Slave States*. New York: Da Capo Press.

Patterson, Orlando (1982) *Slavery and Social Death: A Comparative Study*. Cambridge, MA: Harvard University Press.

Phillips, U. B. (1918) *American Negro Slavery: A Survey of the Supply, Employment, and Control of Negro Labor as Determined by the Plantation Regime*. Baton Rouge: Louisiana State University Press.

Potkay, Adam and Burr, Sandra (eds.) (1995) *Black Atlantic Writers of the Eighteenth Century: Living the New Exodus in England and the Americas*. New York: St. Martin's Press.

Price, Richard and Price, Sally (1999) *Maroon Arts Cultural Vitality in the African Diaspora*. Boston: Beacon Press.

Proceedings of the Meeting in Charleston, S.C., May 13–15, 1845, on the Religious Instruction of the Negroes, together with the Report of the Committee and the Address to the Public (1845) Charleston, SC.

Puckett, Newbell Niles (1926) *Folk Beliefs of the Southern Negro*. New York: Negro Universities Press.

Raboteau, Albert (1978) *Slave Religion: The "Invisible Institution" in the Antebellum South*. New York, Oxford University Press.

—— (1995) *A Fire in the Bones: Reflections on African American Religious History*. Boston: Beacon Press.

—— (1999) *Canaan Land: A Religious History of African Americans*. New York: Oxford University Press.

Rainwater, Lee and Yancey, William (eds.) (1967) *The Moynihan Report and the Politics of Controversy*. Cambridge, MA: MIT Press.

Sernett, Milton (ed.) (1999) *African American Religious History: A Documentary Witness*. Durham, NC: Duke University Press.

Stampp, Kenneth (1956) *The Peculiar Institution: Slavery in the Ante-bellum South.* New York: Vintage.

Starobin, Robert (ed.) (1970) *Great Lives Observed: Denmark Vesey, The Slave Conspiracy of 1822.* Englewood Cliffs, NJ: Prentice-Hall.

Stuckey, Sterling (1968) "Through the prism of folklore: the black ethos in slavery," *Massachusetts Review* 9 (3, Summer).

—— (1987) *Slave Culture: Nationalist Theory and the Foundations of Black America.* New York: Oxford University Press.

—— (1994) "Through the prism of folklore" in *Going through the Storm: The Influence of African American Art and History.* New York: Oxford University Press.

—— (2000) "Time . . . Africa and the Diaspora," The Marion Thompson Wright Lecture Series: Rutgers University.

Turpin, Thomas (1834) "Missionary sketch," *Christian Advocate and Journal,* January 31.

Walker, David ([1829] 1830) *David Walker's Appeal to the Coloured Citizens of the World, but in particular, and very expressly, to those of the United States of America.* Baltimore: Black Classic Press, 3rd edn.

Washington [Creel], Margaret (1988) *A Peculiar People: Slave Religion and Community-Culture among the Gullahs.* New York: New York University Press.

Wesley, Charles (1935) *Richard Allen: Apostle of Freedom.* Washington, DC: Associated Publishers.

White, Deborah Gray (1985) *Ar'n't I A Woman? Female Slaves in the Plantation South.* New York: W. W. Norton.

Wright, Kai (ed.) (2001) *The African-American Archive: The History of the Black Experience in Documents.* New York: Black Dog & Leventhal.

Suggestions for Further Reading

Berlin, Ira (1998) *Many Thousands Gone: The First Two Centuries of Slavery in North America.* Cambridge, MA: Belknap Press of Harvard University Press.

David, Brion Davis (1988) *The Problem of Slavery in Western Culture.* New York: Oxford University Press.

Earl, Riggins (1993) *Dark Symbols, Obscure Signs: God, Self, and Community in the Slave Mind.* Maryknoll, NY: Orbis Books.

Elia, Nadia (2003) "'Kum buba yali kum buba tambe, ameen, ameen, ameen': did some flying Africans bow to Allah?," *Callaloo* 26: 182–202.

Fisher, Miles Mark (1953) *Negro Slave Songs in the United States.* Ithaca, NY: Cornell University Press for the American Historical Association.

Frazier, E. Franklin (1963) *The Negro Church in America.* New York: Schocken.

Frey, Sylvia (1991) *Water From the Rock: Black Resistance in a Revolutionary Age.* Princeton, NJ: Princeton University Press.

Frey, Sylvia and Wood, Betty (1998) *Come Shouting to Zion: African American Protestantism in the American South and British Caribbean to 1830.* Chapel Hill: University of North Carolina Press.

Fulop, Timothy and Raboteau, Albert (eds.) (1997) *African-American Religion: Interpretive Essays in History and Culture.* New York: Routledge.

Guthrie, Patricia (1996) *Catching Sense: African American Communities on a South Carolina Sea Island.* Westport, CT: Bergin and Garvey.

Gutman, Herbert (1976) *The Black Family in Slavery and Freedom, 1750–1925.* New York: Vintage.

Heywood, Linda (2002) *Central Africans and Cultural Transformations in the American Diaspora.* New York: Cambridge University Press.

Holloway, Joseph (ed.) (1990) *Africanisms in American Culture*. Bloomington: University of Indiana Press.

Hurston, Zora Neal (1981) *The Sanctified Church*. Berkeley, CA: Turtle Island.

Johnson, Alonzo and Jersild, Paul (1996) *Ain't Gonna Lay My 'Ligion Down: African American Religion in the South*. Columbia: University of South Carolina.

Johnson, Clifton (1969) *God Struck Me Dead: Religious Conversion Experiences and Autobiographies of Ex-Slaves*. Philadelphia: Pilgrim Press.

Johnson, Paul E. (1994) *African-American Christianity: Essays in History*. Berkeley: University of California Press.

Jones, Norrece T., Jr (1990) *Born a Child of Freedom, Yet a Slave: Mechanisms of Control and Strategies of Resistance in Antebellum South Carolina*. Hanover, NH: University Press of New England.

Lincoln, C. Eric and Mamiya, Lawrence (1990) *The Black Church in the African American Experience*. Durham, NC: Duke University Press.

McCurry, Stephanie (1995) *Masters of Small Worlds*. New York: Oxford University Press.

McKivigan, John and Snay, Mitchell (eds.) (1998) *Religion and the Antebellum Debate over Slavery*. Athens: University of Georgia Press.

Mathews, Donald (1965) *Slavery and Methodism*. Princeton, NJ: Princeton University Press.

—— (1977) *Religion in the Old South*. Chicago: University of Chicago Press.

Murphy, Larry (2000) *Down by the Riverside: Readings in African American Religion*. New York: New York University Press.

Simpson, George Eaton (1978) *Black Religions in the New World*. New York: Columbia University Press.

Sobel, Mechal (1987) *The World They Made Together: Black and White Values in Eighteenth-Century Virginia*. Princeton, NJ: Princeton University Press.

—— (1988) *Trabelin' On: The Slave Journey to an Afro-Baptist Faith*. Princeton, NJ: Princeton University Press.

Thompson, Robert Farris (1983) *Flash of the Spirit*. New York: First Vintage Books.

Whelchel, Love Henry, Jr (2002) *Hell without Fire: Conversion in Slave Religion*. Nashville, TN: Abingdon Press.

Wilmore, Gayraud (1989) *African-American Religious Studies: An Interdisciplinary Anthology*. Durham, NC: Duke University Press.

Wimbush, Vincent (2000) *African-Americans and the Bible*. New York: Continuum.

Woodson, Carter G. (1921) *The History of the Negro Church*. Washington, DC: Associated Publishers.

CHAPTER ELEVEN

Slave Rebels and Black Abolitionists

STANLEY HARROLD

The first recorded slave rebellions in North America occurred during the late 1600s. The first black abolitionists, who called for emancipating all slaves in their states or throughout the United States, became active during the American War for Independence. Historians have always recognized that slave rebels were part of this country's history. No one ever disputed that such black leaders as Frederick Douglass and Sojourner Truth contributed to the pre-Civil War antislavery movement. Yet not until the late 1930s was there systematic evaluation of the role of slave rebels and black abolitionists. It has only been since the 1950s that slave resistance, slave rebellions, and the relationship of African Americans to the antislavery movement have been the subjects of sustained investigation and debate among historians.

This chapter focuses on the transformation of historians' views of slave rebels and black abolitionists. It has two goals. The first is to demonstrate how an understanding of slave rebellion and other forms of black resistance to slavery developed hand-in-hand with an increasingly sophisticated portrait of the black experience in slavery. The second goal is to examine a growing awareness among historians of the importance of black abolitionists, who have progressed from the fringe of historical consciousness to a position at or near the center of antislavery studies. Expanding historical interest in and changing interpretations of these topics reflect events and intellectual developments in the twentieth and twenty-first centuries. The civil rights movement's successes and failures in particular stimulated new approaches to earlier black activists. More recently, growing appreciation of the impacts of gender, violence, memory, and globalization on human behavior have widened historians' perspectives. Increasingly, historians place slave rebels and black abolitionists in broad contexts and thereby change how both groups are perceived.

When, during the late 1930s and early 1940s, Harvey Wish, Joseph C. Carroll, and most notably Herbert Aptheker began writing about North American slave revolts, they were themselves rebels against major assumptions concerning American slavery and African American character. Although black historians of the late-nineteenth and early-twentieth centuries had shown African Americans to be active agents in a variety of contexts, this had not been the case among white historians, who dominated the American historical profession. They rarely included African

Americans in their histories and, when they did, they usually portrayed them as passive recipients of white benevolence.

From the 1910s to the 1950s, the writings of Ulrich B. Phillips provided the dominant view of slavery and the black experience in it. Phillips, a southern-born historian who taught at the University of Michigan, described slavery as a benevolent, paternalistic, and benign institution. People of African descent, he maintained, took naturally to enslavement, were generally content in that condition, and "quite possibly" benefited from being brought as slaves to America (Phillips 1918: 45, 291–4, 342–3). A few dissenters, such as Raymond A. Bauer and Alice H. Bauer (1942), described the many instances in which slaves faked illness, deliberately misunderstood commands, broke tools, and abused farm animals in patterns of "day to day resistance" against masters. But most historians of that time accepted Phillips's emphasis on the "natural amenability of the blacks" (Phillips 1918: 454) and his contention that slavery "maintained order and a notable degree of harmony" between the two races (ibid: 401). Phillips was not entirely consistent in this interpretation. His history of American slavery provides a thorough account of slave revolts and conspiracies in North America and the Caribbean islands from the seventeenth century to the Civil War. It also notes the disquiet the revolts caused among white people (ibid: 463–88).

In *American Negro Slave Revolts* (1943), Aptheker began the attack on the myth of black passivity in slavery and on the contradictions that Phillips and many others indulged. But Aptheker, who relied on a Marxist analysis of the reports of slave revolt that had circulated widely in the Old South, undertook no thorough analysis of American slavery or black culture. Kenneth M. Stampp went a step further. In *The Peculiar Institution* (1956), he portrayed slavery in the United States as having been unredeemably brutal and emphasized that slaves persistently resisted through a variety of tactics, ranging from suicide to large-scale revolts. Short of rebellion and homicide, escape was their most extreme measure.

Stampp, however, did not provide a context for understanding why slaves resisted, what gave them the wherewithal to do so, and what were their precise goals. It was Stanley M. Elkins's 1959 comparison of conditions on southern plantations to those in Nazi concentration camps that stimulated other historians to investigate these crucial issues. Like Stampp, Elkins denied that people of sub-Saharan African descent were inherently docile, but he questioned the existence of widespread slave rebelliousness, arguing that conditions similar to those in concentration camps reduced African Americans to child-like "Sambos," utterly dependent on their masters and incapable of resistance.

Elkins's stark portrayal of black submissiveness within a brutal slave system clashed with the perspective of an increasingly assertive civil rights movement. His book led a diverse group of historians to investigate what became known as the slave community. As early as 1941, anthropologist Melville J. Herskovits contended, against the wisdom of his time, that elements of African culture – religion, folklore, family structure, dance, music, and etiquette – had survived the Atlantic slave trade and endured among American slaves. During the 1960s and 1970s, historians found that these cultural legacies served as the basis for a community that gave enslaved men and women some control over their lives and created long-term patterns of resistance to masters (Blassingame 1979; Genovese 1974; Gutman 1976). It may be that these studies exaggerate the autonomy of slave communities (Shore 1986: 147–64; Wyatt-Brown 1988: 1228–52). They remain, nevertheless, the basis for understanding slave resistance and revolt. In turn, as Norrece T. Jones, Jr puts it, slave rebels forced masters to constantly devise "new modes of control" (Jones 1989: 193).

During the seventeenth and eighteenth centuries, African men and women who arrived as slaves in North America often resisted by openly defying their masters and refusing to work. When Africans attempted to escape from slavery they did so in groups made up of individuals who shared a common homeland or language (Mullin 1972: 34–5, 39–47). Those who succeeded became either *outliers* or *maroons*. The former remained near the plantation they had escaped from and survived by stealing from it. The latter established their own settlements in inaccessible regions, such as mountainous areas or swamps. The largest maroon settlement in North America began in Spanish Florida as a refuge for slaves who had escaped from South Carolina and Georgia. Smaller maroon settlements existed in South Carolina, Georgia, and Virginia (Franklin and Schweninger 1999: 100–3; Aptheker 1939: 167–84, 1947: 452–60; Mulroy 1993).

Africans – as opposed to those American-born of African descent – predominated not only among slaves who escaped but also among the leaders of early slave revolts in British North America (Genovese 1979: 42). There were two waves of rebellion. The first occurred between 1710 and 1722; the second between 1730 and 1740. The most notable rebellion among the first wave took place in New York City in 1712, when approximately 35 Africans, who had some American Indian and white supporters, rose up against "hard usage" (Scott 1961: 43–74). During the second wave, the Stono Rebellion, which took place near Charleston, South Carolina in 1739, was most important, although a revolt conspiracy in New York City in 1741 has produced more controversy among historians.

No one has fundamentally challenged Peter H. Wood's account of how about one hundred slaves, led by recent arrivals from Angola, stole guns at Stono, rallied other slaves, and killed about thirty white people in a failed attempt to flee to Florida (Wood 1974: 308–26). But historians have disagreed concerning the New York trials that led to "four whites hanged, thirteen Negroes burned, eighteen hanged, and seventy shipped out of the colony" for plotting revolt (Jordan 1968: 118). During the 1960s, Ferenc M. Szasz contended that the conspiracy was one of robbers not rebels (Szasz 1967: 215–30), and Winthrop D. Jordan argued that white insecurities and political factionalism led to unwarranted charges against alleged plotters (Jordan 1968: 116–20). In contrast, Thomas J. Davis found evidence of a widespread conspiracy to fight slavery and gain freedom (Davis 1985: xii). In 1999, Graham Russell Hodges contended that poor whites participated with slaves in planning to rise up against wealthier classes. The most recent account of the event posits that, while there was a conspiracy, local authorities greatly exaggerated its extent and the danger it posed to the city (Hoffer 2003). This continuing disagreement is part of a broader debate among scholars, framed by differing perspectives concerning black agency in slavery as well as by fragmentary and often contradictory evidence.

As increasing numbers of American slaves were *creoles* – people of African descent born in America – forms of resistance became subtler. Rather than openly defy masters as their African forebears had, creoles engaged in the various forms of day-to-day resistance that were less likely to result in punishment. Meanwhile, as Gerald W. Mullin points out, escape increasingly became an option exercised by young men who departed not in groups but individually (Mullin 1972). Often they were skilled and acculturated people who used their wits to pass as free. Their destinations also changed. Instead of seeking to reach maroon settlements, they headed for the South's few cities, towns, or regions where there were few slaves. The most extensive account of the different motives and destinations of escapees is John Hope Franklin's and Loren Schweninger's *Runaway Slaves* (1999), which – while focusing mainly on the nineteenth century – provides a multitude of examples.

While most escapees were men, interest in how enslaved women challenged their condition has been increasing since the 1970s. Mullin contends that female escapees demonstrated more aplomb than males (Mullin 1972: 103–5). Gerda Lerner, in her documentary history of black women, emphasizes accounts of how enslaved women resisted their condition by clandestinely learning to read and teaching others (Lerner 1972: 27–33). Darlene Clark Hine and Kate Wittenstein analyze the economic motives of black women who sought to improve their condition (Hine and Wittenstein 1981: 289–99). Elizabeth Fox Genovese investigates how church and community shaped their means of resistance (1986: 143–65). Melton A. McLaurin's *Celia, A Slave* (1991) is a dramatic account of how one slave woman killed her master after he repeatedly raped her.

In a wider context, Eugene D. Genovese most explicitly contends that everyday resistance was designed neither to undermine the slave system nor to gain freedom. Instead slaves used resistance as a tactic to force concessions from masters. These included improvements in working conditions, increased food rations, and social autonomy. In Genovese's view, resistance was one of several ways slaves shaped plantation life in tension with masters' desire for control (Genovese 1979: 594–8, 620–1). More recently Philip D. Morgan has maintained similarly that through day-to-day resistance African Americans created "a coherent culture" and "eased the torments of slavery" (Morgan 1998: xxii). These motives for resistance predominated throughout slavery's existence in North America. Therefore, slaves who engaged in day-to-day resistance were rebels only to a degree.

It is Genovese, as well, who best establishes that early slave rebellions in British North America and elsewhere in the western hemisphere were, like escape attempts, designed only to free the participants from bondage. Rebels did not have an anti-slavery ideology. Instead Christian or African religious beliefs and a personal desire to liberate oneself from social disgrace provided motivation. They did not so much object to the idea of slavery as to their own subjection to it (Genovese 1979: xiv, xviii–xix, xxi). Sylvia R. Frey notes that maroonage "did not constitute a direct attack on the slave system" (Frey 1991: 51–2), and Lawrence W. Levine goes so far as to maintain that American slave rebels remained "prepolitical" throughout the existence of slavery in the United States (Levine 1977: 54–77). Recent research, nevertheless, provides strong, if not absolute, support to Genovese's contention that modernization and the "bourgeois ideology" associated with the Enlightenment and the Age of Revolution led, by the late eighteenth century, to revolts aimed at violently destroying slavery.

The American, French, and Haitian revolutions – the last of which was a success-ful slave uprising that led to the creation of the independent black Republic of Haiti

– provided American slaves with a revolutionary ideology based on natural rights doctrines (Genovese 1979: xiii–xiv, xix; Hunt 1987; Egerton 1993: 8–11, 47–8). Several studies show how slaves fought during the American Revolution on the side that they believed offered them the best chance for freedom (Quarles 1977; Mullin 1972: 130–6; Kaplan 1976: 243–55). In effect the Revolution was the first of a series of events that encouraged American slave rebels to seek freedom, not merely for themselves but to end slavery itself (Frey 1991: 228).

As revolutionary ideology spread, American slaves became restless (Wright 1993: 225). Between 1800 and 1831 there were many minor uprisings, two major slave revolts, and two major revolt conspiracies in the United States, which, as Merton L. Dillon most thoroughly demonstrates, were linked to broader political developments (Dillon 1990: 45–161). The revolts were led by Charles Deslondes in Louisiana during 1811 and Nat Turner in Virginia during 1831. The conspiracies, which white authorities crushed before the rebels could act, were those led by Gabriel in Virginia during 1800 and Denmark Vesey in South Carolina during 1822. Each revolt or conspiracy had aspects linking it to the Age of Revolution, although more traditional motives may be adduced from relevant (and scant) primary sources. The efforts led by Gabriel, Vesey, and Turner have extended historiographies, while historians have only begun to investigate Deslondes.

Largely through Douglas R. Egerton's insights, it is now accepted that Gabriel, an enslaved blacksmith who organized slaves for violent abolitionist action near Richmond, was part of "an urbanized black elite assimilated to American culture" rather than a premodern messianic leader. Black refugees from Haiti and the natural rights doctrines of the American Revolution influenced him. He was also well aware of international and domestic political alignments that gave slave revolt a chance for success, and he hoped to get support from poor and dissenting white people. Only minimally religious, he planned to attack Richmond, the center of slaveholder power in Virginia, rather than to escape from it (Egerton 1993: x–xi, 34–49, 179–81, 189n).

What is known about Deslondes's Louisiana rebellion rests on the work of James H. Dorman (1977: 389–404) and Junius Rodriguez (1999: 65–88). The product of circumstances similar to those that produced Gabriel's conspiracy, this rebellion was – in terms of the number of slaves involved – the largest servile insurrection in America prior to the Civil War. As white refugees from Haiti settled with their slaves in what was then Orleans Territory, rumors of slave unrest spread. Like Gabriel, Deslondes – who was Haitian – planned to march toward a center of slaveholding power – this time New Orleans – rather than to escape. But a large force of territorial militia, slaveholding vigilantes, and US troops crushed Deslondes's poorly equipped army of about 180 men and women.

While interpretations of Gabriel's and Deslondes's goals support the view that they were abolitionists deeply influenced by the Age of Revolution, the other two major American slave rebels of the early nineteenth century, Vesey and Turner, are more complicated figures. Historians tend to emphasize religious influences on them, and their political objectives remain unclear. In a manner similar to those who dispute the existence of a revolt conspiracy in New York City in 1741, a few historians contend that Vesey was not the leader of a revolt conspiracy at all, but instead the victim of white paranoia or a plot to promote proslavery sentiment

(Wade 1964: 143–61; Johnson 2001: 915–76). These claims, however, are refuted by such historians as Max L. Kleinman (1974: 225–9), Sterling Stuckey (1966: 28–41), William W. Freehling (1966: 54n; and 1994: 44–6), John Lofton (1964), and Egerton (2002: 143–52).

Vesey, a skilled former slave, well understood the significance of the French and Haitian revolutions, as well as of growing antislavery sentiment in the North. But, since his planned revolt aimed at the escape of relatively few slaves and free African Americans from Charleston by sea to Haiti, rather than ending slavery in South Carolina, his stature as a revolutionary abolitionist is uncertain. Egerton establishes that Vesey had come to see himself as an Old Testament prophet and one of his closest associates was Jack Prichard, an East African conjurer. The two melded "African magic and . . . Old Testament tales" (Egerton 1999a: 113–20). Vesey's effort, therefore, appears to have been influenced by both revolutionary and traditional elements.

As Turner's biographer Stephen B. Oates notes, Turner – like Vesey – was politically aware, particularly in regard to slave unrest in Virginia and divisions among white people in that state. Unlike Vesey, Turner clearly intended to destroy slavery (Oates 1975: 41–2, 53–4). He originally planned to initiate his revolt on July 4 and it actually began on August 21, the fortieth anniversary of the start of the Haitian Revolution. Yet Oates and other historians also regard Turner, a slave preacher, as having been more of a religious than a political figure, who believed on the basis of visions and portents that God intended him to lead his people violently to freedom.

In part because of increasing white vigilance, there were after 1831 no major antebellum American slave revolts. Nevertheless, two successful shipboard revolts had important impacts. The first of these, which took place aboard the Spanish slave ship *Amistad* in 1839, was not actually an American slave revolt. The rebels were West Africans led by Cinque; the crew they rose up against was Spanish. But the *Amistad* revolt, which is best described by Howard Jones, is part of African American history in that it influenced how northern abolitionists, both black and white, perceived their relationship to slave rebels, the relationship of the United States to the Atlantic slave trade, and the right to freedom under the US Constitution (Jones 1986).

The second shipboard revolt occurred in late 1841 on the *Creole* as it carried a cargo of slaves from Richmond, Virginia, to the slave markets of New Orleans. Led by Madison Washington, 19 black men took control of the vessel and sailed it to the British Bahamas where all the slaves on board gained freedom. Washington became a hero for black abolitionists. But far less evidence is available concerning the *Creole* than there is for the *Amistad*, and there have been fewer studies of the event. In an article, Jones emphasizes the diplomatic aspects of the incident, which involved United States attempts to have Great Britain return the former slaves (Jones 1975: 28–50). Recently the *Creole* revolt has figured in studies of abolitionist understandings of black masculinity and the morality of slave revolt (Yarborough 1990: 166–88; Harrold 1999: 89–107). George and Willene Hendrick's *The Creole Mutiny* (2003) places the revolt in the broader contexts of the domestic slave trade and slave escapes. The book speculates about Madison Washington, and traces his role in black fiction.

As American slave revolts and conspiracies ceased to reach major proportions after 1831, slave escapes greatly increased (Dillon 1990: 201–2). Franklin and Schweninger estimate in *Runaway Slaves* that by 1860 "the number of runaways annually would exceed 50,000" (Franklin and Schweninger 1999: 282). Most escapees continued to seek refuge in the South and many left only temporarily (ibid: 109–20), but slave escapes to the North and Canada mounted steadily after the late 1830s. Most historians agree with Larry Gara's contention that the great majority of these northward escapes were carried out by the slaves on their own or with informal assistance from other African Americans (Gara 1961: 67–8; Hudson 2002: 4). But there is a considerable body of opinion that links the increased escapes to the operation of organized underground railroad networks, which will be discussed below in relation to the abolitionists.

During the early twentieth century, historians interpreted the impact of slave rebels in an essentially southern context. Ranging from Phillips to Aptheker, they noted that slave resistance and insurrection raised great fear among white southerners, which led to repressive measures that limited white freedom as well as black. But Aptheker helped initiate an important line of enquiry by also linking southern defensiveness to national proslavery measures that, in turn, strengthened antislavery sentiment in the North (Aptheker 1943: 372–3). By the 1990s several historians emphasized violent slave resistance and a white southern reaction to it as major factors in the sectional conflict leading to the Civil War (Freehling 1994: 255–67; Ashworth 1995: 5–8; Link 2003, esp. 1–10).

At the same time, historians more carefully investigated the relationship between slave rebels and northern abolitionists. Because slavery had essentially disappeared in the North by the late 1820s and because Phillips portrayed slavery as mild, historians for much of the twentieth century had contended that something other than the peculiar institution must have motivated a few white northerners to become abolitionists. Evangelical religion, social dislocation, and the emergence of wage labor each attracted attention as a motivating factor. But studies by Aptheker (1989), Dillon (1990), James L. Huston (1990), and John Ashworth (1995) indicate that the harshness of slavery – and black resistance to it – stimulated antislavery sentiment among both black and white northerners in a more direct way than Aptheker had earlier described. Ashworth suggests that had the enslaved not resisted their masters, a radical northern antislavery movement would have been inconceivable.

Genovese in *From Rebellion to Revolution* implies that slaves from Gabriel onward who either plotted or engaged in mass uprisings were abolitionists. Douglas R. Egerton (1999b: 41–2) makes this point more explicitly, and I elaborate in *American Abolitionists* (2001). Slave rebels did not join antislavery societies and were usually far removed from northern centers of organized abolitionism. Nevertheless the links between them and northern abolitionists are clear in a variety of contexts. Peter P. Hinks has drawn attention to the likelihood that influential black abolitionist David Walker of Boston, who published his *Appeal to the Colored Citizens of the World* in 1829, earlier had known Denmark Vesey in Charleston (Hinks 1997: 22–62).

Slave rebels also exercised a decisive role in shaping northern abolitionist attitudes toward violent means. Robert H. Abzug noted that Turner's 1831 revolt motivated abolitionists during the 1830s to advocate immediate emancipation as a precautionary measure (Abzug 1970: 15–28). Black and white abolitionists from the early 1830s onwards regarded slave rebels as likely liberators. For abolitionists of both races, the rebels represented a strain of black masculinity and desire for freedom that slavery's defenders contended did not exist. Black abolitionists, especially, admired Gabriel, Vesey, Turner, Cinque, and Washington for their revolutionary bravery (Harrold 1995: 45–63). Dillon points out that by the early 1840s northern abolitionists sought actively to form an alliance with slaves. They proposed to communicate with slaves and a few northerners went south to help slaves escape (Dillon 1990: 201–23; Harrold 1995: 64–83).

Despite these links between slave rebellion and northern abolitionism, it was not actions by southern slaves that directly led to the initiation of an abolitionist movement by black and white northerners. Like Gabriel and Deslondes, the first black northern abolitionists were products of the Age of Revolution. In *Race and Revolution*, Gary Nash establishes that with the start of the American Revolution some black northerners quickly appreciated how the Declaration of Independence's natural rights principles challenged slavery (Nash 1990: 57–87). They prodded state courts and state legislatures to act against it. Earlier, white Quakers had spoken and acted against slavery within their religious denomination. By the 1770s they had organized the first antislavery societies. But, during the late eighteenth century, black and white abolitionists did not belong to the same organizations, and white abolitionists did not advocate equal rights for African Americans. Also, neither black nor white abolitionists during this period looked far beyond their own states (Harrold 2001: 20–1).

Richard S. Newman argues in *The Transformation of American Abolitionism* that a more racially integrated and more radical antislavery movement grew out of black opposition to the plan of the American Colonization Society (ACS) linking gradual emancipation with sending former slaves to the West African colony of Liberia. Newman provides the most thorough analysis yet of black influences on leading white abolitionist William Lloyd Garrison's decision to endorse immediate emancipation (Newman 2002: 86–130). The key point is that from the late 1820s onward American abolitionism was a biracial effort, albeit one beset by racial tensions. The movement peaked after 1831 when Garrison began publishing his weekly *Liberator* in Boston. It is the latter period, for which there are abundant sources, that has attracted the greatest attention from historians.

Aptheker, in his 1941 article "The Negro in the abolitionist movement," produced the first systematic study of black abolitionists. It took some time, however, for historians to appreciate the relationship of black abolitionists to the broader antislavery movement, their importance in it, and their interaction – intellectually, culturally, institutionally, and physically – with their white associates. The first book-length treatment appeared in 1969 with the publication of Benjamin Quarles's *Black Abolitionists*. Quarles portrays black abolitionists as a crucial part of a biracial effort. Since 1969 there have been two other comprehensive studies of black abolitionists. In *They Who Would Be Free*, Jane H. Pease and William H. Pease emphasize the differences between black and white abolitionists, particularly in regard to violent rhetoric, and judge the entire movement to be ineffective (Pease and Pease 1974: esp. 297–9). In *Building an Antislavery Wall* (1983), R. J. M. Blackett places black abolitionists in the context of antislavery in the Atlantic World. More recently, books by Harry Reed (1994) and by James Oliver Horton and Lois E. Horton (1997) establish black abolitionism as part of antebellum northern black community development. Patrick Rael's *Black Identity and Black Protest in the Antebellum North* provides a cultural setting for the phenomenon (2002).

Historians have also increasingly analyzed black abolitionists in terms of gender. Part of this effort involves explaining the role of black women in the movement. Shirley Yee's *Black Women Abolitionists* (1992) is the first book-length treatment of this subject. Julie Roy Jeffrey in her *The Great Silent Army of Abolitionism* (1998) examines the role of both the black and white women who labored in the movement's rank-and-file. At least as important as these books specifically on women is the increasing attention devoted to black antislavery women in general studies of abolitionism. The prominence that the Hortons give Maria W. Stewart, a briefly influential orator during the early 1830s, in their history of antebellum black northerners reflects this trend (Horton and Horton 1997: 174–6). Like their white counterparts, black women sometimes worked in male-dominated antislavery organizations. Generally they maintained separate and subordinate antislavery societies, which raised money for antislavery projects controlled by men. Nevertheless the women and their organizations were forces for women's rights as well as black rights (Yee 1992: 136–54).

Another aspect of gendered approaches to black abolitionism is appreciating how concepts of black masculinity informed the movement's culture, particularly regarding the advocacy and employment of violence. Historians often portray black male abolitionists as less influenced by feminine values than were white male abolitionists, especially those associated with the Garrisonian faction. Garrison and his white associates called on men to reject pride, ambition, and violence in favor of such feminine values as love, peace, gentleness, faith, and meekness. In contrast, black male abolitionists often appear to have been more traditionally masculine as they sought to counteract common perceptions that they were passive and weak. Pease and Pease, among others, contend that they led in using force and in advocating slave revolt (Pease and Pease 1974: 137–8; Horton and Horton 1993: 127–54). But the contrast between black and white abolitionist men on this point may be too sharply drawn. There were black abolitionist men, such as Frederick Douglass, who endorsed feminized Garrisonian values and clung to nonviolence through most of the 1840s. Conversely, leading nongarrisonian white male abolitionists endorsed violent means during the 1830s (Mabee 1970: 38–50). Nearly all abolitionists, both black and white, recognized the right of slaves to revolt and escape (Harrold 1995: 45–63). Some black male abolitionists were sympathetic to feminism, others were not (Yee 1992: 139).

Historians used to present the northern antislavery movement as an essentially white undertaking, in which some black men and women participated. There are several reasons for this. White people predominated in the leadership, as well as the rank-in-file of the largest and best-known abolitionist organizations – the American Anti-Slavery Society (AASS), the American and Foreign Anti-Slavery Society (AFASS), the Liberty Party, and the American Missionary Association (AMA). This was even more the case in antislavery mass political parties of the late 1840s and 1850s – the Free Soil Party and the Republican Party. Also, sources for formal white abolitionists' activities are far more abundant and accessible than those for formal black abolitionists' activities. In some instances, white abolitionists refused to work with black abolitionists in the same organizations, and black abolitionists charged that they were denied leadership roles in other predominantly white abolitionist organizations. During the 1960s, 1970s, and early 1980s, historians such as Leon F. Litwack (1965: 137–55), Pease and Pease (1974: 68–93), and Lawrence J. Friedman (1982: 160–95) established that white abolitionists fell short of embracing racial equality and patronized their black colleagues.

Since the late 1980s, historians have more often emphasized how, despite white prejudices, black and white abolitionists interacted positively and how black abolitionists helped shape the antislavery movement. Benjamin Quarles in 1969 portrayed abolitionism as a biracial movement. So did Carlton Mabee (Mabee 1970: esp. 91–111). But it was during the 1990s that historians began to stress interracial cooperation as the movement's hallmark. Dillon showed that by the early 1840s both black and white abolitionists had begun to regard themselves as allies of the slaves (Dillon 1990: 201–23). Aptheker in *Anti-Racism in U.S. History* emphasized the ability of white abolitionists to overcome their racism, at least to a degree (Aptheker 1992: 129–46). Paul Goodman, while concentrating on the views of white abolitionists, contended that a belief in human equality was at the core of the movement (Goodman 1998). Donald M. Jacobs described cooperation among black and white abolitionists in Boston (Jacobs 1993: 1–20). Clara Merrit DeBoer showed how black abolitionists exercised a major role in the AMA (DeBoer 1994: xii, 87). John R. McKivigan explored the interracial friendship between Frederick Douglass and white abolitionist leader Gerrit Smith (McKivigan 1990: 205–37). John Stauffer has gone on to analyze a wider interracial friendship that linked white abolitionists Smith and John Brown with black abolitionists Douglass and James McCune Smith. Although Stauffer believes that Smith's interracialism was shallow, he emphasizes the hope shared by black and white abolitionists that racial differences were surmountable (Stauffer 2002).

On the basis of this interest in antislavery biracialism, it seems that the best way to understand the role of black abolitionists is through an interactive narrative spanning the years from the late 1820s through the Civil War into Reconstruction. Since the 1960s, general histories of the antislavery movement have increasingly included African Americans. They contend that black abolitionists in Baltimore, black opposition to the ACS, and David Walker's *Appeal* all influenced Garrison's brand of immediatism. Wealthy black abolitionist James Forten and many poorer African Americans supported Garrison's *Liberator*. Black abolitionist energies, which since 1830 had been channeled into the Black National Convention movement, were by 1833 redirected into Garrison's AASS. Biographies of major northern black abolitionists assist in situating them within a broader antislavery narrative. Among the better are Nell Irvin Painter's biography of Sojourner Truth (1996), Hinks's of David Walker (1997), William S. McFeely's of Frederick Douglass (1991), Julie Winch's of James Forten (2002), William F. Cheek and Aimee Cheek's of John Mercer Langston (1989), Jane Rhodes' of Mary Ann Shadd Cary (1998), and Waldo E. Martin's intellectual biography of Douglass (1984).

When the AASS split in 1840 over such issues as political action, women's rights, the role of churches, and Garrison's social radicalism, most black abolitionists joined most white abolitionists in leaving the "old organization." Although some black abolitionists – such as Douglass, Robert Purvis, and Henry Remond – remained loyal to the AASS, there were others, as historians have pointed out (Litwack 1965:

140; Pease and Pease 1974: 74), who criticized its Garrisonian leaders for deemphasizing the slavery issue in favor of women's rights and antisabbatarianism. Many black abolitionists also objected to condescending attitudes among white abolitionists and to a Garrisonian tendency toward abstraction.

After leaving the AASS, many black leaders – especially clergy – joined the new church-oriented AFASS, organized by wealthy white abolitionist Lewis Tappan of New York City. According to Pease and Pease (1974: 79–82) and DeBoer (1994: 87), the AFASS and the related AMA included more black men as leaders than did the AASS. Some black abolitionists also joined the Liberty Party, founded in 1840 (Sewell 1976: 100–1; Schor 1977: 28–46; Hunter 1993: 180–9). They were especially active in the party's radical New York wing led by Gerrit Smith. But the breakup of the AASS also contributed to a resurgence of black abolitionist autonomy. Although dated and superficial, Howard Holman Bell's *A Survey of the Negro Convention Movement* (1969) provides the best existing account of how these conventions served as forums for black abolitionist opinion during the 1840s and 1850s. In addition, black men usually led in the creation of vigilance associations designed to protect fugitive slaves from recapture and northern free African Americans from kidnapping into slavery (Wilson 1995: 103–20). By the late 1840s black abolitionists, such as Henry Highland Garnet and Martin R. Delany, had revived a black-nationalist agenda focused on migration to Africa as an antislavery measure (Miller 1975: 170–231; Robert S. Levine 1997).

During the late 1840s, issues of black manhood and frustration with peaceful tactics led most black abolitionists to believe that slave revolt might be needed to end slavery (Pease and Pease 1974: 233–50). They, like many of their white colleagues, began to put more faith in action than in rhetoric. As the war against Mexico raised the issue of slavery expansion into the southwest and the northern Free Soil Party organized in opposition, Douglass and several other black abolitionists supported the new party. While they criticized its failure to oppose slavery in the South and objected to the racism of many of its white leaders, Douglass and the others regarded the Free Soil Party to be a step in the right direction. They reacted similarly when, following the passage of the Kansas-Nebraska Act in 1854, the more powerful Republican Party organized (Sewell 1976: 160, 246–7, 336–9). But, from the 1840s onward, black abolitionists' most notable activities involved underground railroading and physical opposition to the fugitive slave laws.

Understandings of underground-railroad escape networks have fluctuated over the past fifty years. From the 1890s through the 1950s, Wilbur H. Siebert's interpretation, most thoroughly articulated in *The Underground Railroad from Slavery to Freedom* (1898), which is based on the reminiscences of white abolitionists, held sway. Siebert includes accounts of black underground railroad agents, but he sometimes portrays escapees as passive beneficiaries of white operatives, who sheltered them and led them northward. Siebert also regards underground-railroad networks as having been secret, well organized, and stable. In 1961 Larry Gara offered an influential corrective to this interpretation by contending that most slaves who escaped did so on their own, that aid they received in the North came mainly from African Americans, and that well-organized escape networks were largely mythical. Unfortunately Gara went too far in minimizing both the involvement of white abolitionists in slave escapes and the degree of organization involved. As popular and scholarly interest in underground-railroad networks increased during the 1990s, there emerged a more balanced view of them as relatively well organized biracial efforts.

David Cecelski (1994) and Kathryn Grover (2001) demonstrate that, from the late eighteenth century into the Civil War years, slaves had organized assistance in northward escapes via coastal Atlantic shipping routes. Grover shows that, while black abolitionists provided most of the aid to escapees who reached the port city of New Bedford, Massachusetts, fugitives often received help from white abolitionists as well. Stuart Seely Sprague's edition of black underground-railroad conductor John P. Parker's memoir demonstrates that interracial cooperation marked assisted slave escapes across the Ohio River from Kentucky to Ohio (Parker 1996). It is also clear that assisted slave escapes in Washington, DC, and its vicinity involved northern white abolitionists cooperating with local African Americans (Harrold 2003). Contrary to Gara, mounting evidence indicates that there were preestablished escape routes from the South to the North and Canada, that black and white abolitionists cooperated in helping escapees on their way, and that there was a great deal of secrecy. In her 1999 book, Jacqueline Tobin describes how slaves and free African Americans used designs on quilts to guide fugitives.

Underground railroading and forceful resistance to the fugitive slave laws were related activities. Slaves and free African Americans, North and South, frequently contested enforcement of the Fugitive Slave Law of 1793. Resistance became more frequent and better publicized following the passage of the harsher Fugitive Slave Law of 1850, as white abolitionists joined African Americans in seeking to prevent masters and federal marshals from capturing alleged fugitives. In some cases, opponents of the law rescued individuals who had been captured. Stanley W. Campbell provides a general account of the resistance (Campbell 1968: 148–69). Among the better histories of specific confrontations are Thomas Slaughter's account of the fatal battle between black abolitionists and Virginia masters at Christiana, Pennsylvania in 1851 (Slaughter 1991), Albert J. Von Frank's of the 1854 Anthony Burns rescue attempt in Boston (Von Frank 1998), and Nat Brandt's of the Oberlin-Wellington rescue of 1858 (Brandt 1990).

Continued slave escapes, abolitionist aid to the escapees, southern white fear of abolitionist-inspired slave revolt, and resistance to the Fugitive Slave Act of 1850 all contributed to the inflamed climate of opinion that led to Civil War in April 1861. A few black abolitionists had joined John Brown's tiny biracial band in briefly capturing the federal arsenal at Harpers Ferry, Virginia in October 1859. When war between the North and South broke out less than two years later, slave resistance and black abolitionism continued to play influential roles. Douglass and other black abolitionists led in insisting that the Union enlist black troops and make emancipation a war aim. By late 1863 the Abraham Lincoln administration had adopted both of these policies. Meanwhile, slaves escaped in massive numbers to Union lines, seeking freedom for themselves and weakening the Confederacy (Freehling 2001: xii–xiii, 115–39). Consequently, some historians argue that the Civil War amounted to a successful slave rebellion. Others, while agreeing that African Americans were instrumental in achieving freedom for themselves, give most of the credit to Lincoln's leadership and the Union armies. As aging black abolitionists realized, however, whoever was responsible for the victory, the freedom that had been won was limited and precarious.

It seems likely that historians will continue to broaden the perspective in which they understand and evaluate the character and significance of slave rebels and black abolitionists. Placing both groups in the context of the Atlantic World's Age of Revolution has already led to significant changes in interpretation. There will be others as relationships between events in the Americas, Africa, and Europe are better understood. Gender studies, literary analysis, demographics, studies of memory, and popular interest in the underground railroad will all produce new vantage points from which to understand those African Americans who resisted and opposed slavery, their friends and enemies, and the meaning of their efforts.

NOTE

I thank Merton L. Dillon, Douglas R. Egerton, and William C. Hine for their helpful suggestions concerning this chapter.

BIBLIOGRAPHY

Works Cited

Abzug, Robert H. (1970) "The influence of Garrisonian abolitionists' fear of slave violence on the antislavery argument," *Journal of Negro History* 55: 15–28.
Aptheker, Herbert (1939) "Maroons within the present limits of the United States," *Journal of Negro History* 24: 167–84.
—— (1941) "The Negro in the abolitionist movement," *Science and Society* 5: 2–23.
—— ([1943] 1974) *American Negro Slave Revolts*. New York: International.
—— (1989) *Abolitionism: A Revolutionary Movement*. Boston: Twayne.
—— (1992) *Anti-Racism in U.S. History: The First Hundred Years*. New York: Greenwood.
Ashworth, John (1995) *Slavery, Capitalism, and Politics in the Antebellum Republic*. New York: Cambridge University Press.
Bauer, Raymond A. and Bauer, Alice H. (1942) "Day to day resistance to slavery," *Journal of Negro History* 27: 388–419.
Bell, Howard Holman (1969) *A Survey of the Negro Convention Movement, 1830–1861*. New York: Arno.
Blackett, R. J. M. (1983) *Building an Antislavery Wall: Black Americans in the Atlantic Abolitionist Movement, 1830–1860*. Baton Rouge: Louisiana State University Press.
Blassingame, John W. (1979) *The Slave Community: Plantation Life in the Antebellum South*, 2nd edn. New York: Oxford University Press.
Brandt, Nat (1990) *The Town that Started the Civil War*. Syracuse, NY: Syracuse University Press.
Campbell, Stanley W. (1968) *Slave Catchers: Enforcement of the Fugitive Slave Law, 1850–1860*. Chapel Hill: University of North Carolina Press.
Carroll, Joseph C. ([1938] 1968) *Slave Insurrections in the United States*. New York: Negro Universities Press.
Cecelski, David S. (1994) "The shores of freedom: the maritime underground railroad in North Carolina, 1800–1861," *North Carolina Historical Review* 71: 174–206.
Cheek, William F., and Cheek, Aimee (1989) *John Mercer Langston and the Fight for Black Freedom, 1829–65*. Urbana: University of Illinois Press.

Davis, Thomas J. (1985) *A Rumor of Revolt: The "Great Negro Plot" in Colonial New York*. New York: Free Press.

DeBoer, Clara Merritt (1994) *Be Jubilant My Feet: African-American Abolitionists in the American Missionary Association, 1839–1861*. New York: Garland.

Dillon, Merton L. (1990) *Slavery Attacked: Southern Slaves and Their Allies, 1619–1865*. Baton Rouge: Louisiana State University Press.

Dorman, James H. (1977) "The persistent specter: slave rebellion in territorial Louisiana," *Louisiana History* 18: 389–404.

Egerton, Douglas R. (1993) *Gabriel's Rebellion: The Virginia Slave Conspiracies of 1800 and 1802*. Chapel Hill: University of North Carolina Press.

—— (1999a) *He Shall Go Out Free: The Lives of Denmark Vesey*. Madison, Wisc: Madison House.

—— (1999b) "The Scenes which are acted in St. Domingo: the legacy of revolutionary violence in early national Virginia" in John R. McKivigan and Stanley Harrold (eds.), *Antislavery Violence: Sectional, Racial, and Cultural Conflict in Antebellum America*, 41–64. Knoxville: University of Tennessee Press.

—— (2002) "Forgetting Denmark Vesey; or, Oliver Stone meets Richard Wade," *William and Mary Quarterly* 59: 143–52.

Elkins, Stanley M. ([1959] 1976) *Slavery: A Problem in American Institutional and Intellectual Life*, 3rd edn. Chicago: University of Chicago Press.

Fox-Genovese, Elizabeth (1986) "Strategies and forms of resistance: focus on slave women in the U.S." in Gary Y. Okihiro (ed.), *In Resistance: Studies in African, Caribbean, and Afro-American History*, 143–65. Amherst: University of Massachusetts Press.

Franklin, John Hope and Schweninger, Loren (1999) *Runaway Slaves: Rebels on the Plantation*. New York: Oxford University Press.

Freehling, William W. (1966) *Prelude to the Civil War: The Nullification Controversy in South Carolina, 1816–1836*. New York: Harper & Row.

—— (1990) *The Road to Disunion: Secessionists at Bay, 1776–1854*. New York: Oxford University Press.

—— (1994) *The Reintegration of American History: Slavery and the Civil War*. New York: Oxford University Press.

—— (2001) *The South vs. the South: How Anti-Confederate Southerners Shaped the Course of the Civil War*. New York: Oxford University Press.

Frey, Sylvia R. (1991) *Water from the Rock: Black Resistance in a Revolutionary Age*. Princeton, NJ: Princeton University Press.

Friedman, Lawrence J. (1982) *Gregarious Saints: Self and Community in American Abolitionism, 1830–1870*. New York: Cambridge University Press.

Gara, Larry (1961) *The Liberty Line: The Legend of the Underground Railroad*. Lexington: University of Kentucky Press.

Genovese, Eugene D. (1974) *Roll, Jordan, Roll: The World the Slaves Made*. New York: Vintage.

—— (1979) *From Rebellion to Revolution: Afro-American Slave Revolts in the Making of the Modern World*. Baton Rouge: Louisiana State University Press.

Goodman, Paul (1998) *Of One Blood: Abolitionism and the Origins of Racial Equality*. Berkeley: University of California Press.

Grover, Kathryn (2001) *The Fugitive's Gibraltar: Escaping Slaves and Abolitionism in New Bedford, Massachusetts*. Amherst: University of Massachusetts Press.

Gutman, Herbert (1976) *The Black Family in Slavery and Freedom, 1750–1925*. New York: Pantheon.

Harrold, Stanley (1995) *The Abolitionists and the South, 1831–1861*. Lexington: University Press of Kentucky.

—— (1999) "Romanticizing slave revolt: Madison Washington, the creole mutiny, and abolitionist celebration of violent means" in John R. McKivigan and Stanley Harrold (eds.),

Antislavery Violence: Sectional, Racial, and Cultural Conflict in Antebellum America, 89–107. Knoxville: University of Tennessee Press.

—— (2001) *American Abolitionists*. Harlow, England: Longman.

—— (2003) *Subversives: Antislavery Community in Washington, DC, 1828–1865*. Baton Rouge: Louisiana State University Press.

Hendrick, George and Hendrick, Willene (2003) *The Creole Mutiny: A Tale of Revolt Aboard a Slave Ship*. Chicago: Ivan R. Dee.

Herskovits, Melville J. (1941) *The Myth of the Negro Past*. Boston: Beacon.

Hine, Darlene Clark and Jenkins, Earnestine (eds.) (2001) *A Question of Manhood: A Reader in U.S. Black History and Masculinity*. Bloomington: Indiana University Press.

Hine, Darlene Clark and Wittenstein, Kate (1981) "Female slave resistance: the economics of sex" in Filomina Chloma Steady (ed.), *The Black Woman Cross-Culturally*, 289–99. Cambridge, MA: Schenkman.

Hinks, Peter P. (1997) *To Awaken My Afflicted Brethren: David Walker and the Problem of Antebellum Slave Resistance*. University Park: Pennsylvania State University Press.

Hodges, Graham Russell (1999) *Root and Branch: African Americans in New York and East Jersey, 1673–1863*. Chapel Hill: University of North Carolina Press.

Hoffer, Peter Charles (2003) *The Great New York Conspiracy of 1741: Slavery, Crime, and Colonial Law*. Lawrence: University Press of Kansas.

Horton, James Oliver, and Horton, Lois E. (1993) "The affirmation of manhood: black Garrisonians in antebellum Boston" in Donald M. Jacobs (ed.), *Courage and Conscience: Black and White Abolitionists in Boston*, 127–54. Bloomington: Indiana University Press.

—— (1997) *In Hope of Liberty: Culture, Community, and Protest among Northern Free Blacks, 1700–1860*. New York: Oxford University Press.

Hudson, J. Blaine (2002) *Fugitive Slaves and the Underground Railroad in the Kentucky Borderland*. Jefferson, NC: McFarland.

Hunt, Alfred N. (1987) *Haiti's Influence on Antebellum America: Slumbering Volcano in the Caribbean*. Baton Rouge: Louisiana State University Press.

Hunter, Carol M. (1993) *To Set the Captive Free: Reverend Jermain Wesley Loguen and the Struggle for Freedom in Central New York, 1835–1872*. New York: Garland.

Huston, James L. (1990) "The experiential basis of the northern antislavery impulse," *Journal of Southern History* 56: 192–215.

Jacobs, Donald M. (1993) "David Walker and William Lloyd Garrison: racial cooperation in the shaping of Boston abolition" in Donald M. Jacobs (ed.), *Courage and Conscience: Black and White Abolitionists in Boston*. Bloomington: Indiana University Press, 1–20.

Jeffrey, Julie Roy (1998) *The Great Silent Army of Abolitionism: Ordinary Women in the Antislavery Movement*. Chapel Hill: University of North Carolina Press.

Johnson, Michael P. (2001) "Denmark Vesey and his co-conspirators," *William and Mary Quarterly* 58: 915–76.

Jones, Howard (1975) "The peculiar institution and national honor: the case of the *Creole* slave revolt," *Civil War History* 21: 33–4.

—— (1986) *Mutiny on the Amistad: The Saga of a Slave Revolt and Its Impact on American Abolition, Law, and Diplomacy*. New York: Oxford University Press.

Jones, Norrece T., Jr (1989) *Born a Child of Freedom, Yet a Slave: Mechanisms of Control and Strategies of Resistance in Antebellum South Carolina*. Middleton, CT: Wesleyan University Press.

Jordan, Winthrop D. (1968) *White over Black: American Attitudes toward the Negro, 1550–1812*. Chapel Hill: University of North Carolina Press.

Kaplan, Sidney (1976) "The 'domestic insurrections' of the Declaration of Independence," *Journal of Negro History* 61: 243–55.

Kleinman, Max L. (1974) "The Denmark Vesey conspiracy: an historiographical study," *Negro History Bulletin* 37: 225–9.

Lerner, Gerda (1972) "The struggle for survival – day to day resistance" in G. Lerner (ed.), *Black Women in White America: A Documentary History*. New York: Pantheon.

Levine, Lawrence W. (1977) *Black Culture and Black Consciousness: Afro-American Folk Thought from Slavery to Freedom*. New York: Oxford University Press.

Levine, Robert S. (1997) *Martin Delany, Frederick Douglass, and the Politics of Representative Identity*. Chapel Hill: University of North Carolina Press.

Link, William A. (2003) *Roots of Secession: Slavery and Politics in Virginia*. Chapel Hill: University of North Carolina Press.

Litwack, Leon F. (1965) "The emancipation of the Negro abolitionist" in Martin B. Duberman (ed.), *The Antislavery Vanguard: New Essays on the Abolitionists*. Princeton, NJ: Princeton University Press, 137–55.

Lofton, John (1964) *Insurrection in South Carolina: The Turbulent World of Denmark Vesey*. Yellow Springs, OH: Antioch Press.

Mabee, Carlton (1970) *Black Freedom: The Nonviolent Abolitionists from 1830 through the Civil War*. London: Macmillan.

McFeely, William S. (1991) *Frederick Douglass*. New York: Simon & Schuster.

McKivigan, John R. (1990) "The Frederick Douglass–Gerrit Smith friendship and political abolitionism in the 1850s" in Eric J. Sundquist (ed.), *Frederick Douglass: New Literary and Historical Essays*. New York: Cambridge University Press, 205–37.

McLaurin, Melton A. (1991) *Celia, a Slave*. Athens: University of Georgia Press.

Martin, Waldo E., Jr (1984) *The Mind of Frederick Douglass*. Chapel Hill: University of North Carolina Press.

Miller, Floyd J. (1975) *The Search for Black Nationality: Black Colonization and Emigration, 1778–1862*. Urbana: University of Illinois Press.

Morgan, Phillip D. (1998) *Slave Counterpoint: Black Culture in the Eighteenth-Century Chesapeake and Lowcountry*. Chapel Hill: University of North Carolina Press.

Mullin, Gerald W. (1972) *Flight and Rebellion: Slave Resistance in Eighteenth-Century Virginia*. New York: Oxford University Press.

Mulroy, Kevin (1993) *Freedom on the Border: The Seminole Maroons in Florida: The Indian Territory – Coahuila and Texas*. Lubbock, TX: Texas Tech University Press.

Nash, Gary B. (1990) *Race and Revolution*. Madison, WN: Madison House Publishers Inc.

Newman, Richard S. (2002) *The Transformation of American Abolitionism: Fighting Slavery in the Early Republic*. Chapel Hill: University of North Carolina Press.

Oates, Stephen B. (1975) *The Fires of the Jubilee: Nat Turner's Fierce Rebellion*. New York: Harper & Row.

Painter, Nell Irvin (1996) *Sojourner Truth: A Life, A Symbol*. New York: Norton.

Parker, John P. (1996) *His Promised Land: The Autobiography of John P. Parker, Former Slave and Conductor on the Underground Railroad*, Stuart Seely Sprague (ed.). New York: Norton.

Pease, Jane H., and Pease, William H. (1972) "Ends, means, and attitudes: black–white conflict in the antislavery movement," *Civil War History* 18: 117–28.

—— (1974) *They Who Would Be Free: Blacks' Search for Freedom, 1830–1861*. New York: Athenaeum.

Phillips, Ulrich B. (1918) *American Negro Slavery: A Survey of the Supply, Employment, and Control of Negro Labor as Determined by the Plantation Regime*. New York: D. Appleton.

Quarles, Benjamin (1961) *The Negro in the American Revolution*. Chapel Hill: University of North Carolina Press.

—— ([1969] 1977) *Black Abolitionists*. New York: Oxford University Press.

Rael, Patrick (2002) *Black Identity and Black Protest in the Antebellum North*. Chapel Hill: University of North Carolina Press.

Reed, Harry (1994) *Platforms for Change: The Foundation of the Northern Free Black Community, 1776–1865*. East Lansing: Michigan State University Press.

Rhodes, Jane (1998) *Mary Ann Shadd Cary: The Black Press and Protest in the Nineteenth Century*. Bloomington: Indiana University Press.

Rodriguez, Junius (1999) "Rebellion on the river road: the ideology and influence of Louisiana's German Coast slave insurrection of 1811" in John R. McKivigan and Stanley Harrold (eds.), *Antislavery Violence: Sectional, Racial, and Cultural Conflict in Antebellum America*, 65–88. Knoxville: University of Tennessee Press.

Schor, Joel (1977) *Henry Highland Garnet: A Voice of Black Radicalism in the Nineteenth Century*. Westport, CT: Greenwood.

Scott, Kenneth (1961) "The slave insurrection in New York in 1712," *New York Historical Society Quarterly* 45: 43–74.

Sewell, Richard H. (1976) *Ballots for Freedom: Antislavery Politics in the United States, 1837–1860*. New York: Oxford University Press.

Shore, Lawrence (1986) "The poverty of tragedy in historical writings on southern slavery," *South Atlantic Quarterly* 85: 147–64.

Sidbury, James (1998) *Ploughshares into Swords: Race, Rebellion, and Identity in Gabriel's Virginia, 1730–1810*. New York: Cambridge University Press.

Siebert, Wilbur H. ([1898] 1968) *The Underground Railroad from Slavery to Freedom*, reprint. New York: Arno.

Slaughter, Thomas (1991) *Bloody Dawn: The Christiana Riot and Racial Violence in the Antebellum North*. New York: Oxford University Press.

Stampp, Kenneth M. ([1956] 1972) *The Peculiar Institution: Slavery in the Antebellum South*. New York: Knopf.

Stauffer, John (2002) *The Black Hearts of Men: Radical Abolitionists and the Transformation of Race*. Cambridge, MA: Harvard University Press.

Stuckey, Sterling (1966) "Remembering Denmark Vesey," *Negro Digest* 15: 28–41.

Szasz, Ferenc M. (1967) "The New York slave revolt of 1741: a re-examination," *New York History* 28: 215–30.

Tobin, Jacqueline (1999) *Hidden in Plain View: The Secret Story of Quilts and the Underground Railroad*. New York: Doubleday.

Von Frank, Albert J. (1998) *Trials of Anthony Burns: Freedom and Slavery in Emerson's Boston*. Cambridge, MA: Harvard University Press.

Wade, Richard C. (1964) "The Vesey plot: a reconsideration," *Journal of Southern History* 30: 143–61.

Wilson, Carol (1995) *Freedom at Risk: The Kidnapping of Free Blacks in America, 1780–1865*. Lexington: University Press of Kentucky.

Winch, Julie (2002) *A Gentleman of Color: The Life of James Forten*. New York: Oxford University Press.

Wish, Harvey (1937) "Slave insurrections before 1861," *Journal of Negro History* 22 (July): 299–320.

Wood, Peter H. (1974) *Black Majority: Negroes in Colonial South Carolina from 1670 through the Stono Rebellion*. New York: Knopf.

Wright, Donald R. (1993) *African Americans in the Early Republic, 1789–1831*. Arlington Heights, IL: Harlan Davidson.

Wyatt-Brown, Bertram (1988) "The mask of obedience: male slave psychology in the old South," *American Historical Review* 93: 1228–52.

Yarborough, Richard (1990) "Race, violence, and manhood: the masculine ideal in Frederick Douglass's 'The heroic slave,'" in Eric J. Sundquist (ed.), *Frederick Douglass: New Literary and Historical Essays*, 166–88. New York: Cambridge University Press.

Yee, Shirley J. (1992) *Black Women Abolitionists: A Study in Activism, 1828–1860*. Knoxville: University of Tennessee Press.

Suggestions for Further Reading

Berlin, Ira (1983) *Slavery and Freedom in the Age of the American Revolution*. Charlottesville: University Press of Virginia.

—— (2003) *Generations of Captivity: A History of African-American Slaves*. Cambridge, MA: Harvard University Press.

Brown, Richard Maxwell (1975) *Strain of Violence: Historical Studies of American Violence and Vigilantism*. New York: Oxford University Press.

Fox-Genovese, Elizabeth (1988) *Inside the Plantation Household: Black and White Women in the Old South*. Chapel Hill: University of North Carolina Press.

Kaplan, Sidney, and Kaplan, Emma Nogrady (1989) *The Black Presence in the Era of the American Revolution*. Amherst: University of Massachusetts Press.

Kilson, Marion (1964) "Towards freedom: an analysis of slave revolts in the United States," *Phylon* 25: 175–87.

Mullin, Michael (1992) *Africa in America: Slave Acculturization and Resistance in the American South and the British Caribbean, 1736–1831*. Urbana: University of Illinois Press.

Schwartz, Philip J. (2001) *Migrants against Slavery: Virginia and the Nation*. Charlottesville: University of Virginia Press.

Stewart, James Brewer (1997) *Holy Warriors: The Abolitionists and American Slavery*, revised edn. New York: Hill & Wang.

PART IV

Transculturation

PART IV

CHAPTER TWELVE

The Americanization of Africans and the Africanization of America

SAMUEL T. LIVINGSTON

The historic encounters between Africans, Native Americans, and Europeans have laid a cultural foundation in North America that has been the subject of much scholarship, yet the debt owed to African cultural agency remains unsettled. Understanding African cultural survivals and adaptations within the North American cultural milieu is a formidable task. Hundreds of books and articles have been written in the disciplines of anthropology, sociology, and history to characterize Africana Culture in North America. The obvious question is how should one organize a relatively brief chapter on the history of tri-directional cultural interchange and devote proper attention to disciplinary priorities within History and African American Studies.

Creating a periodization in the manner of Woodyard (1991), one could trace major developments in Africana Studies and their historic context in the following five periods:

1 pre-disciplinary accounts of the Africana cultural dialectic
2 early professional accounts of the Africana cultural dialectic
3 modernist accounts of the Africana cultural dialectic
4 postcolonial accounts of the Africana cultural dialectic
5 Afro-Atlantic accounts of the Africana cultural dialectic

Ostensibly, this periodization suggests order; however, the disciplines have not followed the same rate of change in each epistemic era. Therefore, the chosen path is to use the eras as a general order within a broad discussion of social-cultural and linguistic reciprocity. Central to histories of African diasporic culture have been the contributions of anthropologists and sociologists who have set the terms for the discussion of the Africanization of America and the Americanization of Africans.

The present discussion addresses how African-Americanists have characterized the reciprocal relationship between Africans and other cultures of North America during slavery. Fundamental to an understanding of this interaction are the concepts of culture and diaspora. African American Culture, considered broadly as a complete way of life including worldview, religion, music, dance, and art, has been subject to cross-currents from Africa, America, and Europe. African American Culture and social life, including institutions such as family, marriage, mutual aid societies and religious orders, have exerted an influence on America, while displaying variation due to the particular local political and socioeconomic conditions combined with a distinct mix of Africans in a given locale.

Joseph Harris (1993) posits the diaspora as a heuristic tool in Africana Studies that addresses three primary issues: first, the willed and unwilled dispersion of Africans throughout the globe; second, the development of a cultural identity rooted in notions of origin and social standing; and, third, the idea of return (psychologically and materially) to Africa. Harris' sense of diaspora captures traditional notions of forced dispersion and recent Africa-centered and Afro-Atlantic versions, which respectively have documented and analyzed various aspects of the return. African American Studies-based approaches and the traditional disciplines of anthropology, history, linguistics, and sociology have addressed the relationship between these three aspects of diaspora with special attention to the formation of an identity based on an African foundation and informed by Native and European cultural influences.

Before delving into the major focus of the chapter, we should consider Ivan Van Sertima's *They Came Before Columbus* (1976) as a point of departure for a historical context. His work – which pursues Weiner's thesis (1922), arguing the pre-Columbian African presence in the Americas – is significant because it questions traditionally held notions of chronology, cultural heritage, and epistemology. Epistemologically, the approach of Van Sertima (1976; 1992) draws from sources that characterize the interdisciplinary nature of Africana Studies: oral literature, archival research, botanical studies, and so on. The issue of ways of knowing is relevant to the epistemic tension within Africana Studies and its constituent disciplines. Just as Van Sertima's principal claims have been increasingly accepted, his epistemology has also seen increasing acceptance and validity within interdisciplinary studies. For example, Pollitzer's history of *The Gullah* (1999) is an example of what Keto (1995: 69) terms a "social science history" in its use of a varied epistemology.

Concerning the historical significance of Van Sertima's thesis, it remains to be verified whether pre-Columbian encounters between Africans and Native Americans were significant in creating a lasting historical and cultural legacy. While this contact may not have established a significant cultural base in North America, knowledge of African interaction with other Atlantic cultures contributes to our understanding of the historic context when African ethnics become racial Africans, who then become African Americans. Nonetheless, those attempting to assert a long view of the Africana cultural heritage and historical chronology in North America (Keto 1995) must examine the culture of the diaspora in light of the history subsequent to the transatlantic Slave Trade post-1526.

The roots of the people who would shape the Americas into their own image and simultaneously incorporate American (Native and European) cultural features into their collective way of life were in West Africa. Contrary to early histories of African Americans, which have discussed Jamestown, Virginia, in 1619 as the starting point (Franklin and Moss 1947; Bennett 1975; Quarles 1976), more recent histories have discussed the importance of enslaved Africans brought to the southeast in 1526 by Lucas Vasquez de Ayllon. Vasquez's expedition was one of six major Spanish *conquistas* to colonize the southern part of North America. These *conquistas* involved Africans to varying degrees. Vasquez's party, including one hundred Africans, settled in the Peedee Region of Chicora (South Carolina). The settlement was called San Miguel de Gualdape and was the site of the first slave revolt in North America (Huck and Moseley 1970: 5).

As early as Vasquez's Chicora expedition and increasingly in the seventeenth century, Africans in America encountered Native Americans in the southeast, thus initiating cultural interaction with the Five Civilized Tribes. May has characterized the relationship between Africans and Native Americans as varying from tolerance and acceptance among the Seminoles, to quasi-pariahs and strangers among the Creeks and Cherokees, through to marginalized outsiders amongst the Choctaws and Chickasaws (May 1996: 4–7). The marked increase in the number of enslaved African laborers during the eighteenth century among the Cherokees and Creeks encouraged a shift from matrilineality to patrilineality, as Native American women were displaced as agricultural workers by *ahutsi* (Cherokee for male {African} captives).

Littlefield has shown that the *estelusti* (Africans enslaved by Muskogees) and the Seminoles both developed their identity after the series of events leading to the Seminole War of 1812–18. African fugitives struck common cause with the outcast Muskogees (Creeks) and became prominent and indispensable members of Seminole society, as evidenced by African–Seminole interpreters and soldiers such as Juan and John Cowaya (Littlefield 1977: 7, 18). Halliburton confirms that, in the southeast, Native Americans adopted slave labor as an adaptation to European hegemony in the antebellum era (Halliburton 1977: ix, 11, 12). This cultural adaptation was facilitated by the existence of Native American social categories that defined persons without the benefit of the kinship system. Although some African captives of the Civilized Tribes were adopted into clans, the *atsi nahsa'i* social feature was applied in response to the demographic rise of Africans in the southeast, resulting in a form of slavery not as harsh as European enslavement of Africans, but nonetheless dehumanizing.

Linguistic Cross-Currents

The most obvious process of Americanization that enslaved Africans underwent was the adoption of English. Enslaved Africans transformed their languages, primarily those of Congo-Angola, the Bight of Biafra (Igbo/Kwa), and Senegambia into a creole of English known pejoratively as "baby talk," but Afrogenically as Gullah and Geechee. Newbell Puckett's (1926) work clearly demonstrated that formerly enslaved African Americans possessed a vast heritage that enriched the linguistic and cultural variety of America. The impact of Puckett's pioneering work is borne out in his massive study of *Black Names in America*. He documented 340,000 African American names from 1619 to the 1940s, tracing naming practices from their African origin and the Slavery Era to the cultural and social adjustments made in Segregation Era America (Puckett 1937 and 1975). This study is significant because it demonstrates how African American naming practices have direct origins in what Walker (2001) describes as an "Afrogenic" rationale – that is, African American naming practices developed out of traditions originating in Africa, but reconfigured to the demands of American slavery. These practices are accepted unquestioningly as a part of the American cultural heritage. Names of enslaved Africans included those expressing sound personal character or day names such as "Fortune," "Monday," "Cuffe," as well as famous, but latter-day, examples such as Thurgood Marshall, whose given name, "Thoroughly Good Marshall," was shortened to the form known to history.

Lorenzo Dow Turner advanced the Africanism thesis by conducting a comprehensive study of African American language patterns, particularly of linguistic Africanisms in the Sea Islands of South Carolina and Georgia. His research confirmed the thesis of his mentor, Melville Herskovits, by documenting almost 3,600 "basket names" that were in use amongst the descendants of enslaved Africans (Turner 1949: ch. 3). Many of these names are forms of West African names or words, although Turner did not claim a specific ethnic origin for these because of the inability of his subjects to recall an African linguistic origin. However, he did document the meanings of these words in the languages of the west coast of Africa. Turner's study also examined syntactical and morphological concurrences between Gullah and West African languages.

Subsequent studies have refined Turner's findings. Holloway and Vass (1997) found a vast Bantu heritage in American English among the Gullah, the American South in general, and in "black English." Their study found over 230 words in common American English usage that are African in origin. Mufwene (1993) argues that during the 1700s Gullah and Geechee underwent a gradual process of becoming a single language distinct from its dominant linguistic neighbors. This process of basilectalization was facilitated by the fact that the slave trade through ports such as Charleston, Georgetown SC, and Savannah constantly replenished the enslaved population with Africans before 1739 from Congo-Angolan ports and afterwards variously from Senegambian, Gold Coast, and increasingly from Sierra Leonian slave factories (Wood 1974; Gomez 1998).

The fact that linguistic studies have examined the language of the descendants of enslaved Africans suggests that the basilectalization or linguistic distinctiveness of enslaved Africans in some areas (South Carolina, Georgia, and Louisiana) was even greater during enslavement. Gullah, Geechee, and Louisiana Creole based informed America with words such banjo, gumbo, okra, okay, wow, and tote, as well as the lilt of English spoken in the Lowcountry of Georgia and South Carolina by African and European Americans.

The Cultural Dialectic

The present section discusses African American culture in terms of its worldview and philosophy, religion, music, dance, and art as discussed in the anthropological and sociological literature. In his introduction to *Darkwater*, W. E. B. Du Bois poignantly revealed the significance of the cultural heritage of enslaved Africans, noting that his great-great-grandmother was Bantu and evidently bequeathed an African song to the Burghardt clan. Du Bois' reminiscence is not simple emotionalism. It signals that the scholarly topic of African cultural retention represents a record of loss and dislocation that has reverberated through American social and cultural history. The present section examines how scholars have approached the cultural dialectic between the African American Diasporic community and their homeland

and host nation as informed by prevailing social movements and ideologies of the time.

In their own respective ways, David Walker, Martin Delaney, Anna J. Cooper, Edward W. Blyden, and W. E. B. Du Bois pioneered Africana cultural studies by suggesting the potential of African (American) culture as a redemptive tool for black people in their troubled condition from the nineteenth to the twentieth centuries. Walker's polemic stands out as the major critique of American slavery (Walker [1830] 1994). Delaney's *Condition* and Cooper's *A Voice from the South* both consciously set out to analyze the social costs of slavery for African Americans as racial and gendered beings. Less considered in the literature is Blyden's attempt to "describe the way [the African] has constructed for himself his portion of the world" in the wake of slavery (Blyden 1908: 10). In attempting to construct a normative model of African society and culture to be applied within the pan-African world, Blyden relied on first-hand observations of Africans in North America, the Caribbean, and in Africa, where, he argues, existed "the so-called Pagan African – the man untouched either by European or Asiatic influence" (Blydon 1908: 10). Blyden's views, through his influence on Garvey (Martin 1983: 8, 17) and the genealogy of cultural nationalism, presaged and influenced present-day Africa-centered activism and scholarship. Although Blyden was a member of the academy, his early work represents an extra-disciplinary attempt to analyze African American culture.

John Edward Philips (quoted in Holloway 1990: 225) asserts that disciplined examinations of the depth and dimension of African cultural influence in North America from the Frazier–Herskovits debate to today's Afrocentric–Afro-Atlantic discourse have taken two general approaches. The majority of these studies have identified specific cultural survivals retained by Africans and, increasingly, have observed the degree of influence of these survivals in American cultural life in general. Both of these scholarly thrusts suggest the historic importance of African cultural agency and, together, serve as signposts amongst scholarly approaches to Africana Culture in North America. Africana Studies scholars as diverse as Carter G. Woodson ([1936] 1968), Molefi Asante and Kariamu Welsh-Asante (1987), Paul Gilroy (1993), Vincent B. Thompson (2000), and Sheila Walker (2001), commonly direct our gaze to the importance of cultural agency as a heuristic tool for understanding the African diasporic process and acculturation in the Afro-Atlantic world.

Several challenging issues have handicapped studies of African diasporic culture from within academic disciplines. Lorenzo Turner suggests some of these challenges in his linguistic examination of Africanisms in Gullah speech (Turner 1949: 11). On the part of the descendants of enslaved African subjects, distrust of strangers, progressive acculturation, and the tendency to downplay divergence from the mainstream have hampered scholarly attempts to examine Africanisms. One legacy of slavery for African Americans (and the Gullah/Geechee) has been distrust of strangers, including researchers, that has developed in a prevailing sociopolitical climate that has been exploitative. Ironically, the removal of the Gullah off their lands from Waccamaw, South Carolina, to Daufuskie Island, Florida, has occurred while Gullah culture has been celebrated, researched, and viewed as an oddity by their usurpers (Pollitzer 1999: 3). As for researchers, their lack of linguistic familiarity, cultural sensitivity, and outright chauvinism have alienated more than one intended African subject. These obstacles are relevant to other disciplines as well.

Works by anthropologists – Newbell Puckett, Zora Neale Hurston, Melville and Frances Herskovits – as well as "lay-scholar" E. C. L. Adams have all shaped early understandings of African culture developed during slavery. After World War 1, Ulrich Phillips' historical interpretation of African American cultural life during slavery dominated the American intellectual scene. Phillips' studies asserted the cultural deficiencies of African Americans (Phillips 1918). Appealing to American racism, he declared that African Americans had no culture outside of that which imitated white culture. The African cultural legacy was, in a word, barbarism. However, anthropologists and folklorists of the time responded to Phillips' thesis by suggesting that, where sociopolitical conditions allowed, Africans in America resisted acculturation and developed their own culture based on African cultural retentions and influenced by European and Native American elements.

"Lay-folklorist" Edward C. L. Adams (1927) documented Africanisms in the Congaree region of the South Carolina midlands. This was the site of one of the largest Slavery-Era maroon communities in the southeast. His recording of stories passed down from the Slavery Era by an African American named Thaddeus Goodson (Tad), and references to other storytellers – Napoleon and a local cultural hero, Mensa – denote the persistence of African language, worldview, and way of life in the American South. Adams's volume demonstrated that the Gullah and Geechee coastal regions of South Carolina, Georgia, and Florida did not hold a monopoly on Africanisms. However, Adams' lack of knowledge of the African background hindered his analysis. For example, in recording an African American description of the afterlife in the popular midlands tale, "The Hopkins nigger," Adams misses the point that Tad is relating an Africanism – upon dying, the Hopkins man transforms into a bird (with wings, a beak, and claws) and not into an anthropomorphic angel as is suggested (Adams 1927: 2). Historian Sterling Stuckey in *Slave Culture* explores this specific Africanism (the importance of birds as metaphors for the soul), which has roots at least amongst the Igbo of Nigeria. Additionally, Adams' description of the cultural hero, Mensa – a man of tremendous vital force – ignores the fact that Mensa is an African name – Ewe and Twi for the third son (Adams 1927: 114; Turner 1949: 131). Of equal importance, "Mensa" also approximates the Mandinka term (Mansa) for king, which matches Adams' own description of Mensa's personality. The significance of these cultural survivals is in their usage as socializing tools within various African communities from maroon to slave.

The pioneering writer of the Harlem Renaissance, Zora Neale Hurston also contributed to our understanding of the cultural gifts bestowed upon America by enslaved Africans. Neither Puckett, Adams, nor Du Bois achieved Hurston's degree of groundedness in their culture of study. A closeness to her subject yielded insights that were groundbreaking at their time. Her book *The Sanctified Church*, compiled from her writings in the 1920s, 1930s and 1940s, typifies her pioneering efforts to document African American culture in a naturalistic manner. Using simple descriptive and narrative structures colored by Gullah and Geechee dialect, Hurston characterizes African American culture in terms of its herbal lore and herbalists, the "characteristics of Negro Expression," and the Africanized or "sanctified church." Much of her research is based on first-hand observations of cultural practices in their natural setting of southern black communities (Holloway 1990).

Her description of Shouting, which she describes as a "survival of African 'possession' by the gods" demonstrates her appreciation of African culture and the place and significance of Africanisms in the culture of the diaspora (Hurston 1983: 91). Her ability to pierce the veil of distrust of researchers, as she compiled African American folklore, provided an unobtrusive analysis, letting the stories speak for themselves. Hurston's work is of particular value because of her ability to avail herself of an emic perspective into her subject and her attempt to aggregate and analyze elements of African American cultural life. Whereas Adams collected folklore that was repeated out of context, Hurston gathered much of her data in their natural setting. Hurston attended black church services, Voodoo ceremonies, Hoodoo consultations, and hung out at Jook joints to get her information. She also contributes to our understanding of the Africana Oral Tradition (Hurston 1983: 50–3) in her description of rural expressive characteristics such as using concrete predicates, "nouns from verbs," or "verbal nouns," – objects vivified in African American communication. Hurston's analysis of black linguistic flourishes represents an early attempt to appreciate the canons of African American oral literature in an unpatronizing manner.

Hurston wrote from within the outpouring of black creativity in the 1920s and 1930s alongside bibliophile Arturo Schomburg, and scholars such as Alain Locke, Drusilla Dunjee Houston, and W. E. B. Du Bois, who shared the burden of unfettering the Africana cultural legacy from the racist scholarship of Phillips and others. Du Bois' *The Souls of Black Folk*, written between 1897 and 1903, is the most recognized consideration of African American cultural transformation subsequent to enslavement. Du Bois' essays also offered great insight into African American history and culture. Sociologists Robert Park (1919) and E. Franklin Frazier (1939) responded to celebrations of Africanity and Negritude during the New Negro Era, by arguing that enslavement had completely divested African Americans of social and cultural retentions from Africa. Their view, supported by Ulrich Phillips and others who claimed that African Americans were cultural "blank slates," downplayed the importance of Puckett and Hurston's early work and betrayed the perspective that Africanisms were an obstacle to progressive assimilation.

This was the dominant perspective until two studies published in 1940 and 1941 shook the foundations of the "catastrophe" model. It is interesting that a meltdown of the modern capitalist economy gave rise to America's greatest concerted effort at documenting Africana folk culture. The Savannah Unit of the Georgia Writers' Project, part of the Works Project Administration, employed scholars and artists during the Great Depression in an attempt to record African cultural survivals in the Georgia Sea Islands. The results were published in a volume entitled *Drums and Shadows*, a comprehensive documentary study of Africanisms. The folktales, historical recollections, lore, and photographs of African-inspired implements and artifacts document the cultural presence of Africa in these remote islands, which once housed at least one maroon community at Sapelo Island. The study is limited by its lack of analysis and interpretation and its frequent patriarchal tone toward its African American subjects. However, *Drums and Shadows* offers a rich source of data, which support at least 70 distinct African retentions in its appendix (Georgia Writers' Project 1940).

Against the backdrop of early twentieth-century scholarship which, like its historical contemporary, the Jim Crow system, negated African American cultural agency,

Melville Herskovits attempted to redress several myths of "the Negro past" (Herskovits 1941). His anthropological study (a review of previously published works), published under the title *The Myth of the Negro Past*, sought to create a scientific basis for what Gunnar Myrdal described as "the American dilemma" of racial division. Rejecting the Social Darwinism of his era, Herskovits (ibid: 1, 2) outlined several mythic traits proffered by Eurocentric historians to describe the African American as possessed of debilitating cultural and historical traits:

1   a childlike character, naturally accommodating to southern white paternalism;
2   evolutionary inferiority – African enslavement was the result of a form of socio-historical Darwinism – so that only inferior Africans were enslaved, while "the more intelligent raided (for slaves) having been clever enough to elude the slavers' nets";
3   a pattern of linguistic and cultural dispersion and wide variation, which militated against the creation of a common African-based culture in North America;
4   a sense of awe at the superiority of their enslaver's culture, which led them to abandon their "savage ways" in favor of the European's.

Consequently, the African American is without a past worth remembering. Herskovits refutes the racist opinions of the most often quoted scholars on the African American cultural heritage during the first half of the twentieth century – Tillinghast, Dowd, and Weatherford, who never studied amongst Africans and based their conclusions primarily on secondary sources and textbooks with little special knowledge of specific African cultures. Notably relevant to the second myth listed above, Herskovits confirms that there was no process that selected the inferior for enslavement by the superior (Herskovits 1941: 107).

   Further, *The Myth of the Negro Past* contradicted previously biased scholarship by citing the presence of a profound African cultural heritage amongst African Americans. He prosecuted his argument by identifying the "tribal origins" of African Americans in Western Africa along with a description of the cultural heritage of the ancestors of African Americans. He described the culture of West Africa as complex and dynamic. Interestingly, Herskovits' construction of the "African world view" as a pattern against which we may view ethnic variations presages the Afrocentric concept and its emphasis on the cultural unity of Africa (Herskovits 1941: 70). Contrary to the facile description of African religion as nothing but "fetishism," he characterizes its religious life and worldview as ancestor-oriented, conceptually centered around a supreme deity, concerned with fate, and in most cases flexible.

   After creating this cultural baseline, he observes the African's reaction to enslavement and details the acculturation process, which encouraged the valorization of Euro-American cultural traits and discouraged Afrogenic traits from entering into the American public sphere, except for a few segregated spaces. He then discusses the presence of Africanisms in American secular and religious life and observes the special contribution that Afrogenic culture has made regarding language and the arts. While a detailed discussion of his evidence is beyond the scope of this brief discussion, it may be summarized in two major categories – uninstitutionalized and institutionalized behaviors. Uninstitutionalized behaviors include motor habits such as walking, dancing, singing, sitting, and working; decorative behavior, such as hairdressing, head-dressing, and clothing styles; codes of good and bad manners, especially respect for the elders; concepts of time; and the "complex of indirection," especially in the company of cultural outsiders. Institutionalized practices include the creation of mutual aid societies, fraternal orders, burial societies, and other social edifices. Herskovits' observation that the presence of Africanisms in the United States must be considered a part of the continuum of Africanisms in the Americas augurs for the scholarly validity of the Afro-Atlantic World as a unified field of study.

In contrast to the assertions of Herskovits, sociologist E. Franklin Frazier gave voice to an assimilationist imperative – arguing that the African-European cultural dialectic represents the "second racial frontier" occasioned by the forced importation of enslaved Africans into the West (Frazier 1957: 13). For Frazier, the heuristic issue was assimilation – a standard by which African American Culture was to be evaluated. He pointed to the lack of social institutions, originating in Africa and surviving the trauma of slavery amongst African Americans as proof of progressive cultural assimilation. Africanisms were to be viewed as social aberrations – flawed social forms that have failed to keep apace with progressive integration. Frazier observed the black family as a dysfunctional version of the American nuclear family, instead of viewing it as an African institution transformed by centuries of slavery.

The Frazier–Herskovits debate was based in the distinct disciplines that each scholar pursued. Anthropologists, outfitted for the task of observing nuanced cultural expressions, such as Africanisms, noticed these retentions, particularly amongst less developed and assimilated African American populations. Herskovits' work is populated by cultural comparisons between the likes of Gullahs, Geechees, Surinamese, and Asantes. Whereas Herskovits saw Africanisms as evidence of black cultural adaptation, Frazier viewed them as relics of a past era bound for extinction. Interestingly enough, Frazier and Herskovits shared ideological space with K. Gunnar Myrdal's *American Dilemma*, in their common attempt to lend a scientific approach to an understanding of the African American situation.

Pollitzer – in a detailed and complex study that posits a vibrant African biological, cultural, social, and linguistic heritage of the Gullah people – credits Herskovits in his idea of an African cultural heritage (Pollitzer 1999). His study may shape future interpretations of African American cultural life in his solid documentation that such a cultural heritage has survived not only slavery, but also the rigors of social integration and acculturation.

Scholars in the postcolonial era have addressed Africana cultural adaptation in North America as a means of clarifying the race and class dialectic in North America. Interestingly enough, their ideological bent has raised questions (among the postmodernists) of diminished scholarly rigor. Jahn (1961), Genovese (1981), Levine (1983), and Stuckey (1987), among others, all share the impetus of the Civil Rights/anti-colonial era as epochal epistemic factors affecting their scholarship. Along with Aptheker and Gomez (1998), they have suggested that Africans in antebellum North America created a common society and culture rooted in resistance and self-preservation.

Drawing from Herskovits' retention thesis, Peter Wood (1974) pointed out that, in the seventeenth and eighteenth centuries, the Lowcountry of South Carolina developed an African material cultural hegemony. This was due to the numerical African majority in the region. From 1700 to 1740, the African population in South Carolina grew from just under 3,000 – half of the total population – to 39,155 or twice the number of whites. The African populace in the Lowcountry grew as the amount of rice grown increased (Pollitzer 1999: 88–9). Wood observed that Congo-Angolan Africans up to the Stono revolt of 1739 established a substratum of cultural retention and outright resistance to oppression.

African contributions to American agriculture were particularly apparent. The hoe was central to southern agriculture, and enslaved Africans held great reverence for the hoe's spiritual qualities (Georgia Writers' Project 1940: 137). The successful cultivation of rice in the Carolina and Georgia Lowcountry was the single most important factor in the commercial success of the area (Wood 1974: 35; Littlefield 1981: 114). Lowcountry rice plantations used precise techniques imported from Africa, as practiced by the Kissi, Mende, Serer, and Temni peoples of the Gambia River, Liberia, and Sierra Leone regions, along with fewer numbers of Bambara, Fula, Malinka, and Somanke from the Niger River area (Pollitzer 1999: 89). Other food products introduced from Africa during slavery were okra, benne (sesame) seeds, cowpeas, yams, Guinea corn (sorghum), and the peanut, which came originally from South America (Pollitzer 1998: 66). Also of great importance were Africans captured from the Gambia River region after 1670 who were noted for their open-grazing of cattle. These "cow boys" introduced this method over the objections of whites who favored enclosed pastures (Wood 1974: 30–2). These African techniques enriched southern culture and resulted in the great wealth of the southern United States.

Eugene Genovese (1981) discusses the progression of enslaved African uprisings from reactive isolated events to more expansive plots aimed at overturning the planter class. This progression, Genovese argued, placed African slave rebels abreast of the revolutionary movements of the transatlantic world. This is significant when one considers the historical materialist perspective that has placed great emphasis on the progressive nature of African American historical agency. Genovese's use of the Marxist paradigm is of particular interest since it placed slave revolts in national and international contexts. Prior to writing *From Rebellion to Revolution*, Genovese had directed his scholarly attention to how the perceptions, goals, and aspirations of the enslaved and the paternalistic enslaver combined to create a conflicted southern society – simultaneously dependent upon black subservience and, paradoxically, limited autonomy. The most important conclusion of Genovese's work is that enslaved Africans' freedom of movement and, perhaps, cultural autonomy were indispensable in the everyday functioning of antebellum southern society (Genovese 1974: bk 3, pt 2).

Unfortunately, the Americanization of Africans involved what Charsee McIntyre referred to as the criminalization of an entire race. McIntyre's paradigm reflects the race-first analysis of Africa-centered scholarship. Her study suggests that whites consciously chose to enslave Africans in a society based ideologically on racism – that is, on white supremacy and African oppression. After failing to establish the majority of free blacks in colonies in Africa or any other location, African Americans were described by the Moral Reform Movement as degenerates requiring imprisonment. Additionally, by 1865, all but five states reserved political rights to white men only, a pattern that extended through other indicators of social and political power (McIntyre 1993 [1984]: 82).

In his book *Slave Culture*, Sterling Stuckey demonstrated that, after the Middle Passage, African Culture was a significant means of forming identity and unity among enslaved Africans. Stuckey maintained that the culture developed by enslaved Africans was at once a unifying factor, a reminder of African identity and an informing source for critiques of whites and enslavement (1987). Stuckey further posited that:

> The final gift of African "tribalism" in the nineteenth century was its life as a lingering memory in the minds of American slaves. That memory enabled them to go back to the sense of community in the traditional African setting and to include all Africans in their common experience of oppression in North America . . . African ethnicity [. . .] was in this way the principal avenue to Black unity in antebellum America. (Stuckey 1987: 3)

Essential to the formation of this culture was the experience of the Middle Passage and indigenous African philosophy and spirituality as communicated through storytelling, songs, fables, and poems. These cultural forms affirmed an African-based cultural identity and drew from African culture as a conduit of values and priorities. Wherever the Diaspora was created, African descendants used their culture and art to preserve their identity and enhance their life chances.

Joseph Holloway's edited work *Africanisms in American Culture* discusses the African influence on America in terms of language, music, religion, and folk culture in general (Holloway 1990). Maultsby's chapter is particularly interesting: its "genealogy" of black music represents a virtual history of American popular music from Rhythm and Blues to Rock and Roll and of course, Hip-Hop. Phillips concludes the book with his interesting synthesis of the anthropological study of "traditional" cultures and the sociological study of modern societies. He suggests that white America needs to be studied anthropologically to yield information about cultural influences on America and reversal of the reification of European culture. Maultsby and Phillips taken together suggest that American popular culture largely is an African culture. In this area, the weight (near-hegemony) of African cultural influence on musical traditions stands clear. The appropriation of the banjo during the enslavement in particular is evidence of this influence (Holloway 1990: 229).

Afrocentric scholars, in the attempt to continue the cultural reevaluations of the 1960s and 1970s, have taken the position that African Americans should be studied as Africans in America with little distinction between Diasporic populations. Africa-centered cultural-anthropologist Marimba Ani (1980) has described cultural survivals afrogenically as *kuzinduka* (Kiswahili for "reawakening"), though the existence of Kiswahili as a "genetic" linguistic heritage of African Americans is doubtful. Richards (in Welsh-Asante 1994) and black psychologists such as Linda James Myers (1993), Kobi Kambon (*née* J. Baldwin) and Daudi Azibo (both in Burlew 1992) posit that cultural change since the sixteenth century has occurred in the realm of superficial cultural practices. These scholars adopt a structuralist approach by discussing culture as existing in three concentric layers: surface, intermediate, and deep structures of one organic whole. While the approach is logically plausible, more research bearing out the Africanity of these structures needs to be conducted. Ironically, many

Afrocentrists have avoided the slavery era, which could demonstrate the greatest period of African cultural continuity in African American history.

Melville Herskovits presaged the Afro-Atlantic school by suggesting that the culture of African Americans in the United States should be compared with less rigorous acculturation schemes in the Caribbean and Central and South America (Herskovits 1941: 7, 110). Mintz and Price (1976) attempted to direct studies of Black culture away from a perceived ideological polarization by suggesting an anthropological approach to the study of African American cultural history. In the 1992 reprint, the authors respond to some of their colleagues' negative reactions to their assertion that cultural retentions were not pervasive amongst African Americans. They argue that enslaved Africans did not import institutions into America, but had to create their own institutions in America. This claim, coupled with the assertion that enslaved Africans did not share a common culture in North America, in the way that European colonists did, has been the basis of negative reactions to their thesis (Mintz and Price 1992: 2). Mintz and Price see fallacies in the "Encounter Model" suggested by "historically minded Afro-Americanists" in two areas that would give rise to the possibility of cultural transfers into North America. First, the authors question whether a West African cultural heritage existed at all. Secondly, citing Haiti's population as an example of cultural heterogeneity, Mintz and Price (ibid: 8–9, 15–16) raise doubts about the "cultural homogeneity" of enslaved African populations as suggested by authors such as Herskovits (1941), Harrison (1972), and Stuckey (1987). Their distinction between social and cultural subjects provides a helpful explanation of divergent sociological and anthropological findings (Mintz and Price 1992: 19–22).

Michael Gomez's meta-analysis of previous transatlantic Slave Trade studies offers a fresh look at primary documents, such as slave narratives and fugitive slave advertisements (Gomez 1998). He contends that the majority of enslaved Africans in North America came directly from Africa, the remainder being resold from the Caribbean (ibid: 29). Directly contradicting the Catastrophe School (Mintz and Price, Frazier, et al.), he suggests that in the eighteenth and nineteenth centuries, North America was populated by Africans from the following regions: West Central Africa 26.1 percent; Bight of Biafra 24.4 percent; Sierra Leone 15.8 percent; Senegambia 14.5 percent; Gold Coast 13.1 percent; Bight of Benin 4.3 percent; Mozambique-Madagascar or unknown 1.8 percent (Gomez 1998: 29). Gomez also suggests that a common identity developed from these African ethnic enclaves, in three major regions of the colonial and antebellum North America.

The Virginia–Maryland region was "the preserve of the Igbo" from the Bight of Biafra and Calabar, with significantly fewer Akans, Senegambians, and Congo-Angolans. The Louisiana territory during their Spanish and French colonization saw early numbers of Africans from Senegambia (Mande-, Bamana-, Wolof-, and Jola-speakers) and the Bight of Benin (Fon-, Ewe-, and Yoruba-speakers). From 1780 to 1820, a large number of enslaved Congo-Angolans were imported leading to their numerical majority amongst Africans in the territory. In order of importance, Congo-Angolan, Sierra Leonean, Akan, and Senegambian Africans populated the Lowcountry of South Carolina and Georgia. The Congo-Angolan base from the late seventeenth to the early eighteenth centuries proved an unmanageable mix as the Bantu-speakers struck out in revolt in 1739 at Stono near Charleston, South Carolina (Gomez 1998: 151; Wood 1974: 308–17). The goal of achieving a more ethnically heterogeneous slave labor force led to the increased numbers of Senegambians and, particularly Sierra Leonean Africans, after the Stono revolt of 1739 until the end of the antebellum period. The social conditions, culture, and resistance in these three African American "cultural cradles" provided the matrices of African American identity. Additionally, resistance in these areas encouraged the militarization of the South as discussed in Franklin (1956). This tradition is evident in the military schools of the South such as the Citadel and Virginia Military Institute. Enslaved Africans from these three cultural cradles forged a common African American culture under the duress of slavery and hostile treatment in the North.

Afro-Atlantic scholars such as Robert Farris Thompson and Sheila Walker have refused to let national boundaries obfuscate their understandings of the Africana cultures of the Americas. Thompson (1983) construes Afro-American Culture in all of the societies of North, Central and South America, and the Caribbean, where African-descendants have populated. His study of Diasporic-African visual art documents are not only significant Africanisms, but also the reinterpretation of the cultural philosophies of Yoruba-, Kongo-, and Mande-related cultures in the Americas. Thompson's *Four Moments of the Sun* documents the influence of the Kongo civilization in the Americas. Of particular interest is Thompson's 1983 discussion of the Ejagham *nsibidi* script amongst the Afro-Cuban Ngbe religious order. The Ejagham were brought to the Americas from eastern Nigeria and western Cameroon, and with them a symbolic script system that explodes "the myth of Africa as a continent without a tradition of writing" (Thompson 1983: 227).

Similar to Mintz and Price, Paul Gilroy (1993) discusses trends of essentialism in reference to Black Culture and identity. His discussion classifies scholars of Afrogenic subjects as traditionalists and originalists. Gilroy questioned the essentialism of Afrocentric African Studies, and the validity of nationalist ideology. Gilroy's analysis may be relevant in dialogue with Stuckey (1987) and Thompson (2000), who both argue that African consciousness and nationalism are the foundations of African American and all African diasporic identities. Gilroy's contribution to Afro-Atlantic thought is his consideration of nationalism, which emerged as an ideology during enslavement, as an obstacle to racial harmony.

The African heritage of America is pervasive in such areas as language, agriculture, music, dance, speech, and social philosophy. The processes of Africanization and Americanization from the mid-sixteenth to the nineteenth century witnessed cultural, political, and economic encounters and consequent realignments that would alter the historic trajectories of not only Europe and Africa, but of North American history as well. Histories of the intercultural exchange, and of race- and classcharged encounters, in North America must revise their view of an imposed European culture that has dominated those of all others. As Genovese (1974) suggested, even during the enslavement era whites were dependent upon Africans not just for their labor, but also in creating a culture and social order. African American agency transcended the goal of creating the South's patriarchal society. Through the attempt to retain and build a culture, Africans in America bequeathed their most basic legacy of struggle.

BIBLIOGRAPHY

Works Cited

Adams, Edward C. L. (1927) *Congaree Sketches: Scenes from Negro Life in the Swamps of the Congaree and Tales by Tad and Scip of Heaven and Hell with Other Miscellany*. Chapel Hill: University of North Carolina Press.
Ani, Marimba (1980) *Let the Circle Be Unbroken: The Implications of African Spirituality in the Diaspora*. New York: Nkonimfo.
Asante, M. K. (1987) *The Afrocentric Idea*. Philadelphia: Temple University Press.
—— (1990) *Kemet, Afrocentricity and Knowledge*. Trenton, NJ: Africa World Press.
Bennett, Lerone (1975) *The Shaping of Black America*. Chicago: Johnson.
Blyden, E. W. ([1908] 1994) *African Life and Customs*. Baltimore: Black Classics Press.
Burlew, A. K. (ed.) (1992) *African American Psychology: Theory Research and Practice*. Newbury Park, CA: Sage.
Cruse, H. (1967) *The Crisis of the Negro Intellectual*. New York: Quill.
Dillard, J. L. (1972) *Black English: Its History and Usage in the United States*. New York: Vintage Books.
Du Bois, W. E. B. ([1903] 1997) *The Souls of Black Folk*. [Atlanta] Boston: Bedford Books.
—— ([1920] 1969) *Darkwater: Voices from within the Veil*. [New York] New York: Schocken Books.
Franklin, J. H. (1956) *The Militant South*. Boston: Beacon Press.
Franklin, J. H. and Moss, A. ([1947] 2000) *From Slavery to Freedom: A History of African Americans*, 8th edn. [New York: Alfred Knopf] Boston: McGraw-Hill.
Frazier, E. F. (1939) *The Negro Family in America*. Chicago: University of Chicago Press.
—— (1957) *Race and Culture Contacts in the Modern World*. Boston: Beacon Press.
Genovese, E. (1974) *Roll, Jordan, Roll: The World the Slaves Made*. New York: Vintage Books.
—— (1981) *From Rebellion to Revolution*. Baton Rouge: Louisiana State University.
Georgia Writers' Project, Savannah Unit (1940) *Drums and Shadows: Survival Studies among the Georgia Coastal Negroes*. Athens: University of Georgia Press.
Gilroy, Paul (1993) *The Black Atlantic*. Cambridge, MA: Harvard University Press.
Gomez, Michael A. (1998) *Exchanging Our Countrymarks*. Chapel Hill: University of North Carolina Press.
Halliburton, R., Jr (1977) *Red over Black: Black Slavery among the Cherokee Indians*. Wesport, CT: Greenwood Press.
Harris, Joseph E. (1993) *Global Dimensions of the African Diaspora*. Washington, DC: Howard University Press.
Harrison, Paul C. (1972) *The Drama of Nommo*. New York: Grove Press.
Herskovits, M. ([1941] 1958) *The Myth of the Negro Past*. [New York] Boston: Beacon Press.
Holloway, J. E. (ed.) (1990) *Africanisms in the American Culture*. Bloomington: Indiana University Press.
Holloway, J. E. and Vass, W. K. (1997) *The African Heritage of American English*. Bloomington: Indiana University Press.
Huck, E. R. and Moseley, E. H. (eds.) (1970) *Militarists, Merchants and Missionaries*. Tuscaloosa: University of Alabama Press.
Hurston, Zora Neale (1983) *The Sanctified Church*. Berkeley, CA: Turtle Island.
Jahn, Jahnheinz ([1961] 1990) *Muntu*. New York: Grove Weidenfeld.
Keto, C. T. (1995) *Vision, Identity and Time*. Dubuque, IA: Kendall Hunt.
Lewis, D. L. (ed.) (1995) *W. E. B. Du Bois: A Reader*. New York: Henry Holt.

Levine, L. (1987) *Black Culture and Black Consciousness: Afro-American from Slavery to Freedom*. London: Oxford University Press.

Littlefield, D. F. (1977) *Africans and Seminoles: From Removal to Emancipation*. Westport, CT: Greenwood Press.

Littlefield, D. C. (1981) *Rice and Slaves: Ethnicity and the Slave Trade in Colonial South Carolina*. Baton Rouge: Louisiana State University.

Locke, A. L. (ed.) ([1925] 1992) *The New Negro*. [Washington, DC] New York: Atheneum.

McGary, H. (1983) "Racial integration and racial separation: conceptual clarifications" in Leonard Harris (ed.), *Philosophy Born of Struggle*, 199–211. Dubuque, IA: Kendall/Hunt.

McIntyre, C. C. (1993) *Criminalizing a Race: Free Blacks during Slavery*. New York: Kayode.

Martin, T. (1983) *The Pan-African Connection*. Dover, MA: Majority Press.

May, K. (1996) *African Americans and Native Americans in the Creek and Cherokee Nations, 1830s to 1920s: Collision and Collusion*. New York and London: Garland.

Mintz, S. and Price, R. ([1976] 1992) *The Birth of African American Culture: An Anthropological Perspective*. Boston: Beacon Press.

Mufwene, Salikoko S. (ed.) (1993) *Africanisms in Afro-American Language Varieties*. Athens and London: University of Georgia Press.

Mullin, M. (1992) *Africa in America: Slave Acculturation and Resistance in the American South and the British Caribbean, 1736–1831*. Urbana and Chicago: University of Illinois Press.

Myers, L. J. (1993) *Understanding an Afrocentric Worldview*. Dubuque, IA: Kendall/Hunt.

Park, Robert E. (1919) "The conflict and fusion of cultures with special reference to the Negro," *Journal of Negro History* 4: 111–33.

—— (1950) *Race and Culture: Essays in the Sociology of Contemporary Man*. New York: Free Press.

Perdue, Theda (1979) *Slavery and the Evolution of Cherokee Society, 1540–1866*. Knoxville: University of Tennessee Press.

Phillips, U. B. ([1918] 1952) *American Negro Slavery*. New York: Peter Smith.

Pollitzer, W. S. (1998) "The relationship of the Gullah-speaking people of coastal South Carolina and Georgia to their African ancestors" in M. Goodwine (ed.), *The Legacy of Ibo Landing: Gullah Roots of African American Culture*. Atlanta: Clarity Press.

—— (1999) *The Gullah People and Their African Heritage*. Athens and London: University of Georgia Press.

Poplack, S. and Tagliamonte, S. (2001) *African American English in the Diaspora*. Malden, MA: Blackwell Publishers.

Puckett, N. N. (1926) *Folk Beliefs of the Southern Negro*. New York: Dover.

—— (1937) "Names of American Negro slaves" in G. P. Murdock (ed.), *Studies in the Science of Society*. New Haven, CT: Yale University Press.

—— (1975) *Black Names in America*, Murray Heller (ed.). Boston: G. K. Hall.

Quarles, Benjamin ([1964] 1976) *The Negro in the Making of America*. New York: Collier Books.

Stewart, J. B. (1996) "Africana studies: new directions for the 21st century," *International Journal of Africana Studies* 4 (December): 1–21.

Stuckey, S. (1987) *Slave Culture: Nationalist Theory and Foundation of Black America*. New York and Oxford: Oxford University Press.

Thompson, R. F. (1983) *Flash of the Spirit*. New York: Vintage Books.

Thompson, V. B. (2000) *Africans of the Diaspora*. Trenton, NJ: Africa World Press.

Turner, L. D. ([1949] 1973) *Africanisms in the Gullah Dialectic*. [Chicago] Ann Arbor: The University of Michigan Press.

Van Sertima, I. (1976) *They Came before Columbus*. New York: Random House.

—— (1992) *African Presence in Early America*. New Brunswick, NJ: Transaction.

Walker, D. and Garnet, H. H. (1994) *Walker's Appeal and Garnet's Address to the Slaves of the United States of America*. Nashville, TN: James C. Winston.

Walker, S. (ed.) (2001) *African Roots/American Cultures: Africa in the Creation of the Americas*. Lanham, MD: Rowman Littlefield.

Weiner, L. ([1922] 1972) *Africa and the Discovery of America*. Philadelphia: Innes & Sons.

Welsh-Asante, K. (ed.) (1994) *The African Aesthetic*. Westport, CT: Praeger.

Wood, P. (1974) *Black Majority: Negroes in Colonial South Carolina from 1670 through the Stono Rebellion*. New York: Knopf.

Woodson, Carter G. ([1936] 1968) *The African Background Outlined*. New York: Negro Universities Press.

Woodyard, J. L. (1991) "Evolution of a discipline: intellectual antecedents of African American studies," *Journal of Black Studies* 22: 239–51.

Suggestions for Further Reading

Fabre, G. and O'Meally, R. (eds.) (1994) *History and Memory in African American Culture*. London: Oxford University Press.

Gayle, Addison (ed.) (1971) *The Black Aesthetic*. Garden City, NY: Anchor Books.

Gilroy, P. (1993) *Small Acts*. London: Serpent's Tail.

Goodwine, M. (ed.) (1998) *The Legacy of Ibo Landing: Gullah Roots of African American Culture*. Atlanta: Clarity Press.

Holloway, J. E. (ed.) (1990) *Africanisms in the American Culture*. Bloomington: Indiana University Press.

Martin, T. (1991) *African Fundamentalism*. Dover, MA: Majority Press.

Stuckey, S. (1994) *Going through the Storm: The Influence of African American Art in History*. New York and Oxford: Oxford University Press.

CHAPTER THIRTEEN

African Americans and an Atlantic World Culture

WALTER C. RUCKER

Few topics have generated as much scholarly interest in the past decade as Atlantic World history. As a relatively new approach to regional history, the Atlantic World is geographically defined as the economic, political, social, and cultural connections forged between Africa, the Americas, and Europe beginning in the fifteenth century (Thornton 1992). In the assessment of Kristin Mann (2001: 13), this approach to history seeks "to consider the Atlantic basin as a single integrated unit of analysis." A ground swell of interest in this field has led to a number of recent developments. The Du Bois Institute dataset, which includes detailed information for close to 70 percent of all Atlantic slave voyages, is currently available on CD-ROM and is already producing a flood of scholarly reassessments. *Slavery and Abolition*, the *William and Mary Quarterly*, *Contours* and other refereed journals publish the latest research in Atlantic World and African Diaspora history. A dizzying number of articles, essay collections, and book-length monographs have appeared on the topic in just the last five years. In addition, a few university presses – Louisiana State, Indiana, South Carolina, and Michigan State – have created special book series for works encompassing elements of Atlantic World history, while a growing number of research centers continue to expand scholarly understandings of this field.

The formation of the historical Atlantic World was no less dynamic than the creation of the corresponding field of study. The Iberian *Reconquesta* of the early to mid-fifteenth century led to a series of events that brought the Portuguese to the West African coast for the first time. In their search for Prester John – a mythical East African defender of Christianity – Portuguese navigators encountered powerful West African kingdoms with an expansive trade network, which linked West Africa to much of the known world. Massive quantities of gold and other commodities inspired the Portuguese to establish trading posts from Senegal to Angola in the years after 1482. This opening act in the establishment of the Atlantic World trade network set in motion the Atlantic slave trade, the formation of colonies in the western hemisphere, the economic decline of East African polities and the emergence of Portugal as a truly global power.

As a site of massive intercontinental migrations and trade networks, and also as a conceptual space, the Atlantic World is larger in scope and scale than the African

Diaspora. While the African Diaspora is typically defined by the geographic regions that Africans were dispersed to as a result of the Atlantic slave trade – the Americas, and arguably Europe – by definition it excludes continental Africa and the Atlantic islands from historical analyses. Only recently has the concept of the Diaspora been expanded to encompass the dispersal of Africans across the Sahara to Arabia, and North and East Africa; indeed, it appears that a series of diasporas existed in Africa, which predated the arrival of Europeans and the growth of the Atlantic slave trade (Mann 2001).

In addition to its more significant geographic scope, the Atlantic World began close to a century before the creation of the African Diaspora. While obvious differences between these two approaches are evident, there is at least one area where scholars of the Atlantic World and the African Diaspora have seemingly forged a consensus. Researchers working in both fields have granted subject-positioning or agency to peoples of African decent. No longer are scholars contending that Africans were either victims, bystanders, or objects of historical processes that shaped the world around them. From its very inception, the African Diaspora concept saw Africans as agents of history largely because, as Mann notes, "the idea of the African diaspora developed first among Africans and their descendants, a point not sufficiently recognized in most academic discussions of the subject" (Mann 2001: 3). The notion of viewing Africans as active historical agents has been slow in development among Atlantic World historians. In his analysis of the pioneering works in this field, John Thornton recounts that "the Atlantic still appeared [in the literature] largely from a European perspective . . . The Atlantic, it seems, unlike the Mediterranean, was regarded by all these researchers as being particularly dominated by Europeans" (Thornton 1992: 2).

This Eurocentric approach is epitomized in a number of works, including Pierre and Hugette Chaunu's nine-volume *Séville et l'Atlantique, 1504–1650* (1955–60), James Duffy's *Portuguese Africa* (1961), Charles R. Boxer's *The Dutch Seaborne Empire, 1600–1800* (1965), and Fernand Braudel's *Civilization and Capitalism* (1982–4). Working from the context of the post-colonial world, many of these scholars simply projected current realities and power relationships back through time. By the 1970s and 1980s however, concerted challenges to these views began to alter scholarly approaches to Atlantic World history.

In direct response to Eurocentric approaches, nationalist historians, dependency theorists, revisionists, neo-revisionists, post-modernists, and advocates of world systems analysis filled the interpretive void. Some of these interpretations still emphasized the relatively passive role that Africans played in the formation of the Atlantic World. Borrowing from dependency theory developed largely by Latin Americanists, Walter Rodney (1974) contends in *How Europe Underdeveloped Africa* that colonial and neo-colonial economic links to Europe can be traced back to the era of the slave trade. Thus, in this view, Africans played a subordinate and relatively passive role to Europeans as early as the fifteenth century. Other scholars, including Eric Williams (1944), André Gunder Frank (1967), Immanuel Wallerstein (1974–80) and Chancellor Williams (1976), seemingly concur with this approach. While these studies were generally more sympathetic, emphasizing the victimization of Africans by repressive European powers, the results were the same as the scholarship generated by Eurocentric scholars: Africans were still denied agency and subject-positioning.

These denials of black agency were mirrored in scholarship that focused on North American slavery. During the early twentieth century, a scholarly consensus among American historians emerged to claim that the enslaved African was effectively a *tabula rasa* denuded of any African culture. Once exposed to the "superior" attributes of European and Euro-American culture, Africans – generally assumed to be primitive and savage – readily and willingly adopted European cultural norms and values. Again, these notions essentially denied African agency while emphasizing the sheer inability of Africans to resist this acculturative process. These ideas resonated in the works of scholars such as U. B. Phillips (1918), Kenneth Stampp (1956), Stanley Elkins (1959), and others. In addition, among folklorists and sociologists analyzing African American folk culture, a dominant paradigm emerged in the 1920s known as the "white-to-black" school of acculturation. This interpretive school held the opinion that Africans in North America borrowed so heavily from European and Euro-American culture that slave folklore was ultimately a syncretic matrix of butchered European values and beliefs. Addled by limited intellectual capacity and a barbaric past, Africans in this view were incapable of fully comprehending the complexities of European culture.

Neo-revisionist scholars like Thornton (1992), George Brooks (1993), and others published works detailing a number of elements related to the formation of the Atlantic World; importantly, these scholars approached the issue of African agency seriously. Even before these innovations, however, scholars like Carter G. Woodson (1936), Melville Herskovits (1941), and Lorenzo Dow Turner (1949) had given significant consideration to African agency in the creation of African American culture. Together, both sets of scholars demonstrated a continuum of activities that Africans and their descendants engaged in, including the formation of powerful kingdoms and cities in West Africa, the active role they played in the Atlantic trade network and their creation of Afro-Atlantic societies and cultures throughout the Americas. With this emphasis on African agency, the need to connect Diasporic communities with their homelands in Africa has become an increasing focus in recent scholarship.

The works of Sterling Stuckey (1987), Margaret Washington [Creel] (1988), Joseph Holloway (1990), Michael Gomez (1998), Sheila S. Walker (2001), and Linda Heywood (2002) have done a great deal to facilitate current understandings of important historical connections and cultural continuities. The maintenance of particular "Africanisms" – or discrete systems of African thought and belief – demonstrated to many that Africans were not simply uncultured bodies, which had to be assimilated or Europeanized in order to properly function. This view is epitomized in the work of Sterling Stuckey (1987) who provides strong evidence for the African influences on slave culture. The conditions that facilitated cultural retentions and continuities required resistance on the part of enslaved Africans, as well as a conscious set of decisions to maintain connections to the land of their ancestors. Stuckey (1987) posits a dynamic process by which Africans became a single people, laying the foundation for the development of a black nationalist/ Pan-Africanist consciousness.

Another recent trend, highlighted in Paul Gilroy's *The Black Atlantic* (1993), recognizes African agency while focusing on cultural hybridity and amalgamation. In this post-modernist approach, Gilroy forwards a "black Atlantic" culture that is not

African, American, Caribbean, or European, but a syncretic blending or hybrid of all of these national and ethnic identities. Black Atlantic culture, then, is a polyglot, which transcends "race," ethnicity, and nation; according to Gilroy, this cultural concept belongs to no one set of localities in Africa (Gilroy 1993). Instead he emphasizes the transnational and intercultural nature of identity, focusing almost exclusively on contemporary Anglo-America. Hence, Gilroy tends to place a greater emphasis on cultural discontinuities and disconnections. This approach is not without its problems. As Mann notes, Gilroy "ignores both the rich and dense world of the predominantly Lusophonic and Spanish South Atlantic and the roots of the transnational, intercultural black perspective in the pre-modern era" (Mann 2001: 15).

Geography and Culture in Atlantic West and West-central Africa

Anthropologist Melville Herskovits published *The Myth of the Negro Past* (1941), which at the time was a watershed effort on the topic of African cultural transmissions and continuities. In an attempt to undermine race prejudice in America, his work sought to counter a number of myths about Africa, and about Africans residing in all parts of the Diaspora. By demonstrating tangible cultural links between Africa and Diasporic communities, Herskovits took full aim at the myth that "The Negro is thus a man without a past" (Herskovits 1941: 2). Other myths he addressed in this work included the idea that Africans were brought to America from extremely diverse cultures and were distributed in a fashion that destroyed their cultural identity, and the idea that African cultures were so savage and unredeeming that European customs were readily preferred by enslaved Africans.

In answering these flawed perceptions, he posits what seems to be a problematic homogeneous and monolithic West African cultural heritage. Indeed, Herskovits does not give much consideration to West-central Africa, making passing references to the "Congo" in his analysis of African cultural influences. Most problematic are certain assumptions, guided no doubt by his disciplinary focus, that assume an unchanging African cultural past. Despite these shortcomings, the lasting importance of his research is in noting several examples of Africanisms in both the secular and sacred ethos of African Americans. Herskovits' argument was not a claim that African Americans were Africans culturally, but that "this group, like all other folk who maintained a group identity in this country, have retained something of their cultural heritage, while at the same time accommodating themselves . . . to the customs of the country as a whole" (Herskovits 1941: 145). This research, and subsequent studies by other scholars, helped put to rest various myths and forwarded the idea that "African American" culture was something rich, unique, and worthy of serious and significant scholarly contemplation.

When Sidney Mintz and Richard Price (1976) published *The Birth of African-American Culture*, it was intended to critique and revise Herskovits' 1941 findings. They argued that Africans who were transported across the Atlantic to become slaves in the Americas developed and created a culture that cannot be characterized simply as "African." Essentially, the very nature of the slave trade and enslavement in the Americas made the continuity of African culture nearly impossible. To further this claim, they state that, "[h]erded together with others with whom they shared a common condition of servitude and some degree of cultural overlap, enslaved

Africans were compelled to create a new language, a new religion, indeed a new culture" (Mintz and Price 1976: xi). While African culture may have been crucial in the creation of African American culture, Mintz and Price contend that it was by no means central and not independent of European influences or new cultural developments in the Americas.

This conclusion finds resonance in the claims made by Gilroy (1993), who asserts that black Atlantic culture, itself a "counterculture" of modernity, is not part of a Manichean dichotomy situated between monolithic "black" and "white" cultures. Instead, like Mintz and Price, Gilroy emphasizes the creole, hybrid, and fluid nature of black Atlantic culture; as a combination of European and African cultures, African American culture was a new creation and can be best understood, according to Gilroy, using W. E. B. Du Bois' concept of double consciousness. As Du Bois articulates it, "One ever feels his twoness, – an American, a Negro; two souls, two thoughts, two unreconciled strivings; two warring ideals in one dark body whose dogged strength alone keep it from being torn asunder" (Du Bois 1903: 45). This duality encapsulates the nature of African American culture for Gilroy, Mintz, and Price.

In terms of Herskovits' interpretations, Mintz and Price oppose his theory of West African cultural homogeneity by noting the sheer amount of cultural diversity in Atlantic Africa and by asserting that a number of enslaved Africans exported to the Americas came from West-central Africa (Mintz and Price 1976). They also oppose the notion that specific African cultural enclaves formed in the Americas. Instead, Mintz and Price claim that deliberate ethnic "randomization" – actively engaged in by slave traders, ship captains, and slave owners – ensured diverse populations of enslaved Africans throughout the Americas. Most of their conclusions are based on the same premise – the vastly numerous and diverse cultural heritages of West and West-central Africa. While there is little doubt that major cultural differences indeed existed in Atlantic Africa, what can be contested is the degree of this diversity.

On one end of the debate, Herskovits (1941) and Joseph Holloway (1990) support ideas of cultural homogeneity. Holloway, in his introduction to *Africanisms in American Culture* (1990), asserts that since most North American slaves originated from West-central Africa, the idea of a monolithic Bantu cultural heritage and its links to the birth of African American cultures would be quite applicable. Although there might be flaws with this sort of approach, the idea of a monolithic Bantu culture or its significant contribution to African American culture finds support in the works of a number of scholars (Vansina 1990; Vass 1979; Thompson 1983). On the other end of the spectrum, Mintz and Price likely exaggerate the amount of diversity by using African languages as a tool of measurement. The truth probably lies between the two extremes and ample evidence for this conclusion can be found in recent scholarship.

John Thornton (1992), in *Africa and Africans in the Making of the Atlantic World*, demonstrates that ethnographers have tended to overestimate the amount of cultural diversity in Atlantic Africa – an area encompassing the coastal regions from Senegambia in the north to Angola in the south – because they often ascribe an ethnic identity to every distinct language and regional dialect. The problem with this is the fact that many Atlantic Africans were multilingual, and certain languages and regional dialects were so related that they could be mutually understood throughout vast areas. Thornton concludes that, instead of Atlantic Africa being composed of hundreds of cultural groupings, the region should instead be divided into three cultural zones and further separated into seven "subzones": Upper Guinea, which included the Mande language family and two variants of the West Atlantic language family (northern and southern West Atlantic); Lower Guinea, which included two variants of the Kwa language family (Akan and Aja); and the Angola zone, which included two variants of the western Bantu language family (Kikongo and Kimbundu).

Another issue of major importance in Thornton's assessment is the claim that European traders, slave-ship captains, and plantation owners engaged in active and conscious efforts to ethnically randomize enslaved Africans. If practiced, this measure could effectively have undermined the ability of enslaved Africans to foment rebellion on slave ships or plantations in the Americas, since they would not have an effective means of communication or collaboration. According to Thornton (1992) however, cultural randomization was not a significant aspect of the slave trade. In sociological terminology, he contends that the enslaved Africans on the average transport ship were indeed a group as opposed to an aggregate. In other words, most enslaved Africans on European slave ships had some prior connection to each other and were likely enslaved at the same time from the same geographic region. In addition, he states, "[s]lave ships drew their entire cargo from only one or perhaps two ports in Africa and unloaded them in large lots of as many as 200–1,000 in their new Atlantic homes" (Thornton 1992: 192). Shuffling and randomizing slaves was simply not feasible. While doing so made perfect logic, achieving the goal of cultural randomization could result in longer stays on board ships by enslaved Africans and this would invariably lead to increased mortality rates. Tracing the slave trade from the sixteenth through the early eighteenth century, Thornton concludes that "there were limits on the ability to achieve a random linguistic distribution of slaves, and what this meant was that most slaves on any sizable estate were probably from only a few national groupings" (Thornton 1992: 196).

Michael Gomez (1998), in *Exchanging Our Country Marks*, expands on Thornton's conclusion by claiming that significant African cultural enclaves developed in the Americas as a result of a number of factors. One of these factors would be the lack of cultural diversity in Atlantic West and West-central Africa; again, the conclusion of Mintz and Price (1976) – that hundreds of distinct cultures existed in Atlantic Africa – has stood neither the test of time nor intense scholarly inquiry. While Thornton contends that Atlantic Africa could be divided into three culturally distinct zones and seven subzones, Gomez shows that in fact there were roughly six cultural zones in this region, with a number of subzones in each: Senegambia, Sierra Leone, the Gold Coast, the Bight of Benin, the Bight of Biafra, and West-central Africa. In addition, Africans from certain regions shared cultural affinities, which facilitated the process of hybridization between African groups. Even if randomization was attempted on North American plantations, Gomez contends that this only facilitated the creation of a group consciousness, a group identity and collaborative resistance efforts: "Africans of varying ethnicities, who had never considered their blackness a source of reflection let alone a principle of unity, became cognizant of this feature perhaps for the first time in their lives" (Gomez 1998: 165). This idea finds resonance in the pioneering work of Sterling Stuckey who states in *Slave*

Culture that "slave ships were the first real incubators of slave unity across cultural lines, cruelly revealing irreducible links . . . , fostering resistance thousands of miles before the shores of the new land appeared on the horizon" (Stuckey 1987: 3).

While they still clung to their ethnic identities, enslaved Africans began to shape a new set of cultures in the Americas. These new cultures were not simply a hybrid of "European" and "African" cultural milieus as a number of scholars contend. Instead, Gomez makes a convincing claim that the first step towards the birth of an African American culture was intra-African cultural syncretism or, in his words, the formation of an "African sociocultural matrix" (Gomez 1998: 5). This notion even serves as the guiding intelligence for the structure of *Exchanging Our Country Marks*. Gomez, for example, discusses the cultural links between Africans from Senegambia and Benin, Sierra Leone, and the Gold Coast (the Akan), the Bight of Biafra (the Igbo), and West-central Africa in separate chapters of this important work. He concludes by noting that "[t]he development of African American society through 1830 was very much the product of contributions made by specific ethnic groups . . . varying mixes of ethnicities in each colony/state resulted in communities and cultural forms that were distinctive though related" (Gomez 1998: 291).

With recent efforts to demonstrate that Atlantic Africans were multilingual and separated into just a handful of culturally distinct zones, reassessments of the nature of African American culture have become increasingly frequent (Berlin 1996; Gomez 1998; Morgan 1998; Walker 2001; Heywood 2002). While the work of Sterling Stuckey (1987) has been pivotal in the contemporary scholarship about the formation of African American culture, only at the start of the twenty-first century have Africanists begun to corroborate his findings. Recent trends, however, have moved away from generalizations about "African" cultural continuities, to emphasizing instead the contributions that specific African ethnic groups (such as Igbo, Yoruba, Fon, Mande, and the like) made to African American culture.

In creating an accurate depiction of cultural diversity in Atlantic Africa, using the separate discussions of cultural zones by Thornton (1992) and Gomez (1998) becomes instructive. As Thornton contends, "Africans brought with them a cultural heritage in language, aesthetics, and philosophy that helped to form the newly developing cultures of the Atlantic world" (Thornton 1992: 129). With this being the case, a clear depiction of the cultural geography of Atlantic Africa is necessary. The first of these cultural zones, Upper Guinea, was one of the more ethnically diverse regions in Atlantic Africa. In geographic terms, this area reached from the Senegal River in the north to the region near Cape Mount in modern Liberia and included two important slave-trading regions – Senegambia and Sierra Leone. Culturally, Sengambia was home to a number of ethnic groups representing both the West Atlantic and Mande language families, including the Bambara, the Malinke (Mande-speakers), the Sereer, the Soninke, the Wolof, and the Fulbe. The various ethnonyms used by Europeans to describe Africans from this region – Mandingo, Gambian and Senegambian – were employed to designate people who were primarily from the Bambara linguistic group. The Bambara likely represented the largest population of enslaved Upper Guinean Africans imported to the Americas, but other groups from Senegambia were important in the creation of African American culture (Thornton 1992; Rodney 1969; Gomez 1998; Curtin 1969; Hall 1992). As Gomez recounts, "the Senegambian contingent was both early and substantial. In fact, it can be argued that the Senegambian presence provided a significant portion of the foundation for the consequent African American population" (Gomez 1998: 38–9).

Sierra Leone, a region of Upper Guinea extending from the Casamance River in the north to Cape Mount in the south, was even more heterogeneous than Senegambia. While Gomez contends that the people of Sierra Leone "did not see themselves as ethnicities during the slave trade [and] a number of groups had indeed developed a shared identity," certain cultural patterns can be discerned (Gomez 1998: 89). Among the many ethnicities and other "collective groupings" were the Mande-speakers – the Mandinka, the Susu, the Gola, the Kissi, the Jallonke, the Vai, and the Kono – and the non-Mande West Atlantic language groups, including the Temne, the Landuma, the Bulom, and the Krim (Thornton 1992; Gomez 1998; Curtin 1969). The sheer amount of cultural diversity in this region was balanced by the fact that the forms of Mande spoken in Sierra Leone "were almost mutually intelligible, at least in the seventeenth century" (Thornton 1992: 187). Even the non-Mande groups in Sierra Leone spoke "closely related languages" (Gomez 1998: 88), a concept which finds corroboration in Thornton (1992), who emphasizes the amount of multilingualism and cultural sharing that occurred as a consequence of numerous commercial networks and political interconnections.

The second major cultural zone, Lower Guinea, stretched from modern Ivory Coast in the west to Cameroon in the east and represented the largest geographic region of the three major cultural zones in Atlantic Africa. This area encompassed the regions that Europeans referred to as the Ivory Coast, the Windward Coast, the Gold Coast, and the Slave Coast. Despite its geographic scale, Lower Guinea was much more culturally homogeneous than Upper Guinea and included only one major language family – Kwa. While this region was relatively less culturally diverse, the Kwa language family had two vastly different branches – Western Kwa (Akan, Ewe and Ga) and Eastern Kwa (Yoruba, Fon, Edo, and Igbo). Dominating the eastern portion of Lower Guinea and the region generally known as the Gold Coast, the Akan language subgroup included Baule-speakers in the eastern Ivory Coast (the Sefwi and the Ahanta) and Twi-speakers in the region coterminous with modern-day Ghana (the Asante, the Fante and the Bron). Due to the large number of Akan-speakers leaving Fort Kormantse along the Gold Coast, they became known by the false ethnonym "Cormantee" or "Kromantin" throughout the Americas and were highly prized captives by a number of European slave traders (Thornton 1992; Gomez 1998; Curtin 1969).

Among the most significant Eastern Kwa subgroups were the Fon, the Yoruba, the Edo, and the Igbo (Thornton 1992; Gomez 1998; Curtin 1969). In the case of the Yoruba and the Igbo, Gomez (1998) and Northrup (2000) demonstrate that these ethnic and national terms were more applicable in the American context than in pre-colonial Atlantic Africa. Yoruba, for example, was a term of possible Hausa origin and referred to the people living in the town of Oyo Ile. As Gomez contends, "[t]he Yoruba emerged as a 'nation' not only in North America but also in the West Indies and Brazil" (Gomez 1998: 55). While the Yoruba were a very real group in the Americas, this ethnolinguistic identity emerged only recently in Africa and as a direct result of British colonial administration in Nigeria. Likewise, the "Igbo" did not exist as a distinct ethnicity in Atlantic Africa until they were "created" in the twentieth century (Northrup 2000: 1–2). Simply put, "twentieth-century colonial forces and post-colonial politics fostered solidarity among the millions of Yoruba-and Igbo-speaking peoples that had no pre-colonial counterpart" (ibid: 1). Like a number of ethnonyms used by Europeans during the slave trade era, Calabar, Moko, and Igbo were imprecise and, at times, overlapping identities that Africans in this region did not create or embrace. However, "*Igbo* was a name Igbo-speaking people seem to have readily accepted abroad" (ibid: 13).

The Fon of Dahomey and the Edo of Benin were relatively stable ethnolinguistic groups centered around strong and expansive states in Lower Guinea (Thornton 1992; Gomez 1998; Curtin 1969; Wax 1973). The Bight of Benin, stretching from the Volta to the Benin River, was culturally more diverse than Thornton (1992) contends, but the spreading political influence and domination of the kingdoms of Dahomey and Benin along this region of the coast led to an impressive amount of cultural diffusion and integration. Gomez claims that this cultural sharing was caused by a large number of factors, including "wars, raids, demographic shifts, displacements, diplomatic missions, and trade" (Gomez 1998: 56). Thus, by the mid-seventeenth century, the use of commercial and political *lingua francas* as well as shared religious beliefs in the Bight of Benin proved that "African populations succeeded in borrowing aspects of each other's culture" (ibid: 56).

The third major cultural zone was the Angola coast in West-central Africa. The home of roughly 40 percent of all Africans transported to the Americas as a result of the slave trade, this region was the most significant of the three cultural zones. Importantly, this was one of the most homogenous regions in Atlantic Africa – though there were more than just two language groups (Kikongo and Mbundu) in Angola, as Thornton (1992) claims. Most Africans living in Angola spoke a variant of Bantu (Kikongo, Duala, Bakweri, Isubu, Bassa-Bakoko, Yambassa, Bafia, Ewondo, Bene, and Bulu). Other language groups in this region included semi-Bantu (Bamilike, Banyang and Tikar), Aka, Fulbe, and Podoko. Gomez contends that "[t]hose slaves who found themselves bound for the Western Hemisphere mostly came from Bantu and semi-Bantu populations organized politically into smaller units" (Gomez 1998: 134). It was primarily in the area of politics that the Angola region was diverse, with the proliferation of a number of smaller states. The two larger polities in the Angola coast – the Kikongo state of Kongo and the Mbundu state of Ndongo – because of their size and expansive scope were significant factors in forging a sense of cultural unity in the region by the mid-seventeenth century, though the latter was defeated by Portuguese forces in 1671 (Thornton 1992; Gomez 1998; Curtin 1969; Wax 1973).

The Atlantic Slave Trade and the Birth of African American Culture

Cramped into the numerous factories and slave castles dotting the Atlantic coast of Africa, enslaved Africans awaited the arrival of European-owned slave ships to transport them to the Americas. This second leg of the triangular trade connecting Europe, Africa, and the Americas, known as the Middle Passage, was one of the most terrifying experiences in human history. In the midst of this tragic story, Stuckey (1987) contends that the slave ships crossing the Atlantic were crucibles that helped forge a single people out of numerous African ethnicities. This was an ongoing process, beginning with the enslavement experience in Atlantic Africa and continuing in certain regions of the Americas well into the nineteenth century. Both Gomez (1998) and Douglas Chambers demonstrate that, throughout the Americas, enslaved Africans "identified themselves, or were so identified by others, as members of African-derived named groups" (Chambers 2001: 25). They readily identified themselves as members of separate "nations" initially, until a more unified identity was forged as a result of the common circumstances and conditions of enslavement.

The initial sense of national identity was facilitated by the formation of large ethnic enclaves, which were direct results of import patterns in the Atlantic slave trade. As Daniel Littlefield (1991) notes, European planters developed a number of ethnic preferences based on perceptions of traits that certain enslaved African groups supposedly had. He contends that "European colonists concerned themselves quite closely with distinctions among African peoples, and paid great attention to such things as size, color, and cultural or other characteristics" (Littlefield 1991: 8). Thus, Europeans created alternating hierarchies of ethnic and regional preferences, which were employed and gave some shape to import patterns in locales throughout the Americas. In colonies like Jamaica, Barbados, and South Carolina, Gold Coast Africans were coveted by some planters for their alleged propensity for loyalty and hard work; in other colonies, or even among other planters in colonies that seemingly coveted Gold Coast Africans, these slaves were considered unruly and rebellious. Igbos, and others from Calabar or the Bight of Biafra, were reviled because of an alleged propensity for suicide. Angolans were supposedly paradoxically prone to docility and flight (Littlefield 1991; Gomez 1998; Wax 1973).

European preferences for certain African ethnic groups were likely due to a range of factors – the cost of importing enslaved Africans from certain regions, limited access to certain slave markets on the Atlantic African coast, or the demand for Africans from specific regions with expertise in the cultivation of certain crops and other skills (Littlefield 1991; Gomez 1998; Washington [Creel], 1988; Carney 2001). Certainly among slave traders and plantation owners, there was no clear consensus on the behavioral characteristics of any African group. This reflects what seems obvious from the vantage point of hindsight: the reason why African groups do not fit into generalized behavioral categories is because, like the rest of humanity, Africans can and will display a broad spectrum of behavior. Whether real or imaginary, these perceptions of African behavioral characteristics did contribute to the formation of ethnic enclave communities in North America as well as elsewhere.

The Du Bois Institute database bears out this conclusion. This important project significantly modified the findings of Philip Curtin (1969) and provides a more accurate picture of the slave trade. The Du Bois database, for example, demonstrates that of 101,925 enslaved Africans from identifiable locations sent to Virginia, 44.8 percent came from the Bight of Biafra. In South Carolina, enslaved Africans from the Bight of Biafra accounted for just 9.89 percent of identifiable imports; in the US as a whole, Bight of Biafra exports were 18.6 percent of the 317,748 enslaved Africans recorded in the Du Bois database (Eltis et al. 1999). So it is possible to discuss a Bight of Biafra (Igbo) enclave in Virginia as a phenomenon unique in North America. Not only does this database corroborate many of the findings of Stuckey (1987), Gomez (1998), Washington [Creel] (1988) and others, but it opens new possibilities in the study of the formation of African American culture.

Although the nature of African ethnic enclaves varied over time, it is now possible to pinpoint the nature of these concentrations and track specific cultural influences. Between 1701 and 1800, 26.4 percent of enslaved Africans from identifiable regions and embarking on ships to the Carolinas came from West-central Africa. The 1739 Stono Revolt, initiated principally by enslaved Angolans from West-central Africa, forced the proprietors and slave owners of South Carolina to reduce their reliance on Africans from this region. Also, due to the emphasis on rice cultivation in the South Carolina Lowcountry and sea islands, Africans from rice-producing regions of Upper Guinea – Senegambia (24.9 percent) and Sierra Leone (9.48 percent) respectively – became important demographic factors and largely replaced the earlier West-central African import stream. These three cultural contingents played active roles in the formation Gullah and Geechee culture.

Elements of the West-central African, Senegambian, and Biafran (11.3 percent) contingents of South Carolina's slave population apparently created an alliance in 1822, under the leadership of Denmark Vesey, in an attempt to foment a rebellion. While the details of this conspiracy are currently in dispute, it is clear that separate bands of Gullahs, Igbos, Mande-speakers, French-speaking Saint-Domingans, and American-born slaves had formed and found between them areas of commonality. In some ways, this could have been an early expression of Pan-Africanism (Eltis et al. 1999; Gomez 1998; Washington [Creel], 1988; Carney 2001; Stuckey 1987; Brown 2002; Littlefield 1981; Wood 1974; Thornton 1991; Vass 1979; Rucker 2001a; Johnson 2001; Starobin 1970).

Between 1701 and 1800, 45.1 percent of Africans entering Virginia from identifiable regions were embarked on ships leaving ports in the Bight of Biafra. Thus, Virginia imported a disproportionately large number of Igbo-speakers and others from Calabar and surrounding regions. As Lorena Walsh (1997) and James Sidbury (1997) contend, this emphasis on Igbo imports played a significant factor in the rise of Afro-Virginian culture. One cultural implication of the presence of so many Igbo-speakers was the proliferation of Igbo terms and concepts – *okra, buckra, obia* – or discrete Igbo cultural practices (for example, the Jonkonu celebration, funerary customs and spiritual beliefs) in Jamaica, Virginia, and other regions of the Anglophone Americas that imported significant numbers of Africans from the Bight of Biafra. Another implication, discussed by Sidbury (1997), was the possibility that Gabriel Prosser – leader of a failed Richmond slave revolt in 1800 – was accorded a great deal of respect and veneration because of his blacksmithing skills and the spiritual powers associated with this trade among the peoples living near the Niger River delta. In fact, three separate blacksmiths were claimed to have been part of the leadership core of this attempt to capture and raze the capital of Virginia (Walsh 2001; Walsh 1997; Sidbury 1997; Chambers 1997; Stuckey 1999; Gomez 1998).

Information regarding imports into areas like North Carolina, Georgia, Maryland, the Middle Colonies (with the exception of New York), and the New England colonies is scanty at best and scholars can only detail the slave trade in these regions through inference and suggestive evidence. As the principal port of entry for enslaved Africans, Charleston satisfied most of the demand for forced labor in North Carolina and Georgia. The result of this commercial connection meant that both colonies/states likely had similar demographic patterns and ethnic enclaves to those found in South Carolina (Gomez 1998). Maryland imported a large number of

Africans from Senegambia (49.4 percent) and did not mirror the reliance on imports from the Bight of Biafra found in its Chesapeake neighbor, Virginia (Eltis et al. 1999). For the remainder of the slaveholding regions of North America, Gomez notes that "states such as Alabama, Mississippi, Kentucky, Tennessee, and North Carolina all boasted significant slave populations, derivative, in turn, of the five core colonies/states: Virginia, Maryland, South Carolina, Georgia, and Louisiana" (Gomez 1998: 24).

While there has been a major problem in tracking African imports into certain regions, the Du Bois Institute database and other sources reveal much about imports in colonial New York and Louisiana. The Dutch colony of New Netherland – which became New York after 1664 – witnessed two different waves of African immigrants. The first, lasting for the initial few decades of Dutch rule, was dominated by the importation of West-central Africans. The second wave focused on Africans from the Gold Coast. Combined, these contingents may have contributed to such cultural formations as the Pinkster festivals, the "Congo" dances in Albany and specific funerary practices associated with the African Burial Ground in New York City (for example, carved symbols on coffins, the use of burial shrouds and interment with earthware, beads, and other objects). A definite Gold Coast presence is noted in both the 1712 New York City revolt and the alleged conspiracy of 1741: in both instances, enslaved Africans with Akan day-names predominated among the leadership core (Thornton 1998; Boxer 1965; Postma 1990; Goodfriend 1992; Stuckey 1994; Stuckey 1999; Foote 2001; Blakey 1998; Rucker 2001b).

Although Louisiana shifted from French to Spanish, and finally to American control after 1803, the demographics of the slave trade are relatively easy to trace. The principal import groups into Louisiana were Africans from Senegambia, the Bight of Benin and West-central Africa. As the most numerically significant African group in Louisiana, the Congolese and other West-central Africans contributed to expressive culture (such as dance contests in New Orleans' Congo Square and baton twirling), cuisine (for example, gumbo and jumbalaya) and even body gestures or poses (among them, arms akimbo with both hands on the hips) in Louisiana. The significant African contingent from the Bight of Benin, as well as enslaved Santo Dominguans arriving in New Orleans in the wake of the 1791 revolution, brought with them spiritual beliefs that became Voodoo and Hoodoo in Louisiana. The Voodoo/Hoodoo complex is a syncretic blend of Fon and Yoruba metaphysical and religious concepts and, in Louisiana, it likely incorporated Catholic icons and elements from West-central African and Senegambian belief systems (Mulira 1991; Thompson 1991; Caron 1997; Gomez 1998; Hall 1992).

During her reign as Voodoo Queen in New Orleans from 1830 to 1869, Marie Laveau routinely evoked the names of Fon and Yoruba deities – *Legba* and *Damballa* – in her ritual ceremonies (Gomez 1998; Mulira 1991). Finally, according to Gwendolyn Midlo Hall, "African religious beliefs, including knowledge of herbs, poisons, and the creation of charms and amulets of support or power, came to Louisiana with the earliest contingent of slaves" (Hall 1992: 162). The Bambara from Senegambia played an important role in these areas. While the term "Bambara" has a number of meanings and ethnic connotations, in the context of Louisiana it referred specifically to non-Muslim Africans from Senegambia who were captured in *jihads* and sold to European merchants. However defined, this group significantly influenced the nature of slave culture in Louisiana. For example, *zinzin* – the word for an amulet of power in Louisiana Creole – has the same meaning and name in Bambara. *Gris-gris* and *wanga* were other Bambara or Mande words for charms referred to in colonial and antebellum Louisiana. Even the Arabic-derived Mande word for spiritual advisor or teacher – *marabout* – appears in the records of colonial Louisiana (Hall 1992; Gomez 1998; Caron 1997).

Based on the reality of ethnic enclaves and the information regarding the pattern and structure of the Atlantic slave trade revealed by the Du Bois Institute database, Douglas Chambers notes that "the evidence is mounting that the transatlantic slave-trade was much more patterned and much less random (and randomizing) than previously had been simply assumed, thereby resulting in a greater likelihood of historical influences of groups of Africans in the formation . . . of particular cultural patterns in the Americas" (Chambers 2002: 101). The fact is that randomization was not feasible on either side of the Atlantic and patterns of ethnic concentration that emerged in the Caribbean and South America also emerged in North American colonies/states (Gomez 1998; Chambers 2001 and 2002).

In spite of this mounting evidence however, a number of scholars remain skeptical about the close cultural connections between Africa and the Americas. Among the many critics of the notion of cultural continuities is Philip D. Morgan. In seeming agreement with the interpretations of Paul Gilroy, Mechal Sobel, Ira Berlin, Michael Mullin, Sidney Mintz, and Richard Price, he forwards the notion of ethnic ran-domization – on both sides of the Atlantic – which, in turn, served as a facilitating factor for creolization and acculturation (Morgan 1997; Morgan 1998; Gilroy 1993; Sobel 1987; Mintz and Price 1976; Berlin 1996; Mullin 1994). Using the preliminary results of the Du Bois Institute database, Morgan finds in "much of the Caribbean and North America . . . the absence of a dominant single African provenance zone" (Morgan 1997: 125). He further claims that "contrary to one interpretation, North American plantation slaves generally could not practice 'African religion,' nor did they appropriate only those values that could be absorbed into their 'Africanity.' This is to make excessive claims for the autonomy of slaves and the primacy of their African background" (Morgan 1998: 657).

A spectrum of opinions on the issue of African cultural retention and continuities has emerged among historians and other scholars of the Atlantic World experience. On one end of this spectrum would be the "annihilationist" school epitomized in the work of Jon Butler (1990), who argues that Africans in North America suffered a "spiritual holocaust" between 1680 and 1760, which facilitated their immersion into Euro-American Christianity. This idea – that Africans were stripped of their culture – resonates in the earlier approaches of Phillips (1918), Stampp (1956), Elkins (1959), and E. Franklin Frazier (1964). On the other end of the spectrum would be the work of the "Africanist" school, which includes Herskovits (1941), Stuckey (1987), and Gomez (1998). This school emphasizes direct African cultural influences and the presence of important Africanisms in African American culture.

The interpretive middle ground between the annihilationists and the Africanists, what can be referred to as the "creolization" school, is epitomized in the work of Morgan (1998), Mullin (1994), and Gilroy (1993). Although they largely agree that certain African cultural elements persisted in the Americas, these scholars place more emphasis on cultural hybridity, heterogeneity, and fluidity. While a consensus may never be forged on these important issues, Mann offers a useful and construct-ive model for future studies of Atlantic World culture. She contends that scholars will need to:

> represent the African diaspora beyond simple oppositions, unitary models and static constructions to more varied, complex and fluid accounts that come close to capturing the unfolding experiences of Africans and their descendants throughout the Atlantic world. At the same time, they will challenge us to rewrite Atlantic history and rethink Atlantic culture. (Mann 2001: 16)

What is quite clear is that research on the birth of African American culture has advanced dramatically over the past sixty years and new developments in this area will continue to demonstrate the high level of interconnectedness existing between Atlantic Africa and the Diaspora of peoples created by the slave trade.

BIBLIOGRAPHY

Works Cited

Berlin, Ira (1996) "From creole to African: Atlantic creoles and the origins of African-American society in mainland North America," *William and Mary Quarterly* 53: 251–88.

Blakey, Michael L. (1998) "The New York burial ground project: an examination of enslaved lives, a construction of ancestral ties," *Transforming Archaeology: Journal of the Association of Black Anthropologists* 7: 53–8.

Boxer, Charles R. (1965) *The Dutch Seaborne Empire, 1600–1800*. New York: Oxford University Press.

Braudel, Fernand (1982–4) *Civilization and Capitalism: Fifteenth to Eighteenth Centuries*, 3 vols. New York: Harper & Row.

Brooks, George (1993) *Landlords and Strangers: Ecology, Society, and Trade in Western Africa, 1000–1630*. Boulder, CO: Westview Press.

Brown, Ras M. (2002) "'Walk in the Feenda': West-Central Africans and the forest in the South Carolina–Georgia lowcountry" in Linda M. Heywood (ed.), *Central Africans and Cultural Transformations in the American Diaspora*, 289–318. Cambridge: Cambridge University Press.

Butler, Jon (1990) *Awash in a Sea of Faith: Christianizing the American People*. Cambridge, MA: Harvard University Press.

Carney, Judith A. (2001) *Black Rice: The African Origins of Rice Cultivation in the Americas*. Cambridge, MA: Harvard University Press.

Caron, Peter (1997) "'Of a nation which others do not understand': Bambara slaves and African ethnicity in colonial Louisiana, 1718–1760," *Slavery and Abolition* 18: 98–121.

Chambers, Douglas (1997) "'My own nation': Igbo exiles in the Diaspora," *Slavery and Abolition* 18: 72–97.

—— (2001) "Ethnicity in the diaspora: the slave-trade and the creation of African 'nations' in the Americas," *Slavery and Abolition* 22: 25–39.

—— (2002) "The significance of Igbo in the Bight of Biafra slave-trade: a rejoinder to Northrup's 'myth Igbo,'" *Slavery and Abolition* 23: 101–20.

Chaunu, Pierre and Chaunu, Hugette (1955–60) *Séville et l'Atlantique, 1504–1650*, 9 vols. Paris: A. Colin.

Creel *see* Washington

Curtin, Philip (1969) *The Atlantic Slave Trade: A Census*. Madison: University of Wisconsin Press.

Du Bois, W. E. B. ([1903] 1982) *The Souls of Black Folk*. [New York]. New York: NAL Penguin.

—— ([1939] 1975) *Black Folk Then and Now: An Essay in the History and Sociology of the Negro Race*. [New York] Millwood, NY: Kraus-Thomson.

Duffy, James (1961) *Portuguese Africa*. Cambridge, MA: Harvard University Press.

Elkins, Stanley (1959) *Slavery: A Problem in American Institutional and Intellectual Life*. Chicago: University of Chicago Press.

Eltis, David, Behrendt, Stephen, Richardson, David, and Klein, Herbert (eds.) (1999) *The Trans-Atlantic Slave Trade: A Database on CD-ROM*. Cambridge: Cambridge University Press.

Foote, Thelma (2001) "'Some hard usage': the New York City slave revolt," *New York Folklore* 28: 147–59.

Frank, Andre Gunder (1967) *Capitalism and Underdevelopment in Latin America: Historical Studies of Chile and Brazil*. New York: Monthly Review Press.

Frazier, E. Franklin (1964) *The Negro Church in America*. New York: Schocken Books.

Gilroy, Paul (1993) *The Black Atlantic: Modernity and Double Consciousness*. Cambridge, MA: Harvard University Press.

Gomez, Michael (1998) *Exchanging Our Country Marks: The Transformation of African Identities in the Colonial and Antebellum South*. Chapel Hill: University of North Carolina Press.

Goodfriend, Joyce (1992) *Before the Melting Pot: Society and Culture in Colonial New York City, 1664–1730*. Princeton, NJ: Princeton University Press.

Hall, Gwendolyn Midlo (1992) *Africans in Colonial Louisiana: The Development of Afro-Creole Culture in the Eighteenth Century*. Baton Rouge: Louisiana State University Press.

Herskovits, Melville (1941) *The Myth of the Negro Past*. Boston: Beacon Press.

Heywood, Linda M. (ed.) (2002) *Central Africans and Cultural Transformations in the American Diaspora*. Cambridge: Cambridge University Press.

Holloway, Joseph (ed.) (1990) *Africanisms in American Culture*. Bloomington: Indiana University Press.

Johnson, Michael P. (2001) "Denmark Vesey and his co-conspirators," *William and Mary Quarterly* 58: 915–76.

Levine, Lawrence (1977) *Black Culture and Black Consciousness: Afro-American Folk Thought from Slavery to Freedom*. New York: Oxford University Press.

Littlefield, Daniel (1991) *Rice and Slaves: Ethnicity and the Slave Trade in Colonial South Carolina*. Baton Rouge: Louisiana State University.

Mann, Kristin (2001) "Shifting paradigms in the study of the African Diaspora and of Atlantic history and culture," *Slavery and Abolition* 22: 3–21.

Mintz, Sidney and Price, Richard (1976) *The Birth of African-American Culture: An Anthropological Perspective*. Boston: Beacon Press.

Morgan, Philip (1997) "The cultural implications of the Atlantic Slave Trade: African regional origins, American destinations and New World developments," *Slavery and Abolition* 18: 122–145.

—— (1998) *Slave Counterpoint: Black Culture in the Eighteenth-Century Chesapeake & Low Country*. Chapel Hill: University of North Carolina Press.

Mulira, Jessie Gaston (1991) "The case of Voodoo in New Orleans" in Joseph Holloway (ed.), *Africanisms in American Culture*, 34–68. Bloomington: Indiana University Press.

Mullin, Michael (1994) *Africa in America: Slave Acculturation and Resistance in the American South and the British Caribbean, 1736–1831*. Chicago: University of Illinois Press.

Northrup, David (2000) "Igbo and myth Igbo: culture and ethnicity in the Atlantic world, 1600–1850," *Slavery and Abolition* 21: 1–20.

Phillips, Ulrich B. ([1918] 1966) *American Negro Slavery*. [Baton Rouge, LA] Baton Rouge: University of Louisiana Press.

Postma, Johannes M. (1990) *The Dutch in the Atlantic Slave Trade, 1600–1815*. Cambridge: Cambridge University Press.

Rodney, Walter (1969) "Upper Guinea and the significance of the origins of Africans enslaved in the New World," *Journal of Negro History* 54: 327–45.

—— (1974) *How Europe Underdeveloped Africa*. Washington, DC: Howard University Press.

Rucker, Walter (2001a) "'I will gather all nations': resistance, culture, and pan-African collaboration in Denmark Vesey's South Carolina," *Journal of Negro History* 86: 132–47.

—— (2001b) "Conjure, magic, and power: the influence of Afro-Atlantic religious practices on slave resistance and rebellion," *Journal of Black Studies* 32: 84–103.

Sidbury, James (1997) *Ploughshares into Swords: Race, Rebellion, and Identity in Gabriel's Virginia, 1730–1810*. New York: Cambridge University Press.

Sobel, Mechal (1987) *The World They Made Together: Black and White Values in Eighteenth-Century Virginia*. Princeton, NJ: Princeton University Press.

Stampp, Kenneth (1956) *The Peculiar Institution: Slavery in the Antebellum South*. New York: Alfred Knopf.

Starobin, Robert S. (ed.) (1970) *Denmark Vesey: The Slave Conspiracy of 1822*. Englewood Cliffs, NJ: Prentice-Hall.

Stuckey, Sterling (1987) *Slave Culture: Nationalist Theory and the Foundation of Black America*. New York: Oxford University Press.

—— (1994) *Going through the Storm: The Influence of African American Art in History*. New York: Oxford University Press.

—— (1999) "African spirituality and cultural practice in colonial New York, 1700–1770" in Carla D. Pestana and Sharon V. Salinger (eds.), *Inequality in Early America*, 160–81. Hanover, NH: University Press of New England.

Thompson, Robert Farris (1983) *Flash of the Spirit*. New York: Vintage Books.

—— (1991) "Kongo influences on African-American artistic culture" in Joseph Holloway (ed.), *Africanisms in American Culture*, 148–84. Bloomington: Indiana University Press.

Thornton, John (1991) "African dimensions of the Stono rebellion," *American Historical Review* 96: 1101–13.

—— (1992) *Africa and Africans in the Making of the Atlantic World, 1400–1680*. New York: Cambridge University Press.

—— (1998) "The Coromantees: an African cultural group in colonial North America and the Caribbean," *Journal of Caribbean History* 32: 161–78.

Turner, Lorenzo Dow (1949) *Africanisms in Gullah Dialect*. Chicago: University of Chicago Press.

Vansina, Jan (1990) *Paths in the Rainforests: Toward a History of Political Tradition in Equatorial Africa*. Madison: University of Wisconsin Press.

Vass, Winifred K. (1979) *The Bantu-Speaking Heritage of the United States*. Los Angeles: University of California Press.

Walker, Sheila S. (ed.) (2001) *African Roots/American Cultures: Africa in the Creation of the Americas*. New York: Rowman & Littlefield.

Wallerstein, Immanuel (1974–80) *The Modern World System*, 2 vols. New York: Academic Press.

Walsh, Lorena S. (1997) *From Calabar to Carter's Grove: The History of a Virginia Slave Community*. Charlottesville: University of Virginia Press.

—— (2001) "The Chesapeake slave trade: regional patterns, African origins, and some implications," *William and Mary Quarterly* 58: 139–69.

Washington [Creel], Margaret (1988) *"A Peculiar People": Slave Religion and Community-Culture among the Gullahs.* New York: New York University Press.

Wax, Darold (1973) "Preferences for slaves in colonial America," *Journal of Negro History* 58: 371–401.

Williams, Chancellor (1976) *The Destruction of Black Civilization: Great Issues of a Race from 4500 B.C. to 2000 A.D.* Chicago: Third World Press.

Williams, Eric (1944) *Capitalism and Slavery.* Chapel Hill: University of North Carolina Press.

Wood, Peter (1974) *Black Majority: Negroes in Colonial South Carolina from 1670 through the Stono Rebellion.* New York: W. W. Norton.

Woodson, Carter G. (1936) *The African Background Outlined.* Washington, DC: Association for the Study of Negro Life and History.

Suggestions for Further Reading

Abrahams, Roger D. (1992) *Singing the Master: The Emergence of African-American Culture in the Plantation South.* New York: Pantheon.

Berlin, Ira (1980) "Time, space, and the evolution of Afro-American society on British mainland North America," *American Historical Review* 85: 44–78.

—— (1981) "The slave trade and the development of Afro-American society in English mainland North America, 1619–1775," *Southern Studies* 20: 122–36.

Berlin, Ira, and Morgan, Philip D. (eds.) (1993) *Cultivation and Culture: Labor and the Shaping of Slave Life in the Americas.* Charlottesville: University Press of Virginia.

Blassingame, John (1972) *The Slave Community: Plantation Life in the Antebellum South.* New York: Oxford University Press.

Carretta, Vincent (1999) "Olaudah Equiano or Gustavus Vassa? New light on an eighteenth-century question of identity," *Slavery and Abolition* 20: 96–105.

Dalby, David (1972) "The African element in black American English" in Thomas Kochman (ed.), *Rappin' and Stylin' Out*, 170–86. Urbana: University of Illinois Press.

Dusinberre, William (1996) *Them Dark Days: Slavery in the American Rice Swamps.* New York: Oxford University Press.

Egerton, Douglas (1993) *Gabriel's Rebellion: The Virginia Slave Conspiracies of 1800 and 1802.* Chapel Hill: University of North Carolina Press.

Fenn, Elizabeth A. (1984) "Honoring the ancestors: Kongo-American graves in the American South," *Southern Exposure* 13: 42–7.

Ferguson, Leland (1992) *Uncommon Ground: Archaeology and Early African America, 1650–1800.* Washington, DC: Smithsonian Institution Press.

Fett, Sharla M. (2002) *Working Cures: Healing, Health, and Power on Southern Slave Plantations.* Chapel Hill: University of North Carolina Press.

Genovese, Eugene (1976) *Roll, Jordan, Roll: The World the Slaves Made.* New York: Vintage Books.

Georgia Writers' Project (1940) *Drums and Shadows: Survival Studies among the Coastal Negroes.* Athens: University of Georgia Press.

Gutman, Herbert G. (1976) *The Black Family in Slavery and Freedom, 1750–1925.* New York: Pantheon.

Heckscher, Jurretta Jordan (2000) "'All the mazes of the dance': black dancing, culture, and identity in the greater Chesapeake World from the early eighteenth century to the Civil War." PhD dissertation, George Washington University.

Hine, Darlene Clark and McLeod, Jaqueline (eds.) (1999) *Crossing Boundaries: Comparative History of Black People in Diaspora.* Bloomington: Indiana University Press.

Holloway, Joseph and Vass, Winifred (1993) *The African Heritage of American English.* Bloomington: University of Indiana Press.

Hurston, Zora Neale (1935) *Mules and Men: Negro Folktales and Voodoo Practices in the South*. New York: J. B. Lippincott.

Ingersoll, Thomas (1996) "The slave trade and the ethnic diversity of Louisiana's slave community," *Louisiana History* 37: 133–61.

Jamieson, Ross W. (1995) "Material culture and social death: African-American burial practices," *Historical Archaeology* 29: 39–58.

Jones-Jackson, Patricia (1987) *When Roots Die: Endangered Traditions on the Sea Islands*. Athens: University of Georgia Press.

Leaming, Hugo P. (1979) "Hidden Americans: Maroons of Virginia and South Carolina." PhD dissertation, University of Illinois.

Linebaugh, Peter, and Rediker, Marcus (2000) *The Many-Headed Hydra: Sailors, Slaves, Commoners, and the Hidden History of the Revolutionary Atlantic*. Boston: Beacon Press.

Olwell, Robert (1998) *Masters, Slaves, and Subjects: The Culture of Power in the South Carolina Low Country, 1740–1790*. Ithaca, NY: Cornell University Press.

Palmie, Stephan (ed.) (1995) *Slave Cultures and the Cultures of Slavery*. Knoxville: University of Tennessee Press.

Piersen, William D. (1988) *Black Yankees: The Development of an Afro-American Subculture in Eighteenth-Century New England*. Amherst: University of Massachusetts Press.

—— (1993) *Black Legacy: America's Hidden Heritage*. Amherst: University of Massachusetts Press.

Potkay, Adam and Burr, Sandra (eds.) (1995) *Black Atlantic Writers of the 18th Century: Living the New Exodus in England and the Americas*. New York: St. Martin's Press.

Rawley, James (1981) *The Transatlantic Slave Trade: A History*. New York: Norton.

Rodney, Walter (1969) "Upper Guinea and the significance of the origins of Africans enslaved in the New World," *Journal of Negro History* 54: 327–45.

Rucker, Walter (1999) "'The river floweth on': the African social and cultural origins of black resistance in North America, 1712–1831." PhD dissertation, University of California-Riverside.

Samford, Patricia (1996) "The archaeology of African-American slavery and material culture," *William and Mary Quarterly* 53: 87–114.

Schuler, Monica (1974) "Afro-American slave culture," *Historical Reflections* 6: 121–37, 138–55.

Suttles, William C., Jr (1971) "African religious survivals as factors in American slave revolts," *Journal of Negro History* 56: 97–104.

Thompson, Robert Farris and Cornet, Joseph (1981) *The Four Moments of the Sun: Kongo Art in Two Worlds*. Washington, DC: National Gallery of Art.

Thornton, John (1998) "The African experience of the '20 and odd Negroes' arriving in Virginia in 1619," *William and Mary Quarterly* 55: 421–34.

—— (2000) "War, the state, and religious norms in 'Coromantee' thought: the ideology of an African American nation" in Robert Blair St. George (ed.), *Possible Pasts: Becoming Colonial in Early America*, 181–200. Ithaca, NY: Cornell University Press.

Vlach, John M. (1977) "Graveyards and Afro-American art," *Southern Exposure* 5: 61–5.

—— (1978) *The Afro-American Tradition in Decorative Arts*. Cleveland, OH: Cleveland Museum of Art.

—— (1991) *By the Work of Their Hands: Studies in Afro-American Folklife*. Ann Arbor: UMI Research Press.

Watson, Richard L. (1978) "American scholars and the continuity of African culture in the United States," *Journal of Negro History* 63: 375–86.

Wax, Darold (1978) "Black immigrants: the slave trade in colonial Maryland," *Maryland Historical Magazine* 73: 30–45.

—— (1984) "'New negroes are always in demand': the slave trade in eighteenth-century Georgia," *Georgia Historical Quarterly* 68: 193–220.

White, Shane (1989) "Pinkster: Afro-Dutch syncretization in New York City and the Hudson Valley," *Journal of American Folklore* 102: 23–75.

—— (1994) "'It was a proud day': African Americans, festivals, and parades in the North, 1741–1834," *Journal of American History* 81: 13–50.

White, Shane and White, Graham (1998) *Stylin': African American Expressive Culture from Its Beginnings to the Zoot Suit.* Ithaca, NY: Cornell University Press.

—— (1999) "'Us likes a mixtery': listening to African-American slave music," *Slavery and Abolition* 20: 22–48.

Wood, Betty and Frey, Sylvia (eds.) (1999) *From Slavery to Emancipation in the Atlantic World.* London: Frank Cass.

PART V

The Civil War, Emancipation, and the Quest for Freedom

CHAPTER FOURTEEN

African Americans and the American Civil War

OSCAR R. WILLIAMS III AND HAYWARD "WOODY" FARRAR

Fought from April 1861 to April 1865, the American Civil War is the bloodiest war in US history. Over 620,000 American lives were lost in this tragic event. Fought between the North and South, the war found its origins in fundamental debates over the continued existence of slavery throughout the United States. In the 1850s, the debates came to a head, when proslavery forces became more aggressive in their defense of their plantation slavery-based economy. In late 1860, South Carolina was the first southern state to secede from the Union. By February 1861, seven seceded southern states had formed the Confederate States of America (CSA). In April, Fort Sumter in Charleston, South Carolina, fell to the Confederacy, signaling the beginning of the war.

Most standard histories of the Civil War – such as those of Bruce Catton, Douglas Southall Freeman, Allan Nevins, and Shelby Foote – mention African Americans in the Civil War in passing, but there is also an extensive literature describing the African American struggle for freedom in the Civil War era. Among these works are James McPherson's *Battle Cry of Freedom*, *The Negro's Civil War*, and *Marching toward Freedom*, Benjamin Quarles' *The Negro in the Civil War*, Dudley Taylor Cornish's *The Sable Arm: Negro Troops in the Union Army, 1861–1865*, Louis S. Gerteis' *From Contraband to Freedman: Federal Policy toward Southern Blacks: 1861–1865*, *Freedom's Soldiers* edited by Ira Berlin, Joseph Reidy, and Leslie Rowland, Bernard Nalty's *Strength for the Fight: A History of Black Americans in the Military*, Jack D. Foner's *Blacks and the Military in American History*, Michael Lee Lanning's *The African American Soldier*, and Gerald Astor's *The Right to Fight*. All of these works are consistent in their assertions and descriptions of the bravery of African American soldiers in the face of northern indifference and skepticism, and southern hatred.

Few are aware that, during the first two years of the war, African Americans were not officially included in the Union forces. Despite the fact that the war was fought over the issue of slavery, neither enslaved African Americans nor their free counterparts were permitted to enlist. For them, there was the fight for inclusion and respect.

According to McPherson in his *Battle Cry of Freedom*, immediately after the fall of Fort Sumter, newly elected President Abraham Lincoln made a call for 75,000 state militia volunteers to be placed into federal service to put down an insurrection "too powerful to be suppressed by the ordinary course of judicial proceedings" (McPherson 1988: 274). However, African Americans were excluded. Lincoln's position was that the war was for the preservation of the Union, not for the abolition of slavery. One of Abraham Lincoln's leading biographers, David Herbert Donald asserts that in actuality Lincoln wished for a peaceful reconciliation with the South, leaving slavery intact (Donald 1995: 284).

Dudley Cornish in *Sable Arm* says that – since the Union needed the support of Upper South states such as Maryland, Kentucky, Missouri, and West Virginia (made up of 48 Unionist counties in western Virginia) – they were allowed to keep slavery in return for their loyalty (Cornish 1966: 10–11). Additionally, Lincoln assured white northerners that the war would not free slaves who, they feared, would migrate to northern cities and push working-class and low-income whites out of jobs. Cities such as New York, Boston, and Philadelphia had long histories of bitter racial strife between free blacks and whites competing for the same menial and domestic jobs. Depending on those same whites to make up the bulk of the Union forces, Lincoln and the War Department enforced the ban against African American soldiers. Ohio Governor David Todd summed up the situation when asked to recruit an African American regiment. Jack Foner, in *Blacks and the Military in American History*, quotes Governor Todd as saying that "Do you know that this is a white man's government; that the white men are able to defend and protect it; and that to enlist a Negro soldier would be to drive every white man out of the service?" (Foner 1974: 32).

John Hope Franklin in *From Slavery to Freedom* believed that Lincoln, personally, felt that enslaved African Americans should be freed, but that they did not have a future in the United States. Colonization was sought as an answer. He conveyed his message to a visiting delegation of African Americans in 1862: "Your race suffer greatly, many of them, by living among us, while ours suffer from your presence. In a word we suffer on each side. If this is admitted, it affords a reason why we should be separated," advised Lincoln (Franklin 1982: 189). The following year, the US Government sponsored a colonization experiment with 453 African Americans sent to an island near Haiti. However, McPherson points out that the experiment failed when disease and starvation plagued the colonists. The surviving members were brought back to the USA in 1864 (McPherson 1988: 509).

In spite of Lincoln's ban, African Americans offered their services to defend the Union and defeat slavery. Frederick Douglass opposed Lincoln's ban and argued for their participation. "Let the slaves and free colored people be called into service, and formed into a liberating army, to march into the South and raise the banner of emancipation among the slaves," argued Douglass (Cornish 1966: 5). Benjamin Quarles described how African Americans met at Twelfth Street Baptist Church in Boston to discuss their pledge to defend the USA as well as free their enslaved brethren. "Our feelings urge us to say to our countrymen that we are ready to stand by and defend the Government with our lives, our fortunes and our sacred honor," stated the resolutions committee. Quarles stated that black women volunteered as "nurses, seamstresses, and warriors if need be" (Quarles 1953: 27). He added that, in Cleveland, African Americans pledged at a meeting to form a military corps. This also happened in Pittsburgh, where an African American organization called "Hannibal's Guards offered their services to the Pennsylvania state militia" (McPherson 1965: 19–20).

In New York and Philadelphia, African Americans held similar meetings, pledging their loyalty to the Union and offering to form regiments. The *New York Tribune* reported that, in Philadelphia, "The blacks here are drilling on their own hook. They could muster 5000 here easily" (Quarles 1953: 27). Despite the vigorous patriotism of African Americans, their services were declined, sometimes in vulgar fashion. Peter Clark in his study of African Americans in Cincinnati recorded that, when African Americans in that city tried to form a regiment, police were sent to break up meetings. One policeman bluntly told a group, "We want you dammed niggers to keep out of this; this is a white man's war" (Clark 1969: 5). These examples bolster Gerald Astor's assertion in *The Right to Fight* that "The offer of men, even women, to bear arms, the assertion of fealty to the Union failed to impress either the authorities or much of the white population who scorned blacks as inferior in intelligence and ineffective as warriors" (Astor 1998: 23).

Despite the ban, there were exceptions that helped to break down racial barriers. When the Tidewater Virginia region came under Union control in 1861, fugitive slaves flocked to Union lines and forts with hopes of being free. Fort Monroe in Hampton Roads became the focus of the area's fugitive slaves. In May 1861, Union forces under the command of General Benjamin Butler arrived to occupy the fort. Shortly after their arrival, three slaves arrived at Fort Monroe in the dead of night, and immediately offered their services to the Union. Officially, slaves were to be returned to their owners. General Butler decided to claim the slaves as contraband, arguing that their masters were in rebellion against the Union, and that their property would be considered as such (Nalty 1986: 31). From a practical stance, Butler had justifiable cause to declare such a policy. Butler wrote to his superior officer: "I am credibly informed that the Negroes in this neighborhood are now being employed in the erection of [Confederate] batteries" (Gerteis 1973: 13). Word of the new policy circulated rapidly among the slave population. Within two days, 59 slaves came to Fort Monroe, causing Butler to remark that approximately $60,000 worth of slaves had arrived in a three-day period (Quarles 1953: 61).

In July 1861, Congress addressed the issue by passing the first of two confiscation acts. The first Act stated that any property used in rebellion against the Union would be subject to confiscation by the Union. In the case of fugitive slaves, their status would not change, nor would it affect slaves in areas already under Union or loyalist control (Gerteis 1973: 17). Nonetheless, fugitive slaves labeled contraband would be free from seizure by their masters and under the auspices of federal law. Consequently, fugitive slaves were put to work by Union forces as laborers, teamsters, cooks, and other types of menial and domestic labor. In July 1862, the second Confiscation Act was passed, declaring that slaves "in any city occupied by our troops and previously occupied by rebels were declared free" (ibid: 71–2). Ira Berlin in his *Freedom's Soldiers: The Black Military Experience in the Civil War* asserts that these laws appealed to northerners as ways to punish the Confederacy by depriving it of its slaves, use confiscated slave labor against the South and change the war into a fight against slavery, giving it a moral dimension it had not had before (Berlin

1998: 4–5). Although both acts were designed as war measures, the confiscation acts precipitated the Emancipation Proclamation and the inclusion of African Americans in the Civil War (ibid: 6).

One question regarding contraband slaves was whether they could be incorporated into American society as responsible, self-sufficient citizens. Gerteis and Quarles examine this question through their accounts of the Port Royal Experiment, a federally supported social and economic program which tried to answer this question. Centered at Port Royal, South Carolina, the program focused on the Sea Islands coastal areas of lower South Carolina, Georgia, and parts of upper Florida. When Union forces conquered the region, planters fled the area, leaving behind their slaves and land. Quarles describes how the Union government, needing a labor force to harvest the valuable cotton crop, instructed the Secretary of the Treasury, Salmon P. Chase, to send Edward L. Pierce to Port Royal to construct and supervise a free labor program (Quarles 1953: 123). Pierce did this in 1862, in official cooperation with Mansfield French of the American Missionary Association (AMA), and the program served as a rehearsal for Reconstruction (Gerteis 1973: 52).

The Port Royal Experiment divided the Sea Islands region into military districts headed by superintendents. The plantation labor system was retained, yet the contraband slaves worked under a free labor system and were allowed to supervise themselves (Quarles 1953: 123–5; Gerteis 1973: 52–3). They were required to harvest the area's cotton crop for the US Treasury and allowed to grow foodstuffs such as corn and potatoes. In addition, contraband slaves were eligible to purchase the planters' abandoned lands. The AMA sent missionaries and teachers to establish schools for the contraband slaves (Quarles 1953: 124). To assist in the transition from slaves to freedmen, the federal government, the AMA, and other private organizations established relief agencies. The experiment proved to be a success in demonstrating that former slaves could be productive, educated citizens. In the first year, approximately 4,000 laborers planted and harvested 6,500 acres of corn, 1,000 acres of potatoes, and 3,000 acres of cotton (Gerteis 1973: 52). In the same period, 30 freedmen schools were established, and relief agencies distributed over 35,000 books and pamphlets (Quarles 1953: 125). Sadly, the experiment ended after the war when the abandoned lands were given back to the planters. Nonetheless, the Port Royal Experiment inspired the creation of the Freedmen's Bureau, a federal relief agency for the former slaves. It also inspired the unsuccessful effort to reward former slaves with the abandoned lands of planters, defined by the cry, "forty acres and a mule" (Franklin and Moss 1982: 214).

Another development occurred in April 1862, when Union General David Hunter assumed control of the Sea Islands region. Hunter, aware of the Port Royal Experiment, felt that the contraband slaves could be used militarily for the Union effort (Nalty 1986: 24; Astor 1998: 23). General Hunter, on April 13, 1862, after capturing the Confederate strongholds Fort Pulaski and Cockspur Island, declared: "All persons of color lately held to involuntary service by enemies of the United States in Fort Pulaski and on Cockspur Island, George, are hereby confiscated and declared free, in conformity of law, and shall hereafter receive the fruits of their own labor." Later that month, Hunter placed the Sea Islands region under martial law and declared that "The persons in these three states, Georgia, Florida, and South Carolina, heretofore held as slaves are therefore declared forever free" (Cornish 1966: 35). In conjunction with the radical proclamation, Hunter issued an order to form an armed regiment of freed slaves. Composed of able-bodied men from the Sea Islands area, the regiment was formed into the 1st South Carolina Volunteers Regiment.

Hunter's actions went beyond the first Confiscation Act and directly challenged Lincoln's policy. Although the War Department gave free rein to high-ranking officers to do what they felt was necessary for the war effort, it did not envision the use of fugitive slaves as soldiers. In addition, Lincoln feared that Hunter's actions would cause him to lose support in the Border States and among northern supporters who did not want the war effort to become an abolitionist cause. On May 19, Lincoln countered Hunter with his own proclamation, declaring "The Government of the United States had no knowledge, information, or belief of intention on the part of General Hunter to issue such a proclamation; nor has it any authentic information that the document is genuine" (Cornish 1966: 35). Lincoln rescinded the order, stating that "neither General Hunter nor any other commander or person has been authorized by the Government of the United States to make proclamations declaring the slaves of any State free; and that the supposed proclamation now in question, whether genuine or false, is altogether void" (Cornish 1966: 36). General Hunter then lobbied Lincoln and the War Department to let him continue to recruit runaway and captured slaves (Astor 1998: 23). This effort failed as the War Department, under the leadership of Edwin M. Stanton, ordered the regiment disbanded, with the exception of one unit, which was used for the purpose of constructing Union defenses (ibid: 23; Foner 1974: 35).

Despite the disbanding of the 1st South Carolina Volunteer Regiment, Lincoln was faced with a dilemma in the summer of 1862. Hunter's orders and the Port Royal Experiment proved that the slave population could be used for the Union effort economically and militarily. Simultaneously, Lincoln struggled with keeping the abolition of slavery and the war effort separate. Earlier in the year, Lincoln appealed to representatives in the Border States to gradually abolish slavery and receive financial aid in return. McPherson describes how twice the delegates rejected his appeal, the second time by a vote of 20 to 9 (McPherson 1982: 272). Faced with a stalling Union war effort and constant pressure from abolitionists, Lincoln decided that the abolition of slavery was a necessary war measure.

The distinguished Lincoln biographer David Herbert Donald told how on July 22, 1862 Lincoln held a meeting with his full cabinet to discuss a new plan. Pledging support for those states that would gradually abolish slavery, Lincoln declared that on January 1, 1863, he would declare "all persons held as slaves within any state . . . wherein the constitutional authority of the United States shall not then be practically recognized, . . . forever . . . free" (Donald 1995: 365). Predictably, members of his cabinet expressed doubt and concern. Secretary of State William Seward was most critical, suggesting that the proclamation would harm foreign relations, mentioning Great Britain's sympathies towards the Confederacy. Seward said that additionally, the proclamation would appear as "a cry for help; the government stretching forth its hands to Ethiopia instead of Ethiopia stretching forth her hands to the government" (Quarles 1953: 159). Despite his criticisms, he grudgingly supported the plan, but cautioned Lincoln to issue it after a military success.

The military success came in September 1862, when Union forces defeated Confederate troops at the bloody battle of Antietam in Maryland. Two months to the day after his cabinet meeting, he gathered them once again to read his plan, now called the Emancipation Proclamation. Short and direct, the proclamation stated the following:

> That on the 1st day of January, A.D. 1863, all persons held as slaves within any state or designated part of a state the people whereof shall then be in rebellion against the United States shall be then, thenceforward, and forever free; and the executive government of the United States, including the military and naval authority thereof, will recognize and maintain the freedom of such persons and will do no act or acts to repress such persons, or any of them, in any efforts they may make for their actual freedom. (Franklin 1982: 532)

In practice, the proclamation would abolish slavery in any rebel state or territory that fell under Union control. The proclamation had no effect on slavery in the Border States and those areas already conquered by the Union. In fact, one might go further and say that the proclamation was quite calculated in its limitations: it gave the Confederate states over three months to submit and thereby keep their slaves. It seems surprising that they did not do this and end the war more quickly.

There have been various interpretations of the Emancipation Proclamation. Quarles, Astor, and Nalty assert that it immediately turned the war into a fight for black freedom and opened up the Union Army to black troops (Quarles 1953: 181; Nalty 1986: 36; Astor 1998: 27). Berlin and Cornish take a more measured view, asserting that Lincoln and his advisors had not totally made up their minds on whether or how black troops would be used (Cornish 1966: 96–7; Berlin 1998: 8–10). Nonetheless, the Emancipation Proclamation changed the course of the war. Not only did it challenge the Confederacy to surrender, it made the slave population free to join the Union armed forces, giving Lincoln the boost he needed to win the war.

Predictably, African Americans were the most enthusiastic supporters of Lincoln's proclamation, and showed their appreciation by holding celebrations on New Year's Day in 1863. Quarles describes how at Port Royal, a huge all-day celebration was held, where African Americans sang "My Country 'tis of Thee" (Quarles 1953: 178–9). McPherson, in *The Negro's Civil War*, quotes the African Americans of Harrisburg, Pennsylvania, who held a meeting to commemorate the Emancipation Proclamation and made the resolution, "That we, the colored citizens of the city of Harrisburg, hail the 1st day of January, 1863, as a new era in our country's history – a day in which injustice and oppression were forced to flee and cower before the benign principles of justice and righteousness" (McPherson 1965: 51).

Shortly after the Emancipation Proclamation, the War Department approved the enlistment of African Americans in the Union armed forces, creating the United States Colored Troops (USCT), the division of the US Army for African American soldiers. In response, African American military units were created in northern states. Massachusetts Governor John Andrew received permission to establish the all-African American 54th Massachusetts Regiment. Frederick Douglass, Henry Highland Garnet, Charles Redmond, and other prominent African Americans assisted in recruiting for the regiment. Most impassioned was Douglass, who, in March 1863, published an editorial encouraging African American enlistment. Under the title "Men of Color to Arms," Douglass made the following emotional plea:

Action! Action! Not criticism is the plain duty of this hour. Words are now useful only as they stimulate to blows. The office of speech now is only to point out when, where, and how to strike to the best advantage. There is no time to delay. The tide is at its flood that leads on to fortune. From East to West, from North to South, the sky is written all over, NOW OR NEVER! Liberty won by white men would lose half its luster. Who would be free themselves must strike the blow. Better even die free, than to live slaves. This is the sentiment of every brave colored man amongst us. . . . (Douglass 1892: 414–15)

The fight for inclusion proved to be half the battle for African American soldiers. Sadly, they found themselves fighting a war on two fronts: against the Confederacy, and against their fellow white soldiers. From the beginning, African American soldiers were subject to brutal racism in policy and practice. Only white officers would lead African American soldiers. Most African Americans rose no higher in rank than sergeant, with the exception of some African American chaplains. The most irritating policy was unequal pay between white and African American soldiers. White privates were paid $13 a month plus $3.50 for a clothing allowance. African Americans, regardless of rank, were paid $10 a month, with $3 deducted for clothing allowance (Astor 1998: 29–30; Nalty 1986: 39; Quarles 1953: 200; Foner 1974: 41–2). Many African American soldiers, rankled at their treatment, refused to accept the pay out of principle. The men of the 54th Massachusetts Regiment went without pay for over a year. The Massachusetts state legislature passed provisions to make up the difference in pay, but the regiment refused the offer, arguing that it was the responsibility of the federal government (Astor 1998: 29–30; Nalty 1986: 39; Foner 1974: 41–2). The pay scale was corrected for African American soldiers in 1864, but not before it caused some bitterness. Foner describes how an African American soldier, in a letter to President Lincoln, asked, "We have done a soldier's duty. Why can't we have a soldier's pay?" (Foner 1974: 42).

Most historians of African American soldiers in the Civil War found that African Americans were more subject to backbreaking labor than their fellow white soldiers (Foner, Nalty, Quarles, Cornish). White commanders, feeling that they were better laborers than soldiers, forced them to work on fortifications, roads, and loading docks while under fire. Fellow white soldiers were often resentful of African Americans, feeling that the war was their fault. Redkey quotes an African American soldier who remembered that, when a former white playmate was called off to war, he stated, "Why you niggers are the cause of my having to leave my home. If it had not been for the Negroes this war never would have been" (Redkey 1992: 266). The same soldier recalled another instance where a group of African American and Irish soldiers were having dinner. When finished, the black soldiers paid the bill, whereupon one Irish soldier screamed, "Damn the black soul of you, you must get out or we will give you the shillelagh" (ibid: 268).

Conditions for African American soldiers were rather squalid and unsanitary, as described by one soldier in 1865 in South Carolina. "We are encamped on the old hospital ground, where they buried all their dead. We had to dig wells in the graveyard, and drink the water off the putrid bodies, and it is killing our men" (Redkey 1992: 258). Commenting that the rations they received were those rejected by white troops, he describes their condition:

You ought to see the hard tack that we have to eat. They are moldy and musty and full of worms, and not fit for a dog to eat and the rice and beans and peas are musty and the salt horse (salt beef I mean) is so salt that after it is cooked we can't eat it. Some days the men are sent on fatigue in the hot sun, and when they come home to dinner, there is nothing to eat but rotten hard tack and flat coffee, without sugar in it. (ibid: 260–1)

Redkey and Cornish state that one of the most humiliating experiences for African American soldiers was serving under incompetent racist commanders who shamelessly abused and mistreated their men. Redkey includes a soldier's comment on such instances: "They strike the men with their swords, and jog and punch them in their side to show them how to drill . . . I do not think it right that soldiers should be cuffed and knocked around so by their officers, especially as we colored soldiers are" (Redkey 1992: 261). Another soldier recalled how his white company commander knocked a soldier to the ground with a sword, when the soldier made a mistake while marching in the funeral procession for President Lincoln. "How long is this to be endured? How long must the government strain at gnats and swallow camels . . . With such a man for commander, brutality like that which we have described would find instantaneous redress, and the perpetrator be fitly punished" (ibid: 264).

African American soldiers were not immune to abuse from white civilians. African Americans, resented by working-class and low-income whites in the North and South, were subject to violent attacks (Quarles 1953: 235–7). Redkey published a letter describing how, in Baltimore, an African American surgeon was attacked and robbed on a train by a white mob while in full uniform. When the surgeon and an armed escort cornered the perpetrators, a fight ensued, whereupon the surgeon was punched in the face. Fortunately, they were arrested and prosecuted (Redkey 1992: 253–5). White civilian violence often went beyond targeting African American soldiers. In July 1863, New York City erupted into three days of violence centered in lower and midtown Manhattan. Predominantly Irish immigrant mobs, angered over the military draft, burned and looted hundreds of businesses and other establishments in protest. However, their human targets were African Americans, whom they blamed for the war and viewed as an economic threat. Mobs chased and cornered African Americans, screaming "Kill all niggers!" Many were killed in the sight of policemen, who either stood by and watched, or joined the rioters. Most chilling was the burning of the Colored Orphan Asylum. Rioters surrounded the orphanage with the children inside and set fire to the building, screaming, "Burn the niggers' nest!" (Burrows 1999: 890). Fortunately, all of the children, except one, were able to escape the fire. The riot finally stopped when Union troops returning from the Battle of Gettysburg arrived in the city. Using cannon fire and bayonet charges, the soldiers were able to bring the city under control. The final toll was over 100 killed, although various studies have claimed that the death toll was over 1000 (Quarles 1953: 238–47; Nalty 1986: 42; Burrows 1999: 895).

Despite brutal racism in the North and in the Union Army, the most feared fate of African American soldiers was being in the hands of the Confederate soldiers. Officially, the CSA Legislature recognized African American soldiers as runaway slaves and their white commanders as leaders of slave rebellions. CSA President Jefferson Davis in December 1862 signed into law the proclamation that "all Negro slaves captured in arms be at once delivered over to the executive authorities of the respective states to which they belong to be dealt with according to the laws of said states" and that "like orders be executed in all cases with respect to all commissioned officers of the United States when found serving in company with all slaves" (Westwood 1992: 87). In practice, African American soldiers were either imprisoned and forced to work as laborers for the Confederacy, or sold into slavery. White commanders were either imprisoned or executed. In addition, it was customary for the Confederacy not to exchange African American Union prisoners for Confederate prisoners. The practice, coupled with other types of abuse of African American soldiers, caused the Union to suspend the exchange of Confederate and Union prisoners of war in 1864 (Astor 1998: 31; Nalty 1986: 45; McPherson 1988: 793).

Although the official Confederate policy was reason enough for African American soldiers to fear capture, it was the unofficial and terrifying practice of murdering African American captives that appalled and infuriated them. Incensed by the presence of African American Union soldiers, Confederate officers (many of whom were slave owners) and soldiers felt insulted when confronted by them (Nalty 1986: 44). Consequently, some of the most appalling war atrocities occurred when African American captives were in the hands of Confederate soldiers. Two infamous events that illuminated this horrible practice were the Battle of the Crater and the Fort Pillow Massacre.

In July 1864, during the Siege of Petersburg, Virginia, Union forces attempted a bold plan to detonate explosives under the main Confederate line and send in Union soldiers to capture it (Quarles 1953: 300; Cornish 1966: 273). African American soldiers were to be sent in first to surround the crater, but Union officers pulled them hours before the attack and sent in inexperienced white soldiers. When the explosives blew a huge crater in the line, the white soldiers, unfamiliar with the plan, surged into the crater, instantly becoming open targets for the regrouping Confederate troops. In a state of confusion and desperation, Union officers sent in the African American troops, much to the rage of Confederate soldiers. What ensued was an indiscriminate killing of African American troops who were wounded or tried to surrender. Many were bayoneted and shot at point-blank range by Confederate soldiers who desired instant revenge for their dead comrades. To add insult to injury, some white Union soldiers, fearful of Confederate soldiers, killed African American soldiers in an attempt to save their own lives. The toll was 3,800 casualties, 1,400 of whom were African American. An investigation ruled that the Union officers were at fault for the failure of the plan by pulling the African American soldiers. The findings also revealed that the general of the African American soldiers cowered in the rear getting drunk while they fought (Quarles 1953: 301–4; Cornish 1966: 271–3; Jordan 1995: 276–8).

The Fort Pillow Massacre in Tennessee, three months earlier, was another incident of horrors that outdid the atrocities at Petersburg. Fort Pillow on the Mississippi River was a former Confederate stronghold that was in Union hands at the time of the battle. Approximately 600 Union soldiers, half of whom were African American, were in the fort, as well as African American refugees and Confederate deserters from the area. Surrounded and outnumbered by Confederate forces under the command of General Nathan Bedford Forrest, the fort fell when it was stormed after the Union commander refused to surrender. What followed, according to survivors, was an indiscriminate killing of surrendering troops (McPherson 1967: 82–5; Cornish 1966: 173–6; Nalty 1986: 74).

As with the Battle of the Crater, African American soldiers were the principal targets of enraged Confederate soldiers. Williams and Edgerton describe how African American troops were shot after surrendering and how wounded soldiers were put in tents and other quarters and burned alive (Edgerton 2001: 31–3). Civilians and deserters caught in the fort were not spared: a Confederate lieutenant later testified how he tried to save an African American child, but was ordered by a general to kill the child (Edgerton 2001: 31–3; Williams 1888: 260). Union soldiers who tried to escape to Union gunboats were chased and shot in the river (Williams 1888: 262).

Contemporary estimates placed the death toll near 300, the majority of them African American soldiers. General Nathaniel Forrest, a slave trader before the war and one of the earliest members of the Ku Klux Klan after the war, was investigated for war crimes but was cleared of any charges. The incident shocked and incensed African American soldiers, inspiring them to fight more intensely and giving inspiration to the rallying cry, "Remember Fort Pillow!" (Cornish 1966: 176; Quarles 1953: 222).

Despite suffering from the hands of white Union and Confederate soldiers and officers, African American soldiers fought against adversity and distinguished themselves in the heat of battle. Numerous studies recount the bravery and courage of troops that fought against the odds. The 54th Massachusetts Regiment is one example of bravery in the face of fire. Many historians have described the incredible bravery at the battle of Fort Wagner, and their sacrifice was immortalized in the movie *Glory*. In July 1863, Union forces attempted to take Fort Wagner, a Confederate fort south of Charleston, SC, with a full assault. After an initial attempt to take the fort failed, Colonel Robert Gould Shaw, Commander of the 54th, volunteered to lead the second charge with his troops (Quarles 1953: 13; McPherson 1965: 75; Cornish 1966: 153; Hine et al. 2000: 242). The 54th had experienced wartime combat for only a few days, and now they were asked to charge one of the most impenetrable forts of the war.

After a severe Union bombardment, the 54th led a nighttime advance of 5,000 Union troops. Despite the bombardment, the regiment met heavy fire during the advance and immediately suffered casualties. Nonetheless, the 54th continued their advance, until they were in full view of the parapet. At this point they were fully exposed to the murderous fire of the Confederate artillery and infantry of Fort Wagner. Yet, the 54th advanced on the parapet and took it, to the surprise of the Confederate forces. However, the 54th's valiant and courageous advance was in vain: the Confederate forces pushed back the Union advance and the fort remained in their hands. The Union's casualties were heavy, but the 54th suffered the worst. Over 40 percent of the 54th were killed or injured. Among the killed was Colonel Shaw, who was buried in a mass grave with his men (Quarles 1953: 114–16; McPherson 1965: 76–8; Cornish 1966: 153–6; Hine et al. 2000: 242–3).

Although the advance was unsuccessful, the 54th impressed and amazed white officers and soldiers who witnessed the human tragedy. Edward Pierce, a correspondent of the *New York Tribune*, wrote to Governor Andrew of Massachusetts of the regiment: "The fifty-forth did well and nobly; only the fall of Colonel Shaw prevented them from entering the fort. They moved up as gallantly as any troops could, and with their enthusiasm they deserved a better fate" (quoted in Emilio 1891: 94). One Confederate officer was moved to comment on the 54th's effort. "The Negroes fought gallantly, and were headed by as brave a colonel as ever lived" (ibid: 95). Though their ranks were depleted, the 54th Massachusetts marked their place in American history and continued their service throughout the war.

African American soldiers distinguished themselves in other military battles, such as the Battle of Port Hudson. In May 1863, African American soldiers participated in a Union assault on Port Hudson, a Confederate fort on the Mississippi River in Louisiana. The attempt was unsuccessful but, as with Fort Wagner, the soldiers earned the respect of their white officers. One officer commented, "You have no idea how my prejudices with regard to Negro troops have been dispelled by the battle the other day. The brigade behaved magnificently and fought splendidly" (McPherson 1965: 185; Quarles 1953: 218–20; Cornish 1966: 142–4).

Robert Smalls was a black naval hero of the Civil War. His heroism is described in numerous accounts. Smalls, who was 23 years old in 1862, was a slave on the Confederate warship *Planter*. In May of that year, Smalls enacted a daring plan of escaping to Union lines with his family. When the captain and white crew members went onshore one night in Charleston, South Carolina, Smalls donned a Confederate uniform, smuggled his family on the ship and, relying on his seafaring experience, piloted the ship out of the harbor and to the Union blockade. Smalls was praised and celebrated for his ingenuity and bravery, serving as a Union Navy pilot throughout the war (Quarles 1953: 73–4, 91–3; Astor 1998: 26–7; Nalty 1986: 48–9; Foner 1974: 47; Lanning 1997: 59, 63, 64; Edgerton 2001: 25). Afterward, he returned to his home in South Carolina, where he went on to a distinguished political career as a US congressman (Westwood 1992: 74–85).

Earlier studies were somewhat ambivalent as to African American participation in the Confederacy. However, Ervin Jordan in his *Black Confederates and Afro Yankees in Civil War Virginia* states emphatically that the rebel government and military immediately recognized the enormous slave population as one of the most valuable resources in the Confederate war effort. Jordan describes how slaves were used by the Confederacy primarily as cheap labor in the form of laborers, teamsters, cooks, and other supporting occupations. In Richmond, Virginia, slave labor composed the majority of workers at the Tredegar Iron Works, the main supplier of cannon, shot, and cast-iron plates for the Confederacy during the war (Jordan 1995: 51).

African Americans participated in the Confederate forces militarily as well. Whether out of loyalty to their masters or their homeland, or for self-serving reasons, many slaves and free blacks volunteered their services to the Confederacy. According to James Hollandsworth's *The Louisiana Native Guards: The Black Military Experience during the Civil War*, in New Orleans approximately 1,500 free blacks offered their services to protect the city. Known as the Louisiana Native Guards, the group pledged that "the population to which we belong . . . will be ready to take arms and form themselves into companies for the defense of their homes, together with the other inhabitants of this city, against any enemy who may come and disturb its tranquility" (Hollandsworth 1995: 2). Although they were enthusiastically received by city officials and included in city parades, the Confederate Army refused their services. Ironically, when the city fell in 1862, Union General Benjamin Butler quickly incorporated the regiment into his forces. Body servants were known to participate in battle as well. During the Seven Days' Battles in Virginia, Westley, a body servant described as "a good-looking darkey," was put in place of a Confederate soldier who refused to go into battle. He killed a number of Union soldiers and was held in high regard by his white counterparts (Jordan 1995: 191).

As the Confederate forces suffered heavy losses and desertion from their ranks, some officers contemplated the use of African American soldiers. Confederate General Patrick Cleburne was one of the first officers to suggest it. In an 1863 letter to President Jefferson Davis, he called for the creation of a reserve of slaves to refresh depleted ranks, guaranteeing freedom to slaves "who shall remain true to the Confederacy in this war" (Foner 1974: 49). Cleburne's proposal was largely ignored and forgotten until early 1865, when General Robert E. Lee wrote a letter urging the use of slaves as soldiers (ibid: 50).

Following Lee's request, the Confederate Congress in March 1865 approved the enlistment of 300,000 slaves. With the approval of their masters and home states, the soldiers would be granted freedom after their service. Some studies suggest that African American soldiers did not see any combat, since the Civil War ended a month later. However, others assert that a few soldiers did see action. One Virginia Military Institute cadet reported being relieved by Confederate African American soldiers in March 1865 prior to the fall of Richmond. In addition, 60 African American soldiers reportedly served under the command of Confederate Colonel Scott Shipp in Petersburg during the same month (Jordan 1995: 246).

Lee's request for African American soldiers reflected a universal fundamental change in Civil War military policy. As Douglass had prophesied, slavery became the principal issue of the war and African American soldiers were an integral part in the victory of the Union forces. This fact was perfectly demonstrated in the fall of Richmond in April 1865, when the 5th Massachusetts Cavalry of the 36th United States Colored Troops were the first Union soldiers to enter the burning city. Under the command of General Alonzo Draper, the 36th marched into Richmond and assumed control, much to the delight of cheering African Americans (Blackett 1989: 290; Edgerton 2001: 38).

The consensus of what has been written on African Americans in the Civil War is that their saga is a compelling history of a group of people fighting for respect, dignity, and freedom. Whether they are documentary accounts such as Berlin's *Freedom's Soldiers*, McPherson's *The Negro's Civil War* and *Marching toward Freedom*, and Redkey's *A Grand Army of Black Men: Letters from African American Soldiers in the Union Army, 1861–1865*, or chapters in larger works such as McPherson's *Battle Cry of Freedom*, Nalty's *Strength for the Fight*, Astor's *The Right To Fight*, and Franklin's *From Slavery to Freedom*, or monographs such as Quarles' *The Negro In The Civil War*, and Cornish's *The Sable Arm*, all agree on the exceptional loyalty to freedom and union and the incredible bravery of African Americans of the Civil War era.

Benjamin Quarles' *The Negro in the Civil War* still remains the best monograph on the subject. However, it was published in 1953 and a new study along those lines needs to be made, particularly in light of the findings of the Freedom Project. Indeed new editions of such works as *The Battle Cry of Freedom* are called for. Still the literature, while getting rather mossy, gives a vivid portrayal of how – though scorned and abused by their own country, and unwanted and unloved by white Union and Confederate soldiers – yet African Americans fought against adversity and proved to be courageous, loyal, dedicated, and intelligent soldiers. Their sacrifice and efforts resulted in the abolition of slavery by way of the 13th Amendment, and the birth of a long and proud history of African Americans in the US armed forces. Although future African American soldiers would have to struggle with their own battles of respect and dignity, their way was paved by their predecessors' fight for inclusion in the Civil War.

BIBLIOGRAPHY

Works Cited

Astor, Gerald (1998) *The Right to Fight*. Cambridge, MA: Da Capo Press.

Berlin, Ira, Reidy, Joseph, and Rowland, Leslie (eds.) (1998) *Freedom's Soldiers: The Black Military Experience in the Civil War*. New York: Cambridge University Press.

Burrows, Edwin G. and Wallace, Mike (1999) *Gotham: A History of New York City to 1898*. New York: Oxford University Press.

Clark, Peter H. (1969) *The Black Brigade of Cincinnati*. New York: Arno Press.

Cornish, Dudley Taylor (1966) *The Sable Arm: Negro Troops in the Union Army, 1861–1865*. New York: W. W. Norton.

Donald, David Herbert (1995) *Lincoln*. New York: Simon & Schuster.

Douglass, Frederick (1892) *The Life and Times of Frederick Douglass*. Boston: DeWolfe and Fiske; available from University of North Carolina online collection *Documenting The American South*. http://docsouth.unc.edu/neh/dougl92/dougl92.html#p408.

Edgerton, Robert B. (2001) *Hidden Heroism: Black Soldiers in America's War*. Boulder, CO: Westview Press.

Emilio, Luis F. ([1891] 1990) *A Brave Black Regiment: History of the Fifty-Fourth Regiment of the Massachusetts Volunteer Infantry, 1863–1865*, 3rd edn. Salem, NH: Ayer.

Foner, Jack D. (1974) *Blacks and the Military in American History*. New York: Praeger.

Franklin, John Hope and Moss, Alfred A. (1982) *From Slavery to Freedom: A History of Negro Americans*, 6th edn. New York: Alfred A. Knopf.

Gerteis, Louis S. (1973) *From Contraband to Freedman: Federal Policy toward Southern Blacks: 1861–1865*. Westport, CT: Greenwood Press.

Hine, Darlene C., Hine, William C., and Harrold, Stanley (2000) *The African American Odyssey*, vol. 1. Upper Saddle River, NJ: Prentice-Hall.

Hollandsworth, James G. (1995) *The Louisiana Native Guards: The Black Military Experience during the Civil War*. Baton Rouge: Louisiana State University Press.

Jordan, Ervin L., Jr (1995) *Black Confederates and Afro Yankees in Civil War Virginia*. Charlottesville: University of Virginia Press.

Lanning, Michael Lee (1997) *The African American Soldier*. Secaucus, NJ: Birch Lane Press.

McPherson, James M. (1965) *The Negro's Civil War: How American Negroes Felt and Acted During the War for the Union*. New York: Pantheon Books.

—— (1967) *Marching toward Freedom*. New York: Knopf.

—— (1982) *Ordeal by Fire: The Civil War and Reconstruction*. New York: McGraw-Hill.

—— (1988) *Battle Cry of Freedom: The Civil War Era*. New York: Ballantine Books.

Nalty, Bernard C. (1986) *Strength for the Fight: A History of Black Americans in the Military*. New York: Free Press.

Quarles, Benjamin (1953) *The Negro in the Civil War*. Boston: Little, Brown.

Redkey, Edwin S. (ed.) (1992) *A Grand Army of Black Men: Letters from African American Soldiers in the Union Army, 1861–1865.* New York: Cambridge University Press.

Westwood, Howard C. (1992) *Black Troops, White Commanders, and Freedmen during the Civil War.* Carbondale, IL: Southern Illinois University Press.

Williams, George W. ([1888] 1969) *A History of the Negro Troops in the War of the Rebellion, 1861–1865.* New York: Negro Universities Press.

Suggestions for Further Reading

Bennett, Lerone, Jr (2000) *Forced into Glory: Abraham Lincoln's White Dream.* Chicago: Johnson.

Berlin, Ira et al. (eds.) (1982) *Freedom: A Documentary History of Emancipation 1861–1867,* Series II. *The Black Military Experience.* New York: Cambridge University Press.

—— (1985) *Freedom: A Documentary History of Emancipation 1861–1867,* Series I, vol. I. *The Destruction of Slavery.* New York: Cambridge University Press.

—— (1990) *Freedom: A Documentary History of Emancipation 1861–1867,* Series I, vol. III. *The Wartime Genesis of Free Labor: The Lower South.* New York: Cambridge University Press.

Berry, Mary Frances (1977) *Military Necessity and Civil Rights Policy: Black Citizenship and the Constitution 1861–1865.* Port Washington, NY: Kennicat Press.

Blackett R. J. M. (ed.) (1989) *Thomas Morris Chester, Black Civil War Correspondent: His Dispatches from the Virginia Front.* Baton Rouge: Louisiana State University Press.

Blight, David (1989) *Frederick Douglass' Civil War: Keeping Faith in Jubilee.* Baton Rouge: Louisiana State University Press.

Brewer, James E. (1969) *The Confederate Negro, Virginia's Craftsmen and Military Laborers.* Durham, NC: Duke University Press.

Burrows, Edwin G. and Wallace, Mike (1999) *Gotham: A History of New York City to 1898.* New York: Oxford University Press.

Catton, Bruce (1953) *A Stillness at Appomattox.* New York: Doubleday.

—— (1960) *The Civil War.* Boston: Houghton, Mifflin.

—— (1969) *Grant Takes Command.* Boston: Little, Brown.

Eaton, John (1969) *Grant, Lincoln, and the Freedmen.* New York: Greenwood Press.

Emilio, Luis F. ([1891] 1990) *A Brave Black Regiment: History of the Fifty-Fourth Regiment of the Massachusetts Volunteer Infantry, 1863–1865,* 3rd edn. Salem, NH: Ayer.

Leckie, Robert (1991) *None Died in Vain: The Saga of the American Civil War.* New York: Harper Collins.

McFeely, William S. (1981) *Grant, A Biography.* New York: W. W. Norton.

Mitchell, Joseph B. (1955) *Decisive Battles of the Civil War.* New York: Fawcett Premier.

Roland, Charles P. (1991) *An American Iliad: The Story of the Civil War.* New York: McGraw-Hill.

Wiley, Bell I. (1938) *Southern Negroes.* New Haven, CT: Yale University Press.

CHAPTER FIFTEEN

Jim Crowed – Emancipation Betrayed: African Americans Confront the Veil

CHARLES W. MCKINNEY, JR AND RHONDA JONES

African Americans emerged from the ashes of the Civil War with a mixed spirit of uncertainty and jubilee. The promises and expectations of the emancipation, however, overall instilled a sense of expectation of full enjoyment of American citizenship. But, within a decade of the declaration that they would be "henceforth and forever free" and the guarantees of the Fourteenth Amendment that no state "shall make or enforce any law" denying them full citizenship, the emancipation had been betrayed. Within 15 years of the emancipation, most of the southern states had, indeed, codified the new state of un-freedom in a system of segregation, discrimination, and disenfranchisement that became known as Jim Crow (taking its name from a popular minstrel show of a previous era).

The rise, manifestations, and implications of Jim Crow have been the subject of numerous volumes and essays in United States, southern, and African American historiography. C. Vann Woodward, in such works as *Origins of the New South* and *The Strange Career of Jim Crow* started the debate and, to a certain extent, remains at the center of the historical debate. The Woodward thesis, principally on the origins and "strange career" of Jim Crow, has been challenged in many forms and fashions, most prominently by Howard Rabinowitz. In *Race Relations in the Urban South, 1865–1890* (1978), Rabinowitz argued persuasively that African Americans faced discrimination, exclusion, and segregation in public facilities immediately after emancipation, rather than beginning in the 1880s and 1890s as Woodward had argued. He also suggested that the discrimination was directly linked to African American assertiveness, or agency, in the postbellum period. Thus, as African Americans attempted to claim their newly granted freedoms, the South constructed a *de jure* wall of segregation and discrimination to supplement the customs and practices that had previously been in place.

This chapter acknowledges the thorough treatment of the Woodward thesis and its challenges in many other places, including a volume edited by John Boles in the series of Blackwell Companions to American History, *A Companion to the American*

South (2001). Hence, this chapter will focus on more recent subjects of scholarly inquiry and debate, class, gender, and agency among African Americans.

Numerous historical perspectives on African American life in the Jim Crow South have centered on how, at the close of the nineteenth century, the fluidity of paternalistic race relations diminished and the separation between whites and African Americans drastically increased. By the 1890s, the developing stringency of racist Jim Crow practices served as the ultimate form of social control. The complex system of racial laws that promoted "separate but equal" social customs, ensured white domination and African American oppression.

The primary focus of historical inquiry has centered on all forms of institutionalized discrimination and disenfranchisement. Subjected to white racism, disenfranchisement, violence, and exclusion, African Americans experienced segregation from the "cradle to the grave." They strove for citizenship and respectability, but most recognized they needed shared goals and collective agency to achieve this, even just to survive. New access to oral history and primary documents has brought to light more compelling examples and stimulated wider interpretations. Emphasizing such themes as upward mobility, self-help, thrift, education, philanthropy, and Victorian piety, contemporary scholarship saliently demonstrates that – despite their abject poverty, limited access to education, and repression of their political and civil liberties – African Americans continued to make great strides for freedom in the form of institutional development, accommodation, direct confrontation, migration, religion, entrepreneurship, and the production of race leaders. As the level of scholarship has increased, the infusion of studies that center on class, gender, or regional differences within the African American Community has illustrated that their opinions and strategies for advancement were more various than many have supposed.

As they continued to contend for plausible solutions, they maintained strong core values and aspirations for an educated citizenry. Personal memories such as Mamie Garvin Fields' *Lemon Swamp and Other Places* (1983) and Dorothy Redford's *Somerset Homecoming* (1988) denote tender memories of family pride and the importance of kinship during the formidable times of enslavement and beyond. While the perimeters of African American communities were not impenetrable, they did manage to provide a modicum of sanctity and security. Maintaining schools, lodges, churches, civic and social clubs, and community refuges provided a safe space for affirmation and celebration.

Several studies have demonstrated how the pressures of diverse social and economic backgrounds were often accommodated at the expense of racial solidarity and that leaders were only effective within the limited social space allowed. Lynn B. Feldmen's *A Sense of Place: Birmingham's Black Middle Class Community, 1890–1930* (2000) makes a significant contribution to the growing list of studies on racial uplift and institutional development. Centering on the workers and the educated elites, the study illustrates how the black middle-class mixture of racial pride, social conservatism, and accomodationist agenda distinctly exposed class distinctions and class conflict. Studies about ordinary, everyday heroes have offered new perspectives on African American activism. Greta de Jong's *A Different Day: African American Struggles for Justice in Rural Louisiana, 1900–1970* (2002) illuminates the connections between informal strategies of resistance in the early twentieth century and the mass protests that emerged in the 1950s and 1960s. Oral histories conducted with rural blacks demonstrate the subtle methods that were utilized to resist oppression. Displaying everyday forms of resistance, creating schools and institutions, and defending themselves against white violence in the wake of the Second World War, such activities became more open and culminated in voter registration drives.

Social scientists C. Eric Lincoln and Lawrence H. Mamiya's *The Black Church in the African American Experience* (1990) and E. Franklin Frazier's *The Negro Church in America* (1974) posit how religious institutions served as the central life of the community. Most numerous were the Baptist, African Methodist Episcopal (AME), and the Colored Methodist Episcopal (CME) communities: they were largely independent of white dominance, and their autonomous nature provided spiritual sustenance and represented a safe haven from the intensity of racist oppression. Largely shielded from vicious and lecherous whites, who referred to African American men as "boys" or "uncle" and women as "gals" or "aunty," the confines of this solaced environment fostered social cohesion, sustained morale, self-esteem, and social values, and provided a platform for the training and development of new leaders. Welding personal salvation with social activism, the body of individuals respectably addressed as "Mr," "Mrs," "Dr," "deacon," and "deaconess" advanced the notion of philanthropic agency and active charitable mutual-aid campaigns. Bridging sacred and secular traditions, fraternal organizations and lodges – such as the Elks, Masons, and the Eastern Star – also sustained the cause of communal stability.

With the assistance of northern white missionaries, industrialists, and African American churches, thousands of schools were constructed throughout rural areas of the South. The role of educators was vital to the community, for not only did they provide the intellectual foundations for learning, but they contributed to the development of the religious character and moral fiber of its people. Whether the curriculum offered instruction in domestic skillfulness, or classic liberalism, educators such as Booker T. Washington, Charlotte Hawkins Brown, John Hope, Mary McLeod Bethune and Lucy Haney stressed the utility and dignity of labor, and the importance of personal hygiene, nutrition, and self-discipline, along with Christian values. Offering encouragement and support, teachers provided practical instruction that would prepare students for the larger world. Local residents affirmed their commitment to educators and their schools by aiding in building construction, providing such in-kind donations as food, room, and board for teachers and students, and participating in fundraising campaigns. As the success of historically black colleges and universities increasingly produced more graduates, so the doctors, lawyers, educators, ministers, dentists, and skilled tradesmen further enhanced the community.

Political and social movements, like the Civil Rights Movement and the Women's Rights Movement, have profoundly affected the way scholars identify and assess historical issues. Thus, in the 1960s and 1970s, a new focus on previously marginalized groups emerged. In this context, the characteristic portrayals of these groups as victims in a white, male-dominated society began to give way to more positive pictures of independence, self-help, and assertiveness – the combination we call agency. As to the Jim Crow era, clearly the leading study, capturing the new mood, is Leon Litwack's *Trouble in Mind: Black Southerners in the Age of Jim Crow* (1998). Among other things, Litwack's study places the African American working classes at the center of his inquiry. He shows us an amazing culture of resiliency, resistance, and self-help among both rural and urban blacks.

Since the 1970s, revisionist historians have made valiant attempts to interpret the critical relationship of African American women's history to the dichotomies of both African American and women's history. While both African American and women's history reflect the complexities of being part of American history, the intersection of the two is culturally unique, and of separate consciousness. This newly revised social history examines women's influence on household and family structures, religion, education, labor, and political and social movements, and defines the concept of womanhood, all the while unlimited by the dual constraints of race and gender in such a way that the role of women has not been emphasized at the expense of emasculating the role of men. Mirroring the reformist efforts of the Progressive Movement, African American women's club associations such as the National Association of Colored Women (NACW) and the National Council of Negro Women (NCNW) were formed in the attempt to eradicate negative images of their virtue and sexuality. Echoing the mission to preserve the family and community, these organizations were led by such formidable women as Anna Julia Cooper, Nannie Helen Burroughs, Mary Church Terrell, Mary McLeod Bethune, and Ida B. Wells, to name a few. Serving as domestic missionary societies, the women's associations stressed feminine modesty, self-determination, self-reliance, hard work, temperance, and benevolence, but they also provided a platform from which women could publicly speak out against gender oppression and racial exploitation.

Although the clubs so created were akin to their white counterparts – and their subordination by the white, patriarchal system of power presented more commonalities than differences – *de jure* segregation made their motivations quite different and more direct. African American clubwomen challenged the idea of the "silent helpmate" and illustrated that they were equally obligated to advance not only their race, but also themselves. Discussing the activities of the middle-class club women who acted on behalf of their communities, Cynthia Neverdon-Morton's *Afro-American Women of the South and the Advancement of the Race, 1895–1925* (1989), and Stephanie Shaw's *What a Woman Ought to Be and Do: Black Professional Women Workers During the Jim Crow Era* (1996) focused on social activism – in the form of education, medical care, racial consciousness, temperance, philanthropy or charitable aid – as well as racial uplift, which overlapped with the progressive reform movement. Rosalyn Terborg-Penn's *African American Women in the Struggle for the Vote, 1850–1920* (1998) championed the cause for female suffrage in the continued struggle for political freedom.

Despite racial and economic hindrances, African American women felt a communal responsibility to strike a fair balance between their professional careers and their social obligations. Several studies explore the variety of ways in which women became bridge builders, as in the growing body of literature on the role of African American women in the Civil Rights Movement. Merline Pitre's *In Struggle Against Jim Crow: Lulu B. White and the NAACP, 1900–1957* (1999) chronicles the political techniques and strategies of community activist Lulu Belle Madison White. Serving as executive director, director of branches, and national field worker in the Houston chapter of the NAACP, White is credited by Pitre with playing a crucial role in such landmark cases as *Smith v. Allwright* (1944) and *Sweat v. Painter* (1950).

Other scholars have included African American women in a broader discussion of gender during the Jim Crow era. Among the more important works are Glenda Gilmore's *Gender and Jim Crow: Women and the Politics of White Supremacy in North Carolina, 1896–1920* (1996) and Grace E. Hale's *Making Whiteness: The Culture of Segregation in the South, 1890–1940* (1998). Gilmore's case-study of North Carolina and Hale's larger examination of much of the South show agency among African American men and women, and reinforce Rabinowitz's findings of their assertiveness in fighting Jim Crow. More specifically, Gilmore offers a political analysis that disagrees in part with both Woodward and Rabinowitz. She contends that Jim Crow was not a restructuring of existing custom and law, but a reordering of southern society using both gender and race.

Gilmore uses the events in the 1890s in Wilmington, North Carolina, that culminated in the infamous race riot there, to illustrate her claims. Hale, on the other hand, traces the rise of Jim Crow to a perception by white supremacists that freedpersons in some way represented national forces, the North, *versus* them, the South. This construct, she further argues, was in large measure a pretext to attack the growing economic prosperity of African Americans as well as a reaction to social issues, including the newly elevated position of African American women. Hence, a value-laden racial designation, a culture – whiteness – was introduced. The use of the African American experiences in Wilmington and North Carolina by both Gilmore and Hale has found recent support in Angela Hornsby's works (Hornsby 2003; and Chapter 23 of this volume). She demonstrates the roles of gender, class, and African American assertiveness in the struggles against Jim Crow. Hornsby, however, has a greater focus on African American males than many of the previous works in this area.

A focus on the role of males and masculinity in the rise of Jim Crow first found major prominence in the work of Joel Williamson, *The Crucible of Race: Black–White Relations in the American South since Reconstruction* (1984). Williamson posited that Jim Crow emerged in the determination of white men to foster their masculinity in the face of economic woes and alleged assaults by black men on their women. Thus, racial oppression – both legal and extra-legal, such as lynchings – grew as a major element of the new milieu.

White domination limited African American employment opportunities to sharecropping, tenancy, unskilled manual labor, and domestic work. The tyranny of exploitative capitalism coupled with punitive vagrancy laws maintained a repressed system of labor that harked back to the days of enslavement. Recent labor historiography illustrates how industrialization and urbanization not only altered the conditions of African American work experiences, but also spearheaded resistance and organized mechanisms for protest.

With their aspirations to participate in politics dashed, African American wage earners continued to struggle for advancement. Dwindling opportunities to acquire farmland and the fluctuations of the southern agrarian economy incited them to seek economic self-sufficiency. Understanding that business and commerce signaled not only promising signs of racial progress, but also financial autonomy, scores of African Americans secured membership in such organizations as Booker T. Washington's Negro Business League. Alexa Henderson illustrates in *Atlanta Life Insurance Company: Guardian of Black Economic Dignity* (1990) the story of Alonzo

Franklin Herndon, once enslaved and employed as a barber, who had risen to become the chief architect of one of the most successful African American business enterprises by 1905. The development of Atlanta Life and other institutions, such as North Carolina Mutual Life Insurance Company in Durham, represented the functional link between religious institutions, penny savings clubs, and mutual aid societies. Successful institutions such as these served as symbolic role models of the possibilities of the American dream.

Interestingly enough, amid these new emphases on African American agency, a countervailing element – that of anti-black violence – persists in newer studies as well. "Between 1890 and 1917," writes Alexander Byrd, "white gangs and mobs murdered two to three black southerners a week" (Byrd 2004). Seeking to quantify the phenomenon of lynching from the 1880s to 1968, scholars at Tuskegee Institute in Alabama estimated that nearly five thousand African American men, women, and children died by the collective hand of white mob violence. The codification of Jim Crow law and custom was reinforced by violence. Indeed, violence lay at the heart of Jim Crow life. Violent interracial interactions in general, and lynching in particular, served as the ultimate form of social control throughout the South. Violence in all its forms (physical, psychosocial, economic, and so forth) was the tangible manifestation of white supremacy, a racist code of existence that was written in blood.

Yet, however dire these statements may seem, they only begin to plumb the impact, depth, and pervasive nature of violence perpetrated against African Americans during the Jim Crow era. Violence committed against black bodies cast a pall over every aspect of African American life. The White South's efforts to maintain white supremacy and black subordination were not just occasionally but frequently violent. As Leon Litwack states in his masterwork on the Jim Crow era, *Trouble in Mind*, "the cheapness of black life reflected in turn the degree to which so many whites by the early twentieth century had come to think of black men and women as inherently and permanently inferior, as less than human, as little more than animals" (Litwack 1998: 284). Within the historical literature, several scholars remark on what William Chafe and his fellow editors in *Remembering Jim Crow* call the "dailiness of the terror blacks experienced at the hands of capricious whites" (Chafe et al. 2001: xxx). African Americans who came of age behind the veil of segregation understood the consequences of real or perceived transgression and governed themselves accordingly.

In fact, scholars are still contending with the daily nature of violence and the ways in which its presence informed black life during the Jim Crow era. Efforts since the 1980s to understand African American history "from the ground up" have resulted in the generation of a critical mass of scholarship focusing on local life. Interviews compiled by Duke University's Center for Documentary Studies' *Behind the Veil* Project reveal to both historians and the casual reader how violence affected daily black life. In several of the interviews, respondents recall with chilling clarity the murder of a loved one, the burning of homes and the mutilation of pregnant women – acts committed in the wake of alleged "insolence" on the part of blacks. In her autobiography, *Proud Shoes: The Story of an American Family*, Pauli Murray recalls the murder of a playmate, committed by a white man after her friend ran through his watermelon patch (Murray 1999: 263). Autobiographical works by

Benjamin Mays, Mamie Garvin, C. Eric Lincoln, Richard Wright, and others illumine the pervasive nature of violence in the beginning and middle of the century. Legal transgressions, whether minor (such as chicken stealing) or major (rape and/or murder), were frequently given as the underlying cause of violence. In almost all cases however, the true reason usually turned out to be a perceived refusal on the part of an African American to adhere to the racial etiquette of the White South.

Autobiographical works by blacks and historical studies both reveal the frequently arbitrary nature of violence. In his work on Mississippi, *I've Got the Light of Freedom*, Charles Payne recounts the murder of Malcolm Wright in Mississippi in 1949. Three white men killed Wright because they could not pass his wagon with their car. The men stopped their car, pulled him from his wagon, and beat him to death in front of his family. As Payne tells us, "the point was that there did not have to *be* a point; Black life could be snuffed out on whim, you could be killed because some ignorant white man didn't like the color of your shirt or the way you drove a wagon" (Payne 1995: 15, emphasis added). The work of Payne and others also shows that the tenuous nature of black life was also tied to economic dependency on whites.

Increased scholarly focus on local life serves to further illumine the role that violence played in black life during the Jim Crow era; it has also challenged many traditional notions of lynching. Work by W. Fitzhugh Brundage – in particular his book *Lynching in the New South* – argues persuasively that lynching was not a form of exceptional behavior: the mobs were not merely constituted by crazed, rural, bloodthirsty whites. Rather, lynch mobs were frequently composed of the "best" men in town, included both men and women, and often had the sanction of the local authorities (Brundage 1997). James Allen's work, *Without Sanctuary: Lynching Photography in America* (2000), catalogues decades of lynching postcards: photographs that feature both men and women lynched, and the massive crowds that attended the ghoulish events.

African Americans did not endure this period without responding in various ways. Just as the stories of violence against blacks are legion, so too are the stories of both overt and covert resistance to the starkest element of the Jim Crow regime. Ted Rosengarten's book, *All God's Dangers*, features the turbulent life of Nate Shaw, a sharecropper in Alabama who frequently defied white authority. Robin Kelley's writings on working-class blacks – *Hammer and Hoe* and *Race Rebels* – highlight insurgency during the Jim Crow period and challenge traditional notions of political engagement (or disengagement) by non-elites. Black newspapers in both the North and South spoke out against lynching. African American southerners created organizations to fight against lynching and to challenge local, state, and federal elected officials to defend them against mob violence. Scholarship that re-centers black women in the struggle for equality and safety has also greatly informed (and improved) historical examination of this period. Glenda Gilmore's book, *Gender and Jim Crow* (1996), offers a comprehensive portrait of activism by black and white women during the height of the white supremacy movement in North Carolina. Her work, along with Evelyn Brooks Higginbotham's *Righteous Discontent* (1993), Deborah Gray White's *Too Heavy a Load* (1999), and Jacqueline Jones's *Labor of Love, Labor of Sorrow* (1995) highlight the oft-neglected organizing work of black women. Organizations such as the National Association of Colored Women emerge in these texts as a crucial network in the African American civic universe.

For the vast majority of African Americans living under Jim Crow, economic reality was intimately connected to agricultural concerns. After the dismantling of slavery, millions of newly freed black men and women had few resources of their own. They quickly found themselves working for white elites in an effort to carve out a basic existence. To insure their own economic viability, former masters and landowners quickly developed several methods to keep blacks firmly ensconced in the South. Sharecropping, tenancy, and convict-leasing were the major means by which black workers remained tied to the land, where they often struggled to carve out an existence that, in many ways, resembled slavery. Yet, despite the dire conditions in which many African Americans found themselves, black folks constantly sought to improve their economic lot in life with both collective and individual action.

Historical works that emphasize the agency of poor and working-class African Americans abound. Rosengarten's *All God's Dangers* (1974), Kelley's *Hammer and Hoe* (1990) and Nell Irvin Painter's *The Narrative of Hosea Hudson: His Life as a Negro Communist in the South* (1979) offer compelling testimony to the determination, strength, and intelligence of southern blacks who sought to change the economic realities that they faced. Pete Daniel's works, *Breaking the Land: The Transformation of Cotton, Tobacco and Rice Cultures Since 1880* (1985) and *The Shadow of Slavery: Peonage in the South, 1901–1969* (1990), provide a comprehensive view of the varied economic cultures that the South produced, with rich details of the ways black workers navigated often treacherous terrain. Tera Hunter's *To Joy My Freedom: Southern Black Women's Lives and Labors after the Civil War* (1997) deftly charts the hazards faced by black women of the post-Civil War South. Using race, class, and gender as categories of analysis, Hunter illuminates the efforts of working-class black women to carve out social and economic spaces for themselves and their families. Steve Hahn's study of rural African American life, *A Nation Under our Feet* (2003) boldly posits that blacks were "central political actors" in the country's major political and economic developments from the end of the Civil War to the Great Migration. His repositioning of black people as proactive participants in the nation's economic development challenges historians to view African Americans in this period as something other than simple respondents to the world around them.

Labor unions, thought by many to be solely the domain of white workers in the South, have recently garnered considerable scholarly attention. To be sure, W. E. B. Du Bois' massive study of the black working class, *Black Reconstruction* (1935), and Abram Harris' *The Black Worker: The Negro and the Labor Movement* ([1931] 1972) stand as two of many towering works in the field of African American labor history, and they pointed the way towards a further, more critical examination of black labor in the Jim Crow South. Philip Foner's *Organized Labor and the Black Worker* (1974) meticulously chronicles the seemingly intractable barriers to organizing unions on an interracial basis, by charting African Americans' frequently tortured relationship with the labor movement from the antebellum period to the present.

Within the last two decades, scholars have heeded the call for further analysis by focusing on a vibrant African American organizing tradition, much of which was located in the South. One of the most significant of these works is Tera Hunter's *To Joy My Freedom* (1997). Hunter uses a strike by black female laundry workers in Atlanta in 1881 as a case-study of gender and racial agency in the workplace.

Contradicting other scholars, such as Rabinowitz, she demonstrates that the strike was a successful effort to overcome both gender assumptions and limitations as well as racism. On a larger scale, Jacqueline Jones in *Labor of Love, Labor of Sorrow: Black Women, Work, and the Family from Slavery to the Present* (1985) reaches similar conclusions to those offered by Hunter. Jones, however, differs from Hunter in that her focus is on the rural South and she points up the nexus between the family responsibilities of black women and their work.

Eric Arnesen's *Brotherhoods of Color: Black Railroad Workers and the Struggle for Equality* (2001) is a well-researched effort that highlights the brutal conditions that black railway workers suffered while trying to ply their trades. While Arnesen's work does a wonderful job illuminating many lesser-known railway leaders, Beth Tompkins Bates's study, *Pullman Porters and the Rise of Protest Politics in Black America, 1925–1945* (2001) focuses squarely on the union headed by A. Philip Randolph and shows the reader how the union fused labor organizing with protest politics to create a social movement that would eventually serve as a model for the Civil Rights Movement three decades later. Michael Honey's work, *Black Workers Remember: An Oral History of Segregation, Unionism, and the Freedom Struggle* (1999) offers further testimony that black workers often did not view civil rights and economic rights as two separate struggles. In *Civil Rights Unionism: Tobacco Workers and the Struggle for Democracy in the Mid-Twentieth Century South* (2003), Robert Rogers Korstad provides an eloquent narrative that chronicles the birth, life, and demise of a black working-class-led labor uprising in Winston-Salem, North Carolina. Confronting what Korstad terms "racial capitalism," members of Local 22 mobilized "roughly 10,000 workers" to challenge the racist employment practices of the R. J. Reynolds Tobacco Company, one of the largest companies in the world.

Central to all of the works discussed in this chapter are the themes of assertiveness and resistance, rather than passivity and victimization, independent actions, and self-help – agency – in the efforts of blacks to readjust their lives, fortunes, and futures in the Jim Crow world. But there is still much work to be done. Gender issues, particularly state and local studies and particularly those focusing on black male agency, deserve expanded study. In this regard, specific and urgent attention needs to be directed towards the issue of black masculinity, and homosexuality and homophobia. Fresh studies of agency in political activities, especially in rural areas, should be explored. Finally, new examinations of the role of the Black Church in African American agency during the Jim Crow era are needed to shed additional light on the preeminent role of this institution in African American life and history.

BIBLIOGRAPHY

Works Cited

Allen, James (2000) *Without Sanctuary: Lynching Photography in America*. New York: Twin Palms.

Arnesen, Eric (2001) *Brotherhoods of Color: Black Railroad Workers and the Struggle for Equality*. Cambridge, MA: Harvard University Press.

Ayers, Edward L. (1992) *The Promise of the New South: Life after Reconstruction*. New York: Oxford University Press.

Bates, Tompkins Beth (2001) *Pullman Porters and the Rise of Protest Politics in Black America, 1925–1945.* Chapel Hill: University of North Carolina Press.

Brundage, W. Fitzhugh (1997) *Lynching in the New South: Georgia and Virginia, 1880–1930.* Urbana: University of Illinois Press.

Byrd, Alexander (2004) "Studying lynching in the Jim Crow South," *Organization of American Historians Magazine of History*, 18, pp. 31–5.

Cartwright, Joseph H. (1976) *The Triumph of Jim Crow: Race Relations in the 1880s.* Knoxville: University of Tennessee Press.

Chafe, William, Gavins, Raymond, and Korstad, Robert (eds.) (2001) *Remembering Jim Crow: African Americans Tell about Life in the Segregated South.* New York: New Press.

Daniel, Pete (1985) *Breaking the Land: The Transformation of Cotton, Tobacco and Rice Cultures since 1880.* Urbana: University of Illinois Press.

—— (1990) *The Shadow of Slavery: Peonage in the South, 1901–1969.* Urbana: University of Illinois Press.

De Jong, Greta (2002) *A Different Day: African American Struggles for Justice in Rural Louisiana, 1900–1970.* Chapel Hill: University of North Carolina.

Dittmer, John (1977) *Black Georgia in the Progressive Era.* Urbana: University of Illinois Press.

Dollard, John (1937) *Caste and Class in a Southern Town.* New Haven, CT: Yale University Press.

Fairclough, Adam (1995) *Race and Democracy: The Civil Rights Struggle in Louisiana.* Athens: University of Georgia Press.

Feldman, Lynne B. (2000) *A Sense of Place: Birmingham's Black Middle Class Community, 1890–1930.* Tuscaloosa: University of Alabama Press.

Fields, Mamie Garvin with Fields, Karen (1983) *Lemon Swamp and Other Places.* New York: Free Press.

Flynn, Charles L. (1983) *White Land, Black Labor: Caste and Class in Nineteenth Century Georgia.* Baton Rouge: Louisiana State University Press.

Foner, Philip ([1974] 1982) *Organized Labor and the Black Worker, 1619–1973.* New York: International Publishers.

Frazier, E. Franklin (1974) *The Negro Church in America.* New York: Schocken Books.

Gavins, Raymond (2004) "Literature on Jim Crow," *Organization of American Historians Magazine of History*, 18, pp. 13–16.

Gilmore, Glenda Elizabeth (1996) *Gender and Jim Crow: Women and the Politics of White Supremacy in North Carolina, 1896–1920.* Chapel Hill: University of North Carolina Press.

Goldfield, David R. (1990) *Black, White and Southern: Race Relations and Southern Culture, 1940 to the Present.* Baton Rouge: Louisiana State University Press.

Goodwyn, Lawrence C. (1976) *Democratic Promise: The Populist Moment in America.* New York: Oxford University Press.

Hahn, Steve (2003) *A Nation under Our Feet: Black Political Struggles in the Rural South from Slavery to the Great Migration.* Cambridge, MA: Harvard University Press.

Hale, Grace Elizabeth (1998) *Making Whiteness: The Culture of Segregation in the South, 1890–1940.* New York: Pantheon.

Harris, Abram with Spero, Sterling D. ([1931] 1972) *The Black Worker: The Negro and the Labor Movement.* New York: Atheneum.

Haws, Robert (ed.) (1978) *The Age of Segregation: Race Relations in the South, 1890–1945.* Jackson: University Press of Mississippi.

Henderson, Alexa B. (1990) *Atlanta Life Insurance Company: Guardian of Black Economic Dignity.* Tuscaloosa: University of Alabama Press.

Higginbotham, Evelyn Brooks (1993) *Righteous Discontent: The Women's Movement in the Black Baptist Church, 1880–1920.* Cambridge, MA: Harvard University Press.

Honey, Michael K. (1999) *Black Workers Remember: An Oral History of Segregation, Unionism, and the Freedom Struggle*. Berkeley: University of California Press.

Hornsby, Angela M. (2003) "Cast down but not out: black manhood and racial uplift in North Carolina, 1900–1930." PhD dissertation, University of North Carolina at Chapel Hill.

Hunter, Tera W. (1997) *To Joy My Freedom: Southern Black Women's Lives and Labor after the Civil War*. Cambridge, MA: Harvard University Press.

Janiewski, Delores E. (1985) *Sisterhood Denied: Race, Gender, and Class in a New South Community*. Philadelphia: Temple University Press.

Jones, Jacqueline (1985) *Labor of Love, Labor of Sorrow: Black Women, Work, and the Family from Slavery to the Present*. New York: Basic Books.

Kelley, Robin D. G. (1990) *Hammer and Hoe: Alabama Communists during the Great Depression*. Chapel Hill: University of North Carolina Press.

—— (1995) *Race Rebels: Culture, Politics, and the Black Working Class*. New York: Free Press.

Korstad, Robert Rogers (2003) *Civil Rights Unionism: Tobacco Workers and the Struggle for Democracy in the Mid-Twentieth Century South*. Chapel Hill: University of North Carolina Press.

Lincoln, C. Eric (1984) *Race, Religion and the Continuing American Dilemma*. New York: Hill & Wang.

Lincoln, C. Eric and Mamiya, Lawrence H. (1990) *The Black Church in the African American Experience*. Durham, NC: Duke University Press.

Litwack, Leon (1998) *Trouble in Mind: Black Southerners in the Age of Jim Crow*. New York: Vintage.

—— (2004) "Jim Crow Blues," Organization of American Historians, *Magazine of History*, 18: 7–12.

McMillan, Neil (1989) *Dark Journey: Black Mississippians in the Age of Jim Crow*. Champaign: University of Illinois Press.

Mandle, Jay R. (1992) *Not Slave, not Free: The African American Economic Experience since the Civil War*. Durham, NC: Duke University Press.

Mays, Benjamin (1971) *Born to Rebel: An Autobiography*. New York: Scribner.

Murray, Pauli (1999) *Proud Shoes: The Story of an American Family*. Boston: Beacon.

Neverdon-Morton, Cynthia (1989) *Afro-American Women of the South and the Advancement of the Race, 1825–1925*. Knoxville: University of Tennessee Press.

Painter, Nell Irvin (1979) *The Narrative of Hosea Hudson: His Life as a Negro Communist in the South*. Cambridge, MA: Harvard University Press.

Payne, Charles (1995) *I've Got the Light of Freedom: The Organizing Tradition and the Mississippi Freedom Struggle*. Berkeley: University of California Press.

Pitre, Merline (1999) *In Struggle against Jim Crow: Lulu B. White and the NAACP, 1900–1957*. College Station: Texas A & M University Press.

Powdermaker, Hortense (1968) *After Freedom: A Cultural Study of the Deep South*. New York: Atheneum.

Rabinowitz, Howard N. (1978) *Race Relations in the Urban South, 1865–1890*. New York: Oxford University Press.

Redford, Dorothy Spruill and Dorso, Michael (1988) *Somerset Homecoming: Recovering a Lost Heritage*. New York: Anchor Books.

Rosengarten, Theodore (1974) *All God's Dangers: The Life of Nate Shaw*. Chicago: University of Chicago Press.

Shapiro, Herbert (1988) *White Violence and Black Response: From Reconstruction to Montgomery*. Amherst: University of Massachusetts Press.

Shaw, Stephanie (1996) *What a Woman Ought to Be and Do: Black Professional Women Workers During the Jim Crow Era*. Chicago: University of Chicago Press.

Terborg-Penn, Rosalyn (1998) *African American Women in the Struggle for the Right to Vote, 1850–1920.* Bloomington: University of Indiana Press.

Tyson, Timothy and Cecelski, David (eds.) (1998) *Democracy Betrayed: The Wilmington Race Riot of 1898 and Its Legacy.* Chapel Hill: University of North Carolina Press.

White, Deborah Gray (1999) *Too Heavy a Load.* New York: W. W. Norton.

Williamson, Joel (1984) *The Crucible of Race: Black–White Relations in the American South since Reconstruction.* New York: Oxford University Press.

Woodward, C. Vann (1951) *Origins of the New South, 1877–1913.* Baton Rouge: Louisiana State University Press.

—— (1955) *The Strange Career of Jim Crow.* New York: Oxford University Press.

Wright, Gavin (1986) *Old South, New South: Revolutions in the Southern Economy since the Civil War.* New York: Basic Books.

Wright, Richard (1945) *Black Boy: A Record of Childhood and Youth.* New York: Harper & Brothers.

PART VI

The Maturation of African American Communities and the Emergence of Independent Institutions

CHAPTER SIXTEEN

African American Religious and Fraternal Organizations

DAVID H. JACKSON, JR

From slavery to the present, the Black Church has served as a cornerstone of African American life and culture. After slavery, a number of black political leaders doubled as ministers of the gospel. The Black Church is a critical institution for African Americans. It became the first institution in the United States wholly controlled by blacks, and the major vehicle used in their struggle for black liberation. For more than 150 years it has remained free of white control. This chapter will examine some of the historical literature pertaining to black religious life in America. To a lesser degree, it will survey literature written about black fraternal organizations, particularly those on college campuses. Like the Black Church, those institutions too have remained exclusively under the control of African American leaders since their inception and have played a major role in black life.

As Darlene Clark Hine, William Hine, and Stanley Harrold point out in their recent study, *The African-American Odyssey* (2000), the Black Church has provided for not only the spiritual needs of the masses but also their social, political, and cultural needs. Independent black churches emerged in the antebellum period and their growth accelerated after the end of the war. The desire to establish these churches resulted from black people being treated as "second-class Christians" at white churches. For example, black parishioners attending white churches typically had to sit together in a rear corner of the church or in the balcony. In fact, the earliest examples of organized segregation against African Americans in the United States are found in the church. Moreover, most black people did not have opportunities to serve in leadership capacities at white churches; that is, as deacons, trustees, stewards or stewardesses (Hine et al. 2000: 263–4).

This type of rank discrimination in white churches inspired black people to create an alternative. Although white churches served the spiritual needs of their white members and provided them with theological support for their racist political and social beliefs and practices, African Americans often deemed the white churches' message irrelevant to their needs. Hence they created a variety of churches for themselves. Indeed, a great deal of variety existed within black churches. As Willard Gatewood explains in *Aristocrats of Color: The Black Elite, 1880–1920* (1990), the more prosperous members of the African American Community, the black elite, tended to join the Presbyterian, Catholic, Methodist Episcopal, Congregational, and Episcopal churches.

African Americans who were free before the Civil War usually affiliated with these "elite" congregations and continued to do so through the Jim Crow era. As David Jackson's *A Chief Lieutenant of the Tuskegee Machine: Charles Banks of Mississippi* (2002) has shown, in some cases the particular church attended meant more than the denomination. The Baptist Church, the African Methodist Episcopal (AME) Church, and the African Methodist Episcopal Zion Church, among others, all had elite churches and members. Green Grove Baptist Church and Bethel AME Church in the all-black town of Mound Bayou, Mississippi, were the churches attended by the town's elite at the turn of the twentieth century (Jackson 2002: 21).

Services among the elite tended to be more formal and solemn, as Jackson illustrates with a story that Booker T. Washington frequently told. An older black woman in Mississippi went into an Episcopal church and took a seat in the rear. During the service, the lady started clapping her hands and moaning, so an usher went over to see if she was ill. "No, sir, I'se happy; I'se got religion. Yes, sir, I'se got religion!" The usher looked at the woman in shock and told her: "Why, don't you know that this isn't the place to get religion." Washington won many a laugh by telling this story, which he used to demonstrate the difference between Episcopal Church worship and typical black church services (Jackson 2002: 20). By contrast, as Joe Richardson has shown in his examination of Florida blacks in *The Negro in the Reconstruction of Florida* (1965), the black masses usually attended church services that were emotional and spirit-filled, and most black worship services manifested African influence (Richardson 1965: 88).

W. E. B. Du Bois was one of the first to attempt to survey the church in the lives of African Americans. Du Bois' *The Negro Church*, published in 1903, grew out of proceedings from the Atlanta University Conferences for the Study of Negro Problems, but never received the attention of his *The Souls of Black Folk* published the same year. According to sociologist Phil Zuckerman, Du Bois' *The Negro Church* was a pioneering study: it "was the first book-length sociological study of religion ever published in the United States; it was the first in-depth analysis of black religious life; and it was the first sociological, historical, and empirical study of black religious life to be undertaken by blacks themselves" (Du Bois 1969: vii).

Du Bois published the first scholarly study of the Black Church; Carter G. Woodson, another Harvard-trained historian, was not far behind. In 1921, Woodson published one of the first comprehensive histories, *The History of the Negro Church*, a much more readable narrative. Although some writers, like Daniel Alexander Payne (1891), had written histories of their own denominations, Woodson wanted to evaluate and assess the accomplishments of all the groups and show their evolution. His work was to be revised and reissued several times, most recently in 1992.

Another widely-read survey of the Black Church was produced several decades later by respected sociologist, E. Franklin Frazier. In 1964 Frazier wrote *The Negro Church in America*, in which he references Woodson's work several times. Nonetheless, Frazier gave a fresh, but controversial perspective on black church life in America. Perhaps the most controversial aspect of his book is Frazier's attempt to disassociate anything "African" from African American religious life. Frazier begins his study by arguing that "one must recognize from the beginning that because of the manner in which the Negroes were captured in Africa and enslaved, they were practically stripped of their social heritage" (Frazier 1964: 9).

Many scholars, however, disagreed with Frazier and argued for the continual presence of African cultural retentions in black life, including aspects of their religion. To name a few, Melville Herskovits' *The Myth of the Negro Past* (1924), Lorenzo Turner's *Africanisms in the Gullah Dialect* (1949), Peter Wood's *Black Majority* (1974), John Blassingame's seminal study, *The Slave Community: Plantation Life in the Antebellum South* (1979), and more recently Joseph Holloway's *Africanisms in American Culture* (1991). These studies persuasively argue for the existence of African retentions in general and they point to specific examples of African religious retentions.

Unlike Du Bois's, Woodson's, and Frazier's comprehensive studies, other writers have taken a different approach to studying and preserving the history of black religion by examining individual congregations. Daniel A. Payne, an African Methodist Episcopal (AME) bishop, produced one of the earliest such studies in 1891. He wrote the first of several volumes on the history of the AME Church called *A History of the African Methodist Episcopal Church* and he focused on the years 1816 to 1856. His study was followed by Charles S. Smith's 1922 study, which focused on the years 1856 through 1922. Then a third (undated) volume was written by church historiographer, McCoy Ransom, which traced the church's history from 1922 to 1967 – presumably the year of publication.

After many years of research, William J. Walls wrote a more concise church history, *The African Methodist Episcopal Zion Church: Reality of the Black Church* in 1974. Walls, a bishop in the AME Zion Church, developed a thoughtful narrative. Similarly, Othal H. Lakey has written *The History of the CME Church*, published in 1985. Although all of these writers deal with some of the controversies that emerged within the churches, their studies are generally sympathetic and uncritical, as the writers are members and in some cases leaders of the denominations. So, while these books are informative, they lack necessary scholarly rigor.

The church served many purposes for blacks. It became a theater, a forum, a social center and general gathering place for the black community. Simultaneously, it provided charity to the needy, provided enriching music, developed community and political leaders, and served as the location for some early black schools. Since black ministers provided for many needs of the masses, they became the social and political leaders in the black community. The Black Church worked as an institution, not just for the spiritual concerns of African Americans, but also to better their social conditions (Hine et al: 263–5).

Historian Canter Brown in *Florida's Black Public Officials, 1867–1924* (1998) shows that many of Florida's black elected leaders were also members of the clergy. He examines a number of these leaders. For example, Charles Pierce an elder and AME minister, also served in the Florida Senate and as a Leon County Commissioner and county superintendent from 1868 to 1872. Likewise Jonathan Gibbs, a Presbyterian minister who studied at Princeton Theological Seminary, became involved in Florida politics. He served as Florida's Secretary of State and as state superintendent of education for Florida (Brown 1998: 115).

Other scholars have analyzed black religion through biography. Stephen Angell's *Bishop Henry McNeal Turner and African-American Religion in the South* (1992) shows the political activism of black clergymen. Bishop Turner answered the social and political call from the African American community: he helped organize the Republican Party for blacks in Georgia and in 1867 called the first Republican State Convention. During Reconstruction he served in the Georgia House of Representatives and he even utilized his position within the AME Church to encourage national and international racial consciousness. Turner also served as a bishop in the AME Church for 35 years and as Senior Bishop for the last 20. During his term he extended the AME Church into Sierra Leone, Liberia, and South Africa and helped to place the needs of Africa on the black American agenda for racial uplift.

However, years before Angell published his study, historian Charles Harris Wesley wrote a significant work on Richard Allen, who founded the AME Church in 1816 and became an anti-slavery leader in the North. In 1935, Wesley's work appeared under the title *Richard Allen: Apostle of Freedom*, from the Associated Publishers. In recording the religious endeavors of Allen, Wesley also managed to highlight Allen's concern for the social uplift of African people. Allen urged Africans to fight against slavery, to own their own businesses and to start their own schools. In fact, Wesley asserted that "Richard Allen was in the front rank of those who were leading in the education of both children and adults. It was said that no man of his group was more interested than he in the education of his people" (Wesley 1935: 92). Other scholars have written on Allen, among them E. Curtis Alexander, who however still relies heavily on Wesley's work.

Black ministers like Allen, Pierce, Gibbs, and Turner used the church to effect political and social change, and encourage racial uplift in the black community. If they had belonged to white churches, these black preachers would have been limited in terms of addressing the needs of the community as they saw them. Having the Black Church as a parallel institution, however, served a critical function for African Americans and helped them in more ways than just spiritual ones.

In 1993 William E. Montgomery produced *Under Their Own Vine and Fig Tree: The African-American Church in the South, 1865–1900* in which, in a fashion similar to Woodson and Frazier, he examined developments among multiple denominations within the Black Church, but within a much more narrow period. There is scarcely any period more important to African American religious history than the years Montgomery examined in his book. He discussed the organizing of black churches throughout the South after slavery ended and the churches' role in Reconstruction, among other things. Montgomery even revealed that a number of the church missionaries discussed in his study also founded schools to help elevate the race. Montgomery closed with a provocative analysis of black preachers and their preparation or lack thereof, and their role in the struggle for black equality and salvation. With the advantage of more recent scholarship, Montgomery's study provided fresh insight into topics tackled by Woodson decades earlier.

Following a format similar to Montgomery's, but on a statewide level, new scholarship is beginning to emerge on the role of black denominations in individual states. Larry Rivers and Canter Brown in their *Laborers in the Vineyard of the Lord: The Beginnings of the AME Church in Florida, 1865–1895* effectively accomplish this. The authors examine African American ministerial involvement in politics, the rivalries between the bishops and the local church authorities, the effects of the temperance movement on black churches and the forming of the AME Church, which they see as an example of social and cultural solidarity among blacks as well as a demonstration of independence in the African American community during that era (Rivers and Brown 2001: xix). The same authors have completed a similar study on the African Methodist Episcopal Zion Church, entitled *For A Great and Grand Purpose: The Beginnings of the A.M.E.Z. Church in Florida, 1864–1905*, to be published in 2004 by the University Press of Florida.

Evelyn Brooks Higginbotham has also made a significant contribution to African American religious historiography. Her *Righteous Discontent: The Women's Movement in the Black Baptist Church, 1880–1920* filled a gap in the literature on black churches. While she acknowledges that much has been written on the Black Church, she asserts that "much less has been written about black women's importance in the life of the church" (Higginbotham 1993: 1). She shows that, although black women have been frequently overlooked, they were "crucial to broadening the public arm of the church and making it the most powerful institution of racial self-help in the African American community" (ibid: 1). Higginbotham has provided an excellent model and scholars should follow her example to ascertain the role of black women in the Methodist, Episcopalian, Pentecostal, and other black denominations.

In examining black religion, scholars have also studied the Nation of Islam, founded by Elijah Muhammad, especially after Malcolm X popularized it in the 1950s. Muhammad's *Message to the Blackman in America* (1965) is widely read by members of the sect. However, the first black scholarly study of the subject was written by C. Eric Lincoln. His work *The Black Muslims in America* first appeared in 1961 and scholar James H. Cone recognized it as being the definitive text on black Muslims in America. Since then, there have been different biographical and general studies on the Nation of Islam, although far fewer than those on the black Christian experience. Karl Evanzz has written a critical, yet thought-provoking biography in *The Messenger: The Rise and Fall of Elijah Muhammad* (1999). Others have done broader studies: for instance, Martha Lee's *The Nation of Islam: An American Millenarian Movement* argues that millenarianism is deeply rooted in the ideology of The Nation of Islam. She states that, at the core, members believe that "the White world and its oppressive political institutions would fall; from their ashes would rise the Black millennium" (Lee 1996: 2). Studies of this sort have certainly added to the literature on this subject, but there remains much to be done. Scholars have not focused nearly as much on the African American Muslims that are not in the Nation of Islam, the so-called "orthodox" Muslims.

Perhaps second only to black churches as independent institutions were African American fraternal organizations. The first of these was the Prince Hall Masons, founded in Boston in 1787 by Prince Hall (a minister and businessman). By 1815 other Grand Lodges of Prince Hall Masons were organized in Boston and elsewhere. Following the establishment of Prince Hall masonry, other male groups appeared. These included the Odd Fellows, the Knights of Pythias, the Knights of Tabor, the Ancient Sons of Israel, the Grand United Order of True Reformers and the Improved Benevolent and Protective Order of Elks of the World (commonly known as the Elks). The first major groups for black females were the Order of the Eastern Star and the Sisters of Calanthe (Franklin and Moss 1994).

One of the earliest biographies of Hall by a professional historian was Charles H. Wesley's *Prince Hall: Life and Legacy* (1977). Wesley, a Prince Hall Mason, provided a rather obsequious narrative of his order's founder. George Williamson Crawford in *Prince Hall and His Followers: Being a Monograph on the Legitimacy of Negro Masonry* (1971) and Joseph A. Walkes' *Black Square and Compass – 200 Years of Prince Hall Freemasonry* (1979) both offer a similar treatment. C. H. Brooks has provided a laudatory study of the Odd Fellows and E. A. Williams et al. offers a similar view on the Pythians. More critical treatments of Hall and his lodge can be found in Arthur Diamond and Nathan I. Huggins (eds.), *Prince Hall: Social Reformer* (1992); William A. Muraakin, *Middle-Class Blacks in a White Society: Prince Hall Freemasonry in America* (1975) and David T. Beito, *From Mutual Aid to the Welfare State: Fraternal Societies and Social Services, 1890–1967* (2000). Although the latter is a general work, a chapter is devoted to black fraternal orders. Beito seeks to raise the visibility of these orders, particularly their work in social welfare.

A few other works go beyond Prince Hall and the Prince Hall Masons, providing biographical studies as well as state case-studies. These include D. Webster Davis' biography of William Washington Browne, a leader of the True Reformers, David Fahey's *Black Lodge in White America* (1994), and Joe William Trotter's chapter on the True Reformers in *Coal, Class, and Color: Blacks in Southern West Virginia, 1915–32* (1990). Although much of the activities of these "secret societies" was beyond the purview of non-members and scholars at the time and subsequently, their benevolent and business activities were characteristically and commonly prominent in their communities. They generally offered sick and burial insurance, aided widows and children (particularly of their deceased members), and owned their meeting sites as well as other properties.

Other examples of black fraternal life can be seen in college social life, especially on white college campuses. Since African American college students generally could not join white Greek-lettered college fraternities and sororities, they created their own parallel organizations, starting early in the twentieth century. Founded in Philadelphia, Pennsylvania in 1904, Sigma Pi Phi (known as "the Boule") was the first of these organizations. However, this group remained very exclusive and did not open itself to the general black college population (Graham 1999: *passim*). Thus the emergence of the first really mainstream black college fraternity did not happen until two years later at Cornell University in Ithaca, New York, in 1906. When sociologist E. Franklin Frazier studied these groups in his classic work *Black Bourgeoisie: The Rise of a New Middle Class* (1957), he remained very critical of them regardless of the parallel alternative they provided for African American college students.

However, Charles Wesley's *The History of Alpha Phi Alpha: A Development in College Life* (Wesley 1981: 28–31, 40–4) is more sympathetic to the black college fraternity movement. He describes how several black students at Cornell, many of whom were scattered throughout different departments at the University, wanted to create a venue for closer contacts with each other outside of the classroom. Being at a white-majority institution, blacks were excluded from many of the opportunities for mutual help that white students took full advantage of. Seven of these students – Henry A. Callis, Charles H. Chapman, Eugene K. Jones, George B. Kelley, Nathaniel A. Murray, Robert H. Ogle, and Vertner W. Tandy – came together and created Alpha Phi Alpha Fraternity, Incorporated, on December 4, 1906, "the first national inter-collegiate Greek letter fraternity established for black college men."

Interestingly, Alpha really began to expand after it established its second chapter in December 1907 at the historically black Howard University in Washington, DC (ibid: 28–31, 40–4).

This move seems to have been the catalyst for other African Americans interested in starting college fraternities and sororities, as all the other black Greek-lettered organizations that began in the early 1900s were founded at Howard University, with the exception of Kappa Alpha Psi fraternity founded at Indiana University and Sigma Gamma Rho Sorority founded at Butler University, also in Indiana. Although Kappa Alpha Psi began in Indiana, two of its main founders had transferred from Howard University in 1910. Omega Psi Phi, Phi Beta Sigma, Alpha Kappa Alpha, Delta Sigma Theta, and Zeta Phi Beta all had their beginnings at Howard University (Ross 2000).

Journalist Lawrence Ross's *The Divine Nine* (2000), a study of the most notable African American college fraternities and sororities, shows that the organizations had common objectives and all stressed the significance of scholarship, networking, and community service. They served as a shield against the racism and isolation that black college students experienced, particularly on white college campuses. Members also had opportunities to serve in leadership capacities in these groups and could groom future leaders. Many black leaders and scholars that emerged in the early twentieth century belonged to these organizations, including W. E. B. Du Bois, Carter G. Woodson, A. Philip Randolph, Mary Church Terrell, Mary McLeod Bethune, and Zora Neal Hurston.

These organizations joined the struggle for black equality in an effort to make life better for all African Americans. As a trained historian, Wesley (1981) chronicles fraternity development within the context of the Jim Crow era. He explains that they participated in voter registration drives and campaigns to encourage black children to go to high school and college. Moreover, when the United States entered the First World War "to make the world safe for democracy," black fraternities and sororities supported the war effort. African Americans wanted to serve as officers not just as enlisted men, so black college students – led by members of these fraternities at Howard University, Atlanta University, Fisk University, and Tuskegee Institute, among others – began to agitate for the training of black military officers. Although some African Americans denounced the idea of a separate camp, the government ultimately established a separate training ground at Fort Des Moines, Iowa where 639 black men received commissions, a large portion of whom were black fraternity men (Wesley 1981: 107–9; Franklin and Moss 1994: 326–7).

One thing that distinguished black fraternities and sororities from similar white college organizations was the active participation of their members after they had finished their undergraduate studies. Following a pattern similar to Wesley's are Paula Giddings' *In Search of Sisterhood: Delta Sigma Theta and the Challenge of the Black Sorority Movement* (1988) and Dorothy Height's memoir, *Open Wide the Freedom Gates* (2003). Both works illustrate how members of these African American organizations realized the need for service to the race after graduation and the need for organization to mobilize for change. They learned this lesson well after successfully forcing the government's hand to establish the officers' training camp at Fort Des Moines. Perhaps what is most significant is that by establishing graduate or alumni chapters across the country, older members of these organizations still actively communicated, mentored, and interacted with younger college-level members and by doing this they were able to keep them focused on social and political issues of the day and groom them for future endeavors. It also allowed the members to network with a broad spectrum of other people with similar interests.

Walter Kimbrough has published a more recent study of black fraternities and sororities in his *Black Greek 101: The Culture, Customs, and Challenges of Black Fraternities and Sororities* (2003). He examines the founding of these organizations and their development. He also discusses black pledging rituals and the contemporary movement away from pledging – called "membership intake" – resulting from hazing and various lawsuits faced by the organizations. Moreover, he discusses the future of Greek Life for fraternity and sorority members and their aspirants. More recently Ricky Jones has also done a similar, but broader analysis in *Black Haze: Violence, Sacrifice, and Manhood in Black Greek-Letter Fraternities* (2004).

Because of the secrecy involved in many of these groups, there is no simple way for non-members to obtain certain intimate details. Hence, there continues to be room for scholars to explore additional state studies, significant black clergymen, and the membership of prominent blacks in secret societies, as these organizations continue to hold great significance in the African American community today.

BIBLIOGRAPHY

Works Cited

Alexander, E. Curtis (1985) *Richard Allen: The First Exemplar of African American Education*. New York: ECA Associates.

Angell, Stephen W. (1992) *Bishop Henry McNeal Turner and African-American Religion in the South*. Knoxville: University of Tennessee Press.

Blassingame, John W. (1979) *The Slave Community: Plantation Life in the Antebellum South*. New York: Oxford University Press.

Brown, Canter, Jr (1998) *Florida's Black Public Officials, 1867–1924*. Tuscaloosa: University of Alabama Press.

Brown, Canter, Jr, and Rivers, Larry E. (2004) *For A Great and Grand Purpose: The Beginnings of the A.M.E.Z. Church in Florida, 1864–1905*. Gainesville: University Press of Florida.

Du Bois, W. E. B. ([1903] 1969) *The Souls of Black Folk*. New York: Signet.

—— (ed.) ([1903] 2003) *The Negro Church*. New York: Altamira Press.

Evanzz, Karl (1999) *The Messenger: The Rise and Fall of Elijah Muhammad*. New York: Pantheon.

Feldman, Lynne B. (1999) *A Sense of Place: Birmingham's Black Middle-Class Community, 1890–1930*. Tuscaloosa: University of Alabama Press.

Franklin, John H., and Moss, Alfred A. (1994) *From Slavery to Freedom: A History of African Americans*. New York: McGraw-Hill.

Frazier, E. Franklin ([1964] 1974) *The Negro Church in America*. New York: Schocken.

Gatewood, Willard B. (1990) *Aristocrats of Color: The Black Elite, 1880–1920*. Bloomington: Indiana University Press.

Giddings, Paula (1988) *In Search of Sisterhood: Delta Sigma Theta and the Challenge of the Black Sonority Movement*. New York: William Morrow & Co.

Height, Dorothy (2003) *Open Wide the Freedom Gates*. New York: PublicAffairs.

Herskovits, Melville J. ([1924] 1958) *The Myth of the Negro Past*. Boston: Beacon Press.

Higginbotham, Evelyn B. (1993) *Righteous Discontent: The Women's Movement in the Black Baptist Church, 1880–1920*. Cambridge, MA: Harvard University Press.

Hine, Darlene C., Hine, William C., and Harrold, Stanley (2000) *The African-American Odyssey*. Upper Saddle River, NJ: Prentice-Hall.

Holloway, Joseph E. (1991) *Africanisms in American Culture*. Bloomington: Indiana University Press.

Jackson, David H., Jr (2002) *A Chief Lieutenant of the Tuskegee Machine: Charles Banks of Mississippi*. Gainesville: University Press of Florida.

Jones, Ricky L. (2004) *Black Haze: Violence, Sacrifice, and Manhood in Black Greek-Letter Fraternities*. Albany: State University of New York Press.

Kimbrough, Walter M. (2003) *Black Greek 101: The Culture, Customs, and Challenges of Black Fraternities and Sororities*. Madison, NJ: Dickinson University Press.

Lakey, Othal H. (1985) *The History of the CME Church*. Memphis, TN: CME Publishing House.

Lee, Martha F. (1996) *The Nation of Islam: An American Millenarian Movement*. Syracuse, NY: Syracuse University Press.

Lincoln, C. Eric (1961) *The Black Muslims in America*. New York: Kayode Publications.

Montgomery, William E. (1993) *Under Their Own Vine and Fig Tree: The African-American Church in the South, 1865–1900*. Baton Rouge: Louisiana State University Press.

Muhammad, Elijah (1965) *Message to the Blackman in America*. Chicago: Muhammad's Temple of Islam No. 2.

Payne, Daniel A. (1891) *History of the African Methodist Episcopal Church, 1816–1856*. Nashville, TN: AME Sunday School Union.

Ransom, McCoy (n.d.) *A History of the African Methodist Episcopal Church, 1922–1967*. Nashville: AME Sunday School Union.

Richardson, Joe M. (1965) *The Negro in the Reconstruction of Florida, 1865–1877*. Tallahassee: Florida State University Press.

Rivers, Larry E., and Brown, Canter, Jr (2001) *Laborers in the Vineyard of the Lord: The Beginnings of the AME Church in Florida, 1865–1895*. Gainesville: University Press of Florida.

Ross, Lawrence C. (2000) *The Divine Nine: The History of African American Fraternities and Sororities*. New York: Kensington.

Smith, Charles S. (1922) *A History of the African Methodist Episcopal Church, 1856–1922*. Philadelphia: D. M. Baxter.

Turner, Lorenzo ([1949] 1968) *Africanisms in the Gullah Dialect*. New York: Arno Press.

Walls, William J. (1974) *The African Methodist Episcopal Zion Church: Reality of the Black Church*. Charlotte, NC: AME Zion Publishing.

Wesley, Charles H. ([1935] 1969) *Richard Allen: Apostle of Freedom*. Washington, DC: Associated Publishers.

—— (1977) *Prince Hall: Life and Legacy*. Washington, DC: United Supreme Council, Southern Jurisdiction, Prince Hall Affiliation.

—— (1981) *The History of Alpha Phi Alpha: A Development in College Life*. Chicago: Foundation Publishers.

Wood, Peter (1974) *Black Majority: Negroes in Colonial South Carolina from 1670 through the Stono Rebellion*. New York: Knopf.

Woodson, Carter G. ([1921] 1992) *The History of the Negro Church*. Washington, DC: Associated Publishers.

Suggestions for Further Reading

Cone, James H. (1984) *For My People: Black Theology and the Black Church*. New York: Orbis.

Fulop, Timothy E. and Raboteau, Albert J. (1997) *African-American Religion: Interpretive Essays in History and Culture*. New York: Routledge.

Graham, Lawrence O. (1999) *Our Kind of People: Inside America's Black Upper Class.* New York: HarperPerennial.

Hamilton, Charles V. (1972) *The Black Preacher in America.* New York: William Morrow.

Johnson, Paul E. (1994) *African-American Christianity: Essays in History.* Berkeley: University of California Press.

Pipes, William H. (1992) *Say Amen, Brother! Old-Time Negro Preaching: A Study in American Frustration.* Detroit, MI: Wayne State University Press.

Raboteau, Albert J. (1995) *A Fire in the Bones: Reflections on African American Religious History.* Boston: Beacon Press.

Richardson, Harry V. (1976) *Dark Salvation: The Story of Methodism as it Developed among Blacks in America.* New York: Anchor Press.

Sernett, Milton C. (ed.) (1985) *Afro-American Religious History: A Documentary Witness.* Durham, NC: Duke University Press.

Titon, Jeff T. (ed.) (1989) *Reverend C. L. Franklin, Give Me This Mountain: Life History and Selected Sermons.* Urbana: University of Illinois.

Wilmore, Gayraud S. (1995) *Black Religion and Black Radicalism: An Interpretation of the Religious History of Afro-American People.* New York: Orbis.

CHAPTER SEVENTEEN

The Quest for "Book Learning": African American Education in Slavery and Freedom

CHRISTOPHER M. SPAN AND JAMES D. ANDERSON

Education has always been a core value in the African American experience. As an ideal, it has historically been equated with freedom and empowerment, and has served as a strategy to combat discrimination, exclusion, slavery, segregation, and other systemic forms of oppression. The history of education in the African American experience is one of unremitting struggle and perseverance; it is a history that details the determination of a people to use schools and knowledge for liberation and inclusion in the American social order. The collective strivings and educational history of African Americans in the South before and after enslavement epitomize this contention. Their quest for book learning is arguably one of the better illustrations of their long struggle to affirm their humanity and to persevere amid overtly oppressive and dehumanizing conditions. This chapter traces that educational history. It highlights how the law and societal conditions shaped some of the earliest educational opportunities of African Americans, how historians have chronicled and analyzed this history, and how African Americans – freeborn, manumitted, enslaved, fugitive, freed, and otherwise – attempted to obtain an education before and after the Civil War.

In the African American experience, the quest to acquire book learning for liberation began the day the first Africans were brought to Virginia in 1619. These first Africans and their descendants learned early on that literacy and knowledge of English language, law, and custom were absolutely necessary in a slave-sanctioning society where freedom, indentured servitude, and enslavement were predicated on matters of contract law, property, literacy, and conversion to Christianity. One classic example of the importance of understanding the written word was Anthony Johnson, an enslaved African brought to Virginia in 1621. According to ship records, Johnson's name upon arrival on Virginia's eastern shores was "Antonio the Negro," and historians who have studied his life agree that he arrived not as an indentured servant, but as a slave (Breen and Innes 1980).

Even so, within the next twenty years Johnson would purchase his own freedom and become a significant landowner. He would frequently use the court in colonial

Virginia to protect his property and insure that his wife and daughters were not classified as tithable – that is, obliged to pay taxes. In addition, Johnson would have all his children baptized because he was aware of a Virginia statute that did not allow Christians to be enslaved. Whether Johnson became literate – meaning he could read and write in the English language – is not apparent from the historical record. What is obvious, however, is Johnson's recognition of the importance of learning and self-improvement for the protection of his family, understanding the system of taxation, acquiring and protecting his property and investments, and ultimately for his freedom. Such knowledge and respect for literacy as a way of liberation and protection – in a society that was increasingly enslaving and segregating people on the basis of skin color – was passed down generation to generation, and became a widespread cultural value among African Americans by the American Revolution.

Notwithstanding, this cultural appreciation for learning arose concomitantly with a series of anti-literacy laws aimed to deny African Americans – enslaved or free – access to an education. Nearly every American colony, and later state, prohibited or stridently restricted teaching free and enslaved African Americans in the South to read or write. South Carolina was the first. As early as 1740, the colony enacted a law that prohibited any person from teaching or causing a slave to be taught to read or write (Raffel 1998: xiii). Arguably, this statute was in response to the increased teaching of slaves by Christian ministers. The first school established for enslaved African Americans by South Carolina parishioners was in 1695 at Goose Creek Parish in Charleston.

Believing that all children of God should be baptized and believing that literacy was a prerequisite to baptism, the Society for the Propagation of the Gospel trained thousands of enslaved African Americans in the rudiments of Christian principles and literacy, not just in South Carolina, but in Virginia, North Carolina, and Maryland as well. Fearing baptism equated manumission, and that time spent learning catechism meant time away from plantation work. South Carolina slaveholders pressured the colony's governing body to pass a law that made it a crime to teach slaves to read and write. Thirty years later, colonial Georgia followed South Carolina's precedent and enacted similar legislation that forbade the teaching of slaves to read or write (Cornelius 1991: 18).

Restrictions on African American literacy grew worse during the antebellum era. As noted by one historian, "local ordinances supplemented state laws, and in some places it became a crime merely to sell writing materials" to enslaved African Americans or even establish a school for free blacks (Genovese 1974: 562). The laws against teaching enslaved African Americans to read and write during the antebellum era grew out of a variety of fears and concerns, the most straightforward being the use of literacy as a means to freedom (such as the forging of passes for escape). By 1830, the state of Georgia imposed fines, public whippings, and/or imprisonments to anyone caught teaching enslaved or free African Americans. In that same year, North Carolina and Louisiana also enforced such punishments on persons willing to teach the rudiments of literacy to enslaved African Americans. In its 1830–1 legislative sessions, Virginia provided penalties for teaching enslaved blacks to read or write. In 1832, Alabama's Digest of Laws prohibited under fine the teaching of enslaved African Americans; its legislation arose from the panic following the Nat Turner revolt in Southampton, Virginia. In 1834, South Carolina responded similarly, and revised its 1740 statute to penalize all persons who taught African Americans, even freeborn blacks, how to read or write. Arkansas, Kentucky, and Tennessee never legally forbade the teaching of enslaved African Americans, but public opinion against African American literacy had so hardened that the actual opportunities for enslaved blacks and free persons of color to learn decreased as much as in states where illiteracy was legally mandated. Correspondingly, Mississippi, Missouri, and Maryland never statutorily penalized anyone associated with teaching African Americans. Rather they barred public assemblages of African Americans for educational purposes and strongly discouraged whites from assisting blacks in learning the written word (Cornelius 1991: 32–3).

Local sentiment served as an additional impediment to becoming literate during the antebellum era. Proslavery ideologues assumed only "madmen would risk having their slaves read" or mingle with literate free blacks (Genovese 1974: 561). Most believed that slaves should receive instruction only in that which would qualify them for their "particular station" in life. These sentiments were ingrained points of view by the 1840s, and they complemented the growing number of laws banning or restricting African American literacy in the antebellum South. Similarly, these views served as a rationale for the continued maintenance of hereditary slavery and the denial of civil and political rights to free African Americans in a democratic society. They also became a "self-fulfilling prophecy" for the pseudo-science of the day, which saw African Americans as genetically inferior and by their nature incapable of learning.

Testimony by antebellum African Americans themselves shows that the law, while restrictive, was less of a problem than local sentiment and opposition. To slaves and slaveholders alike, literacy was equated with empowerment and freedom. Enslaved black Charles Ball was certain that slaveholders were always "careful to prevent the slaves from learning to read," because "They fear that they [the slaves] may be imbibed with the notions of equality and liberty" from such teaching (Ball 1837: 164). After he escaped from slavery, Frederick Douglass offered a similar assessment. He reasoned thus:

> It is perfectly well understood at the south, that to educate a slave is to make him discontented with slavery, and to invest him with a power which shall open to him the treasures of freedom; and since the object of the slaveholder is to maintain complete authority over his slave, his constant vigilance is exercised to prevent everything which militates against, or endangers, the stability of his authority. Education being among the menacing influences, and, perhaps, the most dangerous, is, therefore, the most cautiously guarded against. (Douglass 1855: 432)

Many enslaved African Americans knew firsthand the horrors that awaited a slave able to obtain some book learning. As a child during slavery, William Heard personally witnessed the punishment inflicted on a slave who secretly learned the rudiments of literacy. Heard starkly remembered that "any slave caught writing suffered the penalty of having his forefinger cut from his right hand" (Heard 1924: 31). Disfigurement was to ensure that a literate slave never wrote again, because a slave able to write could literally write his or her own pass to freedom. Former slave Lucindy Jurdon had similar recollections. "Ef us tried to learn to read or write," she recalled, "dey would cut your forefingers off" (Rawick 1972: 14). Correspondingly, Arnold Gragston of Macon County, Kentucky remembered when his master suspected his slaves of learning to read and write he would call them to the big house. He continued, "if we told him we had been learnin' to read, he would beat the day-lights out of us" (Irons 2002: 1). Still, as historian Janet Duitsman Cornelius stated, "despite the dangers and difficulties, thousands of slaves learned to read and write in the antebellum South" (Cornelius 1983: 171).

Free blacks in the South desiring a formal education also faced challenges. Their very existence proved to be an anomaly in a nation premised upon a white supremacist ideology and the hereditary and lifelong enslavement of people of African descent. In some locales, free blacks barely maintained a quasi-free status and, consequently, fared little better than their enslaved brethren. Such fate was all too familiar to the Reverend William Troy, who left his birth state for Canada when he and his family could no longer endure life in the United States. Born free in Essex County, Virginia, Troy recalled the immense difficulty he had in procuring an education for himself and his family because of the strict legal and customary proscriptions against free persons of color. "Personally, I have suffered on account of my color in regard to education. I was not allowed to go to school publicly, had to learn pri-vately . . . Further, I could not educate my children there [Virginia], and make them feel as women and men ought – for, under those oppressive laws, they would feel a degradation not intended by Him who made of one blood all the people of the earth" (Drew 1856: 355). Though they never met, Thomas Hedgebeth, a freeborn black from Halifax County, North Carolina, could easily understand Troy's frustra-tion and his migration to Canada. He wrote: "The law there does not favor colored people . . . A free-born man in North Carolina is as much oppressed, in one sense, as the slave. I was not allowed to go to school . . . and I think it an outrageous sin and shame, that a free colored man could not be taught" (ibid: 276).

A Review of the Historiography of African American Education before and after the Civil War

Historians who have studied the specifics of the mass movement for book learning and schooling in the South before and after the Civil War agree that African Ameri-cans everywhere considered education a paramount and invaluable acquisition. The standard histories on African American education document educational norms and values among antebellum and postbellum southern blacks that are complex, adapt-ive, and extremely supportive of learning and self-improvement. Still, historians debate the extent of learning African Americans actually received during these eras and what it was that motivated both free and enslaved (soon thereafter, freed) blacks to seek out book learning in a society that aimed to keep them illiterate. This is especially true of historical analysis concerning slave literacy. For nearly a century historians have debated the approximate percentage of literate slaves in the antebel-lum era.

Carter G. Woodson initiated the debate in 1916. He figured that at least 10 percent of enslaved African Americans "had the rudiments of education in 1860" (Woodson 1916: 139). "But the proportion," he concluded "was much less than it was near the close of the era of better beginnings about 1825" (ibid: 139). Woodson estimated that slave literacy rates declined by almost half after the 1820s, given the series of strict legal measures aimed at deterring the teaching of enslaved African Americans. Nearly two decades after Woodson, W. E. B. Du Bois estimated that only 5 percent of enslaved African Americans in the South were literate prior to emancipation (Du Bois 1935: 638). Du Bois' assessment was drawn primarily from his considerations of the educational and governmental activities of literate freedmen in the first decade after the Civil War. Eugene Genovese in his seminal publication, *Roll, Jordan, Roll: The World the Slaves Made*, took the middle ground on the debate. While he agreed that Du Bois's 5 percent estimate was "entirely plausible," he was also quick to comment that this approximation "may even be too low" (Genovese 1974: 563). What was apparent to Genovese from the historical record was the fact that throughout the South "slaveholders, travelers, and ex-slaves agreed that many plantations had one or more literate slaves" (ibid: 563). This fact alone served as the foundation for Genovese's claim that literacy was an ever-present feature in the antebellum slave community.

Historian Janet Duitsman Cornelius offered her own assessment on the extent of slave literacy during the antebellum era, and she supported Woodson's higher estimate. Cornelius reviewed the testimony of ex-slaves interviewed between 1936 and 1938 by the Works Progress Administration (WPA) and over 200 autobiographical narratives of formerly enslaved African Americans. In her book, *When I Can Read My Title Clear*, Cornelius concluded that more enslaved African Americans learned to read and/or write after 1825 than Woodson or Du Bois could have known (Cornelius 1991). At least 5 percent of the ex-slaves interviewed by the WPA explicitly stated that they learned to read and/or write during enslavement. Given the fact that these interviews were conducted approximately 65 years after slavery's abolition, virtually every ex-slave professing their ability to read and/or write had to have attained these skills post-1825. Notwithstanding, Cornelius is correct in forewarning her readers that as in other cultures "there can never be exact measurements of the extent of literacy among enslaved African Americans" (ibid: 8). One of the primary reasons for the uncertainty has already been alluded to throughout this essay: "Neither slaves nor those slaveholders and others who taught them could proclaim their activities safely" or publicly without the possibility of punishment (Cornelius 1983: 173.)

Still, historians tend to agree on the motivations of slaves to become literate. Enslaved African Americans who learned to read and/or write "gained privacy, leisure time, and mobility. A few wrote their own passes and escaped from slavery. Literate slaves also taught others and served as a conduit for information within a slave communication network. Some were even able to capitalize on their skills in literacy as a starting point for leadership careers after slavery ended" (Cornelius 1983: 171). Most historians are of the same opinion that learning to read and write reinforced an image of self-worth and community empowerment among enslaved African Americans and that literacy in itself was the first step to freedom. As one historian inferred, the acquisition of literacy in the slave community was "a communal act" and "a political demonstration of resistance to oppression and of self-determination for the black community . . . through literacy the slave could obtain skills valuable in the white world . . . and could use those skills for special privileges or to gain freedom" (Cornelius 1991: 3). Thomas Webber's classic, *Deep Like the*

Rivers: Education in the Slave Quarter Community, 1831–1865, which documented the cultural and informal education of slaves during the antebellum era, offered an equally interesting perspective. Webber reasoned that a slave who could read was a very important person in the slave community. Webber adamantly stressed: "Not only could such persons keep other slaves abreast of the news, write them passes, and read to them straight from the Bible, but they disproved the racist notion promulgated by whites that blacks were incapable of such learning" (Webber 1978: 136).

James Olney argued that enslaved African Americans viewed literacy as a "mechanism for forming an identity;" its acquisition confirmed their humanity and gave hope to the possibility of slaves obtaining freedom, even citizenship in American society, through the written word (Olney 1985: 153). To historian V. P. Franklin, literacy signified an additional skill to protect and assist enslaved African Americans in surviving the immeasurable vices of American slavery. "Education and literacy," stated Franklin, "were greatly valued among Afro-Americans enslaved in the United States because they saw in their day-to-day experiences – from one generation to the next – that knowledge and information helped one to survive in a hostile environment" (Franklin 1984: 164). Accordingly, enslaved African Americans considered reading and writing as necessary skills for enduring and possibly escaping enslavement.

Research by Ivan McDougle on runaway slaves strongly supports the contention that enslaved African Americans attempted to use their secretly-gained understanding of the written word to earn their freedom. McDougle documented that 71 of the 350 advertised runaways in antebellum Kentucky, 20.2 percent, were listed as being able to read, and 37 or 10.5 percent were also reported as being able to write (McDougle 1918: 289). Arguably, the high percentage of literate runaway slaves in Kentucky may have existed because there was not a law in Kentucky prohibiting the teaching of slaves. Similarly, almost 9 percent of the 625 runaway slaves interviewed in William Still's *The Underground Railroad* (approximately 56 escapees) were recorded as learning how to read and/or write while enslaved (Still 1872). While these figures may be perceived as low or insignificant in the greater analysis, they serve as excellent examples of literate African Americans in the antebellum slave community. Moreover, they illustrate that enslaved African Americans desired – and sometimes used – these skills to resist enslavement and earn their freedom. To reiterate a previous contention, such ambitions for literacy – whether gained or not – were passed down for generations until freedom universally came in 1865.

Perhaps the most dramatic expression of enslaved African Americans' great longing for education came after emancipation. For freedpeople, as for slaves, literacy and schools were equated with empowerment and freedom: they "represented the Keys of the Kingdom" (Genovese 1974: 565). Historian James D. Anderson was correct in asserting that freedpeople in general "emerged from slavery with a strong belief in the desirability of learning to read and write" (Anderson 1988: 5): "This belief was expressed in the pride in which they talked of other ex-slaves who learned to read and write in slavery and in the esteem in which they held literate blacks" (ibid: 5). The historiography of African American education following the Civil War strongly supports these arguments. Historians James D. Anderson (1988; 1995), Henry Bullock (1967), Ronald Butchart (1980), W. E. B. Du Bois (1897; 1935),

Herbert Gutman (2000), Jacqueline Jones (1980), James L. Leloudis (1996), Robert C. Morris (1982), Christopher M. Span (2001; 2002b), and Heather Williams (2002) have all documented through their research the connections that freed African Americans made between education and citizenship. Further, they have demonstrated how the efforts and educational enthusiasm of former slaves served as the catalyst to the South's first comprehensive public school system.

For both individual and collective reasons, freed blacks sought an education because it represented a previously prohibited means of control, empowerment, and autonomy, as well as a practical means of personal and professional improvement. Moreover, in freedom, as in slavery, the quest for learning was part and parcel of the larger struggle for real freedom and equality. It is difficult to overemphasize the enthusiasm of formerly enslaved African Americans and the expectations they had of education and its usefulness in emancipation. Practically every contemporary, friend or foe, of the ex-slave witnessed their determination in acquiring an education for themselves and their children. "In its universality and intensity," one New England Freedmen Aid Society missionary recounted, "they [formerly enslaved African Americans] believe that reading and writing are to bring with them inestimable advantages" (Fleming 1906: 174). As in slavery, education was perceived as a means to progress and societal uplift: ex-slaves perceived book learning as an investment, a passageway to a better day for themselves and their children. It was considered a priority, a necessary investment for citizenship and the overall advancement of the emergent ex-slave community.

As mentioned, such aspiration for learning was a deeply entrenched cultural value in the African American experience and was virtually universal in the ex-slave community. It sharply differed from the expectations that poor southern whites had of education and the emphasis they placed on it. Where poor whites, according to W. E. B. Du Bois, viewed schooling as a "luxury connected to wealth" and did not demand an opportunity to acquire it, African Americans – both during and after slavery – demanded it, connecting education with freedom, social mobility, and self-sufficiency. Du Bois concluded that formerly enslaved African Americans firmly "believed that education was a stepping-stone to wealth and respect, and that wealth, without education, crippled" a person's prospects of attaining equality, self-reliance, landownership, the vote, and full citizenship (Du Bois 1935: 641). Had he been aware of Du Bois's contention, Charles Whiteside most likely would have agreed. The very day Whiteside's owner informed him that he was free, he also informed him that his freedom was "essentially meaningless" and that he "would always remain a slave" because he had "no education" (Litwack 1998: 56). "Education," the former slaveowner decreed, was "what makes a man free" (ibid: 56). Impressed, but not discouraged, by the words of the man who had hitherto held him in bondage, Whiteside made up his mind, then and there, to insure that his children received the type of education he was systematically denied. He sent each of his 13 children to school, determined, as he said, "to make them free" (ibid: 56).

How enslaved African Americans acquired the skills of reading and writing, with minimal guidance and under the constraints of American slavery, truly characterized ability and determination to learn despite the odds against them. With few options for instruction, minimal resources – pencils, paper, books, and the like – and under the most constraining circumstances, numerous enslaved African Americans haphazardly and defiantly learned to read and write. No matter how discouraging these conditions seemed, the situation was not entirely hopeless. As Carter G. Woodson pointed out:

> The ways in which slaves acquired knowledge are significant. Many picked it up here and there, some followed occupations which were in themselves enlightening, and others learned from slaves whose attainments were unknown to their masters. Often influential White men taught Negroes not only the rudiments of education but almost anything they wanted to learn. Not a few slaves were instructed by the White children whom they accompanied to school. While attending ministers and officials whose work often lay open to their servants, many of the race learned by contact and observation. Shrewd Negroes sometimes slipped stealthily into back streets, where they studied under a private teacher, or attended a school hidden from the zealous execution of the law. (Woodson 1916: 125–6)

How the notable Frederick Douglass learned to read and write as a slave during his childhood is an excellent illustration. At about the age of 10 he was taught by his mistress how to read and "in an incredibly short time" Douglass "had mastered the alphabet and could spell words of three or four letters" (Douglass 1881: 70). Soon thereafter, his master discovered the activities of his wife and Douglass, and brought them to a halt. Before Douglass, he scolded his wife stating, "if you give a nigger an inch he will take an ell. Learning will spoil the best nigger in the world. If he learns to read the Bible it will forever unfit him to be a slave. He should know nothing but the will of his master, and learn to obey it" (ibid: 70). This outburst had a profound effect on Douglass. He remarked:

> His iron sentences, cold and harsh, sunk like heavy weights deep into my heart, and stirred up within me a rebellion not soon to be allayed . . . he underrated my comprehension, and had little idea of the use to which I was capable of putting the impressive lesson he was giving to his wife. He wanted me to be a slave; I had already voted against that on the home plantation of Col. Lloyd. That which he most loved I most hated; and the very determination which he expressed to keep me in ignorance only rendered me the more resolute to seek intelligence. In learning to read, therefore, I am not sure that I do not owe quite as much to the opposition of my master as to the kindly assistance of my amiable mistress. (Douglass 1881: 70–1)

Thenceforth, attempting to learn how to read and later write became an obsession for young Douglass. Filled with the determination to become literate at any cost, and unable to rely anymore on his mistress as a potential resource, Douglass sought out differing avenues to develop his new ability. One opportunity that repeatedly seemed available involved the support of his white plantation playmates. "I used to carry almost constantly a copy of Webster's spelling-book in my pocket," Douglass recalled, "and when sent on errands, or when play-time was allowed me, I would step aside with my young friends and take a lesson in spelling" (Douglass 1881: 74). Douglass would learn to write in much the same manner. While at work on the docks, Douglass secretly sketched the various words he identified on the barrels he loaded and in the evenings or on Sundays he would coax his unsuspecting white playmates into competitive games involving the alphabet and writing. "With play-mates for my teachers, fences and pavements for my copy-books, and chalk for my pen and ink," Douglass proudly recollected, "I learned to write" (ibid: 86).

Douglass' informal educational attainment typified the earliest learning opportunities for the majority of enslaved African Americans who obtained some degree of literacy. Most accounts indicate that enslaved African Americans learned to read before the age of 12, usually with some assistance from whites, and well before they learned – if at all – to write. Learning to read before writing should not come as a surprise since writing required the mastery and acquisition of special equipment. As Cornelius deduced, "writing was harder to learn than reading, and presented the challenge of finding or making materials in a mostly rural society which had little use for these tools" (Cornelius 1991: 61). Nonetheless, enslaved African Americans made the most of their chances to learn to read or write when such opportunities arose, whether at work or home, publicly or secretly. Future congressional senator Blanche K. Bruce was a great example. While enslaved, Bruce educated himself when he was at work at a printer's trade shop in Brunswick, Missouri (Woodson 1916: 128). Another was Benjamin Holmes. As an apprentice tailor in Charleston, South Carolina, Holmes "studied all the signs and names on the doors" of his employment (Cornelius 1991: 69). Thereafter, he would ask people to tell him – one or two at a time – the words he observed on the signs and/or doors. By the age of 12 he discovered that he could read newspapers.

Another common characteristic associated with slave literacy was the exchanging of goods for instructional lessons. Many slave children, for example, bartered trinkets, fruits, and other goods to their white peers to secure a rudimentary education. Young Richard Parker, for example, exchanged marbles to any youth willing to teach him the alphabet (Blassingame 1977: 465). James W. Sumler of Norfolk, Virginia, obtained an elementary education this way as well (Woodson 1916: 130). Tabb Gross learned to read by promising his eight-year-old master an orange every time he taught him the alphabet (Blassingame 1977: 347–8). Uncle Cepahs, "a slave of Parson Winslow of Tennessee," recalled how white children secretly taught him to read in exchange for food cooked for them by Dinah, Winslow's cook (Albert 1890: 126). Robert Adams acquired his first reading lessons in similar fashion. As a child "he would get all the nice fruit he could and bartered it off in the evening and on Sundays to any white child willing to teach him from a book he secretly possessed" (Adams 1872: 9–10). His brother John Quincy Adams recalled that that was "the way many poor slaves learned to read and write" before emancipation (ibid: 10).

Virginia-born Louis Hughes was somewhat of an exception. Like Douglass, Hughes also recalled "learning off the wall;" however, he was not a child, but a young adult when he obtained his first reading lessons. Moreover, a fellow adult slave, Tom, who was the coachman for the plantation, taught him his first lessons. Tom secretly acquired his learning from some neighboring plasterers and workmen. According to Hughes, "they saw that he was so anxious to learn that they promised to teach him every evening if he would slip out to their house" (Hughes 1896: 100). Hughes was also anxious to learn, but being a house servant could not get away as easily. Tom recognized Hughes' inconvenience and ambitions. He secretly taught Hughes by writing numerals and the alphabet on the side of a barn for him to copy (ibid: 100). These lessons lasted for months before the plantation overseers finally discovered and put an end to them. By this time Hughes had already obtain the rudiments of book learning.

The ingenious methods used by ambitious enslaved African Americans to acquire some degree of literacy are recognizable in other ways as well. In his autobiography Lucius Holsey recalled selling old rags for books, so many that he was able to buy five books: two Webster's blue-back spellers, a school dictionary, Milton's *Paradise Lost*, and the Bible. These books "constituted his full stock of literary possessions;" a library, boasted Holsey, "more precious than gold" to him (Holsey 1898: 17). Like many others, Holsey acknowledged that some white children and an African American man taught him the alphabet, after which:

> I fought my way unaided through the depths of my ponderous library. Day by day I took a leaf from one of the spelling books, and so folded it that one or two of the lessons were on the outside as if printed on a card. This I put in the pocket of my vest or coat, and when I was sitting on the carriage, walking the yard or streets, or using hoe or spade, or in the dining room, I would take out my spelling leaf, catch a word and commit it to memory. When one side of the spelling leaf was finished by this process, I would refold it again with a new lesson on the outside. When night came, I went to my little room, and with chips of fat pine, and pine roots . . . I would kindle a little blaze in the fire-place and turn my head toward it while lying flat on my back so as to get the most of the light on the leaves of the book . . . I reviewed the lessons of the day from the unmaimed [*sic*] book. By these means I learned to read and write a little in six months. Besides, I would catch words from the white people and retain them in memory until I could get to my dictionary. Then I would spell and define the words, until they became perfectly impressed upon my memory. (Holsey 1898: 17–18)

Holsey was fortunate that it only took him six months to master the art of reading. For most literate enslaved African Americans, given their restricted circumstances, such attainment was a laborious, extremely dangerous, and time-consuming process. For even the most determined slave, oftentimes it took years of clandestine self-instruction in order to comprehend the English written language well enough to claim the right of knowing how to read. The determination and raw intellectual abilities of Holsey and others, to acquire the rudiments of even an elementary education with so little time and guidance and under the stresses and penalties of slave life, demonstrated incontestably their impressive individual accomplishments. As one historian commented, "with fragmented time, few teacher guides, and limited vocabulary . . . [it is] no wonder it could take even a determined slave years to read. Add the physical threats to other obstacles and the process becomes heroic" (Cornelius 1991: 68).

Some enslaved African Americans, however, did not have to go through the trouble of self-education in secrecy or in fear of severe punishment. According to historian John Hope Franklin (2000), schools for enslaved blacks are known to have existed – despite the law or public sentiment – throughout the South. For example, the enslaved black "Patrick Snead of Savannah, Georgia was sent to a private institution until he could spell quite well and then to a Sunday-school for colored children" (Woodson 1916: 132). On some estates, slave owners actually helped African Americans to learn the written word. Reasons varied. W. S. Scarborough, the future president of Wilberforce College, remembered in his slave childhood receiving permission to attend a school in Bibb County, Georgia (Simmons 1887: 411). I. T. Montgomery, later the founder of Mound Bayou, Mississippi – the first black settlement established in the state – was instructed by his owner, Joseph Davis, in reading, writing, and arithmetic. Joseph and his brother Jefferson Davis attempted to train their slaves to be the accountants of the plantation (Woodson 1916: 131). Aaron Robinson recalled how his owner actually required his own children to teach Robinson how to read, so that he could avoid taking them rabbit hunting (Blassingame 1977: 498). Mississippi native Smart Walker learned to read from his master's son, who had asked his father if he could teach Walker his school lessons (ibid: 517). Frederick Law Olmsted, while touring Mississippi in 1852, found a group of literate enslaved African Americans, all owned by a person entirely illiterate. The slave owner, according to Olmsted, took great pride in possessing such "loyal, capable, and intelligent Negroes" (Woodson 1916: 128).

All the same, the most impressive history of African Americans attempting to educate themselves came after emancipation. Between 1863 and 1870, countless former slaves would rush to the schoolhouse in hopes of learning how to read and write. Booker T. Washington, a part of this movement himself, described most vividly his people's struggle for education: "Few people who were not right in the midst of the scenes can form any exact idea of the intense desire which the people of my race showed for education . . . It was a whole race trying to go to school. Few were too young, and none too old, to make the attempt to learn" (Washington 1901: 30–1). Most attended what were called freedmen schools, started by northern teachers who moved south to assist freedpeople in their transition from slaves to citizens. By 1870, more than 9,500 teachers, with the assistance of the Bureau of Refugees, Freedmen, and Abandoned Lands – a governmental agency commonly referred to as the Freedmen's Bureau – taught nearly 250,000 pupils in over 4,300 schools.

Another type of grassroots school that arose in the earliest emancipation years was what the late historian Herbert Gutman (2000) called "schools of freedom." "Freedom schools" were established, financed, and maintained by former slaves, with only the minimal assistance of others. These virtually self-sufficient schools arose in every locale following the Civil War and historians are finally giving them the attention they deserve (Anderson 1988 and 1995; Gutman 2000; Span 2002a and 2002b; Williams 2002). They began in the South's most prominent cities – Charleston, Nashville, Richmond, New Orleans, Savannah, and Little Rock – as well as in the backwoods and on the most secluded cotton and tobacco plantations, and the first opened well before the outcome of the Civil War was determined.

One of the first schools for the benefit of southern black freedmen opened in Alexandria, Virginia, during the Civil War. On September 1, 1861, Mary Chase and another freedwoman opened a pay school for wartime runaways. Less than a month later, "one of them joined Mrs. Mary Smith Peake, daughter of an English father and a free black woman who had taught at an antebellum Hampton, Virginia school" (Gutman 2000: 389). Together they opened a second school for contrabands at Fortress Monroe, Virginia. The actions of these three black women preceded those of northern white missionaries by nearly a year. In fact, by the time northern white teachers started teaching freedpeople in Virginia, there were already three more schools in Alexandria opened by African Americans. The Freedmen's Inquiry

Commission, an agency established by President Lincoln to investigate the needs of former slaves, was quick to note the pro-activities of freed blacks in Alexandria. "One of the first acts of the negroes when they found themselves free," the commission declared, "was to establish schools at their own expense" (National Freedmen's Aid Union 1867: 4). Union Army Lieutenant C. B. Wilder was astonished at the pace at which former slaves and their children learned in these grassroots Virginia schools. "Scarcely one could be found who could read as they came in," Wilder reported. "Now very few but can read some, and all are getting books and with or without teachers are striving to learn themselves and one another" (*Facts concerning the Freedmen* 1863: 5). By 1867, two years after the Civil War, the push for schooling among freedpeople in Virginia was truly a spectacle. One white Virginian promptly recognized this upon his visit to a school attended by free and freed black children in Norfolk. "We cannot express," he said, "our satisfaction more fully than by saying that we were literally astonished at the display of intelligence by the pupils. Abstruse questions in arithmetic were promptly answered, difficult problems solved, the reading beautifully rhetorical, and the singing charming." Given the pace of learning among former slave children, the onlooker concluded: "more encouragement must be given by our city council to our public schools to prevent white children from being outstripped in the race for intelligence by their sable competitors" (Alvord 1867: 15).

Around the time that missionary schools for freedpeople arose in Virginia in 1862, it was reported by Union Army officials that free and contraband blacks in Nashville, Tennessee, had already independently established a number of schools for more than 800 children. The primary impetus for this educational push in Nashville came from ex-slaves themselves and from Daniel Watkins, an antebellum free black who had maintained, for nearly a decade, a school for the children of free blacks. By summer's end 1864, several schools managed and taught by African Americans in Nashville had "sprung up," and black children outnumbered white children in school attendance (Gutman 2000: 390–1). By 1869, freed African Americans in Tennessee had established a total of 22 private schools throughout the state and were financially assisting northern teachers and the Freedmen's Bureau in maintaining 59 other schools. As the superintendent of education for Tennessee's freedpeople C. E. Compton observed, the private schools established were "wholly supported by the freedmen without any aid from the bureau, State, or from benevolent societies" (Alvord 1869: 62).

Equally impressive efforts were seen elsewhere, particularly in Baltimore, Washington, DC, and Little Rock, Arkansas. By winter 1865, the Society of Friends – based in Philadelphia – and the New York-based American Missionary Association (AMA), in collaboration with Baltimore blacks, had established 16 schools with nearly 2,000 pupils. The city's black population, however, promoted the push for schools even further and independently established and managed seven more schools for freedpeople. A capstone to these efforts came in January 1866, when freeborn and formerly enslaved African Americans in Maryland hosted a state convention in Baltimore to assess and address their overall needs. An advisory board convened and urged each and every Maryland black to "use every exertion to contradict the predictions of [their] enemies, which were uttered previous to the emancipation of the States that if the slaves were freed they would become a pest to society" (Foner and Walker

1986: 228). They advised formerly enslaved African Americans to feel and act as if they were free and independent, to be industrious, to purchase land, and to acquire an education. Specifically, the assembly advised black Marylanders to educate their children for equality, self-sufficiency, and citizenship. "Educate your children and give them trades, thereby making them equal for any position in life, for if ever we are raised to the elevated summit in life for which we strive, it must be done by our own industry and exertion . . . No one can do it for us," they concluded (ibid: 227–8).

Several schools in and around Washington DC were established with similar vigor by newly emancipated blacks. For example, the African Civilization Society of New York, founded in 1858 to promote colonization by African Americans in Africa, reconstituted itself during the Civil War as a freedmen's aid society. Between 1864 and 1867, with the help of former slaves, the organization opened six schools for African Americans. Freeborn African American Catholics of the Blessed Martin de Porres parish in the nation's capital also founded five schools for freedpeople; and 22 African Americans individually started private schools for former slaves and other blacks during the 1860s (McPherson 1965).

In Little Rock, Arkansas, freed African Americans – in addition to establishing private schools for their children – formed the Freedmen's School Society in March 1865, in order to collect monies for educational purposes. "By their own exertions," as reported by one Union Army official, freedpeople in Arkansas "made the city schools free for the rest of the year," an astonishing feat considering the relative impoverishment of a people just removed from enslavement (McPherson 1965: 142). By November 1865, many of these same freed blacks and others reconvened in Little Rock to demand that state legislators acknowledge them as citizens. They also appealed to elected representatives to provide a system of schools for their children. "We do most earnestly desire and pray," their request began:

> That you clothe us with the power of self protection, by giving us our equality before the law and the right of suffrage, so we may become *bona fide* citizens of the State in which we live . . . Believing, as we do, that we are destined in the future, as in the past, to cultivate your cotton fields, we claim for Arkansas the first to deal justly and equitably for her laborers . . . That we are the substrata, the foundation on which the future power and wealth of the State of Arkansas must be built . . . we respectfully ask the Legislature to provide for the education of our children. (Foner and Walker 1986: 194)

Amid this mass movement for literacy and schools, following the end of slavery, few missionary or military personalities from the North recognized and appreciated the educational zeal of the South's freedpeople better than the superintendent of education for the Freedmen's Bureau, John W. Alvord. Alvord was appointed to this commission in July 1865 and made it his first priority to tour the region to assess its needs. He observed firsthand the strides and sacrifices former slaves had made to acquire an education, even if it was only rudimentary instruction. Everywhere Alvord traveled he discovered, with surprise, "a class of schools" that he identified as "native schools." These independent or self-sustaining schools were managed and "taught by colored people, rude and imperfect, but still groups of peoples, old and young, *trying* to learn" [original emphasis] (Alvord 1866: 8). In his first of ten semi-annual reports, Alvord estimated that at least 500 of these independent black schools existed in the South, the vast majority never before visited by a white person. Flabbergasted by the educational motivation and pro-activities of the South's freedpeople, Alvord made it a point to pen his observations. He wrote, "throughout the entire south an effort is being made by the colored people to educate themselves . . . [and] in the absence of other teachings they are determined to be self-taught" (ibid: 10).

What should be apparent in this overview of the history of African American education before and after slavery is the resilience and determination of a people to become literate, as part of a long historical struggle against slavery and racism, in pursuit of freedom and equality. The desire for literacy was in itself an act of resistance. During slavery, the quest for book learning was a direct challenge to the repressive law and social customs that strove to keep African Americans – enslaved or free – illiterate, for literacy was equated with empowerment and freedom from enslavement. Such appreciation for the written word was passed down for generations in the slave community until slavery's abolition. After slavery, this cultural appreciation for book learning among freed southern blacks flourished and took on new forms. As an ideal, literacy was still equated with freedom, but now it related to the extension of personal freedoms as citizens in a democracy and it served as the foundation for citizenship, and individual and collective improvement.

The value that African Americans placed on learning and self-improvement, distinctive as it was, did not necessarily have a natural or "instinctive" cause. However, in the context of slavery and racism, literacy – and the way they acquired it – inevitably developed the way they thought about education. That experience for slaves and free persons of color was vastly different in most respects from all other classes of American citizens, both "native" whites and immigrants. During the decades before the Civil War, slaves and free blacks in the South lived in a society in which literacy was forbidden to them by law and custom; but literacy symbolized freedom and it contradicted the condition of slavery and servitude. At the dawn of the Civil War about four million enslaved African Americans lived in a society where they could be whipped, maimed, or killed for the pursuit of learning. This repression is recorded vividly in the autobiographies and narratives of slaves. Slaves everywhere understood the penalties and extreme difficulties in the pursuit of education as further forms of oppression. "There is one sin that slavery committed against me," professed one former slave, "which I will never forgive. It robbed me of my education" (Anderson 1988: 5). Emancipation released an ex-slave class whose parents, grandparents, and great-grandparents viewed reading and writing as both a challenge to oppression and an expression of freedom. One of the first schools founded by slaves at the onset of the Civil War was established in New Orleans in 1860. They named it the "Pioneer School of Freedom." The very naming of this school epitomized African Americans' belief in education as a means to liberation.

The descendants of both slaves and free persons of color inherited a distinctive orientation toward learning that made education inseparable from the struggle for freedom. This heritage is expressed in the struggle of each generation since the post-emancipation period and has persisted into our own present. The symbolic continuity between the "Pioneer School of Freedom" of 1860 and the "Mississippi Freedom Schools" of the 1960s represents a long-standing and indivisible relationship between the quest for book learning and the quest for freedom in the African American experience. In vital respects, education was viewed as the first act of resistance. "Get an education, boy," African American grandmothers often said, "because that's the one thing that whites can't take away from you" (Patterson 2001: xxiv).

BIBLIOGRAPHY

Works Cited

Adams, John Quincy (1872) *Narrative of the Life of John Quincy Adams, when in Slavery, and Now as a Freeman.* Harrisburg, PA: Sieg.

Albert, Octavia V. Rogers (1890) *The House of Bondage, or Charlotte Brooks and Other Slaves Original and Life-Like, as They Appeared in the Old Plantation and City Slave Life; Together with Pen-Pictures of the Peculiar Institution with Sights and Insights into Their New Relations as Freedmen, Freemen, and Citizens.* New York: Hunt & Eaton.

Alvord, John (1866) *First Semi-Annual Report on Schools for Freedmen, January 1, 1866.* Washington, DC: Governmental Printing Office.

—— (1867) *Fourth Semi-Annual Report on Schools for Freedmen, July 1, 1867.* Washington, DC: Governmental Printing Office.

—— (1869) *Eighth Semi-Annual Report on Schools for Freedmen, July 1, 1869.* Washington, DC: Governmental Printing Office.

Anderson, James D. (1988) *The Education of Blacks in the South, 1860–1935.* Chapel Hill: University of North Carolina Press.

—— (1995) "Literacy and education in the African-American experience" in Vivian Gadsden and Daniel Wagner (eds.), *Literacy among African-American Youth: Issues in Learning, Teaching, and Schooling,* 19–37. Cresskill, NJ: Hampton Press.

Ball, Charles (1837) *Slavery in the United States: A narrative of the life and adventures of Charles Ball, a Black man, who lived forty years in Maryland, South Carolina, and Georgia, as a slave, under various masters, and was one year in the navy with Commodore Barney, during the late war.* New York: John S. Taylor.

Blassingame, John (ed.) (1977) *Slave Testimony: Two Centuries of Letters, Speeches, Interviews, and Autobiographies.* Baton Rouge: Louisiana State University Press.

Breen, Timothy H. and Innes, Stephen (1980) *"Myne Owne Ground:" Race and Freedom on Virginia's Eastern Shore, 1640–1676.* New York: Oxford University Press.

Bullock, Henry (1967) *A History of Negro Education in the South from 1619 to the Present.* Cambridge, MA: Harvard University Press.

Butchart, Ronald (1980) *Northern Schools, Southern Blacks, and Reconstruction: Freedmen's Education, 1862–1875.* New York: Greenwood Press.

Cornelius, Janet (1983) "We slipped and learned to read: slaves and the literacy process, 1830–1865," *Phylon* 44, 171–86.

—— (1991) *When I Can Read My Title Clear: Literacy, Slavery, and Religion in the Antebellum South.* Columbia: University of South Carolina Press.

Douglass, Frederick (1855) *My Bondage, My Freedom.* New York: Miller, Orton & Mulligan.

—— (1881) *Life and Times of Frederick Douglass, Written by Himself.* Hartford, CT: Park.

Drew, Benjamin (1856) *A North-Side View of Slavery. The Refugee: or the Narratives of Fugitive Slaves in Canada Related by Themselves.* Boston: J. P. Jewett.

Du Bois, W. E. B. (1897) "Strivings of the Negro people," *Atlantic Monthly* 80: 194–8.

—— (1935) *Black Reconstruction: An Essay toward a History of the Part which Black Folk Played in the Attempt to Reconstruct Democracy in America.* New York: Harcourt, Brace.

Facts concerning the Freedmen: Their Capacity and Their Destiny (1863) Boston: Press of Commercial Printing House.

Fleming, Walter L. ([1906] 1966) *Documentary History of Reconstruction: Political, Military, Religious, Educational and Industrial, 1865 to 1906*, reprint. New York: Peter Smith Publication.

Foner, Philip S. and Walker, George E. (eds.) (1986) *Proceedings of the Black National and State Conventions, 1865–1900*, vol. I. Philadelphia: Temple University Press.

Franklin, John Hope (2000) *From Slavery to Freedom*, 8th edn. New York: McGraw-Hill.

Franklin, Vincent P. (1984) *Black Self-Determination: A Cultural History of the Faith of the Fathers*. Westport, CT: Lawrence Hill.

Genovese, Eugene (1974) *Roll, Jordan, Roll: The World the Slaves Made*. New York: Pantheon Books.

Gutman, Herbert G. (2000) "Schools for freedom" in Thomas C. Holt and Elsa Barkley Brown (eds.), *Major Problems in African-American History*, 388–401. New York: Houghton Mifflin.

Heard, William (1924) *From Slavery to the Bishopric in the A.M.E. Church*. New York: Arno Press.

Holsey, Lucius (1898) *Autobiographies, Sermons, Addresses and Essays*. Atlanta, GA: Franklin.

Hooker, Charles E. (1876) *On Relations between the White and Colored People of the South: A Speech of Hon. Chas. E. Hooker of Mississippi Delivered in the United States House of Representatives, June 15, 1876*. Washington, DC: U.S. Governmental Printing Office.

Hughes, Louis (1896) *Thirty Years a Slave*. Milwaukee: South Side Printing.

Irons, Peter (2002) *Jim Crow's Children: The Broken Promise of the Brown Decision*. New York: Viking Press.

Jones, Jacqueline (1980) *Soldiers of Light and Love: Northern Teachers and Georgia Blacks, 1865–1873*. Chapel Hill: University of North Carolina Press.

Leloudis, James L. (1996) *Schooling the New South: Pedagogy, Self, and Society in North Carolina, 1880–1920*. Chapel Hill: University of North Carolina Press.

Litwack, Leon (1998) *Trouble in Mind: Black Southerners in the Age of Jim Crow*. New York: Vintage.

McDougle, Ivan (1918) "Slavery in Kentucky," *Journal of Negro History* 3: 211–328.

McPherson, James (1965) *The Negro's Civil War: How American Negroes Felt and Acted during the War for the Union*. New York: Pantheon Books.

Morris, Robert C. (1982) *Reading, 'Riting, and Reconstruction: The Education of Freedmen in the South, 1861–1870*. Chicago: University of Chicago Press.

National Freedmen's Aid Union (1867) *The Industry of the Freedmen of America*. Birmingham, AL: [unknown].

Olney, James (1985) "'I was born': slave narratives, their status as autobiography and literature" in Charles Davis and Henry Louis Gates, Jr (eds.), *The Slave's Narrative*, 148–74. New York: Oxford University Press.

Patterson, James T. (2001) *Brown v. Board of Education: A Civil Rights Milestone and Its Troubled Legacy*. New York: Oxford University Press.

Raffel, Jeffrey (1998) *Historical Dictionary of School Segregation and Desegregation: The American Experience*. New Haven, CT: Greenwood Press.

Rawick, George (1972) *The American Slave: A Composite Autobiography*. 19 vols. Westport, CT: Greenwood Press.

Simmons, William J. (1887) *Men of Mark: Eminent, Progressive, and Rising*. New York: Arno Press.

Span, Christopher (2001) "Citizen or laborer?: the social purposes of black schooling in reconstruction Mississippi, 1862–1875," PhD dissertation: University of Illinois, Urbana-Champaign.

—— (2002a) "Alternative pedagogy: the rise of the private black academy in early postbellum Mississippi, 1862–1870" in Nancy Beadie and Kim Tolley (eds.), *Chartered Schools: Two Hundred Years of Independent Academies in the United States, 1727–1925*, 211–27. New York: Routledge Falmer.

—— (2002b) " 'I must learn now or not at all': social and cultural capital in the educational initiatives of formerly enslaved African Americans in Mississippi, 1862–1869," *Journal of African American History* 87, 196–205.

Still, William (1872) *The Underground Railroad*. Philadelphia: Porter & Coates.

Washington, Booker T. ([1901] 1967) *Up from Slavery*, reprint. New York: Airmont.

Webber, Thomas (1978) *Deep Like the Rivers: Education in the Slave Quarter Community, 1831–1865*. New York: W. W. Norton.

Williams, Heather A. (2002) "Self-taught: the role of African Americans in educating the freedpeople, 1861–1871," PhD dissertation: Yale University.

Woodson, Carter G. ([1916] 1998) *Education of the Negro prior to 1861,* reprint. New York: A+B Publisher Group.

CHAPTER EIGHTEEN

The Growth of African American Cultural and Social Institutions

DAVID H. JACKSON, JR

When Reconstruction ended and African Americans moved into what some historians call the Nadir, they turned more and more to themselves for support and encouragement. Black people were disillusioned with the political system and any faint hopes that racial equality was on the horizon were dashed away. After the effecting of the Compromise of 1877, which led to the end of "Radical Reconstruction" in the South, the following decades were unrelentingly demoralizing, repressive, bloody, and brutal for blacks. Perhaps the most tragic reminder of their precarious position was lynching.

As Philip Dray (2002), Stewart Tolnay and E. M. Beck (1995), and W. Fitzhugh Brundage (1993) have shown, from 1880 to 1930 thousands of African American men and women were lynched throughout the South (black men most often being the victims). They were killed for minor infractions – or even merely being accused of stealing, say – though many times no trial was held to determine their guilt or innocence. The charge of raping or assaulting a white woman would almost invariably lead to lynching. For many, the accusation alone became a death sentence.

As the system of Jim Crow emerged and "separate but equal" became the order of the day with the Supreme Court decision in *Plessy v. Ferguson* (1896), African Americans were systematically shut out of many basic American institutions. If blacks wanted religious fulfillment they had to attend "black" churches. If blacks wanted an education, they had to attend "black" schools. If blacks desired social and cultural endeavors, they had to form their own "black" institutions to facilitate those activities, and they developed a pattern of self-help that carried over from at least the early 1800s with the founding of the Prince Hall Masons and black churches.

In response to the repressive system of Jim Crow, African Americans did not lethargically wait for the doors of white social and cultural institutions to open. Instead, they created their own institutions, which allowed them to live a "parallel" existence. "Without the parallel institutions that the black professional class created," historian Darlene Clark Hine wrote, "successful challenges to white supremacy would not have been possible. The formation of parallel organizations . . . proved to be far more radical, far more capable of nurturing resistance, than anyone could have anticipated in the closing decade of the nineteenth century and opening decades of the twentieth" (Hine 2003: 1279). Furthermore, "segregation provided blacks the chance, indeed, the imperative, to develop a range of distinct institutions they controlled."

In 1967, Charles Kellogg wrote an authoritative history of the National Association for the Advancement of Colored People (NAACP). An examination of Philip Dray's recent study (2002) on racial violence and inequality in America continues to emphasize the work of groups like the NAACP, which is viewed as the institutional leader in the movement for racial justice in America. However, many lesser-known professional organizations served a critical role in the struggle too. Unfortunately, the record of their efforts is not as widely known, understood, or appreciated. This chapter examines how historians have written on these institutions that sustained, propelled, and guided blacks as they struggled for racial equality in America from Reconstruction through the 1930s, under the rubric of "parallelism." The parallel perspective has become a fresh interpretive lens through which historians can assess examples of agency and self-help among blacks during the Age of Jim Crow. While this sort of agency was forced on blacks, it remained "the best hand they had in an all-around bad deal" (Hine 2003: 1280).

Although it is not the author's intent to give here an exhaustive analysis of all the black self-help institutions created during the Jim Crow era, this chapter examines a representative selection of these core institutions, black fraternities and sororities, the National Association of Colored Women (NACW), the National Negro Business League (NNBL), the National Bar Association (NBA), the National Medical Association (NMA), the National Hospital Administration (NHA), and the National Association of Colored Graduate Nurses (NACGN). There remains a need for more studies on these professional organizations and the black professionals who created them.

Stephanie Shaw in *What a Woman Ought to Be and to Do: Black Professional Women Workers During the Jim Crow Era* (1996), Cynthia Neverdon-Morton in *Afro-American Women of the South and the Advancement of the Race* (1989), and Paula Giddings in *When and Where I Enter: The Impact of Black Women on Race and Sex in America* (1985) have produced works that focus on agency and self-help among African American women. During the Jim Crow era, the needs of the urban poor became more acute. In response to these growing needs, white women in 1887 formed a national organization called the General Federation of Women's Clubs (GFWC); however, this organization discriminated against black women. Southern white women particularly found black women objectionable. They impugned the character of black women, asserting that black women were immoral. In fact, one of the catalysts for the forming of the black parallel to the GFWC, the National Association of Colored Women (NACW), was a letter written by James W. Jack, a white American journalist, to Florence Belgarnie in England, the secretary of the Anti-Slavery Society. In his letter Jack wrote that black Americans were "wholly devoid of morality, the women were prostitutes and were natural thieves and liars" (Jones 1982: 22–3).

In her 1982 essay, Beverly Jones shows that these types of pernicious stereotypes and myths about African American women caused them to unite and form a national organization to counter these insidious assertions (Jones 1982: 23). After the merging of several black women's clubs, the NACW was founded on July 21, 1896. This group patterned itself after the GFWC, but there were differences. While both organizations worked to better the lives of women and to provide social services, black women had to struggle against the character assassination harpooned at them by whites. Ultimately, "white women did not have the severe problems of racial discrimination that compounded the plight of black women in employment and education" (ibid: 23).

Black women's clubs throughout the country addressed the social welfare needs of the community by establishing health centers, kindergartens, nurseries, homes for girls and the elderly, and mother's clubs (Lerner 1974: 159, 160, 167). At the mothers' meetings they gave advice on child care, vegetable gardening, home economics and sewing, and conducted inspiring educational discussions. Other clubs set up health centers, began home improvement and clean-up campaigns, and promoted education, race pride, and race advancement. The special circumstances of black women created special needs for the black community that would not have been addressed under the white GFWC. The freedom among these black women to develop leadership skills, along with real opportunities to lead, led to tremendous growth in the aspirations and achievements of black women during the Age of Jim Crow.

Early writers on the NACW tended to focus on general patterns at the national level; thus a closer look at the work of the organization on the state and local levels is still needed. Charles Wesley's *The History of the National Association of Colored Women's Clubs, Inc.* (1984) is a broad survey of the NACW. However, Jacqueline Rouse (1989) in her biography of Lugenia Burns Hope, wife of Atlanta University President John Hope, focuses on the impact of a local affiliate. Hope served as president of the Atlanta Neighborhood Union, a local branch of the NACW, from 1908 to 1935. During that time the group provided classes on personal hygiene, nursing, infant care and prenatal care, among others. It also provided recreational centers and a health care program. Rouse's work serves as a pioneering example of studies that discuss the work of black clubwomen at the local level.

More recently, David Jackson examined the NACW's network in Mississippi, particularly in Mound Bayou, in *A Chief Lieutenant of the Tuskegee Machine: Charles Banks of Mississippi* (Jackson 2002: 23–4). The Mississippi State Federation of Colored Women's clubs served as the state affiliate of the NACW. One local chapter connected with this group was the Silone Yates Federation (SYF), organized in February 1909 in Mound Bayou, Mississippi, and headed by Trenna Banks. It was named after Josephine Silone Yates, who served as the second president of the NACW from 1901 to 1906. For a woman to join the SYF, she had to be willing to work for the civic and social betterment of the community and be of good moral character. Membership certainly denoted high social standing within the community. Although black women's clubs were headed by middle-class women, their leaders were more successful than white women in bridging the class barrier (Lerner 1974: 160).

Jackson found that the Mound Bayou club met weekly or bi-weekly, depending on the needs of the community, and was considered "the intellectual organization of the town" (Jackson 2002: 24). Its members were reputedly some of the "brightest women of the race in the state." Following the general trend of other local clubs, the women visited the elderly, the sick, and the indigent, and provided for their needs in all ways possible. When they visited the sick and shut-in, they typically carried their hymnbooks and Bibles along with them. The SYF engaged in fund-raising for many reasons: for instance, they raised money to build a fence around the Mound Bayou cemetery at a time when many black cemeteries in Mississippi were unkempt.

Most African Americans living in the South around the start of the twentieth century found it difficult to earn a living. Many were forced into tenancy, sharecrop-ping, and peonage. In other words, many ended up back on the same plantations their forefathers had worked for years. The decided majority of blacks worked in agriculture during this era because many other mainstream economic opportunities were closed to them. Most whites thought that blacks were best suited for menial labor and other types of work that required little thought. Consequently it became imperative that the promotion of black business be placed on the agenda for racial uplift. W. E. B. Du Bois intellectualized about this in 1899, but Booker T. Wash-ington, the most prominent black leader during that time, founded an association to promote business and economic development among African Americans, because he realized that blacks were shut out of white-controlled business leagues, chambers of commerce and other economic enterprises (Marable 1986: 29).

When discussing agency and self-help among African Americans, one must con-sider the organization that Booker T. Washington founded in 1900, but very little scholarly work has been published on the National Negro Business League or NNBL (Burrows 1977; Harlan 1988). Entrepreneurs, black professionals, and others interested in starting businesses attended the first meeting. The program issued at the third annual session in 1902 announced that "the object [of the League] is to inform, as best we may, the world of the progress the Negro is making in every part of the country, and to stimulate local business enterprises through its annual meetings and in any other manner deemed wise; to encourage the organization of local business for the purpose of furthering commercial growth in all places where such organizations are deemed needful and wise" (Jackson 2002: 91).

Although it is difficult to quantify the exact impact of the League, it is safe to say that a number of black business people were inspired and spurred on to create businesses because of their affiliation with the NNBL. This provided a number of cultural and social benefits for African Americans. In places like Mississippi, called "the heartland of American apartheid," black people owned and operated 11 banks by 1909, and the Mississippi Negro Business League, led by Charles Banks, was reputedly the strongest state chapter in the national association. As with local affi-liates of the NACW, little has been written on the state and local affiliates of the NNBL. Kenneth Hamilton, editor of the National Negro Business League Papers (1995), has helped put some of this material at the public's disposal, but more needs to be done. Recent scholarship is just beginning to uncover information on the critical role served by these state and local affiliates and their leaders (Jackson 2002: 98, 156).

Juliet E. K. Walker (1998), Lynne Feldman (1999: 78–111), and Jackson (2002: 34–6) have shown a kaleidoscope of black businesses that sprang up during this era. In addition to banks, African Americans created their own dry goods and grocery stores, newspapers, shoe shops, pharmacies, hotels, cemeteries, cotton gins, and cotton mills. Moreover, there were black photographers, physicians, dentists, undertakers, tailors, lumber dealers, cotton brokers, architects, and builders. Out of necessity, those people and institutions were created to serve the needs of the black community and had the additional effect of creating a successful black business class and an emerging black middle class. These factors seriously impacted the social and cultural advancement of African Americans.

Another untapped scholarly area concerning the NNBL is the role that black women served in the organization. Along with this discussion one must consider the various businesses pursued by black women during the Jim Crow era. Walker (1998) has studied the history of African Americans in business. However, her comprehensive work focuses on a myriad of businesses owned by black men and women, including Madam C. J. Walker and Maggie Lena Walker. By contrast, Madam C. J. Walker has been the subject of two, more narrow studies. A'Lelia Bundles, Walker's great-great-granddaughter, wrote *On Her Own Ground: The Life and Times of Madam C. J. Walker* (2001) and Beverly Lowry wrote *Her Dream of Dreams: The Rise and Triumph of Madam C. J. Walker* (2003). Although these studies are useful, historians assessing black women's role in the NNBL will find many other black businesswomen who deserve consideration. African American women participated in the programs at the annual business league meetings, where they discussed entrepreneurial endeavors such as dressmaking, the hair care and beauty parlor business, catering, and even less traditional occupations for women like pharmacy and the ice-cream business.

Black women representatives took full advantage of the platform given them at League meetings to push for social and cultural development among other women. While they talked about relevant business issues, black women also discussed basic skills of womanhood like childcare, cooking, and cleaning. The women also addressed the importance of proper dress, proper hygiene, and physical appearance. Moreover, they tried to impress upon black domestics that there was dignity in all work and that they should revere honest labor.

Alberta Moore-Smith of Chicago organized businesswomen's leagues for the NNBL. In addition to encouraging women to become entrepreneurs, local businesswomen's leagues served as support groups that addressed the particular needs of their members. For instance, African American women were concerned with how the larger society perceived them. They recognized the need to work against baseless racial stereotypes that labeled them as lazy and as poor business risks. So women in the League encouraged training and education as the solution to the crisis. Black businesswomen acting in concert with black businessmen sent a strong message of their commitment to racial uplift.

Not only did the NNBL stimulate business in the African American Community, it also served as an incubator for other black organizations like the National Negro Press Association, the National Negro Funeral Directors' Association, the National Negro Bankers' Association, the National Association of Negro Insurance Men and the National Negro Bar Association. The NNBL offered black business owners an opportunity to network with black lawyers and enabled the latter to develop corporate law practices. Founded in Little Rock, Arkansas, in 1909 the National Negro Bar Association (NNBA), an auxiliary of Booker T. Washington's NNBL, was created in response to black lawyers' exclusion from white law associations like the American Bar Association (ABA) founded in 1868, the Federal Bar Association, and the National Association of Women Lawyers. In fact, black lawyers were barred from the ABA for 66 years; thus, from 1878 to 1944, they had no part in shaping ABA policies, although they were directly affected by them. Hence the NNBL effectively "set in motion the first black national bar movement in the world," J. Clay Smith concluded, and "this movement brought the black lawyer and the black businessman together and strengthened both" (Smith 1993: 555–6, 541–85).

Smith has very extensively chronicled the history of black lawyers during the Age of Jim Crow. At the 1914 annual meeting of the NNBL in Muskogee, Oklahoma, Perry W. Howard – a lawyer and Mississippi race man who made a name for himself in the Republican Party – articulated the importance of the NNBA. He asserted that, first, the group allowed individual black lawyers to meet and become educated on issues that would increase their economic well-being. And, second, they could come together to find ways to protect the race. When the meeting closed, Howard became president, a position he held for nine years (Smith 1993: 553–4).

As Smith contends, credit for forming the National Bar Association (NBA), an outgrowth of the NNBA, is given to George H. Woodson, head of the Iowa Negro Bar Association (INBA) and a graduate from Howard University's law school. At the February 1925 INBA national meeting, he led the movement to create the NBA. Six months later, black lawyers from as many as seven states convened in Des Moines, Iowa, formed the NBA and elected its first officers, with Woodson as president. The only woman in attendance at this first meeting was Gertrude Elzora Durden Rush, a former president of the INBA (Smith 1993: 555–6).

African American lawyers in the country, very small in number, faced a formidable task. According to a study that the NBA released in 1937, there were only about 1,250 black lawyers to service almost 12,000,000 African Americans. Even in Washington, DC, where the greatest concentration of black lawyers existed, there were only around 225. In New York City there were only 112 and shockingly, throughout the entire South, there were only about 200 African American lawyers. To make matters worse, because of Jim Crow and white supremacy, more than half of all black lawyers were "sundowners," meaning most of them had "day" jobs and worked as lawyers by night (Smith 1993: 565).

Over the years the NBA took up many issues, one being civil rights for blacks. At the 1938 meeting of the NBA, New York Judge James S. Watson asserted that while black lawyers had the same responsibilities as other lawyers, they still had to take up the mantle and help liberate African Americans from the oppressive system of Jim Crow. In many ways this was a social and cultural imperative. The NBA went on record in condemning numerous cases that involved police brutality and tried to bring pressure upon different American presidents to appoint African Americans to federal judgeships and even to the Supreme Court (Smith 1993: 566).

Significantly, because black lawyers had a parallel legal institution for themselves, they were not muzzled. They could take positions of leadership within their own organization and could have frank discourse without worrying about violating codes of racial etiquette. Moreover, at the local level, the NBA provided black lawyers with the support they needed when they were excluded by the white Bar. But most important, by forming a separate organization, African American lawyers were able to keep race and black liberation at the top of their agenda (Smith 1993: 572).

Similar difficulties existed for African Americans in the medical profession. This is a subject that has been overlooked by most scholars who have written on the history

of American medicine. Despite the efforts of Darlene Clark Hine (1989), Edward
H. Beardsley (1987), and David McBride (1989), more research is needed. By
1890, approximately 900 practicing black physicians in the United States had to
service a population of some 7.5 million African Americans. The overwhelming
majority of these African American doctors were trained at ten black medical schools,
including the Howard University School of Medicine, in Washington, DC; Meharry
Medical College in Nashville, Tennessee; and the Leonard Medical School at Shaw
University in Raleigh, North Carolina (Hine, Hine, and Harrold 2000: 352;
Gamble 1995: 207).

In the early 1900s, the Carnegie Foundation commissioned Abraham Flexner, an
influential figure in medical education and an official at the General Education
Board, to assess the status of medical education in the United States and make
recommendations on how it could be improved. He issued the so-called Flexner
Report on medical education in 1910 and called for improving medical education
through the closing of "weaker medical schools." For the stronger schools, he
recommended higher admission standards and expanded requirements for clinical
and laboratory training. After his suggestions were implemented, 60 of 155 white
medical schools closed and all the black medical schools closed except for two,
Howard and Meharry (Hine et al. 2000: 352; Gamble 1995: 36, 76).

Even earlier than African American lawyers, black medical doctors realized the
paramount need to have their own, parallel professional association. After a long
unsuccessful battle to integrate the American Medical Association (AMA), black
physicians founded the National Medical Association (NMA) in Atlanta in 1895.
The organization held its first meeting during the Atlanta Cotton States Exposition
a few weeks before Booker T. Washington gave his famous "Atlanta Compromise"
speech. The NMA's goals "gibed well" with those of the Tuskegee leader especially
as they related to self-help and racial solidarity. To better assist NMA members, the
organization held yearly conventions, at which clinical demonstrations and scholarly
research papers were presented, and members were updated on the most recent
developments in the medical field (Gamble 1995: 37).

In an effort to establish this parallel institution, NMA members created not only
a professional association, but also medical schools, professional medical journals,
and hospitals for African Americans. Dr. Miles V. Lynk, a graduate of Meharry
Medical College, created the nation's first black medical journal called *The Medical
and Surgical Observer* in 1892, three years before the founding of the NMA. Unfortunately, because of financial problems, the publication only lasted a year. Members
of the NMA never forgot the significance of their own scholarly journal, however,
and established the *Journal of the National Medical Association* in 1909. This effort
coincided with the NMA's charter, which called for its members to "subscribe to
medical publications, and to buy and study the latest works pertaining to their
professions" (Gamble 1995: 36–7).

The NMA's charter called for "a strong organization among Negro physicians,
dentists, and pharmacists . . . in order that they may have a voice in matters of public
health and medical legislation in general, and in as such matters may affect the
Negro race in particular; and to develop a profound race consciousness." Further, it
aimed to "stimulate professional development by contact, by reading, and discussion
of papers, by reports of cases and by demonstrations." African American physicians

were simultaneously charged with bettering the "health and living conditions of the Negro people by educating them in matters of public health and hygiene" (Gamble 1995: 37).

After all but two black medical schools closed, African American physicians wanted to ensure that black hospitals did not suffer a similar fate. "These doctors realized that their careers depended on access to hospitals, and feared that changes in medical care and hospital practice would lead to the elimination of black hospitals, and with it, the future of the black medical profession" (Gamble 1995: xiii). Vanessa Gamble has written extensively on this subject in her insightful study *Making A Place for Ourselves: The Black Hospital Movement* (1995). Other studies, such as Rosemary Stevens' *In Sickness and In Wealth* (1989), Charles Rosenberg's *The Care of Strangers* (1987), David Rosner's *A Once Charitable Enterprise: Hospitals and Health Care in Brooklyn and New York* (1982), echo the point that hospitals were not just medical institutions as earlier studies depicted, but were "social institutions that reflect and reinforce the beliefs and values of the wider society" (Gamble: xiv). This is a very important consideration when covering the black hospital movement during Jim Crow.

In August of 1923, members of the NMA created the National Hospital Association (NHA) in Saint Louis, Missouri, to ensure that black hospitals had proper educational standards and were efficient. But more important, they wanted to ensure their survival. African American doctors were very much cognizant of the adverse effects that the growing standardization and accreditation movement in medicine could have on them. The American College of Surgeons and the AMA spearheaded this effort. Doctors Henry M. Green, John A. Kenney, Midian O. Bousfield, and Peter M. Murray all played significant roles in the black hospital movement, with Green serving as the first president of the NHA. All of these men were visible and outspoken advocates of black hospital reform (Gamble 1995: 35, 36).

John Kenney, the resident physician at Tuskegee Institute under Booker T. Washington, endorsed Washington's self-help ideology and viewed the establishment of black hospitals as an example of African American self-help. There were many issues the NHA needed to tackle. For example, in 1923 there were around 202 black hospitals in the country; however, none of them had residency programs and only six had internship programs. By 1929 the number of black hospitals had fallen by 33 to 169. Of that number only two had been approved for residencies and 14 for internship training by the AMA. Altogether, 17 were given general accreditation by the American College of Surgeons. That only 70 internship slots were available to around 125 African American medical students compounded this situation. By way of contrast 4,814 white medical students had 6,044 internship opportunities available to them at 682 hospitals. Black NHA and NMA leaders worked to improve the quality of the internship programs at those few hospitals that already had them (Gamble 1995: 42, 43).

The health needs of African Americans also moved black physicians to action. One of the most pressing health problems facing blacks was the lack of an adequate number of hospital beds of acceptable quality. Black people knew too well the consequences of not having appropriate hospital facilities conveniently at their disposal. Any minor accident could become a death sentence in places where there were no black hospitals, nor even segregated black wards at white hospitals. According to

Gamble, "the color line in hospital care was so rigid that even medical emergencies did not bend it" (Gamble 1995: 45). The father of NAACP leader Walter White, for example, died shortly after being evicted from the white ward of an Atlanta hospital and then transferred to the Jim Crow ward, where he suffered in conditions of squalor (Janken 2003: 69).

Spencie Love (1996: 49) and Kenneth Janken (2003: 168) point to the example of Juliette Derricotte, Dean of Women at Fisk University, who in 1931 had an automobile accident in Dalton, Georgia. The segregated George W. Hamilton Hospital refused her care, so she received treatment at the office of a white physician. Shortly afterwards she was moved to the private residence of an African American woman who had no medical training; black patients in Dalton were routinely taken to this woman's home. After several hours, drivers took Derricotte to the black ward of a hospital in Chattanooga, Tennessee, fifty miles away, where she later died. This type of incident reminded the black middle class that race remained a major obstacle before them and reinforced the fact that African Americans had to unite and provide quality services for themselves (Gamble 1995: 46, 47).

Gamble (1995: 47, 48), McBride (1989), and Beardsley (1987) clearly show that health issues among African Americans were always more severe than among whites. In 1925, the death rate for whites was 52 percent lower than that for blacks, while infant mortality was 62 percent higher for blacks than for whites. One hospital bed existed for every 139 whites in America in 1928, in contrast to one for every 1,941 blacks. In Mississippi, a state with almost one million African Americans, that same year there were only four black hospitals with just 42 beds. African American medical leaders were inspired to fight against these conditions and struggle to improve the overall health and health-consciousness of the black race.

The NHA stopped functioning in the early 1940s and was replaced by the National Conference of Hospital Administrators, founded by professional hospital administrators who were not physicians. Although the overall contribution of the NHA was limited by the lack of full-time professional staff and sufficient funds, the NHA had provided black doctors with two major benefits. First, it worked with the NMA to articulate and publicize problems experienced by African American hospitals and their physicians. Second, the NHA provided African American doctors with a forum to examine and discover recent trends in hospital care, when they were excluded by white groups from any other access (Gamble 1995: 55).

Black nurses in the USA were also closely involved with the black medical movement. Like Vanessa Gamble's work on blacks in the hospital movement, Darlene Hine's *Black Women in White: Racial Conflict and Cooperation in the Nursing Profession* (1989: 90, 92) and Mary Carnegie's *The Path We Tread: Blacks in Nursing* (1986) are informative works on blacks in nursing, although Hine's study focuses specifically on the Jim Crow era. Their works significantly show how black female professionals responded to the impositions and restrictions of Jim Crow. They found themselves shut out of white nursing organizations and restricted professionally because of their race. In August 1908, scores of black nurses met and founded the National Association of Colored Graduate Nurses (NACGN). White nurses had set up their own institutions, such as the Society for Superintendents of Training Schools for Nurses in the United States and Canada founded in 1894, which they renamed the National League of Nursing Education in 1912. They created the Nurses' Associated Alumnae of the United States and Canada in 1896, renamed the American Nurses' Association in 1911. They also organized the National Organization for Public Health Nursing in 1912. White nurses used these organizations to promote their interests in the nursing profession. However, none of these groups admitted black nurses except for the National Organization for Public Health Nursing. That group even allowed people who were not nurses to join, in an effort to secure financial support for various endeavors. Lay persons could not vote, however, which effectively muted them in terms of influence within the organization.

There were two principal reasons why African American nurses created their own parallel nursing organization: first, to improve their status as professionals while simultaneously guiding their own personal and professional advancement; second, to improve their career mobility and to meet to discuss recent developments in the profession. While black nurses never openly declared that they had started the NACGN in response to rejection from white nursing groups, Hine asserts that they undoubtedly used these organizations controlled by African Americans to shield them from "the excessive racism, hostility, and denigration of their white colleagues, behind which they developed and honed leadership skills essential to attaining the ultimate objective of integration and acceptance into the mainstream of American nursing" (Hine 1989: 94–5).

Martha Minerva Franklin became the first president of the NACGN in 1908. She graduated from the Woman's Hospital Training School for Nurses in Philadelphia, Pennsylvania in 1897. Franklin put out the call for a national meeting by sending letters to over 1,500 black nursing graduates, superintendents of nursing schools, and the like, to ascertain if they were interested in starting such a group. Ultimately, 52 black nurses met in August 1908 and founded the NACGN at Saint Mark's Episcopal Church in New York City. By 1920 the organization had grown to 500 members. Carrie E. Bullock, a 1909 graduate of Provident Hospital, in 1928 founded and became editor of the official organ of the NACGN, the *National New Bulletin* (Hine 1989: 95, 97).

The NACGN worked on a number of objectives, including higher admission standards at nursing schools. They urged black nurses to qualify for positions in public-health nursing and wanted them to pursue advanced nursing training so they would be better poised to attack job and wage discrimination along with the racial exclusion practiced by white nursing organizations. Unfortunately, white nurses were determined to view black nurses as inferiors. Darlene Clark Hine asserted that "black nurses found it impossible to change white nurses' negative opinions of their professional competence." Moreover, "the fact that blacks as a group occupied a subordinate position in American society influenced the negative assessments of their overall leadership and intellectual abilities." White nurses also resented black nurses because they were a source of competition for jobs, especially private duty nurses. Ultimately, people tended to view black nurses as little more than trained domestics (Hine 1989: 95, 98; Hine et al. 2000: 352, 353).

There were a number of other issues covered by the NACGN. For instance, they addressed the great disparity in the number of nurse training schools for blacks and whites. Whites had 2,150 nursing schools by 1920, while blacks had only 36. Also, these African American nurses-in-training had to contend with exploitation by black doctors who ran nursing schools. Some of these physicians hired out their students for private work duty as part of their school requirement, but made the students give their money back to the schools. Among other things, the NACGN led a tremendous fight to reverse these practices (Hine et al. 2000: 352–3). While African American doctors, nurses, and hospital administrators condemned segregation, they realized that racial discrimination in the medical field left them with no immediate alternative but to establish their own parallel medical and nursing schools, hospitals, and private practices if they were to address the health needs of the race (Gamble 1995: 55).

The fact that African Americans were shut out of white institutions made life difficult, to say the least. However, in developing parallel institutions among their group, black people were able to nurture and develop leaders. Moreover, while segregation was injurious to African Americans, it had unintended benefits in fostering businesses and a professional and middle class among them. Through these businesses the black middle class created institutions to secure their future and provide for their needs, which trickled down to the masses of African Americans. If black people did not have their own institutions, they would not have had the opportunity to develop leaders or exercise organizational control to the extent they did at that juncture in history. They also would have missed the opportunity for networking and social interaction.

Even if whites allowed them to become members of organizations, as the YMCAs and YWCAs did, those groups still discriminated against and marginalized them, limiting black members' growth and development, as convincingly shown by Mjagkij and Spratt (1997) and Weisenfeld (1997). For example, black female college students showed tremendous interest in the YWCA, but "the association's National Board remained ambivalent about and at times insensitive to the concerns of black women." Further, "its local and national structures essentially protected prevailing segregationist practices. Separate branches served black women, and the National Board had no black representation" (Mjagkij and Spratt 1997: 160–1). Although African Americans created parallel YMCAs and YWCAs, they were still ultimately controlled and restricted by the national organization (ibid; Weisenfeld 1997).

Segregation constantly reminded African Americans that they had to do for themselves and not wait for others. While they looked at segregation with contempt, they still had to live with it. As Gordon Blaine Hancock, a prominent black leader of the Jim Crow era in Richmond, Virginia, put it: "racially speaking . . . we oppose segregation, but economically speaking it forms the basis of our professional and business life" (Gavins 1977: 69); and Hine concluded: "parallel institutions offered black Americans not only private space to buttress battered dignity, nurture positive images, sharpen skills, and demonstrate expertise. These safe havens sustained relationships and wove networks across communities served" (Hine 2003: 1280).

While scholars, particularly in the last twenty years, have studied and assessed many of black America's leading social and cultural institutions – focusing increasingly on their significance for self-help, agency, and parallelism – much remains to be done. For example, more work is needed on African American professional organizations and the professionals who created them and much more research is needed on women and their roles in developing black business associations and organizations in the health professions.

BIBLIOGRAPHY

Works Cited

Beardsley, Edward (1987) *A History of Neglect: Health Care for Blacks and Mill Workers in the Twentieth-Century South*. Knoxville: University of Tennessee Press.

Brundage, W. Fitzhugh (1993) *Lynching in the New South: Georgia and Virginia, 1880–1930*. Urbana: University of Illinois Press.

Bundles, A'Lelia (2001) *On Her Own Ground: The Life and Times of Madam C. J. Walker*. New York: Scribner.

Burrows, John H. (1977) "The necessity of myth: a history of the National Negro Business League, 1900–1945," PhD dissertation, Auburn University.

Carnegie, Mary E. (1986) *The Path We Tread: Blacks in Nursing, 1854–1984*. Philadelphia: J. B. Lippincott.

Dray, Philip (2002) *At the Hands of Persons Unknown: The Lynching of Black America*. New York: Random House.

Feldman, Lynne B. (1999) *A Sense of Place: Birmingham's Black Middle-Class Community, 1890–1930*. Tuscaloosa: University of Alabama Press.

Gamble, Vanessa N. (1995) *Making a Place for Ourselves: The Black Hospital Movement, 1920–1945*. New York: Oxford University Press.

Gavins, Raymond (1977) *The Perils and Prospects of Southern Black Leadership: Gordon Blaine Hancock, 1884–1970*. Durham, NC: Duke University Press.

Giddings, Paula (1985) *When and Where I Enter: The Impact of Black Women on Race and Sex in America*. New York: Bantam Books.

Hamilton, Kenneth (1995) *Guide Introduction: Records of the National Negro Business League*. Bethesda, MD: University Publications of America.

Harlan, Louis R. (1988) "Booker T. Washington and the National Negro Business League" in Raymond W. Smock (ed.), *Booker T. Washington in Perspective: Essays of Louis Harlan*. Jackson: University Press of Mississippi.

Height, Dorothy (2003) *Open Wide the Freedom Gates: A Memoir*. New York: Public Affairs.

Hine, Darlene C. (1989) *Black Women in White: Racial Conflict and Cooperation in the Nursing Profession, 1890–1950*. Bloomington: Indiana University Press.

—— (2003) "Black professionals and race consciousness: origins of the civil rights movement, 1890–1950," *Journal of American History* 89: 1279–94.

Hine, Darlene C., Hine, William C., and Harrold, Stanley (2000) *The African-American Odyssey*. Upper Saddle River, NJ: Prentice-Hall.

Jackson, David H., Jr (2002) *A Chief Lieutenant of the Tuskegee Machine: Charles Banks of Mississippi*, 23–4. Gainesville: University Press of Florida.

Janken, Kenneth R. (2003) *White: The Biography of Walter White, Mr. NAACP*. New York: New Press.

Jones, Beverly W. (1982) "Mary Church Terrell and the National Association of Colored Women, 1896 to 1901," *Journal of Negro History* 67: 20–33.

Kellogg, Charles F. (1967) *NAACP: A History of the National Association for the Advancement of Colored People*. Baltimore: Johns Hopkins University Press.

Lerner, Gerda (1974) "Early community work of black club women," *Journal of Negro History* 59: 158–67.

Lewis, David L. (1993) *W. E. B. Du Bois: Biography of a Race, 1868–1919*. New York: Henry Holt.

Love, Spencie (1996) *One Blood: The Death and Resurrection of Charles R. Drew*. Chapel Hill: University of North Carolina Press.

Lowry, Beverly (2003) *Her Dream of Dreams: The Rise and Triumph of Madam C. J. Walker*. New York: Alfred A. Knopf.

McBride, David (1989) *Integrating the City of Medicine: Blacks in Philadelphia Health Care, 1910–1965.* Philadelphia: Temple University Press.

Marable, Manning (1986) *W. E. B. Du Bois, Black Radical Democrat.* Boston: Twayne.

Mjagkij, Nina and Spratt, Margaret (eds.) (1997) *Men and Women Adrift: The YMCA and the YWCA in the City.* New York: New York University Press.

Neverdon-Morton, Cynthia (1989) *Afro-American Women of the South and the Advancement of the Race.* Knoxville: University of Tennessee Press.

Rosenberg, Charles E. (1987) *The Care of Strangers.* New York: Basic Books.

Rosner, David (1982) *A Once Charitable Enterprise: Hospitals and Health Care in Brooklyn and New York, 1885–1915.* Cambridge: Cambridge University Press.

Rouse, Jacqueline A. (1989) *Lugenia Burns Hope: Black Southern Reformer.* Athens: University of Georgia Press.

Shaw, Stephanie J. (1996) *What a Woman Ought to Be and to Do: Black Professional Women Workers during the Jim Crow Era.* Chicago: University of Chicago Press.

Smith, J. Clay, Jr (1993) *Emancipation: The Making of the Black Lawyer, 1844–1944.* Philadelphia: University of Pennsylvania Press.

Stevens, Rosemary (1989) *In Sickness and in Wealth.* New York: Basic Books.

Tolnay, Stewart and Beck, E. M. (1995) *A Festival of Violence: An Analysis of Southern Lynchings, 1882–1930.* Urbana: University of Illinois Press.

Walker, Juliet E. K. (1998) *The History of Black Business in America: Capitalism, Race, Entrepreneurship.* New York: Twayne.

Weisenfeld, Judith (1997) *African American Women and Christian Activism: New York's Black YWCA, 1905–1945.* Cambridge, MA: Harvard University Press.

Wesley, Charles H. (1984) *The History of the National Association of Colored Women's Clubs, Inc. A Legacy of Service.* Washington, DC: National Association of Colored Women's Clubs.

Suggestions for Further Reading

Franklin, John H. and Moss, Alfred A. (1994) *From Slavery to Freedom: A History of African Americans.* New York: McGraw-Hill.

Frazier, E. Franklin (1957) *Black Bourgeoisie: The Rise of a New Middle Class.* New York: Free Press.

Gaines, Kevin K. (1996) *Uplifting the Race: Black Leadership, Politics, and Culture in the Twentieth Century.* Chapel Hill: University of North Carolina Press.

Gatewood, Willard B. (1990) *Aristocrats of Color: The Black Elite, 1880–1920.* Bloomington: Indiana University Press.

Ingham, John N. and Feldman, Lynne B. (1994) *African-American Business Leaders: A Biographical Dictionary.* Westport, CT: Greenwood Press.

Litwack, Leon F. (1999) *Trouble in Mind: Black Southerners in the Age of Jim Crow.* New York: Vintage Books.

Salem, Dorothy (1994) "National Association of Colored Women" in Darlene Clark Hine, Elsa B. Brown, and Rosalyn Terborg-Penn (eds.), *Black Women in America: An Historical Encyclopedia,* vol. 2. Bloomington: Indiana University Press.

Savitt, Todd L. and Rogers, William W. (eds.) (1988) *Disease and Distinctiveness in the American South.* Knoxville: University of Tennessee Press.

Summerville, James (1987) *Educating Black Doctors: A History of Meharry Medical College.* Tuscaloosa: University of Alabama Press.

Terborg-Penn, Rosalyn (1997) "Discriminating against Afro-America women in the woman's movement, 1830–1920" in Sharon Harley and Rosalyn Terborg-Penn (eds.), *The Afro-American Woman: Struggles & Images.* Baltimore: Black Classic Press.

CHAPTER NINETEEN

African American Entrepreneurship in Slavery and Freedom

ANNE R. HORNSBY

African American participation in American business and commerce began in the colonial period with a few free black-owned enterprises in major cities of the North and black artisans and craftsmen in the South. Paul Cuffe in Massachusetts was a shipbuilder and trader; James Forten of Pennsylvania became a wealthy shipbuilder in Philadelphia; and Frank McWorter ("Free Frank") manufactured saltpeter on the Kentucky frontier and operated several enterprises in Chicago. Despite the fact that black businesses – such as barber shops, and other service institutions like banks and insurance companies – expanded in the post-emancipation era, the number and type of African-American-owned businesses remained small until recent times. Furthermore, individual proprietorships, the type of business in which blacks were principally engaged, had a short life-span (Hine, Hine, and Harrold 2000; Higgs 1976; Hornsby 1980; Walker 1983).

Most of the early scholarly studies of black entrepreneurship deplored the paucity of such enterprises and sought to understand the factors behind this. W. E. B. Du Bois published one of the first, major scholarly studies in 1899. In *The Negro in Business*, he made distinctions among black businesses along caste and class lines. He claimed that black bondspersons who had been house servants, field hands, or semi-skilled workers, became barbers, gardeners, and builders, respectively, in the post-emancipation era. Bankers, manufacturers, and merchants, he contended, generally came from those blacks who had been free before the Civil War. As to the small number of black-owned firms, Du Bois concluded that blacks themselves were largely to blame. They were too prone to act out of "spontaneity" than from "concerted guided action" (Du Bois 1899; Green and Pryde 1990).

Eight years after Du Bois wrote, Booker T. Washington also published a work entitled *The Negro in Business*. His, however, was a promotional and inspirational work rather than a scholarly analysis. In their classic study of American race relations, *An American Dilemma*, Gunnar Myrdal and his associates largely ignored black businesses (devoting less than ten pages to the subject). They did conclude, however, that the reason black firms remained so few was because blacks were unable to compete with white concerns on account of size, higher prices, and poor choices of location (Myrdal 1944).

Another respected black scholar treated the subject in 1949. E. Franklin Frazier, operating from an integrationist perspective, downplayed racism as a factor in the poor state of black business. Instead, he emphasized the unwise practice of "buying and selling within the context of everyday life in the black community." Some, however, have postulated that a segregated society could serve as a buttress to black businesses and make for large profits because of the absence of external competition. Becker, for example, in his *The Economics of Discrimination* (1957) suggested that segregation would result in higher returns to the black capitalist because of the relative scarcity of capital in the productive process within the segregated black community. This was, perhaps, best exemplified in the insurance industry, although similar examples could be seen in barbering, catering, and transportation – in the case of hackmen (Frazier 1949; Green and Pryde 1990; Henderson 1990).

Attitudes toward black entrepreneurship, like many other things, were significantly affected by the "Civil Rights Revolution" of the 1960s and 1970s. Black activists and scholars, although often from very different backgrounds, began to extol the virtues of "Black Capitalism." The principal aim of the movement was to secure black control over the economic activities of black communities. Activists and scholars were divided, however, over strategies for business development. Under the concept of "Black Power" and black separatism, many advocated exclusively black involvement in the process. Others felt that outsiders, particularly the federal government, should aid in the new thrust. In 1974, Cross argued that black entrepreneurs should come from – and into – the insular black communities. The building of wealth in black communities, he contended, should be led by business and not by government. However, he was willing to have the federal, state, and local governments aid the process through tax incentives.

The idea of building black wealth within black communities, however, ran into one of the major contradictions of the Civil Rights Movement. Desegregation led to an end to black domination or monopolies in such businesses as banking, catering, and transportation. They had previously lost the monopoly in barbering. In addition, changing technology and business organization (the development and expansion of large-scale business operations such as chain and department stores) in the late nineteenth and early twentieth centuries impacted adversely on the black proprietor (Du Bois 1899; Meier and Lewis 1959; Pierce 1947; Meier 1968; Higgs 1976; Hornsby 1980: 19).

Also, during this period more optimistic assessments of the state and future of black entrepreneurship appeared. Bates and Fusfeld argued in 1984 that racism had played the principal role in the failure of significant black business development. Yet, they argued that the "historical limitations" were being overcome. They found, in the 1960s and 1970s, greater diversity among black enterprises, greater profits and more integration into the larger marketplace (Bates and Fusfeld 1984; Green and Pryde 1990). Swinton and Handy also saw prospects for growing entrepreneurship in black communities. With adequate capital, labor, and markets, black businesses could prosper, they believed, even in a segregated environment (Swinton and Handy 1983; Green and Pryde 1990).

Although Brimmer, pointing to black banks specifically, had earlier predicted that black banks, mainly because of their small size, could never have a significant impact in America, Bates, also representing the Optimistic School, countered that, since

1945, several black banks had prospered because of government-guaranteed loan protection and other stimuli (Brimmer 1985; Bates 1978; Green and Pryde 1990). Rounding out these assessments, Green and Pryde felt that a major impediment to black entrepreneurship was the fear among blacks of risk-taking. Yet, they insisted that black America had enough capital to take financial risks and that it could develop measures that would be attractive to white investors. The impediments to development, then, were largely rooted in black cultural attitudes toward entrepreneurship (Green and Pryde 1990).

Among more recent works, most argue for the growing possibilities for success as well as actual cases of success of black business. Among these are: Hunt and Hunt, *The History of Black Business: The Coming of America's Largest African-American Owned Businesses* (1999); Todd, *Innovation and Growth in an African American Owned Business* (1996); Boston, *Affirmative Action and Black Entrepreneurship* (1999); and Jalloh and Falola, *Black Business and Economic Power* (2002). The Hunts are successful businesspersons who write in the inspirational and promotional mode of Booker T. Washington. Boston makes an impressive case for the potential for black entrepreneurial success. Focusing on Atlanta, he claims that black businesses are growing at a very significant pace. He largely attributes this phenomenon to affirmative action programs at federal, state, and local levels. Jalloh and Falola, and their contributors, write about current developments in African American agency as well as the role of globalization in current discourses. They identify significant pre-colonial black-managed enterprises in Africa – some controlled by women – as well as in colonial and antebellum America. They conclude that it was the slave trade, colonialism, slavery, and segregation – not black cultural failures – that stifled early black entrepreneurship in Africa and among African Americans. Although they decry the fact that political office is too often the road to wealth in Africa, they note promising signs of revival since the 1960s there and in the United States (Hunt and Hunt 1999; Boston 1999; Jalloh and Falola 2002).

Perhaps, the best and most comprehensive of recent works is Juliet Walker's *The History of Black Business in America: Capitalism, Race, Entrepreneurship* (1998). Walker too traces successful managers and managerial skills brought from Africa, which continued to be apparent during the period of African American bondage and into present times. She, too, debunks the notion that African and African American cultural factors led to business failures on the African continent and in America. It was American racism, which denied opportunities and resources, that was the culprit in the slow growth, small number and poor quality of black businesses. Yet she cites a number of individual success stories, ranging from Anthony Johnson, in colonial times, to Amos Fortune, Eleanor Woldridge, and Lucy McWorter in the nineteenth century, and Robert Church, Heman Perry, Harry H. Pace and Madam C. J. Walker in the early twentieth century. Interestingly and significantly, she challenges the classic view of Rayford Logan and others that the post-reconstruction period witnessed a "nadir" in black life and history. Instead, at least when it comes to business, it was rather a "golden age" that lasted until the Great Depression.

Since the publication of her *Free Frank*, an examination of a pioneering African American businessman, Walker has, perhaps, become the leading authority on African American entrepreneurship. In recent years, in addition to her highly acclaimed

1998 history, she has edited a directory of black businesses and established a center for the study of black business at The University of Texas at Austin.

In her black business directory, Walker and her contributors have provided dozens of sketches of individual black businesses, as well as biographical sketches of leaders in black business and commerce. Several useful case-studies of black business firms and individuals, however, predated Walker's work. The more useful, and scholarly, of them include Walter Weare on North Carolina Mutual Insurance Company and its founders and Alexa B. Henderson on the Atlanta Life Insurance Company and its founder, Alonzo Herndon. Both books demonstrate how the principal founders of these firms emerged from slavery and endured Jim Crow to establish multi-million dollar enterprises.

They also reinforce the importance of black churches, black fraternal orders, and other self-help groups in the founding and sustenance of these enterprises. Furthermore, they point to a social and cultural role for the institutions in African American community development. Another scholarly work, Robert E. Weems' *Black Business in the Black Metropolis: The Chicago Metropolitan Assurance Company, 1925–1985* (1996) is one of the few works to detail and assess the role of a major black business enterprise in a northern city. Lerone Bennett, the journalist and historian, has also given us a glimpse of a major northern-based African American firm and its leader in *John H. Johnson: Succeeding against the Odds* (1989). Although quite laudatory of his boss, Bennett shows how racism prevented Johnson and his company from becoming even more successful.

All of the stories of black businesspersons have a Horatio Alger aspect to them, but, perhaps none is as passionately related as that of the Birmingham millionaire A. G. Gaston. Gaston himself details his rise to economic success in *Green Power: The Successful Way of A. G. Gaston* (1968); and two of his relatives, Elizabeth Gardner Hines and Carol Jenkins, offer a useful, well-researched account in *Black Titan: A. G. Gaston and the Making of a Black American Millionaire* (2003).

Spurred, no doubt by the feminist and womanist movements in the Civil Rights and post-Civil Rights era, there has been a growing focus on the cultural and economic role of women in the origins, development, and growth of African American entrepreneurship. Two women, Madam C. J. Walker and Maggie Lena Walker, have received the bulk of attention from scholars. Walker's great-great-granddaughter A'Lelia Bundles wrote the first book-length treatment of the first African American multi-millionaire, *Madam C. J. Walker – Entrepreneur* (1991), a narrative meant primarily for young people, and later wrote *On Her Own Ground: The Life and Times of Madam C. J. Walker* (2001). This latter work has become the definitive scholarly study of Madam Walker, and is largely free of the platitudes of earlier works.

Two works by Gertrude Woodruff Marlowe provide the best studies on Maggie Lena Walker, the first African American woman to head a bank – *Ransom for Many: A Life of Maggie Lena Walker* (1997) and *Right Worthy Grand Mission: Maggie Lena Walker and the Quest for Black Economic Empowerment* (2003). In the latter work, Walker is portrayed as an ideal representative of the "race woman" – dedicated to activism, hard work, and charitable endeavors. As Nannie Helen Burroughs, a contemporary in the black clubwomen's movement, put it, she "gave her life as a ransom for many." Nevertheless, Marlowe finds that conventional terms like "charismatic leader" or "cultural heroine" are inadequate to define Walker. She was, in a larger sense, a pioneer in African American womanist agency and transcended race in some respects, winning respect and praise from powerful white interests in Richmond, Virginia. Another significant work on Walker, although not book-length, is Elsa Barkeley Brown's study of Walker's role in the Grand United Order of St. Luke. This fraternal, cooperative insurance society was plagued with financial woes – largely the result of mismanagement – when Walker came to the rescue. Starting in 1890, using her considerable oratorical skills and other aspects of her charisma as well as her considerable financial acumen, by 1924 Walker had increased membership in the order to more than 70,000, with assets of nearly a half million dollars. This feat, according to Barkeley Brown, represented a perfect example of African American womanist agency in the post-emancipation South (Brown 1989).

Prior to the 1960s, scholars tended to posit that, since black business enterprises were marginalized in the American economy, they were not a major area of inquiry in African American historiography. However, beginning in the Civil Rights era and on into the post-Civil Rights era, several major studies have appeared, reflecting new interests in race, class, gender, and globalization. Yet, there remains much to be done to explore and explain this important aspect of African American – as well as American – history. Many more historical black firms and their leaders, North as well as South, deserve study. Particularly pressing is the need for further examinations of the leadership of African American women in the funeral industry; the social and cultural roles of black businesses in the post-Jim Crow era; and African based businesses, particularly in East Africa, and their relationships to African American businesses.

BIBLIOGRAPHY

Works Cited

Bates, Timothy (1978) *An Analysis of the Portfolio Behavior of Black-owned Commercial Banks*, Minority Economic Development Series. Berkeley, CA: UCLA Center for Afro-American Studies.
—— (1985) "An analysis of minority entrepreneurship: utilizing the consensus of public use samples," *Fourth Progress Report on MBDA Contract*. Burlington, VT: MBDA.
Bates, Timothy and Fusfeld, Daniel R. (1984) *The Political Economy of the Urban Ghetto*. Carbondale, IL: Southern Illinois University Press.
Becker, Gary (1957) *The Economics of Discrimination*. Chicago: University of Chicago Press.
Bennett, Lerone (1989) *John H. Johnson: Succeeding against the Odds*. New York: Warner Books.
Boorman, John (1979) "New minority-owned commercial banks" in Timothy Bates and William Bradford (eds.), *Financing Black Economic Development*. New York: Academic Press.
Boston, Thomas D. (1999) *Affirmative Action and Black Entrepreneurship*. New York: Routledge.
Brimmer, Andrew (1985) "The future of blacks in the public sector," *Black Enterprise* (November).
Brown, Elsa Barkeley (1989) "Womanist consciousness: Maggie Lena Walker and the Independent Order of Saint Luke," *Signs* 14.
Bundles, A'Lelia (1991) *Madam C. J. Walker – Entrepreneur*. New York: Chelsea House.

—— (2001) *On Her Own Ground: The Life and Times of Madam C. J. Walker*. New York: Scribner.

Cole, John A., Edwards, Alfred L., Hamilton, Earl G. and Reuben, Lucy J. (1985) "Black banks: a survey and analysis of the literature," *Review of Black Political Economy* 14 (1).

Cross, Theodore (1969) *Black Capitalism*. New York: Atheneum.

Du Bois, W. E. B. ([1899] 1971) *The Negro in Business*, reprint. New York: SMS Press.

Foley, Eugene (1968) *The Achieving Ghetto*. Washington, DC: National Press.

Fratoe, Frank (1986) "A sociological analysis of minority business," *Review of Black Political Economy* 15 (2).

Frazier, E. Franklin (1949) *The Negro in the United States*. New York: Macmillan.

Gaston, A. G. (1968) *Green Power: The Successful Way of A. G. Gaston*. Birmingham, AL: Southern University Press.

Green, Shelley and Pryde, Paul (1990) *Black Entrepreneurship in America*. New Brunswick, NJ: Transaction.

Handy, John W. (1990) *An Analysis of Black Business Enterprises*. New York: Garland.

Henderson, Alexa B. (1990) *Atlanta Life Insurance Company: Guardian of Black Economic Dignity*. Tuscaloosa: University of Alabama Press.

Higgs, Robert (1976) "Participation of blacks and immigrants in the American merchant class, 1890–1910: some demographic relations," *Explorations in Economic History* 13.

Hine, Darlene C., Hine, William C., and Harrold, Stanley (2000) *The African American Odyssey*, vol. 1. Upper Saddle River, NJ: Prentice-Hall.

Hines, Elizabeth Gardner and Jenkins, Carol (2003) *Black Titan: A. G. Gaston and the Making of a Black American Millionaire*. New York: Macmillan.

Hornsby, Anne R. Lockhart (1980) "Shifts in the distribution of wealth among blacks in Georgia, 1890–1915," PhD dissertation, Georgia State University.

Hornsby, Anne R. (1989) "The accumulation of wealth by black Georgians," *Journal of Negro History* 79 (4, Fall): 13–20.

Hunt, Martin K. and Hunt, Jacqueline E. (1996) *Black Business*. New York: Knowledge Express.

—— (1999) *The History of Black Business: The Coming of America's Largest African-American Owned Businesses*. New York: Knowledge Express.

Jalloh, Alusine and Falola, Toylin (eds.) (2002) *Black Business and Economic Power*. Rochester, NY: University of Rochester Press.

Kijakazi, Kilio and Bruchey, Stuart (1997) *African American Economic Development and Small Business Ownership*. New York: Garland.

Marlowe, Gertrude Woodruff (1997) *Ransom for Many: A Life of Maggie Lena Walker*. New York: Carlson.

—— (2003) *Right Worthy Grand Mission: Maggie Lena Walker and the Quest for Black Economic Empowerment*. Washington, DC: Howard University Press.

Meier, August (1968) *Negro Thought in America, 1880–1915*. Ann Arbor: University of Michigan Press.

Meier, August and Lewis, David (1959) "History of the Negro upper class in Atlanta, 1890–1958," *Journal of Negro Education* 28 (Spring): 128–39.

Myrdal, Gunnar (1944) *An American Dilemma*. New York: Harper & Brothers.

O'Hare, William (1986) "Wealth and economic status: a perspective on racial inequality," monograph. Washington, DC: Joint Center for Political Studies.

Pierce, Joseph A. (1947) *Negro Business and Business Education*. New York: Harper & Brothers.

Swinton, David and Handy, John (1983) *The Determinants of Growth and Black Owned Businesses: A Preliminary Analysis*. Washington, DC: US Department of Commerce (September).

Todd, Gwendolyn Powell (1996) *Innovation and Growth in an African American Owned Business*. New York: Taylor & Francis.

Walker, Juliet E. K. (1983) *Free Frank: A Black Pioneer on the Antebellum Frontier*. Lexington: University Press of Kentucky.

—— (1998) *The History of Black Business in America: Capitalism, Race, Entrepreneurship*. New York: Twayne.

Washington, Booker T. ([1907] 1968) *The Negro in Business*, reprint. Chicago: Afro-American Press.

Weare, Walter B. ([1973] 1994) *Black Business in the New South: A Social History of the North Carolina Mutual Life Insurance Company*, reprint. Urbana: University of Illinois Press.

Weems, Robert E. (1996) *Black Business in the Black Metropolis: The Chicago Metropolitan Assurance Company, 1925–1985*. Bloomington: Indiana University Press.

CHAPTER TWENTY

The Black Press

SHIRLEY E. THOMPSON

In 1944, the "Dean of the Negro Press" P. Bernard Young wrote a set of guidelines for the National Newspaper Publishers Association (NNPA). In this "credo for the Negro Press," Young, editor of the *Journal and Guide* of Norfolk, Virginia, wrote in the voice of the committed black journalist: "I Shall be a crusader and an advocate, a mirror and a record, a herald and a spotlight, and I Shall not falter. So help me God." The black press was to be an agent of protest, pushing America to realize its highest moral principles. It was to be double-voiced, speaking to and for America's black population. Written amidst a delicate but strident wartime campaign of black journalists for racial justice in America, Young's statement reaffirmed the range of functions claimed by African American print journalism since its inception over a hundred years earlier. Furthermore, it described the terms upon which historians would continue to consider the black press. For historians, the press has provided evidence of black protest, a glimpse into black life, and a record of the African American quest for freedom and success. After briefly tracing the contours of the history of the African American press, this article will discuss the evolution of black press scholarship, detailing the impact of other disciplines on black press historiography and the connections between academic inquiry and its political and social contexts.

Typically, the history of the black press in America begins with the founding in 1827 of *Freedom's Journal* by John Brown Russwurm and Samuel Eli Cornish, two of New York's prominent free blacks. As crusader and advocate, mirror and record, *Freedom's Journal* protested against the efforts of the American Colonization Society, founded a decade earlier by some of America's leading white citizens, to force free blacks to leave American shores and emigrate to Liberia. "We wish to plead our own cause," the editors announced in the first issue, directing their message outward to their oppressors. However, the journal also sought to identify a "common cause" for black Americans and perform various educational and self-help functions, claiming as well a goal internal to the free black community. *Freedom's Journal* lasted only until 1829, but it inaugurated a flurry of antebellum black newspapers and periodicals. By the eve of the Civil War, black Americans had edited at least forty newspapers and periodicals, including the *Colored American* (1837–42), Frederick Douglass' *North Star* (1847–50), and *Frederick Douglass'*

Paper (1851–60). Most of these publications had been at the forefront of abolition-ist and anti-emigrationist agitation.

After emancipation, a southern black press emerged, detailing the complex rela-tionship of freedmen and women to the Republican Party and charting the efforts of newly freed blacks to establish their communities and to acquire literacy. By the end of the nineteenth century, there were hundreds of black newspapers and periodicals of all stripes for each region of the country. Many of these newspapers, such as Louis Martinet's *Crusader*, the New Orleans' newspaper that spearheaded Homer Plessy's 1892–6 challenge to segregation, and Ida B. Wells Barnett's *Memphis Free Speech*, which led the anti-lynching campaign in the early 1890s, were primarily organs of protest. Other newspapers and periodicals – such as the *Christian Recorder* (1841–present), the publication of the African Methodist Episcopal Church, and T. Thomas Fortune's *New York Age* (1885), eventually owned by Booker T. Washington – detailed the concerns of black institutions and chronicled black economic and social achievement.

Beginning in the 1910s, the black press spawned and chronicled the massive migration of black Americans from the South to northern urban industrial areas. Newspapers such as the *Chicago Defender* (1905–present) and the *New York Amsterdam News* served the growing needs of a segregated, constantly mobile black population. However, they also facilitated the urbanization of African Americans and the social changes accompanying this process, by communicating opportunities to southern blacks and providing them with the impetus and the means to relocate. As the Great Migration ensued, several of these urban newspapers such as the *Defender*, the *Pittsburgh Courier* (1910–present), and the *Baltimore Afro-American* (1892–present) gained prominence beyond their immediate locales, creating in effect a national black press. Claude Barnett's Associated Negro Press, which pro-vided access to national and international news, and improved distribution and production strategies, aided this process.

Thus, when African American soldiers began to experience discrimination and other forms of mistreatment, the press was uniquely poised to launch a vocal cam-paign for desegregation and equal political and social rights. This mobilization began in the First World War with Asa Philip Randolph's *Messenger* (1917–28) and blossomed in the Second World War when the *Courier* articulated a "double-V" campaign, urging victory against the Axis abroad and against American oppression against blacks at home. These wartime protests have prompted many historians to label the Second World War era as the "golden age" of the black press.

Although the black press played a significant role in the Civil Rights Movement, many historians mark this period as ushering in the press's gradual demise. Indeed, one of the questions posed by black press scholarship of the early 1970s was "Will/should the black press survive?" (Wolseley 1971). The black press previously existed to cover issues that the mainstream press had not thought important. Suddenly black news was national news. In order to provide adequate coverage of the Civil Rights Movement, mainstream press organizations began to hire black journalists, taking them away from the black press. Furthermore, civil rights legislation brought down barriers to integration, facilitating the integration of the national news media in the 1970s and beyond. While many of the traditional black newspapers fell on hard financial times and struggled to maintain their readership, some black publications, primarily those chronicling entertainment and "lifestyle" issues have thrived in a post-integrationist setting.

John H. Johnson's Johnson Publishing, the most successful black publishing company in the world, represents the towering example of this kind of black press venture. Johnson created *Ebony* magazine in 1945 and has offered a range of other publications from *Jet*, a pocket-sized weekly, to *Negro Digest*, a more literary venture. Other niche publications include *Black Enterprise*, chronicling blacks in corporate America, and *Essence*, a monthly magazine geared towards black women. *O!* magazine, launched by Oprah Winfrey, is black-owned, but appeals to Americans across racial and ethnic lines. Alongside these corporate ventures, the closing decade of the twentieth century has perhaps witnessed a resurgence of a more popular and "populist" black press. Just as new technologies facilitated an explosion of black publishing in the early twentieth century, the digital age of the late twentieth and early twenty-first century has suggested opportunities for new forums of black expression. Web publications such as *Black Commentator, AfroAmeric@*, and BlackPressUSA.com, the official website of the NNPA, continue to shape black identity and to offer forms of political critique and cultural expression for a new generation.

Sociology and Early Black Press Historiography

Much of the historiography of the black press has been guided by the goals set forth by the press's spokespeople. How well, decades of historians have asked, has the black press lived up to its role as both an agent of protest and a forum for black expression? What has been the quality of its protest? And what can the black press tell us about the cultural practices of black Americans across various historical periods? In the late nineteenth century and the early twentieth, the black press entered scholarly discussion as a subject of inquiry for both historians and other social scientists engaged in the vibrant debate over the "Negro Problem" reverberating not only through academia but also through American society as a whole. After emancipation, American writers and thinkers had to address the issue that they had anticipated for decades. How could the nation possibly incorporate black Americans into its body politic, and how would race relations proceed now that African Americans were nominally free?

American social critics turned their anxious attention to the black population, with certain questions in mind. How would blacks fare in America without the "protective" institution of slavery? Would the race become extinct? If not, what methods of social control must be employed in order to mediate racial difference and govern social relations? Armed with Social Darwinist theories, cultural critics predicted the disintegration of black America and pathologized black culture, juxtaposing it with a "civilized" White America. Black scholars and leaders, ranging from Booker T. Washington to W. E. B. Du Bois, sought in their various and often conflicting ways to defend the black community and to suggest strategies of racial "uplift," promoting the improvement and advancement of black Americans.

These concerns form the immediate context for the first history of the black press, I. Garland Penn's *The Afro-American Press and Its Editors*. For Penn, writing in 1891, the black press was indispensable to the case of black fitness for American citizenship. Not only had the black press recorded black achievements and provided a forum for the political development and social and moral instruction of blacks, but the press and its editors exemplified "black progress." In this hagiographic account of the "journalistic career" of the Afro-American, Penn predicted that the "Nineteenth century will close with a halo of journalistic sunshine about [the Afro-American's] head" (Penn 1891: 26). For Penn, the black press – and the editors who defined it – loomed above the "Negro Problem" as beacons of civilization and respectability.

In fact, his study was a history with work to accomplish. Not only did he review the history of black print journalism from 1827 to 1891, but he also conducted an extensive survey of active journalists and other black leaders in order to align the activities of journalistic leadership with the expressed and projected needs of black Americans. "The Afro-American editor should, most assuredly know for what he is striving, and the public, in whose welfare he is interested, should know, through this medium, in what way he is using his freedom in their behalf" (Penn 1891: 479). Some of the questions Penn asked of the leadership of the black community included: "Do you think the Press in the hands of the Negro has been a success? What achievements have been the result of the Afro-American editor?" (ibid: 431). As a secondary source, but also as an artifact of the period, Penn's *History* complements the uplift and protest functions of the black press, creating the case for black civil and political rights.

Penn's history was an auspicious beginning for the historiography of the black press, but it did not seem to inspire other historians to take up the subject. Through the first half of the twentieth century, histories of the black press were encapsulated within sociological considerations of black America, explicitly tying black press history to presentist concerns about race in America. The growth of sociology in America accompanied the growth of American cities with their extensive racial, ethnic, and class diversity. The immigration of southern and eastern Europeans to America, the migration of African Americans from the South to the urban north and midwest, and the technological and industrial changes attending these demographic shifts, drew the attention of social scientists seeking ways to control and direct this change. Grounded in anxiety over the implications of cultural difference, urban anonymity, and industrial technology, American sociologists approached urban populations, claiming "objectivity" but wishing effectively to mediate the impact of pluralism.

The first sociological treatment of the black press, Frederick G. Detweiler's *The Negro press in the United States*, aimed to dispel "the utter ignorance of the great mass of white Americans as to what is really going on among the colored people of the country" (Detweiler 1922: 3). A student of Robert Park, whose *The Immigrant Press and Its Control* (1922) served as an inspiration and model, Detweiler accessed the "mirror" function of the black press, offering (in his terms) an "objective" account and appraisal of black journalistic activity. His study built on Robert Kerlin's *The Voice of the Negro* (1920), a compilation of editorials and articles from black newspapers during the First World War, a book which for many white Americans was an introduction to the very existence of a black press.

One of the fears in the USA in both world wars was that the black press could be an agent of anti-American sentiment. Many Americans feared an isolated, oppositional community of black Americans in the context of a polarizing international scene, in which America would play a dominant, galvanizing role. In the First World War, a young J. Edgar Hoover warned that blacks were "seeing red" and he attempted to place the press under censorship. This atmosphere of alarm certainly informs Detweiler's presentation of the "Negro press." Driving the sociological inquiry were three interrelated questions: What are black Americans like? What do black Americans want? Can other Americans trust the black population to be loyal? Detweiler concluded that, despite the warnings of Hoover and others, the attitude of the black press was a "far cry from socialism or bolshevism" (Detweiler 1922: 158). Ultimately, Detweiler's study is a vindication of the protest role of the black press, but this protest is reassuringly American in tone. Echoing W. E. B. Du Bois' request in the First World War that black Americans support fully America's war effort, Detweiler wrote "The essential Americanism of the Negro Press is proved by the fact that its appeal is always to American constitutional rights" (ibid: 157).

The scrutiny focused on the black press during the First World War and the subsequent Red Scare period only hinted at the controversy the press would inspire in the Second World War era. The stakes rose with the volume of the debate, as the government voiced their accusations against the black press and pursued their investigations in earnest. The director of "Negro Relations" for the "Council of Democracy," Warren H. Brown, a black critic, claimed that the press was "Negro first and American second," that it was race-conscious before being American-conscious, thereby increasing rather than alleviating the effects of segregation. As part of *An American Dilemma*, his massive study on race and the black community in America, Gunnar Myrdal devoted a chapter to the black press where, building on Detweiler's study, he called on the "objectivity" of sociology and the "mirror function" of the press to provide a "balanced" account of this "fighting press." It was true, he conceded, that the black press was interested in the "advancement of the race" (Myrdal 1944: 910); however, he placed the protest in an American tradition stretching back to *Freedom's Journal*, noting that the papers were invariably edited to "prove the theory that they [blacks] are similar and they should be treated as ordinary Americans" (ibid: 912).

Other defenders of the black press during this period included Vishnu Oak, a professor at Wilberforce University in Ohio, who claimed in 1948 that in addition to supporting American ideals, the black press rendered "an invaluable service in crystallizing Negro thought and action. In serving as a necessary outlet to the Negro's otherwise thwarted ambitions and repressed anger against the injustices of his white compatriots, it is also preventing the birth of more 'Bigger Thomases'" (Oak 1948: 133). In other words, the press allowed blacks to let off steam so that they could continue to live peacefully and relatively profitably in America. Maxwell Brooks, writing in 1959, sought to put an end to charges that black newspapers were "radical" and "communistic" with a scientific analysis of the press that measured references in the black press "favorable to American symbols" against those supportive of "Red" ideas. In *The Negro Press, Re-examined*, Brooks confirmed that the newspapers' values were consistent with the "American tradition." Furthermore, Brooks concluded, the press could not properly be considered an organ of protest. Instead, he characterized these papers as "journals of reform," promoting typically American or middle-class values within the black community (Brooks 1959: 31, 98–9).

Even as they drew upon the press's "mirror" quality, these sociologists and critics generally read the historical trajectory of the black press as one of decline. Placing the "classical age" of black journalism in the antebellum period, James Weldon Johnson, in *Black Manhattan* (1930) describes the era somewhat nostalgically: "There was the great cause, the auspicious tone, and by some curiously propitious means, there were, too, the men able to measure up to the cause and the time. There were among the editors of these papers, especially in New York, men of ability and men of learning" (Johnson 1930: 15). In contrast, scholarly readers of twentieth-century black newspapers felt compelled to render judgment on the editorial quality and the non-protest goals of the black press. Oak, for example, claimed that the press offered a "materialistic journalism where the profit motive is such a dominant factor" (Oak 1948: 52). Many scholars accused the press of sensationalism, lacking the "objectivity" of mainstream newspapers. Others, such as Myrdal, claimed as well that the black press was frivolous. "Few features of the Negro press seem more ridiculous to ordinary white Americans than the display of Negro society" (Myrdal 1944: 919–20).

Criticisms of the frivolity of the black press culminated in E. Franklin Frazier's scathing critique, found in his influential study of the black middle class, *The Black Bourgeoisie* (1957). For Frazier, black press protest did not go far enough. The black press supported an increasingly isolated middle class of African Americans more concerned with conspicuous consumption, protecting its delicate social status and indulging in a world of "make-believe." As the "chief medium of communication" for this group, the press's arguments for equality and inclusion of blacks in American life represented primarily a claim for "opportunities which [would] benefit the black bourgeoisie economically and enhance the social status of the Negro" (Frazier 1957: 146). Examples of race leadership and actions of exceptional black individuals not only buttressed the ideology of uplift for Frazier, but in doing so revealed "the inferiority complex of the black bourgeoisie" and provided "a documentation of the attempts of this class to seek compensation for its hurt self-esteem and exclusion from American life" (ibid: 146). In his account, Frazier gives a cursory recounting of the history of the black press, more concerned instead with how the black press reflected and directed black values. When taken as a whole, these twentieth-century sociologists left scholars with a legacy of concern over the quality and ideology of the black press.

Historians and the Black Press

From this springboard in sociology and the debate over its contemporary function, the black press entered historians' field of vision relatively gradually. The press has had its greatest impact on the writing of black history in its role as a primary source. A survey of social and cultural histories of the African American experience proves the claim of black press scholar Henry Suggs that the black press is a "window" for historians and that "all serious scholarship about the black experience, both past and present, is incomplete without a detailed analysis of the black press" (Suggs 1996: 2). However, the press as such has not been a primary concern of historians. In fact, since Penn's 1891 study, there has only been one comprehensive history, Armistead Pride and Clint C. Wilson II's *History of the Black Press* (1997). Much of the historiography of the black press has been driven by the same concern driving other areas of African American Studies, especially since the establishment in the late 1960s of Black Studies departments and curricula – the need to recover the materials and documents relating to the African American Experience.

The question of recovery is especially acute in studying the black press, given the fragility of newspapers. Intended as temporary and immediate, copies of newspapers have been handled over and over again and few have survived. In recent years, as organizations such as Accessible Archives, the University of Wisconsin's Center for the Study of Print Culture in Modern America, and the Library of Congress have placed the texts of black newspapers on the internet, new technologies have offered the chance to preserve these valuable primary resources and yet make them accessible to researchers. Historians and archivists of the black press have struggled to maintain and create a comprehensive list of African American newspapers and periodicals. From Martin Delany who prepared, in the 1850s, a list of 40 or so antebellum newspapers to James Danky and Maureen E. Hady's *African-American Newspapers and Periodicals: A National Bibliography* (1998), which provides informa- tion on over 6,500 extant or defunct black periodicals and newspapers, recovering the black press tradition has been a major task. In order to add a narrative voice to these lists, many histories of the black press have been descriptive, fleshing out the scope and context of black journalism. One of the most active historians in this vein is Henry Suggs, whose works when taken together provide perhaps the most com- prehensive narrative account of black journalistic activity after the Civil War. His geographically organized volumes on the black press, including *The Black Press in the South, 1865–1979* (1983) and *The Black Press in the Midwest, 1865–1985* (1996), promise to leave no stone unturned.

Historians are not the only ones undertaking, and benefiting from, this recovery project. Scholars of African American literature also rely on the black press and have been at the forefront of this process of recovery. Starting in the antebellum period with the *Colored American* and *Anglo-African* (1859–62), black periodicals and newspapers have offered a rich forum for African American writers of poetry and fiction. African American literary works which first appeared in newspapers, serials, and journals include Martin Delany's *Blake, or the Huts of America* (1859–61); Pauline Hopkins's *Contending Forces* (1900) and *Of One Blood* (1903); Langston Hughes' "Simple" tales of the 1950s, and the poetry of Armand Lanusse (1817– 67), Claude McKay (1890–1948), Gwendolyn Brooks (1917–2000) and LeRoi Jones/Amiri Baraka (1934–) among others. Several scholars from Detweiler to the present have also addressed the black press as a site for black literary activity. The Black Periodical Literature Project, conducted at Yale and Harvard universities in the 1980s and early 1990s, recovered more than 40,000 specimens of serialized fiction, poetry, and other literature from black periodicals.

In his article from an edited text, *Perspectives of the Black Press: 1974*, Henry LaBrie saw an intimate link between black literature and black journalism, asking such questions as, "What has been the relationship between black fiction writers and black poets and the black press?" and "Were any of these black literary figures journalists first?" He listed a number of influential writer-journalists including James Weldon Johnson, Langston Hughes, and George Schuyler. Abby Johnson and Ronald Johnson fleshed out LaBrie's merely speculative work in their 1979, *Propaganda and Aesthetics*. This study, reissued in 1991, remains the most comprehensive and authoritative literary history of the black press in the twentieth century. The authors explore the creation of black literary criticism in twentieth-century journals such as *Opportunity* (1923–49), *The Crisis* (1910–present), *Negro Digest* (late 1960s), and *Calallo* (1970s–present), where countless black intellectuals have debated the relationship between art and politics and have developed methods of reading black texts.

In their assessments and analyses of the black press, historians have been engaged in an implicit conversation with the suspicious and critical sociological accounts outlined above, adopting some of their chief concerns. What has been the nature of black leadership as exemplified by the press? To what extent and to what end have blacks used their newspapers for protest? Whether or not a particular study focuses explicitly on the period of 1880–1915, historical interpretations of the black press have generally been grounded in a paradigm common to other subfields of black history, the early-twentieth-century debate between accommodationists and integrationists. Many black press histories have viewed its leadership and political ideology along a spectrum stretching from W. E. B. Du Bois' support of social integration and political participation, on the one hand, to Booker T. Washington's articulation of a social policy that accommodated racial segregation on the other. Since the 1950s, an implicit goal of historians of the black press has been to rescue it from the popular notion that Washington's policies predominated in black journalism in the early twentieth century in the same way that his financial support did.

Beginning with August Meier's 1953 argument in the *Journal of Negro History* that Washington's influence may not have been so extensive, most historians have stressed the militancy of the black press. In the 1970s, this historical interest manifested itself in an attention to the antebellum period and the Second World War, times when black press protest was most demonstrable. In *The Black Press, 1827–1890: The Quest for National Identity* (1971), Martin Dann echoed the themes and concerns of the 1960s Black Power Movement. Dann situated the early development of a black national identity, replete with a philosophy of black pride and black self-determination, in the middle of the nineteenth century. In the 1970s, historians also expanded on Penn's 1891 study by identifying and assessing exemplary black leaders. Following on from this, they responded to the Civil Rights and Black Power movements with biographies of the late-nineteenth-century editors T. Thomas Fortune and William Monroe Trotter who, in these accounts, demonstrated for this age of integration an uncompromising black leadership.

Perspectives that place heavy emphasis on politics, ideology, and activism continue to inform black press scholarship, though a concern for the other functions of the press has gradually resurfaced. In the 1990s, Bernell Tripp and Frankie Hutton sought to reassess the antebellum press as something more than an anti-slavery force. According to Tripp, early black journalists "placed a greater emphasis on civil rights, pride, unity and the progress of the black race" (Tripp 1992: 10). Likewise, Hutton's study hoped to "quell the pervasive view of this press as primarily or solely abolitionist [and] . . . to make room for a broader understanding of this important institution." Her study emphasized the middle-class identity of early black journalists, but without the stigma placed by E. Franklin Frazier on decades of black editors and newspaper writers. She depicted middle-class free blacks as "a beleaguered free people striving for vindication, uplift and, idealistically, for acceptance" (Hutton 1993: ix). Hutton utilized the reflective or, rather, the refractive, function of the black press. For her, newspapers are "prisms" through which to witness "a group of middle class blacks in remarkable patterns of social responsibility" (ibid: ix).

From its earliest years, the black press included women journalists and editors, and their prevalence has made the black press a major resource for African American women's history. In preparation for his history, I. Garland Penn wrote to a number of prominent African Americans with a list of questions and topics concerning the black press. He recorded their responses in his study. Penn asked Nellie F. Mossell, a prominent black writer and journalist, soon to be author of *The Work of the Afro-American Women* (1894), to expound on the issue of "Our Women in Journalism." Mossell responded: "They are admitted to the press association and are in sympathy with the male editors; but few have become independent workers in this noble field of effort, being yet satellites revolving around the sun of masculine journalism" (Penn 1891: 490). This picture is bleak; however, it is significant that Penn considered "women journalists" to be a topic at all and instructive that Mossell saw the black press as a forum to discuss publicly the issue of gender equity. Elsewhere she explained the reasons for this freedom: "Our men are too much hampered by their contentions with their white brothers to afford to stop and fight their black sisters" (quoted in Streitmatter 1994: 10).

Thus freed from excessive hindrance, black women established a tradition of public activism that came to a head as part of the larger women's movement in the 1970s. Scholars of black women's history looked to the black press for predecessors and role models. Accordingly, Alfreda Duster edited and reissued *Crusade for Justice: The Autobiography of Ida B. Wells* in 1970. The 1980s witnessed a flurry of publications on black women writers and public figures, such as Maria Stewart (1803–1879), Frances E. W. Harper (1825–1911) and Mary Ann Shadd Cary (1823–1893). In *Raising Her Voice* (1994), Rodger Streitmatter offered a very celebratory biographical study of eleven black women journalists, ranging across time from Maria Stewart to Charlayne Hunter-Gault (1941?–), and a synthetic treatment of how these women approached their journalistic endeavor. In this first comprehensive treatment of these women as journalists, Streitmatter asked such questions as "Why did these women choose to become journalists? How did they succeed in a competitive and demanding field traditionally dominated by white men? How have black women journalists differed from other journalists?" (Streitmatter 1994: 11).

While scholars have been interested in black women editors and journalists for their value as role models and exemplars of black women's spirit and activism, they have also looked at these journalists as fellow theorists. Scholars have fortified their own gender analyses with the journalists' specific social critiques. Work on Ida B. Wells-Barnett illustrates this interest in black women journalists most clearly. In her widely read article, "'On the threshold of women's era': lynching, empire and sexuality in black feminist theory," Hazel Carby builds upon Wells-Barnett's bold claim that the practice of lynching reflected white men's fears of black political and economic advancement, and that the rape of black women by white men defined the sexual landscape of the South rather than vice versa (Carby 1985). In her important study of gender, race, and national identity, *Manliness and Civilization* (1996), Gail Bederman similarly relies on Wells-Barnett as a key theorist of race and gender in the late nineteenth century. In her study of the life of Mary Ann Shadd Cary, editor of the *Provincial Freeman*, an antebellum antislavery newspaper published in Canada, Jane Rhodes underscores the importance of Shadd Cary's life to gender history, claiming that "an evaluation of Shadd Cary's career as a publisher and editor transforms the traditional conceptual framework of nineteenth century journalism as a white male-centered enterprise where women and persons of color existed only at the margins" (Rhodes 1998: xii). Furthermore, Rhodes' study of Shadd Cary's lifelong activism illuminates gender relationships within the black community, addressing the conundrum of "black men's desire to keep women within the cult of domesticity and their encouragement of black women's political labor" (ibid: xii).

New Trends in Black Press Scholarship

If historians in the 1970s and 1980s took on the project of recovery and historians of the early 1990s began to synthesize the historical themes of the press, scholarship of the late 1990s and early twenty-first century has taken an interdisciplinary, cultural historical approach to the press. Todd Vogel, editor of *The Black Press: New Literary and Historical Essays* (2001), opened with the bold claim that the essays would "rewrite our understanding of the black press" (Vogel 2001: 1). Indeed, the collection maps out some interesting new territory that departs from scholarship that views the press in terms of the accomodationist/protest paradigm and uses the press as a mirror reflecting black cultural experience. In the expanded 1990 edition of his *Black Press U.S.A.*, Roland E. Wolseley argued that the chief functions of the black press were "preserving identity, accepting the plurality that exists culturally and racially, bringing about more harmony between the two" (Wolseley 1990: xv). Likewise, much of the scholarly work on the black press has rested on the assumption that the press represents and speaks to a community defined by a fixed sense of its racial identity. In 1944, Gunnar Myrdal claimed in what seemed like an offhand comment: "The Press defines the Negro group to the Negroes themselves ... [It] has created the Negro group as a social and psychological reality to the individual Negro" (Myrdal 1944: 911). Recently, scholars have begun to explore the full implications of the idea that instead of merely reflecting or preserving black life, the black press actually produces racial meaning. In this view, the black press is an important agent in the social construction, not only of race but of a host of other social categories and their attending values.

Drawing on the work of critical race theorists, scholars have begun to demonstrate ways in which the press "redefined class, restaged race and nationhood, and reset the terms of public conversation" (Vogel 2001: 1). Focusing on the reflexivity of black journalistic efforts, historians and literary scholars chronicle and analyze the journalists' active and conscious construction of racial identity. For example, in *Returning the Gaze* (2001b), Anna Everett has unearthed early black film criticism and details how black journalists, by challenging cinematic representations of African Americans, actively participated in the processes of racial formation in the United States. Americans therefore came to understand the symbolism of blackness in part because the black press helped to interpret it. In his contribution to Vogel's volume, Robert Fanuzzi provides an antebellum example of how the press created racial meaning. In Fanuzzi's analysis, the race of a paper's editor did not necessarily determine its identity as a "black" newspaper. William Lloyd Garrison, white publisher of the *Liberator*, and Frederick Douglass, his former protégé and editor of the *North Star*, competed in the late 1840s for the status of editing the premier "colored newspaper."

Along similar lines, scholars of the black press have addressed work on the social construction of race in their characterizations of the black press. What does it mean to study a "black press" if racial boundaries are to be understood as porous, allowing identities to shift back and forth with evolving historical and cultural contexts? William G. Jordan's recent work on the black press during the First World War, *Black Newspapers and America's War for Democracy* (2001), advances this more flexible understanding of the impact of the black press on racial categorization. Far from merely reflecting black life, the press for Jordan "served as a frontier between white and black in which the terms of racial coexistence were negotiated and renegotiated through written and verbal exchanges" (Jordan 2001: 5). Conscious attention to the various practices and identities constituting race is especially pertinent to a study of black journalism in the digital age. What does "black" mean in cyberspace, a disembodied realm where identity is not determined by phenotype?

Another trend in black press scholarship of the past decade or so has been to read the black press as a crucial institution defining and shaping the "black public sphere." This scholarship grows out of philosopher Jürgen Habermas' formulation of the "public sphere" as a realm in which free and rational individuals come together and, through debate and discussion, arrive at a democratic consensus. Scholars of African American culture and that of other marginalized groups have challenged Habermas' conception of a free public sphere, to which all citizens have equal access, and modified his claims to describe the public activities of those groups denied full citizenship status. These groups create alternative public spheres that operate as spaces of group-identity formation and critique of the dominant society. Seeing the black press as a constituent of a black public sphere has led scholars to reconceptualize the nature of the press's protest function.

Earlier scholars wondered why blacks would adopt and promote "American ideals." For example, in her 1993 treatment of the early black press, Frankie Hutton ponders over what she takes to be the antebellum editors' political idealism and naïveté, demonstrated by the extent to which they "bore the spirit of republicanism, democracy and morality" (Hutton 1993: xi). While still sustaining the claim that the black press concentrated on advocating full inclusion in American society, more recently scholars have also examined how the black press entered the fray of national debate over the fundamental values of American society, not as politically immature imitators but as full-fledged social critics. Historians have addressed the ways in which editors have critiqued black public practices as well. For example, Rhodes' biography of Mary Ann Shadd Cary describes how she "demanded that the black public sphere be accessible to both men and women" (Rhodes 1998: 213).

In addition to providing a rubric for discussing African American critique, scholars have focused attention on a black public sphere that overlaps with – but doesn't fully correspond with – the national public sphere. In this vein, scholars have reassessed the international aspects of the black press, distancing their studies from scholarship that has measured protest in terms of its relationship to American national identity. In his contribution to *Black Press*, Robert S. Levine predicts that "a reconceived literary history that puts [*Freedom Journal*'s Authorized Agent David] Walker's writings at the center of a tradition of African American writing will pay greater attention to writers such as Martin Delany and Mary Ann Shadd Cary who similarly addressed connections between nationalism and transnationalism and racial and geographical borders" (Levine 2001: 34).

In her study of African American anticolonialism, *Race against Empire* (1997), Penny M. Von Eschen demonstrates the implications of uncoupling the black press from the "American" identity that its Cold War proponents fought so hard to obtain. Whereas other scholars of the black press have discussed the anti-imperialist views of the press or stressed its critique of American foreign policy, Von Eschen reads the press in terms of its journalistic efforts to craft a "new international political language and new political strategies" (Von Eschen 1997: 8). Far from the isolationists that Frazier described in *Black Bourgeoisie*, the black press and its journalists, in Von Eschen's account, "formed a dense nexus with journalists and publishers from London to Lagos and Johannesburg, marshalling the resources of important black middle-class and entrepreneurial institutions to create an international anticolonial discourse" (ibid: 8). In *The Practice of Diaspora* (2003), his study of the rise of black internationalism in the 1920s and 1930s, Brent Edwards describes an African American press that cuts across national and linguistic lines, collaborating and corresponding with Afro-French editors and intellectuals. In these studies, the black press constitutes nothing less than the public sphere of the black Diaspora.

Drawing upon recent work on the history of print culture, another current trend in black press historiography expands the scope of the black press, bringing an interdisciplinary approach to bear on the production, dissemination, and reception of the printed word. The circulation of newspapers through the population prods print-culture scholars towards interesting questions. Under what circumstances are these newspapers disseminated from reader to reader? Is hearing a newspaper read aloud in a group the same kind of experience as reading it silently alone? What happens to the content of editorials and features when it is communicated orally instead of by the printed word? On the threshold of the twenty-first century, when digital communication and internet technology have transformed the way readers and writers communicate, scholars have become particularly conscious of the historical and social context of the printed word. In her contribution to Vogel's *Black Press*, Anna Everett outlines the concerns this new technology raises. "How then to define the particularities of the black press in cyberspace now that the drastically revolutionized nature of 'the text,' of publication, of authorship, of information dissemination and retrieval, and of the reader all signify so significant a shift in the basic terms and concepts of our topic?" (Everett 2001a: 247).

Scholars interested in the black press in the wider context of print culture consider the "circulation" of the press, its movement through various levels of public and private discourse across boundaries of class, race, gender, and literacy. "A complex understanding of production, distribution, regulation and reception allows us to grasp a more textured public discourse, one that exchanges ideas within not just the black community but in the nation at large" (Vogel 2001: 2). The authors in Vogel's collection view the press in terms of its "cultural work." In addition to being a commodity bought and sold, the black press, for these historians, names a complex of social performances, a series of staged acts that tie local issues and fleeting events to larger questions of freedom, equality, and justice. The black press plays a major role in *Forgotten Readers* (2002), Elizabeth McHenry's recovery and exposition of African American reading practices in the nineteenth and early twentieth centuries. McHenry demonstrates that a consideration of the production and circulation of black newspapers and periodicals is essential to reconstructing a history of black literacy, literature, and literary conversation.

From *Freedom's Journal* to BlackPressUSA.com, black journalism has assumed myriad forms and articulated a vast array of social commentary. A particularly pliable source, the black press has formed the backbone of scholarship across the disciplines from sociology to literary, social, and cultural histories. At various times and in its varied ways, the black press has advocated freedom and justice; it has chronicled African American economic achievement; it has knit together highly mobile black populations; it has advocated specific religious, spiritual, and moral practices for black people; it has provided entertainment and gossip; it has translated black culture for the rest of the world; it has created racial discourse and practice; and it has guided national and international policy. Ultimately the historiography of the black press illustrates the ongoing struggle of scholars to live up to the full range of the press's implications by expanding methods of inquiry and by rethinking notions of the "black community."

BIBLIOGRAPHY

Works Cited

Bederman, Gail (1996) *Manliness and Civilization*. Chicago: University of Chicago Press.
Brooks, Maxwell R. (1959) *The Negro Press, Re-examined*. Boston: Christopher.
Carby, Hazel (1985) " 'On the threshold of woman's era': lynching, empire and sexuality in black feminist theory," *Critical Inquiry* 2 (1, Autumn).
Danky, James and Hady, Maureen E. (1998) *African-American Newspapers and Periodicals: A National Bibliography*. Cambridge, MA: Harvard University Press.
Dann, Martin E. (ed.) (1971) *The Black Press, 1827–1890: The Quest for National Identity*. New York: G. P. Putnam and Sons.
Detweiler, Frederick G. (1922) *The Negro Press in the United States*. Chicago: University of Chicago Press.
Edwards, Brent Hays (2003) *The Practice of Diaspora: Literature, Translation and the Rise of Black Internationalism*. Cambridge, MA: Harvard University Press.
Everett, Anna (2001a) "The black press in the age of digital reproduction" in T. Vogel (ed.), *The Black Press: New Literary and Historical Essays*, 244–57. New Brunswick, NJ: Rutgers University Press.
—— (2001b) *Returning the Gaze: A Genealogy of Black Film Criticism, 1909–1949*. Durham, NC: Duke University Press.
Frazier, E. Franklin ([1957] 1962) *The Black Bourgeoisie*. New York: Collier Books.
Hutton, Frankie (1993) *The Early Black Press in America, 1827–1860*. Westport, CT: Greenwood Press.
Johnson, Abby Arthur and Johnson, Ronald Mayberry (1979) *Propaganda and Aesthetics*. Amherst: University of Massachusetts Press.
Johnson, James Weldon (1930) *Black Manhattan*. New York: Alfred A. Knopf.

Jordan, William G. (2001) *Black Newspapers and America's War for Democracy, 1914–1920.* Chapel Hill: University of North Carolina Press.

Kerlin, Robert T. (1920) *The Voice of the Negro.* New York: E.P. Dutton.

Levine, Robert S. (2001) "Circulating the nation: David Walker, the Missouri compromise, and the rise of the black press" in T. Vogel (ed.), *The Black Press: New Literary and Historical Essays*, 17–36. New Brunswick, NJ: Rutgers University Press.

McHenry, Elizabeth (2002) *Forgotten Readers: Recovering the Lost History of African-American Literary Societies.* Durham, NC: Duke University Press.

Myrdal, Gunnar (1944) *An American Dilemma.* New York: Harper.

Oak, Vishnu (1948) *The Negro Newspaper.* Yellow Springs, OH: Antioch Press.

Park, Robert (1922) *The Immigrant Press and Its Control.* New York: Reprint Services Corp.

Penn, I. Garland (1891) *The Afro-American Press and Its Editors.* Springfield, MA: Willey.

Pride, Armistead and Wilson, Clint C., II (1997) *A History of the Black Press.* Washington, DC: Howard University Press.

Rhodes, Jane (1998) *Mary Ann Shadd Cary: The Black Press and Protest in the Nineteenth Century.* Bloomington: Indiana University Press.

Streitmatter, Rodger (1994) *Raising Her Voice: African-American Women Journalists Who Changed History.* Lexington: University Press of Kentucky.

Suggs, Henry Lewis (ed.) (1983) *The Black Press in the South, 1865–1979.* Westport, CT: Greenwood Press.

Suggs, Henry Lewis (ed.) (1996) *The Black Press in the Midwest, 1865–1985.* Westport, CT: Greenwood Press.

Tripp, Bernell (1992) *Origins of the Black Press: New York 1827–1847.* Northport, AL: Vision Press.

Vogel, Todd (ed.) (2001) *The Black Press: New Literary and Historical Essays.* New Brunswick, NJ: Rutgers University Press.

Von Eschen, Penny M. (1997) *Race against Empire: Black Americans and Anti-Colonialism, 1937–1957.* Ithaca, NY: Cornell University Press.

Wolseley, Roland E. ([1971] 1990) *The Black Press, U.S.A.* Ames: Iowa State University Press.

Suggestions for Further Reading

Bullock, Penelope L. (1981) *The Afro-American Periodical Press, 1838–1909.* Baton Rouge, LA: Louisiana State University Press.

Danky, James and Weigand, Wayne (eds.) (1998) *Print Culture in a Diverse America.* Urbana: University of Illinois Press.

LaBrie, Henry G., III (1974) *Perspectives of the Black Press: 1974.* Kennebunkport, ME: Mercer House Press.

Meier, August (1953) "Booker T. Washington and the Negro press: with special reference to the *Colored American Magazine*," *Journal of Negro History* 38: 67–90.

Potter, Vilma Raskin (1993) *A Reference Guide to Afro-American Publications and Editors, 1827–1946.* Ames: Iowa State University Press.

Pride, Armistead and Wilson, Clint C., II (1988) *P. B. Young, Newspaperman: Race Politics and Journalism in the New South, 1910–1962.* Charlottesville: University of Virginia Press.

Washburn, Patrick S. (1986) *A Question of Sedition: The Federal Government's Investigation of the Black Press during World War II.* New York: Oxford University Press.

PART VII

African Americans and Wars "For Democracy"

CHAPTER TWENTY-ONE

The Black Soldier in Two World Wars

HAYWARD "WOODY" FARRAR

Black soldiers were marginalized in both the First and Second World Wars. In neither war were black servicemen accorded the attention, fairness, and respect paid to their white counterparts. Rather, the armed forces only grudgingly allowed their participation. When given the opportunity, African American soldiers, sailors, and aviators fought bravely and well, but in both wars the prevailing doctrine in the military was racial segregation and exclusion. According to the high commands of the Armed Forces, African Americans were too lazy, stupid, and cowardly to make good soldiers, sailors or aviators. If they were good for anything it was to load, unload, and move cargo, and cook and serve food to white officers and enlisted personnel. Combat for blacks was out of the question, except perhaps in racially segregated units and squadrons.

This marginalization has been reflected in the historiography of the First and Second World Wars. The best-known historians of the world wars – John Keegan, Stephen Ambrose, Gerhard Weinberg, Michael Lyons, and Paul Fussell – either do not mention the contributions of African Americans or devote only a page or two in their massive works to such contributions. For example, Gerhard Weinberg, in his almost 1200-page history of the Second World War *A World at Arms* devotes just two pages to African Americans (Weinberg 1994: 495–6).

Despite the slighting of African Americans in most general histories of the world wars, there have been a number of monographs, starting from the 1970s, detailing the African American experience in the military in general and in the First and Second World Wars in particular. While not as numerous or as analytical as on other topics in African American history, the major works in the field (Edgerton 2001; Buckley 2001; Cooper 1997; Lanning 1997; Nalty 1986; Foner 1974; Henri and Stillman 1970; Dalfiume 1969) rescue from obscurity the African American contributions to the world wars. Blacks fought these wars on two fronts. One front was the war against the enemy, be it the Germans in the First World War or the Germans, Italians, and Japanese in the Second World War. The other front was a war against the racism that infested America and its armed forces in the first half of the twentieth century. That war was a frustrating and debilitating one and it very much influenced how black soldiers, sailors, airmen, and marines fought the enemy.

The historiography concerning black soldiers in the First and Second World Wars is more descriptive than analytical. Many of the authors in this field say the same things and draw the same conclusions. They all exhibit a remarkable consensus that despite, the military's low opinion of them, African Americans fought bravely and well. Furthermore, the historiography specific to African Americans in the military has changed little over time. Richard M. Dalfiume's *Desegregation of the Armed Forces: Fighting on Two Fronts, 1939–1953* (1969) was one of the earliest works to deal with the African American experience in the world wars. Jack Foner's *Blacks and the Military in American History* (1974) was the most comprehensive and factual account of black participation in the First and Second World Wars. All succeeding works on the subject built on this one. The most comprehensive and analytical account of black soldiers in the two world wars is Bernard Nalty's *Strength For The Fight: A History of Black Americans in the Military* (1986), which is considered the standard work. Black military history is in its infancy, with its first stage still correcting the marginalization of black soldiers in the historiography of the two world wars.

Black Service in the First World War

The literature (Dalfiume 1969; Henri and Stillman 1970; Foner 1974; Nalty 1986; Lanning 1997; Edgerton 2001; Buckley 2001; Cooper 1997) devoted to black soldiers in the First World War all agrees that black soldiers fought with courage, despite their racist mistreatment, and that accounts of black heroism were downplayed while instances of black cowardice were overblown to reinforce racist attitudes towards black soldiers. These authors take different approaches to come to these conclusions. Henri, Cooper, Foner, and Lanning all give straightforward narratives of African American military participation in the First World War. Edgerton and Nalty weave in accounts of black civilian efforts to mitigate military racism. Buckley uses vignettes of individual black soldiers to make her points.

When the United States entered the First World War in April 1917, African American soldiers were confined to the 9th and 10th cavalry and the 24th and 25th infantry regiments, plus several black national guard units scattered throughout the country. The Conscription Act of 1917 authorized a colorblind draft. Consequently, according to Lanning, the numbers of blacks in the Army increased exponentially as southern draft boards, eager to rid their communities of potentially disruptive black men, inducted a disproportionate number of African Americans into the Army (Lanning 1997: 131). Overall, 13 percent of all draftees were African American, though they were just 10 percent of the US population (ibid: 131).

Meanwhile, the Navy refused to enlist or employ African American men for any jobs other than messman and steward. Messmen cooked and served food to enlisted sailors, while stewards were servants to officers. According to Lanning, Nalty, and Foner, the Navy believed these jobs were all that blacks were capable of doing, but it also made it easier to segregate the races aboard warships because the messman and steward divisions could be accommodated separately from the combat sections (Lanning 1997: 146–7; Nalty 1986: 83–4; Foner 1974: 106). The Marine Corps and infant Army Air Corps completely barred blacks.

The army initially planned to employ the first 75,000 black draftees in 16 combat regiments set aside for them. The Houston Riot in late August 1917 changed that, however. This disturbance resulted from a rumor that the police had killed a member of Company L of the 24th black regiment, which was temporarily based in Houston. That unit then went on a rampage on the night of August 23, 1917, shooting up the city, killing 15 whites and wounding 20 more (Nalty 1986: 102–4).

The Army court-martialed 118 black soldiers for mutiny and murder in three trials, beginning in December 1917. The result was that 19 of the 24th regiment were hanged, 41 were sentenced to life, and 9 more were imprisoned for shorter terms. More black soldiers would have been executed had it not been for pressure placed on the War Department by the black press, the NAACP and other black organizations (Foner 1974: 115; Lanning 1974: 127). Nalty states that the Army refused to acknowledge the racist provocation behind the Houston Riot, attributing it to the inherent criminality of African American soldiers. Lanning, while acknowledging the existence of this provocation, does not excuse the mutinous soldiers (Nalty 1986: 102–4; Lanning 1997: 128).

As a result the Army scrapped its plan to create 16 all-black combat regiments. Instead it created a black division (the 92nd) of four regiments, to be commanded and officered by whites, and assigned the rest of the black draftees to service and supply units, which would load and unload trains, trucks, and ships. Foner, Edgerton, Nalty, and Lanning state that to ease southern paranoia, the 92nd division was neither to train as a unit nor to train with weapons. According to these historians, this had disastrous consequences for the combat effectiveness of the division (Foner 1974: 116; Edgerton 2001: 90; Lanning 1997: 134; Nalty 1986: 108).

The Army was reluctant to commission new black officers. According to Lanning, Nalty, and Foner, the Army allowed no black officer to command whites and few to be promoted to high rank. Whites commanded black regiments and divisions. The most senior black officer, Lt Colonel Charles Young, was prematurely retired for bogus health reasons, rather than be given charge of the 92nd division, where he might have commanded white officers. The black press and the NAACP protested against Young's retirement, and Young himself proved he was fit for further duty by riding on horseback from Ohio to Washington, DC. Though he was promoted to full colonel, Charles Young never got the chance to command troops in battle (Edgerton 2001: 80; Nalty 1986: 110–11; Foner 1974: 113; Lanning 1997: 132).

Buckley, Foner, Lanning, and Nalty describe how pressure from the NAACP, especially its president Joel Spingarn, and the black press forced the Army to open an Officer's Candidate School for blacks at Camp Des Moines, Iowa. This camp was to commission junior officers to command small black units in service battalions and the 92nd division or to serve as doctors or chaplains. Over 600 blacks received commissions through this camp (Foner 1974: 117–18; Lanning 1997: 132; Nalty 1986: 110; Buckley 2001: 178).

The 92nd Division, commanded by Major General Charles Ballou, was composed of the 365th, 366th, 367th, and 368th infantry regiments. The 369th, 370th, 371st, and 372nd black National Guard regiments were organized into the 93rd division. This division never operated as a unit, but was broken up by regiments and assigned to fight with French army units (Foner 1974: 197: 116–17; Nalty 1986: 112; Lanning 1997: 133–4).

The black combat units of the Army during the First World War totaled 42,000, 11 percent of all the blacks that served in the Army. The rest were assigned to non-combat units, where they served as ammunition handlers, longshoremen, steve-dores, truck drivers, and railroad workers (Nalty 1986: 112). According to Michael Cooper in *Hellfighters* – his study of blacks in the First World War – these service troops' labor made it possible for the US military to embark and supply over 2,000,000 soldiers in France, but they were never accorded the recognition they deserved (Cooper 1997: 26).

According to the literature on the subject (Foner 1974; Buckley 2001; Lanning 1997; Nalty 1986), the 92nd and 93rd divisions were neither adequately trained for combat in France, nor properly commanded. This was especially true of the 92nd division, whose command was composed of racist southern officers who routinely debased, denigrated, and degraded their black troops. According to the authors mentioned, many of these officers felt that command of black soldiers was demean-ing and not career-enhancing, so they refused to provide the leadership and care they would give to white soldiers. Most white officers held the prevailing view that blacks were lazy, stupid, cowardly, and prone to sexually assault white women. White supremacy forbade equal relationships between white and black officers and encouraged gross mistreatment of black officers by their white counterparts. Fur-thermore, white commanders refused to protect their black troops from racist treat-ment by white civilians in stateside training camps where they were trained. In fact Major General Ballou, the commanding officer of the 92nd division, ordered his black troops to accept racial discrimination and segregation in public accommoda-tion, even where this was illegal (Edgerton 2001: 80; Lanning 1997: 135; Nalty 1986: 113; Foner 1974: 116).

The command of the American Expeditionary Force (AEF) actually instructed the French that black troops assigned to their army units should not be treated with the same respect and dignity they accorded to French soldiers (Foner 1974: 122; Lanning 1997: 136). Lanning tells how the French, remembering how well their black troops from their African empire fought for them, disregarded these instructions and treated the African American soldiers assigned to them far better than the US Army. It is the consensus of Nalty, Lanning, and Buckley that it was no coincidence that the black regiments assigned to the French fought better than those commanded by white Americans.

The historiographical consensus (Foner 1974; Cooper 1997; Nalty 1986; Buckley 2001; Lanning 1997) is that the 92nd fought as well as could be expected, despite constant racist assaults on its dignity. One of its regiments, the 368th, was accused of cowardice because of their disorganized withdrawal in the face of a German assault. The division commander Major General Charles Ballou then court-martialed 30 black junior officers (Foner 1974: 123; Nalty 1986: 115–16; Lanning 1997: 141). Ignored was the fact that the regiment lacked training for trench warfare, detailed orders, and necessary combat equipment (Dalfiume; Foner; Nalty; Lanning 1997: 141). Edgerton, in his study *Hidden Heroism*, maintains that white regiments and officers who conducted retreats as disorderly as that of the 368th were not punished (Edgerton 2001: 93–5). The 367th regiment of the 92nd division did perform well, pushing the Germans back from their positions in the last days of the war.

Despite the last-minute improvement in its performance, the 92nd division was blasted for its alleged cowardice by the commander of the US 2nd Army, Lt General Henry Bullard (Lanning 1997: 142). Both Ballou and Bullard blamed the 92nd division's problems on the alleged deficiencies of black troops, not on their racist leadership and lack of support for these soldiers, according to those who have studied the 92nd (Cooper 1997; Nalty 1986; Lanning 1997). Nalty, in his study, downplays Bullard's racism and claims that he really wanted black soldiers to succeed, but was disillusioned by their less-than-stellar performance in the 92nd division. Lanning states that General Bullard from the beginning never believed in black soldiers. Nevertheless, 21 members of the 92nd won the Distinguished Service Cross, the Army's second-highest award. According to Edgerton, that was more than was achieved by several all-white divisions in the 2nd Army, to which the 92nd was assigned (Edgerton 2001: 98). Those accomplishments, according to the historiography of this era, were ignored.

The regiments of the 93rd division assigned to the French army were issued with French weapons and rations, and treated more equally than black soldiers under American command. They remained under French command until the end of the war and participated in the Meuse-Argonne and Oise-Aisne campaigns (Lanning 1997: 139). One of these regiments, the 369th, distinguished itself. Due to its exploits, historians of the African American experience in the First World War have paid the most attention to the 369th (Henri and Stillman 1970; Foner 1974; Buckley 2001; Lanning 1997; Nalty 1986).

The regiment was originally the 15th Colored National Guard Regiment from New York. Commanded by a liberal white, Colonel William Hayward, the regiment became legendary for its bravery. Called the "Men of Bronze" by the French and the "Hellfighters" by the Germans, the 369th spent over six months on the front lines, had none of its men taken prisoner, and surrendered no ground to the Germans. The 369th received a group Croix de Guerre citation and 171 officers and men received individual Croix de Guerres or Legions of Merit (Foner 1974: 123; Buckley 2001: 209; Lanning 1997: 139; Cooper 1997: 32–45).

Two members of the regiment, Privates Henry Johnson and Neeedham Roberts, especially distinguished themselves. On May 14, 1918, on their own they repulsed a 24-man German attack on their observation post, despite both being seriously wounded (Lanning 1997: 139). The 369th was also distinguished by its regimental band, led by Lt James Reese Europe, who recruited numerous talented black musicians from New York. The band played jazz as well as more traditional music and was said to have introduced jazz to European audiences (Lanning 1997: 139). Other 93rd division regiments attached to the French also fought with courage, but were not as heralded as the 369th.

The Inter-War Period

Foner, Edgerton, Lanning, and others who have studied the period all agree that the heroism and contributions of black soldiers in the First World War went unheralded by White America (Edgerton 2001: 99; Foner 1974: 125; Lanning 1997: 150). African American soldiers were not included in the victory parades held in Paris and London right after the war, though black African and West Indian soldiers who fought with the French and British were included (Buckley 2001: 220–1). Only in African American communities were black troops celebrated with parades. The exception was New York City, where – due to the insistence of its commander Col. William Hayward – the 369th regiment staged a gala parade down 5th Avenue (Lanning 1997: 146).

Once home, black veterans faced a country driven to madness by racism. Lynchings greatly increased in the South and race riots infested the North. Racist southern whites – frightened by the specter of thousands of black men with ideas and experiences of social equality gained from their overseas service, as well as armed combat experience – stopped at nothing to strengthen white supremacy and black subordination. In 1919, for example, 77 blacks were lynched. Of these victims, 10 were veterans lynched while still in uniform. In the North, returning white veterans found that many of their jobs had been taken during the war by black migrants from the South. The resulting tensions culminated in a series of race riots from 1919 to 1921. New York, Washington, DC, Chicago, Omaha, and Tulsa were among the places where riots occurred (Nalty 1986: 125–6; Lanning 1997: 151–2; Henri and Stillman 1970: 116–18; Edgerton 2001: 110–12).

The Armed Forces were not immune from the hyperracism that swept the country. The Army strongly denigrated the performance of black combat troops. According to Edgerton, several "studies" concluded that blacks were physically unfit for combat duty because their brains were smaller than whites' (Edgerton 2001: 119). A rough consensus developed in the Army that in any future war black combat units were to be kept to a minimum, with the vast majority of black enlistees and draftees assigned to menial tasks. No advanced branch, such as the Signal Corps or Air Corps, was to accept blacks. The Navy, which had confined its black sailors to messmen and stewards, decided to accept no new black enlistees. This ensured an all-white Navy in the future. The Marines continued to bar blacks altogether.

In the 1920s, black army enlistees were confined to the traditional black regiments: the 24th and 25th infantry and 9th and 10th cavalries. These units, however, were not combat trained. Rather they were used as service labor pools or garrison troops. As for black officers, their numbers steadily dwindled in the Regular Army until less than a half dozen remained (Lanning 1997: 155). It was difficult to impossible for a black to win appointment to the service academies, and only one – Benjamin O. Davis, Jr – survived the racism and abuse to graduate from West Point in 1936.

During the 1930s, African Americans continued to fall to insignificance in the Armed Forces. In 1930 there were less than 4,000 in the Army and 450 in the Navy (Foner 1974: 129–31; Lanning 1997: 157–8). The Army Air Force and Marines remained lily-white. The situation was little better in the National Guard and Reserves, as only 2 percent of soldiers in those branches were black. After 1933 the Navy began enlisting blacks again, but only as stewards and messmen. This was in response to an anticipated shortage of Filipinos to fill those ratings, due to the coming of independence in the Philippines (Lanning 1997: 158). By 1939 the numbers of black sailors had reached 2,400 (Foner 1974: 130–2; Lanning 1997: 158).

The Second World War Approaches

Dalfiume, Foner, Nalty, and Edgerton all pay close attention to the efforts of America's black community, speaking through their newspapers and groups such as the NAACP, to put pressure on the government to lift the restrictions placed on their participation in the Armed Forces, as the world lurched towards war in the late 1930s. By 1940 black votes in the North were important enough to force President Franklin D. Roosevelt to broaden black participation in the Armed Forces. However, he was not willing to antagonize a southern-dominated Congress, Army, and Navy by racially integrating the Armed Forces. The government's military racial policy was issued in October 1940. It stipulated that blacks were to be drafted in proportion to their percentage in the population and would be employed in every branch of the Army, including the Air Force. Nevertheless, black and white soldiers would still serve in racially segregated units commanded by whites (Dalfiume 1969: 29–33; Foner 1974: 135–7; Edgerton 2001: 129; Nalty 1986: 136–42).

These policies angered many black leaders who saw it as an expansion of military segregation. With the 1940 election imminent and black voters leaning to the liberal Republican Wendell Willkie, who hinted at ending Armed Forces segregation, President Roosevelt made further concessions by appointing Judge William Hastie, Dean of Howard University Law School, to be a Special Assistant to the Secretary of War, Campbell Johnson to be the Special Assistant to General Lewis Hershey, Director of the Selective Service, and promoting the Army's highest ranking black officer, Colonel Benjamin O. Davis, Sr, to brigadier general. Davis was the first black appointed to that rank (Lanning 1997: 165; Edgerton 2001: 130). These advances were enough to keep black voters in the Democratic fold in 1940. Black leaders had to accept what was offered, in the hope of future advances in the desegregation of the armed forces (Dalfiume 1969: 29–33; Foner 1974: 135–7; Edgerton 2001: 129; Nalty 1986: 136–42).

Blacks in the Second World War Army

The published works (Foner 1974; Nalty 1986; Lanning 1997; Edgerton 2001; Buckley 2001) devoted to black soldiers in the Second World War replicate those of the First World War in approach and conclusions. They discuss how, despite promises to open up all its branches to black enlistees and draftees, the Army at the beginning of the war treated its black soldiers as it had in the First World War. The plan was to assign the majority of blacks to service and engineer units, loading and unloading cargo ships, trains, trucks, and airplanes, or building roads. For example, African Americans helped build the Alaska Highway and the Burma Road (Lanning 1997: 174). Although the Army reactivated the First World War 92nd and 93rd black combat divisions and established the 2nd cavalry division, it took its time assigning them to combat, preferring to keep them stateside in auxiliary roles (Nalty 1986: 166–7; Lanning 1997: 175).

Adding insult to injury was the racist treatment that black officers and men received at army bases in the South and elsewhere. The Army rigidly segregated the races on base. Conditions off base were no better, as black soldiers were just as rigidly segregated. Black soldiers were also targets for police brutality and lynchings. Base and unit commanding officers, mindful of keeping good relations with their surrounding communities, refused to use their power to prevent or mitigate off-base racist treatment of their black soldiers. According to Nalty and Foner, the Army claimed it could do nothing to disturb long-established patterns of racial segregation and for it to try would degrade its combat effectiveness. According to the Army high command, the service was no place for "social experimentation" (Foner 1974: 141–2; Nalty 1986: 146–7; Lanning 1997: 170).

In 1942 the Army not only reactivated the 1918 black combat divisions – the 92nd and 93rd – but also organized the traditionally black 9th and 10th cavalry regiments into the 2nd Cavalry Division. When the 2nd Cavalry was sent to North Africa in 1944, the Army deactivated it and scattered its personnel among non-combatant service units. However, the Army – true to its racist practices – retrained personnel in deactivated white cavalry units for infantry and other combat roles (Edgerton 2001: 147). The 92nd and 93rd infantry divisions might also have been deactivated, since the Army was reluctant to use either in combat, had it not been for pressure from the black community, insistent on their soldiers going into action (Nalty 1986: 167–9; Dalfiume 1969: 93–6; Foner 1974: 158–60; Lanning 1997: 174–7; Edgerton 2001: 147–8). The 93rd Infantry division was the first to see combat. However, the division was poorly prepared and trained for the fighting. Edgerton, Nalty, and others state that the white officers and commanders of this and other black units expected, as they had in the first war, that black troops would fail and therefore gave them little leadership or inspiration.

In any event the 93rd went to the South Pacific in early 1944. Its first three regiments, the 25th, 368th, and 369th, arrived on islands already taken from the Japanese, so they were used in non-combatant roles (Lanning 1997: 175). This did not sit too well with stateside black leaders and their complaints led to the 25th regiment of the 93rd division seeing combat on Bougainville Island in March 1944 (Lanning 1997: 175). The 25th infantry performed well although its achievements were ignored because of the failure of one of its units to conduct an orderly retreat in the face of Japanese fire. This isolated incident was used to slander the entire division as being cowardly and incompetent. The Army during the Second World War, as in the previous world war, was eager to use any failure by black troops to justify its racist beliefs in their inferiority. For the rest of the war in the Pacific, the 93rd division was used in service activities in rear echelon fronts, only very occasionally seeing combat. This they did very well, since the division as a whole did receive a campaign battle star ribbon (Lanning 1997: 176).

Its exploits more publicized than the 93rd, but treated with no more dignity, the 92nd infantry fought in the Italian campaign. It was commanded by Major General Edward Almond (Lanning 1997: 178). He and his white command staff were southerners, true to the Army's tradition of appointing those types to command black units. According to one military historian, the rationale for such assignments was that southerners were more familiar with, and better understood, African Americans (ibid: 178). Actually they were less likely to treat black officers and enlisted men properly. McGuire, in his *Taps for a Jim Crow Army*, shows how black soldiers in their letters home and to black newspapers continually complained of racist treatment from white officers (McGuire 1993: 99–117). That this seriously degraded the combat effectiveness of black soldiers mattered little to the Army since, according to Nalty, these soldiers were not expected to see combat (Nalty 1986: 167). Only black community protests forced the Army to use the 92nd in the role for which it was trained (Nalty 1986: 167–9; Dalfiume 1969: 93–6; Lanning 1997: 174; Foner 1974: 158–60).

The division was sent to Italy, which by the fall of 1944 was already a secondary front in the European Theater of Operations. In October, units of the 92nd attacked heavily fortified German positions along the "Gothic Line." The Germans repulsed the attack, causing the 92nd to retreat in a somewhat disorderly fashion. As in the First World War, the soldiers in the 92nd were tarred with the coward's brush. Nalty, Dalfiume, Lanning, and Foner all give accounts of this disaster that emphasize poor training and racist leadership as accounting for the division's poor performance. Paul Fussell's most recent book on the Second World War, *The Boy's Crusade*, tells how white divisions – poorly trained and led – broke and ran in the face of German assaults during the Battles of the Bulge and Huertgen Forest. Unlike the 92nd, they had their cowardice either explained away or covered up (Fussell 2003).

Escaping criticism for the 92nd's performance was their commanding officer General Almond, whose racist attitudes certainly did not inspire his men. For example, he welcomed one of the 92nd's regiments by stating that he did not want them and they were there only at the insistence of black politicians and newspapers, and "white friends" (Edgerton 2001: 151). With leadership like that, it was no wonder that the 92nd initially failed to perform up to standard.

As the Italian campaign wore on, however, the 92nd division's performance steadily improved, despite the disdain these commanders had for its black soldiers. It took 3,000 casualties and received 12,000 decorations for its troops. Among the brave soldiers of the 92nd division were 1st Lt Vernon Baker, who led a platoon assault on a German position in Italy that resulted in the destruction of six machine-gun bunkers and the killing of 26 German soldiers, and 1st Lt John Fox, who called down artillery fire on his own position and destroyed an attacking German force in doing so (Lanning 1997: 186). Their heroism merited the Congressional Medal of Honor, which – due to Army racism – they belatedly received only in 1997 (Lanning 1997: 186). There were also other black units, not assigned to the 92nd division, that distinguished themselves in Europe. The most notable of these was the 761st Tank Battalion, which, by its brave fighting across Europe, convinced a skeptical General George Patton that blacks could excel at armored warfare. This unit received a much belated Presidential Unit Citation in 1978 (Lanning 1997: 181).

In late 1944, manpower shortages caused the Army to call for black volunteers from non-combatant units to serve in depleted white combat units. The Army high command decided to organize all-black rifle platoons commanded by white officers, and then attach them to white companies and battalions. This new policy was as desegregated as the Army would get during the war. The black platoons fought alongside white platoons for the remainder of the war, impressing their white counterparts with their courage and skill (Nalty 1986: 178; Foner 1974: 162–3; Lanning 1997: 181–2).

This performance was reflected by the following heroes: SSgt Ruben Rivers, who with his tank single-handedly stopped a German assault; Pfc. Willy James, who died while rescuing his commanding officer, 1st Lt Charles Thomas, who himself, though mortally wounded, still directed the successful defense of his company's position; and SSgt Edward Carter, who killed six German soldiers in hand-to-hand combat (Lanning 1997: 186). These soldiers finally received the Congressional Medal of

Honor in 1997. According to the historiography of blacks in the military (Foner 1974; Nalty 1986; Lanning 1997; Edgerton 2001; Buckley 2001), this experience helped pave the way for the eventual end of racial segregation in the Army in the post-war years.

Blacks in the Second World War Army Air Force

The most memorable black participants in the Second World War were the "Tuskegee Airmen," who made up the 99th Pursuit (Fighter) Squadron of the US Army Air Force. Access to military aviation was the most prized goal of those who wanted blacks to fight in the war. The Army Air Force initially resisted giving flight training to blacks. Nevertheless, First Lady Eleanor Roosevelt, the NAACP, and the black press reminded the Army of its promise to open all its branches to blacks. Consequently the Army Air Force in January 1941 opened a flight-training school at Tuskegee Institute to form the 99th Pursuit Squadron of black combat pilots (Lanning 1997: 191). When enough black pilots had been trained, Capt. Benjamin O. Davis, Jr, who had passed the flight course, was promoted to colonel and chosen to command the squadron. According to Lanning, he was the obvious choice since he was the most senior black officer qualified to fly (Lanning 1997: 192).

By October 1942, the 99th squadron was ready for combat, but the Army Air Force, true to its belief in black inferiority, would not send it to battle. Again the NAACP and other black leaders protested. Judge Hastie resigned his War Department position in protest and Eleanor Roosevelt applied backstage pressure to force the Army to send the black aviators to combat (Lanning 1997: 193). This protest plus manpower shortages caused the Army to send the renamed 99th Fighter Squadron to North Africa in April 1943. It was attached to the 33rd Fighter Group, who ignored it, scorned it, and refused to train with it. Despite this, the black pilots showed their mettle, engaging German aircraft on 80 percent of their missions. This performance refuted the Army's contention that the 99th squadron's pilots were lazy and cowardly. Despite this, the Army Air Force attempted to disestablish the 99th or take it out of combat. That was stopped by domestic political considerations and by Benjamin Davis' testimony to a War Department advisory committee on black soldiers, skillfully refuting charges made against his command (Lanning 1997: 195; Nalty 1986: 151–2).

The 99th fighter squadron distinguished itself in the invasion of Anzio, Italy, by shooting down eight enemy aircraft, more than any other squadron. Meanwhile, more black aviators and ground crew had been trained at Tuskegee and elsewhere, and they formed the 100th, 301st, and 302nd fighter squadrons. Along with the 99th, these squadrons comprised the 332nd fighter group with the now-veteran combat pilot Benjamin Davis commanding it. This black fighter unit escorted US bombers deep into German territory and lost no bombers to German fighters. They were the only air group with this distinction. The 99th fighter squadron itself won three distinguished unit citations and the 332nd fighter group won one. During the war, black fighter pilots flew close to 1,600 missions and shot down 261 enemy aircraft (Lanning 1997: 196). They accomplished this despite an Army Air Force high command that continually degraded them and used them in combat only due to pressure from the black community.

Black Sailors and Marines

The historiography of the black naval experience in the Second World War emphasizes the demeaning and frustrating existence of blacks in that service. Most accounts tell the story of Dorie Miller, one of the initial heroes of the Second World War, as an example of the Navy's racist attitudes. Miller, a messman aboard the battleship USS *West Virginia,* during the Pearl Harbor attack pulled his mortally wounded commanding officer to a safe place, then manned a nearby anti-aircraft gun and shot down at least two Japanese aircraft. Miller's heroism disproved the Navy's contention that the stupidity and cowardice of blacks fitted them only for servant duty aboard warships. Instead of publicizing Dorie Miller's heroic acts, the Navy covered them up for almost a year. Then, after pressure from the black press, the Navy awarded Miller its second highest honor, the Navy Cross. Yet the Navy kept him in the messman branch. He, along with hundreds of other sailors, died in 1943 in the sinking of the escort carrier *Liscombe Bay* (Lanning 1997: 198–9).

In 1942 the navy reluctantly agreed to enlist blacks in a wider array of specialties. These included radioman, boatswain's mate, radarman, gunner's mate, and similar ratings. Yet the navy was adamant about preserving racial segregation aboard its ships, something it could do with black messmen, who could be berthed in remote parts of the ship. Therefore, enlisted blacks enlisted under the new more open policy were confined to shore duty, where they could be more easily segregated. Not surprisingly, black enlistments remained low. In 1943 there were only 26,000 blacks in the Navy, only 2 percent of the total. Two-thirds were still stewards; the rest were confined to shore duty or labor jobs (Lanning 1997: 201). Most of these laboring jobs involved the loading and unloading of ammunition ships.

As more blacks were drafted into the Navy, that service somewhat relaxed its rigid policies of racial exclusion and segregation. For example, in January 1944 a special all-black Navy Officer's Candidate School opened at the Great Lakes, Illinois Naval Station. Nalty and Lanning explain that the Navy could open this school because it now had enough black men for black officers to command. Paul Stilwell's *The Golden Thirteen* (1993) is a moving oral history of the black naval officer candidates, the story told by the graduates themselves. As the war went on, more black officers were commissioned, including such future notables as Carl Rowan and Samuel Gravely, later the first black admiral. Buckley pays special attention to Carl Rowan (Buckley 2001: 309; Lanning 1997: 207). The war ended before many of them could see combat.

In 1944 Secretary of the Navy James Forrestal, a liberal attorney and member of the Urban League, provided blacks with more opportunities for service. By now there were enough black sailors to man the destroyer escort *Mason* and the submarine chaser *PC-1264.* These ships were commanded by white officers but had all-black crews. Both performed very well in the North Atlantic, protecting convoys from German U-boats, and convinced the Navy that blacks could handle at-sea combat jobs. To see whether at-sea integration would work, blacks were assigned on a desegregated basis to a number of naval auxiliary vessels. According to Nalty, this experiment was a success, and prompted Secretary Forrestal to believe that racial segregation in the Navy was the least efficient use of manpower and it intensified rather than eased racial tensions (Nalty 1986: 193–5). As the war ended the Navy assigned black and white recruits to racially desegregated boot camps.

The Marine Corps reluctantly accepted black enlistees in the spring of 1942. Lanning, Nalty, and Foner explain that the Marines assigned the vast majority of black enlistees to racially segregated service and labor units. Though non-combatant, these units did come under fire in the Pacific as they unloaded supplies and ammunition on island beaches like Tarawa and Iwo Jima, which the Marines had wrested from the Japanese. The Marine Corps did form two black combat battalions, the 51st and 52nd air defense battalions, but these units saw no combat as they were sent to islands the Marines had already captured. The Marines enlisted less than 20,000 blacks, making up 5 percent of their total force (Foner 1974: 173; Nalty 1986: 199–202; Lanning 1997: 212–13).

Black Women and the Military during the Second World War

Black women were even more marginalized in the armed forces during the First and Second World Wars than black men. The literature reflects this, as the major works on blacks in the military make only passing mention of black women. Martha Putney's *When the Nation Was in Need: Blacks in the Women's Army Corps During World War II* (1992) is the most known work on the topic. *Bitter Fruit: Black Women in World War II*, an anthology edited by Maureen Honey (1999), while only indirectly touching on black military women, is another major work.

Only 18 black women were allowed to serve in the Army Nurse Corps during the First World War and only in segregated hospitals. In the Second World War, although the Women's Army Corps (WACS) was supposed to have a quota of 10 percent black female officers and enlisted women, the numbers of black women never exceeded 6 percent. In the last months of the war, just 120 black female officers and 3,961 black enlisted were serving in the WACS (Lanning 1997: 183). Like their male counterparts, they were racially segregated in Army facilities and job assignments, and excluded from promotion and overseas duty. They were confined to menial stateside clerical jobs (ibid: 183; Foner 1974: 165). Only after much protest from black leaders was a black female unit sent overseas. This was the 688th Central Postal Directory Battalion, which was sent to Europe in February 1945 to assist in mail delivery to US troops in Europe (Foner 1974: 166; Lanning 1997: 183).

The Army Nurse Corps was as unwelcoming in the Second World War as in the first. By 1945, less than 500 black women were Army nurses. This was only 1 percent of the total number of nurses (Lanning 1997: 184). Again they were confined to racially segregated army hospitals and denied choice assignments and promotions (Foner 1974: 166). Only a few black nurses made it overseas, 30 going to Liberia and 63 going to England. This latter group cared for German prisoners of war (Lanning 1997: 184). Black women were less welcome in the Navy, as their Women Accepted for Volunteer Emergency Service (WAVES) refused to accept black enlistees until late 1944 when President Roosevelt, needing black votes for his reelection, ordered the WAVES to accept black applicants. The WAVES did not vigorously recruit blacks, and black women were reluctant to join. Consequently at the war's end there were only 2 black female officers and 70 black enlisted women in the WAVES (ibid: 185).

The historiographical consensus (Edgerton 2001; Buckley 2001; Lanning 1997; Nalty 1986; Foner 1974; Dalfiume 1969) is that the repression of black troops did not prevent them from fighting well in both world wars. According to these authors, most black soldiers hoped that their bravery on the battlefield would convince whites that blacks were equal and could take advantage of the opportunities provided in the Armed Forces. This hope came true as the courage black soldiers showed in fighting for a country that disdained them, plus the unremitting support of the black leadership, persuaded the Armed Forces to desegregate in the immediate post-war era. This consensus has remained little changed over the years.

More work needs to be done in the field of twentieth-century black military history, especially in explaining why whites were so adamantly against full African American participation in the First and Second World Wars, and why this prospect terrified them so much. There should be more studies on the day-to-day activities of black soldiers and sailors. Even more work needs to be done on black female personnel in the Armed Forces. There is a need for more works such as Stilwell's *The Golden Thirteen*, Honey's *Bitter Fruit*, Motley's *The Invisible Soldier*, and McGuire's *Taps for A Jim Crow Army* – all first-hand accounts from blacks serving in the Armed Forces during the Second World War. This need is more urgent than ever as the Second World War generation is dying out. There should be more accounts of how and why blacks responded as they did to the treatment they received in wartime service. Nevertheless, the historiography of black soldiers in both world wars has performed an invaluable service in restoring their brave struggle to historical memory.

BIBLIOGRAPHY

Works Cited

Buckley, Gail (2001) *American Patriots: The Story of Blacks in the Military from the Revolution to Desert Storm*. New York: Random House.
Cooper, Michael (1997) *Hellfighters: African American Soldiers in World War I*. New York: Lodestar Books.
Dalfiume, Richard M. (1969) *Desegregation of the Armed Forces: Fighting on Two Fronts, 1939–1953*. Columbia: University of Missouri Press.
Edgerton, Robert B. (2001) *Hidden Heroism: Black Soldiers in America's War*. Boulder, CO: Westview Press.
Foner, Jack (1974) *Blacks and the Military in American History*. New York: Praeger.
Fussell, Paul (2003) *The Boy's Crusade*. New York: Modern Library.
Henri, Florette and Stillman, Richard Joseph (1970) *Bitter Victory: A History of Black Soldiers in World War I*. Garden City, NY: Doubleday.
Lanning, Michael Lee (1997) *The African American Soldier*. Secaucus, NJ: Birch Lane Press.
McGuire, Phillip (1993) *Taps for a Jim Crow Army*. Lexington: University Press of Kentucky.
Nalty, Bernard C. (1986) *Strength for the Fight: A History of Black Americans in the Military*. New York: Free Press.
Stilwell, Paul (1993) *The Golden Thirteen: Recollections of the First Black Naval Officers*. Annapolis, MD: U.S. Naval Institute Press.
Weinberg, Gerhard L. (1994) *A World at Arms*. Cambridge: Cambridge University Press.

Suggestions for Further Reading

Barbeau, Arthur E. and Florette, Henri (1974) *The Unknown Soldiers; Black American Troops in World War I*. Philadelphia: Temple University Press.

Biggs, Bradley (1986) *The Triple Nickels: America's First All-Black Paratroop Unit*. Hamden, CT: Archon Books.

Brandt, Nat (1996) *Harlem at War: The Black Experience in WW II*. Syracuse, NY: Syracuse University Press.

Buchanan, A. Russell (1977) *Black Americans in World War II*. Santa Barbara, CA: Clio Books.

Davis, Benjamin O., Jr (1991) *Benjamin O. Davis, American*. Washington, DC: Smithsonian Institution Press.

Dunn, James A. (1996) *On Board the USS Mason: The World War II Diary of James A. Dunn*, Mansel G. Blackford (ed.). Columbus: Ohio State University Press.

Farrar, Hayward (1998) *The Baltimore Afro-American, 1892–1950*. Westport, CT: Greenwood Press.

Ferguson, William C. (1987) *Black Flyers in World War II*. Cleveland, OH: W. C. Ferguson.

Finkle, Lee H. (1975) *Forum for Protest: The Black Press during World War II*. East Rutherford, NJ: Fairleigh Dickinson University Press.

Fleming, Thomas (2003) *The Illusion of Victory: America in World War I*. New York: Basic Books.

Fletcher, Marvin (1974) *The Negro Soldier and the United States Army, 1891–1970*. Columbia: University of Missouri Press.

Francis, Charles E. (1955) *The Tuskegee Airmen: The Story of the Negro in the U.S. Air Force*. Boston: Bruce Humphries.

Hargrove, Hendon (1985) *Buffalo Soldiers in Italy: Black Americans in World War II*. Jefferson, NC: McFarland.

Harris, Paul N. (1963) *Base Company 16*. New York: Vantage Press.

Harrod, Frederick S. (1979) "Integration of the Navy (1941–1978)," *U.S. Naval Institute Proceedings* 105 (October): 41–7.

Honey, Maureen (1999) *Bitter Fruit: Black Women in World War II*. Columbia: University of Missouri Press.

Kellogg, Charles Flint (1967) *NAACP: A History of the National Association for the Advancement of Colored People, Vol. 1: 1909–1920*. Baltimore: Johns Hopkins University Press.

Kelly, Mary Pat (1995) *Proudly We Served: The Men of the* USS Mason. Annapolis, MD: U.S. Naval Institute Press.

Kirby, John (1982) *Black Americans in the Roosevelt Era*. Knoxville: University of Tennessee Press.

Lee, Ulysses (1994) *The Employment of Negro Troops*. Washington, DC: Center for Military History.

Luszki, Walter A. (1991) *A Rape of Justice: MacArthur and the New Guinea Hangings*. Lanham, MD: Madison Books.

McGregor, Morris J. (1989) *Integration of the Armed Forces 1949–1965*. Washington, DC: Center for Military History.

Mead, Gary (2000) *The Doughboys: American and the First World War*. New York: Overlook Press.

Motley, Mary P. (ed.) (1975) *The Invisible Soldier: The Experience of the Black Soldier, World War II*. Detroit: Wayne State University Press.

Murphy, John D. (1997) *The Freeman Field Mutiny: A Study in Leadership*. Maxwell Airforce Base, AL: Air Command and Staff College.

Nalty, Bernard C. (1995) *The Right to Fight: African-American Marines in World War II*. Washington, DC: History and Museums Division, Headquarters, U.S. Marine Corps.

Nelson, Dennis D. (1948) *The Integration of the Negro into the U.S. Navy 1776–1947.* Washington, DC: Navy Department.

Parrish, Noel Francis (1947) *The Segregation of Negroes in the Army Air Forces.* Maxwell Airforce Base, AL: Air Command and Staff College, May.

Perret, Geoffrey (1991) *There Is a War to Be Won: The United States Army in World War II.* New York: Ballantine Books.

Potter, Lou, Miles, William, and Rosenblum, Nina (1992) *Liberators: Fighting on Two Fronts in World War II.* New York: Harcourt Brace Jovanovich.

Putney, Martha S. (1992) *When the Nation Was in Need: Blacks in the Women's Army Corps during World War II.* Metuchen, NJ: Scarecrow Press.

Samuelson, Hyman (1995) *Love, War, and the 96th Engineers (Colored): The World War II New Guinea Diaries of Captain Hyman Samuelson,* Gwendolyn Hall (ed.). Urbana: University of Illinois Press.

Smith, Graham A. (1988) *When Jim Crow Met John Bull: Black American Soldiers in World War II Britain.* New York: St. Martin's Press.

Sweeney, William Allison (1969) *History of the American Negro in the Great World War; His Splendid Record in the Battle Zones of Europe.* New York: Negro Universities Press.

—— *This Is Our War* (1945) Baltimore: Afro-American Company.

Trice, Craig A. (1997) *The Men that Served with Distinction: the 761st Tank Battalion.* Fort Leavenworth, KS: Army Command and General Staff College, School of Advanced Military Studies.

Washburn, Patrick (1986) *A Question of Sedition: The Federal Government's Investigation of the Black Press during World War II.* New York: Oxford University Press.

Williams, Charles Halston (1970) *Negro Soldiers in World War I: The Human Side.* New York: AMS Press.

Wynn, Neil A. (1975) *The Afro-American and the Second World War.* New York: Holmes & Meier.

CHAPTER TWENTY-TWO

Identity, Patriotism, and Protest on the Wartime Home Front, 1917–19, 1941–5

HAYWARD "WOODY" FARRAR

Fighting for one's country is one of the markers of citizenship. Since American citizenship for African Americans has always been problematic for the white majority, black participation in the armed forces has been problematic as well. African American servicemen were either not welcome in America's armed forces or grudgingly enlisted to serve in secondary and racially segregated roles. This made it difficult for many blacks to feel as patriotic as whites.

Nevertheless, the black elite – speaking through the black press and protest organizations such as the NAACP – agitated for full African American participation in the armed forces during the First and Second World Wars. They believed that brave service in these wars would convince whites to grant civil and social equality to African Americans. Despite continuing and frustrating opposition from "the white power structure" in both world wars, and apathy in the black community, black leaders went on struggling to expand opportunities for blacks in the military.

The historiography of blacks on the home front in the First and Second World Wars parallels that of black soldiers in the military. The major works in that field describe the civilian black community's responses to these wars. In all these works, the black community's ambivalence towards fighting for a country that disdained them is highlighted. There are more detailed accounts of the black community's attitudes towards the military in Jordan's *Black Newspapers and America's War for Democracy, 1914–1920* (2001), Finkle's *Forum For Protest: The Black Press during World War II* (1975), and Washburn's *A Question of Sedition: The Federal Government's Investigation of the Black Press During World II* (1986). These historians chronicle black newspapers' coverage of the First and Second World Wars and the response they received from their readers and the federal government. The black press represented the views of the black elite and the community that they aspired to lead. The dilemmas that blacks faced in dealing with the wars were reflected in the pages of black newspapers. Of the major studies, Jordan's is the most comprehensive look at the black press in wartime. Three studies of individual black publishers and newspapers are Buni's *Robert L. Vann of the* Pittsburgh Courier, Farrar's *The Baltimore* Afro-American, *1892–1950* and Suggs' *P. B. Young, Newspaperman: Race, Politics, and Journalism in the New South*. They detail how these newspapers shaped and reflected black community opinion of the two world wars. Nat Brandt's *Harlem at War* takes that community as representative of black America's response to the Second World War.

African American Attitudes Towards the First World War

According to Jordan's *Black Newspapers and America's War for Democracy*, "historians have been deeply divided over how to characterize the black response to this [the First World War] war" (Jordan 2001: 5). He contends that some historians, such as Barbeau and Henri in *The Unknown Soldiers: Black American Troops in World War I* (1974), state that the black community generally approved of W. E. B. Du Bois' idea of "closing ranks" behind America's war effort in the hope of winning post-war racial equality (ibid: 192). In contrast, Jordan cites other historians such as Kornweibel, who in "Apathy and dissent: black America's negative responses to World War I" (1981) estimated that almost half of America's black community opposed the war (Jordan 2001: 172).

Farrar (1998) points out that the Baltimore *Afro-American* expressed the ambivalence of African Americans towards the First World War when the newspaper commented that blacks were not as willing to fight for the United States as they had been at the start of the Spanish American War (Farrar 1998: 158). Jordan states that black newspapers such as the New York *Age* and the Chicago *Defender* blasted President Woodrow Wilson for hypocrisy in fighting against German atrocities and for democracy in Europe, while allowing white racist tyranny and violence in the South (Jordan 2001: 76–7). On the other hand, Buni points out that the Pittsburgh *Courier* strongly supported America's entry into the war (Buni 1974: 101–3). So did P. B. Young, publisher of the Norfolk *Journal and Guide* (Suggs 1988: 37). Historian Lewis Suggs asserts that "blacks throughout Virginia reacted favorably to Young's philosophy and supported the war effort in the hope that their loyalty would be rewarded by an improvement in their conditions" (ibid: 37).

Testing the patriotism of African Americans was the riot in East St. Louis, Illinois, in early July 1917, which was marked by open combat between blacks and whites. At least 39 blacks and 8 whites were killed, hundreds more were injured and millions of dollars' worth of damage was done. Henri's *Black Migration* explains that the riot was the result of animosity between black migrants and white workers, competing for jobs in a city already straining to meet the demands of wartime production (Henri 1975: 224). Black leaders traveled to Washington to petition President Woodrow Wilson to deal with the causes of the riot (Farrar 1998: 125), but he refused to see them. Then in late July 1917 black New Yorkers conducted a "silent march" to question the nation's commitment to fighting for democracy overseas while denying it to blacks at home (Jordan 2001: 98). Meanwhile black newspapers, such as the Norfolk *Journal and Guide*, New York *Age*, Chicago *Defender*, and Baltimore *Afro-American*, denounced the government's inaction concerning the riot, again pointing out the government's hypocrisy in fighting a war for democracy overseas while ignoring it at home (ibid: 86–9). Oddly, neither Farrar nor Suggs mentions these denunciations in their studies of the *Afro-American* and the *Journal and Guide* (Farrar 1998: 125; Suggs 1988: 37).

All this time the activities of black leaders, such as Chicago black journalists Robert Abbott and Ferdinand Barnett who spoke out against the violence, were monitored by the Bureau of Investigation (Kornweibel 2002: 120–1; Fleming 2003: 108–12). In such a climate it was no wonder that blacks were lukewarm about fighting in the First World War. Not helping matters were the plans by the War Department and the Navy Department to minimize black participation. For example, no plans were made for training or commissioning black army officers. Only those black officers attached to the traditional black units would be retained. The Marine Corps barred black enlistments and the Navy restricted blacks to service as stewards or messmen. White southerners were aghast at the idea of armed black soldiers and treated those in their midst with disdain and hatred. This was seen in the Houston, Texas incident in the summer of 1917, where black soldiers of the 24th infantry regiment, who were taunted and goaded beyond reason by racist Houstonites, went berserk and shot up the city, leaving 15 dead and 20 wounded (Jordan 2001: 92–3; Nalty 1986: 102–4).

Jordan asserts that black leaders had to walk a tightrope concerning the Houston riot. While they understood that white racist behavior goaded the black troops into shooting up Houston, they could not openly condone the troops' actions. They did not want "the white power structure" to question the loyalty of African Americans in wartime, yet they did not want to alienate their readers who were enraged at the treatment of black soldiers in the South. The Richmond *Planet*, Norfolk *Journal and Guide*, Cleveland *Gazette,* Chicago *Defender*, Baltimore *Afro-American*, and Pittsburgh *Courier* denounced the mutinous soldiers (Jordan 2001: 96). Jordan quotes the *Courier* stating "That soldiers who participate in lawlessness must take the consequences" (ibid: 96). Nevertheless, they also blamed the Houston police and racist Houstonites for goading the soldiers to riot (ibid: 97). The Baltimore *Afro-American* called the soldiers "victims of southern copperheads and crackers who baited them on" (Farrar 1998: 158), while Jordan quotes the Cleveland *Gazette* as blaming the riot on a "Texas mob of lynch-murderers" (Jordan 2001: 97).

Following the Houston riot, 118 black soldiers were charged with mutiny and court-martialed, beginning in December 1917. The result was that 19 of the regiment were hanged and 41 sentenced to life. These harsh sentences enraged blacks, who through their newspapers expressed their opposition (Nalty 1986: 101–6). Had the NAACP and the black press not intensely lobbied the Army, more black soldiers would have been executed for their part in the Houston riot (Nalty 1986: 105–6). This was an example of how pressure from the black leadership elite during the First World War influenced, however slightly, the US military high command.

The armed forces' indifference to African Americans did not prevent the NAACP and other elements of the black elite from agitating for greater black participation in the war. For example, in response to the Army's plans not to commission new black officers, Joel Spingarn of the NAACP led efforts to persuade the War Department to open a racially segregated training camp to train black Army officers. The War Department did so, but the black community responded with indifference as only 250 men volunteered for this camp (Farrar 1998: 158). Quite a few black newspapers, including the Washington *Bee*, Chicago *Defender*, Cleveland *Gazette*, Baltimore

Afro-American and New York *Age,* opposed Jim-Crow training camps and approved of the lack of black volunteers for Army officer training.

Racial segregation in the armed forces continued to alienate African Americans throughout this period. The *Age* said: "We do not deem it wise on our part to voluntarily segregate ourselves or permit our friends to do it for us" (Jordan 2001: 81). According to Jordan, this opposition masked a dilemma facing the black leadership. Although they wanted a racially integrated army, they also wanted greater black participation in the war, even if segregated. Faced with segregated training camps for black officers or none at all, black leaders accepted the War Department's decision. They pointed out that African Americans had to have a role in the armed forces, even a racially segregated one, if they were to credibly pursue their demands for full citizenship and equality (ibid: 81–2). Black newspapers such as the Cleveland *Gazette* and the Baltimore *Afro-American*, which opposed the camp, changed their minds and enthusiastically supported those blacks accepted for officer training. For example, the *Gazette* proclaimed that each black officer trainee would "have a proud heritage to pass down to one's children," while the *Afro-American* ran weekly articles describing the activities of black officer candidates (ibid: 81; Farrar 1998: 158).

Black leaders continued to agitate to open the armed forces to black participation and to get their constituents to take advantage of the new opportunities. The NAACP, especially, supported the war effort. Its president Joel Spingarn helped establish the black officers' training camp, while W. E. B. Du Bois, editor of the NAACP's magazine *The Crisis*, published numerous articles supporting African American participation in the war. Du Bois believed that the war was a struggle for worldwide democracy and that an Allied victory would bring self-determination to the world's people of color. Full black participation in this struggle would ensure their gaining freedom and equality in post-war America. He best expressed this sentiment in his famous "Close ranks" editorial in June 1918:

> We of the colored race have no ordinary interest in the outcome. That which the German power represents today spells death to the aspirations of Negroes and all the darker races for equality freedom and democracy. Let us not hesitate. Let us while this war lasts, forget our special grievances and close our ranks shoulder to shoulder with our white fellow citizens and the allied nations that are fighting for democracy. We make no ordinary sacrifice, but we make it gladly and willingly with our eyes lifted to the hills. (W. E. B. Du Bois, "Close ranks," *The Crisis*, 16 (July 1918): 111, cited in Lewis 1993: 556)

Those comments provoked a significant amount of criticism, reflecting the ambivalence of the black community towards the war. Some black newspapers, such as the New York *Age* and the Washington *Bee*, considered Du Bois' words an attack on their criticisms of racism in the armed forces and accused him of currying favor with the Army so that he could secure an officer's commission (Kellogg 1967: 271–2). Other newspapers, such as the *Journal and Guide* and the Richmond *Planet*, supported Du Bois (Suggs 1988: 37; Jordan 2001: 131).

One of the reasons why Du Bois wrote the "Close ranks" editorial, some scholars speculate, was that *The Crisis* was targeted for investigation by the Justice Department, which was monitoring black newspapers' expressions of the black community's attitudes towards the war. The Bureau of Investigation (BI) investigated Robert Abbott, publisher of the era's leading black newspaper, the Chicago *Defender* (Washburn 1986: 17). The *Defender* loudly condemned all instances of domestic and military racism. It vociferously encouraged southern blacks who were the victims of Jim-Crow, peonage, disfranchisement, lynchings, or race riots to come north, where jobs and freedom awaited them. Millions heeded the *Defender's* call. This made the newspaper very unpopular in the South as African American migration from that area deprived it of its cheap labor force and racial scapegoats. Only after Abbott offered to encourage *Defender* readers to buy war bonds and purchased some himself as proof of his patriotism did he and his newspaper avoid prosecution for sedition (ibid: 17).

However, the government was not through with Abbott. In 1918, Major Walter Loving, a black officer in charge of monitoring the black community for the Military Intelligence Branch of the Army, again warned the *Defender* of terrible consequences if it did not tone down its criticisms of military racism (Washburn 1986: 17–18). Abbott wrote a contrite letter to Loving that defused the situation. Meanwhile the Baltimore *Afro-American* and the St Louis *Argus* were both told by the Justice Department to reduce their militancy concerning the war (ibid: 17–18). As a result the *Afro*, in an editorial dated July 26, 1918, defended Du Bois' "Close ranks" position. It stated that, since the Justice Department was strictly enforcing the Espionage Act by prosecuting what it thought were seditious newspaper statements, the *Afro*, *The Crisis*, and other black publications had to tone down their comments concerning race relations. According to the newspaper, "For the present he [Du Bois] and we [the *Afro*] have got to be quiescent even tho [*sic*] not acquiescent in the government's programs for the Negro" (Farrar 1998: 152).

On two occasions the government did more than just warn black journalists. In 1917 G. W. Bouldin, editor of the San Antonio *Inquirer,* was sentenced to two years in a Federal penitentiary for sedition, for an article his newspaper published that harshly criticized the Army's handling of the Houston riot. Then, in 1918, A. Phillip Randolph and Chandler Owen, editors of the black socialist magazine *The Messenger*, were charged with treason for their magazine's anti-war articles. Although the charges against it were dropped, *The Messenger* lost its second-class mailing privileges.

Realizing that a supportive African American population would enhance the war effort, the Creel Committee on Public Information, along with the War Department, sponsored a conference in Washington DC in June 1918 to discuss how the black press could best aid the war effort. This conference, chaired by Emmett J. Scott, special assistant for Negro affairs to the Secretary of War, was attended by nearly every prominent black publisher and journalist. The conference also resulted in an anti-lynching statement by President Wilson and the commissioning of Ralph Tyler, a black journalist from Columbus, Ohio, to serve as a war correspondent for the black press. From then on most, if not all, of the stories in the black press concerning the First World War extolled the bravery of black soldiers. When black troops went overseas in 1918, black newspapers such as the *Afro-American* used articles sent by black soldiers, and by war correspondent for the black press Ralph Tyler, to cover their activities (Farrar 1998: 159; Jordan 2001: 122–3).

Despite persecution the black press continued, though in a more muted fashion, to protest against civilian and military racism (Washburn 1986: 20–1). This government muting of black newspaper criticism deprived more militant opponents of the war a voice. Yet, Washburn asserts that the black press was viewed by the government, particularly the Justice Department, as radical and subversive (Washburn 1986: 29).

It was the hope of blacks and their leaders that their display of patriotism during the First World War would be rewarded. Such was the case, as the United States erupted in a series of race riots and lynching. Riots in Washington, DC, and Chicago, among other places, left scores of African Americans killed or injured, and made problematic the black community's physical survival in America. Especially demoralizing was the lynching of returning black soldiers, some while still in uniform. The economic gains made by northern blacks during the war were crippled by the displacement of black workers by returning white veterans, while the South rededicated itself to excluding and segregating its black population. The black community, speaking through its newspaper, vigorously condemned the racism that caused the riots. Their criticisms subjected them to continuous scrutiny by the Justice Department, which in 1919 was conducting a witch-hunt against all those suspected of leftist thought and leanings (Jordan 2001: 144–55; Washburn 1987: 20–9).

Jordan, whose book is the most comprehensive account of the black press's representation of black community attitudes during the First World War, contends that while some historians considered the black press too acquiescent during the First World War but militant during the Second World War, the reality is far more complex. He asserts that these newspapers had to express their readers' dissatisfaction with military and domestic racism, but do it in such a way that it would not discourage the community from supporting the war or cause the government to shut these newspapers down. To resolve this dilemma, Jordan claims that black publishers conducted an early version of the "Double V" campaign carried on by the black press in the Second World War (Jordan 2001: 163–8). Publicizing and criticizing domestic and military racism, while supporting black soldiers and the war effort in general, was the way out and the black press succeeded in gaining some concessions from an intransigent system (ibid: 163–8).

After the First World War, the armed forces continued to marginalize African Americans. The Army disbanded the 92nd and 93rd divisions. The four traditional all-black regiments were retained, though stationed in remote forts. The Navy, which had enlisted blacks to be only stewards or mess cooks, decided to bar African Americans from enlisting altogether, while the Marines continued to bar blacks. Racial segregation and exclusion in the armed forces continued in the 1930s. All the services justified this exclusion by stating that, since racial segregation and exclusion were the norm in American life, to go against that would degrade military efficiency as white soldiers would never serve alongside black soldiers nor would they take orders from black officers. Furthermore the armed forces believed that blacks were too lazy, stupid, and cowardly to make good soldiers; marines, sailors, or aviators.

These policies incensed the black leadership, who, as the Second World War approached the United States, strongly believed that full black participation in the military was necessary for black advancement. Guided by these principles, African

American organizations pressured the Army to recruit its quota of blacks. The Baltimore *Afro-American* and the Pittsburgh *Courier* led the advocacy of quotas to ensure black participation in the Army. While not approving of racial segregation in the Army, the *Courier*, for example, was willing to accept it if the Army opened up 10 percent of its force to blacks. Their segregation in all-black units was preferable to complete exclusion. In pursuit of that goal, the *Courier* organized the Committee for the Participation of Negroes in the National Defense. This committee – consisting of representatives from black fraternities, American Legion Posts, the YMCA, the Negro Reserve Officers Association, and the Association for the Study of Negro Life and History – lobbied the government for the establishment of black Army recruiting quotas (Dalfiume 1969: 26; Finkle 1975: 130, 132).

The Norfolk *Journal and Guide*, the New York *Amsterdam News*, and the Savannah *Tribune* initially supported the draft, with its black quota. The *Tribune* commented that, since segregation was still the norm, the establishment of black combat jobs and units was a great advance for the black community (Finkle 1975: 147). The Chicago *Defender*, however, opposed the draft. It claimed that conscription would not ensure full black participation in the armed forces but would be used as a tool to silence black opposition to domestic and military racial abuses (Farrar 1998: 166). The Baltimore *Afro-American*, a fervent supporter of the draft to achieve both preparedness and racial justice, began to have second thoughts once the Draft Act was passed (ibid: 166).

The *Afro-American* was not alone in its about-face on the issue of black participation in the armed forces. Indeed the President's acceptance of racial segregation was opposed by most black newspapers and community organizations, such as the NAACP, and black leaders such as A. Phillip Randolph and Mary McLeod Bethune. This opposition seemed puzzling since they had, for three years, placed a higher priority on increasing the numbers of blacks in the Army than on ensuring that these blacks served in racially-mixed units. Yet once the goal of increased black participation had been reached, the black community now crusaded for what it *really* wanted [*italics mine*], which was a complete end to racial segregation in the armed forces (Farrar 1998: 166–7).

Roosevelt's endorsement of racial segregation in the Army, and the Navy's refusal to change its Jim-Crow policies, threatened to drive black voters into the arms of the Republican Party for the 1940 presidential elections. Their candidate, Wendell Willkie, called for an end to racial segregation in the armed forces. Consequently, the *Courier* and the *Afro-American* endorsed Willkie for President. Meanwhile Walter White, head of the NAACP, complained to Roosevelt about his failure to move the armed forces further towards desegregation. Fearful of losing his grip on the black vote, which could be decisive in closely contested northern states, President Roosevelt just before the election reiterated that all branches of the Army would be open to black soldiers. He then promoted Colonel Benjamin O. Davis, Sr to brigadier general and appointed the Dean of Howard Law School, William Hastie, to the post of civilian aide to the Secretary of War. Hastie had worked very closely with the NAACP and was considered their representative at the War Department. Both appointees were to be advisors on African American issues in the Army. This was enough to retain the black vote for Roosevelt (Foner 1974: 135–7; Nalty 1986: 136–42).

In 1935, African Americans were concerned not only by the approaching war from Europe but also by the Italian conquest of Ethiopia. The black leadership, as represented by the NAACP and the black press, was generally supportive of Ethiopia's fight with the Italians. However, there was some ambivalence as expressed by the *Courier, Afro-American, Amsterdam News* and *Defender*. These papers felt that black Americans must make their problems at home the priority. The *Defender* asked why should black Americans "go to a country in which you have neither friend, nor kin, nor common tongue . . . Is there enough here to fight for?" Also, they considered Ethiopia a backward civilization. Meriweather recounts how the *Courier* called Ethiopia's army "semi-barbaric" and the *Amsterdam News* called that army's leaders "savage chieftains." But the rank and file in the black community saw things differently. They were more Afro-centric than the black elite and saw the Italian takeover of Ethiopia as a threat to the freedom of blacks everywhere. They pressured their leaders to more vigorously support Ethiopia's defense (Meriweather 2002).

Meriweather quotes an NAACP member asking why its leaders "remain idle and the golden opportunity pass to regain our Black Kingdom" (Meriweather 2002: 43). As a result, according to Meriweather, the black press responded with intensified coverage of the Ethiopian invasion that gave a positive and optimistic spin on events (ibid: 46). The *Afro,* for example, secured first-hand reports from its on-scene reporter, A. B. Abdelmalik, who regularly sent reports of the fighting. The *Courier,* which earlier had disparaged efforts to aid Ethiopia, sent J. A. Rogers to cover the war (ibid: 44; Farrar 1998: 163). After the Italian conquest of Ethiopia in 1936, the black community's concern diminished. Still, as Meriweather contends, Ethiopia's plight did strike a responsive chord in African Americans and laid the foundation for a growing interest in African affairs (Meriweather 2002: 53–6).

As injurious to the wartime African American community as racial exclusion and segregation in the Armed Forces was the exclusion from employment in the fast-growing defense industries. These industries were lifting the country out of the Great Depression, and African Americans had to be included in this process if they too were to recover economically. With that in mind, A. Phillip Randolph, head of the Brotherhood of Sleeping Car Workers, campaigned against racial discrimination in defense industries. This campaign culminated in the March On Washington Movement, which planned a mass march of African Americans on the capital in the summer of 1941. The *Afro-American* called on black organizations, such as the NAACP and the Elks, to hold their conventions in Washington on the date of the march so their members could join it (Farrar 1998: 95). The NAACP did endorse the March On Washington at its annual meeting and promised to mobilize its members in support (Lanning 1997: 168).

Fearful of the disruption the march would cause, the Federal government in early 1941 started dealing with racial exclusion in defense industries. For example, in June 1941 President Roosevelt directed the Office of Production Management to end the exclusion of blacks from defense employment. This was not enough to satisfy A. Phillip Randolph, the chief coordinator of the March on Washington Movement, or his supporters and they continued organizing the march (Lanning 1997: 168). The March on Washington was called off after President Roosevelt, on the eve of the event, issued Executive Order 8802, which directed all government departments and agencies concerned with defense preparedness to eliminate any racial discrimination in employment (Farrar 1998: 95). It also ordered all defense contractors to carry a clause in their contracts pledging not to discriminate on the basis of race in their employment practices (ibid: 95). It established the Fair Employment Practices Committee (FEPC), which was to hear complaints of violations of Executive Order 8802, redress grievances, and recommend enforcement measures to federal agencies (Finkle 1975: 97; Farrar 1998: 95; Lanning 1997: 168).

Blacks hoped Executive Order 8802 and the FEPC would force defense contractors to hire black workers. However, they were not enough to immediately open defense employers to black employment. The committee had little real power to compel defense contractors to hire blacks since the government's first priority was to have no disruptions in defense production. Firm enforcement of Executive 8802, the government feared, would alienate defense contractors and white labor (Finkle 1975: 97–9). Therefore little more than persuasion was used to compel contractors to hire blacks. Black organizations struggled for the remainder of the war, and afterwards, to put some backbone into the FEPC (ibid: 97–9). Even so, this effort helped black men find more job opportunities during the Second World War than in any other era. However, black women did not see the increase in employment that white women did (Honey 1999: 7–9).

The Black Home Front in the Second World War

The major problem confronting "the Black establishment" throughout the Second World War was the lukewarm attitude their constituents had towards the fighting. America's racist treatment of black soldiers and sailors, its failure to end racial discrimination in defense employment, and its preservation of racial disfranchisement and segregation in the South, all instilled this apathy. Their leadership, however, as it had during the First World War, strongly believed that blacks had to participate fully in the war effort if they were to press claims to full citizenship in American society. They expressed this belief through the black press. With the entry of the United States into the Second World War, many black newspapers – such as the Pittsburgh *Courier*, New York *Amsterdam News*, California *Eagle*, and Norfolk *Journal and Guide* – called on their readers to wholeheartedly support the war. According to the *Journal and Guide*: "We are Americans – We're at War" (Suggs 1983: 407). The California *Eagle* best expressed the idea – that full participation in the war would bring dividends in the post-war period – when it said, on December 11, 1941, that: "So long as our service remains complete and unsullied, the cry for total emancipation is just inevitable" (Finkle 1975: 109).

This notion was the same as W. E. B. Du Bois' call during the First World War for black America to "close ranks" with White America in a common fight against the enemy; but this did not lead to an end to racial discrimination and segregation after the First World War. Consequently, black Americans were reluctant to believe that loyalty to the nation in the Second World War would bring them rewards either during or after that conflict. For example, the NAACP's Walter White, in an article he wrote in 1942 for the *Annals of the American Academy of Political and Social Science*, recounted the applause a black audience gave to comments by a black college student implying that Hitler could not do more damage to black folk than

American racial segregation, exclusion, and lynching (Finkle 1975: 211). This sentiment was not that unusual in the black community, especially among the young. In a poll taken in one southern city, 83 percent of 150 black college students – when asked about the war – said that blacks should not fight in it; and, at a conference in early 1942 of black leaders, held by William Hastie, black assistant to the Secretary of War, 64 percent believed that the black community would not support the war (ibid: 103, 107, 209). Consequently, the elite of the black community and the press that spoke for them faced a huge challenge in selling the war to the black masses (ibid: 114, 119–20).

The spectacle of the United States fighting a worldwide crusade against racist German, Italian, and Japanese fascism – when the US civilian and military social order was racially segregated and treated African Americans in a fascist manner – created an enormous morale problem in the black community. Many African Americans tepidly supported the war effort or expressed their protest through draft dodging, desertion, or violence against white authority figures and each other (Brandt 1996: 132–43). The most notorious instance of black resistance to the draft came in 1942 when Elijah A. Muhammad, the head of the Nation of Islam (NOI), was arrested and charged with "inciting his followers to resist the draft (Essien Udom 1962: 67). He was sentenced to five years in Federal prison, and 100 NOI members were sentenced to lesser terms, for failing to register for the draft. Essien Udom, in his study of the Nation of Islam, *Black Nationalism*, states that it was the NOI's theology prohibiting members from bearing arms in the military that caused the organization to defy the draft. The government suspected the NOI of collaboration with Japanese secret agents. No firm evidence of this was found (ibid: 67), but many in the black community did resent having to fight for the right to fight for a country that treated them so badly. Myrdal noted this when he quoted black journalist Earl Brown, who explained black attitudes by saying: "Because he must fight discrimination to fight for his country and to earn a living, the Negro today is angry, resentful and utterly apathetic about the war" (Myrdal 1944: 1006).

Black protest organizations, such as the NAACP, and black newspapers were aware of this anger and tried to channel it into militant non-violent protest against wartime civilian and domestic racism. This strategy was the "Double V" campaign. First popularized by the Pittsburgh *Courier* in 1942, this strategy was to propagate in the black community the idea that the Second World War was a struggle against racism and tyranny *at home [italics mine]* as well as abroad. Black protest movements and the newspapers hoped to do this by intensive coverage of the exploits of black servicemen and the constant exposure of any and all racial abuse of those soldiers. The black press, NAACP, National Urban League, and leaders such as A. Phillip Randolph, also agitated against domestic racism through the constant exposure of racial discrimination in jobs, housing, and civil rights. Through these tactics, black organizations and newspapers endeavored to enlist their members and readers in an effort which, they believed, would lead to an ending of racial discrimination in the post-war era (Finkle 1975: 120–1).

That they were not completely successful can be seen in the race riots of 1943. These riots put the Double V strategy to its severest test. That year the nation suffered a series of race riots – in Detroit, Harlem, and elsewhere – that cast doubt on why blacks should be fighting for America overseas. Brandt, in his *Harlem at*

War, examines these riots and states that they were caused by racial tensions, intensified by the competition between whites and blacks for jobs in defense plants and for scarce housing – especially in Detroit, a magnet for poor southern whites and blacks. In the last week of June 1943, this flammable racial mixture exploded in a riot that devastated large sections of Detroit and killed 34 people (Brandt 1996: 144–52; Farrar 1998: 126).

Then in New York City, in August 1943, a riot erupted in Harlem, which left six dead, and two million dollars' worth in property damage (Farrar 1998: 126; Brandt 1996: 183–206). The *Afro-American* called the Detroit riot a warning that the black masses would resort to violence to bring about an end to racial oppression (Farrar 1998: 126). The *Amsterdam News*, commenting on the Harlem riot, blamed it on a "few irresponsible and misguided individuals" (Brandt 1996: 209). This indicated divisions within the black elite concerning the morale of the masses. After the riots, proposals for a national commission on race relations were voiced, but President Roosevelt ignored these calls (Dalfiume 1969: 130–1).

The black press's intense coverage of racial abuse in the armed forces worried government agencies such as the Office of War Information, the FBI, and the Justice Department. They were concerned that such coverage would weaken the black community's support for the war. This concern evidently reached the White House, since President Roosevelt in 1942 asked Walter White of the NAACP to use that organization to muzzle the black press. White then called a meeting of black newspaper publishers to convey the President's sentiment and warn the publishers against going too far in their criticism of racism in the war effort. There was even talk in high government circles about charging some black newspapers, particularly the Baltimore *Afro-American*, with sedition. The Attorney General, Francis Biddle, a strong supporter of free speech, squelched such talk, however (Washburn 1986: 3–10, Finkle 1975: 76; Farrar 1998: 169).

Nevertheless the *Afro-American,* Pittsburgh *Courier,* Detroit *Tribune,* Chicago *Defender,* Philadelphia *Herald,* and other black newspapers were the subjects of intense surveillance from the FBI and the Post Office. These newspapers' exposure of armed forces racism prompted the FBI to spy on it throughout the Second World War. No seditious material was found. J. Edgar Hoover, if he had had his way, would have closed the *Afro* and other black newspapers (Washburn 1986: 96, 178, 180–2).

Prominent civilians also thought the wartime black press was subversive. Some of this criticism came from southern white liberals such as Mark Ethridge and Virginius Dabney, who believed that the militant integrationism expressed by such black newspapers as the *Afro-American*, the *Courier*, the *Defender*, and the *Amsterdam News* would undo their efforts, along with those of "responsible" blacks, to effect a gradual amelioration of southern racial policies. In their opinion, the militance expressed by black newspapers would encourage white racist extremists to resort to violence to preserve the South's racial order. By the end of 1942, this criticism had reached the pages of the *Atlantic Monthly* (Finkle 1975: 69). In the January 1943 issue of *Atlantic Monthly*, Virginius Dabney, editor of the Richmond *Times-Dispatch*, harshly criticized the black press for "demanding an overnight revolution in race relations." Such journalism, in Dabney's view, encouraged blacks to militant protest, thereby disturbing the delicate balance of southern race relations (ibid: 71–3).

Dabney's criticism of the wartime black press was unfounded. He did not understand that the unrest in America's black communities was not created by a sensation-mongering black press, but by justified anger over white oppression. Black newspapers, by exposing and denouncing white domestic and military mistreatment of blacks, provided their readers with an outlet for their rage. Without this outlet, blacks might well have found other, more violent expressions of their anger. This point was lost on whites such as Virginius Dabney, who believed that if the black press kept quiet about racial segregation and discrimination then the black community would do the same, thus allowing "enlightened liberals" like themselves to work for a gradual, peaceful easing of racial tension (Finkle 1975: 73).

In any event black newspapers were not deflected from their coverage and criticism of racism in the armed forces. Black newspapers such as the *Afro American, Journal and Guide, Courier,* and *Defender,* and the *Atlanta Daily World,* regardless of government retaliation, covered the reluctance of the Army to use black soldiers in combat roles in France, the mistreatment of black Army/Air Force officers at Freeman Field, Indiana, and racial abuse of black soldiers in southern Army camps, among other racial wrongs.

As a result of the black press's exposure of armed forces racism, the Army decided to cooperate with black newspapers in efforts to boost black morale. In the summer of 1942 it opened a special Negro section in its Bureau of Public Relations. This office, staffed by black public information personnel, was the Army's liaison with the black press. The Army helped black newspapers to set up pooling arrangements, so that individual war correspondents could cover wider areas for more newspapers. The Army also sent representatives to the conventions of the National Newspaper Publishers Association, the trade association for the black press, and in 1944 established a special European clearing office for news of black soldiers. This agency followed troops in the European Theater and provided war correspondents from black newspapers with news of their exploits. Even the Navy cooperated, hosting a group of black journalists for a two-day visit in 1944 to the Great Lakes Naval Base, where the first-ever officer candidate school for blacks was located (Finkle 1975: 83, 85).

Resulting from this cooperation was an endless stream of stories in black newspapers stressing the heroism of black soldiers. The *Afro-American's* pages particularly were filled with this kind of news, since the newspaper sent six of its reporters overseas as war correspondents – more than any other black newspaper (Farrar 1998: 171). The *Journal and Guide,* among other black newspapers, also sent reporters overseas and filled its pages with stories of black combat heroism (Suggs 1988: 132–6). These stories fulfilled the Double V mission, as they were a powerful inspiration to the civilian black community to support the fight against fascism abroad and racism at home. There were small, though welcome improvements in the lot of black soldiers as the armed forces eased their segregationist policies towards the end of the war. This was due to the constant agitation by black organizations, especially as they expressed themselves through the black press. This was done in the face of the black community's overall ambivalence towards the war and the White Community's indifference to domestic and military racial justice. For those reasons, the Double V strategy was a qualified success.

The historiographical consensus (Finkle 1975; Jordan 2001; Farrar 1998; Kornweibel 2001; Farrar 1997; Dalfiume 1969, and others) is that, in both world wars, the black community on the home front was ambivalent in its attitudes. The absurdity of a nation fighting for democracy abroad while not practicing it at home or in the military was not lost on America's black communities. Their leaders, however, believed that full black participation in America's wars was a prerequisite for full citizenship. This created a tension between black leaders and their followers, which they tried to resolve through criticizing racism and tyranny at home and in the military while encouraging blacks to fight against it abroad. This strategy was covertly practiced in the First World War and was the basis of the Double V program in the Second World War. In both wars this strategy caused the government to consider the black press subversive and a subject for investigation and suppression. Some historians (Farrar 1998; Jordan 2001) claim that the Double V campaign did produce some gains. Finkle on the other hand asserts that the Double V campaign was a throwback to the past and it did not reconcile the rift between the black community and its leaders, and did not radicalize blacks to create the post-war Civil Rights Revolution (Finkle 1975: 221). In his words, "It substituted militant rhetoric for its lack of innovative direction" (ibid: 223).

More study needs to be done of the black community's attitudes towards the two world wars. Finkle urged that those seeking the origins of the Civil Rights Revolution in the Second World War must study the black masses. Consequently, there is a need for more studies of black communities in the Second World War, such as Brandt's *Harlem at War*. Also more attention needs to be paid to black women's attitudes towards the Second World War. Honey's *Bitter Fruit* is an invaluable pioneering contribution in this regard. Finkle's *Forum for Protest* (1975), still the standard account of the black press during the Second World War, needs to be updated in the manner of William Jordan's treatment of the black press during the First World War. There also needs to be an update of the histories of the Chicago *Defender* and Pittsburgh *Courier* since both end in 1940. The *Courier's* promotion of the Double V campaign, particularly, needs further study. Nevertheless, the current literature on the black home front in the world wars admirably spotlights a neglected topic in African American history.

BIBLIOGRAPHY

Works Cited

Barbeau, Arthur E. and Henri, Florette (1974) *The Unknown Soldiers: Black American Troops in World War I*. Philadelphia: Temple University Press.

Brandt, Nat (1996) *Harlem at War: The Black Experience in WW II*. Syracuse, NY: Syracuse University Press.

Buni, Andrew (1974) *Robert L. Vann of the Pittsburgh Courier*. Pittsburgh: University of Pittsburgh Press.

Dalfiume, Richard M. (1969) *Desegregation of the Armed Forces: Fighting on Two Fronts, 1939–1953*. Columbia: University of Missouri Press.

Essien Udom, E. U. (1962) *Black Nationalism*. Chicago: University of Chicago Press.

Farrar, Hayward (1998) *The Baltimore Afro-American, 1892–1950*. Westport, CT: Greenwood Press.

Finkle, Lee H. (1975) *Forum for Protest: The Black Press during World War II*. East Rutherford, NJ: Fairleigh Dickinson University Press.

Fleming, Thomas (2003) *The Illusion of Victory: America in World War*. New York: Basic Books.

Foner, Jack (1974) *Blacks and the Military in American History*. New York: Praeger.

Henri, Florette (1975) *Black Migration: Movement North, 1900–1920*. Garden City, NY: Anchor Press.

Honey, Maureen (1999) *Bitter Fruit: Black Women in World War II*. Columbia: University of Missouri Press.

Jordan, William G. (2001) *Black Newspapers and America's War for Democracy, 1914–1920*. Chapel Hill: University of North Carolina Press.

Kellogg, Charles Flint (1967) *NAACP: A History of the National Association for the Advancement of Colored People, Vol. 1: 1909–1920*. Baltimore: Johns Hopkins University Press.

Kornweibel, Theodore, Jr (1981) "Apathy and dissent: black American's negative responses to World War I," *South Atlantic Quarterly* 80 (Summer): 322–38.

—— (2002) *"Investigate Everything": Federal Efforts to Compel Black Loyalty during World War I*. Bloomington: Indiana University Press.

Lewis, David Levering (1993) *W. E. B. Du Bois: Biography of a Race, 1869–1919*. New York: Henry Holt.

Meriweather, James H. (2002) *Proudly We Can Be Africans: Black Americans and Africa, 1935–1961*. Chapel Hill: University of North Carolina Press.

Myrdal, Gunnar (1944) *American Dilemma*. New York: Harper & Bros.

Nalty, Bernard C. (1986) *Strength for the Fight: A History of Black Americans in the Military*. New York: Free Press.

Suggs, H. Lewis (ed.) (1983) *The Black Press in the South, 1865–1979*. Westport, CT: Greenwood Press.

—— (1988) *P. B. Young, Newspaperman: Race, Politics, and Journalism in the New South*. Charlottesville: University Press of Virginia.

Washburn, Patrick (1986) *A Question of Sedition: The Federal Government's Investigation of the Black Press During World War II*. New York: Oxford University Press.

Suggestions for Further Reading

Buchanan, A. Russell (1977) *Black Americans in World War II*. Santa Barbara, CA: Clio Books.

Cayton, Horace and St. Clair, Drake (1945) *Black Metropolis*. New York: Harcourt Brace.

Cronon, David E. (1962) *Black Moses: The Story of Marcus Garvey and the Universal Negro Improvement Association*. Madison: University of Wisconsin Press.

Cruse, Harold (1967) *The Crisis of the Negro Intellectual*. New York: Morrow.

Davis, Benjamin O., Jr (1991) *American*. Washington, DC: Smithsonian Institution Press.

Dunn, James A. (1996) *On Board the* USS Mason*: The World War II Diary of James A. Dunn*, Mansel G. Blackford (ed.). Columbus: Ohio State University Press.

Greenberg, Cheryl Lynn (1991) *Or Does It Explode? Black Harlem in the Great Depression*. New York: Oxford University Press.

Kirby, John (1982) *Black Americans in the Roosevelt Era*. Knoxville: University of Tennessee Press.

Lee, Ulysses (1994) *The Employment of Negro Troops*. Washington, DC: Center for Military History.

McGregor, Morris J. (1989) *Integration of the Armed Forces 1949–1965*, Washington, DC: Center for Military History.

Mead, Gary (2000) *The Doughboys: American and the First World War*. New York: Overlook Press.

Motley, Mary P. (ed.) (1975) *The Invisible Soldier: The Experience of the Black Soldier, World War II*. Detroit: Wayne State University Press.

Murphy, John D. (1997) *The Freeman Field Mutiny: A Study in Leadership.* Maxwell Airforce Base, AL: Air Command and Staff College.

Nelson, Dennis D. (1948) *The Integration of Negro into the U.S. Navy, 1776–1947.* Washington, DC: Navy Department.

Parrish, Noel Francis (1947) *The Segregation of Negroes in the Army Air Forces.* Maxwell Airforce Base, AL: Air Command and Staff College, May.

Perret, Geoffrey (1991) *There Is a War to Be Won: The United States Army in World War II.* New York: Ballantine Books.

Potter, Lou, Miles, William, and Rosenblum, Nina (1992) *Liberators: Fighting on Two Fronts in World War II.* New York: Harcourt Brace Jovanovich.

Putney, Martha S. (1992) *When the Nation Was in Need: Blacks in the Women's Army Corps during World War II.* Metuchen, NJ: Scarecrow Press.

Samuelson, Myman (1995) *Love, War and the 96th Engineers (Colored): The World War II New Guinea Diaries of Captain Hyman Samuelson,* Gwendolyn Hall (ed.). Urbana: University of Illinois Press.

Smith, Graham A. (1988) *When Jim Crow Met John Bull: Black American Soldiers in World War II Britain.* New York: St. Martin's Press.

Suggs, H. Lewis (ed.) (1996) *The Black Press in the Middle West, 1865–1985.* Westport, CT: Greenwood Press.

Thompson, Julius E. (1993) *The Black Press in Mississippi, 1865–1985.* Gainesville: University Press of Florida.

Williams, Charles Halston (1970) *Negro Soldiers in World War I: The Human Side.* New York: AMS Press.

Wynn, Neil A. (1975) *The Afro-American and the Second World War.* New York: Holmes & Meier.

Part VIII

Gender and Class

CHAPTER TWENTY-THREE

Gender and Class in Post-Emancipation Black Communities

ANGELA M. HORNSBY

The period characterized by historian Rayford Logan as the "nadir" in American race relations (c.1880–1920) presented gender and race challenges to black men and women, North and South. The nadir was marked by lynchings, black peonage, disfranchisement, race riots, and white supremacist ideology. Between 1886 and 1900, more than 2,500 lynchings of blacks occurred as whites resorted to violence to enforce black subordination. This era of "radical" race relations also popularized the image of the "black beast rapist," which rationalized violence against black men for presumed sexual assaults on white women. Between 1900 and 1931, 566 lynchings were reported in the South, in which 97 percent of the victims were black. Throughout the Jim Crow era, hundreds of blacks were maimed, jailed, intimidated, or otherwise terrorized for racial dissent – or even just for being black (Woodward 1971; Raper 1933; Hall 1993; Williamson 1986).

Much of the scholarship on Jim Crow has reflected the grave effects of the "nadir" on black communities, especially in the South. Stressing black victimization and accommodation, such accounts have, ironically, served to deny black men and women agency and self-determination (Litwack 1998; Packard 2002). These works, which focus on black oppression, have muted a contrasting theme of black empowerment. And yet, despite innumerable obstacles, many of both sexes determined to remain in the South and establish themselves as dynamic race and civic leaders. Indeed, increasingly, scholars have demonstrated the varied ways in which blacks continued to act "in their own interests" during and after Reconstruction through community-building – social, political, religious, and economic activism (Lewis 1991; Chafe et al. 2001; Trotter 1990; Brown 1997; Hampton-Miller 1981; Greenwood 1994; Edwards 1997; Bercaw 2003; Schwalm 1997; Gavins 1989; Payne and Green 2003).

Of continuing interest to scholars in this regard is the emergence of the black women's club movement, and with it the increased visibility of black middle-class women race activists. The period following disfranchisement was one of intense activity and productivity for black women. The year 1892 saw not only the publication of Frances Harper's *Iola Leroy* but Anna Julia Cooper's *A Voice From the South* and Ida B. Wells' *Southern Horrors: Lynch Law in All Its Phases*. The black women's club movement began that same year when Mary Church Terrell, Anna Julia Cooper, and Mary Jane Patterson formed the Colored Women's League in Washington, DC. The League, which established branches in the South and the West, urged black women to play a role in solving the race problem. Three years later, the first Congress of Colored Women of the United States met in Boston; the Congress later developed into the National Federation of Afro-American Women. In 1896, the National Federation and the National League of Colored Women merged to form the National Association of Colored Women (NACW) in Washington, DC. This group comprised a coalition of two hundred clubs across the country. Black women's immersion in race activity converged with the dawning of a "Woman's Age," which proclaimed women's superiority in issues concerning the moral welfare of the black community, but the equality of men and women in all other matters.

While historians of women and gender generally have focused on black women's subversion of Jim Crow, through their social, religious, and political activities (including interracial alliances with white women) within their communities after disfranchisement, the localized, grassroots work of black men during this period has received less sustained inspection. This lack of emphasis can be attributed, in part, to the tendency of some scholars to view black men's identity through a narrow prism, that of formal politics. The assumption on the part of some historians has been that black women's orientation to race activism and politics is primarily grounded in their relationship to community while men's stems largely from political ideology. Several narratives have thus held that, as black men confronted the cumulative strains of disfranchisement, racial violence, and segregation, black women positioned themselves to shoulder the race problem. Historians such as Glenda Gilmore, Deborah Gray White, and others have eloquently and convincingly argued how black women stepped forward after disfranchisement to lift up the race, build community institutions and serve as ambassadors to the White community (Gilmore 1996; Shaw 1996; White 1999; Hunter 1997; Rouse 1989; Neverdon-Morton 1989; Salem 1990; Giddings 1984; Frankel and Dye 1991).

Although black men never completely disappear from historians' interpretive radar, the impression is left that they prematurely "retired" from their role as race leaders. According to this narrative, black women believed themselves to be the primary instruments to ensure the race's moral uplift. Scholars further emphasize that, though at times women felt compelled to explain and justify their race work to black men, they experienced increased clout and independence as they formed their own network of "para-political" community organizations (Baker 1984; Scott 1970; McGerr 1990; Freedman 1979; Sims 1997). As a result, historians of African American life have largely left uninterrogated black women's supposed ascendance to leadership at the turn of the twentieth century. They have also failed to examine fully the position of southern black men in relation to this ascendance. While studies have revealed black and white women's views of each other in the early twentieth-century South, scholars have failed to tackle in depth black men's attitude towards, and their relationship with, black women during this time.

Increasingly, however, scholars are reassessing and expanding concepts of gender as applied to the post-Emancipation experience of African Americans. Historians are investigating more vigorously the intra-racial and gendered dimensions within black communities. Recent scholarship has revealed the importance of black men and women's collective engagement in race issues as key to defining their public and private selves. For example, while black women did come into their own as an autonomous force at the dawn of the Jim Crow era, historians stress the importance of internal, gendered dynamics within the black community as key to black women's emergence as prominent race activists. That is, they point to the long tradition of shared civic and political activism by both sexes in African American communities that allowed for black women's entry into politics well prior to women's "great age" (Brown 1994; Shaw 1991; Higginbotham 1993).

Elsa Barkley Brown's work on the black community in Richmond, Virginia, and her numerous theoretical essays have demonstrated the necessity of placing black men and women within the same sphere of analysis. Brown and sociologists such as Andrea Hunter, moreover, support applying feminist methodology (women's role as "kin keepers," culture carriers, and stewards of morality) – which has broadened our understanding of black women's everyday lives – to black men. That is, they suggest that questions be raised about black men similar to those posed of black women within gender and feminist studies. Black men and women, these scholars assert, should be placed in dialogue with one another, with the understanding that they occupy the same historical and cultural ground (Brown 1989, 1993, 1994; Hunter and Davis 1992, 1994; Shaw 1991; Hine and Jenkins 1999).

While scholars have acknowledged black men's ideological, institutional, and sociological perspectives, a focus underlying this research has been black men's continual striving to reclaim their political standing. Even within the strictures of segregated life, black men did not abandon the role of political actor. Through non-political institutions such as businesses and the church, black men persisted in flexing their political muscle. In rhetoric and in deed, black men sought to demonstrate their economic and moral clout as evidence of their right to the franchise. Walter Weare has referred to this as the "politics of no politics" (Weare 1993; L. Brown 1997). While the assertion of black men's political mobilization is a truthful one, it is only a partial truth. The ongoing struggle by black men to reclaim their franchise and citizenship rights did not, in and of itself, define them or their manhood. Black men's activities during Jim Crow reflected a spectrum of identity. Not unlike black women, they acted for themselves, their families, and communities.

Thus, while studies have investigated African American male identity, these works have often been segregated from the community-based, moral emphasis attached to black women's work. Sociological studies examining black men's experience have also ignored the multifaceted dimensions of black manhood and instead have projected an image of black identity that has gone unfulfilled or awry (Hunter and Davis 1994). Other scholars have undertaken the task of defining a generic "American Manhood." These studies have utilized a solitary model, that of white middle-class men, to frame their analysis, thus obscuring the different conceptions of male identity held by African Americans (Kimmel 1996; Carnes and Griffen 1990; Rotundo 1993). Moreover, while a number of scholars have explored black male identity within the context of the Civil Rights Movement of the latter half of the twentieth century, the terrain of African American manhood in the early-twentieth-century South has yet to be extensively mapped (Ling and Monteith 1999; Estes 2000).

Borrowing from feminist methodology – which has made visible black women's labors – and from recent scholarly insights, this chapter furthers the dialogue of gender, class, and race activism after Emancipation with a focus on the community-building activities of North Carolina's "best" black men and women during Jim Crow. Using gender as the lens, what emerges from this collaborative exploration is a complex portrait of commonality and difference, gender cooperation and tension, and much negotiation by both sexes. The "nadir" of race relations in North Carolina saw the exodus of about 57,000 blacks in the first three decades of the twentieth century. The start of the twentieth century signaled the return of disfranchisement for most of the state's African American men. Increasingly concerned about blacks' growing political power, Democrats launched a virulent white supremacist campaign. Playing on fears of "Negro domination," the campaign resulted in the 1898 Wilmington Race Riot, in which a mob of prominent and armed businessmen who opposed power-sharing rioted in the streets, effectively driving black and white Republicans from the city. Three white men were wounded and eleven blacks killed in the incident. A successful disfranchisement amendment campaign followed in 1900. Faced with suffrage restrictions such as poll taxes, literacy tests, and the grandfather clause, black men were effectively driven from electoral politics.

After the passage of the disfranchisement amendment, several of the state's race leaders invoked the rhetoric of manhood as they denounced the measure. George White exclaimed "I cannot live in North Carolina and be a man." Another black leader compared disfranchisement to the "shock of an earthquake," adding that some black men "are only waiting to see just how greatly they are damaged, before making a move" (Marby 1940; Edmonds 1951; Gilmore 1996; Prather 1984; Anderson 1981; Cecelski and Tyson 1998; Crow and Hatley 1984, 1992).

While the disfranchisement campaign and subsequent institutionalization of legalized segregation inspired "leading" black men to leave North Carolina, it also motivated those African American men who stayed to affirm a manly identity and expand their role within their communities. Such men included Charles B. Dusenbury of Lexington, North Carolina. Dusenbury's labors both in and outside the church garnered him a reputation as one who, though overworked, devoted his life in faithful service to others. Dusenbury founded Asheville's Calvary Presbyterian church in 1881, Catholic Hill school in 1891, and the Presbyterian Parochial School in 1894. Dusenbury also played an instrumental role in founding the Young Men's Institute (YMI), a social, educational, spiritual, and cultural haven for blacks. White citizens dubbed him a race diplomat, with many proclaiming him a "peace-maker and peace-keeper." In all that he did, his wife shared in his work. Dusenbury's union with Lula Martin Dusenbury, a graduate of Scotia Seminary in Concord, produced seven children. They reputedly worked "side by side in complete sympathy." Towards the end of his life, Dusenbury remarked that, though his life had been hard, his life's work had been a delight. He had been "cast down, but not out" (Hornsby 2003).

In North Carolina, black men generally viewed black women as their "partners" in race work. By and large, they understood the racial legacy that both sexes shared, dating back to slavery, a legacy which undercut the inclination to bifurcate race and gender roles into distinctly "feminine" and "masculine" categories. With disfranchisement, however, men were denied an important avenue for expressing their manhood; and, with the construction of black men as dangerous potential rapists, they also found themselves saddled with a definition of self that they had to respond to in one way or another. Just as the symbolism of "the lady" both circumscribed and defined black women's activism, so too did the projection of the "black beast rapist" and "emasculated" male influence black men's role in race uplift. Not unlike black women who sought to improve the status of their race, by turns playing up their "feminine" side and then asserting their feminist side in community work, so too black men pondered what best defined their manhood. Were they to be tough and manly, or compassionate and gender-inclusive?

In the aftermath of disfranchisement and the legalization of segregation, black men in North Carolina and elsewhere labored alongside black women to uplift the race and their sex through institution-building. Confronted with a racially defined middle-class status that restricted them occupationally, politically, and legally, black elites formulated a "moral economy" that stressed moral privilege and patriarchal conventions within black communities. The black middle class during Jim Crow became increasingly defined by certain characteristics: occupation, wealth, and skill, but also culture and education. This elite corps of black entrepreneurs, skilled workers, and professionals began to compete with the nineteenth century's "Negro vanguard," which had stressed the importance of ancestry (mixed race) and character – honesty, self-restraint, thrift, industry, and sobriety. For this black vanguard, genealogy became the fundamental measure of social status.

Willard Gatewood and other scholars have observed, when assessing the black middle class as a whole, how status and adherence to social values, including a self-conscious distancing from the working classes, held more lasting currency among the old and newer black elite than markers of wealth or occupation. And yet, as historians also point out, by the early 1900s, it was a newly educated and economically stable black elite that began aggressively campaigning against racism, in part by joining the NAACP and other civil rights groups (Bardolph 1959; Gatewood 1990).

The values and behavior of the black middle class, and its role in race advancement, have inspired both praise and criticism from black intellectuals. Where W. E. B. Du Bois praised the "talented tenth," a select group of upwardly mobile, educated African Americans endowed with the responsibility of uplifting the race, sociologist E. Franklin Frazier castigated the black bourgeoisie as largely self-absorbed and exclusionary, having mythologized much of its economic and institutional development, and wishing to imitate whites and their value system. Recent appraisals of the black middle class have served to mediate Frazier's critiques by further illuminating the customs, social organizations, learning institutions, leisure activities, and values of the black elite. While Frazier considered the black bourgeoisie as lacking content and significance, Lawrence Otis Graham's work on the black upper class reveals a group of people committed to preserving and cultivating their black identity, in part through their participation in black institutions – churches, fraternal organizations, institutions of higher learning, and the Civil Rights Movement (Frazier 1957; Gaines 1996; Graham 2000).

Additionally, scholars have acknowledged the cross-class alliances that informed black middle-class race activism and community building. In his examination of black coal miners in West Virginia, Joe Trotter reveals the ways in which the black bourgeoisie was dependent upon coal operators to support its various institutions – schools, churches, and newspapers. Inter-class alliances also illuminated black middle-class women's social reform activity. Historian Tera Hunter's work on Atlanta's black working class, in part, uncovered examples where working-class women don-ated monies, participated in fund-raising events like bake sales and baby contests, or provided "in-kind labor" to support charitable, reform, and community groups. Such groups included Atlanta's Gate City Kindergarten, which relied heavily on such donations. These organizations, in turn, provided services to poor blacks (Trotter 1990; Hunter 1997).

Hunter's study is one of a growing number to explicate the gender and race consciousness/activism of working-class blacks after Reconstruction. Hunter illum-inates how Atlanta's black women workers engaged in multiple acts of resistance to counter race oppression and retain their independence. While the majority of black women subsisted as domestic workers, most chose not to live with their white employers. Also, black working-class women sought release from the daily drudgery of labor by seeking out entertainments like dance halls, public sites that encouraged creative and unfettered self-expression. Elizabeth Clark-Lewis' rich examination of black domestic workers in Washington, DC, is one of several works to address how gender shaped the Great Migration. Using oral histories, Clark-Lewis provides insight into the "subtle process of women's migration," from the rural South to northern cities. This process, the author informs, included relying on female friends and family members to assist in the journey. Black female migrants were also dependent upon an array of female-based folk customs and rituals, all designed to guarantee good luck and safety. Clark-Lewis also discusses how domestics choosing to "live out" – that is, work as day laborers rather than live in their employer's residence – fostered a "collective consciousness" among the women; that is, that they could effect personal and social change (Hunter 1997; Clark-Lewis 1994).

Robin D. G. Kelley's *Hammer and Hoe* assesses the impact of communism on black workers in Alabama in the 1930s, examining how the Communist party became a means for black workers to organize themselves. His exploration juxtaposes the southern environment of Jim Crow and lynch law with an equally formidable tradi-tion of biracial labor unity and black resistance. Mitchell Duneier's sociological study *Slim's Table*, moreover, focuses on the class and gender perspectives of black working-class men in southside Chicago. Contradicting urban black male stereo-types, *Slim's Table* portrays a group of elderly, working-class black males as caring, morally upstanding, and stewards of the community. Dismissing urban social theory that fails to recognize the existence of ethical, black role-models in ghettos, Duneier uses his book's male subjects to demonstrate black moral leadership and respons-ibility. While men in Duneier's study discuss and critique black women, what is missing from this otherwise powerful account is analysis of intra-class gender dyna-mics by integrating black women's perspectives within the narrative (Kelley 1990; Duneier 1992).

African Americans thus asserted their class and gendered concerns publicly and privately – through work, religion, leisure, and the cultivation of familial and kinship ties. Much has been revealed concerning the linkages between gender, race, and community upbuilding among the working classes during Jim Crow; yet exploration of the meaning and performance of gender among black middle-class men during this time and, equally important, their relationship to black women race activists have been under-analyzed. This chapter now turns to address these matters.

Race uplift for black middle-class men assumed a multitude of dimensions and approaches, rooted in a commitment to community and the fostering of a respectable manhood. As Martin Summer's recent work on black middle-class manhood illustrates, black men "imagined and performed a gendered subjectivity" in the early twentieth century. By his excavation of the social and cultural worlds of Prince Hall freemasonry, the nationalist Universal Negro Improvement Association (UNIA), the Harlem Renaissance, and black college campuses after the First World War, Summers explains how both black and African Caribbean immigrant men constructed their gendered selves through language, organizational activities, literature, and "daily public rituals of performance." Summers also gleans how this identity formation was shaped in relation and opposition to white men, youth, black women, and dominant or hegemonic constructions of manhood.

Indeed, black middle-class men and women figured prominently in addressing the black community's internal needs. Like black women, whose community activism tackled the girl problem, men grappled with the "boy problem" by stewarding young boys into manhood. Male organizers also sought to promote interracial cooperation with white men. Yet, while race activism could be a porous domain for men and women, in other ways such permeability was challenged. Patriarchy, at times, became a necessary ingredient in black men's conception of race uplift and progress, from the perspective of black men and some women alike. Such recognition of patriarchal authority, accompanied by stresses on masculinity and civilization, posed continual challenges to black men on how, and to what extent, black women should be recognized as equal partners in the race fight (Hornsby 2003; Summers 2004).

Influenced by numerous factors, including race uplift ideology and the activity/ discourse of their white counterparts, middle-class black men defined and displayed their manhood in various and sometimes competing ways. For example, black middle-class men and women subscribed to white beliefs regarding the "separate spheres" ideology, a belief system inscribed in the South's racial and gender hierarchy, and which dictated distinct social roles for both sexes. Black men's activist agenda and attitudes towards black women, while acted out within the black community, were thus shaped in relationship to prevailing notions about what it meant to be a man in American society. Their gendered perspectives reflected a cultural interdependency that cut across the black/white racial binary. As American and black men, they adopted and experimented with values and broader trends from a variety of "cultural fields" (Hutchinson 1995; Higginbotham 1993). Evelyn Brooks Higginbotham argues that black women in particular fashioned a "politics of respectability," in which they sought to conform to the posture of a "lady." By demonstrating to whites that they were just as virtuous, nurturing, and genteel as white women, that they too merited protection from insult and assault, black women hoped to erase negative stereotypes ascribed to their morality and the race as a whole. Black men were also invested in such politics.

"Civilization" as a racial and gendered discourse for the aspiring and elite classes also held currency among black men. To be manly and civilized meant the exhibition of self-control and self-restraint, characteristics which on the surface privileged class status over race. However, the trope of civilization also became the marker of race supremacy as whites appropriated the term and its stress on Social Darwinism to cast blacks, and in particular, black men, as primitive. When white men charged black men with the crime of rape against white women, they affixed labels of "barbarism" and "savage" to the banner of black manhood. The concept of civilization as held by whites fed the propagandizing of American imperialism; white and black religious institutions, moreover, felt it their duty to civilize other peoples through their domestic and foreign missions (Bederman 1995).

Black middle-class men were thus influenced by broader masculine rhetoric and other cultural imperatives of the day, which, among other things, called for high moral character and conduct, less individualistic, material consumption on the part of citizens and separate spheres of activity for men and women. Black women activists, not surprisingly, figured directly into men's self-imaging (Gaines 1996; Landry 1987). Moreover, the First World War, the "New Negro" movement, Garveyism, and Harlem Renaissance reasserted and revised notions of black manhood. Some male activists began to rebel against accommodationism, the reign of the clubwoman, and Victorian manliness (with its exercise of respectability, and patriarchy) as they adopted a more militant, confrontational approach towards race inequity (White 1999; Carby 1998; Douglas 1995; Summers 2004). Boxed in by a myriad of ideological pressures arising from within and outside the black community, black men's ongoing dialogue with black women activists produced moments both of consensus and tension as each group campaigned for similar goals: the uplift of the race and their sex.

While Summers' new work sheds light on the gendered tensions among black men and women, his focus, which tends towards nationalist black movements and cultural brokers (Claude McKay, Langston Hughes) obscures the localized, and complicated, gendered dynamics occurring within black southern communities (Summers 2004).

A glimpse at the community-building activities of North Carolina's race men and women underscores these complex gender dynamics and negotiations. Working in religious, educational, and community-based institutions such as the Baptist Sunday School Convention, the Mary Potter Institute, and the Young Men's Institute, North Carolina's black men endeavored to groom black boys into respectable, industrious, useful citizens who embraced both their racial and gendered selves. While histories of African American communities have revealed in great detail the rhetoric and strategies used by black women to enhance the morality and respectability of young black girls during Jim Crow, less attention has been paid to the collective efforts of both sexes to bolster the character and gender identity of boys. North Carolina's churchmen's efforts to stem the "boy problem" included proposing wholesome alternatives to urban youth culture, encouraging a softer church discipline for boys, stressing traditional gender roles in the home, and improving the structure and quality of Sunday School instruction. Fearing that their churches were becoming feminized, Baptist Convention leaders worked to make their churches and themselves more manly, in part, by weakening black church women's home missionary work. At the same time, black men campaigned to assume more of "women's" work by engaging in social service activity (Higginbotham 1993; Hornsby 2003; McMillen 2002).

Black secret societies such as the Prince Hall Masons, moreover, were privatized spaces wherein lodge men set about the business of crafting a respectable manhood.

Proceedings of North Carolina's Grand Lodge of Prince Hall Masons reveal the importance of gender to men and how it was retooled over time to allow for uplifting images of black manhood, and ostensibly, black womanhood. This gender task proved challenging for Prince Hall Masons: they struggled to define what constituted a respectable manhood amidst the perceived threat of rival factions within their ranks, growing demands on fraternity men to exercise more militant politics, and, most notably, squabbles with women in their auxiliary (Order of the Eastern Star) over issues of work autonomy (Hornsby 2003; Kenzer 1997; Muraskin 1975; Williams 1980; Bazemore 2001; Wallace 2002).

Although black men typically dominated public events as spokespersons, black women nonetheless played critical roles in the communal enterprises. Their unique contributions demonstrate the ways in which black men and women both shaped the occasions and how their race strategies worked to unify and divide each other. Further, as interracial gatherings, Emancipation Day, and state fair events spoke simultaneously to black and white audiences, often producing multiple and conflicting messages about the meaning of race progress and equality. Over time, racial progress, as codified within African Americans' community institutions, evolved from a philosophy touting "good feelings" between the races to one that endorsed more militant, non-compromising approaches. But the self-help leadership preferred by some black men fell to disfavor in the wake of the First World War and the "New Negro" ideology of the 1920s (Clark 2000; Wiggins 1987; Haley 1987; Weare 1991).

Despite black middle-class women becoming an autonomous force at the end of the nineteenth century, in part because of the stripping of black men's formal political identities, the degree to which black women exercised this autonomy has been exaggerated. Rather than being driven from the field of race activism completely, black men held firm to their community work and the validation that such labor conferred on their gender. This chapter has situated gender (analysis of black womanhood and manhood) more firmly within the discourse of race activism prior to and during the emergence of the Jim Crow South. Such an approach furthers the goal of expanding the vocabulary of black manhood and illuminates the relationship between black male and female activists during an era of heightened race repression.

Gender matters consistently framed black middle-class men's and women's communal partnerships, public and private. To celebrate black women's independence and activism in race work, to proclaim them indispensable instruments in Jim Crow's demise, encouraged race solidarity and a status equal to men in public affairs. Yet it also promoted the erosion of masculine authority and security. Thus, while male leaders of North Carolina's Young Men's Institute, for example, accommodated black women's activity through the use of shared space and resources, YMI's black men, in their need to reach and uplift male youth, restricted black women's access to, and activities within, the Institute in efforts to fortify a manly dominance. While women still retained a place within the YMI, their activism was circumscribed enough that the organization's primary, or authentic, identification as a black male institution remained intact. The cooperative, communal traits nurtured and ritualized within privatized black fraternal spaces also remained in a state of fragility. Order of the Eastern Star's primary identity as the familial relations of Prince Hall men reinforced patriarchal tenets of provider and protector; thus the range of autonomy and leadership women could exercise proved tenuous.

Contestations over gender authority also resonated in the most private of matters, that of romantic love. Historian Eleanor Alexander's recently published work examining the tempestuous courtship and marriage of literary figures Paul Lawrence Dunbar and Alice Moore disclosed the meaning and conflicts inherent in African American courtship and love rituals (Hornsby 2003; Clawson 1989; Carnes 1991; Alexander 2001). Cultural and race ideologies internal and external to the black community also shaped the relationship of black male and female activists. A tradition of shared public space within the black community competed with the ideology of separate spheres. Adherence to this ideology and its attendant stress on strict gender roles undermined an African American value system that had viewed public spaces as sites of active, and necessary, engagement for both sexes. It was in these black public spaces, protected from the harsh reality of Jim Crow politics, that black men and women strengthened communal bonds, nurtured race unity, exercised democratic principles and plotted race strategy.

This tradition of shared public space within the black community was tested by southern race ideology, which stressed not only conventional gender roles but also white patriarchy. The First World War and the New Negro Movement of the 1920s, moreover, fostered intra-racial debate about the appropriate course for race uplift and the realization of a respectable black manhood. These two developments prompted many black men to shift from race accommodation to race militance. Previous admonitions from black male leaders to "labor and wait" were now supplanted by spirited calls for the restoration of denied manhood rights, including the franchise. By the 1930s, race observers began to chronicle the demise of the fabled "race man" of the nineteenth and early twentieth centuries (Young 1973; Meier 1982; Weare 1991).

Gender, class, and race considerations, taken together, formed a dialectic within black communities that was simultaneously uplifting and divisive. As North Carolina's middle-class black men sought to reconcile themselves with the outer, Jim Crow world, they were equally attentive to coming to terms with their gendered selves. Such weighty aims illuminate the challenge confronting black men as they attempted to fashion a race vocabulary that could prove uplifting both to their manhood and the black community overall (Hornsby 2003).

By placing black manhood and womanhood within the broad discourse of race and race activism prior to and during the "nadir," a multitude of scholarly fields are enriched, including women's, southern, gender, American, and African American history. Indeed, a deeper look at black men helps sharpen analysis of black women's public and private lives. Moreover, given that black manhood is still a problematic concept in America today, thoughtful analysis of black manhood and womanhood provides historical context useful to current debates about the "endangered" state of African American males. As evidenced by the "Million Man March," performances of African American manhood still resound loudly. Led by Nation of Islam minister Louis Farrakhan, speakers extolled the need for manhood, self-respect, respect for women, family, and repentance. The march invited lingering questions over the role and appropriateness of black women's participation at such events and is a reminder of the potency and divisiveness inherent in gendered activism among African Americans (Smooth and Tucker 1999; Alexander 2000).

Additional investigations addressing gender and race during the "nadir" are ripe for pursuit. How are black maleness and femaleness conceptualized and understood? How is manhood defined within varying geographical contexts, urban *versus* rural? Working-class notions of what it meant to be a man – in concert with, or in opposition to, middle-class models – also deserve further analysis, as does the impact that race/gender has had in shaping US public policy towards African Americans. The use of institutional spaces in the black community and the extent of opportunities for men and women within them also merit further study. Did certain institutional spaces, such as the church, complicate the question of black women's activism more so than other black public spaces? What accounts for such variation? Eleanor Alexander's probing of Paul Laurence Dunbar and Alice Moore also encourages additional inquiry into how respectability, sexuality, and romantic love manifested themselves among the ebony elite and working classes. Scholarly illumination of all these critical issues will further amplify the essential role that the race/gender/class nexus has played, and continues to play, in African American communities.

BIBLIOGRAPHY

Works Cited

Alexander, Eleanor (2001) *Lyrics of Sunshine and Shadow: The Tragic Courtship and Marriage of Paul Laurence Dunbar and Alice Ruth Moore*. New York: New York University Press.

Alexander, Nikol Gertrude (2000) "From endangerment to atonement: reading gender, race, and nationalism in the Million Man March," PhD dissertation, Rutgers State University.

Anderson, Eric (1981) *Race and Politics in North Carolina, 1872–1901: The Black Second*. Baton Rouge: Louisiana State University Press.

Baker, Paula (1984) "The domestication of politics: women and political society, 1780–1920," *American Historical Review* 89 (June): 620–47.

Bardolph, Richard (1959) *Negro Vanguard*. New York: Vintage Books.

Bazemore, Corey (2001) "The Freemasonry of the race: the cultural politics of ritual, race, and place in post-emancipation Virginia," PhD dissertation, College of William and Mary.

Bederman, Gail (1995) *Manliness and Civilization: A Cultural History of Gender and Race in the United States, 1880–1917*. Chicago: University of Chicago Press.

Bercaw, Nancy (2003) *Gendered Freedoms: Race, Rights and the Politics of Household in the Delta, 1861–1875*. Gainesville: University Press of Florida.

Brown, Elsa Barkley (1989) "Womanist consciousness: Maggie Lena Walker and the Independent Order of St. Luke," *Signs* 14 (Spring).

—— (1993) "Mapping the terrain of black Richmond," *Journal of Urban History* 21 (3, March): 296–346.

—— (1994a) "Uncle Ned's children: negotiating community and freedom in post-emancipation Richmond, Virginia," PhD dissertation, Kent State University.

—— (1994b) "Negotiating and transforming the public sphere: African American political life in the transition from slavery to freedom," *Public Culture* 7: 107–46.

Brown, Leslie (1997) "Common spaces, separate lives: gender and racial conflict in the 'capital of the black middle class,'" PhD Dissertation, Duke University.

Carby, Hazel (1998) *Race Men*. Cambridge, MA: Harvard University Press.

Carnes, Mark (1991) *Secret Ritual and Manhood in Victorian America*. New Haven, CT: Yale University Press.

Carnes, Mark and Griffen, Clyde (1990) *Meanings for Manhood: Constructions of Masculinity in Victorian America*. Chicago: University of Chicago Press.

Cecelski, David S. and Tyson, Timothy B. (1998) *Democracy Betrayed: The Wilmington Race Riot of 1898 and Its Legacy*. Chapel Hill: University of North Carolina Press.

Chafe, William H., Gavins, Raymond, and Korstad, Robert (2001) *Remembering Jim Crow: African Americans Tell about Life in the Segregated South*. New York: New Press, in association with Lyndhurst Books of the Center for Documentary Studies of Duke University.

Clark, Kathleen (2000) "Celebrating freedom: emancipation day celebrations and African American memory in the early reconstruction South" in W. Fitzhugh Brundage (ed.), *Where These Memories Grow: History, Memory, and Southern Identity*. Chapel Hill: University of North Carolina Press.

Clark-Lewis, Elizabeth (1994) *Living-In, Living Out: African American Domestics in Washington, DC, 1910–1940*. Washington, DC: Smithsonian Institution Press.

Clawson, Mary Ann (1989) *Constructing Brotherhood: Class, Gender, and Fraternalism*. Princeton, NJ: Princeton University Press.

Crow, Jeffrey J. and Hatley, Flora J. (eds.) (1984) *Black Americans in North Carolina and the South*. Chapel Hill: University of North Carolina Press.

—— (1992) *A History of African Americans in North Carolina*. Raleigh: Division of Archives and History, NC Dept of Cultural Resources.

Douglas, Ann (1995) *Terrible Honesty: Mongrel Manhattan in the 1920s*. New York: Farrar, Straus, & Giroux.

Duneier, Mitchell (1992) *Slim's Table: Race, Respectability, and Masculinity*. Chicago and London: University of Chicago Press.

Edmonds, Helen G. (1951) *The Negro and Fusion Politics in North Carolina, 1894–1901*. Chapel Hill: University of North Carolina Press.

Edwards, Laura (1997) *Gendered Strife and Confusion: The Political Culture of Reconstruction*. Urbana: University of Illinois Press.

Estes, Steve (2000) "'I AM a man!': race, masculinity, and the 1968 Memphis sanitation strike," *Labor History* 41 (2, Spring): 153–70.

Firor-Scott, Anne (1990) "Most invisible of all: black women's voluntary associations," *Journal of Southern History* 56 (February): 3–22.

Frankel, Noralee and Dye, Nancy S. (eds.) (1991) *Gender, Class, Race, and Reform in the Progressive Era*. Lexington: University of Kentucky.

Frazier, E. Franklin ([1957] 1997) *Black Bourgeoisie*, reprint. New York: Free Press.

Freedman, Estelle (1979) "Separatism as strategy: female institution building and American feminism, 1870–1930," *Feminist Studies* 5 (Fall): 512–29.

Gaines, Kevin K. (1996) *Uplifting the Race: Black Leadership, Politics, and Culture in the Twentieth Century*. Chapel Hill: University of North Carolina.

Gatewood, Willard B. (1990) *Aristocrats of Color: The Black Elite, 1880–1920*. Bloomington: Indiana University Press.

Gavins, Raymond (1989) "The meaning of freedom: black North Carolina in the nadir, 1880–1900" in Jeffrey J. Crow and Paul D. Escott (eds.), *Race, Class, and Politics in Southern History: Essays in Honor of Robert F. Durden*. Baton Rouge: Louisiana State University Press.

Giddings, Paula (1984) *When and Where I Enter: The Impact Of Black Women on Race and Sex in America*. New York: Morrow.

Gilmore, Glenda (1996) *Gender and Jim Crow: Women and the Politics of White Supremacy in North Carolina, 1896–1920*. Chapel Hill: University of North Carolina Press.

Graham, Lawrence Otis (2000) *Our Kind of People: Inside America's Black Upper Class*. New York: HarperCollins.

Greenwood, Janette Thomas (1994) *Bittersweet Legacy: The Black and White "Better Classes" in Charlotte, 1850–1910*. Chapel Hill: University of North Carolina Press.

Haley, John (1987) *Charles N. Hunter and Race Relations in North Carolina*. Chapel Hill: University of North Carolina Press.

Hall, Jacquelyn Dowd (1993) *Revolt against Chivalry: Jessie Daniel Ames and the Women's Campaign against Lynching*. New York: Columbia University Press.

Hampton-Miller, Bertha (1981) "Blacks in Winston-Salem, North Carolina in 1895–1920: community development in an era of benevolent paternalism," PhD dissertation, Duke University.

Higginbotham, Evelyn Brooks (1993) *Righteous Discontent: The Women's Movement in the Black Baptist Church, 1880–1920*. Cambridge, MA: Harvard University Press.

Hine, Darlene Clark and Jenkins, Earnestine (eds.) (1999) *A Question of Manhood: A Reader in U.S. Black Men's History and Masculinity*. Bloomington: Indiana University Press.

Hornsby, Angela M. (2003) "Cast down but not out: black manhood and racial uplift in North Carolina, 1900–1930," PhD dissertation, University of North Carolina at Chapel Hill.

Hunter, Andrea and Davis, James Earl (1992) "Constructing gender: an exploration of Afro-American men's conceptualization of manhood," *Gender and Society* 6 (3, September): 464–79.

—— (1994) "Hidden voices of black men: the meaning, structure, and complexity of manhood," *Journal of Black Studies*, 25 (1, September): 20–40.

Hunter, Tera (1997) *To 'Joy My Freedom: Southern Black Women's Lives and Labors after the Civil War*. Cambridge, MA: Harvard University Press.

Hutchinson, George (1995) *The Harlem Renaissance in Black and White*. Cambridge, MA: Harvard University Press.

Kelley, Robin D. G. (1990) *Hammer and Hoe: Alabama Communists during the Great Depression*. Chapel Hill: University of North Carolina Press.

Kenzer, Robert (1997) *Enterprising Southerners: Black Economic Success in North Carolina, 1865–1915*. Charlottesville: University Press of Virginia.

Kimmel, Michael (1996) *Manhood in America: A Cultural History*. New York: Free Press.

Landry, Bart (1987) *The New Black Middle Class*. Berkeley: University of California Press.

Lewis, Earl (1991) *In Their Own Interests: Race, Class, and Power in Twentieth-Century Norfolk, Virginia*. Berkeley: University of California Press.

Ling, Peter and Monteith, Sharon (eds.) (1999) *Gender in the Civil Rights Movement*. New York: Garland.

Litwack, Leon (1998) *Trouble in Mind: Black Southerners in the Age of Jim Crow*. New York: Knopf.

McGerr, Michael (1990) "Political style and women's power, 1830–1930," *Journal of American History* 77 (December): 864–85.

McMillen, Sally G. (2002) *To Raise up the South: Sunday Schools in Black and White Churches, 1865–1915*. Baton Rouge: Louisiana State University Press.

Marby, William A. (1940) *The Negro in North Carolina Politics since Reconstruction*. Durham, NC: Duke University Press.

Meier, August (1982) *Black Leaders of the Twentieth Century*. Urbana: University of Illinois Press.

Muraskin, William (1975) *Middle-Class Blacks in a White Society: Prince Hall Freemasonry in America*. Berkeley: University of California Press.

Neverdon-Morton, Cynthia (1989) *Afro-American Women of the South and the Advancement of the Race, 1895–1925*. Knoxville: University of Tennessee Press.

Packard, Jerrold M. (2002) *American Nightmare: The History of Jim Crow*. New York: St. Martin's Press.

Payne, Charles and Green, Adam (eds.) (2003) *Time Longer than Rope: A Century of African American Activism, 1850–1950*. New York: New York University Press.

Prather, Henry Leon (1984) *We Have Taken a City: Wilmington Racial Massacre and Coup of 1898*. Rutherford, NJ: Associated Universities Press.

Raper, Arthur F. (1933) *The Tragedy of Lynching*. Chapel Hill: University of North Carolina Press.

Rotundo, Anthony (1993) *American Manhood: Transformations in Masculinity from the Revolution to the Modern Era*. New York: Basic Books.

Rouse, Jacqueline (1989) *Lugenia Burns Hope, Black Southern Reformer*. Athens: University of Georgia Press.

Salem, Dorothy (1990) *To Better Our World: Black Women in Organized Reform, 1890–1920*. Brooklyn, NY: Carlson.

Schwalm, Leslie (1997) *A Hard Fight for We: Women's Transition from Slavery to Freedom in South Carolina*. Urbana: University of Illinois Press.

Scott, Anne Firor (1970) *From Pedestal to Politcs, 1830–1930*. Chicago: University of Chicago Press.

Shaw, Stephanie (1991) "Black Club women and the creation of the National Association of Colored Women," *Journal of Women's History* 3 (Fall): 10–25.

—— (1996) *What a Woman Ought to Be and to Do: Black Professional Women Workers During the Jim Crow Era*. Chicago: University of Chicago Press.

Sims, Anastatia (1997) *The Power of Femininity in the New South: Women's Organizations and Politics in North Carolina, 1880–1930*. Columbia: University of South Carolina Press.

Smooth, Wendy G. and Tucker, Tamelyn (1999) "Behind but not forgotten: women and the behind-the-scenes organizing of the Million Man March" in Kimberly Springer (ed.), *Still Lifting, Still Climbing: Contemporary African-American Women's Activism*. New York: New York University Press.

Summers, Martin (2004) *Manliness and Its Discontents. The Black Middle Class and the Transformation of Masculinity, 1900–1930*. Chapel Hill: University of North Carolina Press.

Thomas-Greenwood, Janette (1994) *Bittersweet Legacy: The Black and White "Better Classes" in Charlotte, 1850–1910*. Chapel Hill: University of North Carolina Press.

Trotter, Joe (1990) *Coal, Class and Color: Blacks in Southern West Virginia, 1915–32*. Urbana: University of Illinois Press.

Wallace, Maurice (2002) *Constructing the Black Masculine: Identity and Ideality in African American Men's Literature and Culture, 1775–1995*. Durham, NC: Duke University Press.

Weare, Walter B. (1991) "New Negroes for a new century: adaptability on display" in Betsy Jacoway et al. (eds.), *The Adaptable South*. Baton Rouge: Louisiana State University Press.

—— (1993) *Black Business in the New South: A Social History of the North Carolina Mutual Life Insurance Company*. Urbana: University of Illinois Press.

White, Deborah Gray (1993) "The cost of club work, the price of black feminism" in Nancy A. Hewitt and Suzanne Lebsock (eds.), *Visible Women: New Essays on American Activism*. Urbana: University of Illinois Press.

—— (1999) *Too Heavy A Load: Black Women in Defense of Themselves, 1894–1994*. New York: Norton.

Wiggins, William H., Jr (1987) *O Freedom! Afro-American Emancipation Celebrations*. Knoxville: University of Tennessee Press.

Williams, Loretta (1980) *Black Freemasonry and Middle-Class Realities*. Columbia: University of Missouri Press.

Williamson, Joel (1986) *A Rage for Order: Black/White Relations in the American South since Emancipation*. New York: Oxford University Press.

Woodward, C. Vann (1974) *The Strange Career of Jim Crow*, 3rd edn. New York: Oxford University Press.

—— ([1971] 1994) *Origins of the New South, 1877–1913*, reprint. Baton Rouge: Louisiana State University Press.

Young, James O. (1973) *Black Writers of the Thirties*. Baton Rouge: Louisiana State University Press.

CHAPTER TWENTY-FOUR

African American Women since the Second World War: Perspectives on Gender and Race

DELORES P. ALDRIDGE

African American women have sought many things, among them an authentic paradigm that could explain their lives and act as a template for their becoming all they are capable of being. The focus, then, of this chapter is on the various concepts and perspectives that have been presented to provide an understanding of what has meaning and importance to black women as they have sought fulfilling lives since the Second World War. Could African American women fit into a women's or feminist movement that originally scorned traditional female roles – ones which were promoted as ideal not only in white society, but in black society as well? How did black females view the Women's Movement in the 1960s and 1970s, a movement led by a group which heretofore had subjugated and humiliated them? Is feminism interchangeable with black feminism, or womanism, or Africana womanism? What are the values of contemporary feminism and what is the African American woman's fit in contemporary feminism? Is the new or contemporary feminism the key to black women's agency and will it serve to form a union among all women and not just among white women? Where will black women put their priorities? In other words, do they see their future more with the black male or the white female? How will black women's priorities impact on the African American family and community? These are among the questions this chapter seeks to answer.

African American women have shared various perspectives on the concept and development of feminism and feminist theory, both of which became the subject of much discussion in the 1970s with the emergence of the Africana/Black Studies Movement and the Feminist/Women Studies Movement. Many African American women were slow to embrace the terminology, while a minority became very active in identifying with a feminist movement. In order to effectively understand the dynamics of the Africana and Feminist movements one must consider not only changes in individuals, but cultural changes as well. A social movement is not just a mass of individuals, but an ongoing social process. In relation to social change, the African American woman is also part of American society. Her propensity to embrace or reject a social movement led and controlled by white women, such as the feminist movement, has thus been partly a function of what her society has made of her and she of it.

Black Women and their Views on the
Women's Movement/Feminism

Willa Hemmons, writing on the Women's Movement, noted:

> One cannot say that Black women will have positive attitudes or negative attitudes toward the movement without specifying the characteristics of the woman. We found that Black women who were committed to the Black liberation movement were also committed to the women's liberation movement. Further, Black women who took traditional attitudes toward the roles of women were less likely to embrace the ideas and values of the women's movement. Surprisingly, Black women were more "feminine" in their values than white women, but this did not decrease the percentage of women who showed a positive attitude toward the women's liberation movement. We have suggested that this inconsistency may result from the various non-traditional roles that Black women have played. In short, it is a result of Black women having a different history than white women. (Hemmons 1980: 296)

Hemmons goes on to say that

> many Black women say they are unconcerned with giving up feminine behavior; they still want men to open doors for them and take them to dinner. At the same time, these women do not mind washing dishes, cooking, and taking care of children. What they want is the same economic benefits enjoyed by the white man. Black women do not want to invade all-male clubs because they do not want men to invade their clubs. Black women enjoy the sisterhood of other women; it is a part of their culture. Black women say they want the same education and job opportunities of white males. (ibid: 296)

Finally, Hemmons posits that the primary reason for black women's failure to join the Women's Movement was grounded in the priorities of the movement. When white women were into consciousness-raising sessions, trying to come to grips with who they were apart from their husbands and children, black women were seeking ways to address unemployment and underemployment among black people in general and black women in particular. When white women were trying to find time to write or do research, black women were searching for organizations and groups that would address the quality of education their children were receiving. When white women were crafting strategies for moving into the labor market and out of the house, large numbers of black women were suggesting that they would gladly return home and take care of their families if the economic system were not so oppressive for black men. At the same time, black women were saying to black men that to be in the home would not make them become subservient to black men (Hemmons 1980: 297). Data from Hemmon's study show that black women were indeed aware of their status as women. However, major issues for black women were not being addressed by the Women's Movement – issues of economic and racial oppression, issues that involved her men and her children, the very centrality of her existence.

A black Feminist Statement by The Combahee River Collective provides another perspective on black women, the Women's Movement, and feminism. In a statement dated April 1977, it raises the issue of differences among women and their perception of their relationship to the Women's Movement:

> We are a collective of black feminists who have been meeting together since 1974. During that time we have been involved in the process of defining and clarifying our politics, while at the same time doing political work within our own group and in coalition with other progressive organizations and movements. The most general statement of our politics at the present time would be that we are actively committed to struggling against racial, sexual, heterosexual, and class oppression and see as our particular task the development of integrated analysis and practice based upon the fact that the major systems of oppression are interlocking. The synthesis of these oppressions creates the conditions of our lives. As black women we see black feminism as the logical political movement to combat the manifold and simultaneous oppressions that all women of color face. . . . Although we are feminists and lesbians, we feel solidarity with progressive black men and do not advocate the fractionalization that white women who are separatists demand. Our situation as black necessitates that we have solidarity around the fact of race, which white women of course do not need to have with white men, unless it is their negative solidarity as racial oppressors. We struggle together with black men against racism, while we also struggle with black men about sexism. (Combahee River Collective 1977: 13)

They then link Feminism and the Black Movement with their political and economic positions:

> We realize that the liberation of all oppressed people necessitates the destruction of the political-economic systems of capitalism and imperialism as well as patriarchy. We are socialists because we believe the work must be organized for the collective benefit of those who do the work and create the products and not for the profit of the bosses. Material resources must be equally distributed among those who create these resources. (ibid: 14)

It is clear that the women of The Combahee River Collective understood the interrelationship between race, class, and gender. But not only did they articulate theory in identifying issues particularly relevant to black women, they were also involved in organizing and actively working toward elimination of inequity with the inclusiveness of their politics. Issues and projects that collective members actually worked on included workplace organizing at a factory, sterilization abuse, abortion rights, battered women, rape, and health care. One issue of major concern that they addressed was racism in the white women's movement:

> As black feminists we are made painfully aware of how little effort white women have made to understand and combat their racism, which requires among other things that they have a more than superficial comprehension of race, color, and black history and culture. Eliminating racism in the white women's movement is by definition work for white women to do, but we will continue to speak to and demand accountability on this issue. (Combahee River Collective 1977: 15)

In *All the Women Are White, All the Blacks Are Men, But Some of Us Are Brave*, three Africana women scholars wrote:

> Women's Studies focused almost exclusively upon the lives of white women. Black Studies, which was much too often male-dominated, also ignored Black women... Because of white women's racism and Black men's sexism, there was no room in either area for a serious consideration of the lives of Black women. And even when they have considered Black women, white women usually have not had the capacity to analyze racial politics and Black culture, and Black men have remained blind or resistant to the implications of sexual politics in Black women's lives. (Hull, Scott, and Smith 1982: xx–xxi)

Clenora Hudson-Weems says that the emergence of black feminism in the 1970s, an offshoot of white feminism, has witnessed the response of many black women who have not readily embraced the concept of feminism for a variety of reasons, in spite of its legitimacy in the academy and the desire of many to be a legitimate part of the academic community. To be sure, embracing an established, acceptable theoretical methodology – feminism – is one of the most reliable, strategic means of ensuring membership into that powerful, visible community of academic women, which extends far beyond itself and secures for its supporters not only job possibilities and publications, but also prestige and high visibility. While many other black women naively adopted feminism early on, because of the absence of an alternative and suitable framework for their individual needs as Africana women, more are reassessing the historical realities and the agenda for the modern feminist movement, and have bravely stood firm in their outright rejection of it (Hudson-Weems 2000: 205).

Hudson-Weems strongly resists labeling all black women activists as feminists. According to her, while feminism – an agenda designed to meet the needs and demands of white women – is quite plausible for that group, placing all women's history under white women's history, thereby giving the latter the definitive position, is problematic. In fact, it demonstrates the ultimate of racist arrogance and domination, suggesting that authentic activity of women resides with white women. It is, therefore, ludicrous to claim as feminists such Africana women activists as Maria W. Stewart and Frances Watkins Harper, abolitionist Sojourner Truth, militant abolition spokesperson and universal suffragist; Harriet Tubman, Underground Railroad conductor, Ida B. Wells, early twentieth century anti-lynching crusader; and Anna Julia Cooper, who proclaims in *A Voice from the South* that "Woman's cause is man's cause: [we] rise or sink together, dwarfed or godlike, bond or free" (ibid: 209).

In fact, black women got there first, long before feminists:

> In considering the race-based activities of these early Africana women and countless other unsung Africana heroines, what white feminists have done in reality was to take the lifestyle and techniques of Africana women activists and use them as blueprints for framing their theory. They then proceed to name, define, and legitimize it as the only substantive women's movement. Thus, in defining the feminist and her activity, they are identifying with independent African women, women whom they both emulated and envied. (Hudson-Weems 2000: 210)

Bettina Aptheker, a white feminist herself, even sees the feminist priority as un-workable for the black woman:

> When we place women at the center of our thinking, we are going about the business of creating an historical and cultural matrix from which women may claim autonomy and independence over their own lives. For women of color, such autonomy cannot be achieved in conditions of racial oppression and cultural genocide. In short, "feminist," in the modern sense, means the empowerment of women. For women of color, such an equality, such an empowerment, cannot take place unless the communities in which they live can successfully establish their own racial and cultural integrity. (Aptheker 1981: 13)

She recognizes the importance of prioritizing the race factor for the black woman as a prerequisite for dealing with the question of gender. This is not to say that gender issues are not important: they are real concerns for all women, black women included, as we are yet operating within a patriarchal system and therefore must confront this issue head on.

However, attacking gender biases does not translate into mandating one's identi-fication with or dependency upon feminism as the only viable means of addressing them. Feminists have no exclusivity on gender issues. According to Vivian Gordon – in her book *Black Women, Feminism, and Black Liberation: Which Way?* –

> To address women's issues, therefore, is not only to address the crucial needs of black women, it is also to address the historic primacy of the African and African American community; that is the primacy of its children and their preparation for the responsibili-ties and privileges of mature personhood. (Gordon 1991: viii)

Gordon's approach in dealing with women's issues is to bring out the historical reality of Africana people and the centrality of family for the security of future generations. Aldridge takes this a step further in her *Focusing: Black Male-Female Relations*, contending that derailing our race-based struggle for a gender-based one poses serious consequences:

> One might argue . . . that the women's liberation movement – as it is presently defined and implemented – has a negative impact on the Black Liberation movement . . . [for] Women's liberation operates within the capitalist tradition and accepts the end goals of sexist white males. (Aldridge 1991: 35)

Clearly, Aldridge understands well the perspective from which the feminist comes. In "Cultural and agenda conflicts in academia," Hudson-Weems succinctly puts it as "mainstream feminism is women's co-opting themselves into mainstream patriarchal values" (Hudson-Weems 1989: 187). The key issue for Hudson-Weems, Aptheker, Gordon, and Aldridge – three of them black and one white – is not the exclusion of gender issues, but rather the manner in which they are addressed.

From the perspectives emerging – from Hemmons' empirical study of African American women's attitudes toward the Women's Movement and feminism, and the self-defined black feminists of The Combahee River Collective, as well as from theorists Aptheker, Aldridge, Gordon, and Hudson-Weems – there exist strong

positions about black women's fit in a racist, white-women-led movement or one
defined as feminist. The Women's or Feminist Movement in the first several decades
of existence was perceived as not embracing black women's major concern of the
intersection of race, class, and gender.

The women whose views were analysed by Hemmons (1980), The Combahee
River Collective, and other women critics are not unlike outspoken African American women intellectuals before them, who viewed the struggles of women of
African descent in America as part of a wider struggle for human dignity and empowerment. As early as 1893, Anna Julia Cooper in a speech to women provided this
perspective:

> We take our stand on the solidarity of humanity, the oneness of life, and the unnatural-
> ness and injustice of all special favoritisms, whether of sex, race, country, or con-
> dition . . . The colored woman feels that woman's cause is one and universal; and that
> not till race, color, sex, and condition are seen as accidents, and not the substance of
> life, not till the universal title of humanity to life, liberty, and the pursuit of happiness
> is conceded to be inalienable to all, not till then is woman's lesson taught and woman's
> cause won – not the white woman's nor the black woman's, not the red woman's, but
> the cause of every man and of every woman who has writhed silently under a mighty
> wrong. (quoted in Loewenberg and Bogin 1976: 235)

The perspectives addressed above speak to the lives of African American women.
And, some focus directly on concepts or terms in an effort to give clarity in defining
black womanhood. However, it is important to move further into a discussion of
some of the various terms and/or paradigms used in naming and defining black
women's lives.

Feminism, Black Feminism, Womanism, Africana Womanism – The Same or Different?

The terms feminism, black feminism, womanism, and Africana womanism – as
explainers of the realities of black women's lives – have been proposed and defined
by numerous critics and scholars. Some use one term giving it the meaning that
someone else attributes to another term. Thus, some confusion exists about what is
meant when the terms are used. Smith explains:

> Feminism is the political theory and practice that struggles to free *all* women: women
> of color, working-class women, poor women, disabled women, lesbians, old women –
> as well as white, economically privileged, heterosexual women. Anything less than this
> vision of total freedom is not feminism, but merely female self-aggrandizement. (Smith
> 1982: 49)

If this definition is to be accepted, then it must be conceded that feminism does not
exist, as it has not embraced in theory or practice all women. According to Vivian
Gordon,

> if Africana women were to elect to do so, they could lay an unprecedented historic
> claim to the lexicon "feminist" by simply citing the conditions over which they have

struggled in the Americas, such as: (1) the right to control one's own reproduction; (2) freedom from sexual harassment; (3) equality before the law; (4) the right to vote; (5) equal pay for equal work (or historically, pay for work); (6) equal opportunity for a quality education; (7) quality housing; (8) quality health care, including preventive and rehabilitation services; (9) survivors' benefits for families; (10) old age security; (11) nonpunitive assistance programs for the qualified poor; and (12) the abolition of racism and sexism in the criminal justice system. (Gordon 2000: 166)

Gordon stresses that

their rebellion during the enslavement; their devotion to family; their copartnership with men in the fight against oppression; their demonstrated ability to do work, including "traditional man's work;" their historic organization, which demonstrates an ability to organize on behalf of the elevation of positions of women; their involvement in the development of educational and business institutions, as well as their contributions to science, medicine, and technology from the times of the ancients to the present; more than qualify Africana women as the first "feminists." That they have continuously elected to not compartmentalize their identity into categories of race versus gender bars further discussion. (Gordon 2000: 166)

Gordon continues:

The lexicon of feminism is conceptually exclusive. It is seated in a gender-specific identity, which is a female response to the unique experiences of a male supremacy that America is justified by a culturally rooted belief system that traces back to a Greco-Roman legacy. African American women linked to their ancestral past grounded in collective consciousness are guided by their identification with the total community – which is ultimately the extended kin, as opposed to an ongoing isolated gender-specific identity. (ibid: 167)

In African cosmology, proper naming – *nommo* – says it all, as it is essential to existence, which makes it all the more difficult to accept an improper name for oneself. In 1983, Alice Walker identified with the term womanist, of which she says "womanist is to feminist as purple is to lavender," addressing the notion of the solidarity of humanity. She defines "womanist" in her book *In Search of Our Mothers' Gardens: Womanist Prose*. For Walker, a "womanist" is one who is "committed to the survival and wholeness of an entire people."

Clenora Hudson-Weems (1993) provides us with another concept that differs subtly from womanism – Africana womanism. The Africana refers not only to continental Africans, but also to people of African descent worldwide. The concept, Africana, perhaps first received national visibility as a descriptor of Africana Studies with the naming of the Africana Studies and Research Center at Cornell University. In the book, *Africana Womanism: Reclaiming Ourselves*, Hudson-Weems explores the dynamics of the conflict between the mainstream feminist, the black feminist, womanism, and the Africana womanist. In this work, she sets forth 18 principles in the African womanism paradigm. Among these are self-naming, self-defining, family centered, and cooperative male–female relationships.

According to Hudson-Weems, Africana womanism is neither an outgrowth nor an addendum to mainstream feminism, but rather a concept grounded in the culture of

– and which focuses on the experiences, needs, and desires of – Africana women. Africana womanists and feminists have separate agendas. Feminism is female centered; Africana womanism is family centered. Feminism is concerned primarily with ridding society of sexism; Africana womanism is concerned with ridding society of racism first, then classism, and sexism. Many feminists say their number one enemy is the male; Africana womanists welcome and encourage male participation in their strug- gle. Feminism, Hudson-Weems says, is incompatible with Africana women, as it was designed to meet the needs of white women.

Black feminism is a paradigm designed to bring black women into the fold of white feminism. These new black feminists now emphasize race, as well as gender and class, as critical to understanding the lives of black women – an orientation long shared by many other black women who did not identify with feminism. Those black women who continue to use the term feminism as a theoretical construct for their analysis receive considerable support for their research. Aligning themselves with the framework of feminism has proved to be a relevant strategy for acceptance into that established community – a membership which carries many benefits, such as visibility, numerous employment possibilities, and publications. Such a reward system can not be dismissed or minimized, because it is highly influential on black feminists and their allegiance to, and identification with, dominant feminist ideologies. Often these same feminists, under the guise of a "new feminism," have duplicated work and/or misappropriated practical and theoretical constructs of scholars and critics who have stressed race, gender, and class, with a focus on the family and community survival of black people.

New Black Feminism

Contemporary scholars, black and non-black, who write on women's lives concede that the development of an intersectional perspective on gender and race is rooted in the work of scholars studying women of color. Several prominent black female historians have focused on the frustration and triumph of black women who have been faced with the double burden of race and sex (Brown 1989; Rouse 1989; Shaw 1996). This body of work on gender and race is usually referred to under the rubric of multiracial feminism, multicultural feminism, or postcolonial feminism (Zinn and Dill 1996; Lorber 1998; Mohanty 1991). As part of this endeavor, contemporary or new feminist theory has become pivotal in proposing treatment that is inclusive of race and gender in determining labor market outcomes (Brewer 1993; Collins 1999; James and Busia 1993). Relying on an experience-based epistemology, black women revealed that not only were both race and gender implicated in shaping their lives, but neither the extant theories of gender as "simultaneous and linked" social iden- tities or race as paramount or sufficient to explain their lives, rather "both and . . . was necessary (Cade 1970; Brewer 1993; Glenn 1999; hooks 1989; Hull et al. 1982; Spelman 1988).

Sara Evans (1979) wrote one of the first books to underscore the invaluable role of women in the Civil Rights Movement. *Personal Politics: The Roots of Women's Liberation in the Civil Rights Movement and the New Left* was a triumph in establish- ing black women as role models in organizing young white women workers from the South and the North. Interestingly, however, white women borrowing from black women became the definers and leaders of the Women's Movement. And while black women historians contend that scholars on the South's white women and black women have found common ground, other black women scholars differ (Crawford, Rouse and Woods 1999). For example, both Gordon (2000) and Hudson-Weems (2000), who identify with Africana womanism, have insisted on the importance of naming and defining one's paradigms to provide understanding of and direction for the lives of black women, their families, and communities. Both insist the proper naming of a thing will in turn give it essence. They, as does Toni Morrison in *Beloved*, maintain: "Definitions belong to the definers not the defined. Self naming and self defining is crucial" (Morrison 1987).

On the other hand, Collins – in "What's in a name . . . ?" – asserts:

> Rather than developing definitions and arguing over naming Practices – for example, whether this thought should be called Black feminism, womanism, Afrocentric Feminism, Africana womanism, and the like – a more useful approach lies in revisiting the reasons why black feminist thought exists at all. (Collins 1996: 22)

Clearly, from this quotation, she is not in agreement with Gordon, Hudson-Weems, and Morrison. Obviously she does not embrace the concept of *nommo*, or she would not have ended by proposing such a question. More importantly, why does Collins retain the term "feminist," rejecting a more authentic one? This is the dilemma within which black feminism finds itself. Holding on to a term but yet incorporating facets of a paradigm or paradigms that they have not acknowledged as more authentic for black women, indeed black people. They have too often camouflaged their so-called "new black feminism," as introduced by Hortense Spillers at the 2000 Du Bois Conference in Philadelphia. The new black feminism will allow women, according to its advocates, to more equitably deal with gender and race issues. With their revised feminist theory, they position themselves such that they remain ideologically acceptable by the dominant culture.

The resistance to the term "feminism" by many African American women appears not to be their misunderstanding of the definition. Rather, the resistance suggests a selective and deliberate avoidance of an association with a social movement led by a white female majority in America, grounded in a struggle against their cultural roots in the Greco-Roman male patriarchy. While it is an appropriate struggle for white women who have been denied their equality by the men of their historic ties, this is not the same struggle for African American women. The fundamental issue is whether gender-specific theory addresses the race-specific and culture-specific issues of women who might wish to work against sexism, but who are not predisposed to substituting their historic cultural identities for a collective women's culture.

Values of Contemporary White Feminists

What does contemporary feminism dominated by white women offer, that is similar to or different from that of the past? And does it embrace the needs and aspirations of black women? Is it moving toward an active race-gender-class focus with equity and humanism for all? And is the new black feminism compatible with contemporary or new feminism as advocated by white women? According to Mary Rogers, in her edited volume *Contemporary Feminist Theory*, "feminist theory takes shape around the dialectic between its partnered terms. 'Feminist' connotes activism and shaking things up, while 'theory' connotes dispassionate scholarship and abstract ideas. Feminist theory defeats that divergence by making theory and practice collateral projects." Rogers writes that "theorists have been grouped using names like 'standpoint theorist' or 'materialist feminist' or 'womanist theorist' among other nomenclature. A women-centered approach is necessary for feminist theorizing, but it is insufficient" (Rogers 1998: 3). What are some of the commonalities for explaining what "feminist" involves?

Feminists maintain that women and men are equally entitled to all the good things a society makes available to its members – all the opportunities, rewards, respect and status, power, and responsibilities. Feminists thus believe that gender should not be a distributive mechanism in society, a basis for social hierarchy, or a means whereby some parts of people get stunted and other parts get overdeveloped. Feminism serves, then, as an "intervention in the ideology of gender" (Grant 1993: 179). Not all feminists simply seek parity with relatively privileged men. Some challenge what gender itself embodies: namely, hierarchy. Some common values driving contemporary feminists are embedded in questions about six issues:

First – Standards used to justify why some people get to the top and other people get trapped at the bottom of various hierarchies. These standards end up as preferences that get widely institutionalized (Williams 1991: 103).

Second – Hierarchical approaches to a group's problem-solving or projects. In theory and in practice, they often turn to alternative approaches such as collaborative decision-making, agreement by consensus, and cooperative modes of dividing labor and rewards. Thus, feminists often believe that hierarchy has been overdone in societies like that of the USA and seek fairer ways of getting jobs done (Rogers 1998: 4).

Third – Social justice is crucial to that of hierarchal elimination whether it is called distributive justice, equality, fairness, or equal rights. Social justice advocates that each person's dignity is being honored with their needs recognized and addressed, and they or their group's claims to extras are anchored in merits or needs widely agreed upon and open to debate among members. Closely allied to social justice is the democratic process, which requires that each person's voice be heard or at least effectively represented (ibid: 4).

Fourth – Extension of responsibility beyond oneself and one's circle of loved ones, especially to those who depend heavily on the rest of us for sustenance and nurturing.

Fifth – Inclusive thinking that would embrace all women. Given the attacks on the women's movement and white feminists as racist and elitist, the reality of inclusive practices appears to be debatable.

However, some developments may have moved feminists toward inclusive stances and interactions. A part of the development of the inclusive posture has been the movement away from dualistic, binary, either/or thinking – the very thinking that pits male against female as superior against inferior, strong against weak, and rational against emotional. By and large, contemporary feminist theorists made it their business to overcome "prefeminist, either/or, polarized thinking" (Casto 1984: 169). But while feminist theorists commonly recognize that women are both old and young, monosexual and bisexual, low income and middle income, they often do not consider that "both" is problematic. Such designations suggest a pair of realities where usually there are multiple ones, such as red, yellow, brown, black, and white, or inner city, urban, suburban, rural and frontier, and the like.

Even though some contemporary feminist theorists recognize that inclusive perspectives must extend beyond dualistic usages, others have lapses. For example, in the feminist journal *Gender & Society* appeared the article "Wives and husbands: perceptions of why wives work" (Spade 1994). All the participants in the study were white. Accordingly, the article's title should have referred to *white* spouses' attitudes. This certainly would have occurred had all the participants been black.

The inclusive intentions of contemporary feminist theory attempt to embrace multiculturalism, which mandates curricular attention to the experiences, historical and contemporary, of women and men of color, lesbians and gay men of all racial and ethnic groups, and women with diverse sexual, racial, and ethnic identities. To the extent that its inclusive intentions succeed, contemporary feminist theory both feeds into and draws on multiculturalism. That connection makes for rich but problematic theorizing insofar as "many of the factors which divide women also unite some women with men" (Hartsock 1990: 158). As Joan Wallach Scott observes, feminism is "a site where differences conflict and coalesce, where common interests are articulated and contested, where identities achieve temporary stability . . . where politics and history are made" (Scott 1996: 13).

Sixth – Freedom and its close allies, liberation and self-actualization. As Mary Rogers says:

> In the long run and across diverse domains, feminists aim to enhance women's freedom to choose the circumstances and purposes of their lives. For a variety of reasons, rooted in their experiences of androcentric (male-centered) institutions, feminists mostly abhor doctrine, orthodoxy, and anything else that decontextualizes people's choice making. Disinclined to prescribe or proscribe anything specific for women, feminists commonly lean toward nonjudgmental stances about women's actual choices, even those they themselves may not favor. Feminism is not about "enlightened" women who, having raised their consciousness, then tell other women how they should live.
>   Yet feminist theory is normative. How might these two perspectives be reconciled, at least in principle? (Rogers, 1998: 6)

Sandra Lee Bartky says feminism involves both critique and resistance (Bartky 1993: 13). Characteristically, feminists challenge whatever demeans, hurts, impedes, or otherwise treats unfairly large numbers of women. Thus, most feminist writing includes critique among its defining features. At the same time, most such writing delineates how women resist and can further resist such unfair circumstances. All these normative concerns are macro-level. That is, they address a society's or community's social structure, its culture (values, norms, beliefs), and diverse female groupings' opportunities and outcomes. While normative, these concerns are large-scale and impersonal: they have to do with systemic patterns and aggregated human activities.

In the personal and interpersonal spheres, where selfhood and relationships are embodied, feminists turn away from normative thinking. Like many other contemporary theorists, they recognize that each person makes choices within a biographical situation of which one is a product that no one else can fully apprehend; that she chooses by drawing on the resources available. Thus, one might hear a feminist protest about the objectification of women but never hear her criticize a real-life person who works as a fashion model. Feminists recognize, then, that women lead "lives of multiple commitments and multiple beginnings" (Bateson 1990: 17).

Drawing on work from the sociology of knowledge, proposed by Peter L. Berger and Thomas Luckmann's *The Social Construction of Reality* (1967), and recent work of feminist theorists such as Dorothy E. Smith (1990), it appears that all knowledge is socially constructed and variously linked to what Smith calls the "relations of ruling" in society. Their work suggests that theory is a product of the real world, not a creation of "pure" ideas. Zillah R. Eisenstein extends on that notion as she posits "Theory must grow out of reality, but it must be able to pose another vision of reality as well" (Eisenstein 1979: 30). If these writers are correct, then feminists are first and foremost shaped by the American society of which they are a part – either those privileged by their white skin or those not privileged because of lack of white skin.

African American Women, Their Men, Families, and the Contemporary/New Feminism

What relevance does the contemporary or new feminism hold for African American women, based on the values being espoused by its advocates? Do these values embrace African American women, their men, and their families? Does the new/contemporary feminism encourage action on behalf of self and community? Does it raise difficult questions, suggest relevant alternatives, hold powerful people account-able, and empower those who desire change? Or, is it simply a way of usurping an existing paradigm? While the discussion on values of contemporary or new feminists – including those new black feminists – are informative and useful, perhaps, the only true paradigms set forth for explaining and giving direction to/for black women's lives are those set forth before the new black feminists or contemporary white feminists – those provided by Hudson-Weems, Gordon, and other Africana womanists.

The long-standing focus on the woman and her role in the greater society contin-ues to be at the center of controversy today. Even prior to the Civil War and the Emancipation Proclamation, women were engaged in shaping their role within the context of a particular social reality, one in which white males dominated within a racist patriarchal system. Although racism is clearly the bedrock of oppression, white women in general, and the feminist movement in particular, have both been driven almost exclusively by issues related solely to gender oppression. However, the vast majority of black women have necessarily focused their energies on combating racism first, before addressing the gender question. As a consequence, it is clear that the two groups ultimately have disparate goals for meeting their specific needs. In short, for most black women, who are family-centered, it is race empowerment; for white women, many of whom are female-centered, it is female empowerment. Because of this difference in agendas, distinct lexicons of names and definitions are critical.

Julia Hare makes a comment on the reality of the difference in the politics of black life and that of white life, particularly in terms of the difference in certain meanings and ideals relative to the two parallel groups:

Women who are calling themselves black feminists need another word that describes what their concerns are. Black feminism is not a word that describes the plight of Black women. In fact, . . . black feminists have not even come to a true core definition of what black feminism is. The white race has a woman problem because the women were oppressed. Black people have a man and woman problem because Black men are as oppressed as their women. (quoted in Crawford 1993: 15)

In the late 1960s the Civil Rights Movement, which stressed liberation, marked the first time Africana people engaged in a struggle to resist racism where distinct boundaries were established, which separated the roles of women and men. Africana male activists publicly acknowledged expectations that women involved in the movement would conform to a subservient role pattern. This sexist expectation was expressed as women were admonished to manage household needs and breed warriors for the revolution. Toni Cade elaborated on the issue of roles that prevailed in black organizations during the 1960s:

It would seem that every organization you can name has had to struggle at one time or another with seemingly mutinous cadres of women getting salty about having to man the telephones or fix the coffee while the men wrote the position papers and decided on policy. Some groups condescendingly allotted two or three slots in the executive order to women. Others encouraged the sisters to form a separate caucus and work out something that wouldn't split the organization. Others got nasty and forced the women to storm out to organize separate workshops. Over the years, things have sort of been cooled out. But I have yet to hear a coolheaded analysis of just what any particular group's stand is on the question. Invariably, I hear from some dude that Black women must be supportive and patient so that Black men can regain their manhood. The notion of womanhood, they argue – and only if pressed to address themselves to the notion do they think of it or argue – is dependent on his defining his manhood. (Cade 1970: 107–8)

Though many black women activists did not succumb to the attempts of black men to reduce them to a secondary role in the movement, many did. bell hooks writes:

Black women questioning and or rejecting a patriarchal black movement found little solace in the contemporary women's movement. For while it drew attention to the dual victimization of black women by racist and sexist oppression, white feminists tended to romanticize the black female experience rather than discuss the negative impact of oppression. When feminists acknowledge in one breath that black women are victimized and in the same breath emphasize their strength, they imply that though black women are oppressed they manage to circumvent the damaging impact of oppression by being strong – and that is simply not the case. Usually, when people talk about the "strength" of black women they are referring to the way in which they perceive black women coping with oppression. They ignore the reality that to be strong in the face of oppression is not the same as overcoming oppression, that endurance is not to be confused with transformation. (hooks 1981: 6)

Thus, to be an activist in the liberation of black people or women did not necessarily mean there was sensitivity for black women. Now, for black people to move forward as a strong group will require men and women working together to build their families, institutions, and communities (Aldridge 1991, 1992, 1998). Values espoused by contemporary or new feminists – black or white – are relevant for self-affirmation of all people. But it is not feminism that best reflects the current conditions or future needs of black women, men, children, and their communities. Rather, to build upon the paradigm of Africana womanism as a means of moving toward a more humane world may be in the best interest of black people – indeed, all people.

Continuing Issues for African American Women

There is still unfinished business at the intersection of black issues and feminist issues:

- Claiming *nommo* or naming and self defining. Clearly, those who control the naming and defining, control the named and defined.
- Recognition that common usage of feminism or black feminism by many African American women differs within the group as well as from that of many white women, who may or may not be self-defined feminists.
- Commitment to the Black Freedom Movement over the Women's Liberation Movement because of a "best fit."
- Resolution of the tension produced by feminism and its perspective of "women's culture." This requires African women with primary identity in the African diaspora to fend off racism from both white women and white men.
- Participation in coalitions that advocate inclusion of African American women, with a gender-specific focus that obscures race-specific issues.
- Development of strategies for moving toward common grounds on crucial issues that impact women and men from different cultural groups.

Black women had no significant role in the Women's or Feminist Movement of the 1960s, even though their ideas and strategies used in the Civil Rights Movement were appropriated by white women. However, neither black women's major concerns nor historical realities were embraced. As such, a place had to be created for black women. In order to fully include them, there was need for more than writing about them. White women needed to change their attitudes and behavior toward black women, and black women were required to make their concerns known and dealt with. Black women also had to become more active in telling their own stories and moving toward changing their own conditions. It is clear that most black women organizations, writers, and/or activists were not attaching the same meanings to the concept of feminism as were most white women or their various groups.

Numerous black scholars and critics as well as lay individuals have held on to a concept that they had no part in naming or defining, rather than moving to a different one that embodies what they in actuality are now espousing – Africana womanism, or perhaps a new term of "*humanism*" (emphasis mine). The call for an intersection of race, gender, and class is important, but under the rubric of feminism it carries all the nuances of continued control by white women, who named and defined it. The new or contemporary feminism espouses values that embrace politically-correct concepts of inclusiveness, multiculturalism, and diversity. But even if the new feminism takes the uncomfortable positions of actively addressing racism, classism, and other "isms" as passionately as it has battled against sexism, will black women have the "agency" necessary to do what is best for them, their families, and communities? If so, then the quest for an authentic paradigm will have been realized, with a significant intersection of gender and race in the aftermath of the Second World War.

BIBLIOGRAPHY

Works Cited

Aldridge, Delores P. (1991) *Focusing: Institutional and Interpersonal Perspectives on Black Male–Female Relations.* Chicago: Third World Press.
—— (1992) "Womanist issues in Black Studies: toward integrating of Africana women into Africana studies,"*Afrocentric Scholar* 1 (1, May).
—— (1998) "Black women and the new world order: toward a fit in the economic marketplace" in Irene Browne (ed.), *Latinas and African American Women at Work: Race, Gender, and Economic Inequality.* New York: Russell Sage Foundation, 357–79.
Aptheker, Bettina (1981) "Strong is what we make each other: unlearning racism within women's studies," *Women's Studies Quarterly* 9 (4, Winter).
Bartky, Sandra Lee (1993) "Reply to commentators on femininity and domination," *Hypatia: A Journal of Feminist Philosophy* 8 (Winter): 193.
Bateson, Mary Catherine (1990) *Composing a Life.* New York: Penguin Books.
Berger, Peter L. and Luckmann, Thomas (1967) *The Social Construction of Reality: A Treatise in the Sociology of Knowledge.* New York: Anchor Books.
Boxer, Marilyn J. (1982) "For and about women: the theory and practice of women's studies in the United States," *Signs* 7: 160–95.
Brewer, Rose (1993) "Theorizing race, class, and gender: the new scholarship of black feminist intellectuals and black women's labor" in Joy James and A. Busia (eds.), *Theorizing Black Feminisms: The Visionary Pragmatism of Black Women*, 13–30. New York: Routledge.
Brown, Elsa Barkeley (1989) "Womanist consciousness: Maggie Lena Walker and the Independent Order of Saint Luke," *Signs* 14.
Cade, Toni (ed.) (1970) *The Black Woman: An Anthology.* New York: New American Library.
Casto, Ginette ([1984] 1990) *American Feminism: A Contemporary History*, trans. Elizabeth Loverde-Bagwell. New York: New York University Press.
Collins, Patricia H. (1990) *Black Feminist Thought: Knowledge, Consciousness, and the Politics of Empowerment*, 2nd edn. London: HarperCollins Academic.
—— (1996) "What's in a name: womanism, black feminism and beyond," *Black Scholar* 26 (1, March): 9–17.
—— (1999) "Gender, black feminism and black political economy," *Annual of the American Academy of Political and Social Science*, 568: 41–53.
Combahee River Collective ([1977] 1998) "A black feminist statement" in Mary F. Rogers (ed.), *Contemporary Feminist Theory*, 13–15. McGraw-Hill: New York.
Crawford, Ellen (1993) "Feminism in academe: the race factor," *Black Issues in Higher Education* 10 (1, March).
Crawford, Vicki L., Rouse, Jacqueline Anne, and Woods, Barbara (eds.) (1999) *Women in the Civil Rights Movement: Trailblazers and Torchbearers, 1941–1965.* Brooklyn: Carlson.
Eisenstein, Zillah R. (1979) "Introduction" in Zillah R. Eisenstein (ed.), *Capitalist Patriarchy and the Case for Socialist Feminism.* New York and London: Monthly Review Press.
Evans, Sara (1979) *Personal Politics: The Roots of Women's Liberation in the Civil Rights Movement and the New Left.* New York: Alfred A. Knopf.

Glenn, Nakano E. (1999) "The social construction and institutionalization of gender and race: an integrative framework" in M. Marx Ferree, J. Lorber, and B. B. Hess (eds.), *Revisioning Gender*, 3–43. Thousand Oaks, CA: Sage.

Gordon, Vivian V. (1991) *Black Women, Feminism, and Black Liberation: Which Way?* Chicago: Third World Press.

—— (2000) "Black women, feminism, and black studies" in Delores P. Aldridge and Carlene Young (eds.), *Out of the Revolution: The Development of Africana Studies*, 165–75. Lanham, MD: Lexington.

Grant, Judith (1993) *Fundamental Feminism: Contesting the Core Concepts of Feminist Theory*. New York: Routledge.

Hartsock, Nancy (1990) "Foucault on power: a theory for women?" in Linda J. Nicholson (ed.), *Feminism/Postmodernism*. New York: Routledge.

Hemmons, Willa M. (1980) "Black women and the women's liberation movement" in LaFrances Rodgers Rose (ed.), *The Black Woman*, 285–99. Beverley Hills, CA: Sage.

hooks, bell (1981) *Ain't I A Woman: Black Women and Feminism*. Boston: South End Press.

—— (1984) *Feminist Theory: From Margin to Center*. Boston: South End Press.

—— (1989) *Talking Back: Thinking Feminist, Thinking Black*. Boston: South End Press.

Hudson-Weems, Clenora (1989) "Cultural and agenda conflicts in academia: critical issues for Africana women studies," *Western Journal of Black Studies* 13 (4): 185–9.

—— (1993) *Africana Womanism: Reclaiming Ourselves*. Detroit: Bedford.

—— (2000) "Africana womanism: an overview" in Delores P. Aldridge and Carlene Young (eds.), *Out of the Revolution: The Development of Africana Studies*, 205–17. Lanham, MD: Lexington Books.

Hull, Gloria T., Scott, Patricia Bell, and Smith, Barbara (eds.) (1982) *All the Women Are White, All the Blacks Are Men, but Some of Us Are Brave: Black Womens' Studies*. Old Westbury, NY: Feminist Press.

James, Joy and Farmer, Ruth (eds.) (1993) *Spirit, Space, Survival: Africana American Women in (White) Academe*. New York: Routledge.

James, S. and Busia, A. (1993) *Theorizing Black Feminisms: The Visionary Pragmatism of Black Women*. New York: Routledge.

Loewenberg, Bert J. and Bogin, Ruth (eds.) (1976) *Black Women in Nineteenth-Century American Life*. University Park: Pennsylvania State Press.

Lorber, Judith (1994) *Paradoxes of Gender*. New Haven, CT: Yale University Press.

—— (1998) *Gender Inequality: Feminist Theories and Politics*. Los Angeles: Roxbury.

Mohanty, Carolyn (1991) "Under western eyes: feminist scholarship and colonial discourses" in C. Mohanty, A. Russo, and L. Torres (eds.), *Third World Women and the Politics of Feminism*. Bloomington: Indiana University Press.

Morrison, Toni (1987) *Beloved*. New York: Alfred A. Knopf.

Owens, Timothy J., Mortimer, Heylan T., and Finch, Michael D. (1996) "Self-determination as a source of self-esteem in adolescence," *Social Forces* 74 (4, June).

Rogers, Mary F. (1998) *Contemporary Feminist Theory*. New York: McGraw-Hill.

Rouse, Jacqueline A. (1989) *Lugenia Burns Hope: Black Southern Reformer*. Athens: University of Georgia Press.

Scott, Joan Wallach (1996) "Introduction" in Joan Wallach Scott (ed.), *Feminism and History*. New York: Oxford University Press.

Shaw, Stephanie J. (1996) *What a Woman Ought to Be and to Do: Black Professional Women during the Jim Crow Era*. Chicago: University of Chicago Press.

Smith, Barbara (1982) "Racism and women's studies" in G. T. Hull, P. B. Scott, and B. Smith (eds.), *All the Women Are White, All the Blacks Are Men, But Some of Us Are Brave: Black Women's Studies*. New York: Feminist Press.

Smith, Dorothy E. (1990) *The Conceptual Practices of Power: A Feminist Sociology of Knowledge*. Boston: Northeastern University Press.

Spade, Joan V. (1994) "Wives and husbands: perceptions of why wives work," *Gender and Society* 8 (2, June): 170–88.

Spelman, E. (1988) *Inessential Woman: Problems of Exclusion in Feminist Thought*. Boston: Beacon Press.

Stefano, Christine Di (1991) "Who the heck are we? Theoretical turns against gender," *Frontiers* 12 (2): 87.

Walker, Alice (1982) *The Color Purple*. New York: Washington Square Press.

—— (1983) *In Search of Our Mothers' Gardens: Womanist Prose*. New York: Harcourt Brace, Jovanovich.

Williams, Patricia J. (1991) *The Alchemy of Race and Rights*. Cambridge, MA: Harvard University Press.

Zinn, Baca M. and Dill, Thornton B. (1996) "Theorizing difference from multiracial feminism," *Feminist Studies* 22: 321–33.

Suggestions for Further Reading

Baumgardner, Jennifer and Richards, Amy (2000) *Manifesta: Young Women, Feminism, and the Future*. New York: Farrar, Straus, & Giroux.

Bell, Brandi Leigh-Ann (2002) "Riding the third wave: women-produced zines and feminisms," *Resources for Feminist Research*, 29: 3–4.

Dicker, Rory and Piepmeier, Alison (eds.) (2003) *Catching a Wave: Reclaiming Feminism for the 21st Century*. Boston: Northeastern University Press.

Drake, Jennifer (1997) "Third wave feminisms," *Feminist Studies*, 23: 1.

Findlen, Barbara (ed.) (1995) *Listen Up! Voices from the Next Feminist Generation*. Seattle: Seal.

Franklin, V. P. (2002) "Hidden in plain view: African American women, radical feminism, and the origins of women studies programs, 1967–1974," *Journal of African American History*, 87 (Fall): 433–45.

Gordon, Vivian V. (1991) *Black Women, Feminism, and Black Liberation: Which Way?* Chicago: Third World Press.

Green, Karen and Taormino, Tristan (eds.) (1997) *A Girl's Guide to Taking Over the World: Writings from the Girl Zine Revolution*. New York: St. Martin's Press.

Heywood, Leslie and Drake, Jennifer (eds.) (1994) *Teaching to Transgress: Education as the Practice of Freedom*. New York: Routledge.

—— (1997) *Third Wave Agenda: Being Feminist, Doing Feminism*. Minneapolis: University of Minnesota Press.

Hudson-Weems, Clenora (1993) *Africana Womanism: Reclaiming Ourselves*. Detroit: Bedford.

Lotz, Amanda D. (2003) "Communicating third-wave feminism and new social movements: challenges for the next century of feminist endeavor," *Women and Language* 26 (1).

Manzano, Angie (2000) "Charlie's Angels: free-market feminism," *off our backs*, 30 (11).

Walker, Rebecca (ed.) (1995) *To Be Real: Telling the Truth and Changing the Face of Feminism*. New York: Anchor Books.

Chapter Twenty-Five

Striving for Place: Lesbian, Gay, Bisexual, and Transgender (LGBT) People

Juan J. Battle and Natalie D. A. Bennett

When I picketed for Welfare Mother's Rights, and against the enforced sterilization of young Black girls, when I fought institutionalized racism in the New York City schools, I was a Black Lesbian. But you did not know it because we did not identify ourselves, so now you can say that Black Lesbians and Gay men have nothing to do with the struggles of the Black Nation. And I am not alone. When you read the words of Langston Hughes you are reading the words of a Black Gay man. When you read the words of Alice Dunbar-Nelson and Angelina Weld Grimke', poets of the Harlem Renaissance, you are reading the words of Black Lesbians. When you listen to the life-affirming voices of Bessie Smith and Ma Rainey, you are hearing Black Lesbian women. When you see the plays and read the words of Lorraine Hansberry, you are reading the words of a woman who loved women deeply . . . ! (*Lorde, I Am Your Sister* 1986)

Missing! Marginal! Misrepresented! Until the early 1990s, scholarly inquiries into the diversity of Black[1] experiences seemed to proceed much as it had in prior decades, paying little or no attention to how questions of same-sex sexuality might alter or significantly inform the perspectives and interpretations of the research itself. But that has begun to change, albeit slowly.

Several factors, together, have made the issue of same-sex sexuality – despite its being denigrated as a "White thing" by cultural nationalists or altogether ignored by mainstream scholars – directly relevant to the historical and contemporary realities of Blacks: in particular, the devastating impact of the HIV/AIDS epidemic within Black communities, and the increased visibility of Black lesbians and gays on questions of racial and sexual justice.

Within academia, this long overdue attention has begun to occur in two areas. Black feminist theorists, who advance an intersectional approach (that is, race, class, and gender) to understanding Black women's experiences, have taken note of normative sexuality as a part of that matrix of oppression (Collins 1990). New generations of scholars in sexuality studies, including those who use "queer theory," have increasingly probed how sexual identities are raced, gendered, and classed; and have begun to extend this theoretical framework to areas and groups previously unexamined through these analytic lenses.

Outside of academia, but by no means devoid from interactions with it, there is an established (and growing) body of non-fictional writings by and about gays and lesbians of African descent. These writings provide critical and incisive analyses of the relationships between sexuality and Black racial identities, as well as a broad theoretical framework that (ought to) inform and generate in-depth empirical studies on the topic. The mainstream lesbian and gay movement has also been important, providing the political and discursive space for critiquing homophobia, addressing anti-gay violence, and consequently opening up possibilities for discussing the incestuous relationship between homophobia and racism.

In delineating the experiences of Black gay men, lesbians, and bisexuals, this chapter draws on various bodies of scholarship – historical, social scientific, and literary – to reveal the multiple and intersecting social forces that have shaped their place, or lack thereof, in US society. Notably, we also pay attention to how gays, lesbians, and bisexuals themselves have resisted and questioned dominant notions of place, based on the racial and sexual hierarchy. As such, we also discuss the individual and collective strategies that have been used to articulate different visions of racial collectivity, as well as critical interpretations of same-sex sexuality in the context of Black racial identity, both of which – the strategies and the interpretations – have challenged but also enriched Black Studies.

Although throughout this chapter we present separately results from the fields of social science research and cultural production research, we by no means imply that these areas of intellectual development are mutually exclusive. We are clear that they are symbiotic. Presenting them separately – cultural production and the social science research – respects their inherent uniqueness, evolutions, and contributions. Further, it allows for a clearer narrative as we discuss each.

This chapter is by no means definitive of the history, contributions, and knowledge about Black lesbians, gays, bisexuals, and transgender people. As a matter of fact, discussions of transgender persons here will be limited, since it is a relatively new category in gender and sexuality studies. Like the categories "gay," "lesbian," and, "bisexual," we do not apply the term "transgender" uncritically across historical contexts, since the use and meaning of these terms changed dramatically during the twentieth century, most notably from defining deviant behavior to defining identity. Although there were (and are) Black men and women who crossed gender boundaries – living and identifying as another gender – the historical evidence that we review is insufficient for us to provide a meaningful discussion here.

This chapter aims to document what we currently know and, in doing so, to identify areas that need further in-depth research. In short, the "place" of Black gays, lesbians, bisexuals, and transgender persons is not singular nor fixed, and nor is it entirely determined by any single factor such as "culture." Rather, as we show through the following discussion, "place" is always negotiated within the myriad constraints presented by historical context, and articulated through various notions of class, gender, and region. Thus, we look to understand not what is "the" place of Black lesbians, gays, bisexuals, and transgender persons *per se*, but rather, how is "place" constituted by broader social forces and how it is contingent on social and cultural change.

Piecing Together Place: Lesbians, Gays, Bisexuals, and Transgender Persons in *Black* History

Talking about lesbians, gay men, and bisexual persons in the context of Black history inevitably raises questions about identity and disclosure: How can we tell/ know who they were? Did they identify themselves as such? Certainly, it bears repeating here that sexual identities like "gay," "lesbian," and the like are relatively modern constructions, and therefore, cannot be projected backward onto histories and identities. Such terms and identities did not have the same meaning – perhaps had no meaning – for those who participated in and created sexual subcultures well before the watershed moment of the Stonewall uprisings. Nonetheless, since same-sex erotic attraction is transhistorical and transcultural (Peplau 2001), an important question to consider is how scholars' own taxonomy of identities has enabled or constrained the recognition of Black men and women who share same-sex sexuality and, as a result, to what extent they appear as actors in Black historiography.

Reconstructing gay and lesbian Black history of the twentieth century is still in its initial stages, inhibited both by the suspect nature of the subject and the small number of individuals willing and able to pursue the sources that would shed light on the topic. In large part, historians of sexuality occupy centerstage in this venture. And while they have not always asked research questions that directly focused on Black lesbians and gays, their scholarship offers important insight into the social lives of individual gays and lesbians, the communities they participated in, and the institutions they helped to create. As new historical sources become available, or as new questions are being asked of the established scholarship, undoubtedly new inquiries will ensue.

A good example of the nature of new inquiries is Farah Griffin's *Beloved Sisters and Loving Friends* (1999). This edited collection of letters that were exchanged between Rebecca Primus and Addie Brown in the late nineteenth century offers a rare glimpse into the intimate lives of Black women, and particularly the ways in which Black women's emotional and erotic relationships with each other were expressed. The letters also show that love, desire, and relationships are structured by social differences as well as by social similarities. Such expressions of same-sex desire are time-specific and historically bound, sometimes bearing little resemblance to the categories that we currently use to analyze sexuality. Nonetheless, the letters provide concrete evidence of the romantic relationship between these two women. It was being expressed in the context of their commitment to Black equality and "racial uplift," and enables us to "move beyond the silence" about sexuality in Black historiography.

While we await a full-length historical study of Black lesbians, gays, and bisexuals, useful insights can be found in the recent studies on lesbian and gay social history, particularly in New York. In his critical study of the thriving gay male culture in New York from 1890 to 1940, historian George Chauncey (1994) points out that the "closet" was not always *the* defining aspect of men's social interactions with each other and the broader society. Rather, men's abilities to enter and interact with "homosexual society" or "the gay world" were shaped by social hierarchies based on race and class. To the extent that Black gay men participated in the "gay world" they did so in ways limited by their place in the racial order of things.

Similarly, Eric Garber's 1989 research on the lesbian and gay subculture of early twentieth-century Harlem, particularly during the Harlem Renaissance in the period 1920–35, points to the ways African American gays, lesbians, and bisexuals appropriated social and intellectual spaces for their own use and, within these settings, made a palpable mark on African American culture. Indeed, it is arguable whether there would have been a Renaissance at all without the participation of Black lesbians, gay men, and bisexuals. Henry Louis Gates, Jr observes that the Harlem Renaissance was "surely as gay as it was black, not that it was exclusively either of these" (quoted in Wirth 2002: 31). Many of the persons who have attained iconic stature in Black history actively participated in the lesbian and gay subculture of Harlem, whether or not they addressed issues of same-sex sexuality in their writings of the day. These figures include some who are generally known, and others who are less well known: Angelina Weld Grimke, Alice Dunbar-Nelson, Alaine Locke, Langston Hughes, Claude McKay, Wallace Thurman, Countee Cullen, Lorraine Hansberry, Zora Neale Hurston, and Richard Bruce Nugent.

Much ink has been devoted to the literature and politics of this era, which we will not rehash here. Most significant is that the work of these intellectuals has not been thoroughly analyzed within the context of Black lesbian and gay intellectual life. A corrective to this appears in the 2002 anthology *Black Like Us: A Century of Lesbian, Gay, and Bisexual Black Fiction*, edited by Devon Carbado, Dwight McBride, and Donald Weise. Their work highlights the tremendous variations in the intellectual lives of lesbian, gay, and bisexual Black cultural producers. Further, they argue that lesbian and bisexual authors like Grimke and Dunbar-Nelson did not deal with same-sex subject matter at all, nor would they necessarily have identified their sexual orientation as "lesbian" or "bisexual" (cf. Hull 1983).

Other figures, such as Richard Bruce Nugent, did exactly the opposite. In 1926, Nugent – who helped to create the legendary Renaissance publication *FIRE!!* – published an essay entitled "Smoke, lilies and jade" in the first (and only) issue. Deemed by literary scholars to be the "first-known overtly homosexual work published by a Black," the essay was the first of many such works by Nugent, who fully embraced both his racial and sexual identities, and wrote from a "self-declared homosexual perspective." In the edited volume of Richard Nugent's work, friend and colleague Thomas Wirth points out that "little that was printed in *FIRE!!* would have appeared in *Crisis*," the publication of the National Association for the Advancement of Colored People (NAACP). *The Crisis* featured the work of Black writers and artists, but its audience was decidedly middle-class and would have been quite offended at the content (Wirth 2002: 14). However, his artwork, with some stylized sexual undertones, was featured on the cover of the National Urban League's *Opportunity* in March 1926 (no. 66). Through his subject matter and his wide social networks, which crossed the racial and geographic boundaries of New York City, "Bruce Nugent linked the black world of the Harlem Renaissance with the gay world of bohemian New York" (Wirth 2002: xii). Nugent's talent was supported from very early on by luminaries like Angelina Grimke, one of his high-school teachers, and by some of the foremost intellectuals at the time, such as Alain Locke, but did not attract the approval or admiration of others, notably W. E. B. Du Bois. Nugent's exploration of male same-sex desire in writings and drawings also predates – by three decades – James Baldwin's novel *Giovanni's*

Room (1956), another definitive work that explores what it means to be both Black and gay.

The debates around sexual morality and respectability among Blacks at that time, though these debates set the terms of much homophobic discourse later on, do not seem to have resulted in same-sex sexuality being precluded. Rather, the question was about how homoerotic sentiment would be expressed. Many writers and scholars, in the process of questioning how the "Black self" was to be represented, and whether each person could adequately represent the race as a whole, toyed with social conventions of the "open secret" about their same-sex sexuality. At the same time that they invented characters who openly expressed homoerotic sentiments, they did not always follow suit in their public lives, avoiding the stigma of being seen as "fairies" (Wirth 2002: 50). In a similar vein, Gloria Joseph argues that, during the 1920s and 1930s, Black male homosexuality simply did not capture the ire of the broader community in the way that it would after the 1950s. She argues that "the male homosexual was not categorically ostracized, nor did he become totally invisible. [Rather], the extent of derision and/or acceptance depended to a great extent how much he manifested his homosexuality" (Joseph 1981: 191, 188).

George Chauncey offers a more extensive analysis, arguing that in the early twentieth century, fine lines were drawn between "queers/fairies" and "men" on the basis of gender status. In the late twentieth century, lines in American culture would be drawn between "heterosexual" and "homosexual" on the basis of sexual object choice. Chauncey argues that it was only around the middle of the century that homosexual behavior became the primary basis for the labeling and self-identification of men as "queer." Previously, his study shows, they were only so labeled if they assumed sexual or other cultural roles ascribed to women, that is, if they took on effeminate traits rather than abide by masculine gender conventions. This distinction between "heterosexual" and "homosexual," the former as the marker of a "real" man, the latter of the debased anti-man, does not become part of the cultural lexicon of Black gender identity until well after the Second World War. This finding would explain, in part, why this early period as captured by the Harlem Renaissance was such a watershed moment for Black gay and bisexual men (less so for lesbians), and how sexual identity appeared to be far more fluid in its expression than in later decades.

For women, the gendered politics of respectability within Black communities seemed to have a significant impact on their sexual expression. This led many, if not most, women writers of the day to hide their same-sex relationships under the guise of heterosexuality and to refrain from participating in the sexual freedom and openness that seemed possible and available to men. This "culturally imposed self-silencing" has had the effect of preventing subsequent scholars from recognizing the specific contributions that Black women made to discourses about race and sexuality during that period (Smith 1979; Keating 2002).

Homoerotic socializing was a major feature of Harlem life in the 1920s and 1930s. It was also the setting for rent parties and buffet flats – all-night events for gay, lesbian, bisexual, and sexually adventurous persons that were held in private homes and featured food, drink, gambling, sex, and/or any combination thereof. Gay male and lesbian revues and cabarets were also frequent, as were drag balls – what Langston Hughes called "Spectacles in Color" – which were attended by large numbers of Black gay men and lesbians, where both men and women could dress as they desired and dance with whomever they pleased. Gay-friendly speakeasies also provided the setting for blues singers like Bessie Smith, Gertrude "Ma" Rainey, Jackie "Moms" Mabley, and Lucille Bogan to reflect themes and sensibilities about Black women's sexuality in their music (Garber 1989; Davis 1998). These settings also provided important sources of economic support, especially for lesbians who worked as entertainers, and who generally had fewer options for work, especially if they sought to live non-traditional lifestyles. Gladys Bentley, Josephine Baker, and Ethel Waters were among the Black lesbians and bisexual women of this period who carved out an economic niche in show business for themselves.

Oral history accounts and other personal narratives provide important insight into the challenges faced by Black gays and lesbians during this period. For example, through the memories and reconstruction of her own life, Mabel Hampton, a Black lesbian, points out that high rents and housing shortages made privacy a much sought-after luxury for lesbians and gays. State repression increasingly became a feature of Harlem life, as migrant women from the South, especially those who did not live traditional lifestyles, were often mistaken for prostitutes and were often arrested and harassed by the police (Garber 1989). Nonetheless, for Hampton, show business offered a much needed economic respite, while allowing her to socialize within a predominantly Black female world. Mabel Hampton was committed to the preservation of Black lesbian history – she donated her papers and artifacts to the Lesbian Herstory Archives in 1976 and helped to index them. She was also a key source of knowledge about Black lesbian and gay life in the pre-Stonewall era, and was featured in the historic documentary film *Before Stonewall*, which explored the lives, relationships, and communities of self-identified gays and lesbians between the 1920s and the 1960s. She continued to be active in lesbian communities until her death in 1989. As Carbado, McBride, and Weisse note in *Black Like Us* (2002), not all Black lesbians and gays were able or desired to live their entire lives as sexual nonconformists. In later years, Gladys Bentley re-invented herself as a more traditional woman, which, they argue, bespoke the pressure towards "normalcy" and the changing perceptions of lesbians and gays as "dangerous" in the Depression Era as chronicled by Chauncey and others.

Historians of sexuality have drawn more systematically on oral histories to reconstruct the lives of lesbians and gays. Such strategies are only now being used by Blacks to do the same thing. In their 1993 study of the working-class lesbian community of the 1930s to the 1950s in Buffalo, New York, Elizabeth Lapovsky Kennedy and Madeline Davis used an "ethno-historical approach" – combining ethnography, oral histories, and archival research methodology – to analyze the role of public spaces like bars in the development of lesbian communities and identities. Their extensive research showed that, far from the single lesbian identity or politics they expected to find, the racial segregation and economic inequality in the growing industrialized city had helped to generate (at least) two separate lesbian communities – one Black and the other White.

Kennedy and Davis argue that the bold, new participation of groups of Black lesbians in White lesbian bar spaces in the 1950s helped to usher in "changes in lesbian culture and consciousness" in Buffalo. However, that change was neither far-reaching nor long-lasting. On one hand, it is notable that Black lesbians' efforts in the 1950s to challenge their exclusion from public space in Buffalo and to rene-gotiate the terms of lesbian community and identity were taking place at the same time that other Black men and women were desegregating public lunch counters in southern states. On the other hand, Black lesbians were possibly further stigmatized and largely rejected by White women, and found themselves dealing face to face with racist attitudes of White lesbians in the intimate setting of the bars (Kennedy and Davis 1993: 116–19). Outside of Black social contexts, interracial lesbian and gay couples were seen as suspect, subject to harassment from police and from White gays and lesbians, primarily because of the presence of a Black person (D'Emilio 1983: 88; Kennedy and Davis 1993: 119).

Kennedy and Davis provide mixed evidence for how Black women responded to this new backlash; while some returned to socializing primarily within Black homosocial environments, others became involved in disassembling the barriers to Black women's full participation in Buffalo's social life, including in the lesbian bar scene. What appears to have been the typical response was to continue going to bars that were generally perceived as supportive and relatively devoid of racist hostility, while participating fully in the distinct cultural scene offered by "house parties."

Black lesbian culture emerged in Buffalo (and in other places, like Cleveland, Detroit, and New York City) around private, secluded events such as house parties, partly as a response to exclusion from the public lesbian life of White working-class and elite bars. Another reason why these private social events flourished as hubs of Black lesbian life was precisely because they existed *within* the racially segregated neighborhoods where Black lesbians lived, rather than outside them. The significance of house parties and their role in creating community among Black lesbians (and gays) is often repeated in accounts of gay and lesbian life in the early twentieth century. For example, the late Ruth Ellis, who was the oldest *known* lesbian-identified Black woman – 100 years old – lived in Detroit until her death in October 2001.

Through Ellis's narrative, as featured in the documentary film *Living With Pride*, we recognize that her sexual identity as a lesbian was intricately tied to her being born into and living in the violence of racial apartheid in Springfield, Illinois, and Detroit, Michigan. Among Ellis's many achievements was opening her house as "The Spot," one of the few social spaces available to Black gay men and lesbians in Detroit, where they could temporarily escape the vagaries of living in a racist, class-segregated, heterosexist society. Such house parties remained institutions in Detroit's Black lesbian and gay community, and became a significant resource for Ellis well into her later years. They provided access to social networks, resources, and support, and especially an extended family of affinity that few Black elderly persons – especially women – in her circumstances would ordinarily have access to.

The tradition of house parties during this period affirmed Black same-sex sexuality in a collective sense. Certainly, it predated (as well as set the stage for) the emer-gence of Black lesbian and gay organizations in the 1970s and 1980s that replicated and extended the social and political functions of those events. It is also clear that house parties and the like also afforded Black lesbians some protection from racist attacks that public Black gay bars could attract. Nonetheless, there has been little substantive research on these institutions and the people who organized and sus-tained them. One notable exception is a section of *Gay Rebel of the Harlem Renaissance* (Wirth 2002) entitled "Harlem Renaissance personalities." It provides vignettes of several persons – for example, A'Lelia Walker a.k.a. "Mahogany Millionaire" and Mr Winston a.k.a. "Miss Gloria Swanson" – who ought to be the subject of future historical studies.

We also learn something about various individuals in key positions within the early lesbian and gay movement, who do not show up in the historical spotlights as exceptional persons. For example, in his study of the emergence of the modern gay and lesbian civil rights movement, John D'Emilio discusses the significance of Ernestine Eckstein, a Black woman who was elected in 1965 to run the New York chapter of the national homophile organization, Daughters of Bilitis. Her activism in the Black civil rights movement shaped her radical politics, which emphasized direct, political engagement with "the powers that be," especially against the State (D'Emilio 1983: 172–3). The backlash she faced from the "old guard," who were more interested in creating a "social service group, protective of women" than participating in a political movement for civil rights, eventually led to her resignation in 1966. Eckstein was also one of few Blacks who visibly participated in the homophile movement, and the only Black to participate in the 1965 protest in Washington, DC against federal employment discrimination (Carbado, McBride, and Weise 2002).

Black lesbians and gays participated in the major Black social movements in US history, as indicated in the epigraph at the beginning of this chapter, but they have not always been fully welcomed or acknowledged. Among the reasons for this were fears of the "fairy" and "mannish woman," which increasingly became pre-occupations in the Depression era. These fears were replaced by a virulent homophobia that soon became a leitmotif in American politics, as in the McCarthyite anti-Communist era of the 1950s. Clearly, Blacks – whether in the civil rights and literary movements, or gays and lesbians – were not immune to this.

During this period, several Black male authors explored gay themes in their work – including Owen Dodson's *Boy at the Window* (1951), Ralph Ellison's *Invisible Man* (1952), and Chester Himes' *Cast the First Stone* (1952). They did so probably with full awareness of the consequences for themselves, should they be viewed as suspect under the repressive social climate that penalized gay sex as criminal, and assigned guilt by association to others. As such, it is nearly impossible to decipher the historical record of contributions made by Black lesbians, gays, and bisexuals during that period, as many seem to have been driven underground and into the closet, and even worse, alienated from each other (Lorde 1984).

The oral historical record does show that community building remained a key part of Black gay and lesbian life, regardless of where they lived. In this era, house parties and other private events probably took on a more urgent meaning, representing both a symbolic and literal lifeline for many. Nonetheless, two self-identified gay figures emerge as important in this period. Despite being located in different arenas, both inadvertently disturbed the prevailing political discourses about the inherent tension between race and sexual orientation. One was James Baldwin, who emerged as an important Black writer in this period, offering incisive analyses of Black experiences. He engaged the intersections of race and sexuality by critiquing the heterosexism in Black cultural and political projects. For this, he attracted the ire of many who believed that he was a race traitor.

Bayard Rustin's life, his contributions to the Black Civil Rights Movement, his thoughts on the gay and lesbian liberation movement, and his involvement in international struggles until his death in 1987, have been the subject of five full-length studies and a documentary film. Perhaps best known for his role in orchestrating the March on Washington in 1963, Rustin was a Black gay man whose political and social life was embedded in, and strongly shaped by, his participation in the social movements of the day. These movements challenged the orthodoxy of social hierarchies that deprived American citizens of basic freedoms.

As a self-identified radical in a time of intense cultural repression, Rustin found his sexual orientation being placed at the center of ideological power struggles within the Black Civil Rights movement. He stated that "my being gay was not a problem for . . . [Martin Luther] King but it was a problem for the movement" (Redvers 1988: 3). Central to the concerns of movement leaders, about whether his homosexuality would be used to discredit the movement in the face of its opponents, was the lingering notion that homosexuals are unstable, untrustworthy, and an indelible stain on the moral fabric of the Black America they were trying to validate. This idea returned again and again to the forefront of political discourse in the Black Nationalist Movement of the 1960s and 1970s, and served as a lightning rod for criticisms by many Black feminists, lesbians, and gays who were being vilified and pushed out of the movement. As this particular strain of homophobia seemed to become permanently enshrined in the movement for Black Liberation, many gays and lesbians were forced to carve out autonomous spaces that were more inclusive, and which directly addressed the intersections of oppression based on race, gender, and sexual orientation that informed their social experiences.

Our review of the historical scholarship demonstrates that black gays and lesbians were – and are – no more likely to be "in the closet" than their white counterparts. Still, the notion that black gays and lesbians have a particular affinity and interest in masking their non-heterosexual identities continues to reverberate through both scholarly and popular discourse. But, as scholars of modern American sexuality have shown, the "closet" itself is a historical and political construction. On the one hand, it is useful, since it provides both a visual image of the way homosexuality has been criminalized and stigmatized, and also the basis for a shared identity that has persisted over several decades. On the other hand, the "closet" has taken on epistemic significance in the post-Stonewall period, such that most inquiries into same-sex sexuality have focused on "coming out" (Butler 1991; Sedgwick 1993). Framing questions of sexual identity in this way largely ignores the way sexual identities are also defined by race, class, and nationality. The historiography of the "closet" in post-war America has given little attention to the salience of racism in shaping gay and lesbian identities – for whites and blacks alike (cf. Sommerville 2000). That was true even of the path-breaking work by George Chauncey and Esther Newton, published in the 1990s and much cited.

More recent work has begun to address these important gaps. Reimonenq (2002) argues that in the early part of the twentieth century the "closet" functioned as a protective shield for black gays and lesbians, who used the privacy to form gendered networks and coalitions of like-minded intellectuals and as a bridge to the mainstream, while also keeping individual discrimination at bay. These "protective" effects would have been particularly salient for black gays and lesbians in the period immediately after the Second World War. Coincidentally, this is also the period that we know the least about. And, if this was a period of great upheaval and change for

blacks in general – with continued migration from rural to urban areas, growing economic insecurity and class inequality, establishment of new housing developments
and neighborhoods, and the emergence of a distinct urban political culture – then
certainly gays and lesbians participated in, and were affected by, these new conditions.

Rochella Thorpe's work (1996) offers some insight into these questions by in-
quiring into the ways in which black lesbians in post-war Detroit responded to their
marginality within a material context defined by increasing economic inequality and
racial segregation, and whose effects had, and continue to have, different implications for black women than for men. Thorpe's analysis begins to jettison the notion
that Black urban public culture is, by default, masculine and heterosexual, and
points to the various ways that black lesbians used gender-, class-, and race-based
resources to counter their isolation from each other, and to provide economic
avenues that were sustainable for a period of time. But this analysis also extends
questions first raised by Black lesbian feminist scholars like Barbara Smith, and which
still need to be explored in depth. Such questions include: How have the sexual
identities of black gays and lesbians been shaped by the intersections of racism, class
inequality, sexism, and heterosexism? And where and how do gender, class, and
nationality figure in the ways in which black lesbians and gays have responded to
marginalization and invisibility within black families and community contexts?

What is also clear from this review of the evidence is that social and cultural
constructions of gender within Black communities presented different options and
constraints for men and women. The scholarship shows, although not always
by intention, that while Black men and women shared the material conditions of
segregated, economically deprived, and politically disenfranchised communities, their
experiences and outlooks as lesbians and gay men seem to have been strongly
bifurcated along gender lines. When we learn about men's social worlds, women
seem to disappear, and vice versa. Within the historiography, Black gay men are the
subject of analysis and commentary – both academic and popular – far more frequently than are lesbians. Here, the efforts of Black feminists to systematically
inquire into the nature of Black sexual politics have contributed to a more careful
leveling of the historical playing field, and still do so (White 2001).

Re-Visioning Place: Lesbians, Gays, Bisexuals, and Transgender Persons in Black Culture

Black cultural discourses shifted to emphasize racial pride and protest in the 1970s
and the 1980s. The mandate that all energies – creative, political, sexual – be
directed toward the redemption of Black identity (read: heterosexual masculinity)
presented gays and lesbians with a significant obstacle to claiming racial authenticity.
A new Black gay and lesbian identity and politics emerged in this era, one that has
scarcely registered in Black scholarship, but which has continued to breathe life and
direction into the work of activists and scholars alike.

What was this new politics, and how might we identify it? First, it emerged in a
particular cultural context, out of the nexus of the feminist, gay, and Black Civil
Rights movements. Disaffection with the lack of attention to race and sexuality in
these movements prompted many Black lesbians and gays to find new mechanisms
through which to express their political sensibilities. They continued to participate in

Black and (predominantly White) gay and lesbian organizations, embodying dual, warring identities, even as they helped to make civil rights a concrete reality for each group. Increasingly however, their voices were channeled through grassroots organizations that they developed, and through literary and critical writings read primarily by other lesbians and gays.

For example, in 1973, Black feminists organized the National Black Feminist Organization from which splintered the Combahee River Collective, a group of lesbian feminists that included renowned scholar and activist Barbara Smith. The Collective argued that Black feminist work ought to be guided by an intersectional theory of oppression, emphasizing the interconnected nature of racism, economic exploitation, sexism, and heterosexism in Black women's lives. Further, the Collective authored a statement that is a foundation document in Black feminism today (Combahee River Collective 1974). This was one of the first times that same-sex sexuality was explicitly placed on the political agenda of a Black organization. By calling for a more inclusive and radical movement framework for social justice, the literary productions of Black lesbians propelled this criticism onward, and issued a challenge to White mainstream feminism, Black Nationalism, and the gay liberation movement. Although this call never really found an echo in these camps, and resonated more in later years, it continued to be heard and sustained in the writings of Black lesbians.

In this way, the new politics had a decidedly cultural turn and was also distinctly gendered. Much of the political writing produced in this time came from Black lesbians like Cheryl Clarke and Barbara Smith, who were radicalized by participation in the feminist, Black Nationalist, and Black Arts Movements. They also joined key debates and articulated radical ideas that challenged monolithic constructions of Blackness and womanhood. Their political writings were remarkably prescient and continue to offer insight into debates about Black identities and politics. Literary writings were an especially important "catalytic agent" of the Women's Movement, and women's collectives and publications sprung up in major cities, offering numerous venues for Black lesbians to publish their work. It is in this period that the first Black unambiguously lesbian novel is published – Ann Allen Shockley's *Loving Her* (1974) – and the now-oldest Black lesbian organization was founded – Salsa Soul Sisters, now African Ancestral Lesbians United for Societal Change (1974). Years later, the National Coalition of Black Gays (later renamed National Coalition of Black Lesbians and Gays) emerged, and had a key role to play in the first March on Washington for Lesbian and Gay Rights, in 1979.

The autobiographical and fictional work of Audre Lorde, the poetry of Pat Parker, and the journalistic writings of Anita Cornwell together formed the foundation for the Black Lesbian Renaissance of the 1970s. Notwithstanding the differences in their positions relative to feminism and the Black Civil Rights Movement for social justice, all articulated and identified with Black Lesbian Feminism, and focused their work on exploring the myriad social aspects of Black lesbians' lives. In the process, they offered scathing critiques on racism in the women's movement, Black men's sexism, homophobia in Black communities, cultural nationalism, and racial identity – to name only a few issues – that rarely left anyone unprovoked.

During this period, Black lesbians' writings projected new and different visions of inclusive communities, and voices of protest, as well as an ethics of caring that was otherwise unavailable in the political discourse of the day. They also offered ways to understand erotic attraction as more than simply a source of oppression: the erotic was also a source of inspiration and connection to others, the basis of community in the context of marginalization from traditional "home" communities. Through their literary writings, Black lesbians – and later gay men – were able to express values, images, and visions of racial-sexual identities that differed significantly from those being constructed in either mainstream or specifically Black contexts (Keating 2002).

Black gay men's literary and political engagement fully emerged in the early 1980s, and drew heavily on the work and traditions of Black lesbians. The onset of the HIV/AIDS epidemic gave their writings and activism a certain urgency, still present today. At the same time that Black gay men sought to develop and define affirmative sexual identities, they were subject to a particularly virulent form of homophobia. While they were contending with the impact of the disease on a community that was still in formation, they also had to challenge effectively the homophobia in Black political and cultural discourse, which had seeped into most institutions and fueled the widespread denial and negligence towards the HIV/AIDS epidemic (Harper 1996; Cohen 1999).

Whether found in the works of cultural nationalists like Molefe Asante's *Afrocentricity* (1988) or in the new field of "Black Psychology," notably in Nathan and Julia Hare's *The Endangered Black Family* (1984) and Frances Cress Welsing's *The Isis Papers: The Keys to the Colors* (1990), whether in the pulpits or on the streets, the conservative sexual politics and anti-gay rhetoric of the 1980s presented a formidable opponent to the individual and collective well-being of Black gay men. This period also represented a distinct shift in the tenor of "sexual conservatism," to use a term borrowed from Carbado et al. The writings and the activism – of both men and women, but moreso men's – that emerged in this phase took on the challenge of debunking these assumptions and exposing the problems underlying them, notably the assumption of a mythological past that guaranteed men's social superiority and made misogynist and homophobic notions appear entirely natural and unproblematic (White 2001; Ransby 2000).

Since the 1980s, the shift in the visibility of Black gay men and lesbians has been provoked by the impact of multiple social movements that sought to broaden access to civil and social rights, and to destabilize White male hegemony. One consequence of these social movements was the construction of new identities, ones that marginalized groups could use to demand fuller inclusion into society. The emergence of gay, largely White, institutions and infrastructure in the urban centers of the US – neighborhoods, political organizations, and academic programs, for example – helped to open up social discourse about sexual identity. At the same time, Black gays and lesbians tended to create their own spaces to explore questions of racial and sexual identity. Not surprisingly, the organizations (whether social, political, and/or cultural in nature) that emerged during this period embraced a hybrid social identity (Black *and* Gay/Lesbian/Bisexual/Transgender), further institutionalizing the validity of these identities for those oppressed by virtue of their membership in these stigmatized groups.[2] In the process, these organizations offered an opportunity to define a collective identity around which people could be mobilized for greater access to resources, as well as to engage in the broader struggle for civil rights.

Homophobia may be the "last acceptable prejudice;" nonetheless, Black lesbians, gays, and bisexuals – and, increasingly, transgender persons – have not readily conceded this fight. Challenging their social and political marginalization by their racial group and the broader society has occurred in a number of ways. The critical analyses of Black feminists such as Barbara Smith, Cheryl Clarke, Evelyn Hammonds, and Cathy Cohen, and the emergence of Black gay political leaders like Keith Boykin, Mandy Carter, and Phill Wilson have consistently challenged the notion that same-sex sexuality is "at odds" with Black racial identity.

Black lesbians and gays have also responded to the triple dose of silence, indifference, and marginality within both the Black and LGBT communities by developing organizations that reflect the intersection of their racial and sexual identities, while also emphasizing the racial difference from their White LGBT counterparts. Through the development of organizations, marginalized groups have created institutional alternatives that also legitimize their resistance to dominant ideas. In general, organizations serve to represent collective group interests to the public, and illustrate their symbolic ties to the broader group's history and culture through the names they give themselves.

Organizations like Gay Men of African Descent, African Ancestral Lesbians, United Lesbians of African Heritage, SiSTAHS, Black and White Men Together (now Men Of All Colors Together), National Black Lesbian and Gay Leadership Forum, People of Color in Crisis, NIA Collective, Zami, ADODI, Unity Fellowship Church, Griot Circle, and the New York State Black Gay Network, have – and continue to be – important sites for affirming same-sex sexual identities of Black people. Equally importantly, these spaces – whether religious/spiritual or secular, gender- or age-specific, issue-oriented or general support – are also critical to defining oppositional discourses about same-sex desire that directly challenge normative ideas about Black sexualities.

As a way of foregrounding and championing an intersectional approach to sexual identity and racial politics, many of these organizations use symbols and language that draw on cultural nationalist ideals, with a twist. Such strategies include incorporating the red/black/green nationalist flag and African-inspired images into organizations' logos and promotional materials. They also include creating alternative systems of naming – for example, using the term "same gender loving (SGL)" and eschewing the terms "gay," "lesbian," and "queer," as well as incorporating Black cultural celebrations such as Kwanzaa, and African rituals such as the pouring of libations at meetings and events. Many of these organizations serve as political advocates for Black LGBTs, and bring a critical, race-centered analysis to debates about sexual orientation and civil rights.

Since the 1990s, these organizations have helped to sustain Black LGBT counterpublics – that is, arenas that stand in opposition to the racism and homophobia of White mainstream and the Black public sphere. These counterpublics have resisted, and continue to resist, easy uncritical identification with either "camp" and they promote images and understandings of race, gender, and sexuality that support and legitimize *Black* LGBT identities. Functioning in this capacity, these organizations have supported the tremendous groundswell of visibility and activism of Black LGBTs, and rightly, constitute the core elements of a vibrant urban Black LGBT culture in this decade.

If invisibility was the leitmotif of the 1980s, then the 1990s looked remarkably different for Black LGBTs. For one thing, various renditions of LGBT Black Experience began to appear in the mass media and particularly, although not exclusively, among all-Black casts. Television programs featuring butch–femme lesbian relationships in *The Women of Brewster Place*, the highly effeminized finger-snapping gay men on *In Living Color*, and the witty, gay staff assistant on *Spin City*, for the moment, seemed to fill the vacuum of images. So too, did major motion pictures like *Set It Off* (1996) and now-discontinued programs like *Courthouse* (CBS 1995), *Roc* (Fox 1991), and *Linc's* (Showtime 1998), which offer glimpses of lives hanging in the social chasm between "black" and "gay/lesbian." More recently, *Soul Food* (Showtime 2000) and *The Wire* (HBO 2003) feature Black lesbian characters as regular and central to the story lines.

Several documentaries were also released during this time, exploring varied aspects of the Black LGBT identities, albeit to different ends – from Marlon Riggs' *Tongues Untied* (1991) and *Black Is, Black Ain't* (1996) to Cheryl Dunye's *Watermelon Woman* (1996). Using the narrative format of a documentary, Black (primarily) gay and lesbian subject identities were put on display (sometimes in very problematic ways) for the first time, to a national, rather than a specialized (read: minority) audience. This "broader exposure" phenomenon is best exemplified in the cross-over popularity of Jennie Livingston's *Paris is Burning* (1990) and Isaac Julien's *Looking for Langston* (1989). The political significance of these two films in the broader discourse about race, gender, and sexuality has been treated extensively elsewhere (see, for example, Mercer 1993, Harper 1995, and Munoz 1999).

A hostile political climate informed by President Bill Clinton's "Don't ask, don't tell" policies and generalized right-wing backlash against sexual minorities also informed the formation of Black LGBT identities in the 1990s. This backlash ranged from state-level ballot initiatives to repealing existing constitutional protections for lesbians and gays, to challenging the introduction of the Rainbow Curriculum into New York City's public schools, to outcries against the use of public funds via the National Endowment for the Arts to support gay-themed art. Such protest was especially vigorous with regard to works engaging Black gay and lesbian sexuality, or which overtly challenged – or at least raised questions about – normative constructions of race, sexuality, and gender identity, in relation to Black men and women. The films by Marlon Riggs and Cheryl Dunye were a focus of these debates and censorship efforts.

The virtual explosion of (White) gay and lesbian political activism around HIV/AIDS and sexual orientation-based discrimination during this period occurred in tandem with the steadily rising incidence of HIV/AIDS infections, and the increasing discord within Black communities about whether and how to address this problem. The increasing visibility of LGBT persons in American life was accompanied by a new social problem – homophobic violence or "gay bashing" – as well as the development of organizational infrastructure and discourses, such as hate crimes legislation, to document the problem. Nonetheless, the violence that LGBT Blacks face both inside and outside of Black communities rarely appears in these official statistics, on account that the other problem – of "Black homophobia" – is seen as the cause, and as a local, isolated concern.

Urban centers of Black life in the 1990s were also the nerve centers of Black LGBT culture. Drag balls offered young Black men (and to a lesser extent women) opportunities to create art forms and self-styled subjective identities that they used to navigate the strictures of masculinity, poverty, joblessness, and outsider status in their economically depressed, racially segregated communities. The emerging literati composed of college-educated Black gay men created underground magazine and journal outlets such as *Pomo Afro Homos* and *Other Countries* for cultural and political expression. Through their writings, with varied success in mainstream and gay and lesbian markets, they have perceptibly altered the perceptions of Black gay men, making them a little more familiar, while not completely removing that tell-tale shroud of distrust in the age of AIDS. For example, the popular best-selling novels of E. Lynn Harris and James Earl Hardy, which explore Black gay men's multifaceted lives and identities, also introduce the latest figment of the collective Black (hetero-sexual) nightmare – the presumably straight man who has sex with other men and is therefore on the "Down Low."

Black lesbians also created and sustained "wimmin-centered" spaces, which affirm women's sexual identities, primarily by emphasizing the interconnections between spirituality, sexuality, and mental wellbeing. For both Black men and women, rethinking and creating alternative visions of sexual expression were part of this renewal, especially given the impact of HIV/AIDS on the meaning and expression of sexual attraction. Embracing the erotic as a source of personal and collective power, as noted by the late Audre Lorde (1984), clearly spurred the emergence of women's erotic clubs and creative expression, as demonstrated in magazines and edited volumes of fictional and non-fictional writings dedicated to the topic. These provide the most tangible source of insight into the development of Black lesbian identities. Catherine McKinley and L. Joyce Delaney published *Afrekete: An Anthology of Black Lesbian Writing* in 1995, while Lisa C. Moore began a publishing press, RedBone Press, featuring the work of Black lesbians, and has since published *Does Your Mama Know?: An Anthology of Lesbian Coming Out Stories* in 1997, as well as the *Bull Jean Stories* by Sharon Bridgforth in 1998.

For Black gay and bisexual men in the age of AIDS, no respite from the demonization of "gay sex" could be found in public discourse in either White or Black communities. Increasingly, public discussions about same-sex sexuality in the 1990s constructed the issue in terms of a turf war between "Blacks" and "Gays" (Hutchinson 2000; Brandt 1999). Similarly, Black cultural nationalist discourses that associate "gayness" with "whiteness" have expanded to emphasize protecting The Black Family through restoring proper (read: straight) Black masculinity, as the Million Man March in 1995 demonstrated. And while individual gay men did participate, Black gay men continue to be excluded from participation in critical aspects of Black communities, and to be seen as liabilities. For example, many resources and much energy have been expended by organizations like the Balm in Gilead in New York City, which is dedicated to mobilizing Black congregations and religious organizations to respond proactively to the HIV/AIDS epidemic. Nonetheless, many mainstream Black organizations are still hesitant to become involved on account that, even in this stage of the disease pandemic, they still see Black gay men as a scourge on the race, to be considered separate from the larger Black community (Cohen 1999).

Given these repressive social constraints, LGBT Blacks continue to create safe social spaces where the possibilities for sexual agency can be realized, without men and women feeling forced to choose from pre-existing categories, like "being out," "gay," "lesbian," and so on. Black Pride events offer these kinds of social spaces. Billed as multi-day social events organized by Black LGBT groups and individuals, Black Pride events are held in cities that have large, concentrated Black populations. These include Philadelphia, Chicago, Houston, Milwaukee, Detroit, Los Angeles, Washington, DC, New York City and, Atlanta. The first Black Pride event was held in Washington, DC in 1991, and this now consists of workshops and political/educational activities. Some cities also host day-long Black Pride festivals, which feature staged entertainment, vendors selling jewelry and myriad cultural articles, and organizations distributing materials (brochures, key chains, bags, magazines, and the like) that advertise the health, social, political, and spiritual resources they can offer to this captive audience. These events are modeled after Gay Pride events, which,are a celebration of LGBT identity, and usually occur in the summer months to celebrate the Stonewall Riots of 1969. However, Black Pride events tend to be more about the celebration of Black LGBT identity; thus, they are both political and social in nature. The number of locations hosting Black Pride events continues to grow. Currently, more than two dozen cities in various states in the USA as well as in various countries around the world host Black Pride events.

In a parallel vein, new identity categories emerged within Black LGBT urban culture, which rejected the overly behavioral notions of "men who have sex with men" (MSM) coined by the Centers for Disease Control (CDC) and the National Institutes of Health (NIH), and which are defined in the context of everyday experiences of homophobia in Black communities. Reflecting the current shifting landscape of sexuality, even within Black communities, many Black men and women, regardless of age, identify as being "on the down low" or "D.L." with regard to their same-sex sexual orientation. Juxtaposed against the normative standard of "being out, loud and proud" that has been championed by Black and white LGBT organizations alike, being "on the D.L." suggests something shady, secret, to be ashamed of. Yet, "D.L." in current parlance can be understood as an identity, and one that is fluid and subject to change. As a subculture, "D.L." has been most closely identified with a specifically gay, Black, hip-hop culture (Jamison 2001).

Nonetheless, rather than understanding "D.L." as a new and different way of asserting sexual identities, Black media and community leaders – as well as mainstream media, such as the *New York Times*, that have long scrutinized Black urban culture – have repeatedly sought to demonize this "new" population in public discourse, by drawing attention to the "risky" sexual behaviors that men "on the D.L." are presumed to participate in. Such men become, by implication, contaminants of an already imperiled community, and conduits for HIV to the "innocent" Black women that they go home to. It may be that "D.L." is the *nom du jour* to describe variations of sexual expression across the spectrum of human existence. Nonetheless, this new stigmatization seems to imply concern, or something more, with those who live "on the D.L." What is left unexamined – what we believe future attention should be devoted to – is the tenuous position that young Black gay and lesbians find themselves in at this historical moment, given the hegemonic constructions of Black racial identity that still preclude affirmation of non-heterosexuality.

Moreover, how does being on the "D.L." help or hinder both men and women in negotiating the multiple social worlds and constraints they encounter on a daily basis? To answer this question requires attention to the broader context that defines the place of LGBT Blacks, and the effects of the multiple social structural forces on their physical, mental, and social wellbeing. Therefore, a survey of the literature in the social sciences provides valuable insight.

Social Science Research

While Black lesbians, gays, bisexuals, and now transgender persons have strenuously fought for the recognition of their humanity and to be seen as subjects and agents of social change, that struggle did not always register on intellectual agendas of the late twentieth century. Indeed, the same problems that plagued the movements that gave rise to Women's, Black, and LGBT Studies can also be found in the academic disciplines themselves, though to varying degrees. The problem – that is, the interconnections between race, gender, and sexuality as structures of oppression that shape lived experiences and cannot be analyzed separately from each other – has been addressed more thoroughly in Women's Studies and LGBT Studies, and less so within Black Studies, or even in traditional disciplines like Sociology which feed these bodies of knowledge. The notion of "place" for LGBT Blacks in academic discourse is heavily informed by the ideological constructions of Black racial identity (particularly from the early 1970s), which emphasized heterosexuality and a "politics of respectability."

We do not wish to suggest that such a place is stagnant and fixed across time and space. As this chapter aims to show, LGBT Blacks have not (and perhaps never) accepted the "place" designated by heterosexism in African American studies and discourse. Rather, we argue, implicitly, that defining the "place" of LGBT blacks is an intellectual and political process, one that emphasizes the constructed, contested, and shifting boundaries of Black identities. That process of definition is more fully articulated in the dominant questions and categories within social science disciplines like Sociology. Critical social theorists argue that Sociology has always had a problem with "difference." As Seidman argues, "Sociology has refused difference, at times, by assimilating or repressing difference or approaching it as a transient condition or evolutionary phase to be superseded" (Seidman 1997: 102). Patricia Hill Collins makes a similar argument with regard to how the "place" of Black within social science has been defined by the extant categories, which have been resistant to change.

Within Sociology, difference is unreflexively seen as "Other," deviant or dangerous in relationship to its foundational categories of "race," "women," "gay," "lesbian," "immigration," and so on. Thus, despite the call by many sociologists to pay attention to intersectionality of race, gender, and sexual orientation, studies of race or same-sex sexuality tend to follow the conventions of the discipline, and to rank social relations in order to preserve conceptual integrity of the "gay" or "Black" subjectivity. To no one's surprise then, research on LGBT populations within Black communities has not focused on the very issues that emerged in the intertwined social movements for Black, women's, and gay liberation, and remain salient for this group.

In the following section we trace the development of the body of knowledge on LGBT Blacks by following the same general historical trajectory within which this knowledge was produced. Along the way, we identify the core issues that were addressed in each phase (and to some degree, earlier in this text), and how the questions asked were largely shaped by the social and historical context. In doing so, we show how research questions have become more refined, moving from a notion of same-sex sexuality as pathological to exploring how healthy Black LGBT identities are constructed and reinforced.

Homophobia and Heterosexism

On the question of homophobia, early work in the field adopted a decidedly homophobic stance, viewing same-sex sexuality as a mental illness or as a Euro-American strategy for destroying the "Black race." More recent work has taken a critical look at homophobia itself, arguing that this system of meaning is the real problem, and that it has destructive consequences for Blacks.

Until 1973, homosexuality was considered a mental illness by the American Psychiatric Association (APA). This blatant homophobia was realized at new heights in research on gay and lesbian Blacks. Such research tended to adopt cultural nationalist interpretations found in Afrocentric thinking that homosexuality, as a practice, was unknown in Africa and was forced onto peoples of the African diaspora through colonial contact with Europeans. Thus, in an article first published in 1974 entitled "The politics behind black male passivity, effeminization, bisexuality, and homosexuality," Frances Cress Welsing argued that homosexuality was a "strategy for destroying Black people" (Welsing 1990: 91). Haki Madhubuti also argued that Black men were convinced by Whites to practice homosexuality in order to "disrupt Black families and neutralize black men" (quoted in Conerly 2001). The history of the argument that homosexuality is a weapon of mass destruction that was spread in the Black community by Western capitalist influences has been extensively discussed and critiqued (Potgieter 1997; Wekker 1994; Ransby 2000). Supported by the APA's later declaration that homophobia, not homosexuality, is the truly abnormal condition, researchers have begun to look at homophobia as the real cancer in Black communities, although the earlier view has certainly not disappeared.

Even after the gay liberation movement successfully argued that homosexuals, like people of color and women, constitute an official "minority" group (Barron 1975; D'Emilio 1983), research has shown that Blacks retain negative attitudes toward homosexuals (Lorde 1978; Staples 1981; Gates 1993b; Herek and Capitanio 1995). Several sources have been named as the cause/source for homophobia among Blacks. The most often cited is probably Black religious institutions (Bonilla and Porter 1990); however, other research has shown no such relationship (Seltzer 1992). The institutionalization of Black cultural nationalism (Harper 1996) runs a close second in the "blame game." Yet another related and popular explanation in Black contexts resides in the sexual politics of women's relationships to men. This perspective identifies heterosexual Black women as one of the progenitors of the problem (Ernst et al. 1991). According to this perspective, heterosexual women see (male) same-sex sexuality as exacerbating the shortage of available male sexual partners, and contributing to the demise of marriage among Blacks. As such, they reject male same-sex sexuality because it conflicts with their interests. This perspective has not been supported in the research (Tucker and Mitchell-Kernan 1995). Nor does it account for homophobia directed at Black women. Unfortunately, higher levels of education are not an antidote to homophobic attitudes – Blacks with higher education still tend to have more homophobic attitudes than their White counterparts (Chang and Moore 1991).

The effects of culturally sanctioned homophobia are also the focus of study. Black youth engaging in homosexual behavior perceive that their friends and neighbors are not supportive (Siegel and Epstein 1996; Stokes et al. 1996b). They are then often reluctant to disclose their sexuality, even within settings where they can receive appropriate counseling or other supportive services. As such, they are also at higher risk from abuse, suicide, and HIV infection (Cochran and Mays 1988a; Mays 1989; Savin-Williams 1994). Similar results were found when examining older Black gay populations (Adams and Kimmel 1997).

Homophobic attitudes in Black contexts have far-reaching impact. Such attitudes have been linked with mishandling sexual abuse cases by professionals working with racial and sexual minorities (Fontes 1995), to the explosion of HIV/AIDS among Blacks (Stokes and Peterson 1998; Cohen 1999). Not surprisingly, the impact of such attitudes is also palpable among researchers who study Black populations, shaping the questions they are willing to ask, whether because they see same-sex sexuality as unimportant and irrelevant, or because they fear being rejected by their subjects (Bennett and Battle 2001).

A major flaw in much of the thinking and research on homophobia and Blacks has to do with the way questions have been asked. Until now, researchers and laypersons alike have implied that the attitudes, behaviors, and ideologies that we call "homophobic" are unique to Blacks as a group. Put another way, the implication is that Blacks have a monopoly over homophobia. The popularity of this way of thinking is embedded in the now-historic divisions drawn between Black civil rights and gay liberation movements, and has figured significantly in public discourse about HIV/AIDS (Cohen 1999).

However, to simply claim that Blacks are "more" homophobic than Whites or any other racial-ethnic group entirely misses the point, and produces a skewed analysis, which further demonizes Blacks as having the "wrong" values or failing to keep pace in a rapidly changing society. Given the institutional barriers that have been developed and maintained in the USA to marginalize same-sex sexuality, and to limit the full participation and rights of LGBT persons, it becomes evident that homophobia is embedded in the national culture, rather than originating from a specific racial-ethnic group. Recognition of this critical point has led researchers to inquire into the nature of homophobia and how its expression in Black cultural contexts is informed by the intersection of racial and other forms of inequality in broader societal institutions like family, religion, and politics (Cohen 1999). On a related note, researchers also need to pay attention to how heterosexism – the notion that heterosexuality is good, natural, right, and superior – is implicated in and still informs racial group identity in the contemporary United States.

Black Lesbians

Some of the earliest research concerning Black lesbians came from Black feminists in the 1970s (for examples, see Lorde 1978; Smith 1979). Although historically some researchers saw lesbianism as a "choice" in response to the shortage of Black men (Staples 1978), current research recognizes the limits of such a perspective. Research on Black lesbians addresses the multiple manifestations and contexts of same-sex sexuality among Black women. Wekker (1994), for example, suggests that Black mati-ism – the Sranan Tongo word for women who have sexual relationships with women – provides an Afrocentric and working-class alternative to notions of Black lesbianism, which is seen to be more middle-class and Eurocentric in nature.

The experiences of Black lesbians have been explored in various settings – workplaces, healthcare, Black and other communities (Eversley 1981; Cochran and Mays 1988b; Stevens 1998). The largest body of research concerns the negative impact of perceived discrimination on the mental health, health status outcomes, and intimate relationships of Black lesbians. This research began in 1986 with the pioneering work of Vickie Mays and Susan Cochran's Black Women's Relationship Project (Cochran and Mays 1988a). Since then, the majority of the scholarship on Black lesbians has been psychological in nature. For example, researchers have examined the psychological toll of this particular matrix of domination (Collins 1990) and its many implications for Black lesbians (for a discussion, see Greene and Boyd-Franklin 1996). Others have examined the relationships between sexual identity and risk behaviors as well as the role of racism, sexism, and heterosexism in the development of Black lesbians' and bisexual women's sexual identities (Greene 2000; Saewyc 1999). Others have focused on more sociological outcomes, and particularly the effects of inequalities on Black lesbians' life chances.

In a recent study examining health status and outcomes among women of color, sexual minority status emerged as a key variable in exacerbating the impact of racial, gender, and class-based inequalities on Black women's life chances. Mays, Yancey, Cochran, Weber, and Fielding (2002) found that self-identified Black lesbians and bisexuals in Los Angeles County faced greater health risks and worse health status than Black heterosexual women, on indicators such as being overweight, participating in risky behaviors (such as tobacco use and heavy alcohol consumption), access to health insurance, and a regular source of health care. Notably, the authors surmise that both employment and marital status are keys to improved access to quality healthcare for women. That is, while Black lesbian and bisexual women had higher rates of full-time employment, their non-married status limited their access to health insurance through a spouse or relationship partner. Other research has begun to inquire into the ways that Black lesbians counter the effects of discrimination, by exploring the benefits of developing "community" with lesbians of other racial and class backgrounds (Hall and Rose 1996).

Family studies have long shown that race and social class have a strong, persistent effect on patterns of family formation practices among Blacks. Black women are much more likely to parent alone than say, White women. Mays et al. (1998) found that this pattern holds regardless of sexual orientation. In their study, one in four Black lesbians lived with a child for whom she had child-rearing responsibilities, and one in three reported having at least one child. And according to analysis of 1990 census data, Black lesbian couples were more likely than White couples to report having given birth to a child (Ettlebrick et al. 2001). These findings suggest an especially fruitful area for in-depth research on Black lesbians, and the effects of race, social class, sexual orientation, and community support on the well-being of Black lesbian families.

Mental Health Outcomes among Gay and Bisexual Men

Marginalized status based on sexual orientation, as well as fear of disclosure and ostracism, have led many researchers to explore the impact of same-sex sexual orientation on mental health outcomes. Not surprisingly, the preponderance of evidence found that LGBT Blacks have higher levels of negative mental health outcomes than their White counterparts (Siegel and Epstein 1996). A major source of anxiety for non-heterosexual Blacks is fear of disclosure. In a small sample of Black and White gay men, Ostrow et al. (1991) found that their Black respondents were less likely to be open about their sexuality and that they had less affirmative social support than their White counterparts. Stokes et al. (1996a) used a much larger sample of men, and found that among bisexually active men, Blacks were much less likely to disclose their sexual orientation to their female partners than were Whites. Despite this reticence, when Black men do disclose their same-sex sexual orientation, it is usually to women first (Mays et al. 1998). Mays and her colleagues went on to find that two major predictors of disclosure for Black men were current age and age at initial engagement in homosexual behavior. Older and more experienced men were more willing to disclose their sexuality.

Despite the stress surrounding disclosure, some researchers have found that openly gay Black men have developed positive self-esteem and sexual identities. Edwards (1996) examined four areas of social psychological functioning among a sample of Black gay adolescents: self-identity, family relation, school/work relations, and social adjustment. He found that even in the presence of homophobia and racism, his subjects possessed positive social psychological attitudes and survival skills. Peterson et al. (1996) studied a larger sample of Black gay, bisexual, and heterosexual men, examining the relationship between depressive mood, social psychological stressors, psychosocial resources, and coping strategies. They found no significant difference in depression among the three groups. Research has consistently found that Black men of same-sex sexual orientation have significant difficulties in dealing with their sexual orientation (Cochran and Mays 1994). Richardson et al. (1997) who studied 311 HIV-negative Black men, found that gay/bisexual orientation was a primary predictor of anxiety disorder.

Like the question of homophobia, interpreting the causal mechanisms for poor mental health outcomes among LGBT Blacks is easily tainted by problematic notions that it is same-sex sexuality, rather than context-specific interactions and responses, that produces poor coping skills, higher levels of depression, suicide ideation, and so on. Such a perspective completely ignores the possibility that LGBT Blacks do develop affirmative social identities, and can be psychologically well adjusted. The question then becomes, what are the factors and contexts that produce the disparities in mental health outcomes among men? How are these related to economic status, social support, strength of family ties, region, education, and occupational attainment, to name just a few factors? And more importantly, exactly how does sexual orientation *status* contribute to the answer? Far from assuming a pathological model of same-sex sexuality, new research on gay men in general points to the effects of structural discrimination on the basis of sexual orientation on men's social and psychological well-being. Such work ought to be expanded to examine the specific barriers and conditions that Black gay and bisexual men face, that hinder the development of healthy racial and sexual identities.

HIV/AIDS

Without question, the AIDS epidemic in the United States has been instrumental in forcing society in general, and Blacks as a group specifically, to address issues of same-sex sexuality (Cohen 1999). Since the 1980s, Black gay men have been particularly affected by the epidemic, making them the natural choice for research on the social causes and effects of HIV/AIDS, as well as understanding the context-specific nature of prevention efforts.

Black gay men have a significantly higher rate of infection than both their heterosexual and White counterparts (Koblin et al. 1996; Sullivan et al. 1997; Williams et al. 1996). In a recent study conducted by the Centers for Disease Control and Prevention in six major US cities – Baltimore, Dallas, Los Angeles, Miami, New York, and Seattle – the researchers found that more than one-third of young Black gay men were infected with the HIV virus (Centers for Disease Control 2001). The epidemic is growing especially rapidly among Black gay youth in economically depressed urban communities, a problem scholars believe is exacerbated by poverty, violence, lack of social support, lack of resources in families, health, and educational systems, and lack of support from religious institutions.

The body of research on Black gay men (less so for lesbians) is now fairly large, covering various regions (Sullivan et al. 1997; Williams et al. 1996; Lichtenstein 2000). However, the bulk of this research has been conducted in New York City (Koblin et al. 1996; Quimby and Friedman 1989) and San Francisco (Peterson et al. 1996), where there are significant gay male populations, as well as established research institutions and infrastructure for managing the information. Regardless of the region or number of cases in a sample, researchers have concluded that there is an urgent need for culturally sensitive programs that are targeted at gay and bisexual Black men, and which stress prevention and avoidance of risky behaviors (Peterson et al. 1996; Rotheram-Borus, Hunter and Rosario 1994; Myrick 1999). As the epidemic grows, and the body of research stressing the medical model also grows along with it, researchers have begun to emphasize the social and economic, rather than behavioral, factors that contribute to the epidemic, and which should be taken into consideration in prevention programs (Icard, Schilling and El-Bassel 1992; Peterson 1997). What they argue is that individual, interpersonal, and contextual factors, together, help to inform the participation of gay and bisexually-active Black men in "high-risk" behaviors. Arguably, Cathy Cohen's full-length 1999 study of the Black community's response to HIV/AIDS is the best and most comprehensive treatment of this issue.

Still others continue to lay much of the responsibility for the epidemic on the reluctance of Black churches to engage in HIV/AIDS activism. These scholars argue that socially conservative religious ideologies help to legitimize homophobia and an AIDS panic within the Black community, fragmenting both the community politics and retarding an effective response to the epidemic (Blaxton 1998; Fullilove 1999).

Comparisons between Homosexual and Heterosexual Populations

Despite the fact that studies of HIV/AIDS have dominated the social science research agenda on LGBT Blacks, researchers have sought to explore broader comparisons among Blacks of different sexual orientations. Researchers have found that, like the larger heterosexual population, LGBT Blacks are more likely to be distrustful of health care providers (Cochran and Mays 1988b; Siegel and Raveis 1997) and are generally suspicious of social workers (Icard 1985; Icard and Traunstein 1987). In examining the experiences of older Black gay men, research has shown not only diversity within that population, but similarities between them and older Black heterosexual men (Adams and Kimmel 1997).

Beyond the similarities, however, research has discovered some clear differences in life course experiences. Though extremely underutilized in academic scholarship, there is a rich body of work produced by lesbian and gay Black activists and cultural workers who have explored many dimensions of the intersections of race, class, gender, and sexual orientation (Baldwin 1956; Beam 1986; Boykin 1996; Hemphill 1991; Lorde 1982; Smith 1983). Recently, more traditional researchers have entered in the discussion. The work of Peplau et al. (1997), for example, highlighted unique dimensions to the intimate relationships of homosexual Blacks. They found that homosexual Blacks were more likely to engage in interracial dating than were their heterosexual counterparts; and that lesbian and gay Blacks were highly satisfied in their relationships – regardless of the race of the other partner. Crow et al. (1998) conducted a controlled study where they examined biases in hiring against women, Blacks, and homosexuals. They found that Black gay men were most likely to be discriminated against. Doll et al. (1992) conducted interviews with over 1,000 adults in Chicago, Denver, and San Francisco to study patterns of sexual abuse in the life histories of adults; they found higher rates of abuse within the population of Black gay men. Similarly, the findings about suicide ideation and alcoholism among Blacks (Gibbs 1997; Icard and Traunstein 1987) have shown that gay men are at much higher risks for these. As a result of these findings in the empirical research, mental health workers are beginning to develop models that are designed to address minority lesbian and gay populations (Greene 1997).

Arguably, one of the most comprehensive research projects ever conducted on Black LGBT populations is the Black Pride Survey 2000 (Battle et al. 2002). In an effort to gather more information on this understudied population, a group of researchers and the National Gay and Lesbian Task Force's Policy Institute developed one of the largest and most important research documents on Black lesbian, gay, bisexual, and transgender (LGBT) populations in the United States. The study was conducted in nine cities during the summer of 2000 and the sample represents possibly the largest national, multi-city sample of Black LGBT people ever gathered. Over 2,600 Black LGBTs across the country were sampled. The self-administered survey consisted of various questions focusing on basic demographic information, experiences with discrimination, policy priorities, and political behavior, as well as the attitudes of Black LGBT individuals towards both gay and straight organizations that are either predominantly Black or predominantly White. Major findings from this study have been thoroughly explored elsewhere (Battle et al. 2002; Battle et al. 2003).

Re-configuring Place: Future Directions in Black LGBT Studies

Given what research has been and is being done, where should scholarly research on Black LGBT populations next delve? Currently, the social constructionist perspective shapes much of current thinking about identities based on race and sexuality (Howard 2000). This perspective emphasizes how the meanings of categories and the shape of identities are conditioned by the social and historical contexts in which they emerge and, as such, are not fixed, but change over time. From this perspective, a new body of research is emerging demonstrating that social identities are fluid, mobile, and contingent, rather than assigned or derivative of the social structure. As noted above, despite the distinct shift towards an intersectional approach to race, gender, class, and sexuality, inquiry about Black identities has not always given attention to how sexual identities are constitutive of and help to shape racial identities.

The work of critical race theorists and cultural studies scholars has been extremely important in addressing this problem. For example, they argue and show through careful reading of historical evidence, that racial boundaries in the USA have frequently been constructed and maintained along sexual lines (Gilman 1985; Davis 1981; Crenshaw 1989; Collins 1990 and 1994; Cohen 1999; Sommerville 2000; Nagel 2003). Not only are racial categories and identities already sexualized, but sexuality is central to understanding how race categories are formed, defined, and change over time. In a way, this approach has come full circle, reflecting the critical insights from writers like James Baldwin. This area – Black Queer Studies – represents the "cutting edge" of research, and further defines Black sexuality studies as fertile territory for research.

Based on our review of the bodies of scholarship that have explored various aspects of Black LGBT experiences, we note that the research has covered a great deal of ground over the last quarter-century. However, there are a few gaps that ought to be addressed in the next phase of research, and guided by analytic perspectives that emphasize change, fluidity, and context. For example, there is clearly room for research that is focused not so much on how problems of the past continue to haunt Black LGBT – from oppression and its negative effects to HIV/AIDS – but on how these groups participate in contesting and shaping the here and now. Drawing on the themes that emerged from our literature review, we suggest a few fruitful areas of research for the next quarter-century, including family structure, sexual behavior and identity, political issues and attitudes, religion, and immigration and ethnicity.

Family Structure

Despite the growing attention to family issues and sexual orientation, little is known about the family structures and parenting experiences of Black LGBTs (Battle et al. 2003). Documenting the existence of gay, lesbian, bisexual, and transgender parents is important, inasmuch as they reflect the diversity of family arrangements, and provide greater insight into the ways in which social policies and structures affect families on the micro-level. They also show how families, by their very practices, help to engender macro-level social change. Yet family and same-sex sexuality appear as mutually exclusive categories in most treatments of Black family structure and change. However, LGBT people indeed have siblings, care for elderly parents, raise children, and develop mutually beneficial romantic relationships. In short, they develop families of their own, though not always in circumstances of their own choosing.

Why is this important? There is evidence to suggest that lesbian and bisexual women report higher incidences of adolescent pregnancy than their straight counterparts (Saewyc 1999). If Black lesbian couples were more likely than White lesbian couples to be parenting, then that suggests that the "lesbian baby boom," much touted in the media in the late 1990s, really began much earlier, and may well not be a notable phenomenon among Black women. Most importantly, what are the psychological, social, and political ramifications of Black lesbians parenting in communities and contexts that provide far less support than to heterosexual women? One might ask similar questions about Black gay men in families, and particularly how men negotiate gender identities in family contexts that require men to "father" children, if not to actually raise them. Also, how are gay men and lesbians similar to or different from each other, or from their heterosexual counterparts, in the way they build relationships with blood relations and kin, and how they participate in family networks? The life of Ruth Ellis raises some key questions about how Black lesbians (and gay men) create families and communities of affinity, and the challenges and limits of doing so.

Sexual Behavior and Identity

Identity is important as it helps to build and solidify feelings of pride and purpose among the individual and group members. It is important to determine, particularly for Black LGBT people, what terms like "gay," "lesbian," "queer," and "same gender loving," among the many other labels, mean to both the individual and the group. How does identifying as one or the other reflect or shape one's relationships to sexual or racial-ethnic communities, and politics? For whom are these identity categories meaningful, and why? How do social class, age, generation, and political ideology shape how people identify themselves? Does identifying as "queer" suggest that one is more likely to be more politically active in one's community or to work more closely with White LGBT communities? On the other hand, does identifying as "same gender loving" mean that one is more likely to see their sexual orientation and their lives through Afrocentric lenses?

Scholars need to explore further how different identities shape experience, and vice versa. As made evident by the BPS2000 sample (Battle et al. 2002) and the work of Black feminists and theorists (Collins 1990; Davis 1981, Reid-Pharr 2001; Smith 1983), race, gender, class, and sexual orientation are important valences through which identities are forged. They shift in importance and rank, depending on broader political and cultural contexts in which individuals and groups find themselves. In other words, these identities are not separable as they each help define the unique experience of Black LGBT populations. Researching the intersection of these structures of inequality and the identities that emerge can tell us much about the relative replays in oppressing and empowering individuals and communities. Such research findings can then inform research on physical health, mental health, political participation, and a whole host of other life course outcomes.

Political Issues and Attitudes

There are clearly different as well as shared political priorities between the Black LGBT community and the mainstream Black community. What is less clear is how intersecting identities affect how one thinks about politics. More research is needed to determine how being Black *and* lesbian, gay, bisexual, or transgender shapes one's attitudes toward politics, as well as the level and type of political participation. Are Black men more politically concerned about HIV/AIDS than are other Blacks? If so, how do they effect change around this issue? Similarly, are Black transgender people more concerned about discrimination in jobs or in housing? What strategies do they use to make their views and experiences heard? Such questions can only be meaningfully answered through systematic research, whose goal is also to address and alleviate marginalization of LGBT Blacks from the political process.

Religion

Religious institutions have always played a prominent role in Black communities, offering opportunities for leadership, status attainment, comfort, and support that were largely unavailable outside this community. The religious ideologies embodied in many Black churches have played a strong role in the subordination of gays and lesbians. For many, religiosity and affirmative same-sex sexual identity are seen as polar opposites. However, there is also mounting evidence that gays and lesbians participate in and engage religious structures for the purpose of challenging doctrinal hegemony, as well as to affirm their sexual identities. In the years since the AIDS crisis emerged, Black LGBTs have organized themselves into congregations and formal churches to respond to their spiritual, health, and political needs, especially with regard to people with AIDS, who had largely been abandoned by mainstream Black churches.

Black LGBT churches provide much more than formal ministry to the spiritually needy. They also constitute an alternative institutional context that validates LGBT families and communities, and nurtures and mobilizes new forms of identities. Important questions to examine include: what is the role of religion in the lives of Black LGBTs? If they are excluded from traditional religious venues, what are the psychosocial implications of this rejection, and where do Black LGBT people go? Furthermore, what are the political implications of establishing largely LGBT congregations for religious and political empowerment in a culture that encourages separation of church and state? As the larger society moves toward a more liberal stance on (homo)sexuality, how have traditional Black churches coped with, and responded to, this profound cultural change? Far from assuming that Black religious institutions are monolithic, and are in the vanguard of social change, these questions ask for closer and more deeply historical examinations of how, on the question of sexuality, Black churches have been both empowering and oppressive institutions.

Immigration and Ethnicity

Black immigrants – Afro-Caribbean and African – also face distinct challenges that limit their participation in and access to social networks, support, and political resources within Black LGBT organizations. For many Black LGBT immigrants, the terms of participation place limitations on how they can identify themselves racially and ethnically, as well as the meaning of their participation in Black LGBT communities and politics. This is a familiar, yet curious bind in which Black immigrants find themselves, as ethnicity becomes the primary lens through which they understand the dynamics of racial, gender, and sexual politics in the US context. How immigrant men and women negotiate these dynamics ought to be the focus of future studies.

Special attention should also focus on historical as well as current manifestations of Black LGBTs in the African continent. One of the most comprehensive volumes to do so is Murray and Roscoe's *Boy-Wives and Female Husbands: Studies in African Homosexualities*. Across 15 thoroughly presented studies, and while tracing discussion about sexual orientation in Africa back to Edward Gibbon's *History of the Decline and Fall of the Roman Empire* (1781), Murray and Roscoe conclude that "[t]he colonialists did not introduce homosexuality to Africa but rather intolerance of it – and systems of surveillance and regulations for suppressing it" (Murray and Roscoe 1998: xvi).

Research into the lives of LGBT Blacks has come a long way. As questions of sexuality move to the forefront of several academic disciplines – including Sociology, Black Studies, Political Science, and History – and as LGBT Blacks become more visible as both researchers and subjects, the knowledge base from which we understand the complexities of Black experience must continue to expand. In time, we may no longer need to search for the place of LGBT Blacks in history and society.

NOTES

1. Throughout this text, we will use the term "Black" to refer to people of African Diaspora, and to such populations that reside within the United States. To some, African Americans are a subgroup within the larger Black community. Since our discussion purposely includes those who may be first-generation immigrants or who, for whatever reason, do not identify as African American, we employ the term "Black." Furthermore, we capitalize it to distinguish the racial category and related identity from the color. Similarly, we capitalize the word "White" when referring to race.

2. The increased visibility of transgender persons in the mainstream lesbian and gay movement has not always been received well, and has prompted a series of debates about the inclusiveness of the broader social movement. Within Black LGBT communities, recognition of transgender persons has occurred sporadically, primarily through the development of specific support groups, targeted outreach for HIV prevention efforts, and within Black LGBT urban culture. Since the late 1990s, social science researchers have begun to include transgender populations into their research questions and analyses. As a way of recognizing this shift in the terms and debates, and its importance in understanding the various manifestations of Black sexual identities and politics, we include the term, and much of what it implies, in our subsequent discussion.

BIBLIOGRAPHY

Works Cited

Adams, C. and Kimmel, D. (1997) "Exploring the lives of older Black gay men" in B. Greene (ed.), *Ethnic and Cultural Diversity among Lesbians and Gay Men. Psychological Perspectives on Lesbian and Gay Issues*, 132–51. Thousand Oaks, CA: Sage.

Asante, Molefe Kete (1988) *Afrocentricity*. Trenton, NJ: African World Press.

Baldwin, James (1956) *Giovanni's Room*. New York: Dell.

Barron, M. (1975) "Recent developments in minority and race relations," *Annals of the American Academy of Political and Social Science*, 420: 125–76.

Battle, Juan, Cohen, Cathy, Warren, Dorian, Fergerson, Gerard, and Audam, Suzette (2002) *Say It Loud: I'm Black and I'm Proud; Black Pride Survey 2000*. New York: Policy Institute of the National Gay and Lesbian Task Force.

Battle, Juan, Cohen, Cathy, Harris, Angelique, and Richie, Beth (2003) "We really are family: embracing our lesbian, gay, bisexual, and transgender (LGBT) family members," *The State of Black America* (special edition on the Black Family), 93–106. Washington, DC: National Urban League.

Beam, Joseph (ed.) (1986) *In the Life: A Black Gay Anthology*. Boston: Alyson.

Bennett, Michael and Battle, Juan (2001) "We can see them, but we can't hear them: LGBT members of black families" in M. Bernstein and R. Reimann (eds.), *Queer Families, Queer Politics: Challenging Culture and the State*. New York: Columbia University Press.

Blaxton, R. G. (1998) "'Jesus wept': Black churches and HIV," *Harvard Gay and Lesbian Review* 4: 13–16.

Bonilla, L. and Porter, J. (1990) "A comparison of Latino, Black, and non-Hispanic white attitudes toward homosexuality," *Hispanic Journal of Behavioral Sciences* 12 (4): 437–52.

Boykin, K. (1996) *One More River to Cross: Black and Gay in America*. New York and London: Anchor Books/Doubleday Press.

Brandt, Eric (ed.) (1999) *Dangerous Liaisons: Blacks, Gays and the Struggle for Equality*. New York: New Press.

Butler, Judith (1991) "Imitation and gender insubordination" in Diana Fuss (ed.), *Inside/Out: Lesbian Theories, Gay Theories*, 13–31. New York and London: Routledge.

Carbado, Devon, McBride, Dwight, and Weise, Donald (eds.) (2002) *Black Like Us: A Century of Lesbian, Gay and Bisexual Black Fiction*. San Francisco: Cleis Press.

Carbado, Devon and Weise, Donald (eds.) (2003) *Time on Two Crosses: The Collected Writings of Bayard Rustin*. San Francisco: Cleis Press.

Carter, Mandy (1999) "The emperor's new clothes, or how not to run a movement" in Kris Kleindienst (ed.), *This Is What a Lesbian Looks Like*. Ithaca, NY: Firebrand Books.

Centers for Disease Control and Prevention (2000) *HIV/AIDS Among Blacks*. Atlanta, GA: Centers for Disease Control and Prevention.

—— (2001) "Nearly one-third of young Black gays are HIV positive," *Contemporary Sexuality* 35 (3, March): 7–8.

Chang, C. and Moore, A. (1991) "Can attitudes of college students towards AIDS and homosexuality be changed in six weeks? The effects of a gay panel," *Health-Values*, 15 (2): 41–9.

Chauncey, George, Jr (1994) *Gay New York: Gender, Urban Culture, and the Making of the Gay Male World, 1890–1940*. New York: Basic Books.

Clarke, Cheryl (1977) "To a bamboozled soul sister," *Sinister Wisdom* 3 (Spring): 46–8.

—— (1981) "Lesbianism: an act of resistance" in Cherrie Moraga and Gloria Anzaldua (eds.), *This Bridge Called My Back: Writings by Radical Women of Color*. Watertown, MA: Persephone Press.

—— (1983a) "New notes on lesbianism," *Sojourner: The Women's Forum* (31 January): 6–14.

—— (1983b) "The failure to transform: homophobia in the Black community" in Barbara Smith (ed.), *Home Girls: A Black Feminist Anthology*. New York: Kitchen Table, Women of Color Press.

—— (1990a) "Knowing the danger and going there anyway," *Sojourner: The Women's Forum* 16 (31 March): 14–15.

—— (1990b) "The homoerotic other," *The Advocate* (2 February): 42.

—— (1993) "Living the texts out: lesbians and the use of Black women's traditions" in Stanlie M. James and Abena P. A. Busia (eds.), *Theorizing Black Feminisms: The Visionary Pragmatism of Black Women*. New York: Routledge.

Clarke, Cheryl, Gomez, Jewell, Hammonds, Evelyn, Johnson, Bonnie, and Powell, Linda (1983) "Conversations and questions: Black women on Black women writers," *Conditions Nine* 3 (3): 88–94.

Cochran, S. and Mays, V. (1988a) "Disclosure of sexual preferences to physicians by black lesbian and bisexual women," *Western Journal of Medicine* 149: 616–19.

—— (1988b) "Epidemiological and sociocultural factors in the transmission of HIV infection in Black gay and bisexual men" in M. Shernoff and W. Scott (eds.), *The Sourcebook of Lesbian/Gay Health Care*, 202–11. Washington, DC: National Gay and Lesbian Health Foundation.

—— (1994) "Depressive distress among homosexually active Black men and women," *American Journal of Psychiatry*, 151: 524–9.

Cohen, Cathy (1999) *The Boundaries of Blackness: AIDS and Breakdown of Black Politics*. Chicago: University of Chicago Press.

Collins, Patricia (1990) *Black Feminist Thought*. Cambridge, MA: Unwin Hyman.

—— (1994) *Black Sexual Politics: African Americans, Gender, and the New Racism*. New York: Routledge.

Combahee River Collective ([1974] 1983) "Combahee River Collective Statement" in Barbara Smith (ed.), *Home Girls: A Black Feminist Anthology*, 272–82. Albany, NY: Kitchen Table, Women of Color Press.

Conerly, Gregory (2001) "Are you Black first or are you queer?" in Delroy Constantino-Simms (ed.), *The Greatest Taboo: Homosexuality in Black Communities*, 7–23. New York: Alyson Books.

Cornwell, Anita (1983) *Black Lesbian in White America*. New York: Naiad Press.

Crenshaw, Kimberle (1989) "Demarginalizing the intersection of race and sex: a Black feminist critique of antidiscrimination doctrine, feminist theory and anti-racist politics," *University of Chicago Legal Forum*, 139. Reprinted in Joy James and T. Denean Sharpley-Whiting (eds.), *The Black Feminist Reader*. Oxford: Blackwell.

Crow, S., Fok, L., and Hartman, S. (1998) "Who is at greater risk of work-related discrimination: women, Blacks or homosexuals?" *Employee Responsibilities and Rights Journal* 11 (1): 15–26.

D'Emilio, John (1983) *Sexual Politics, Sexual Communities: The Making of a Homosexual Minority in the United States, 1940–1970*. Chicago: University of Chicago Press.

—— (1995) "Homophobia and the trajectory of postwar American radicalism: the case of Bayard Rustin," *Radical History Review* 62: 80–103.

—— (1999) "Bayard Rustin, civil rights strategist," *Harvard Gay and Lesbian Review* (Summer).

—— (2003) *Lost Prophet*. New York: Free Press.

Davis, Angela Y. (1981) *Women, Race, and Class*. New York: Random House.

—— (1998) *Blues Legacies and Black Feminism: Gertrude "Ma" Rainey, Bessie Smith and Billie Holiday*. New York: Random House/Vintage Press.

Denizet-Lewis, Benoit (2003) "Double lives on the down low," *New York Times Magazine*, 3 August: 28–39.

Doll, L., Joy, D., Bartholow, B., Harrison, J., Bolan, G., Douglas, J., Saltzman, L., Moss, P., and Delgado, W. (1992) "Self-reported childhood and adolescent sexual abuse among adult homosexual and bisexual men," *Child Abuse and Neglect* 16 (6): 855–64.

Edwards, W. (1996) "A sociological analysis of an in/visible minority group: male adolescent homosexuals," *Youth and Society* 27 (3): 334–55.

Ernst, F., Francis, R., Nevels, H., and Lemeh, C. (1991) "Condemnation of homosexuality in the Black community: a gender-specific phenomenon?" *Archives of Sexual Behavior* 20 (6): 579–85.

Ettelbrick, P., Bradford, J., and Ellis, J. (2001) *The 21st Century Family: Same-sex Unmarried Partners and the US Census (Characteristics of Same-sex Coupled Households from the 1990 Census Data)*. New York: Policy Institute of the National Gay and Lesbian Task Force.

Eversley, R. (1981) "Out on the job: a Black lesbian feminist takes a courageous stand: an interview with Andrea Canaan," *Catalyst* 4 (12): 13–19.

Faderman, Lillian (1992) *Odd Girls and Twilight Lovers: A History of Lesbian Life in Twentieth-Century America*, 2nd edn. New York: Penguin.

Fontes, L. (ed.) (1995) *Sexual Abuse in Nine North American Cultures: Treatment and Prevention*. Thousand Oaks, CA: Sage.

Fullilove, Mindy T. (1999) "Stigma as an obstacle to AIDS action: the case of the Black community," *American Behavioral Scientist* 42 (7): 1,117–29.

Garber, Eric (1989) "A spectacle in color: the lesbian and gay subculture of jazz age Harlem" in Martin Duberman, Martha Vicinus, and George Chauncey, Jr (eds.), *Hidden from History: Reclaiming the Gay and Lesbian Past*, 318–31. New York: New American Library.

Gates, Henry Louis, Jr (1993a) "The Black man's burden" in Michael Warner (ed.), *Fear of a Queer Planet: Queer Politics and Social Theory*. Minneapolis: University of Minnesota Press.

—— (1993b) "Blacklash? Blacks object to gay rights–civil rights analogy," *New Yorker*, 69 (May 17): 13.

Gibbs, J. (1997) "African-American suicide: a cultural paradox," *Suicide and Life Threatening Behavior* 27 (1): 68–79.

Gilman, Sander (1985) "Black bodies, white bodies: toward an iconography of female sexuality," *Critical Inquiry* 12: 203–42.

Glick, Elisa F. (2003) "Harlem's queer dandy: African-American modernism and the artifice of Blackness," *Modern Fiction Studies* 49 (3): 414–42.

Greene, Beverley (1997) "Ethnic minority lesbians and gay men: mental health and treatment issues" in B. Greene (ed.), *Ethnic and Cultural Diversity among Lesbians and Gay Men. Psychological Perspectives on Lesbian and Gay Issues*, 216–39. Thousand Oaks, CA: Sage.

—— (2000) "Black lesbian and bisexual women," *Journal of Social Issues* 56 (2): 239–49.

Greene, Beverley and Boyd-Franklin, Nancy (1996) "Black lesbian couples: ethnocultural considerations in psychotherapy," *Women and Therapy* 19 (3): 49–60.

Griffin, Farah Jasmine (1999) *Beloved Sisters and Loving Friends: Letters from Rebecca Primus of Royal Oak, Maryland and Addie Brown of Hartford, Connecticut, 1854–1868*. New York: Knopf.

Hall, R. and Rose, Suzanna (1996) "Friendships between African-American and white lesbians" in J. Weinstock et al., *Lesbian Friendships: For Ourselves and Each Other. The Cutting Edge: Lesbian Life and Literature*, 165–91. New York: New York University Press.

Hammonds, Evelynn (1994) "Black (w)holes and the geometry of Black female sexuality," *Differences: A Journal of Feminist Cultural Studies* 6 (2–3): 126–45.

—— (1997) "Toward a genealogy of Black female sexuality" in Jacqui Alexander and Chandra Talpade (eds.), *Feminist Genealogies, Colonial Legacies, Democratic Futures*. New York: Routledge.

Hare, Nathan and Hare, Julia (1984) *The Endangered Black Family: Coping with the Unisexualization and Coming Extinction of the Black Race*. San Francisco: Black Think Tank.

Harper, Philip Brian (1994) "The subversive edge – 'Paris is burning,' social critique, and the limits of subjective agency," *Diacritics: A Review of Contemporary Criticism*, 24 (2, 3): 90–103.

—— (1995) "Walk-on parts and speaking subjects: screen representations of Black gay men," *Callaloo* 18 (2): 390–4.

—— (1996) *Are We Not Men? Masculine Anxiety and the Problem of Black Identity*. New York: Oxford University Press.

Hemphill, Essex (ed.) (1991) *Brother to Brother: New Writings by Black Gay Men*. Boston: Alyson.

Herek, Gregory M., and Capitanio, John P. (1995) "Black heterosexuals' attitudes toward lesbians and gay men in the United States," *Journal of Sex Research* 32 (2): 95–105.

Howard, Judith (2000) "Social psychology of identities," *Annual Review of Sociology* 26: 367–93.

Hull, Gloria (1983) "'Under the days': the buried life and poetry of Angelina Weld Grimke" in Barbara Smith (ed.), *Home Girls: A Black Feminist Anthology*, 73–82. New York: Kitchen Table Press.

Hutchinson, Earl Ofari (2000) "My gay problem, your Black problem: African American men's fear and misconceptions contribute to their homophobia" in Delroy Constantino-Simms (ed.), *The Greatest Taboo: Homosexuality in Black Communities*, 2–6. New York: Alyson.

Icard, L. (1985) "Black gay men and conflicting social identities: sexual orientation versus racial identity," *Journal of Social Work and Human Sexuality* 4 (1–2): 83–93.

Icard, L. and Traunstein, D. (1987) "Black, gay, alcoholic men: their character and treatment," *Social Casework* 68 (5): 267–72.

Icard, L., Schilling, R., and El-Bassel, N. (1992) "Preventing AIDS among Black gay men and Black gay and heterosexual male intravenous drug users," *Social Work* 37 (5): 440–5.

Jamison, Laura (2001) "A feisty female rapper breaks a hip-hop taboo" in Delroy Constantino-Simms (ed.), *The Greatest Taboo: Homosexuality in Black Communities*, 337–41. New York: Alyson.

Joseph, Gloria (1981) "Styling, profiling and pretending: the games before the fall" in Gloria Joseph and Jill Lewis (eds.), *Common Differences: Conflicts in Black and White Feminist Perspectives*, 178–230. Boston: South End Press.

Keating, AnnLouise (2002) "African-American literature: lesbian" in Claude Summers (ed.), *glbtq: An Encyclopedia of Gay, Lesbian, Bisexual, Transgender, and Queer Culture*. On line at: www.glbtq.com/literature/african_am_lit_lesbian.html. Retrieved October 10, 2003.

Keeling, Kara (2003) "Ghetto heaven": *Set It Off* and the valorization of Black lesbian butch–femme sociality," *Black Scholar* 33 (1): 33–46.

Kennedy, Elizabeth Lapovsky and Davis, Madeline D. (1993) *Boots of Leather, Slippers of Gold: The History of a Lesbian Community*. New York: Penguin Books.

Koblin, B., Taylor, P., Avrett, S., and Stevens, C. (1996) "The feasibility of HIV-1 vaccine efficacy trials among gay/bisexual men in New York City: Project ACHIEVE," *AIDS* 10 (13): 1555–61.

Lewin, Ellen (ed.) (1996) *Inventing Lesbian Cultures in America*. Boston: Beacon Press.

Lichtenstein, B. (2000) "Secret encounters: Black men, bisexuality, and AIDS in Alabama," *Medical Anthropology Quarterly* 14 (3): 374–93.

Lorde, A. (1978) "Scratching the surface: some notes on barriers to women and loving," *Black Scholar* 9 (7): 31–5.

—— (1982) *Zami: A New Spelling of My Name*. New York: Persephone Press.

—— (1984) "Manchild: a Black lesbian feminist response" in *Sister Outsider: Essays and Speeches*. Freedom, CA: Crossing Press.

—— (1986) *I Am Your Sister: Black Women Organizing across Sexualities*. Latham, NY: Kitchen Table, Women of Color Press.

—— (1991) "What's at stake in Lesbian and Gay publishing today: the Bill Whitehead Memorial Ceremony," *Callaloo* 14, 1: 65–6.

Lorde, Audre, and Baldwin, James (1982) "A conversation between James Baldwin and Audre Lorde," *Essence* (August): 58–60.

Lorde, Audre and Rich, Adrienne (1981) "An interview with Audre Lorde," *Signs: A Journal of Women in Culture and Society* 6 (3): 713–36.

Mays, V. (1989) "AIDS prevention in Black populations: methods of a safer kind" in V. Mays, G. Albee, and S. Schneider (eds.), *Primary Prevention of AIDS: Psychological Approaches*. Beverly Hills, CA: Sage.

Mays, V., Chatters, L., Cochran, S., and Mackness, J. (1998) "Black families in diversity: gay men and lesbians as participants in family networks," *Journal of Comparative Family Studies* 29 (1): 73–87.

Mays, Vickie M., Yancey, Antronette K., Cochran, Susan D., Weber, Mark, and Fielding, Jonathan (2002) "Heterogeneity of health disparities among Black, Hispanic, and Asian American women: unrecognized influences of sexual orientation," *American Journal of Public Health* 92 (4, April): 632–9.

Mercer, Kobena (1993) "Dark and lovely too: Black gay men in independent film" in Martha Gever, John Greyson, and Pratibha Parmar (eds.), *Queer Look: Perspectives on Lesbian and Gay Film and Video*. New York: Routledge.

Munoz, Jose Esteban (1999) *Disidentifications: Queers of Color and the Performance of Politics*. Minneapolis: University of Minnesota Press.

Murray, Stephen and Roscoe, Will (1998) *Boy-Wives and Female Husbands: Studies in African Homosexualities*. New York: Palgrave.

Myrick, R. (1999) "In the life: culture-specific HIV communication programs designed for Black men who have sex with men," *Journal of Sex Research* 36 (2): 159–70.

Nagel, Joane (2003) *Race, Ethnicity and Sexuality: Intimate Intersections, Forbidden Frontiers*. New York: Oxford University Press.

Ostrow, D., Whitaker, R., Frasier, K., and Cohen, C. (1991) "Racial differences in social support and mental health in men with HIV infection: a pilot study," *AIDS Care* 3 (1): 55–62.

Parkerson, Michelle (1993) "Birth of a notion: towards Black gay and lesbian imagery in film and video" in Martha Gever, John Greyson, and Pratibha Parmar (eds.), *Queer Look: Perspectives on Lesbian and Gay Film and Video*. New York: Routledge.

Peplau, L. (2001) "Rethinking women's sexual orientation: an interdisciplinary, relationship-focused approach," *Personal Relationships*, 8: 1–19.

Peplau, L., Cochran, S., and Mays, V. (1997) "A national survey of the intimate relationships of Black lesbians and gay men: a look at commitment, satisfaction, sexual behavior, and HIV disease" in Beverley Greene (ed.), *Ethnic and Cultural Diversity among Lesbians and Gay Men. Psychological Perspectives on Lesbian and Gay Issues*, 11–38. Thousand Oaks, CA: Sage.

Peterson, J. (1997) "AIDS-related risks and same-sex behaviors among Black men" in M. Levine and P. Nardi (eds.), *In Changing Times: Gay Men and Lesbians Encounter HIV/AIDS*, 283–301. Chicago: University of Chicago Press.

Peterson, J., Folkman, S., and Bakeman, R. (1996) "Stress, coping, HIV status, psychosocial resources, and depressive mood in Black gay, bisexual, and heterosexual men," *American Journal of Community Psychology* 24 (4): 461–87.

Potgieter, C. (1997) "From apartheid to Mandela's constitution: Black South African lesbians in the nineties" in B. Greene (ed.), *Ethnic and Cultural Diversity among Lesbians and Gay Men. Psychological Perspectives on Lesbian and Gay Issues*, 88–116. Thousand Oaks, CA: Sage.

Quimby, E. and Friedman, S. (1989) "Dynamics of Black mobilization against AIDS in New York City," *Social Problems* 36 (4): 403–15.

Ransby, Barbara (2000) "Afrocentrism, cultural nationalism and the problem with essentialist definitions of race, gender and sexuality" in Manning Marable (ed.), *Dispatches from the*

Ebony Tower: Intellectuals Confront the African-American Experience. New York: Columbia University Press.

Redvers, Jeanmarie (1988) "An interview with Bayard Rustin," *Other Countries: Black Gay Voices* 1 (Spring): 1–7.

Reid-Pharr, Robert (2001) *Black Gay Man: Essays.* New York: New York University Press.

Reimonenq, Alden (2002) "The Harlem Renaissance" in Claude J. Summers (ed.), *glbtq: An Encyclopedia of Gay, Lesbian, Bisexual, Transgender, and Queer Culture.* On line at: www.glbtq.com/literature/Harlem_Renaissance.html. Retrieved October 10, 2003.

Richardson, M., Myers, H., Bing, E., and Satz, P. (1997) "Substance use and psychopathology in Black men at risk for HIV infection," *Journal of Community Psychology* 25 (4): 353–70.

Rotheram-Borus, M., Hunter, J., and Rosario, M. (1994) "Sexual and substance use acts of gay and bisexual male adolescents," *Journal of Adolescent Research* 9: 498–508.

Saewyc, E. M. (1999) "Sexual intercourse, abuse, and pregnancy among adolescent women: does sexual orientation make a difference?" *Family Planning Perspectives* 31 (3): 127–31.

Savin-Williams, R. C. (1994) "Verbal and physical abuse as stressors in the lives of lesbian, gay male, and bisexual youths: associations with school problems, running away, substance abuse, prostitution, and suicide," *Journal of Consulting Clinical Psychology* 62: 261–69.

Schiller, Greta (1985) *Before Stonewall,* movie film: 87 minutes.

Sedgwick, Eve Kosofsky (1993) "Epistemology of the closet" in Henry Abelove, Michele Aina Barale, and David Halperin (eds.), *The Lesbian and Gay Studies Reader.* New York: Routledge.

Seidman, Steven (1997) *Difference Troubles: Queering Social Theory and Sexual Politics.* Cambridge: Cambridge University Press.

Seltzer, R. (1992) "The social location of those holding antihomosexual attitudes," *Sex Roles* 26 (9–10): 391–8.

Shockley, Ann Allen (1974) *Loving Her.* Boston, MA: Northeastern University Press.

—— (1979) "The black lesbian in American literature: an overview," *Conditions Five* 2 (1): 133–42.

Siegel, K. and Epstein, J. A. (1996) "Ethnic-racial differences in psychological stress related to gay lifestyle among HIV-positive men," *Psychological Reports* 79 (1): 303–12.

Siegel, K. and Raveis, V. (1997) "Perceptions of access to HIV-related information, care, and services among infected minority men," *Qualitative Health Research* 7 (1): 9–31.

Smith, Barbara (1979) "Toward a black feminist criticism," *Women's Studies International Quarterly* 2 (2): 183–94.

—— (ed.) (1983) *Home Girls: A Black Feminist Anthology.* Albany, NY: Kitchen Table, Women of Color Press.

—— (1984) "Barbara Smith on Black feminism," *Sojourner: The Women's Forum* 31 December: 13–15.

—— (1993) "Homophobia: why bring it up?" in Henry Abelove, Michele Aina Barale, and David Halperin (eds.), *The Lesbian and Gay Studies Reader.* New York: Routledge.

—— (1995) "Whose American history? Gays, lesbians, and American history," *Gay Community News* 20 (4): 9–12.

—— (1998a) "Making history: an interview with Barbara Smith," *Lambda Book Report* 6 (11, June): 1–3.

—— (1998b) "The fight is for social, political and economic justice," *Gay Community News* 23 (4): 40–1.

—— (1998c) "'We refuse to be bought off': an open letter from Barbara Smith," *Gay Community News* 23 (10, June): 8.

—— (1998d) *The Truth that Never Hurts: Writings on Race, Gender and Freedom.* New Brunswick, NJ: Rutgers University Press, 1998.

—— (1999) "Doing it from scratch: the challenge of black lesbian organizing" in Kris Kleindienst (ed.), *This Is What a Lesbian Looks Like*. Ithaca, NY: Firebrand Books.

Smith, Beverly, Stein, Judith, and Golding, Priscillia (1981) "The possibility between us: a dialogue between Black and Jewish women," *Conditions Seven* 3 (1): 25–46.

Sommerville, Siobhan (2000) *Queering the Color Line: Race and the Invention of Homosexuality in American Culture*. Durham, NC: Duke University Press.

Staples, R. (1978) "The myth of black sexual superiority: a re-examination," *Black Scholar*, 9 (7): 16–23.

—— (1981) *The Changing World of Black Singles*. Westport, CT: Greenwood Press.

Steinberg, Stephen (1997) "Bayard Rustin and the rise and decline of the black protest movement," *New Politics* 6 (3, Summer).

Stevens, P. (1998) "The experiences of lesbians of color in health care encounters: narrative insights for improving access and quality" in C. Ponticelli (ed.), *Gateways to Improving Lesbian Health and Health Care: Opening Doors*, 77–94. New York: Harrington Park Press/Haworth Press.

Stokes, J., McKirnan, D., Doll, L., and Burzette, R. (1996a) "Female partners of bisexual men: what they don't know might hurt them," *Psychology of Women Quarterly* 20 (2): 267–84.

Stokes, J., Vanable, P. and McKirnan, D. (1996b) "Ethnic differences in sexual behavior, condom use and psychosocial variables among Black and white men who have sex with men," *Journal of Sex Research* 33 (4): 373–81.

Stokes, J. and Peterson, J. (1998) "Homophobia, self-esteem, and risk for HIV among Black men who have sex with men," *AIDS Education and Prevention* 10 (3): 278–92.

Sullivan, P., Chu, S., Fleming, P., and Ward, J. (1997) "Changes in AIDS incidence for men who have sex with men, United States 1990–1995," *AIDS* 11 (13): 1,641–6.

Thorpe, Rochella (1996) "A house where queers go: African-American lesbian nightlife in Detroit, 1940–1975" in Ellen Lewin (ed.), *Inventing Lesbian Cultures in America*, 40–61. Boston: Beacon Press.

Tucker, Belinda and Mitchell-Kernan, Claudia (eds.) (1995) *The Decline in Marriage among Blacks: Causes, Consequences, and Policy Implications*. New York: Russell Sage Foundation.

Wekker, G. (1994) "Mati-ism and Black lesbianism: two idealtypical expressions of female homosexuality in Black communities of the diaspora," *Journal of Homosexuality* 24 (3–4): 145–58.

Welsing, Frances Cress (1990) *The Isis Papers: The Keys to the Colors*. Chicago: Third World Press.

White, E. Frances (2001) *Dark Continent of Our Bodies: Black Feminism and the Politics of Respectability*. Philadelphia: Temple University Press.

Williams, M., Elwood, W., Weatherby, N., and Bowen, A. (1996) "An assessment of the risks of syphilis and HIV infection among a sample of not-in-treatment drug users in Houston, Texas," *AIDS Care* 8 (6): 671–82.

Wirth, Thomas H. (2002) *Gay Rebel of the Harlem Renaissance: Selections from the Work of Richard Bruce Nugent*. Durham, NC: Duke University Press.

PART IX

Migration, Renaissance, and New Beginnings

CHAPTER TWENTY-SIX

Exodus from the South

MARK ANDREW HUDDLE

The first work of fiction to appear in the famous 1925 "Special Harlem Number" of the magazine *Survey Graphic* was a short story by the physician Rudolph Fisher, "The South lingers on." This edition of the magazine was the result of the great success of the Civic Club dinner organized by Charles S. Johnson of the National Urban League to draw attention to the cultural awakening taking place in Harlem. Johnson transformed the meal – attended by many of New York's brightest literary lights – into a literary symposium, a coming-out party for a new generation of African American writers who had emerged in the months before the gathering. So great was the outpouring of enthusiasm in the wake of the dinner that the *Survey Graphic* editor, Paul Kellogg, asked Johnson to help put together the special number of his magazine as a showcase for this new talent. A longer and more polished presentation of the material became Alain Locke's magnificent anthology, *The New Negro*.

The five vignettes that comprised Fisher's story described the travails of rural black southerners who had left their homes and now struggled to find a niche in the new urban setting. In his sketches, readers met a country preacher who followed his flock to Harlem only to find that they had fallen under the influence of a "jack-leg preacher" who preyed on their superstitions. There is a young migrant laborer wandering from shop to shop searching for work only to find discrimination; not from whites but from northern African Americans appalled at what they perceive as his backwardness. In the third vignette, a young girl rejects the morals and folkways of her grandmother in favor of the hedonism of Harlem's cabarets. Next, a husband and wife argue about whether their daughter has received too much education, only to rejoice when informed she has won a scholarship to Columbia's Teachers College. Fisher ends his tale with the story of two bootleggers who enter a tent-meeting looking to make mischief. Instead, one of the hooligans is overcome by the spiritual and emotional power of the service, explaining to his friend that he was the son of a country preacher. Remembering what had been, this man was overwhelmed by a terrible sense of loss (Fisher 1925). At a moment when the "Negro" celebrated all things "new," Fisher captured the ambivalence of this wrenching, transformative experience of African Americans on the move. History, memory, loss, nostalgia, faith, tradition: whatever the reason, the South lingered on.

The Great Black Migration from the South was arguably the greatest demographic event of the American Century. It reshaped the politics of the rural South and urban North, altered the economic landscape of the nation and transformed American culture. Driven by displacement from the land because of the infamous boll weevil and the mechanization of southern agriculture (Holley 2000), the shifting demands of a wartime labor market, racial discrimination and violence, and often just word-of-mouth descriptions of the "promised land," 400,000 African Americans left the South between 1916 and 1920, followed by another 600,000 over the next ten years (Fligstein 1981). Although the Great Depression distracted many scholars from the phenomenon, the exodus continued throughout the 1930s. This chapter traces the trends in migration scholarship from what might be termed "proto-migration" studies rooted in early-twentieth-century urban sociology to the great syntheses of the 1940s and 1950s, the social histories and community studies of the 1970s and 1980s, and finally the most recent work that extends our knowledge of the culture of migration as well as attempts to "internationalize" our conceptions of the movement by rooting it in the context of the African diaspora. The historiography of the black migration reflects the continuing African American freedom struggle and has been as successful as any historiographical current at moving black America to the center of our national narrative.

Uplifting the Race: Black Sociology and Migration Studies before the First World War

Black migration studies were born with the earliest attempts to delineate a black sociology, specifically with W. E. B. Du Bois' path-breaking *The Philadelphia Negro*. It is hard to overstate the importance of Du Bois' effort, which was one of the first attempts to challenge with empirical data the racist suppositions that were commonplace in much of the scholarly literature of the day (Katz and Sugrue 1998). Much of what passed for social science orthodoxy was rooted in the evolutionary rhetoric of social Darwinism that culminated with Frederick Hoffman's 1896 study *Race Traits and Tendencies*, a work that synthesized much of the racist pseudo-science in concluding that blacks were biologically and culturally inferior and doomed to extinction (Bay 1998).

Du Bois embraced the belief of many progressive reformers that social science methodologies were a necessary tool in combating society's evils and an integral element in the ideology of racial uplift, a complex of ideas and strategies which spanned the African American political spectrum but which held in common the desire to re-appropriate the black image from white supremacy (Gaines 1996). Du Bois spent a year in Philadelphia's Seventh Ward interviewing residents and observing social trends. He concluded that it was a lack of opportunity, accompanied by severe environmental constraints, that afflicted the black community and not some natural inferiority (Du Bois 1899).

However, while *The Philadelphia Negro* laid the foundation for a more objective assessment of the African American situation, Du Bois was unable to shrug off his Victorian sensibilities, especially when discussing the impact of southern migrants. He argued that this migration threatened the moral stability of neighborhoods. Criminal activity emanated from the dysfunctional structure of migrant families.

Single black women posed a particular problem. By attributing to these newcomers a sort of urban pathology, Du Bois touched on a theme that compromised many early sociological studies of black urban communities, some of which devolved into racist stereotyping (Daniels 1914), a theme that has had some staying power to the present. These ideas certainly influenced the important work of the African American sociologist, E. Franklin Frazier, whose study of the black family in Chicago updated many of Du Bois's arguments (Frazier 1939).

Of course there were important exceptions. In 1906, R. R. Wright of the University of Pennsylvania explicitly rejected the social pathology argument. His was one of the first studies to map the geographic origins of the migrants, as well as their destinations. Wright was one of the first scholars to focus on causation, especially the economic dislocations in the South (Wright 1906). Two early studies by George Haynes described the "push-pull" of economic forces transforming the southern economy and drawing migrants northward. Haynes was also quick to attack the violence of southern life and the horrible inequities of Jim Crow, presaging his work for the Department of Labor, the National Urban League and then as a long-time professor of sociology at Fisk University (Haynes 1912, 1913).

Another event of great importance to the study of the black migration was the relocation of Robert E. Park from Tuskegee, where he had served as an aide and ghostwriter to Booker T. Washington, to the University of Chicago in 1913. The timing of Park's move was propitious. His theory of cyclical race relations – which exemplified conflict, change, and accommodation in a biracial society – was eagerly embraced by sociologists and policy-makers struggling to make sense of the demographic revolution taking place around them. He trained many of the most influential sociologists of his generation, including E. Franklin Frazier and Charles S. Johnson, and his ideas held sway in the profession for a quarter-century and did much to displace the racial determinism of earlier scholarship (Stanfield 1982).

Exodus from the South: The First World War, Mass Migration, and the Politics of Uplift

In December 1916, *Chicago Daily News* reporter Junius B. Wood authored a series of articles describing the waves of African American migrants arriving in Chicago. According to Wood, the world war raging in Europe had choked off immigration from that source, fueling labor shortages and drawing black southerners northward in tremendous numbers. Sounding much like a representative from the chamber-of-commerce, Wood extolled black businesses, investments, and professional and political life, praised the contributions of black musicians, artists, and writers, and offered advice to these new Chicagoans on how to secure both employment and housing (Wood 1916). On one level, Wood was simply reporting a story. On another level, however, he and his newspaper – along with other African American newspapers, like the *Chicago Defender* – crafted a primer for these newcomers on what to expect from the urban experience, a primer whose gist was distributed via informal communications networks back to the South.

As many as 400,000 African Americans left the South during the First World War to seek the expanded economic opportunities in northern industries and to escape the political, economic, and social tyranny of Jim Crow. In the process, what many

Americans once termed a "southern problem" was now national in scope. White America viewed the migration with ambivalence. It was obvious to most observers that this was a logical response to wartime necessities and was driven by demand for labor in the war industries. On the other hand, northerners – white and black – looked with alarm at growing African American ghettos while southern employers took a dim view of what was transpiring and often took extraordinary measures to stem the tide, stopping trains, banning labor agents, and even arresting migrants.

Many of the migration studies undertaken during the war – even those undertaken by the federal government – reflected those changing political realities. These studies displayed a much greater depth and sophistication than the pre-war scholarship and showed (during the war) a commitment to national service, while at the same time continuing to reflect a belief in the ideology of racial uplift and the role to be played by social science in that process. Black civil rights leaders sought to use the migration as a "lever for social change" (Cohen 1991; Arnesen 2003), and wartime contingencies forced the Wilson Administration to respond to African American demands for greater representation within the government. In October 1917, Emmett Scott, Booker T. Washington's former secretary, was named Special Adviser to the Secretary of War and in April 1918 sociologist George Haynes was appointed director of the newly created Division of Negro Economics in the Department of Labor. Haynes led one of the first full-scale studies of wartime migration (Department of Labor 1919). His team gave a much more detailed rendering of the economic conditions in the South that led to the out-migration. The ravages of the boll weevil, floods, the inefficiency of land tenancy, poor schools, the corrupt court system, lynching, labor agents, and press coverage in the North were all cited. In the midst of all these economic data, the migrants themselves tended to recede from view, a failing that many of these sociological studies shared.

Emmett Scott quickly emerged as one of the great publicists of this demographic phenomenon. He published the letters of the migrants themselves in Carter Woodson's *Journal of Negro History* to demonstrate that they were active participants in this movement to the industrial North. His own research culminated in the publication of *Negro Migration During the War* (Scott 1920). Scott attempted to capitalize on increasing media attention to lobby for the creation of a permanent Bureau of Negro Affairs. His bid failed, but he was able to capitalize on the surge of interest to secure a grant from the Carnegie Corporation to commission a series of studies from the sociologists Monroe Work and Charles S. Johnson, and from the journalist T. Thomas Fortune (Cohen 1991; Work 1924; Johnson 1925).

As mentioned above, there was a general consensus that economic factors in North and South were the chief reasons for the exodus. However, many of the studies from the First World War into the early 1930s were quick to use this population movement to shine a light on southern racism. Not only did they give detailed explanations of the causes of the migration that included a stinging critique of race relations in the South, many contained prescriptions for improving those relations (Scott 1920; Work 1924; Donald 1921; Kennedy 1930; Kiser 1932), thus rooting those studies in the uplift tradition.

There were dissenters. Charles S. Johnson, for instance, used Georgia census data to show that there was no direct correlation between lynchings and black out-migration in counties where those lynchings took place. In fact, Johnson argued, there was greater out-migration of whites than blacks (Johnson 1923). Thomas Jackson Woofter, Jr, a former Fellow with the Phelps-Stokes Fund and a member of the faculty at the University of North Carolina at Chapel Hill, argued that the migration was the natural result of the post-bellum reorganization of the southern rural economic order. Woofter saw that reorganization unfolding in stages, beginning with the collapse of plantation agriculture, stages that picked up momentum in response to wartime conditions. He saw the wartime migration as "abnormal" in the broader context of this longer historical process (Woofter 1920).

Another important trend in the literature of this period was to focus attention on the impact of the migration on northern cities as well as the difficulties faced by the migrants in their new environs. The migration exacerbated racial tensions across the urban North. In 1917, racial violence erupted in East St Louis (Rudwick 1982) and then, in the so-called "Red Summer" of 1919, riots broke out in more than two dozen cities. The worst violence was in Chicago in July, when 23 African Americans and 15 whites died in three days of street-fighting. There were 520 people injured (Tuttle 1996). Local authorities convened a civil rights commission to investigate the causes of the violence. The final report, authored by Charles S. Johnson, who was then employed by the Chicago Urban League, was one of the first in-depth studies to connect racial violence in northern cities to the dislocations wrought by mass migration. The lengthy final report was accompanied by a discussion of the causes of the migration as well as a massive compendium of information about black life in Chicago. There were sections on population growth, housing shortages, violence against black neighborhoods, medical care, crime, employment opportunities, and work conditions. There were over eighty pages of recommendations to the city to improve race relations (Chicago Commission on Race Relations 1922).

Other studies described the social processes by which rural black southerners became an urban working-class (Kennedy 1930; Lewis 1931). The sociologist Clyde Kiser employed multiple methodologies to trace the migration of a group of St Helena Islanders to Harlem, Boston, Philadelphia, and Savannah. The use of such a control group allowed Kiser to demonstrate the role of kinship networks and informal institutional structures in the migration, as well as the impact of the urban experience on the St Helena migrants (Kiser 1932). These studies of social transformation reached their apogee in this period with E. Franklin Frazier's controversial 1939 work *The Negro Family in Chicago*. According to Frazier, the migration destroyed the only moral foundation these rural folk had ever known. In the cities, black family structures grew unstable. Crime, divorce, and illegitimate birth rates ballooned while the sheer numbers of migrants rendered black institutions in northern cities unable to improve the quality of life. Frazier supported his urban pathology thesis with a mountain of evidence gleaned from much of the major social science research of the period.

A Renaissance in Chicago and an American Dilemma: The 1940s and 1950s

By the end of the 1930s, the study of black migration had fallen out of favor within the academy. Anthropological studies by scholars such as John Dollard and Hortense Powdermaker described black life in southern towns, but there was little or no attention paid to population movements and their effects (Dollard 1937; Powdermaker 1939). Interestingly, however, a young novelist with connections to the University of Chicago Sociology Department was about to give the migration a horrifying, if fictional, face. In 1940, Richard Wright published his searing novel *Native Son*, and the character Bigger Thomas entered the American consciousness. Bigger Thomas, in Wright's rendering, was a measure of how the migration had failed the African American community, as early hopes gave way to almost nihilistic rage. Born near Natchez, Mississippi, Wright was himself a product of the migration, who had moved to Chicago by way of Memphis. He began his writing career in the 1930s as an employee of the Federal Writers Project in Chicago, where he was heavily influenced by Robert Park's School of Sociology at the University (Rodgers 1997). Wright's turn towards social realism in the late 1930s owed much to his connections with the sociologists Horace Cayton and St Claire Drake. Their work influenced not only *Native Son*, but Wright's quirky folk history of rural-to-urban migration, *Twelve Million Black Voices*, and his autobiography, *Black Boy* (Wright 1940, 1941 and 1945).

In 1944, Richard Wright wrote the introduction to Cayton and Drake's epic, *Black Metropolis: A Study of Negro Life in a Northern City*. If "you doubted the reality of Bigger Thomas," Wright wrote, ". . . then study the figures on family disorganization here." In many ways, *Black Metropolis* simply built on Charles S. Johnson's *The Negro in Chicago*. While purporting to describe the impact of the migration into the 1930s and 1940s, little attention was paid to the changing nature of the migration in the 1930s. The focus remained on the period from the First World War through the 1920s. There is a long discussion of southern agricultural practices and demand for labor in northern industries. Especially interesting is Cayton and Drake's discussion of the role played by the *Chicago Defender* in encouraging black southerners to make the trek north. Their analysis of the black family structure during the migration and in Chicago greatly expanded Clyde Kiser's description of kinship networks. The picture that emerges in this massive study is one of urban anomie and social dysfunction, themes that urban historians would explore in the 1960s and 1970s.

When *Black Metropolis* was published, the nation was still at war. Few outside the academy took notice of this massive local study. One major work on American race relations that could not be so easily ignored, however, was Gunnar Myrdal's *An American Dilemma: The Negro Problem and Modern Democracy* published in 1944. Myrdal's international stature combined with timing of his study made its publication a major event. By placing his interdisciplinary analysis in the context of the war against fascism, Myrdal cast America's racial travails as a moral question, as a question of conscience. It was a symptom, again, of the changing politics of race. The Second World War opened social fissures across the American cultural land-scape. The war had touched off another wave of black migration from the South (Lemann 1991) and the racial dilemma was national in scope.

An American Dilemma synthesized much of the earlier literature on the black migration and again focused on the First World War as a catalyst for the exodus. The most important aspect of Myrdal's discussion was his description of the chang-ing nature of the migration in the 1930s. The economic crisis, Myrdal argued, did not dissuade black southerners from coming north. Instead, 300,000 migrants made the journey, safe in the knowledge that public assistance programs under the New Deal were preferable to the suffering in the rural South. This challenged many earlier economic arguments concerning causation. But despite a broad interdisciplinary approach, *An American Dilemma* shared a major weakness with many of these sociological studies. While it paid lip-service to the historical context of the exodus, it never dealt with this population movement as a historical *process*. Instead, the migration was reduced to a "social problem." That would change in the 1960s.

Upheaval: Historical Scholarship in the 1960s and 1970s and the Rise of Social History and Community Studies

In 1918, one of the progenitors of the modern study of African American history, Carter Woodson, published *A Century of Negro Migration*. Written at the height of the wartime out-migration, Woodson urged readers to step back and see the current exodus as the latest phase in a long history of black population movements. He began his study in antebellum America with the establishment of free black communities in the northeast and midwest. He characterized the African colonization movement of the 1820s and 1830s as a response to black migrants in the North. He described the underground railroad as a stage in this history of population movements. He reminded readers of the "Exoduster" migrations to Oklahoma and Kansas in the 1870s and 1880s and the "migration of the talented tenth" – intellectuals, teachers, and skilled artisans – at the turn of the twentieth century. Only then did Woodson discuss the migration during the war years. Woodson's remarkably prescient monograph highlighted the weakness of many of the early sociological studies – the inability to see the broader historical implications of this mass movement.

By the early 1960s, historians had turned their attention to the migration and they did so against the backdrop of civil rights agitation and mounting conflict in America's urban centers. The "ghetto" had entered the consciousness of both the American public and American policy-makers, and a series of important studies sought to make sense of this urban malady. Beginning with Gilbert Osofsky's pioneering 1963 study of Harlem, studies of Chicago, Detroit, and Cleveland appeared in close succession (Osofsky 1963; Spears 1967; Katzman 1973; Kusmer 1976). Echoing Woodson, these studies agreed that many of the earlier studies of the migration were too reductive. All pushed the temporal boundaries of analysis back into the nineteenth century; indeed, David Katzman's study of black Detroit focused primarily on the nineteenth century. These scholars agreed that this pre-war migration created a tenuous infrastructure that awaited the migrants when the exodus from the South began in earnest. More importantly, the patterns of racial prejudice and discrimination were the norm in northern cities long before the wartime demand for labor set off this demographic revolution.

These ghetto studies were important contributions to urban history. However, they tended to portray the migrants themselves as flotsam and jetsam swept along by great historical currents. They demonstrate little agency. In fact, one study invoked Detroit, Chicago, and New York in describing "a tragic sameness in the lives of black people today and in the past" (Katzman 1973). It is a startling renunciation of contingency. There was no discussion of the "southern-ness" of the migration, no discussion of the world the migrants left behind or the important networks they

established and exploited in their journeys, and no discussion of the cultural transformation wrought in this rural-to-urban migration. Nonetheless, these studies of
ghetto-formation finally rooted the black migration more deeply in the broader
historical processes and helped set the research agenda for the future.

The upheavals of the 1960s had a transformative effect on the American academic
world. New voices demanded to be heard. New methodologies challenged the
traditional narrative of American history. The 1970s witnessed the rise of a new
social history that sought to view the past "from the bottom up" and to give agency
to those who had either been left out of the story or who tended to be rendered
only as part of monolithic groups. Much of this social history straddled historiographical boundaries. Many migration studies of the 1970s and 1980s contributed
heavy doses of class analysis to the study of race relations. There were labor histories
and community studies, which contributed to our understanding of the diversity of
experience involved in this historical process. And slowly in this period, the experience of women in the migration became fodder for a new generation of scholarship.

One of the earliest attempts to give voice to black migrants and workers was
William Tuttle's *Race Riot: Chicago in the Red Summer of 1919*, originally published
in 1970. Tuttle rooted the causes of the Chicago riot in the social tensions caused
by the influx of black migrants. At the same time, he told his story from the point-
of-view of working-class blacks who experienced the violence on the streets. Another
attempt to render African Americans as actors in the exodus was Florette Henri's
idiosyncratic *Black Migration: Movement North, 1900–1920*. Henri (1975) incor-
rectly declared that blacks were invisible in the North prior to 1900. However, she
moved the migrants in this period to the center of her analysis, declaring them to be
"choosers, makers, and doers." Henri argued that "Nobody drove the black man
out of the South; he made the decision to leave." Arguably, the best of the migration studies of the 1970s was Nell Irvin Painter's brilliant, *Exodusters: Black Migration to Kansas after Reconstruction* (1977). Painter portrayed the Exoduster movement
as being driven by the black working class, attempting to make a world for itself
outside of the increasingly poisonous atmosphere of the South.

The 1980s witnessed something of an explosion of theses, dissertations, books,
and articles about the Great Migration. Many shed light on African American communities that had garnered little attention. Others re-conceptualized familiar tales
and afforded scholars a wealth of new insights. Joe W. Trotter, Jr's study of black
Milwaukee led the way and was quickly followed by important studies of Pittsburgh,
Chicago, and Norfolk, Virginia (Trotter 1985; Gottlieb 1987; Grossman 1989;
Lewis 1991). If these texts were "a subfield of black urban history" (Trotter 1991),
they also had one foot squarely in African American labor history. They focused on
the "proletarianization" of migrants once they reached the urban setting and paid
little attention to the actual process of migration. James Grossman's *Land of Hope:
Chicago, Black Southerners, and the Great Migration* was a notable exception. In
his painstaking examination of the migration experience, Grossman delineated the
contours of a "grass-roots social movement" with its own indigenous leadership
class and kin networks that facilitated migration and eased the transition to urban
living. He was careful to note that those experiences were filtered through the
prisms of class and gender as well as race.

Two other studies demonstrated the greater diversity in migration studies: Earl Lewis's *In Their Own Interests: Race, Class, and Power in Twentieth-Century Norfolk, Virginia* and Joe W. Trotter, Jr's *Coal, Class, and Color: Blacks in Southern West Virginia, 1915–32.* Lewis's book was one of the first historical studies of black life in a southern city. It showed the connections between black workers in Norfolk and their families in the nearby countryside, further complicating our knowledge of the black exodus. Trotter's *Coal, Class, and Power* left the "urban" out of the migration experience completely, tracing the movement of black agricultural workers into the Appalachian coalfields.

One other text that bears mentioning from this fruitful period is Carole Marks's *Farewell – We're Good and Gone: The Great Black Migration* (1989). Marks's interesting, albeit controversial, book challenged a number of black migration studies' sacred cows. She contended that a "majority" of migrants were actually urban, nonagricultural workers and not rural "peasants." Marks also believed that the catalyst that drove these workers northward was southern industrial development. These workers were relatively skilled and it was institutional racism that blocked upward mobility; not their inability to survive in an industrial system.

Contemporary Migration Studies: Eclecticism and Ferment

Since the early 1990s, black migration studies have spun off in fascinating new directions. We have studies of African American women in the North and South, and their roles in shaping both the migration and their new worlds north of the Mason-Dixon line. New cultural histories describe the integration of black migrants into the urban consumer culture, the role of the Black Church in the exodus, and the impact of the black migration on American literary culture. More recently migration studies have been "internationalized" as the exodus from the South has been integrated into studies of the African diaspora.

In a 1991 essay, Deborah Clark Hine urged historians to consider the "gender dimension" of the black migration. According to Hine, the dearth of material on African American women in this story was an "egregious void" in the literature that needed to be remedied (Hine 1991). Two studies have since appeared that have taken up Hine's call and both have made creative use of a variety of untapped sources to craft works of innovative scholarship. Tera W. Hunter's *To 'Joy My Freedom: Southern Black Women's Lives and Labors After the Civil War* studied black domestic laborers from the end of the Civil War through the Great Migration of the 1920s. With the collapse of plantation slavery after the Civil War, thousands of black women migrated to Atlanta. There they struggled to achieve self-sufficiency as well as a semblance of dignity within a racist system. Hunter's study describes the neighborhood networks of support, the institution-building, and the day-to-day resistance to Jim Crow, and concludes with descriptions of the transplantation of these support networks in the urban North during the Great Migration (Hunter 1997).

Victoria Wolcott's *Remaking Respectability: African American Women in Interwar Detroit* (2001) picks up where Hunter's work leaves off. Studies of Detroit migrants have focused primarily on the men who found work in the smokestack industries of the region. Women have remained largely invisible in those stories.

Wolcott moves women to the center of her analysis by taking her readers into the speakeasies, blues clubs, church groups, and settlement houses to demonstrate the role of women in remaking their post-migration lives. Both Hunter and Wolcott demonstrate the richness of these women's lives; their gendered renderings of the migrant experience have greatly expanded our knowledge of the migration and pointed the way for future scholarship.

Historians have also begun to pay attention to the cultural impact of the migration. In Lizabeth Cohen's brilliant *Making a New Deal: Industrial Workers in Chicago, 1919–1939*, labor history took a cultural turn. Cohen attempted to make sense of the rising political consciousness among Chicago workers in the 1930s, arguing that changes in day-to-day experience contributed to political awareness, in particular, the encounter with mass consumption and mass culture. For African American workers, many of whom had recently migrated to the city, this encounter contributed to the making of a new urban black identity. Participation in commercial life signaled independence to many. Mass culture, Cohen argued, was a site where "black folk culture, black inventiveness, and black talent" entered mainstream popular culture. African Americans were trend-setters and taste-makers. Participation in this consumer culture was a way of turning black vulnerability and dependence into a demand for respect (Cohen 1990).

Historian Milton Sernett has also ventured into the cultural realm, in his study of the impact of the migration on African American religion. In *Bound for the Promised Land: African American Religion and the Great Migration*, Sernett decries the socioeconomic bias of migration studies, noting that cultural considerations in general had been "slighted" and that the church was "missing" from histories of the exodus (Sernett 1997). This is especially egregious given the centrality of the church to the Black Experience. It is interesting, also, because of the wide gulf between northern and southern churches before the migration, a division made more acute by the tensions between the church of the rural South and their more cosmopolitan northern brethren. Sernett argues that despite profound theological differences, a much "more mixed religious culture" emerged as a result of this encounter that made the church more responsive to the needs of its community. Another study that looks to the cultural impact of the migration is Lawrence Rodgers's *Canaan Bound: The African American Great Migration Novel* (1997). Rodgers explores the intersection of the historical migration and the literary significance of the event. He traces the literary treatments of the exodus from the Harlem Renaissance to Richard Wright, to the culmination of the migration novel in Ralph Ellison's *Invisible Man*. Rodgers argues that the "Great Migration novel" has become a viable literary form in American letters that influences writers to the present day.

One last trend in the contemporary literature that bears mentioning is the "internationalization" of migration studies. These studies root the African American flight from the South within the international movements of peoples of African descent. A series of studies have analyzed the impact of Caribbean immigrants on the Great Migration. On the move because of economic dislocations throughout the Caribbean basin, many found their way to the urban centers of the North. Many of those immigrants initially found themselves in conflict with native-born African Americans. And many of the intellectuals who immigrated in this period found their way into American radical organizations (Watkins-Owens 1996; James 1998;

Hathaway 1999; Foner 2001). These newcomers contributed to the making of an urban black identity and these studies do much to complicate our ideas about race-making in the 1920s.

Another important area of migration studies has focused attention on African Americans who migrated to Paris in the 1920s (Fabre 1991; Stovall 1996; Leininger-Miller 2001; Shack 2001). While they most assuredly stretch our conceptions of the "exodus from the South," these studies denote global communities of resistance that responded to many of the same conditions as black southerners. Diaspora-theorists such as Paul Gilroy have posited the emergence of a transnational culture of resistance during the interwar period (Gilroy 1993; Hall 1994). While there has been no shortage of critics of Gilroy's approach, his work does demonstrate an on-going search for a framework through which to view these demographic surges from a global perspective.

This wide-ranging scholarship is indicative of the tremendous impact that the Great Black Migration has had on American society. Each generation has had to wrestle with its legacies. The migration has affected American politics, economics, and culture. At times, it has exacerbated racial tensions in the Republic, reminding Americans of the great distance between their national ideals and national realities. With each methodological innovation, our understanding of this remarkably complex event grows fuller and more complicated, and thus more human. Ironically, as we struggle with its meaning, there is significant evidence that a reverse migration is under way. African Americans have been returning to the South in increasing numbers (Stack 1996; Lemann 1991). As the very first sociologists who took notice of this phenomenon understood all too well, much can be learned about a society by the movement of its peoples. That is why it is certain that students and scholars will continue to return to the "exodus from the South" because it provides us with another tool by which we can try to understand what it means to be "American."

BIBLIOGRAPHY

Works Cited

Adero, Malaika (ed.) (1993) *Up South: Stories, Studies, and Letters of this Century's African-American Migrations*. New York: New Press.

Arnesen, Eric (2003) *Black Protest and the Great Migration: A Brief History with Documents*. Boston: Bedford/St. Martin's.

Bay, Mia (1998) " 'The world was thinking wrong about race': *The Philadelphia Negro* and American science" in M. B. Katz and T. J. Sugrue (eds.), *W. E. B. Du Bois, Race, and the City:* The Philadelphia Negro *and Its Legacy*. Philadelphia: University of Pennsylvania Press.

Chicago Commission on Race Relations (1922) *The Negro in Chicago: A Study of Race Relations and a Race Riot*. Chicago: University of Chicago Press.

Cohen, Lizabeth (1990) *Making a New Deal: Industrial Workers in Chicago, 1919–1939*. Cambridge: Cambridge University Press.

Cohen, William (1991) "The Great Migration as a lever for social change" in Alferdteen Harrison (ed.) *Black Exodus: The Great Migration from the American South*. Jackson: University Press of Mississippi.

Daniels, John ([1914] 1969) *In Freedom's Birthplace: A Study of the Boston Negro*. New York: Arno Press.

Department of Labor, Division of Negro Economics (1919) *Negro Migration in 1916–1917.*
Washington, DC: Government Printing Office.

Dollard, John ([1937] 1957) *Caste and Class in a Southern Town.* Garden City, NY: Doubleday
Anchor Books.

Donald, Henderson H. (1921) "The Negro migration of 1916–1918," *Journal of Negro
History* 6 (October): 383–498.

Drake, St Clair and Cayton, Horace R. (1945) *Black Metropolis: A Study of Negro Life in a
Northern City.* Chicago: University of Chicago Press.

Du Bois, W. E. B. ([1899] 1967) The Philadelphia Negro: *A Social Study.* New York: Schocken.

Fabre, Michel (1991) *From Harlem to Paris: Black American Writers in France, 1840–1980.*
Urbana: University of Illinois Press.

Fisher, Rudolph (1925) "The South lingers on," *Survey Graphic* 6 (March): 644–7.

Fligstein, Neil (1981) *Going North: Migration of Blacks and Whites from the South, 1900–
1950.* New York: Academic Press.

Foner, Nancy (ed.) (2001) *Islands in the City: West Indian Migration to New York.* Berkeley:
University of California Press.

Frazier, E. Franklin (1939) *The Negro Family in Chicago.* Chicago: University of Chicago Press.

Gaines, Kevin K. (1996) *Uplifting the Race: Black Leadership, Politics, and Culture in the
Twentieth Century.* Chapel Hill: University of North Carolina Press.

Gerstle, Gary (1995) "Race and the myth of the liberal consensus," *Journal of American
History* 82 (September): 579–86.

Gilroy, Paul (1993) *The Black Atlantic: Modernity and Double Consciousness.* Cambridge, MA:
Harvard University Press.

Gottlieb, Peter (1987) *Making Their Own Way: Southern Blacks' Migration to Pittsburgh,
1916–1930.* Urbana: University of Illinois Press.

Grossman, James R. (1989) *Land of Hope: Chicago, Black Southerners, and the Great Migration.* Chicago: University of Chicago Press.

Hall, Stuart (1994) "Cultural identity and diaspora" in Patrick Williams and Laura Chrisman
(eds.), *Colonial Discourse and Post-Colonial Theory: A Reader.* New York: Columbia University
Press.

Harrison, Alferdteen (1991) *Black Exodus: The Great Migration from the American South.*
Jackson: University Press of Mississippi.

Hathaway, Heather (1999) "'An essential friendship': African Americans and Caribbean immigrants in Harlem" in Timothy B. Powell (ed.), *Beyond the Binary: Reconstructing Cultural
Identity in a Multicultural Context.* New Brunswick, NJ: Rutgers University Press.

Haynes, George Edmund (1912) *The Negro at Work in New York City.* New York: Columbia
University Press.

—— (1913) "Conditions among Negroes in the cities," *Annals of the American Academy of
Political and Social Sciences* 49 (September): 100–11.

—— (1918) "Negroes move North: I. Their departure from the South," *Survey* 40 (May 4):
118–22.

Henri, Florette (1975) *Black Migration: Movement North, 1900–1920.* Garden City, NY:
Anchor Press.

Hine, Deborah Clark (1991) "Black migration to the urban Midwest: the gender dimension,
1915–1945" in Joe William Trotter, Jr, *The Great Migration in Historical Perspective: New
Dimensions of Race, Class, and Gender.* Bloomington: Indiana University Press.

Hirsch, Arnold R. (1998) *Making the Second Ghetto: Race and Housing in Chicago, 1940–
1960.* Chicago: University of Chicago Press.

Holley, Donald (2000) *The Second Great Emancipation: The Mechanical Cotton Picker, Black
Migration, and How They Shaped the Modern South.* Fayetteville: University of Arkansas
Press.

Hunter, Tera W. (1997) *To Joy My Freedom: Southern Black Women's Lives and Labors after the Civil War.* Cambridge, MA: Harvard University Press.

James, Winston (1998) *Holding Aloft the Banner of Ethiopia: Caribbean Radicalism in Early Twentieth-Century America.* New York: Verso.

Johnson, Charles S. (1923) "How much is the migration a flight from persecution?" *Opportunity* 1: 272–4.

—— (1925) "The Negro migration: an economic interpretation," *Modern Quarterly* 2: 314–26.

Katz, Michael B. and Sugrue, Thomas J. (eds.) (1998) *W. E. B. Du Bois, Race and the City: The Philadelphia Negro and Its Legacy.* Philadelphia: University of Pennsylvania Press.

Katzman, David M. (1973) *Before the Ghetto: Black Detroit in the Nineteenth Century.* Urbana: University of Illinois Press.

Kennedy, Louise Venable (1930) *The Negro Peasant Turns Cityward.* New York: Columbia University Press.

Kiser, Clyde Vernon (1932) *Sea Island to City: A Study of St. Helena Islanders in Harlem and Other Urban Centers.* New York: Columbia University Press.

Kusmer, Kenneth (1976) *A Ghetto Takes Shape: Black Cleveland, 1870–1930.* Urbana: University of Illinois Press.

Leininger-Miller, Theresa (2001) *New Negro Artists in Paris: African American Painters and Sculptors in the City of Light, 1922–1934.* New Brunswick, NJ: Rutgers University Press.

Lemann, Nicholas (1991) *The Promised Land: The Great Black Migration and How It Changed America.* New York: Knopf.

Lewis, Earl (1991) *In Their Own Interests: Race, Class, and Power in Twentieth-Century Norfolk, Virginia.* Berkeley: University of California Press.

Lewis, Edward E. (1931) *The Mobility of the Negro: A Study in the American Labor Supply.* New York: Columbia University Press.

Marks, Carole (1985) "Black workers and the Great Migration North," *Phylon* 46 (Winter): 148–61.

—— (1989) *Farewell – We're Good and Gone: The Great Black Migration.* Bloomington: Indiana University Press.

Meyerowitz, Joanne Jay (1991) *Women Adrift: Independent Wage Earners in Chicago, 1880–1930.* Chicago: University of Chicago Press.

Myrdal, Gunnar (1944) *An American Dilemma: The Negro Problem and Modern Democracy.* New York: Harper & Brothers.

Osofsky, Gilbert ([1963] 1971) *Harlem: The Making of a Ghetto.* New York: Harper Torchbooks.

Painter, Nell Irvin ([1977] 1992) *Exodusters: Black Migration to Kansas after Reconstruction.* New York: W. W. Norton.

Powdermaker, Hortense (1939) *After Freedom: A Cultural Study of the Deep South.* New York: Viking Press.

Rodgers, Lawrence R. (1997) *Canaan Bound: The African American Great Migration Novel.* Urbana: University of Illinois Press.

Rudwick, Elliott (1982) *Race Riot at East St. Louis, July 2, 1917.* Urbana: University of Illinois Press.

Scott, Emmett J. (1919) "Letters of Negro migrants of 1916–1918," *Journal of Negro History* 4 (July and August): 290–340; 412–65.

—— (1920) *Negro Migration during the War.* New York: Oxford University Press.

Sernett, Milton C. (1997) *Bound for the Promised Land: African American Religion and the Great Migration.* Durham, NC: Duke University Press.

Shack, William A. (2001) *Harlem in Montmartre: A Paris Jazz Story between the Great Wars.* Berkeley: University of California Press.

Spears, Allan H. (1967) *Black Chicago: The Making of a Negro Ghetto*. Chicago: University of Chicago Press.

Stack, Carol (1996) *Call to Home: African Americans Reclaim the Rural South*. New York: Basic Books.

Stanfield, John H. (1982) "The 'Negro problem' within and beyond the institutional nexus of pre-World War I sociology," *Phylon* 43 (Fall): 187–201.

Stovall, Tyler (1996) *Paris Noir: African Americans in the City of Light*. Boston: Houghton Mifflin.

Sugrue, Thomas J. (1995) "Crabgrass-roots politics: race, rights, and the reaction against liberalism in the urban North, 1940–1964," *Journal of American History* 82 (Sept.): 551–78.

—— (1996) *The Origins of the Urban Crisis: Race and Inequality in Postwar Detroit*. Princeton, NJ: Princeton University Press.

Sutherland, Edwin and Locke, Harvey J. (1936) *Twenty Thousand Homeless Men*. Philadelphia: J. B. Lippincott.

Trotter, Joe William, Jr (1985) *Black Milwaukee: The Making of an Industrial Proletariat, 1915–1945*. Urbana: University of Illinois Press.

—— (1990) *Coal, Class, and Color: Blacks in Southern West Virginia, 1915–32*. Urbana: University of Illinois Press.

—— (1991) *The Great Migration in Historical Perspective: New Dimensions of Race, Class, and Gender*. Bloomington: Indiana University Press.

Tuttle, William M., Jr (1996) *Race Riot: Chicago in the Red Summer of 1919*. Urbana: University of Illinois Press.

Watkins-Owens, Irma (1996) *Blood Relations: Caribbean Immigrants and the Harlem Community, 1900–1930*. Bloomington: Indiana University Press.

Wolcott, Victoria W. (2001) *Remaking Respectability: African American Women in Interwar Detroit*. Chapel Hill: University of North Carolina Press.

Wood, Junius B. (1916) *The Negro in Chicago: A First-Hand Study*, reprinted from *Chicago Daily News*, December 11–27. Chicago: *Chicago Daily News*.

Woodson, Carter G. (1918) *A Century of Negro Migration*. New York: Russell & Russell.

Woofter, Thomas Jackson (1920) *Negro Migration: Changes in Rural Organization and Population in the Cotton Belt*. New York: W. D. Gray.

Work, Monroe N. (1924) "The Negro migration," *Southern Workman* 53 (May): 202–12.

Wright, R. R. (1906) "Migration of Negroes to the North," *Annals of the American Academy of Political and Social Science* 27 (January–February): 559–78.

Wright, Richard. (1940) *Native Son*. New York: Harper & Row.

—— (1941) *Twelve Million Black Voices*. New York: Viking.

—— (1945) *Black Boy*. New York: Viking.

CHAPTER TWENTY-SEVEN

Development, Growth, and Transformation in Higher Education

ABEL A. BARTLEY

At the close of the Civil War, among the most pressing problems facing the freedpersons was the massive illiteracy inherited from slavery. Both the federal government and northern humanitarians realized that education was a compelling necessity if African Americans were to become productive citizens in the New Order. At both the lower and higher levels of education, the federal government, through the Bureau of Refugees, Freedmen and Abandoned Lands (Freedmen's Bureau) and northern humanitarians, mostly (though not all) missionary societies of the major Protestant denominations stepped in to fill this void.

Most parties were agreed that the moral and economic status of the race was heavily dependent upon education. As to higher education, it was further believed that colleges and universities were needed to insure there would be leaders, primarily teachers and preachers, for the newly freed people. Some, however, North as well as South, had doubts about the educability of the race. Indeed, in the antebellum period, many had argued – on the basis of observation and "scientific studies" – that the race was closer to beast than to man. At best, blacks had "childlike" mental abilities, even into adulthood. Even foreign statesmen, like Lord James Bryce of Britain, had lamented the "pathetic zeal" that blacks exhibited for learning. Additionally, particularly in the South, the concept of universal education was still a novel one. In the post-emancipation South, Du Bois and others argued, universal education was largely "a Negro idea" (Du Bois 1900, 1903; Anderson 1988; Hornsby 1971; Bond 1934, 1939; Curti 1935; Dabney 1936; McPherson 1970).

Among those who conceded the educability of the race, there were questions as to the aims and purposes of such learning. Missionary groups, particularly the American Missionary Society, argued for a type of learning that would foster American citizenship, but would also make blacks into good Calvinists. Almost all agreed that it was necessary to prevent a state of barbarism and to instill good manners and morals. Many southerners, particularly those in the former slavocracy, were hesitant to concede the educability of their former chattels, but when they did, even if grudgingly, they tended to favor agricultural-industrial training that would fit the blacks for farm and semi-skilled industrial labor. This view was also widely shared by many in the North, including humanitarians and philanthropists (Baldwin 1899; McPherson 1970; Bullock 1967; Anderson 1988).

African Americans themselves were also divided over the best approach to take toward their higher education. Earlier studies tended to divide their views into two "warring" camps – those who favored agricultural education and those who favored liberal-classical education. Booker T. Washington of Tuskegee was most often cited as a leader of the former view, while W. E. B. Du Bois of Atlanta University was most often cited as a leader of the latter view. Washingtonians focused on the production of farmers and mechanics, while DuBoisans looked toward a classically educated "Talented Tenth" to lead the masses (Baldwin 1899; Bullock 1967; Anderson 1988; Washington 1901; Du Bois 1900, 1903; Meier 1963). In fact, the institutions – whether "agricultural-industrial" or "liberal-classical" – sprinkled their curricula with both approaches. And, regardless of the emphases, the curricula tended to follow those of most Euro-American colleges and aimed to produce citizens worthy of participation in an American Democracy, with exemplary civility and morality (Bullock 1967; Anderson 1988).

By 1933, Carter G. Woodson had emerged as a major critic of this approach to African American education. He castigated America's educational leaders for developing schooling that failed to meet the educational needs of African Americans. They sought, he said, "to transform the Negroes, not to develop them." They "followed the traditional curricula of the times which did not take the Negro into consideration except to condemn or pity them" (Woodson 1933: 17). He also aimed his fire at African American leaders who, he believed, were ashamed of their past and therefore had become co-conspirators in their educational destruction. He also offered solutions to the basic problems that he identified; many of which presaged the Black Studies Movement of the 1960s. Woodson's criticisms were echoed by another black scholar, J. Saunders Redding nine years later (Woodson 1933; Redding 1942).

By the 1930s, when Woodson wrote his treatise *The Mis-Education of the Negro*, the American educational system was already undergoing a massive overhaul. African Americans were beginning the legal assault on segregation, which would eventually bring them to the verge of equal education. The initial assault on segregated education came from men fired by their 1930s experiences who realized that separation had not produced educational equality (Woodson 1933: 9–16; Kluger 1976). Meanwhile, spurred by the Morrill Act, the southern states began to open colleges and universities for blacks, but – in congruence with thinking in the region on black education – most of these schools were of the agricultural industrial variety (Logan 1969; Du Bois 1935; Lee 1954; Woolfolk 1962; Neyland and Riley 1963; Jenkins 1964; Bullock 1967).

Eventually, more than a hundred colleges and universities became part of the Historically Black Colleges and Universities (HBCUs) network. By the 1960s, many of the state schools became a part of their respective state's university systems. All continue to play a vital role in preparing African Americans for future leadership positions. Some of them are small baccalaureate degree-granting institutions. Others are full-fledged learning institutions offering a variety of degrees with impressive buildings and facilities. By the end of the twentieth century, less than half a dozen were located outside of the South and less than a dozen offered post-baccalaureate degrees. Among the most prominent HBCUs are Howard University, Atlanta University, and Fisk University (Carpenter 1964; Anderson 1988).

Howard was founded in 1866 by ten white members of the First Congregational Society of Washington, DC, as the Howard Normal and Theological Institute for Education of Teachers and Preachers, having been named in honor of Major General Oliver Otis Howard, the commissioner of the Freedmen's Bureau, and received its university charter. The school opened with four white female students, and even though it had prominent African American leaders – such as Frederick Douglass and Booker T. Washington – on its board of trustees, in its first few years it had a predominantly white administration, and white philanthropists provided most of its funding. After the Freedmen's Bureau closed its doors in 1879, the United States Congress agreed to provide a yearly appropriation to the school. The idea was that the nation needed trained African American leaders and the government had a responsibility to ensure this (Dyson 1941; Logan 1969; McFeeley 1968).

Howard was the only African American school receiving an annual federal appropriation. However, the money proved to be both a blessing and a curse. With a stable, dependable cash flow, Howard had a financial stability that other HBCUs could only dream about and was able to develop programs and opportunities that other HBCUs could not match. It was also able to hire the best and brightest of African American intellectuals (Dyson 1941; Logan 1969). However, the money came with strings, including the surrender of academic freedom. University officials monitored faculty members who were considered radical and reported all evidence of un-American activities. The money also had a moderating influence on the student body, faculty, and administration.

When Mordecai Johnson took over in 1926 as Howard's first African American president, it had 1,700 students and a $700,000 annual budget, with eight unaccredited schools and colleges. When he retired some 34 years later, Howard had an $8 million annual budget, with ten nationally ranked accredited schools and colleges, enrolling more than 6,000 students. Howard had the finest African American law and medical schools in the country. It also had dental, pharmaceutical, and science programs that were nationally recognized. Howard's faculty represented a virtual who's who of the African American intellectual community. It was also a leader in training teachers, nurses, and political scientists. There were few other African American schools that could match the work of Howard (Dyson 1941; Logan 1969; Janken 1993).

In Georgia, Atlanta University was developing a reputation as one of the best liberal arts schools for African Americans in the Deep South. Atlanta University was opened in 1865, using abandoned railroad cars as its classrooms. By 1867, when university President Edmund Ware began challenging students to improve, the school faced severe economic difficulty. Atlanta University was modeled after Yale University. It quickly developed a reputation as a premier African American school. Some of the most notable African American leaders, including James Weldon Johnson, were trained there. Atlanta University would eventually become part of the Atlanta University Center, which included Clark, Morehouse, Spelman, and Morris Brown College as well as the Interdenominational Theological Center. The Atlanta University Center became the largest and most prestigious educational consortium for

African Americans in the world (Brawley 1917; Bacote 1969; Read 1961; Jones 1967).

The other school that gained a national reputation in the post-Emancipation period was Fisk University. It was founded in 1866 by Erastus Millo Cravath, Reverend Edward P. Smith, and John Ogden. Cravath and Smith were officers of the American Missionary Association, while Ogden was an official of the Freedmen's Bureau. The school was named after General Clinton B. Fisk, the Assistant Commissioner in charge of the Freedmen's Bureau in Tennessee. It started out as an elementary school providing the rudiments of education for local African Americans around Nashville, Tennessee. In 1867, after Tennessee began offering free public elementary education, Fisk changed its mission and began concentrating on collegiate education (Taylor 1941; Richardson 1980; Anderson 1988).

To raise money, Fisk organized a choir which, beginning in 1871, traveled throughout the country raising funds through concerts. The Fisk Jubilee Singers carried African American spirituals to the broader world and developed a reputation as one of the best college choirs in the country. They were very successful at raising money for the school, which allowed its administrators to build one of the most impressive black schools in the South. They raised more than $150,000 for the school in three years. Fisk developed a reputation as one of the best academic schools in the South. Teachers trained at Fisk University were widely sought by schools throughout the South. Fisk also boasted one of the most impressive black faculties in the country. In 1947, Charles S. Johnson became the school's first African American president. Among the alumni of Fisk are historian John Hope Franklin and writers Nikki Giovanni and Frank Yerby (Bond 1972; Richardson 1980; Anderson 1988; Gilpin 2003).

At first, partly because of the paucity of trained black educators, whites dominated the faculties and administrations of most of the black colleges and universities. Major exceptions were Booker T. Washington at Tuskegee Institute, William H. Crogman at Clark College and John Hope at Atlanta Baptist College (later Morehouse). The schools founded by black denominations, the African Methodist Episcopal (AME) and Colored Methodist Episcopal (CME), were also exceptions to the general rule. But by the 1920s, a movement for black control of black colleges had developed. Students and others even resorted to demonstrations, at places like Fisk and Howard, in their demands for black control (Brawley 1917; McPherson 1970; Wolters 1975). Despite the excellence of these schools, they could educate only a small portion of the African American community. Most blacks had little chance of attending colleges. The educational systems of the South were poorly maintained and many southerners were just not interested in ensuring that African American children received a good education, so it was almost by accident when any of them did (Lee 1954).

Several wealthy northern philanthropists donated money to found and support the early colleges and universities, including John D. Rockefeller and Andrew Carnegie. Possibly the most important development in African American education during this period was the introduction of the Julius Rosenwald Fund. By 1932 this had provided grants for the construction of 5,000 African American schools in 833 counties in 15 southern states. The Rosenwald funds played a pivotal role in expanding African American educational opportunities, accounting for 15 percent of all monies spent on African American education. Even more telling is that another 15 percent of educational spending on African Americans came directly from blacks themselves. Capital spending on African American educational facilities was just 20 percent of that for whites and African American teachers' salaries were generally about half of what their white counterparts earned (Embree and Waxman 1949; Bremmer 1960; Bullock 1967; Leavell 1970; Anderson and Moss 1999; Abels 2000). African American children were generally denied the chance of a secondary education. In 1920, 85 percent of African American students enrolled in school were enrolled in the first four grades. The nation had very few high schools open to blacks and those were generally in poor condition. Less than 20,000 African Americans attended high school in 1916 (Franklin 1999).

Despite the dismal conditions in state-supported schools for blacks at all levels, from 1899 to 1930 the federal courts consistently upheld the doctrine of "separate but equal." This gave African Americans little room to negotiate improvements in their education. Then, in 1935, a court decision gave African Americans some hope of changing the educational landscape. Donald Murray had applied to the Law School at the University of Maryland and had been denied admission simply because of his race. Murray challenged the decision in court, arguing that the out-of-state tuition scholarships offered by the state violated the "separate but equal" policy. The federal court ordered the university to admit Murray (Kluger 1976). Almost immediately, southern states recognized the handwriting on the wall and began to establish graduate programs for their African American citizens. Southerners made dramatic improvements in spending on African American education in a desperate attempt to forestall challenges to the "separate but equal" policy. However, it did not take them long to realize that their spending was too little, too late to repair the years of neglect. The inequalities between African American and white educational facilities were just too great to be made up by some quick spending (Goldman 1963; Jenkins 1964; Kluger 1976).

With the coming of the Second World War, new opportunities opened. African Americans began to wake up to their potential and demand a greater say in society. Although they had gone to Europe and Asia to fight for the rights and freedoms of others, many realized they were being excluded from the very things they had fought for. As a result, they came back from the war determined to keep fighting for their own freedom (Franklin 1999). They were aided by a change in attitude by the federal courts, which began to stand up and recognize their responsibility to demand equality for all American citizens. During the Cold War, in recognition of the fact that African Americans had made equal sacrifices under difficult circumstances, the courts became more sympathetic to African American plaintiffs (ibid; Lawson 1990).

The desire to improve opportunities for African Americans caused leaders trained in these schools to argue an ambivalent position. Even as they tried to convince Americans that lawyers, doctors, and others trained in HBCUs were just as good as people trained in traditionally white schools, they were going to court to argue that their educational experiences were far inferior and that separate could never be equal. They believed that the only way to destroy the assumption by whites that blacks were inferior was by competing with them educationally (Jaffe 1966; Franklin 1999).

The other obstacle HBCUs have faced since legal segregation ended has been maintaining a stable financial base. As some of the better African American students have found places at traditionally white colleges, the Talented Tenth have lost their interest in ensuring that HBCUs survive. African American schools have had a difficult time building their endowments and maintaining enrollment. Financial constraints have made it harder for HBCUs to hold onto their better faculty and to compete when recruiting students, compared to schools with a healthier financial status (Jaffe 1966).

Although state-supported schools were able to hold their own, the smaller private colleges were battered by declining resources. There were calls for consolidation in places like Atlanta, where several black colleges existed side by side. Although the United Negro College Fund has done a wonderful job raising money for scholarships and improved facilities for the HBCUs, the challenge they face is building a national endowment to stabilize the finances of these schools. Also, HBCUs must expand their base and attract some white students to supplement the small proportion of African Americans enrolling for college (McGrath 1965; Jaffe 1966; Jones 1967; Hornsby 2003).

The last hurdle HBCUs faced was the opportunity to compete with whites for economic and educational opportunities. A major step in destroying the Jim Crow system came when Calvert Ambrose of the US Office of Education instituted a program to wipe out illiteracy among African Americans. However, it was a series of court cases that eventually spelled doom for the segregationist educational system in America. In 1938 Lloyd Gaines was admitted into the University of Missouri Law School – the South too was going to have to change. By the end of the Second World War, African Americans could see the changing trends in world relations. Oppressed peoples all around the world began to stand up and fight for their rights (Kluger 1976). In the United States, African Americans, many of whom had traveled thousands of miles away from their homes to fight for the four freedoms for other people, demanded it for themselves. More and more people began to challenge the charade of separate but equal educational systems (Lawson 1990).

Since the 1896 landmark decision in *Plessy v. Ferguson*, America had operated a dual educational system. African Americans were finally challenging that system. In 1946 Ada Sipuel requested admission into the University of Oklahoma Law School. After three years of legal wrangling, she was admitted in 1949 (Goldman 1963; Kluger 1976). At the same time George W. McLaurin, an African American at the University of Oklahoma's graduate school, challenged the segregation enforced on him in the cafeteria, library, and classroom. On the same day that the High Court forced the university officials to end the restrictions on McLaurin, the court forced the University of Texas to admit Heman Sweatt, an African American, to their Law School. This proved to be a very important case. It convinced most southern states that the Supreme Court would eventually open all their graduate programs to African Americans. Arkansas voluntarily did just that, to forestall a costly lawsuit. Those who supported and those who opposed integration realized that the next step would be a challenge to segregation on the elementary and secondary levels. Yet both sides knew that this would be a much more difficult process. Southern leaders, however, saw the evolving pattern and began to make plans to avert this process. They pledged themselves to spend money repairing the damage of the past (Kluger 1976).

Also, by the early 1950s the NAACP had changed strategies and began openly to challenge the inequalities in education on the elementary and secondary level. The South could not stop the coming challenge (Goldman 1963; Kluger 1976; Patterson 2000). The next important phase in the transformation of African American higher education was the long hard struggle to integrate. The African American community were not unanimous in their support of integration. There were several factors to consider as they debated their support for the effort. African American professors were concerned about their jobs. African American students were concerned about losing their cultural heritage in integrated schools. Parents wondered if their sons and daughters would be well served by white professors, who often had precon-ceived ideas about African American intellectual potential (Goldman 1963; Jaffe 1966; Kluger 1976; Patterson 2000).

Many in the South were also determined not to give an inch on the issue of segregation. Southern leaders marshaled all of their resources in a no-holds-barred struggle to hold onto the Jim Crow system. In 1956, 101 prominent southern legislatures signed what became known as the Southern Manifesto, which dedicated them to using all legal measures to block integration. There was a rebirth of several racist organizations such as the Ku Klux Klan, the newly formed National Association for the Advancement of White People (NAAWP) and the White Citizens Council (Goldman 1963; Kluger 1976; Patterson 2000).

Integration created problems for African Americans at both HBCUs and tradi-tionally all-white schools. HBCUs faced the possibility of a loss of students. The years of assaults on the reputation of HBCUs had created the perception that they were not academically equal to white schools. The novelty of having access to opportun-ities traditionally denied to African Americans was very appealing to aspiring young blacks. At the same time, the federal government began to offer incentives to white schools to increase enrollment of African American students (McGrath 1965; Goldman 1963; Jaffe 1966). HBCUs also were at a disadvantage in offering the courses of study available at white schools. African American students had new opportunities to study subjects that had traditionally been the exclusive domain of whites. By using financial incentives, white schools were able to attract some of the best black minds to study in their institutions. The facilities and scholarship opportunities were also generally much better at white schools (McGrath 1965; Jaffe 1966).

The other problem HBCUs faced was a brain drain, the loss of some of their best faculty. White schools once again had an incentive to hire the best black faculty away from the HBCUs, offering them better pay and a more flexible schedule. With the introduction of affirmative action (which soon became a racially and politically divisive concept), white schools aggressively recruited African American faculty, staff, and administrators. The more minority students the White schools recruited, the more minority administrators and faculty they needed (McGrath 1965; Jaffe 1966; Bond 1972).

Soon the African Americans admitted to the white colleges began to protest against the denigration of their past. This developed into a movement to create a culturally relevant curriculum for black students, from which evolved Black Studies, African American Studies and Pan-African Studies. What all of these programs had in common was the introduction of African Americans as developers and thinkers (agents), who had an important story that needed to be told. African American

Studies gave black students an authentic voice not only to assimilate within, but to challenge the American System (Exum 1985; Aldridge and Young 2002).

The increased demand for African American faculty was fueled by Black Studies as a legitimate field of study. African American students who had been seared in the caldron of the Civil Rights Movement demanded courses that met their need to be included in the cultural development of the West and the rest of the world. Black faculty were hired to teach courses in these areas. As Black Studies grew, a competition developed for the best scholars in these fields. Many white schools, although earlier somewhat skeptical about the academic validity of the field, began to compete to offer the best Black Studies programs. Once this process was institutionalized, Black Think Tanks emerged at places like Harvard University, and prominent black faculty like Henry "Skip" Gates and Cornel West became "public intellectuals" (Exum 1985; Clark and Plotkin 1964). But Black Studies programs proved both a blessing and a curse for African American faculty and administrators. One of the major problems they created was that African Americans were generally pigeonholed in these programs. Many of the best African American intellectuals found their opportunities were limited to minority issues only (Aldridge and Young 2002). Colleges and universities that were historically black adjusted to survive the mass exodus of students to white schools. There was an initial loss of enrollment, but some African American students preferred the historically black colleges and universities. However, they soon came to demand that their institutions become truly "black colleges." They demanded, often through public protest, that the curricula, faculty, and trustees be all or predominantly "black" (Foster 1973; Aldridge and Young 2002).

African American students who had been energized by the 1960s Civil Rights Movement also joined white students in protesting against the Vietnam War. African American college campuses often looked like white college campuses, as black students became part of growing national protest movements. The results were similar to those faced by white students at such places as Kent State University. In April 1973, white Mississippi State patrolmen fired 300 shots into a dormitory room at Jackson State University, killing two African American female students and injuring twelve others; the patrolmen said someone in the room had thrown bottles at them. In another sign of increasing political self-confidence, black students also demanded that their schools divest their endowments of investments in companies that did business with governments that oppressed their people, such as the apartheid government of South Africa (Bass and Nelson 1970; Carson 1981; Sellers and Terrell [1973] 1990: 103–4).

The philosophical and theoretical basis of the black demand for educational, social, and political reform, Afrocentricity, tended to divide Americans along racial and generational lines. Even though it had been part of Black Studies programs since the 1970s, Afrocentricity came into the national discussion only in the 1980s and 1990s. Temple University Professor Molefi Asante wrote *Afrocentricity* in 1980 and the *Afrocentric Idea* in 1987, arguing that only by using an African-centered perspective can African Americans ever hope to challenge the dominance of Eurocentric values in education. Other leading scholars, such as John Henrik Clarke, produced studies on Africa to make similar arguments. Martin Bernal even posited a black cultural presence in Ancient Greece (Clarke 1991; Bernal 1987).

As the Afrocentric movement began to spread, many African American scholars jumped on board, making it the major educational movement in black America. Many scholars viewed Afrocentricism as the best way to link the African American struggle to an international African diasporic movement that could unify African Americans with other Africans. Afrocentrists dismissed the notion of America being a melting pot and instead highlighted differences, while denouncing American institutions, arguing that America has been a co-conspirator in the dehumanization of Africans (Asante 1987; Anderson 1990; Keto 1995). Afrocentrists took an aggressive posture as they proselytyzed for converts to their field. They denounced African American scholars, like the historian John Hope Franklin, whom they perceived as refusing to place African at the center of their intellectual discourse. They argued that African American scholars had a responsibility to confront the Eurocentric paradigm so prevalent in American educational settings. Black scholars, they contended, had to push a more favorable picture on Africa, to foster a greater appreciation amongst young people of Africa and her contributions to the world. Afrocentrists tended to vigorously defend their positions, sometimes rejecting all opponents as "sellouts" or intellectually naïve (Anderson 1990; Keto 1995; Aldridge and Young 2002).

African American opponents of the Afrocentric perspective vehemently rejected their notions, often also using vitriolic language to denounce it as anti-progressive and intellectually suspect. They argued that Afrocentrism would lead to greater separatism in the academic community and in the nation. They questioned the attack on Eurocentric scholarship as well as the legitimacy of some of the claims made by Afrocentrists. They accused the Afrocentrists of being overzealous in their analysis and attempting to replace Eurocentric notions with "feel good" interpretations of culture and history. They suggested that Africa's past had to be subjected to the same scholarly scrutiny as other places. Not everything in Africa, they countered, was worthy of reproducing in contemporary society. Furthermore, the African past had to be examined for aspects of racism, sexism, and homophobia (West 1993). White scholars also attacked the movement. Historian Arthur Schlesinger, for example, launched an attack on the idea in *The Disuniting of America*. He accused the Afrocentrists of attempting to manufacture a glorious past for Africans, which did not fit the written record (Bernal 1987; Schlesinger 1992).

The result of these attacks was that the Black Studies Movement splintered into various paths with different goals. On one side were the Afrocentric scholars who attempted to recreate positive aspects of the African past, making them fit into a contemporary setting. On the other side were African American intellectuals who attempted to reintroduce African Americans into the academic discourse of traditional scholarly disciplines and white scholars who debunked the movement as a major threat to national unity and academic integrity (Schlesinger 1992; Aldridge and Young 2002).

The Afrocentricity debate, however, did not diminish the growing transformation of black higher education from HBCUs to white institutions. And as more and more American colleges and universities coped to meet the demands for increased diversity in their student bodies, faculty, and curricula, the number of African American institutions and the students in them steadily decreased. By the 1970s, the majority of African Americans attending college were in non-black institutions. Increasingly, individuals and groups began for various reasons to question the continued existence of these institutions. Some argued that, in view of desegregation decisions, it was illegal for majority-black state schools to continue. Others argued it was too costly to continue to maintain dual systems of higher education. The black institutions should be merged with existing, better financed, better equipped white schools. Many blacks, on the other hand, feared the loss of their cultural heritage in the abolition of their institutions.

Other scholars entered this debate, arguing that the black institutions were anachronistic and inferior, and thus should be phased out. This indictment, most prominently associated with Harvard scholars Christopher Jencks and David Reisman, included the black private colleges as well as the public ones. Black scholars and administrators responded angrily and forcefully, attempting to justify the continuation of their institutions. Critical to the debate was the assumption among some that the black schools were unitary in their purposes, goals, effectiveness, and efficiency. But other scholars, including Addie Butler and Stephen Wright, argued for distinctiveness among the black schools while admitting that, like white institutions, some were weaker than others. Many – including Howard, Fisk, Tuskegee, Talladega, Spelman, and Morehouse – were clearly, particularly in terms of quality, in the upper tiers of American higher education (Clark 1958; Brown 1958; McGrath 1965; Bryant 1982; Jencks and Reisman 1967, 1968; Wright et al. 1967; Sebora 1968; Butler 1977).

The better black colleges survived the controversy. However, the weaker ones, faced with declining enrollments and declining revenues, either reduced services or closed, sometimes after having lost their accreditation. Meanwhile, a new cultural movement among African Americans – Hip-Hop – tended to suggest even more transformations in Black Education, from kindergarten to college. The Hip-Hop Movement, although often anti-intellectual in tone, swept through the ranks of recent generations of black college students. In suggesting that Hip-Hop – with its often vulgar, ungrammatical language, and dress, among other things – represented core Black Culture, the Hip-Hop generation portended the most radical transformation in black education since Reconstruction (Brown 1958; Selden 1960; Bryant 1982; hooks 1994; Kelley 1994; Rose 1994; see also Chapter 30).

BIBLIOGRAPHY

Works Cited

Abels, Jules ([1967] 2000) *The Rockefeller Millions.* New York: Macmillan.
Aldridge, Delores and Young, Carlene (eds.) (2002) *Out of the Revolution: The Development of Africana Studies.* Lanham, MD: Rowman & Littlefield.
Ambrose, Caliver (1970) *A Personnel Study of Negro College Students: A Study of the Relations between Certain Background Factors of Negro College Students and Their Subsequent Careers in College.* Westpoint, CT: Negro Universities Press.
Anderson, Eric and Moss, Alfred A., Jr (1999) *Dangerous Donations: Northern Philanthropy and Southern Black Education, 1902–1930.* Columbia: University of Missouri Press.
Anderson, James D. (1988) *The Education of Blacks in the South, 1860–1935.* Chapel Hill: University of North Carolina Press.
Anderson, Talmadge (ed.) (1990) *Black Studies: Theory, Method, and Cultural Perspectives.* Pullman: Washington State University Press.

Asante, Molefi (1987) *The Afrocentric Idea*. Philadelphia: Temple University Press.

Bacote, Clarence A. (1969) *The Story of Atlanta University: A Century of Service, 1865–1965*. Atlanta, GA: Atlanta University.

Baldwin, William (1899) "The present problem of Negro education," *Journal of Social Sciences* 37.

Bass, Jack and Nelson, Jack (1970) *The Orangeburg Massacre*. Cleveland, OH: World Publishing.

Bernal, Martin (1987) *Black Athena: The Afroasiatic Roots of Classical Civilization: The Fabrication of Ancient Greece, 1785–1985*. New Brunswick, NJ: Rutgers University Press.

Bond, Horace Mann (1934) *The Education of the Negro in the American Social Order*. New York: Prentice-Hall.

—— (1939) *Negro Education in Alabama: A Study in Cotton and Steel*. New York: Associated Publishers.

—— (1972) *Black American Scholars: A Study of Their Beginnings*. Detroit: Balamp.

Brawley, Benjamin (1917) *History of Morehouse College*. Atlanta, GA: Morehouse College.

Bremmer, Robert H. (1960) *American Philanthropy*. Chicago: University of Chicago Press.

Brown, Aaron (1958) "Graduate and professional education in Negro institutions," *Journal of Negro Education* 27 (Summer).

Bryant, Mynora Joyce (1982) "An historical study of factors that have contributed to and/or influenced the mortality of Negro colleges and universities, 1860–1980," DEd dissertation, George Washington University.

Bullock, Henry Allen (1967) *A History of Negro Education in the South from 1619 to the Present*. Cambridge, MA: Harvard University Press.

Butler, Addie Louise Joyner (1977) *The Distinctive Black College: Talladega, Tuskegee and Morehouse*. Metuchen, NJ: Scarecrow Press.

Carpenter, John (1964) *Sword and Olive Branch: Oliver Otis Howard*. Pittsburgh: University of Pittsburgh Press.

Carson, Clayborne (1981) *In Struggle: SNCC and the Black Awakening of the 1960s*. Cambridge, MA: Harvard University Press.

Chambers, Frederick (1972) "Histories of black colleges and universities," *Journal of Negro History* 557 (July).

Clark, Felton G. (1958) "The development and present status of publicly supported higher education for Negroes," *Journal of Negro Education* 27 (Summer).

Clark, Kenneth and Plotkin, Lawrence (1964) *The Negro Student at Integrated Colleges*. New York: National Scholarship Service and Fund for Negro Students.

Clarke, John Henrik (ed.) (1991) *New Dimensions in African History: From the Nile Valley to the New World*. New York: Africa World Press.

Curti, Merle (1935) *The Social Ideas of American Educators*. New York: Charles Scribner's Sons.

Dabney, Charles William (1936) *Universal Education in the South*. New York: Arno Press.

Du Bois, W. E. B. (1900) *The College Bred Negro*. Atlanta: Atlanta University Press.

—— ([1903] 1968) *The Souls of Black Folk: Essay and Sketches*. Greenwich, CT: Fawcett.

—— ([1935] 1976) *Black Reconstruction*. Millwood, NY: Kraus-Thomson.

Dyson, Walter (1941) *Howard University: The Capstone of Negro Education, A History: 1867–1940*. Washington, DC: Howard University.

Edwards, Harry (1970) *Black Students*. New York: Free Press.

Embree, Edwin R. and Waxman, Julia (1949) *Investment in People: The Story of the Julius Rosenwald Fund*. New York: Harper & Brothers.

Exum, William H. (1985) *Paradoxes of Protest: Black Student Activism in a White University*. Philadelphia: Temple University Press.

Foster, E. C. (1973) "Carter G. Woodson's 'The mis-education of the Negro' revisited: Black colleges, Black studies," *Freedomways*, I.

Franklin, John H. (1999) *From Slavery to Freedom*, 8th edn. New York: McGraw-Hill.

Gallager, Buell (1966) *American Caste and the Negro College*. New York: Gordian Press.

Gilpin, Patrick (2003) *Charles S. Johnson: Leadership beyond the Veil in the Age of Jim Crow*. Albany: State University of New York Press.

Goldman, Freda H. (1963) "Integration and the Negro college" in *Educational Imperative: The Negro in the Changing South*. Chicago: Center of Liberal Education for Adults.

Holloway, Lynette (2002) "The angry appeal of Eminem is cutting across racial lines," *New York Times* (October 28).

Holmes, Dwight (1934) *The Evolution of the Negro College*. College Park, MD: McGrath.

hooks, bell (1994) *Outlaw Culture: Resisting Representations*. New York: Routledge.

Hornsby, Alton, Jr (1971) *In the Cage: Eyewitness Accounts of the Freed Negro in Southern Society, 1877–1929*. Chicago: Quadrangle.

—— (2003) *A Short History of Black Atlanta*. Atlanta, GA: Apex Museum.

Jaffe, Walter Adams and Meyers, Sandra G. (1966) *Ethnic Higher Education – Negro Colleges in the 1960s*. New York: Columbia University.

Janken, Kenneth Robert (1993) *Rayford W. Logan and the Dilemma of the African American Intellectual*. Amherst: University of Massachusetts Press.

Jencks, Christopher and Reisman, David (1967) "The American Negro college," *Harvard Educational Review* 37 (Winter).

—— (1968) *The Academic Revolution*. Garden City, NY: Doubleday.

Jenkins, Martin D. (1964) *The Morgan State College Program – An Adventure in Higher Education*. Baltimore: Morgan State College Press.

Jones, Edward A. (1967) *A Candle in the Dark: A History of Morehouse College*. Valley Forge, PA: Judson Press.

Kelley, Robin D. G. (1994) *Race Rebels: Culture, Politics, and the Black Working Class*. New York: Free Press.

Keto, Tsehloane (1995) *Vision, Identity and Time: The Afrocentric Paradigm and the Study of the Past*. Dubuque, IA: Kendall-Hunt.

King, Kenneth James (1971) *Pan Africanism and Education: A Story of Race, Philanthropy and Education in the Southern States of America and East Africa*. London: Oxford University Press.

Kluger, Richard (1976) *Simple Justice: The History of Brown v. Board of Education and Black America's Struggle for Equality*. New York: Alfred A. Knopf.

Kolchin, Peter (1972) *First Freedom: The Response of Alabama's Blacks to Emancipation and Reconstruction*. Westport, CT: Greenwood Press.

Lawson, Steven (1990) *Running for Freedom: Civil Rights and Black Politics in America, 1941–1988*. Philadelphia: Temple University Press.

Leavell, Ullin W. (1970) *Philanthropy in Negro Education*. New York: Negro Universities Press.

Lee, Lurlene Mehan (1954) "The origin, development, and present status of Arkansas' program of higher education for Negroes," PhD dissertation, Michigan State University.

LeMelle, Tilden J. and Lemelle, Wilbert J. (1969) *The Black College: A Strategy for Relevance*. New York: Frederick A. Praeger.

Logan, Frenise A. (1958) "The movement in North Carolina to establish a state supported college for Negroes," *North Carolina History Review* 35 (April).

Logan, Rayford W. (1969) *Howard University, 1867–1967*. New York: New York University Press.

McDaniel, Dennis (1997) *John Ogden, Abolitionist and Leader in Southern Education*. Philadelphia: American Philosophical Society.

McFeely, William S. (1968) *Yankee Stepfather: General O. O. Howard and the Freedmen:* New Haven, CT: Yale University Press.

McGrath, Earl (1965) *The Predominantly Negro Colleges and Universities in Transition*. New York: Teachers College, Columbia University.

McPherson, James M. (1970) "White liberals and black power in Negro education," *American Historical Review* 125 (June).

Mayo, Amory Dwight (1888) *Industrial Education in the South*. Washington, DC: Government Printing Office.

Meier, August (1963) *Negro Thought in America, 1880–1915. Racial Ideologies in the Age of Booker T. Washington*. Ann Arbor: University of Michigan Press.

Miller, Kelly (1926) "The higher education of the Negro is at the crossroads," *Educational Review* 122 (December).

Neyland, Leedell W. and Riley, John W. (1963) *The History of Florida Agricultural and Mechanical College*. Gainesville: University of Florida Press.

Noble, Jeanne L. (1956) *The Negro Woman's College Education*. New York: Teachers College.

Patterson, James T. (2000) *Brown v. Board of Education: A Civil Rights Milestone and Its Troubled Legacy*. New York: Oxford University Press.

Read, Florence Matilda (1961) *The Story of Spelman College*. Princeton, NJ: Princeton University Press.

Redding, J. Saunders (1942) *No Day of Triumph*. New York: Harper & Row.

Richardson, Joe M. (1980) *A History of Fisk University, 1865–1946*. Tuscaloosa: University of Alabama Press.

—— (1986) *Christian Reconstruction: The American Missionary Association and Southern Blacks, 1861–1890*. Athens: University of Georgia Press.

Rose, Tricia (1994) *Black Noise: Rap Music and Black Culture in Contemporary America*. Hanover, NH: Wesleyan University Press.

Schlesinger, Arthur M. (1992) *The Disuniting of America*. New York: W. W. Norton.

Sebora, John (1968) "Our Negro colleges: a reply to Jencks and Reisman," *Antioch Review* 28 (Spring).

Selden, William K. (1960) *Accreditation: A Struggle over Standards in Higher Education*. New York: Harper & Brothers.

Sellers, Cleveland and Terrell, Robert ([1973] 1990) *The River of No Return: The Autobiography of a Black Militant and the Life and Death of SNCC*. [New York: William Morrow] Jackson: University Press of Mississippi.

Spivey, Donald (1978) *Schooling for the New Slavery: Black Industrial Education, 1868–1915*. Westport, CT: Greenwood Press.

Taylor, Alrutheus Ambush (1941) *The Negro in Tennessee, 1865–1880*. Washington, DC: Associated Publishers.

Thompson, Daniel C. (1973) *Private Black Colleges at the Crossroads*. Westport, CT: Greenwood Press.

Washington, Booker T. (1901) *Up from Slavery*. New York: Doubleday.

West, Cornel (1993) *Race Matters*. Boston: Beacon Press.

Wolters, Raymond (1975) *The New Negro on Campus: Black College Rebellions of the 1920s*. Princeton, NJ: Princeton University Press.

Woodson, Carter G. (1933) *The Mis-education of the Negro*. Washington, DC: Associated Publishers.

Woolfolk, George R. (1962) *Prairie View: A Study of Public Conscience, 1878–1946*. New York: Pageant Press.

Wright, Stephen (1973) *The Traditionally Black College, 1966–1972*. Washington, DC: Educational Resources Information Center.

Wright, Stephen J. (1949) "The development of the Hampton–Tuskegee pattern of higher education," *Phylon* 10 (Fall).

Wright, Stephen J., et al. (1967) "'The American Negro college': four responses and a reply," *Harvard Educational Review* 37 (Summer–Fall).

CHAPTER TWENTY-EIGHT

Identity, Protest, and Outreach in the Arts

JULIUS E. THOMPSON

The Early Twentieth Century, 1900–19

The early decades of the twentieth century witnessed a significant growth in the development of African American literary activities, in the form of increased artistic production of novels, plays, poetry, and short stories, in addition to scholarly efforts in the humanities and social sciences. Scholars such as McHenry also note the important role of black literary societies in promoting black citizenship rights, and encouraging skills development and education among black citizens (McHenry 2002: 19). These positive developments, including the growth of the black press during this era, must be viewed against the harsh realities of the Age of Segregation and its proscriptions on the economic, social, and political life of black Americans. During these years, white southern terror resulted in the deaths of hundreds of American citizens, mostly blacks, in the Deep South and the border states of that region (see Tolnay and Beck, *A Festival of Violence*, 1995: 30, 37). Thus, as African Americans fought to advance their contributions to literature, music, the fine arts and scholarly endeavors, they had to wage a constant struggle to protect the black community from violence, discrimination, economic oppression, and psychological warfare. In reality, black literary activities, although complex in nature, were also created to offer a group protest against the inhuman conditions facing African Americans.

There were 21 significant voices among black men and women thinkers, writers, scholars, and leaders of this period. The 11 African American men who dominated the literary period were: W. E. B. Du Bois (1868–1963), Paul Laurence Dunbar (1872–1906), James Weldon Johnson (1871–1938), Charles W. Chestnut (1858–1932), Robert S. Abbott (1870–1940), Carter G. Woodson (1875–1950), Marcus Garvey (1887–1940), William Stanley Braithwaite (1878–1962), Benjamin Griffith Brawley (1882–1939), Booker T. Washington (1856–1915), and Kelly Miller (1863–1939). On the other side of this group stood 10 African American women: Ida B. Wells-Barnett (1862–1931), Mary Church Terrell (1863–1954), Mary McLeod Bethune (1875–1955), Bessie Smith (1894–1937), Georgia Douglass Johnson (1886–1966), Frances Ellen Watkins Harper (1825–1911), Alice Ruth Moore Dunbar-Nelson (1875–1935), Angelina Weld Grimke (1880–1958), Anne Spencer

(1882–1975), and Henrietta Cordelia Ray (1849–1916). Collectively, these men and women represented the giants among black intellectuals of the first two decades of the twentieth century. They were the leading "race men and women of their era," who viewed their personal struggles for success and the building of their careers as part of an ongoing challenge to encourage and strengthen the black community, and to promote the economic, political, and social development of the African American people.

They worked to achieve these goals through education, teaching, writing, publishing, and building black organizations. The key leaders in the organization of protest in this era were W. E. B. Du Bois, Ida Wells-Barnett, James W. Johnson, Marcus Garvey, and (secretly) Booker T. Washington. Du Bois' first efforts bore fruit with the Niagara Movement (1905), a black group attacking white discrimination against black rights in the United States (Frazier 2001: 192). This was followed in 1909–10 by the creation of the National Association for the Advancement of Colored People (NAACP), with support from Du Bois, Wells-Barnett, and J. Johnson Garvey, of course, is given credit for creating the largest black-base movement organization in American history, the Universal Negro Improvement Association, formed in the USA in 1916 (Lewis 1988: 59). Washington was the single most important black leader of this period and, though he stressed in public a position of accommodation to white interests, he also privately sought to reduce the violence and racism suffered by blacks in America (Harlan 1972: 297–8).

Black writers are the most prominent element on this list. In fact, every individual noted above used the written word in some way to advance their leadership position, express their viewpoints to the world, and advance human knowledge and understanding. Among the poets of this group are Dunbar, the leading black male poet of the period, James Weldon Johnson, Georgia Douglass Johnson, Harper, Dunbar-Nelson, Grimke, Spencer, and Ray. Their work expressed the determination of the African American community to achieve personal and group freedom, and the need to give something of beauty to the world, from an African American perspective.

Chestnut was a major novelist of the era; and three important critics are Braithwaite, Brawley, and Miller. Robert S. Abbott was the most important black journalist of his day, and edited the *Chicago Defender* between 1905 and 1940 (Wolseley 1971: 36–8). Bessie Smith was the leading black woman blues singer and composer of her era. Wells-Barnett, Terrell, and Bethune were key players in the black women's club movement of the period, and collectively they did much to advance the causes of black women in America (Hine and Thompson 1998: 94–200, 250–1).

Ten major issues and themes dominated the literary considerations of African Americans during the years 1900–19. Black intellectuals faced and sought answers to all ten:

1   Should blacks support industrial or liberal education for the masses of black Americans?
2   Did black literary activities represent a first commitment to a race consciousness (or black focus) or were they an attempt to seek American integration for black literature?
3   How important was the African past to black Americans?

4   Should black leaders support the migration of blacks from rural to urban areas
    in the South and North?
5   How could black Americans overcome the Color Line in America?
6   When and how could blacks help to end the violence of lynching in America?
7   Should blacks leave the United States *en masse* and return to Africa, or move
    elsewhere in the world?
8   What roles were blacks to play in the First World War?
9   Should black writers use "black" English or traditional "white" English in their
    writing? and
10 What was the greatest problem facing black women in America: racism, sexism,
    or classicism?

Historians have focused on the major issue of black leadership in America during
the period 1900–19. David Levering Lewis, in *W. E. B. Du Bois: Biography of a
Race, 1868–1919* (1993), offers a comprehensive view of the leading black scholar
produced in America. Unlike Booker T. Washington, W. E. B. Du Bois strongly
supported liberal education for the black community, *versus* Washington's emphasis
on industrial education. Like Lewis, V. P. Franklin's *Black Self-Determination: A
Cultural History of the Faith of the Fathers* (1984) also notes the central importance
of leadership in Black History, and in particular the key role of Du Bois. R. Douglas
Hurt's edited collection, *African American Life in the Rural South, 1900–1950*
(2003), places the above issues in the context of the lives of the masses of blacks,
most of whom still lived in the South in 1900–19. A clear pattern of black protest
emerges: "Migrate from the South, if at all possible," became a constant cry of black
people. If this was not possible, then migrate to southern cities, but escape the very
worst of life on the plantations and southern farms.

Finally, the voices of black women historians, such as Melba Joyce Boyd, author of
Discarded Legacy: Politics and Poetics in the Life of Frances E. W. Harper, 1825–1911
(1994), noted the challenges facing black women writers and leaders. No case is
more complex than Harper's. Like many of her contemporaries, she had fought to
bring an end to American slavery, while seeking to advance the cause of black women
in American society. She did this as an abolitionist, lecturer, educator, and writer,
using all of her skills and talents to overcome the problems of her lifetime. Paula
Giddings, in *When and Where I Enter: The Impact of Black Women on Race and Sex
in America* (1984), places Ida B. Wells-Barnett in the midst of the struggles of her
age, with a focus on lynching and issues involving women. Both these studies highlight
the central roles of black women in the early history of the twentieth century.

These issues remained at the forefront of black intellectual concerns for decades.
Each question posed a major challenge to the black community, and there were no
easy solutions to such complex problems. Many black thinkers took the long view,
and worked to achieve gradual change in a very racist society. They focused on
promoting liberal education and the religious traditions of black Americans, developing black organizations (such as the NAACP, the National Urban League, and
the Universal Negro Improvement Association), strengthening the black family,
promoting racial consciousness – especially through black culture, and the study of
history in America and Africa by way of Carter G. Woodson's Association for the
Study of Negro Life and History, formed in 1915 – and encouraging black music
(gospel, blues and jazz, which would help to lift the black community), as well as

writing poetry, novels, plays, and short stories that sought to reflect the complex rural experiences of most blacks, but also the change to urban life and industry that more and more African Americans were making.

The Harlem Renaissance, 1920–1935

A second major black literary period, generally referred to as the Harlem Renaissance era, extended from 1920 to 1935. This cultural movement holds a special place in the history of African Americans. Also called the Black Renaissance, the period witnessed a tremendous outpouring of literary, historical, and artistic productions by black people in the United States; with Harlem, New York, serving as the major vantage point of the movement (Valade, *The Essential Black Literature Guide* 1996: 165–7).

The Black Renaissance occurred during a critical period of modern black American history. Politically, socially, and economically, an Age of Segregation still gripped black life in America, especially in the South. With the increased demand for labor during the First World War and on into the 1920s, many blacks sought to escape the harshest consequences of American racism. Hundreds of thousands left the South, and took their talents and skills with them to the North. When combined with the native northern black populations, the black population in the United States was transformed from a largely rural people to one concentrated in cities. One scholar estimates that "at the end of the 1920s there were 164,566 black people living in Harlem, making it the most densely populated black area in the world" (Marks, *Farewell, We're Good and Gone: The Great Black Migration* 1989: 121).

Black writers, artists, intellectuals, and leaders were especially attracted to New York City, because of its major importance in the economic, cultural, and political life of the nation. New York was the largest city in America, the center of banking and commercial activities, the press, foundations, book publishing, and other cultural institutions; hence its role in bringing together a large range of black talent.

The list of outstanding black figures who contributed to the Black Renaissance – and made New York their home at some stage of their career – reads like a who's who among African Americans of the twentieth century. In addition to those mentioned already – James Johnson, Marcus Garvey, W. E. B. Du Bois, Alice Dunbar-Nelson, Angelina Grimke, Georgia Johnson, and Anne Spencer – other prominent names included Jean Toomer (1894–1967), Jessie Fauset (1882–1961), Walter White (1893–1955), Countee Cullen (1903–1946), Langston Hughes (1902–1967), Eric Walrond (1898–1966), Rudolph Fisher (1897–1934), Nella Larsen (1891–1964), Claude McKay (1890–1948), Wallace Thurman (1902–1934), Arna Bontemps (1902–1973), Zora N. Hurston (1891–1960), May Miller (1899–1995), Alain Locke (1885–1954), Charles W. Chestnutt (1858–1932), Katherine Dunham (1910–), and Ira De A. Reid (1901–1968). Yet, it must be understood that the Black Renaissance also took place in many other cities, such as Chicago, Washington, DC, and Atlanta.

Although the Harlem Renaissance had perhaps its greatest impact in the area of literary production – poetry, stories, plays, and novels – the movement also encouraged expansion of black jazz, gospel, and blues; other fine arts, such as painting, sculpture, and theatre; education; and the study of Africa and blacks outside of the mother continent, especially black history, life, and culture in the United States.

Certainly the impact of the movement was impressive. Scholar Nathan Irvin Huggins notes that the Harlem Renaissance: "left its mark as a symbol and a point of reference for everyone to recall . . . the very name continued to connote a special spirit, new vitality, black urbanity, and black militancy. Through the activities, the writings, the promotion of Negroes in the 1920s, Harlem had become a racial focal point for knowledgeable black men [and women] the world over" (Huggins 1971: 303).

Black poets were central figures in the Harlem Renaissance. Two of the best known black male poets were Countee Cullen and Langston Hughes. Their works were respected for exploring the complexities of the black experience and for writing on universal themes, such as beauty, the search for truth and freedom, and human understanding (Emanuel and Gross 1968: 173; Wagner 1973: 283–347; Rampersad 1986: 50–1). During the highlight years of the Harlem Renaissance, Cullen was famous for such poems as "Heritage," "Shroud of Color," "Yet Do I Marvel," and "Incident." His poem "For A Poet" reflects the richness of his lyric style and mood:

> I have wrapped my dreams in a silken cloth,
> And laid them away in a box of gold;
> Where long will cling the lips of the moth,
> I have wrapped my dreams in a silken cloth;
> I hide no hate, I am not even wroth
> Who found earth's breath so keen and cold;
> I have wrapped my dreams in a silken cloth,
> And laid them away in a box of gold. (Early 1991: 109)

Like Cullen, Langston Hughes was a giant among the figures of the Harlem Renaissance. Examples of his best work from the period include: "The Weary Blues," "Dream Variation," "The South," and "Mother To Son." An early poem of Hughes' which reflected the new mood of the Black Renaissance was "The Negro Speaks of Rivers" (1921):

> I've known rivers;
> I've known rivers ancient as the world and older than the
>   flow of human blood in human veins.
>
> My soul has grown deep like the rivers.
>
> I bathed in the Euphrates when dawns were young.
> I built my hut near the Congo and it lulled me to sleep.
>
> I looked upon the Nile and raised the pyramids above it.
> I heard the singing of the Mississippi when Abe Lincoln
>   went down to New Orleans, and I've seen its muddy
>   bosom turn all golden in the sunset.
>
> I've known rivers:
> Ancient, dusky rivers.
>
> My soul has grown deep like the rivers. (Hughes [1926] 1954: 36)

Three black women novelists were exceptional figures during this era. They were Nella Larsen, author of *Quicksand* (1928) and *Passing* (1929); Jessie Fauset, who wrote *The Chinaberry Tree* (1931); and Zora Neale Hurston, famous for her novels *Jonah's Gourd Vine* (1934) and *Their Eyes Were Watching God* (1937). Such writers were cultural workers in the promotion, growth, and development of the culture, creativity, and spirituality of blacks in America and around the world (Whitlow, *Black American Literature* 1984: 92–6, 104; Hine, King, and Reed, *We specialize in the wholly impossible*, 1995: 509).

During the Harlem Renaissance, black intellectuals were faced with ten major issues and themes. They were:

1   Should black artists continue to seek "respectability" from Americans, or stress their own experiences, growing out of the black experience, and try to first reach a black audience in the struggle for black literary achievement?
2   How should black intellectuals express black pride, racial consciousness, and uplift in their artistic works?
3   What kinds of protest should be employed in black literary production?
4   Should black writers support the continued movement of blacks in the Great Migration?
5   What special role should black Americans play in anti-colonial struggles, especially in Africa?
6   Was there a place for disillusion, militancy, and anger in black arts?
7   How were black women's voices to be heard in the movement?
8   Should black writers focus on racial themes and avoid overt political statements in their artistic creations?
9   How would blacks deal with the new issue of the diversity of the black population in urban centers – local blacks, migrants from the South, and immigrants from Africa and the Caribbean?
10 Where should blacks publish their manuscripts: with all-black publishers, or on the open American market (with white publishers)?

Scholars of the Harlem Renaissance have noted its central place in the advancement of black American culture in the 1920s and early 1930s. In this connection, an early, major work was Nathan Irvin Huggins' *Harlem Renaissance* (1971). A later study, which also places Harlem in historical perspective, but emphasizes the contributions and issues facing black women, is Darlene Clark Hine and Kathleen Thompson's *A Shining Thread of Hope: The Black Women in America History* (1998). Issues surrounding the major black male poet of the movement are refined by Arnold Rampersad in *The Life of Langston Hughes*, Volume 1: *1902–41, I Too, Sing America* (1986). This work is counter-balanced with a treatment of Countee Cullen and other writers, by Houston A. Baker, Jr, in *Long Black Song: Essays in Black American Literature and Culture* (1972).

As in the past, such themes were complex and offered no easy solutions to contemporaries of the 1920s and early 1930s. Group concerns and the realities of living in a segregated society meant that most blacks had to be practical and flexible in their artistic work. Yet, as scholars Robin D. G. Kelley and Earl Lewis note, "The idea of the 'New Negro' took hold in many influential publications in the 1920s, and the term itself was used as the title of a book edited by Howard University professor Alain Locke in 1925. In his introduction Locke proposed two complementary principles underlying this new perspective. New Negroes insisted on the rights embodied in 'the ideals of American institutions and democracy.' They also promoted 'self-respect and self-reliance' among African Americans, with a distinct emphasis on race pride" (Kelley and Lewis, *To Make Our World Anew* 2000: 400). Thus, the Harlem Renaissance brought "a fresh faith in blackness and a fervent racial pride . . . [and] the Harlem Renaissance marked a major watershed in black, and consequently, in American literary history" (Hirsch 1991: 56–7). Indeed, the movement witnessed a national birth of black creativity, and saw the creation of thousands of black artifacts, which reflected the talents and skills of black artists as they sought to speak their minds on the human condition at home and abroad, and to continue and refine the earlier black artistic traditions.

The Age of Richard Wright, 1935–59

The Great Depression of the 1930s was a period of extreme economic hardship for the American people. The bright hopes reflected in the Harlem Renaissance were crushed by the economic crisis of the new period. Nonetheless, black literary efforts continued in the period 1935–59, but at a slower pace. The critic Blyden Jackson called this "the Age of Wright," because Richard Wright emerged as the most outstanding black writer and thinker of his generation and produced a masterful body of creative work (Jackson 1976: 203–4). Wright was especially known for *Uncle Tom's Children* (1938), a collection of short stories; the novel, *Native Son* (1940); *12 Million Black Voices* (1941); and *Black Boy: A Record of Childhood and Youth* (1945), among other works (Rowley 2001: 593).

Wright's work and that of many other black intellectuals reflected a growing radicalism in artistic productions and outlook during this period. For Wright, this took the form of using Marxist analysis to reflect upon society and the human condition. Socialism became a major theme in the work of many artists, when they could secure publication or production of their works. Some, like Wright, were able to turn to publications on the left for support, including *New Masses, New Challenge, Left Front*, and *Partisan Review*. The new mood among black artists was very critical of American society and of the continued harsh realities facing black Americans, due to racism, lynching, and general discrimination against blacks and other marginal groups in American life.

Twenty major black voices can be identified in the life and work of artists during the Age of Wright. Ten significant black male figures were: Richard Wright (1908–1960), Langston Hughes (1902–1967), James Baldwin (1924–1987), John Hope Franklin (1915–), Martin Luther King, Jr (1929–1968), Paul Robeson (1898–1976), Ralph Ellison (1914–1994), Melvin B. Tolson (1898–1966), Sterling A. Brown (1901–1989), and Robert Hayden (1913–1980).

The ten major black women figures of this era were: Zora Neale Hurston (1891–1960), Gwendolyn Brooks (1917–2002), Margaret Walker (1915–1998), Marian Anderson (1897–1993), Lorraine Hansberry (1930–1965), Rosa Parks (1913–), Naomi Long Madgett (1923–), Ella Baker (1903–1986), Alice Childress (1916–1994), and Margaret Danner (1915–1984).

The work of the black intellectuals of the late 1930s through the 1950s signaled a further development of the protest tradition among black artists. Although the artists of this generation created a very complex body of work, they felt a need to demand even stronger statements and works that called for black human and civil rights in the United States and abroad. Thus, their creative works, teaching activities, and organizational work stressed the need for black advancement and achievement, against the odds of American racism, discrimination, and oppression of the black community. Among the creative artists, black novelists, and poets are dominate figures for the period. After Richard Wright came the novels of Langston Hughes, *Not Without Laughter* (1930) and *Tambourines to Glory* (1963), James Baldwin, *Go Tell It On the Mountain* (1953) and *Giovanni's Room* (1956), Ralph Ellison, *Invisible Man* (1952), Zora Hurston, *Moses, Man of the Mountain* (1939) and *Seraph On the Suwanee* (1948), and Gwendolyn Brooks, *Maud Martha* (1953).

A fine selection of black poets were representative of the period, and included: Langston Hughes, Melvin B. Tolson, Sterling A. Brown, Robert Hayden, Gwendolyn Brooks, Margaret Walker, Naomi Long Madgett, and Margaret Danner. Poets called for a new spirit and connection to the African past, in such poems as this one of Danner's:

> This is an African worm
> but then a worm in any land
> is still a worm.
>
> It will not stride, run, stand up
> before the butterflies, who
> have passed their worm-like state.
>
> It must keep low, not lift its head.
> I've had the dread experience, I know.
> A worm can do nothing but crawl.
>
> Crawl, and wait. (Danner, "This Is An African Worm," in Ward 1997: 168)

The search for freedom is also expressed in Robert Hayden's "Frederick Douglass":

> When it is finally ours, this freedom, this liberty, this beautiful
> and terrible thing, needful to man as air,
> useable as earth; when it belongs at last to all,
> when it is truly instinct, brain matter, diastole, systole,
> reflex action; when it is finally won; when it is more
> than the gaudy mumbo jumbo of politicians:
> this man, this Douglass, this former slave, this Negro
> beaten to his knees, exiled, visioning a world
> where none is lonely, none hunted, alien,
> this man, superb in love and logic, this man
> shall be remembered. Oh, not with statues' rhetoric,
> not with legends and poems and wreaths of bronze alone,
> but with the lives grown out of his life, the lives
> fleshing his dream of the beautiful, needful thing. (Robert Hayden, "Frederick
> Douglass," in Ward 1997: 150)

Other intellectuals who significantly influenced their areas of expertise during this era were: John Hope Franklin, historian, and author of *From Slavery To Freedom* (1947); the civil rights activists, Martin Luther King, Jr and Ella Baker; the activist Paul Robeson, who supported many anti-racist causes in his lifetime; Marian Anderson, a concert artist; and the important playwrights, Lorraine Hansberry, author of *A Raisin the Sun* (1959); and Alice Childress, noted for her plays *Florence* (1949) and *Trouble in Mind* (1955), among others.

Black intellectuals were still faced with many of the same major issues and themes as in the Harlem Renaissance era, but for the period 1935–59 their ten main challenges were:

1   What economic, social, and political analysis should black intellectuals employ in their creative works: capitalism, socialism, or communism?
2   How should black separatism or integration influence black literary activities?
3   Should black Americans support the Republican or Democratic parties?
4   What role should protest themes play in black artistic productions?
5   How should the lives of black women, men, and children be reflected in black literature and the arts?
6   What roles should black Americans play in the future development of Africa?
7   Was there a place for race, or black consciousness, in African American literature?
8   Was there a special role for the black press to play in black American affairs and literary activities?
9   What steps should the Civil Rights Movement take to advance black American human and civil rights? and
10 What role should black colleges and universities play in staging black artistic productions?

Historians have noted the controversial, radical positions involving black writers and artists of the Age of Wright, especially on political issues centering around the roles of capitalism, socialism, and communism in black American life and affairs. Certainly the key figure of the period was Richard Wright, in terms of his interests in the American Left and the US Communist Party of the 1930s, though he later lost interest in communism and broke with the party. Such issues are explored by Hazel Rowley in *Richard Wright: The Life and Times* (2001). The work of Langston Hughes during these years is further explored by Arnold Rampersad, in *The Life of Langston Hughes*, Volume II: *1941–1967, I Dream A World* (1988). A major artist, in terms of music, films, and political activism, is studied by Martin Duberman, in *Paul Robeson* (1988). The attempts by black writers to promote their works during the Age of Wright are studied in: A. A. Johnson and R. M. Johnson, *Propaganda and Aesthetics: The Literary Politics of Afro-American Magazines in the Twentieth Century* (1979).

As in earlier artistic periods, black intellectuals in the Age of Wright were faced with many challenges and most adopted a stand of continued protest, combined with faith and hope in the future endeavors and struggles of black people and black culture. The individual and group creative spirits led most black intellectuals to support the Democratic Party, as did a majority of black Americans from 1932 forward; most held out hope for a democratic America, with faith that American institutions could be reformed over time through black struggle and with support from Congress, the justice system (especially the courts), religious institutions, and improved educational opportunities and literary efforts for the American people. Meanwhile, black artistic productions had to reflect the complexities of the black experience in America and, as in the past, draw upon the rural and urban dimensions of that background, while also offering a didactical summary of black life in this nation. Thus, the Black Arts had to advance human understanding, while stressing the beauty and universal nature of black life, and there was a continued place and role for black colleges and universities in this struggle for black advancement. Yet blacks had a right, if not an obligation, to seek the continued desegregation of white-controlled educational, business, and cultural institutions in the United States.

The Black Arts Movement, 1960–79

Like the Harlem Renaissance of the early twentieth century, the Black Arts Movement, at the last quarter of the century, witnessed a significant rebirth of all of the arts in black America. It was a period of tremendous new opportunities for black artists and creative people. Every artistic and scholarly field was impacted. In essence, the Black Arts Movement refers to the period between 1960 and 1979, when black intellectuals began a call for a radical new state of black consciousness in the United States, and with a demand that black artistic production must reflect the black aesthetic. Poet and critic Larry Neal observed that a central reason for the Black Arts Movement was a need to promote "artistic responsibility to a Black community, employing an aesthetic derived from Black experience" (Neal 1989: 222). In a period of rapid social change, it must be observed that the Black Arts Movement was also connected to the Civil Rights Movement and the Black Power Movement. Indeed, the Black Arts Movement can be viewed as the cultural struggle of blacks to seek freedom in America, just as the other movements sought to end American segregation, and the economic, social, and political oppression that blacks suffered in the twentieth-century America.

The Black Arts Movement also had important consequences for related black institutions and life in the 1960s and 1970s. For example, with the increased out-pouring of black poetry, novels, essays, short stories and plays, came developments in African American education, especially noted in the Black Studies Movement of the same period; in fashion design and hair-care concerns; in the expansion of black music, especially jazz, gospel, and rhythm and blues; in a special focus on black American and African history; and in a renewal of black press and publishing companies, which published, distributed, and critiqued the new work.

Thirteen black male figures are especially noteworthy during this period: Amiri Baraka [LeRoi Jones] (1934–), Haki R. Madhubuti [Don L. Lee] (1942–), Dudley Randall (1914–2000), Etheridge Knight (1931–1991), Raymond R. Patterson (1929–2001), Kalamu ya Salaam (1947–), Sterling D. Plumpp (1940–), Eugene B. Redmond (1937–), Larry Neal (1937–1981), Addison Gayle, Jr (1932–1991), Malcolm X (1925–1965), Marvin X (1944–), and Hoyt W. Fuller (1923–1981). Ten women figures are representative of the extraordinary efforts of black women to promote and help develop black arts during the Black Arts Movement. Two have already been mentioned – Gwendolyn Brooks and Margaret Walker – and the others were Maya Angelou (1928–), Mari Evans (1923–), Audre Lorde (1934–1992), Sonia Sanchez (1934–), Nikki Giovanni (1943–), Lucille Clifton (1936–), June Jordan (1936–2002), and Carolyn Rodgers (1945–). These writers were powerful cultural workers in the efforts of African Americans to focus public attention on black literacy, on the social well-being of the black community – with a greater understanding and appreciation of black literature and artifacts – and on the continued relationship between black struggles in the arts, with the political, economic, and social campaigns of blacks in their never-ending search for freedom and liberation in modern America.

Some writers from the 1940s and 1950s were still prominent – James Baldwin, Gwendolyn Brooks, Alice Childress, Lorraine Hansberry, and Margaret Walker – and other members of the Black Arts Movement included Houston A. Baker, Jr (1943–), Toni Cade Bambara (1939–1995), Claude Brown (1937–2002), Sterling Brown (1901–1989), Margaret G. Burroughs (1917–), John Henrik Clarke (1915–1998), Pearl Cleage (1948–), Eldridge Cleaver (1935–), Harold Cruse (1916–), Angela Davis (1944–), Ossie Davis (1917–), Thomas C. Dent (1932–1998), Addison Gayle, Jr (1932–1991), Paula Giddings (1947–), Sam Greenlee (1930–), Alex Haley (1921–1992), Nathan Hare (1934–), Calvin C. Hernton (1934–2001), Jewel Latimore [Johari Aminil] (1935–), Haki R. Madhubuti [Don L. Lee] (1942–), Pauli Marshall (1929–), Anne Moody (1940–), Toni Morrison (1931–), Gloria Naylor (1950–), Larry Neal (1937–1981), Ann Petry (1908–1997), Dudley Randall (1914–2000), Ishmael Reed (1938–), Kalamu ya Salaam (1947–), Ntozake Shange (1948–), Askia Muhammad Toure (1938–), Alice Walker (1944–), and Helen Washington (1941–). In essence, the social backgrounds and lives of such figures are representative of the creative artists who promoted racial identity and protest during this era.

Although the people mentioned were born all over the United States, it is noteworthy that the majority (47) were born in the South. This can be explained by the fact that until the mid-twentieth century, most African Americans continued to live in the South, in spite of the loss of tens of thousands of blacks in the Great Migration, between 1900 and the 1940s. Twelve American cities were significant as birthplaces of Black Art Movement figures. These cities (and the number of births) were: Chattanooga, Tennessee (1); Nashville (2); Greenville, Mississippi (2); St Louis, Missouri (2); New Orleans (2); Washington, DC (2); Birmingham, Alabama (4); Atlanta, Georgia (4); Chicago (4); Detroit (4); Philadelphia (5); and New York City (11). Many of those born in New York City came from Harlem. Many of these American cities were the concentration points of most Black Arts Movement activities in the 1960s and 1970s, and helped to focus the energies of the movement among large numbers of people, both in the North and South.

Four broad categories seem to capture the occupational interests of most Black Arts Movement personalities. Since most were creative writers, they were generally known as poets, dramatists, novelists, short story writers, or non-fiction writers. However, many had long and varied careers, where their artistic interests often expanded over time. Thus, many were journalists, artists, actors, dancers, community activists, directors, commentators, and especially educators, at all levels of the United States educational system. Such flexibility greatly advanced the careers of many movement workers.

The black press and publishers were very important in promoting the achievements of the Black Arts Movement. Key journals, newspapers, and publishers included, from New York City: *Black Creation*, *Black Theatre*, *The Crisis*, Emerson Hall Publishers, *Freedomways*, *Liberator*, and Third Press; from Chicago: *Black Books Bulletin*, *Chicago Defender*, DuSable Museum Press, Johnson Publishing Company, *Negro Digest/Black World*, Nommo, and Third World Press; from California: the *Black Panther*, the *Black Scholar* and Press, the *Journal of Black Poetry*, the *Journal of Black Studies*, *Soulbook*, the *Los Angeles Sentinel*, and Yardbird Press; from Detroit: *Black Arts Magazine*, Broadside Press, Lotus Press, and the *Michigan Chronicle*; and from Washington, DC: the *Afro-American*, Associated Publishers, Drum and Spear Press, *Howard University Magazine* and Press, the *Journal of Negro Education*, and the *Negro History Bulletin*, among many others. These publications and publishers were very active in helping to increase and distribute the artistic and scholarly productions of the Black Arts Movement, including poetry, works for radio, television, and film, book reviews, essays, short stories, novels, reports, plays, biographies, and autobiographies, and scholarly studies across the curriculum in American higher education.

The leading black writer of the Black Arts Movement was Amiri Baraka, especially noted for his poetry, in collections such as *Preface to a Twenty Volume Suicide Note* (1961), and his famous plays, including *Dutchman* (1964), *The Slave* (1964), and *The Toilet* (1964), among others. Baraka's body of work expressed the new radical mood among African American intellectuals, and demanded a change in society, but especially in outlook among blacks themselves on their position in American society. The power of Baraka's best work is shown in "Preface to a Twenty Volume Suicide Note (For Kellie Jones, born 16 May 1959)":

> Lately, I've become accustomed to the way
> The ground opens up and envelops me
> Each time I go out to walk the dog.
> Or the broad edged silly music the wind
> Makes when I run for a bus . . .
>
> Things have come to that.
>
> And now, each night I count the stars,
> And each night I get the same number.
> And when they will not come to be counted
> I count the holes they leave.
>
> Nobody sings anymore.
>
> And then last night, I tiptoed up
> To my daughter's room and heard her
> Talking to someone, and when I opened
> The door, there was no one there . . .
> Only she on her knees, peeking into
>
> Her own clasped hands. (Baraka, "Preface to a Twenty Volume Suicide Note,"
> in Ward 1997: 297–8)

Three important godfathers of the movement were Dudley Randall, Hoyt W. Fuller, and Addison Gayle, Jr. This group of critics and editors helped greatly to promote the movement, to advance the black aesthetic, and to encourage particip-ants. Randall was the founder of Broadside Press, in Detroit in 1965, and published hundreds of poets and other writers. Fuller was editor of *Negro Digest/Black World*, a leading publication which supported the movement, and also published hundreds of its writers. Gayle was a chief theoretician of the movement, who promoted the black aesthetic. These figures were also important creative writers in their own right (Thompson 1999: 25, 30).

Black women were a powerful voice in the Black Arts Movement, and Nikki Giovanni is a representative of the new, revolutionary black poets of the period. Her excellent poetry was best represented in such works as "Nikki-Rosa" –

> childhood remembrances are always a drag
> if you're Black
> you always remember things like living in Woodlawn
> with no inside toilet
> and if you become famous or something
> they never talk about how happy you were to have
> your mother
> all to yourself and
> how good the water felt when you got your bath
> from one of those
> big tubs that folk in Chicago barbecue in
> and somehow when you talk about home
> it never gets across how much you
> understood their feelings
> as the whole family attended meetings about Hollydale
> and even though you remember
> your biographers never understand
> your father's pain as he sells his stock
> and another dream goes
> And though you're poor it isn't poverty that
> concerns you
> and though they fought a lot
> it isn't your father's drinking that makes any difference
> but only that everybody is together and you
> and your sister have happy birthdays and very good Christmases
> and I really hope no white person ever has cause
> to write about me
> because they never understand
> Black love is Black wealth
> and they'll probably talk about my hard childhood
> and never understand that
> all the while I was quite happy. (Giovanni, "Nikki-Rosa," in Ward 1997: 419)

Ten major issues and themes can be identified as significant to participants in the Black Arts Movement during the years 1960–79:

1 Who would support, and who oppose, the black aesthetic philosophy?
2 How would blacks deal with disagreements among themselves over political participation, either in black separatist organizations, such as the Nation of Islam, or in mainstream Democratic and Republican Party politics, and who would win the support of the black masses? Should blacks support an independent black political party?
3 Where should black authors go to publish – to all-black publishers or white publishers?
4 How were blacks to deal with religious division in the community, especially among black Christians, Muslims, and those in traditional African religions?
5 What did the domination of the Black Arts Movement by black men mean for the movement, and for the future roles of black women in the movement?
6 Which major cities would command the best talent and productions of the Black Arts Movement: New York, Chicago, Detroit, Los Angeles, Atlanta, Washington, or Philadelphia perhaps?
7 Should white Americans be encouraged to review black artistic productions, or only black critics and thinkers?
8 How should black Americans approach blacks on the continent of Africa and other areas of the Diaspora, in terms of political, economic, social, and cultural cooperation, to uplift the entire black world?
9 What should be the roles of black intellectuals in the Civil Rights and Black Power Movements of the era? and
10 How would blacks deal with the issue of continued violence against the black community in modern America, including the large number of blacks imprisoned?

Historians and critics of the Black Arts and Aesthetic Movement represent two schools of thought on the figures of the period 1960–79. Scholar Arthur P. Davis was very critical of the writers of the era in a famous essay entitled "The new poetry of black hate" (1970), whereas Eugene B. Redmond generally praised the writers of his generation and earlier times, in a powerful study published as *Drumvoices: The Mission of Afro-American Poetry* (1976). Addison Gayle, Jr, a major supporter of the movement, created the policy manual of the period with his edited volume *The Black Aesthetic* (1972). Several scholars agree that the issue of black leadership, political development, and organized black struggle defines the Black Arts Movement (Boyd 2003; Kent 1990; Melhem 1987; Brown 2003). The key theme of the political roles of black women is discussed in Joanne Grant, *Ella Baker: Freedom Bound* (1998) and two lives of Fannie Lou Hamer – Kay Mills, *This Little Light of Mine* (1993) and Chana Kai Lee, *For Freedom's Sake* (1999). The relationship of African Americans to Africa is considered in Alex Haley's *Roots* (1976) and Lorraine Williams (ed.), *Africa and the Afro-American Experience: Eight Essays* (1977).

In general, black intellectuals of the 1960s and 1970s supported a new radical twist in terms of black political, social, economic, and cultural developments. A central issue was a look inward to focus on black consciousness, and black determination to forge ahead, certainly in the continuing struggle to overthrow segregation and discrimination, but also to support black separatism/nationalism. These were seen as especially reflected in the promotion of black institutions, such as the family, and in economic matters, political activity, self-help, black cultural interests, and the Black Studies Movement.

Many Movement participants were distrustful of white intellectuals, critics, editors, and publishers. Many sought publication of their work with black publishers, such as Broadside Press, Third World Press, and Lotus Press. The worldwide condition of black people became a major focus of black thinkers, and attention was given to black affairs and needs in Africa, the West Indies, South America, and other regions. Black women became more outspoken during this period in demanding their rights, and especially in the long struggle to overcome racism, sexism, and classicism in society. In fact, black women intellectuals emerged during the 1960s and 1970s as major players in the production of black artistic materials, and as master teachers and leaders in black arts. Social issues such as violence and prison conditions in the USA became another source of special concern to black intellectuals, and this was reflected in the body of works produced by the movement. Although the black aesthetics were not adopted by all black intellectuals during this period, the new philosophy certainly had great impact on the way many black artists viewed their artistic creations and their roles in black and American society. This focus on black consciousness and the black community became a major contribution of the Black Arts Movement to black America.

The Hip-Hop Generation and New Cultural Definitions since 1980

In the period after the Black Arts Movement came a new movement called "the hip hop generation and the emergence of a distinctive black youth culture" largely based on a rap style of music, dress, hair care, and outlook (Kitwana 2002: xiv). The Hip-Hop Cultural Movement has had a profound impact upon American youths, as well as youth in other societies. Much of its message has been viewed as controversial, radical, abusive of women, and representative of lower-income blacks who live largely in the major cities. Nonetheless, the new black culture has dominated the artistic scene in the United States from the 1980s to the present. Yet, the spirit and challenges of the Black Arts Movement are still present today, since a large number of the leading participants of the former movement are still alive and continue to be active as artists and writers.

Since 1980, a number of new voices have joined the older generation of black artists in interpreting the Black Experience in the United States. Ten black males are representative of black culture in this period: Tupac Shakur (1971–1996), Houston A. Baker, Jr (1943–), E. Ethelbert Miller (1950–), Quincy Troupe (1943–), Al Young (1939–), Askia Muhammad Toure (1938–), 50 Cent [Curtis Jackson] (1976–), Common [Lonnie Rashied Lynn] (1972–), Nelly [Cornell Haynes, Jr] (1978–), and Haki R. Madhubuti (1942–). Among prominent black women of this era are Alice Walker (1944–), Toni Morrison (1931–), Jayne Cortez (1936–), Ntozake Shange (1948–), Wanda Coleman (1946–), Harryette Mullen (1960–), Rita Dove (1952–), Queen Latifah [Dana Owens] (1970–), and Angela Davis (1944–).

As in the long black past, much of the Hip-Hop Culture and rap music tradition have had to deal with the realities of living in America. Thus, many Hip-Hop artists have focused a considerable body of their work on dealing with black problems in society, poverty, unemployment, racism, the criminal justice system, and the health care system, among other-themes. Other artists have treated topics such as personal relationships, friendships, disagreements between artists, and playing the dozens, often referred to as gangsta rap.

Ten major themes and issues have dominated the Hip-Hop generation since the 1980s:

1 How should traditional African American culture influence the Hip-Hop generation?
2 What should Hip-Hop culture emphasize?
3 How can blacks continue to control the Hip-Hop movement; and is there a major role for whites to play in the movement?
4 Has the gangsta rap segment of Hip-Hop been too negative with many of its rap lyrics on black women?
5 What role should the Hip-Hop movement play in American politics?
6 What is the role of older black artists in the Hip-Hop movement?
7 Have black men been the dominant voices in the Hip-Hop culture?
8 What role should black women play in the movement?
9 Have opportunities for black artists and writers increased or decreased in the United States since the Black Arts Movement era?
10 Will the Hip-Hop cultural movement have a lasting impact on American life and institutions?

Some contemporary scholars have offered praise for the positive achievements of the Hip-Hop generation, while offering a critical review of the shortcomings of the movement, especially the negative treatment of black women by some Hip-Hop artists and a lack of political activity by some artists and their supporters. Bakari Kitwana's study, *The Hip Hop Generation* (2002), is a major contribution to this perspective. Likewise, Nelson George, in *Buppies, Notes On B-Boys, Post-Soul Baps and Black Bohos Culture* (1992), takes up the challenge to study the new Black Culture. Other studies, such as James L. Conyers, Jr, *African American Jazz and Rap* (2001), highlight the continued historical significance of traditional black music, as represented by jazz, but they note the new themes and the impact of rap on all aspects of African American culture.

The continuing influence of the Black Arts Movement, however, is still apparent in the theme of several magnificent studies: Molefi Kete Asante, *Kemet, Afrocentricity, and Knowledge* (1990); Haki R. Madhubuti, *Tough Notes: A Healing Call For Creating Exceptional Black Men* (2002); Joyce Ann Joyce, *Warriors, Conjurers and Priests: Defining African-Centered Literary Criticism* (1994); and Maryemma Graham (ed.), *On Being Female, Black and Free: Essays by Margaret Walker, 1932–1992* (1997). Voices expressing the determination of black women for justice and equality have also been very active in the modern era. These include the works of Alice Walker, *In Search of Our Mothers' Gardens: Womanist Prose* (1983), and Patricia Hill Collins, *Black Feminist Thought: Knowledge, Consciousness, and the Politics of Empowerment* (1991). Even black prisoners have found new attention in Alton Archer, *Black Prison Movements USA* (1995).

Thus, as the Hip-Hop generation continues to dominate contemporary black arts in the United States, the traditional artists – especially from the Black Arts Movement – remain a major force for identity and protest. This is especially true of many black poets, novelists, playwrights, and other artists. Thus, we have a phenomenon in black America, a situation whereby the traditional voices of the past are now mixed with, and in competition with, the new voices (largely from the Hip-Hop generation). A struggle has now ensued to control who can discuss, write on or sing about the complex nature of black life in the United States, as well as how, when, and where they create their works and distribute them in the market place of ideas. As yet, it is not clear who will win the struggle, but it will be a fight to the finish. And the rich and complex nature of African American life suggests there is still a need for a variety of viewpoints, perspectives, and outlooks to explore its questions of identity and protest in the arts.

BIBLIOGRAPHY

Works Cited

Archer, Alton (ed.) (1995) *Black Prison Movements USA*. Trenton, NJ: Africa World Press.
Asante, Molefi Kete (1990) *Kemet, Afrocentricity, and Knowledge*. Trenton, NJ: Africa World Press.
Baker, Houston A., Jr (1972) *Long Black Song: Essays in Black American Literature and Culture*. Charlottesville: University Press of Virginia.
Boyd, Melba Joyce (1994) *Discarded Legacy: Politics and Poetics in the Life of Frances E. W. Harper, 1825–1911*. Detroit: Wayne State University Press.
—— (2003) *Wrestling with the Muse: Dudley Randall and the Broadside Press*. New York: Columbia University Press.
Brown, Scot (2003) *Fighting for Us: Maulana Karenga, The US Organization, and Black Cultural Nationalism*. New York: New York University Press.
Brown, Sterling A., Davis, Arthur P., and Lee, Ulysses (eds.) (1970) *The Negro Caravan*. New York: Arno Press and the New York Times.
Collins, Patricia Hill (1991) *Black Feminist Thought: Knowledge, Consciousness, and the Politics of Empowerment*. New York: Routledge.
Conyers, James L., Jr (ed.) (2001) *African American Jazz and Rap: Social and Philosophical Examinations of Black Expressive Behavior*. Jefferson, NC: McFarland.
Davis, Arthur P. (1970) "The new poetry of black hate," *CLA Journal* 13 (4, June): 382–91.
—— (1981) *From the Dark Tower: Afro-American Writers, 1900–1960*. Washington, DC: Howard University Press.
Duberman, Martin Bauml (1988) *Paul Robeson*. New York: Alfred A. Knopf.
Early, Gerald (ed.) (1991) *My Soul's High Song: The Collected Writings of Countee Cullen: Voice of the Harlem Renaissance*. New York: Anchor Books.
Emanuel, James A. and Gross, Theodore L. (eds.) (1968) *Dark Symphony: Negro Literature in America*. New York: Free Press.
Franklin, John Hope and Moss, Alfred A., Jr ([1947] 2000) *From Slavery to Freedom: A History of African Americans*. Boston: McGraw-Hill.
Franklin, V. P. (1984) *Black Self-Determination: A Cultural History of the Faith of the Fathers*. Westport, CT: Lawrence Hill.
Frazier, Thomas R. (ed.) (2001) *Readings in African-American History*. Belmont, CA: Wadsworth.

Gayle, Addison, Jr (ed.) (1972) *The Black Aesthetic*. Garden City, NY: Anchor Books.

George, Nelson (1992) *Buppies, Notes on B-Boys, Post-Soul Baps and Black Bohos Culture*. New York: HarperCollins.

Giddings, Paula (1984) *When and Where I Enter: The Impact of Black Women on Race and Sex in America*. New York: Bantam Books.

Graham, Maryemma (ed.) (1997) *On Being Female, Black and Free: Essays by Margaret Walker, 1932–1992*. Knoxville: University of Tennessee Press.

Grant, Joanne (1998) *Ella Baker: Freedom Bound*. New York: John Wiley & Sons.

Haley, Alex (1976) *Roots*. Garden City, NY: Doubleday.

Harlan, Louis R. (1972) *Booker T. Washington: The Making of a Black Leader, 1856–1901*. New York: Oxford University Press.

Hine, Darlene Clark, King, Wilma, and Reed, Linda (1995) *We Specialize in the Wholly Impossible: A Reader in Black Women's History*. Brooklyn, NY: Carlson.

Hine, Darlene Clark and Thompson, Kathleen (1998) *A Shining Thread of Hope: The History of Black Women in America*. New York: Broadway Books.

Hirsch, Edward (1991) "Helmet of fire: American poetry in the 1920s" in Jack Myers and David Wojahn (eds.), *A Profile of Twentieth Century American Poetry*. Carbondale, IL: Southern Illinois University Press.

Huggins, Nathan Irvin (1971) *Harlem Renaissance*. New York: Oxford University Press.

Hughes, Langston ([1926] 1954) *Selected Poems*. New York: Alfred A. Knopf.

—— (2001) *The Collected Works of Langston Hughes, Vol. 1: The Poems, 1921–1940*, Arnold Rampersad (ed.). Columbia: University of Missouri Press.

Hughes, Langston and Bontemps, Arna (eds.) ([1949] 1970) *The Poetry of the Negro, 1746–1970*. Garden City, NY: Doubleday.

Hurt, R. Douglas (ed.) (2003) *African American Life in the Rural South, 1900–1950*. Columbia: University of Missouri Press.

Jackson, Blyden (1976) *The Waiting Years, Essays on American Negro Literature*. Baton Rouge: Louisiana State University Press.

Johnson, Abby Arthur and Johnson, Ronald Maberry (1979) *Propaganda and Aesthetics: The Literary Politics of Afro-American Magazines in the Twentieth Century*. Amherst: University of Massachusetts Press.

Jones, LeRoi (1961) *Preface to a Twenty Volume Suicide Note*. New York: Totem Press/ Corinth.

Joyce, Joyce Ann (1994) *Warriors, Conjurers and Priests: Defining African-Centered Literary Criticism*. Chicago: Third World Press.

Kelley, Robin D. and Lewis, Earl (2000) *To Make Our World Anew*. New York: Oxford University Press.

Kent, George E. (1990) *A Life of Gwendolyn Brooks*. Lexington: University Press of Kentucky.

Kitwana, Bakari (2002) *The Hip Hop Generation: Young Blacks and the Crisis in African-American Culture*. New York: Basic Vivitas Books.

Lee, Chana Kai (1999) *For Freedom's Sake: The Life of Fannie Lou Hamer*. Urbana: University of Illinois Press.

Lewis, David Levering (1993) *W. E. B. Du Bois: Biography of a Race, 1868–1919*. New York: Henry Holt.

Lewis, Rupert (1988) *Marcus Garvey, Anti-Colonial Champion*. Trenton, NJ: Africa World Press.

McHenry, Elizabeth (2002) *Forgotten Readers: Recovering the Lost History of African American Literary Societies*. Durham, NC: Duke University Press.

Madhubuti, Haki R. (2002) *Tough Notes: A Healing Call for Creating Exceptional Black Men: Affirmations, Meditations, Readings and Strategies*. Chicago: Third World Press.

Marks, Carole (1989) *Farewell – We're Good and Gone: The Great Black Migration*. Bloomington: Indiana University Press.

Melhem, D. H. (1987) *Gwendolyn Brooks: Poetry and the Heroic Voice*. Lexington: University Press of Kentucky.

Mills, Kay (1993) *This Little Light of Mine: The Life of Fannie Lou Hamer*. New York: Dutton/Penguin.

Neal, Larry with Schwartz, Michael (1989) *Visions of a Liberated Future: Black Arts Movement Writing*. New York: Thunder's Mouth Press.

Rampersad, Arnold (1986) *The Life of Langston Hughes*, Volume I: *1902–1941, I Too, Sing America*. New York: Oxford University Press.

—— (1988) *The Life of Langston Hughes*, Volume II: *1941–1967, I Dream a World*. New York: Oxford University Press.

Redmond, Eugene B. (1976) *Drumvoices: The Mission of Afro-American Poetry*. Garden City, NY: Anchor Press/Doubleday.

Rowley, Hazel (2001) *Richard Wright: The Life and Times*. New York: Henry Holt.

Thompson, Julius E. (1999) *Dudley Randall, Broadside Press, and the Black Arts Movement in Detroit, 1960–1995*. Jefferson, NC: McFarland.

Valade, Roger M. (1996) *The Essential Black Literature Guide*. Canton, MI: Visible Ink Press.

Wagner, Jean (1973) *Black Poets of the United States: From Paul Laurence Dunbar to Langston Hughes*, trans. Kenneth Douglass. Urbana: University of Illinois Press.

Walker, Alice (1983) *In Search of Our Mothers' Gardens: Womanist Prose*. San Diego, CA: Harcourt Brace Jovanovich.

Ward, Jerry W. (ed.) (1997) *Trouble the Water: 250 Years of African-American Poetry*. New York: Penguin.

Whitlow, Roger (1984) *Black American Literature*. Chicago: Nelson Hall.

Williams, Lorraine (ed.) (1977) *Africa and the Afro-American Experience: Eight Essays*. Washington, DC: Howard University Press.

Wolseley, Roland E. (1971) *The Black Press, U.S.A*. Ames: Iowa State University Press.

Suggestions for Further Reading

Bigsby, C. W. E. (1980) *The Second Black Renaissance: Essays in Black Literature*. Westport, CT: Greenwood Press.

Bontemps, Arna (ed.) (1963) *American Negro Poetry*. New York: Hill & Wang.

Chestnutt, Helen M. (1952) *Charles Waddell Chestnut: Pioneer of the Color Line*. Chapel Hill: University of North Carolina Press.

Collins, Patricia Hill (1991) *Black Feminist, Thought, Knowledge, Consciousness, and the Politics of Empowerment*. New York: Routledge.

Conyers, James L., Jr (ed.) (2001) *African American Jazz and Rap: Social and Philosophical Examinations of Black Expressive Behavior*. Jefferson, NC: McFarland.

Dent, Thomas C., Schechner, Richard and Moses, Gilbert (eds.) (1969) *The Free Southern Theater by the Free Southern Theater*. Indianapolis: Bobbs-Merrill.

Ervin, Hazel Arnett (ed.) (1999) *African American Literary Criticism, 1773 to 2000*. New York: Twayne.

Evans, Mari (1970) *I Am a Black Woman: Poems*. New York: William Morrow.

Farnsworth, Robert M. and Tolson, Melvin B. (1984) *1898–1966: Plain Talk and Poetic Prophecy*. Columbia: University of Missouri Press.

Fowler, Carolyn (1976) *Black Arts and Black Aesthetics: A Bibliography*. Atlanta: by the author.

Hughes, Langston (ed.) (1964) *New Negro Poets: U.S.A*. Bloomington: Indiana University Press.

Hull, Gloria, Bell Scott, Patricia, and Smith, Barbara (eds.) (1982) *All the Women Are White, All the Blacks Are Men, But Some of Us Are Brave: Black Women's Studies*. Old Westbury, NY: Feminist Press.

Janken, Kenneth Robert (1993) *Rayford W. Logan and the Dilemma of the African American Intellectual*. Amherst: University of Massachusetts Press.

Jones, LeRoi (1964) *Dutchman and the Slave; Two Plays*. New York: New Editions.

Jones, LeRoi and Neal, Larry (eds.) (1968) *Black Fire: An Anthology of Afro-American Writing*. New York: William Morrow.

Jordan, June (1973) *New Days: Poems of Exile and Return, 1970–1972*. New York: Emerson Hall.

Joyce, Donald Franklin (1991) *Black Book Publishers in the United States: A Historical Directory of the Presses, 1817–1990*. Westport, CT: Greenwood Press.

Killens, John Oliver and Ward, Jerry W., Jr (eds.) (1992) *Black Southern Voices: An Anthology of Fiction, Poetry, Drama, Nonfiction and Critical Essays*. New York: Penguin Books.

Latimore, Jewel C. (1968) *Black Essence*. Chicago: Third World Press.

Lee, Don L. [Haki R. Madhubuti] (1969) *Think Black*! Detroit: Broadside Press.

Lorde, Audre (1973) *From a Land Where Other People Live*. Detroit: Broadside Press.

Madgett, Naomi Long (1970) *Star by Star: Poems*. Detroit: Evenil.

Major, Clarence (ed.) (1969) *The New Black Poetry*. New York: International Publishers.

Melhem, D. H. (1990) *Heroism in the New Black Poetry: Introductions and Interviews*. Lexington: University Press of Kentucky.

Mitchell, Loften (1967) *Black Drama: The Story of the American Negro in the Theatre*. New York: Hawthorne Books.

Moody, Anne (1968) *Coming of Age in Mississippi*. New York: Laurel/Dell.

Tolnay, Stewart and Beck, E. M. (1995) *A Festival of Violence: An Analysis of Southern Lynchings, 1882–1930*. Urbana: University of Illinois Press.

Turner, Darwin T. (ed.) (1970) *Black American Literature: Essays, Poetry, Fiction, Drama*. Columbus, OH: Charles E. Merrill.

Walker, Alice (1968) *Once: Poems*. New York: Harcourt, Brace & World.

—— (1982) *The Color Purple: A Novel*. New York: Harcourt, Brace & World.

Walker, Margaret (1966) *Jubilee, a Novel*. Boston: Houghton Miffin.

—— (1970) *Prophets for a New Day: Poems*. Detroit: Broadside Press.

X, Malcolm with Haley, Alex (1973) *The Autobiography of Malcolm X*. New York: Ballantine Books.

Young, James O. (1973) *Black Writers of the Thirties*. Baton Rouge: Louisiana State University Press.

Part X

Searching for Place

Chapter Twenty-nine

Searching for a New Freedom

Hasan Kwame Jeffries

In the immediate aftermath of emancipation, the lives of former bondsmen and bondswomen failed to meet their basic expectations. Quite simply, their lives too closely resembled the status quo antebellum. Indeed, African Americans remained landless, lacked ownership of the fruits of their labor, lost the vote (through electoral fraud and discriminatory changes to state constitutions) shortly after they had received it, and were subject to vicious, vulgar, and random acts of racial terrorism as a result of the federal government being more interested in protecting the southern economy than in protecting black folk.

In response, African Americans organized to implement their vision of freedom, which differed substantially from that of white southerners and white northerners. By agitating for their civil and human rights, especially for good-quality education, political participation, personal safety, and control of their own labor, the former slaves launched the fight for racial justice that continues to this day (Harding 1981). The most important link in this intergenerational struggle is the modern Civil Rights Movement. It represents the most highly organized manifestation of African Americans' post-emancipation search for a new freedom and, if measured narrowly in legislative terms, the most successful.

Popular interest in the Civil Rights Movement has swelled during the last two decades. Evidence of this trend is the surge in the number of feature-length films that explore aspects and events of the civil rights era, such as *Freedom Song* and *Boycott*. The extensive media coverage given to the trials and convictions of whites involved in the 1963 murders of Medgar Evers and the four little girls killed in the Birmingham church bombing also reflects this trend. Academics have also paid increasing attention to the Black Freedom Struggle. In fact, their interest in the movement has fueled popular interest in it. In the years since 1990, the literature on the movement has grown substantially (Fairclough 1990; Lawson 1991). In the process, scholars have altered their general analytic framework, relying less on top-down, "great man" perspectives, and more on bottom-up, grassroots approaches. They have also broadened their subjects of inquiry, ranging beyond dramatic mobilizing events to examine community organizing (Eagles 1986; Robinson and Sullivan

1991; Lawson and Payne 1998; Davis 2000). Consequently, movement scholarship has become much richer and more complex.

This chapter focuses on the evolution of civil rights inquiry over the last quarter-century. It discusses and analyzes the major shifts in the subjects that historians study. It also looks at the ways the latest analytic approaches to studying social movements have caused scholars to look anew at civil rights events, activists, and organizations. This chapter also identifies and considers areas of the Black Freedom Struggle that remain understudied.

The origin of the Civil Rights Movement has been the focus of intense scholarly debate. Initially, historians tended to locate the starting point of the Black Freedom Struggle in the mid-1950s, arguing that the movement began when the US Supreme Court ruled in *Brown v. Board of Education, Topeka, Kansas* in 1954 that *de jure* segregated education was inherently unequal and unconstitutional (Kluger 1975). For these scholars, the primary catalysts behind the movement were the usual arbiters of power. They argue that the judicial branch of the federal government, followed later by the executive and legislative branches, led the charge for social change (Sitkoff 1978; Weisbrot 1991).

The push to acknowledge African American agency started a gradual shift in the discourse on movement origins. Rather than *Brown*, scholars began to point to the Montgomery bus boycott and the emergence of Dr Martin Luther King, Jr in 1955 as having jumpstarted civil rights struggles (Garrow 1986; Branch 1988). As a result, many scholars centered their studies of the movement around the life and protest activities of the Atlanta-born preacher. Taylor Branch, for example, situates his award-winning works on the Civil Rights Movement wholly around King's public life (Branch 1988, 1998). David Garrow and Adam Fairclough examine King's personal life during his public years even more closely; Garrow accomplishes this by making effective use of Federal Bureau of Investigation (FBI) surveillance records (Garrow 1983, 1986; Fairclough 1995a). More recently, historian Clayborne Carson has edited several volumes of King's personal papers. Although Carson is less committed to a King-centered understanding of the movement's beginning and evolution, he argues forthrightly for King's centrality to the Black Freedom Struggle (Carson 1992–2000, 1998).

Sociologist Aldon Morris complicates the Montgomery–King starting point slightly by beginning his exploration and analysis of the movement's origin with the 1953 Baton Rouge bus boycott. Like the aforementioned scholars, however, he centers the bulk of his study on the protest activities of King and the resource networks of black ministers (Morris 1984). In the years since 1990, increased awareness of the power of ordinary people – the proverbial grassroots – to make the decisions that most affect their lives has prompted scholars to challenge the idea that the Civil Rights Movement began with the bus boycotts of the 1950s and the emergence of King. Robin D. G. Kelley and Eric Arnesen look at organized black protest among southern sharecroppers and railroad workers as antecedents to the civil rights struggles of the 1950s (Kelley 1990; Arnesen 2001). Kelley also points to individual grassroots protest during the Second World War era as evidence of the need to push back the movement's starting point (Kelley 1994). Robert Korstad and Nelson Lichtenstein (1988), Michael Honey (1993), and Bruce Nelson (1993), for their part, test the normative narrative of the movement's origin by examining the intersection of black struggles for equality and southern labor organizing in the 1940s.

Interestingly enough, scholars who position white powerbrokers as the leading catalysts behind the Black Freedom Struggle have also divined earlier roots for the movement. Patricia Sullivan (1996), for example, locates the origins of the Civil Rights Movement in the liberal politics of New Deal southerners. Others have suggested that a liberal ethos permeated the late 1940s and sparked the movement by creating a popular consensus for progressive social change. As evidence, they point to the publication of Gunnar Myrdal's *An American Dilemma* and the Truman Administration's statement on civil rights *To Secure These Rights* (Lawson and Payne 1998). Scholars questioning this analytic trend note that the machinations of Washington insiders had only a limited impact on everyday black life, particularly in the rural South, even during the height of the New Deal. They also point out that Red-baiting McCarthyites and massive white resistance in the wake of *Brown* together limited the space available for public criticism and social activism, extinguishing post-war liberal sentiment and retarding rather than sparking black protest (Klarman 1994; Payne 1995; Lawson and Payne 1998; Dudziak 2000).

Understandings of the origins of the Civil Rights Movement have significantly shaped the study of civil rights organizations. Interest in *Brown* has sparked a handful of monographs on the NAACP's strategy to dismantle Jim Crow and on the Howard University lawyers who engineered and executed it (McNeil 1983; Tushnet 1987; Williams 1998). A number of works investigating the nation's oldest civil rights organization examine aspects of its fight "to reach the conscience of America" such as the crusade against lynching (Zangrando 1980; Goings 1990; Meier and Bracey 1993; Bates 1997). Unfortunately, far fewer studies exist of NAACP operations beyond New York boardrooms and Washington courtrooms. Only in the last decade have historians focused significant attention on the activities of the NAACP's local branches and local leaders. Notable works in this category are Ray Gavins' essay on the NAACP in North Carolina during the Jim Crow era, Tim Tyson's biography of Robert F. Williams, NAACP branch leader in Monroe, North Carolina, and most recently John Kirk's work on black activism in Little Rock, Arkansas, which considers the leadership and struggles of Daisy Bates (Robinson and Sullivan 1991; Tyson 1999; Kirk 2003).

As scholars began to look more closely at the bus boycotts of the 1950s and the emergence of Martin Luther King, Jr, they devoted increasing attention to the Southern Christian Leadership Conference (SCLC) and King-led SCLC campaigns. King biographers David Garrow and Adam Fairclough have both written impressive organizational histories of SCLC that scrutinize King's leadership and look closely at the group's civil rights battles (Garrow 1986; Fairclough 1987). Garrow has also penned a detailed account of SCLC's involvement in the 1965 voting rights drive in Selma, Alabama (Garrow 1978). Not surprisingly, most treatments of SCLC center on King. A refreshing break from this practice is Andrew Manis' 1999 biography of Fred Shuttlesworth. The fiery Rev. Shuttlesworth was the driving force behind the Alabama Christian Movement for Human Rights (ACMHR) and SCLC's man-on-the-ground in Birmingham, Alabama.

Popular perceptions of King *as* the movement, coupled with the NAACP's legal victories, caused scholars to pay only nominal attention to the Congress of Racial

Equality (CORE) or the Student Nonviolent Coordinating Committee (SNCC). They pushed these bodies to the movement periphery, dismissing them as secondary, even irrelevant (Morris 1984). Notable early exceptions are the 1973 history of CORE by August Meier and Elliot Rudwick, and histories of SNCC by Howard Zinn (1964) and Clayborne Carson (1981). To their credit, the works by Carson, and Meier and Rudwick are still the definitive studies of their subjects.

Examinations of CORE remain few in number. The literature on SNCC, however, has exploded. Since the mid-1990s, SNCC has moved from the margins of civil rights inquiry to the center. Studies of SNCC organizing in Mississippi by historian John Dittmer (1994) and sociologist Charles Payne (1995) have been principally responsible for redefining how the academic community looks at SNCC. Their application of a bottom-up approach to the Black Freedom Struggle demonstrated unequivocally that SNCC, and more specifically its African American organizers and the local people working with them, belongs at the center of movement histories, rather than at the margins. These works also reshaped the broader field of civil rights inquiry by drawing attention to the desire of the grassroots to have a say in the decisions that affect their lives and by making clear the essential distinction between movement organizing and movement mobilizing.

A disproportionate amount of the literature on SNCC focuses on Freedom Summer. In 1964, SNCC brought hundreds of white students from the nation's premier universities to Mississippi to draw attention to the desire of Mississippi's black residents to vote, to shine light on the obstacles impeding their ability to exercise the franchise, and to conduct freedom schools (McAdam 1988). Scholarly interest in this particular SNCC project has everything to do with white participation, particularly the participation of white women, and the murder of two white volunteers (Evans 1979). Whites, rather than SNCC's veteran black organizers and the local people who risked life and livelihood to shelter and feed them, are the primary subjects of inquiry. Memoirs by SNCC field secretaries have helped set the record straight, redirecting scholarly attention toward the activism, and heroism, of SNCC's black organizers and their local comrades (Forman 1972; Sellers 1973; King 1987; Lewis 1998; Curry et al. 2000; Moses and Cobb 2001). Former SNCC chairman Stokeley Carmichael's posthumously released autobiography is the most recent addition to this invaluable body of literature, and arguably the most significant (Carmichael 2003).

There remains a need for detailed studies of SNCC organizing that occurred outside Mississippi. Journalist David Halberstam's 1998 look at the Nashville movement and the soon-to-be SNCC activists who led the sit-in campaign in that city in 1960, namely Diane Nash, James Bevel, Bernard Lafayette, and John Lewis, is a step in the right direction. There is a similar need for critical studies of prominent SNCC members. Recent biographies of SNCC activists Fannie Lou Hamer and Ruby Doris Smith Robinson, and influential SNCC adviser Ella Baker, are excellent starting points (Lee 1999; Fleming 1998; Ransby 2003).

Scholars began to look anew at SNCC in the 1990s largely because of lessons they had learned in the 1980s from studying local civil rights movements. Collectively, William Chafe's 1980 examination of the freedom struggle in Greensboro, North Carolina, David Colburn's 1985 look at the movement in St Augustine, Florida, and Robert Norrell's 1985 study of black protest in Tuskegee, Alabama, made clear that the Civil Rights Movement was less a centrally coordinated national campaign and more a diffuse collection of local struggles in which local people played a leading role (Norrell 1985). Realizing that no organization worked in the trenches and on the front lines with the grassroots more than SNCC, scholars began to reevaluate the organization.

Interest in local movements continues. Caroline Emmons and Paul Ortiz have penned excellent articles on voting rights in Florida (Emmons 1997; Ortiz 2003). In 2003, much-needed monographs on the civil rights movements in Cambridge, Maryland, and Little Rock, Arkansas, appeared (Levy 2003; Kirk 2003). These studies reaffirm the idea that local people were the driving force behind the Black Freedom Struggle. At the same time, deconstructing the Civil Rights Movement geographically has prompted scholars to conduct state studies of black protest. John Dittmer's *Local People* (1994) is the foremost state study of the freedom struggle in Mississippi. Adam Fairclough's *Race and Democracy* (1995b) is an exhaustive study of black protest in Louisiana. Its pattern was followed by Stephen Tuck's *Beyond Atlanta* (2001), a broad history of civil rights activism in Georgia. To date, however, no comprehensive study of civil rights activism in Alabama exists – a glaring omission given the history of struggle in the self-styled Heart of Dixie. Glen Eskew's *But for Birmingham* (1997) and J. Mills Thornton's *Dividing Lines* (2002) come closest to filling this void, but these works focus wholly on municipalities and pay scant attention to civil rights activism in Alabama's rural counties.

The tendency to overlook rural protest is not limited to Alabama. Much of the literature on civil rights struggles outside Alabama also ignores rural protest. This oversight is partly a function of academic interest in dramatic mobilizing events, which typically occurred in urban areas. Norrell's 1985 work on Tuskegee is a notable exception, but the presence there of Booker T. Washington's Tuskegee Institute and a Veteran's Administration hospital made Tuskegee less than representative of typical, rural, black towns. Greta de Jong's *A Different Day* (2002), a study of black protest in rural Louisiana from 1900 to 1970, and Nan Woodruff's *American Congo* (2003), which examines the Black Freedom Struggle in Arkansas and the Mississippi Delta during the first half of the twentieth century, are first-rate examples of the types of rural case studies needed.

Black protest in rural areas is just one of several aspects of the Civil Rights Movement pregnant with investigative possibility. Another is black protest outside the South. To date, most studies that examine black activism in the North focus on the Nation of Islam (NOI) (Lincoln 1961; Essien-Udom 1962; McCartney 1992; Sales 1997). Ironically, the NOI, under the leadership of the Honorable Elijah Muhammad, did not identify with the Civil Rights Movement. Muhammad, through his principal spokesperson Malcolm X, preached racial separatism and criticized civil rights activists, particularly Christian ministers, for "trying to integrate into a burning house." Claude Clegg's biography of Elijah Muhammad offers an excellent analysis of the NOI's criticisms of the Civil Rights Movement. It also places the Nation's civil rights critique in the context of its political conservatism (Clegg 1997).

Interest in the Nation of Islam, coupled with the tendency of the southern struggle against Jim Crow and disfranchisement to dominate conceptualizations of the Civil Rights Movement, has caused historians to give much less attention than it deserves to organized northern protest against job discrimination and police brutality, and for fair housing and improved social services. Hopefully *To Stand and Fight*, a study of black activism in post-Second World War New York City, and *Freedom North*, a collection of essays on freedom struggles outside the South, will start a new trend, one in which northern struggles are fully integrated into analyses of the Civil Rights Movement (Biondi 2003; Theoharis and Woodard 2003).

African American armed self-defense is another greatly understudied aspect of the Civil Rights Movement. Popular perceptions of the freedom struggle as a nonviolent crusade obscure the fact that most civil rights activists who subscribed to nonviolence did so as a tactic only, and that the grassroots indulged rather than embraced nonviolent protest. Under constant assault from white reactionaries affiliated with terror organizations and law enforcement, local people did not hesitate to pick up guns in defense of self, family, organizers, and community. Although a full-length study of armed self-defense during the Black Freedom Struggle has yet to be written, there are useful articles on self-defense in Mississippi and on the Louisiana-based Deacons for Defense and Justice that demonstrate the willingness of local people to defend themselves and the ways they did it (Strain 1997; Umoja 1999, 2002; Crosby 2003).

Violence against African Americans has become a regular part of the discourse on southern white resistance, and thus has received more attention than armed self-defense. Lynching dominates the literature on white violence that occurred in the decades up to the 1960s. The lynchings of Mack Charles Parker and Emmett Till in Mississippi have captured the interest of historians above all (Smead 1986; Whitfield 1988; Hudson-Weems 1996, 1998). Much of the literature on violent white behavior during the 1960s examines violence perpetrated by terror groups, particularly the Ku Klux Klan and the White Citizens' Council (McMillen 1971; McWhorter 2001). Urban uprisings, beginning with the Harlem rebellion of 1965, and state-sponsored terrorism, most notably the counter intelligence programs of city police and the FBI, take over the literature on white violence of the late 1960s and early 1970s (Horne 1995; O'Reilly 1989). Although studies of white violence during all three eras are generally balanced – meaning that they incorporate black perspectives – future explorations have to include greater scrutiny of the interplay between violent white behavior and African American armed self-defense. White expectations of African American responses, whether nonviolent or violent, dictated white behavior to a measurable degree. In the rural South, it was common for whites to refrain from violence when they suspected an armed black response. At the same time, urban police often resorted to violence when they believed African Americans would meet force with force.

Until recently, scholars paid little attention to the critical role played by African American women in the freedom struggle. The historiographic tendency to focus on ministerial leadership and movement spokespersons, positions typically occupied by men, rendered the activism of African American women invisible. There are now, however, several excellent studies of African American women's participation and leadership in the movement. *Women in the Civil Rights Movement* was the first major collection of academic essays that looked closely at the struggles of African American women in the movement (Crawford et al. 1990). *Sisters in Struggle* follows a similar format, but delves deeper into the personal lives of the women under study and pushes the temporal boundaries of their activism forward into the Black Power era (Collier-Thomas and Franklin 2001). A spate of biographies on women activists, particularly women affiliated with SNCC, and memoirs by women who were active in the struggle, has vastly improved understandings of the personal and political lives of black women activists (Brown 1986; Robinson 1987; Murray 1989; Lee 1999; Fleming 1998; Ransby 2003). Of greatest need now are monographs synthesizing black women's activism along the lines of Belinda Robnett's *How Long? How Long?* (1997), which offers a usable analytic framework for understanding black women's participation and leadership in the movement.

Exploring the complexity of women's roles in the freedom struggle is part of a broader trend of complicating the movement's evolution. What began with historians reconsidering the starting point of the Black Freedom Struggle has now shifted toward scholarly reassessments of its terminus. Theses positing that the Civil Rights Movement ended with the passage of the 1964 Civil Rights Act and 1965 Voting Rights Act have fallen out of favor. The goal of the Black Freedom Struggle was never, simply, federal legislation. Rather than fighting solely for unfettered access to public accommodations and the ballot box, African Americans in the middle decades of the twentieth century agitated for full civil and human rights, much as their forebears had immediately after emancipation. Theses arguing that the movement ended with the assassination of Martin Luther King, Jr in 1968 have also lost currency. King was big in the movement, but it was bigger than him.

Replacing earlier arguments positing that the Civil Rights Movement ended in 1965 or 1968 is the idea that civil rights struggles continued into the Black Power era. Rather than viewing civil rights and Black Power agitation as unconnected, scholars have begun to see the latter as an extension of the former (Collier-Thomas and Franklin 2001; Joseph 2002). Merging civil rights and Black Power struggles has required scholars to go beyond simplistic understandings of the era. The Civil Rights Movement, for example, was more than what King said and SCLC did. Similarly, the Black Power Movement was more than what Stokely Carmichael said and the Black Panther Party did (Carmichael and Hamilton 1967, 1992; McCartney 1992; Van Deburg 1992). Students of Black Power have taken the lead in reconceptualizing this moment. Recent works by Komozi Woodard on the Black Arts Movement (1999), Rod Bush on Black Nationalism (1999), Scot Brown on the US organization (2003), and Yohuru Williams on the Black Panther Party (2000) have established a template for looking anew at this tumultuous time.

The literature on the Civil Rights Movement has matured substantially over the last quarter-century. Scholars have transcended narrow understandings of the movement's chronology, extending its temporal boundaries both forward and backward in time. They have complicated civil rights leadership, broadening definitions of leaders to incorporate women and the grassroots. No longer is the prototypical civil rights leader the black Baptist minister. They have also placed ordinary black folk, local people, at the center of study, recognizing not only their agency as historical actors, but also their desire and capacity to make the decisions that shape their lives. In addition, they have reevaluated civil rights organizations, finally recognizing the invaluable contributions of SNCC's young radicals.

There remains, however, work to be done. The leadership and participation of women has to be synthesized further, as does African American armed self-defense.

Some significant local movements, in both the South and the North, have yet to be examined, and important state studies have yet to be written. Fortunately, if the period from 1980 to 2004 is any indication of the direction in which movement literature is headed, these gaps will be filled in the very near future. This will enhance our understanding of this critical moment in African Americans' intergenerational search for a new freedom.

BIBLIOGRAPHY

Works Cited

Arnesen, Eric (2001) *Brotherhoods of Color: Black Railroad Workers and the Struggle for Equality.* Cambridge, MA: Harvard University Press.
Bates, Beth Tompkins (1997) "A new crowd challenging the agenda of the old guard in the NAACP, 1933–1941," *American Historical Review* 102 (2, April): 340–77.
Belfrage, Sally (1965) *Freedom Summer.* New York: Viking Press.
Biondi, Martha (2003) *To Stand and Fight: The Struggle for Civil Rights in Post War New York City.* Cambridge, MA: Harvard University Press.
Branch, Taylor (1988) *Parting the Waters: America in the King Years, 1954–63.* New York: Simon & Schuster.
—— (1998) *Pillar of Fire: America in the King Years, 1963–65.* New York: Simon & Schuster.
Brown, Cynthia S. (ed.) (1986) *Ready from Within: Septima Clark and the Civil Rights Movement.* Nevarro, CA: Wild Trees Press.
Brown, Scot (2003) *Fighting for US: Maulana Karenga, The US Organization, and Black Cultural Nationalism.* New York: New York University Press.
Bush, Rod (1999) *We Are Not What We Seem: Black Nationalism and Class Struggle in the American Century.* New York: New York University Press.
Carmichael, Stokeley, with Thelwell, Ekwueme Michael (2003) *Ready for Revolution: The Life and Struggles of Stokeley Carmichael (Kwame Ture).* New York: Scribner.
Carmichael, Stokeley and Hamilton, Charles V. ([1967] 1992) *Black Power: The Politics of Black Liberation in America.* New York: Vintage Books.
Carson, Clayborne (1981) *In Struggle: SNCC and the Black Awakening of the 1960s.* Cambridge, MA: Harvard University Press.
—— (ed.) (1998) *The Autobiography of Martin Luther King, Jr.* New York: Intellectual Properties Management in association with Warner Books.
—— (ed.) (1992–2000) *The Papers of Martin Luther King, Jr.,* 4 vols. Vol. 1, *Called to Serve, January 1929–September 1951,* Ralph E. Luker and Penny A. Russell (eds.); Vol. 2, *Rediscovering Precious Values, July 1951–November 1955*; Vol. 3, *Birth of a New Age, December 1955–December 1956*; Vol. 4, *Symbol of the Movement, January 1957–December 1958,* Susan Carson, Virginia Shadron, Kieran Taylor, and Adrienne Clay (eds.). Berkeley: University of California Press.
Chafe, William H. (1980) *Civilities and Civil Rights: Greensboro, North Carolina, and the Black Struggle for Freedom.* New York: Oxford University Press.
Clegg, Claude Andrew (1997) *An Original Man: The Life and Times of Elijah Muhammad.* New York: St. Martin's Press.
Colburn, David R. (1985) *Racial Change and Community Crises: St. Augustine, Florida, 1877–1980.* New York: Columbia University Press.
Collier-Thomas, Bettye and Franklin, V. P. (eds.) (2001) *Sisters in the Struggle: African American Women in the Civil Rights–Black Power Movement.* New York: New York University Press.

Crawford, Vicki L., Rouse, Jacqueline Anne, and Woods, Barbara (eds.) (1990) *Women in the Civil Rights Movement: Trailblazers and Torchbearers, 1941–1965.* Bloomington: Indiana University Press.

Crosby, Emilye J. (2003) "'You got a right to defend yourself': self-defense and the Claiborne County, Mississippi civil rights movement," *International Journal of Africana Studies* 9 (1, Spring): 133–63.

Curry, Constance, Browning, Joan C., Burlage, Dorothy Dawson, Patch, Penny, Del Pozzo, Theresa, Thrasher, Sue, Baker, Elaine DeLott, Adams, Emmie Schrader, and Hayden, Casey (2000) *Deep in Our Hearts: Nine White Women in the Freedom Movement.* Athens: University of Georgia Press.

Davis, Jack E. (ed.) (2000) *The Civil Rights Movement.* Malden, MA: Blackwell.

De Jong, Greta (2002) *A Different Day: African American Struggles for Justice in Rural Louisiana, 1900–1970.* Chapel Hill: University of North Carolina Press.

Dittmer, John (1994) *Local People: The Struggle for Civil Rights in Mississippi.* Urbana: University of Illinois Press.

Dudziak, Mary L. (2000) *Cold War Civil Rights: Race and the Image of American Democracy.* Princeton, NJ: Princeton University Press.

Eagles, Charles W. (ed.) (1986) *The Civil Rights Movement in America.* Jackson: University Press of Mississippi.

Emmons, Caroline (1997) "'Somebody has got to do this work': Harry T. Moore and the struggle for African American voting rights in Florida," *Journal of Negro History* 82 (2): 232–43.

Eskew, Glenn T. (1997) *But for Birmingham: The Local and National Movements in the Civil Rights Struggle.* Chapel Hill: University of North Carolina Press.

Essien-Udom, E. U. (1962) *Black Nationalism: A Search for an Identity in America.* Chicago: University of Chicago Press.

Evans, Sara (1979) *Personal Politics: The Roots of Women's Liberation in the Civil Rights Movement and the New Left.* New York: Vintage Books.

Fairclough, Adam (1987) *To Redeem the Soul of America: The Southern Christian Leadership Conference and Martin Luther King, Jr.* Athens: University of Georgia Press.

—— (1990) "State of the art: historians and the civil rights movement," *Journal of American Studies* 24 (3): 387–98.

—— (1995a) *Martin Luther King, Jr.* Athens: University of Georgia Press.

—— (1995b) *Race and Democracy: The Civil Rights Struggle in Louisiana, 1915–1972.* Athens: University of Georgia Press.

Fleming, Cynthia Griggs (1998) *Soon We Will Not Cry: The Liberation of Ruby Doris Smith Robinson.* New York: Rowman & Littlefield.

Forman, James (1972) *The Making of Black Revolutionaries: A Personal Account.* New York: Macmillan.

Garrow, David J. (1978) *Protest at Selma: Martin Luther King, Jr. and the Voting Rights Act of 1965.* New Haven, CT: Yale University Press.

—— (1983) *The FBI and Martin Luther King, Jr.* New York: Penguin Books.

—— (1986) *Bearing the Cross: Martin Luther King, Jr., and the Southern Christian Leadership Conference.* New York: Vintage Books.

Goings, Kenneth W. (1990) *The NAACP Comes of Age: The Defeat of Judge J. Parker.* Bloomington: Indiana University Press.

Halberstam, David (1998) *The Children.* New York: Fawcett Books.

Harding, Vincent (1981) *There Is a River: The Black Struggle for Freedom in America.* San Diego: Harcourt Brace Jovanovich.

Honey, Michael K. (1993) *Southern Labor and Black Civil Rights: Organizing Memphis Workers.* Urbana: University of Illinois Press.

Horne, Gerald (1995) *Fire This Time: The Watts Uprising and the 1960s*. Charlottesville: University Press of Virginia.

Hudson-Weems, Clenora (1998) "Resurrecting Emmett Till: the catalyst of the modern civil rights movement," *Journal of Black Studies* 29 (2, November): 179–88.

Hudson-Weems, Clenora and Weems, Robert E., Jr (1996) *Emmett Till: The Sacrificial Lamb in the Modern Civil Rights Movement*. Boston: Bedford.

Joseph, Peniel (2002) "Black liberation without apology: reconceptualizing the Black Power movement," *Black Scholar* 31 (3–4): 2–19.

Kelley, Robin D. G. (1990) *Hammer and Hoe: Alabama Communists during the Great Depression*. Chapel Hill: University of North Carolina.

—— (1994) *Race Rebels: Culture, Politics, and the Black Working Class*. New York: Free Press.

King, Mary (1987) *Freedom Song: A Personal Story of the 1960s Civil Rights Movement*. New York: William Morrow.

Kirk, John A. (2003) *Redefining the Color Line: Black Activism in Little Rock, Arkansas, 1940–1970*. Gainesville: University Press of Florida.

Klarman, Richard (1994) "How Brown changed race relations: the backlash thesis," *Journal of American History* 81 (1, June): 81–118.

Kluger, Richard (1975) *Simple Justice: The History of Brown v. Board of Education and Black America's Struggle for Equality*. New York: Vintage Books.

Korstad, Robert and Lichtenstein, Nelson (1988) "Opportunities found and lost: labor, radicals, and the early civil rights movement," *Journal of American History* 75 (3): 786–811.

Lawson, Steven F. (1985) *In Pursuit of Power: Southern Blacks and Electoral Politics, 1965–1982*. New York: Columbia University Press.

—— (1991) "Freedom then, freedom now: the historiography of the civil rights movement," *American Historical Review* 96 (2, April): 456–71.

Lawson, Steven F. and Payne, Charles (1998) *Debating the Civil Rights Movement, 1945–1968*. New York: Rowman & Littlefield.

Lee, Chana Kai (1999) *For Freedom's Sake: The Life of Fannie Lou Hamer*. Urbana: University of Illinois Press.

Levy, Peter B. (2003) *Civil War on Race Street: The Civil Rights Movement in Cambridge, Maryland*. Gainesville: University Press of Florida.

Lewis, John with D'Orso, Michael (1998) *Walking with the Wind: A Memoir of the Movement*. New York: Simon & Schuster.

Lincoln, C. Eric ([1961] 1994) *The Black Muslims in America*. Grand Rapids, MI: William B. Eerdmans.

McAdam, Doug (1988) *Freedom Summer*. New York: Oxford University Press.

McCartney, John T. (1992) *Black Power Ideologies: An Essay in African-American Political Thought*. Philadelphia: Temple University Press.

McMillen, Neil R. (1971) *The Citizens' Council: Organized Resistance to the Second Reconstruction*. Urbana: University of Illinois Press.

McNeil, Genna Rae (1983) *Groundwork: Charles Hamilton Houston and the Struggle for Civil Rights*. Philadelphia: University of Pennsylvania Press.

McWhorter, Diane (2001) *Carry Me Home: Birmingham, Alabama. The Climactic Battle of the Civil Rights Revolution*. New York: Simon & Schuster.

Manis, Andrew M. (1999) *A Fire You Can't Put Out: The Civil Rights Life of Birmingham's Reverend Fred Shuttlesworth*. Tuscaloosa: University of Alabama Press.

Meier, August and Bracey, John H. (1993) "The NAACP as a reform movement, 1909–1965: to reach the conscience of America," *Journal of Southern History* 59 (1): 3–30.

Meier, August and Rudwick, Elliot (1973) *CORE: A Study in the Civil Rights Movement, 1942–1968*. New York: Oxford University Press.

Morris, Aldon D. (1984) *The Origins of the Civil Rights Movement: Black Communities Organizing for Change*. New York: Free Press.

Moses, Robert P. and Cobb, Charles E., Jr (2001) *Radical Equations: Civil Rights from Mississippi to the Algebra Project*. Boston: Beacon Press.

Murray, Pauli (1989) *Pauli Murray: The Autobiography of a Black Activist, Feminist, Lawyer, Priest, and Poet*. Knoxville: University of Tennessee Press.

Nelson, Bruce (1993) "Organized labor and the struggle for black equality in Mobile during World War II," *Journal of American History* 80 (3, December): 952–88.

Norrell, Robert J. (1985) *Reaping the Whirlwind: The Civil Rights Movement in Tuskegee*. New York: Vintage Books.

O'Reilly, Kenneth (1989) *"Racial Matters": The FBI's Secret File on Black America, 1960–1972*. New York: Free Press.

Ortiz, Paul (2003) "'Eat your bread without butter, but pay your poll tax': roots of the African American voter registration movement in Florida, 1919–1920" in Charles Payne and Adam Green (eds.), *Time Longer than Rope: A Century of African American Activism, 1850–1950*, 196–229. New York: New York University Press.

Payne, Charles M. (1995) *I've Got the Light of Freedom: The Organizing Tradition and the Mississippi Freedom Struggle*. Berkeley: University of California Press.

Ransby, Barbara (2003) *Ella Baker and the Black Freedom Movement: A Radical Democratic Vision*. Chapel Hill: University of North Carolina Press.

Robinson, Armstead L. and Sullivan, Patricia (eds.) (1991) *New Directions in Civil Rights Studies*. Charlottesville: University Press of Virginia.

Robinson, Jo Ann (1987) *The Montgomery Bus Boycott and the Women Who Started It: The Memories of Jo Ann Gibson Robinson*. Knoxville: University of Tennessee Press.

Robnett, Belinda (1997) *How Long? How Long? African American Women in the Struggle for Civil Rights*. New York: Oxford University Press.

Sales, William W. (1997) *From Civil Rights to Black Liberation: Malcolm X and the Organization of Afro-American Unity*. Boston: South End Press.

Sellers, Cleveland with Terrell, Robert (1973) *The River of No Return: The Autobiography of a Black Militant and the Life and Death of SNCC*. New York: William Morrow.

Sitkoff, Harvard (1978) *A New Deal for Blacks: The Emergence of Civil Rights as a National Issue*. New York: Oxford University Press.

Smead, Howard (1986) *Blood Justice: The Lynching of Mack Charles Parker*. New York: Oxford University Press.

Strain, Christopher (1997) "'We walked like men': the Deacons for Defense and Justice," *Louisiana History* 38 (1): 43–62.

Sullivan, Patricia (1996) *Days of Hope: Race and Democracy in the New Deal Era*. Chapel Hill: University of North Carolina Press.

Theoharis, Jeanne F. and Woodard, Komozi, with Countryman, Matthew (2003) *Freedom North: Black Freedom Struggles outside the South, 1940–1980*. New York: Palgrave.

Thornton, J. Mills, III (2002) *Dividing Lines: Municipal Politics and the Struggle for Civil Rights in Montgomery, Birmingham, and Selma*. Tuscaloosa: University of Alabama Press.

Tuck, Stephen G. N. (2001) *Beyond Atlanta: The Struggle for Racial Equality in Georgia, 1940–1980*. Athens: University of Georgia Press.

Tushnet, Mark V. (1987) *The NAACP's Legal Strategy against Segregated Education, 1925–1950*. Chapel Hill: University of North Carolina Press.

Tyson, Timothy (1999) *Radio Free Dixie: Robert F. Williams and the Roots of Black Power*. Chapel Hill: University of North Carolina Press.

Umoja, Akinnyele (1999) "The ballot or the bullet: a comparative analysis of armed resistance in the civil rights movement," *Journal of Black Studies* 29 (4): 558–78.

—— (2002) "'We will shoot back': the Natchez model and paramilitary organization in the Mississippi freedom movement," *Journal of Black Studies* 32 (3): 272–94.

Van Deburg, William (1992) *New Day in Babylon: The Black Power Movement and American Culture, 1965–1975.* Chicago: University of Chicago Press.

Weisbrot, Robert (1991) *Freedom Bound: A History of America's Civil Rights Movement.* New York: Plume.

Whitfield, Stephen J. (1988) *A Death in the Delta: The Story of Emmett Till.* New York: Free Press.

Williams, Juan (1998) *Thurgood Marshall: American Revolutionary.* New York: Random House.

Williams, Yohuru (2000) *Black Politics/White Power: Civil Rights, Black Power, and the Black Panthers in New Haven.* New York: Brandywine.

Woodard, Komozi (1999) *A Nation within a Nation: Amiri Baraka (LeRoi Jones) and Black Power Politics.* Chapel Hill: University of North Carolina Press.

Woodruff, Nan Elizabeth (2003) *American Congo: The African American Freedom Struggle in the Delta.* Cambridge, MA: Harvard University Press.

Zangrando, Robert L. (1980) *The NAACP Crusade against Lynching, 1909–1950.* Philadelphia: Temple University Press.

Zinn, Howard (1964) *SNCC: The New Abolitionists.* Boston: Beacon Press.

Suggestions for Further Reading

Barksdale, Marcellus C. (1984) "Robert F. Williams and the indigenous civil rights movement in Monroe, North Carolina, 1961," *Journal of Negro History* 69 (2): 73–89.

Beifuss, Joan T. (1985) *At the River I Stand: Memphis, the 1968 Strike, and Martin Luther King, Jr.* Memphis, TN: B & W Books.

Bloom, Jack M. (1987) *Class, Race, and the Civil Rights Movement.* Bloomington: Indiana University Press.

Brown, Cynthia S. (2002) *Refusing Racism: White Allies and the Struggle for Civil Rights.* New York: Teachers College Press.

Brown, Elaine (1992) *A Taste of Power: A Black Woman's Story.* New York: Pantheon.

Burns, Stewart (2004) *To the Mountaintop: Martin Luther King Jr.'s Sacred Mission to Save America, 1955–1968.* New York: HarperSanFrancisco.

Carson, Clayborne (ed.) (1990) *The Student Voice, 1960–1965: Periodical of the Student Nonviolent Coordinating Committee.* Westport, CT: Meckler.

Clarke, John Henrik (ed.) (1969) *Malcolm X: The Man and His Times.* New York: Macmillan.

Cone, James H. (1991) *Martin and Malcolm: A Dream or a Nightmare.* Maryknoll, NY: Orbis.

D'Emilio, John (2003) *Lost Prophet: The Life and Times of Bayard Rustin.* New York: Free Press.

Davis, Angela (1976) *Angela Davis: An Autobiography.* New York: Bantam Books.

Egerton, John (1994) *Speak Now against the Day: The Generation before the Civil Rights Movement in the South.* Chapel Hill: University of North Carolina Press.

Farmer, James (1985) *Lay Bare the Heart.* New York: Arbor House.

Grant, Joanne (1998) *Ella Baker: Freedom Bound.* New York: John Wiley & Sons.

Henry, Aaron with Curry, Constance (2000) *Aaron Henry: The Fire Ever Burning.* Jackson: University of Mississippi.

Hill, Lance (2004) *The Deacons for Defense: Armed Resistance and the Civil Rights Movement.* Chapel Hill: University of North Carolina Press.

Levine, Daniel (1999) *Bayard Rustin and the Civil Rights Movement.* New Brunswick, NJ: Rutgers University Press.

Marable, Manning (1991) *Race, Reform, and Rebellion: The Second Reconstruction in Black America, 1945–1990.* Jackson: University Press of Mississippi.

Mills, Kay (1993) *This Little Light of Mine: The Life of Fannie Lou Hamer*. New York: Penguin Books.

Moody, Anne (1968) *Coming of Age in Mississippi*. New York: Dell.

Pfeffer, Paul F. (1990) *A. Philip Randolph, Pioneer of the Civil Rights Movement*. Baton Rouge: Louisiana University Press.

Rachal, John R. (1999) "'The long hot summer': The Mississippi response to Freedom Summer, 1964," *Journal of Negro History* 84 (4): 315–39.

Shabazz, Amilcar (2004) *Advancing Democracy: African Americans and the Struggle for Access and Equity in Higher Education in Texas*. Chapel Hill: University of North Carolina Press.

Tyson, Timothy B. (2004) *Blood Done Sign My Name: A True Story*. New York: Crown.

Wilkins, Roy (1982) *Standing Fast*. New York: Viking Press.

X, Malcolm (1970) *By Any Means Necessary*. New York: Pathfinder.

X, Malcolm, with Haley, Alex (1964) *The Autobiography of Malcolm X*. New York: Ballantine Books.

CHAPTER THIRTY

"Race Rebels": From Indigenous Insurgency to Hip-Hop Mania

MARCELLUS C. BARKSDALE AND
SAMUEL T. LIVINGSTON

By 1935, the National Association for the Advancement of Colored People (NAACP) had launched its legal assault on segregation, discrimination, and disfranchisement. Two major successes came in the area of higher education when Donald Murray (*Murray v. Pearson*) and Lloyd Baines (*Missouri ex. rel. Gaines v. Canada*) integrated the law schools of the University of Maryland in 1935 and Missouri in 1938, respectively. In the area of voting rights, a major victory was achieved in the case of *Smith v. Allwright*, 1944. These victories inspired many African Americans and contributed to the beginning of the modern Civil Rights Movement. The Movement spurted ahead through the 1940s and reached a new zenith in *Brown v. Board of Education* in 1954 (Woodward 1974; Jackson 1990).

These achievements in the federal courts seemed to justify the NAACP's legalistic approach to dismantling Jim Crow. Some, however, continued to believe that this strategy was too slow and too piecemeal. The only major organization at the time to deviate from the NAACP's legalism was CORE, a biracial group founded in Chicago in 1942. It launched restaurant sit-ins in Chicago that year and conducted "freedom rides" as early as 1947. Even NAACP officials, like Florida's Howard Moore and North Carolina's Robert Williams, rebelled against the strategy of the parent organization, leading to their suspension. The activities of Moore and Williams and the long struggle that had brought blacks to *Brown* were partly the result of a psychological revolution that had occurred among African Americans by 1950. This had been intensified by their military experiences and upward social mobility during the 1940s, which helped to poise them to take their fight for inclusion – and that is what the early civil rights movements were about – to another level.

The years immediately after the Second World War saw the emergence of a different, if not new, black America. Some writers – James Baldwin, Gunnar Myrdal, E. Franklin Frazier, and Charles Silberman – attribute this change in the behavior of blacks to the social upheavals brought about by the war. Some scholars – Harold R. Isaacs, Talcott Parsons, and Kenneth B. Clark – describe the increased militancy of blacks in the United States as part of the international struggle for liberation by

Africans and other peoples of the Third World who saw a glaring conflict in the myth and reality – the ideal and practice – of universal democracy; while others – like Lodis Rhodes, S. Rudolph Martin, Jr, and James Robert Bruce – say that increased civil rights activity among blacks was the product of time and the process of conscious awakening. Whatever the causes, one result was clear: blacks did more actively demand their human and civil rights after the Second World War (Myrdal et al. 1944; Silberman 1964; Isaacs 1964; Parsons 1968; Rhodes 1972, 1998; Barksdale 1984; Jackson 1990).

The thesis of conscious awakening as the principal motivation for the escalation of the black struggle for freedom in America is, in itself, an intriguing discussion. Human culture is learned behavior that is internalized on both the conscious and subliminal levels of our minds. The socialization process through which human culture is perpetuated begins very early in life and continues, for all intents and purposes, for the remainder of our lives. In the absence of health issues, humans never get too old to learn new things. According to Lodis Rhodes, black conscious development evolves through identifiable stages characterized by symbolic behavior. At no time are all blacks at the same level of consciousness, but groups of blacks may conform to the same symbolic behavior and share philosophical positions. The more provincial a person's or a group's experiences are, the more conservative and pre-scriptive their thinking and behavior may be. The more cosmopolitan a person's or a group's experiences are, the more liberal and open their thinking and behavior may be. And so it was for black Americans, who for generations had lived very provincial lives on slave plantations and sharecroppers' farms. As they migrated out of the South and served military duty in foreign places, they had new and stimulat-ing experiences, which changed their way of thinking and behaving. They were now more willing than ever before to take up the fight for their freedom (Berelsen and Steiner 1967; Levine 1977; Rhodes 1972, 1998).

It was in the context of awakened consciousness that Howard Moore and the NAACP clashed over tactics, beginning in the 1930s. Moore, head of the Florida State NAACP, won national attention after leading a black registration drive that added 10,000 voters in the state. He also broke with tradition by advising blacks to break with the Republicans and vote Democratic. His militancy led him further into a pivotal role in the Groveland Rape Case ("Florida's Little Scottsboro"), when he intervened to prevent the swift conviction and certain execution of two black defendants. Scholars agree that his involvement in this case led to his murder, along with his wife, in 1951. Moore's story is told best in *Before His Time: The Untold Story of Harry T. Moore, America's First Civil Rights Martyr*; however, this is more of a journalistic account than a historical analysis. A general overview of pre-war challenges to the NAACP hegemony can be found in Beth Tompkins Bates, "A new crowd challenges the agenda of the old guard in the NAACP, 1933–1941" (Bates 1997; Sanders 2000).

The case of Robert F. Williams and the Civil Rights Movement in Monroe, North Carolina, is another example of this conscious change. Williams was born in Monroe in 1925 and in his youth had acted, to some extent, according to the dictates of the local brand of the culture of white supremacy. Although his father provided a comfortable standard of living for his family, Williams' social life was limited by the Jim Crow laws of the time. He lived in a segregated community, attended segregated schools and churches, socialized in segregated settings, and was relegated by the rules of segregation as he encountered whites in the public arena. Williams's mind-set changed after he left Monroe to work for the Ford Motor Company in Detroit, to attend West Virginia State College, and to serve in the US Army and Marines. The Robert Williams who returned to Monroe in the mid-1950s and took command of the black struggle for freedom in that western North Carolina town was not the same Robert Williams that left in the 1940s. There had been a conscious awakening in him and, by 1950, in thousands of other blacks too (Williams 1962; Barksdale 1984; Tyson 1999).

The actions of Moore, Williams, and others were, in fact, a continuation of protests dating back to the era of African American bondage. Runaway slaves and day-to-day resistance were hallmarks of the indigenous phase of abolitionism, to which David Walker, Henry Highland Garnet, and others gave theoretical and textual support. In the Civil Rights Era, such action became national news in December 1955 when Mrs Rosa Parks took a seat designated for Negro passengers on a bus in Montgomery, Alabama, and refused to get up for a white man. Parks' conscious awakening was repeated in thousands of other black citizens of Montgomery, including E. D. Nixon, JoAnne Robinson, Ralph D. Abernathy, and Martin Luther King, Jr. This was the beginning of a new era in the black struggle for freedom in America: blacks moved to became more widely organized and mounted protests through mass meetings, boycotts, marches, and acts of civil disobedience such as sit-in and sit-down demonstrations (Branch 1988, 1998; Garrow 1986).

Perhaps the most telling example of the conscious awakening took place in Sumner, Mississippi. In August 1955, Emmett Till had been lynched by white racists in Money, Mississippi, for violating the culture of white supremacy by making an unwelcome advance to a white woman. The Till murder became a *cause célèbre* when his mother, Mamie Till, directed that his casket be left open during his funeral and *JET* magazine carried color pictures of his mutilated body in its next issue. The world was horrified at what it saw. At the trial for Till's murderers, Mose Wright, his uncle, testified for the prosecution. When asked if he saw the white men who came to his house and took Till away, Wright stood and in a very resolute voice said: "Thar he." Clearly some change had taken place in the mind-set of Wright that allowed him to make this bold statement. He probably would not have taken this stand ten or twenty years earlier; and the stand he took in 1956 would not have been taken by other blacks at that time (Whitefield 1988; Hudson-Weems 2000).

Benjamin E. Mays, one of the most prominent African American educators of this period epitomizes the awakening that took place. He emerged from a life under white terrorism in South Carolina to become a leading spokesperson for civil rights. By 1950 many other prominent blacks had emerged from behind the veil and were making their mark on the world stage. In addition to Mays, there were Dr Mary McLeod Bethune in education, Gwendolyn Brooks and Langston Hughes in literature, Malcolm X and Nannie Helen Burroughs in religion, Marian Anderson and Roland Hayes in black classical music, and Paul Robeson and Dorothy Dandridge in other performing arts. The events of the 1950s brought about a sea-change in the life experiences of black Americans and they began to consciously identify with their blacknesss in the 1960s (Franklin and Moss 1988; Hine, Hine, and Harrold 2000; Levine 1977).

The Southern Christian Leadership Conference (SCLC), formed in 1957, gave structure to the indigenous movement that was then emerging in the South. But it was the student sit-in movement of the 1960s that forcefully and dramatically carried the new movement to greater heights and into new directions (Branch 1988, 1998; Fairclough 1987). Robert Williams captured the attention of the nation when he advocated self-defense against violence in Monroe, North Carolina. But the black struggle for freedom that had gained momentum in the 1950s dramatically escalated after the college students staged a major sit-down demonstration in Greensboro, North Carolina, in 1960.

Most Americans and most scholars had not foreseen the radicalism of the 1960s. For most Americans, the 1950s had been a time of conformity and indulgence. The hysteria of McCarthyism and the Korean conflict had dominated the first half of the fifties; the renewed agitation for civil rights had come to the fore in the second half of that decade. Situation comedies such as *I Love Lucy*, *Leave It to Beaver*, *Father Knows Best*, and *Ozzie and Harriett* depicted an idyllic white family life – whereas life in the segregated South continued much as it had for generations. But on February 1, 1960 four students from North Carolina A & T College in Greensboro committed an act that violated the Jim Crow laws of that state. Ezell Blair, David Richmond, Franklin McCain, and Joseph McNeill entered the Woolworth's Five and Dime store, took seats at the lunch counter and ordered coffee. When they were refused service, they refused to leave. Over the next days, this first major lunch counter sit-down demonstration grew in numbers and intensity; and, as arrests were made, the direct action phase of the Civil Rights Movement began to spread across the South. In almost every community, but especially in those towns and cities where there was a black college or university, or a strong black high school, demonstrations were mounted.

The new abolitionists appeared in Nashville, Tennessee; Atlanta and Albany, Georgia; Durham and Charlotte, North Carolina; Orangeburg, South Carolina; Richmond, Virginia; Baton Rouge, Louisiana; and Tallahassee, Florida. All over the South a conscious awakening rapidly overtook young black Americans. In order to make this new movement more effective, the students organized the Student Non-violent Coordinating Committee on the campus of Shaw University in Raleigh, North Carolina, during Spring Break, April 15–17, 1960. The spirit of the *Brown* decision was now starting to have its full effect and there was no turning back. SNCC took its place alongside the major civil rights organizations – the NAACP, Congress of Racial Equality (CORE), National Urban League (NUL), and SCLC – and became one of the vanguard in the black struggle for freedom in the first half of the 1960s.

SNCC was also involved in the indigenous black struggles for freedom, including the Freedom Rides of the 1960s, Freedom Summer of 1963, the Lowndes County Freedom Organization in 1965, and the "Meredith March against Fear" in 1966 where the first calls for "Black Power" were heard in the movement. In one of the earliest accounts of SNCC, Howard Zinn wrote:

> These young rebels call themselves the Student Nonviolent Coordinating Committee, but they are more movement than an organization, for no bureaucratized structure can contain their spirit, no printed program capture the fierce and elusive quality of their

thinking. And while they have no famous leaders, very little money, and no inner access to the seats of national authority, they are clearly the front line of the Negro assault on the moral comfort of white America. (Zinn 1964: 1–2)

SNCC, however, was no more united in its philosophy and approaches than traditional civil rights actions. Although much of its origins and work can be attributed to women like Ella Baker, the "godmother of the civil rights movement," and Fannie Lou Hamer, who led an indigenous social, economic, and political movement in Mississippi, there were gender as well as racial and class tensions in this wing of the Civil Rights Movement. Only recently have activists and scholars assessed these conflicts (Crawford, Rouse and Woods 1990; Carson 1981; Lee 2000; Ransby 2003; Perkins 2000; Grant 1999; Carmichael 2003). In the end, the Civil Rights Movement was largely a southern crusade. There was segregation – and there were other forms of discrimination – in northern cities like Chicago, Philadelphia, Cleveland, New York and Boston, but they were *de facto* forms of racism. In the South, however, Jim Crow and other forms of discrimination were *de jure* or legal.

In this region there were state statutes, county laws, and city ordinances that worked to relegate Negroes to second-class status. The application of acts of racial discrimination always took place at the local level, in some hamlet, town or city while the hegemonic community was determined to maintain its position. But because the culture of white supremacy did not always show itself in the exact same way in each hamlet, town or city, the character of the indigenous civil rights movement was not the same either. In Monroe, North Carolina, the virulent, venomous, and vexatious nature of racial discrimination caused the black crusaders in that town to take up arms to defend themselves against violent mobs. On the other hand, the civil rights activists in Weldon, North Carolina, worked within the bounds of the established order and achieved some measure of success. Two factors contributed to the different ways the black struggle played out in each town. In Monroe, blacks were largely unskilled workers, poorly educated and in the minority, but in Weldon there were many professionals – doctors, dentists, pharmacists, teachers, undertakers – who were not only better educated but also in the majority (Woodward 1974; Bennett 1969; Barksdale 1984).

The indigenous movements originated, according to sociologist Aldon Morris, in such institutions as black churches and colleges. They sprang up in major cities like Atlanta, Birmingham, Greensboro, and Jackson, but also in smaller cities and areas like Selma, Alabama, and Leflore County, Mississippi. The Birmingham Movement became most notable for the use of children as demonstrators and the vicious response of local officials (with dogs and fire hoses), propelling the movement into the national consciousness. Recent studies have also emphasized class and gender aspects of the Birmingham movement. McWhorter, for example, is highly critical of established, middle-class leaders in Birmingham and largely downplays the Black Church, while focusing on Communist-connected reformers (McWhorter 2001; Branch 1988; Garrow 1986; Barksdale 1984; Hornsby 2003; Lewis 1991; Bayor 1996; Tyson 1999).

The cultural side of the African American freedom struggle, in the pre-Hip-Hop era, has been treated in Vincent Harding, *Hope and History: Why We Must Share the*

Story of the Movement (1990), William L. Van Deburg, *New Day in Babylon: The Black Power Movement and American Culture, 1965–1975* (1992), Barbara Dianne Savage, *Broadcasting Freedom: Radio, War, and the Politics of Race* (1998), Charles W. Eagles, "Toward new histories of the civil rights era" and Brian Ward (ed.), *Media, Culture, and the Modern African American Freedom Struggle* (2001). Ward typifies this school of thought in suggesting that because of the "master narrative" of the Civil Rights and Black Power Movements – an Establishment version of the history of these movements – the significance of freedom songs in the movement has not received its deserved attention in Civil Rights historiography. Thus, Ward and other authors in his volume seek to deconstruct the "master narrative" by introducing new genres and new voices into the discussion (Ward 2001).

Cultural and class dimensions of the Civil Rights Movement were also seen in the Black Studies Movement, the Black Power Movement, and the Nation of Islam, but also in the urban unrest and rioting that affected black neighborhoods in Harlem and other northern cities in 1964 and exploded in Watts in south central Los Angeles in 1965. Using the words said by Willie Ricks earlier, Stokeley Carmichael popularized the phrase when he made "Black Power" the centerpiece of a speech he made shortly after he became the executive director of SNCC in 1966. The belief that black self-defense and black nationalism were critical to the success of the black struggle for freedom was an idea that had been around for decades when Carmichael gave it a new voice in the mid-1960s. But the very uttering of the words was the cause for fear, trepidation, anger, and much debate. The old-guard civil rights activists thought that Black Power would galvanize white supremacists, who would use their hegemonic muscle to block the momentum of the Civil Rights Movement and end its successes. Both black and white liberals thought that black power would result in white power. They did not understand that what the black struggle for freedom was attacking was White Power, which had always been the mainstay of American society (Carson 1981; Zinn 1964; Carmichael 2003).

At the same time that Black Power burst upon the American consciousness, the Black Studies Movement also emerged. The Movement, began at San Francisco State College, a predominantly white school, in 1966. Maulena Karenga sought self-definition "and organized discipline in the university" (Karenga 2002: 5). As one of its founders, Karenga put it:

> In fact, Black Studies, as an intellectual practice, is rooted in and reflects the social visions and social struggles of this period. The critical concerns in struggles for freedom, justice, equality, power, political and cultural self-determination, educational relevance, and for an expanded sense of human possibility are all reflected in both the vision and practice of Black Studies. (ibid: 5–6)

It is important to remember that the Black Studies Movement began at Historically White College and Universities (HWCUs) and, with caution, spread to Historically Black Colleges and Universities (HBCUs). Scholars have assessed why HBCUs trailed in the development of Black Studies and tried to judge its larger meaning in the indigenous civil rights struggles. They have examined the "faddiness" of the movement as well as any social changes that it wrought. At least two major schools have emerged: one contending that it was a positive phenomenon that transcended class and gender and wrought advances in the Black agenda of agency, self-definition and pluralism; others have seen it as a racist and separatist movement aimed at carrying America away from a national cultural synthesis (Anderson 1990; Conyers 1997; Aldridge and Young 1999).

To reiterate, while the Black Studies Movement had profound effects on the academic community, its larger meaning lay in the effects on black identity and agency. There were also two other major developments in the 1970s that would have profound repercussions on black life and thought in the dawning years of the twenty-first century: a dramatic growth of the black middle class, and a widening breach between them and the black working class. The 1970s also saw the emergence of one of the most powerful artistic movements America has ever seen: Hip-Hop.

The militant consciousness that blacks exhibited in the late 1960s and early 1970s was a dramatic psychological shift in their behavior, never seen before in America. This new consciousness was reflected in the "Black Power" cry that could be heard across the land; it was heard in James Brown's popular song "Say It Loud, I'm Black and I'm Proud"; and it was manifested in the raised fist, a gesture of defiance that young blacks frequently used. The new consciousness could also be seen in the popularity of the Afro hairstyle, in African dashikis and denim clothing. Blacks called themselves brothers and sisters, and greeted one another with complicated hand-shakes. They used pejoratives such as "honky" and "whitey" to denigrate whites; and the police were called "pigs." Young black Americans had decided that White America was corrupt and they did not want any part of it, or so their rhetoric would suggest.

Some young blacks resorted to burning their communities down, either as acts of violent protest or as excuses to plunder and pillage. The black rage that erupted in the late 1960s caused the presidential administration of Lyndon Johnson to appoint a commission – headed by Otto Kerner, Governor of Illinois – to investigate the reasons for this new black behavior. In its final report, released in 1968, the commission declared that America was moving toward two societies, one black and one white. But at a time that blacks were scaring the hell out of other Americans, they were also on the move. Middle-class blacks were beginning to leave the inner cities all over the country and they were gradually beginning to return to the South from the North, the midwest, and the west (Grier and Cobb 1968; Kerner 1988).

As race became less of a factor in determining the life chances of blacks, and as affirmative action initiatives opened doors to them, members of the black middle class took advantage of the social and cultural changes that swept the nation in the 1970s. As the black middle class dramatically increased in numbers, out-migration increased from neighborhoods where they lived alongside working-class members of their race. As the black middle class left their working-class neighbors behind, they moved into predominantly white communities or created all-black enclaves of affluence that ringed the major cities of the South. Atlanta is perhaps the best example of this dynamic. Upward social mobility and outward geographical mobility were companions (Wilson 1980; Hunter 1996; Merritt 2002; Hornsby 2003). While windows and doors of opportunity were opening to blacks in general and the middle class in particular, a large segment of the black population remained alienated from mainstream America. Many of these African Americans suffered under high unemployment, which locked many of them into a state of semi-permanent economic and mental depression. Another factor affecting black life in the 1970s was "a new white consensus based on the idea that America had done enough for blacks and that it was time to go back to the old 'morality' and old verities of free enterprise and rugged individualism" (Bennett 1969: 433, 436; Marable 1984).

In 1968 the Kerner Commission on Civil Disorder had reported that the United States was becoming two communities, one white, one black, separate and unequal; by 1980 it was clear that the same process was happening to black America, as it divided into the deserving rich and the undeserving poor. The black middle and upper classes were being recognized for their work ethic and values (which mirrored those of mainstream Americans) while the black working and lower classes were criticized for their antisocial behavior and increasing dependency on social welfare doles for survival. This criticism of the black poor was coming from whites for certain, but it was also coming from members of the black middle class, who had benefited from the strides made by the black struggle for freedom but were now living apart from their brothers and sisters in the "hood" (a word that was coined at this time to refer to the black ghetto). As the gulf between the black haves and have-nots began to widen in the late 1970s, fresh cultural movements began to emerge, whose major expression was Hip-Hop (Marable 1984: Williams 1987).

The Hip-Hop Movement is an artistic movement, but it is also a countercultural movement that defies established conventions and the status quo. The movement began in the late 1970s in several housing projects in the Bronx and Brooklyn in New York City. But its roots are traceable to earlier times and other places. Some look to Jamaica in the 1940s for the origins of the musical genre. Certainly, by the 1960s, "sounds" (as rhythm and blues and other popular recordings were locally known) were being heard coming from trucks parked at street corners in neighborhoods of Jamaican cities. By the 1970s, similar sounds could be heard on street corners in New York housing projects. Street-corner DJs played disco music, and youth responded with "street dancing" or "break dancing." Soon, the movement spread from the street into "house parties" and disco clubs.

Eventually, "MCs" were hired to coordinate and direct the parties and dances. Between interludes of playing music, the MC would often talk to the crowd "to keep the party going." This monologue soon became known as "the rap." The "rap" or "rapping" – rhyming words to the beat of music, with no set of rules except to be original – came to include the words "hip-hop." Thus, a new genre of music and a culture were born (Smith 1994; Nelson 1992, 1996). By 2003, a Hip-Hop think tank (Urban Think Tank, Inc.) and journals (*Source* and *Doula*) had been founded, a Hip-Hop Summit had been held in New York, and a major Hip-Hop Conference held at Harvard. In the latter, the discussion was focused on civic engagement and political action – an area in which critics have charged that the Hip-Hop generation has not been significantly involved (Urban Think Tank 2004).

Some scholars – including those at the Salzburg Conference in 2003 – have suggested that since the 1970s Hip-Hop has become perhaps the most pervasive form of popular culture in the world. And, as such, it has gained increasing attention in scholarly studies. Some works have found it more racist and sexist than socially or politically conscious. Others have contended that it is the most significant social and political movement in black America in the post-Civil War era. Du Bois had argued as early as 1926 that all art is propaganda and that it should be used for "gaining the right of black folk to love and enjoy" (Bracey, Meier and Rudwick 1970: 286). Several decades later, Jones, Cruse, Gayle, Fuller, Harrison, and Hall offered analyses that interpreted African American culture as an indicator of social change or as an *avant garde* force for social change. Jones elaborates on how blues music represented the African Americans' desire to define themselves, rather than being defined by whites. For Jones, African American agency during the Great Migration was a catalyst in the process of identity transformation. He asserts that it was the decision to leave the South that allowed the development of blues and jazz, which created transcripts of cultural and social striving quickly appropriated by the American mainstream as its own (Jones 1963: 95).

In *The Crisis of the Negro Intellectual*, Cruse posited a philosophical tenet adopted by hip-hop activists a decade later. He asserted that it is "the Negro creative intellectual who must take seriously the idea that culture and Art belong to the people – with all the revolutionary implications of that idea" (Cruse 1967: 96). Cruse prescribed community-based cultural and intellectual initiatives that would encourage grassroots black people to define the content of their own culture towards collectively defined goals. His highly political work called for creating institutional vehicles (economic, political, and cultural establishments), which would allow participation in a pluralistic American society and world culture. Gayle argued that the "Black Aesthetic" was "a corrective – a means of helping black people out of the polluted mainstream of Americanism" (Gayle 1972: xxii).

Hoyt W. Fuller continued this argument by contending that artists "of the black ghetto have set out in search of a black aesthetic, a system of isolating and evaluating the artistic works of black people which reflect the special character and imperatives of [the] black experience" (Fuller 1996). Harrison discussed the potential of music to intensely alter the sociopolitical mode of African peoples. His cultural critique observed how Africanisms in urban settings were used as a form of ritual drama that allowed resolution of community issues. Stuart Hall continued this line of analysis in 1996, suggesting that a popular culture movement is based in "the experiences, the pleasures, the memories, the traditions of the people. It has connections with local hopes and local aspirations, local tragedies, and local scenarios that are the everyday practices and the everyday experiences of ordinary folks. Hence, it links with. the vulgar – the popular, the informal, the underside [and] the grotesque" (Dent 1992: 25; Harrison 1972; Potter 1995; Sexton 1995; Shomari 1995; Bradley 1995; Smith 1994; Williams 2001; Guevara Rodriguez 1985; Miller 1990; Stephens 1996; Wilson 1980; Cheyney 2002; Bynoe 2001; Sanneh 2001; Anderson 2003).

One school of thought believes that Hip-Hop is a nationalist or Pan-Africanist movement, while another has portrayed it as a transcultural movement that has infiltrated into White America and extended abroad into Africa, Asia, Australia, and Europe. Several scholars have contributed to an aesthetic approach readily applicable to hip-hop. Kariamu Welsh-Asante discusses the fact that performers and the audience, who feed off each other, create art in the African context: "In traditional African society, the spectators and the artists are one" (Welsh-Asante 1994: 2). This model suggests that in hip-hop the audience and the MC or DJ interact with each other to produce an energy and creative spectacle that is rarely achieved in other genres. Erroll Henderson, on the other hand, discusses hip-hop's connection to the tradition of black nationalist struggle and posits that rap music has the ability to serve as a conduit of African cultural values – through the agency of DJs mixing and sampling – and in the role of a grassroots organization, such as Zulu Nation and Five Percent Nation (Henderson 1996: 315–18). Similarly Livingston examined Hip-Hop in the context of black nationalist struggle in the Nation of Islam and the Africana tradition of utilitarian art. His study characterizes Hip-Hop's deepest significance as that of an art form culturally focused on the power of speech and its relationship to the human condition (Livingston 1998).

Sheila Walker contributes to the Afrocentric approach by synthesizing it with Afro-Atlantic assumptions. She terms Africana cultural forms "Afrogenic" – that is, expressions, interpretations, and scholarly analyses that derive from Africana cultures – in the creation of the Americas. Her embrace of a multilingual agency-oriented approach seeks to reclaim the humanity and sheer existence of Africa-descended populations long ignored in Western societies and bodies politic. She and her contributing authors – representing various disciplines from, *inter alia*, history, linguistics, anthropology, and non-disciplinary approaches – proclaim and expand the Africana World by asserting the presence of African cultural activity in regions where these "second Americans" have been socio-politically, economically, and culturally marginalized.

It is in this trans-regional context that scholars have come to consider the Afrogenic polylectic that is Hip-Hop (Walker 2001: 8). The Hip-Hop Movement, for example, was the major topic of discussion in a seminar on "The politic of American popular culture: here, there and everywhere" among an international gathering of scholars in Salzburg, Austria, in 2002. This global approach concurs with the fact that Hip-Hop developed out of a microcosm of the African diaspora in the Bronx borough of New York City. According to Thompson (1983), African Americans Barbadians, Haitians, Afro-Cubans, Boricuas, and Jamaicans built the culture that would produce Hip-Hop. Caribbean cultural creativity combined with African American funk, jazz, soul, and "ebonics" to produce Hip-Hop. As to language, J. L. Dillard (1972) suggests that the African American appropriation of English evidenced a history of profound cultural influence on the larger linguistic environs of America. African Americans "africanized" English by incorporating words and structural elements from Niger-Congo languages into "mainstream English." Mufwene (1993) concurs with Dillard in encouraging further research and discourse on the African linguistic substratum in American black English vernacular, which forms the core of Hip-Hop, as an aspect of the African oral tradition (Shabazz 1992; Toop 1994; Herz 1998; Rodriguez 1999; Sanneh 2001, 2002; Bynoe 2001; Holloway 2002).

Thompson's (1983) discussion of the centrality of *nsibidi* script among the Abakua orders of Cuba conceptually prefigures an understanding of the complexity of writing in African American Hip-Hop culture. Hip-Hop graphic artists have developed a tradition of symbolic script commonly refered to as graffiti. Each community, crew, and set has its own way of arranging its icons and letters so that few can interpret the ornate writings. Tricia Rose (1994) addresses the significance of writing to the process of constructing rhymes. She attempts to de-link Hip-Hop from essential constructions of the African oral tradition by positing rap lyrics as a form of "Postliterate orality," which "describes the way oral traditions are revised and presented in a technologically sophisticated context" (Rose 1994: 85, 86). Her discussion contributes to our understanding of two aspects of rap music as aspects of cultural activism. First, she discusses central themes in the music, lyrics, and visual images, and secondly, explains these themes within the cultural and institutional contexts from which they emerge (1994: 124). Her study contributes to our understanding of American culture through the history of rap in relation to New York's cultural politics, and hip-hop's musical and technological interventions, which provide a medium for rap's racial politics, institutional critiques, and media and institutional responses. Significantly, she discusses female rappers' critiques of men and the feminist debates within Hip-Hop Culture (Rose 1994: ix–xvi, 85, 86, 124). Forman's recent work observes how race, class, and their spatial signifier, the "hood," frame communication within Hip-Hop (Forman 2002).

Although the Hip-Hop Movement became the most visible expression of indigenous protest in the post-Civil Rights era, scholars had begun to pay closer attention to counter-culture activities among working-class African Americans and black youth at least two decades earlier. Pioneers in this effort were Herbert Gutman and Nell Painter. In *The Black Family in Slavery and Freedom – 1750–1925* (1976), Gutman offered a Marxist view of the history of ordinary, working-class black people. He was one of the first, in the post-Civil Rights era, to give this class of African Americans significant roles as actors in the historical process-agency. In *Exodusters: Black Migration to Kansas after Reconstruction*, Painter details the post-Reconstruction movement of blacks out of the South as "a genuine folk movement" designed to "solve the race problem once and for all." Similarly, in *The Narrative of Hosea Hudson: His Life as a Negro Communist in the South*, she uses class conflict as a model for black indigenous rebellion. However, in Hosea Hudson she shows a rebel against American racism whose activities in the Communist Party represented mutual exploitation.

By the time that the Hip-Hop Movement emerged, Robin Kelley had undoubtedly become the leading scholar of African American popular culture. In such works as *Hammer and Hoe: Alabama Communists During the Great Depression* (1990), *Yo' Mama's Disfunktional: Fighting the Culture Wars in Urban America, Race Rebels: Culture, Politics and the Black Working Class,* and "Identity politics and class struggle" (1997), and *Freedom Dreams: The Black Radical Imagination* (2003), Kelley explores labor movements, socialist organizations, and "street culture" to offer new perspectives on the roots and manifestations of black urban culture. Specifically, he portrays certain working-class African Americans and black youth subverting the capitalist system and challenging existing political orders through such indigenous means as work slowdowns, leaving work early, signifying (joking) and rapping. Of rap, he says, it projects and reflects "the lessons of lived experiences" of youth on the "social and spatial fringes of the post-industrial city" (Lusane 1993: 38). He also makes a call for a resurgence of class politics. It is time, he believes, to "transcend" race and gender and "get to the matter at hand: class warfare against the bosses."

Other recent works focusing on working-class people and movements include Elijah Anderson, *Streetwise: Race, Class and Change in an Urban Community* (1990), Joe William Trotter (ed.), *The Great Migration in Historical Perspective: New Dimensions of Race, Class and Gender* (1991), Kenneth W. Goings and Raymond A. Mohl (eds.), *The New African American Urban History* (1996), and Kimberley L. Phillips' *Alabama North: African-American Migrants, Community, and Working*

Class Activism in Cleveland, 1915–45 (1999). Anderson conducted a 14-year study of a low-income African American community in Philadelphia, which focused on the nature of street life and popular culture. He concluded that while young black males, especially, were powerless in the larger society, where wealth and power dominate, they found self-esteem through their control of street life, including the illegal drugs scene. Goings and Mohl contend that in the 1980s a "new" African American urban history emerged that was defined by "agency." In a series of essays, they portray a black working class actively involved in shaping their own lives and their own future. The essays look at the day-to-day fight by black working-class people against exploitation and oppression, as well as the flight of black women from the South to escape sexual exploitation by both white and black men. Phillips attempts to extend the framework for larger perspectives of the Great Migration, begun by scholars like Trotter, by examining how southern culture in a northern setting created militant working-class political activities. She criticizes the black elite, while extolling working-class black resistance among both males and females.

Recently, a few studies have emerged treating the transcultural aspects of indigenous race rebellion, particularly of Hip-Hop as a forum of intergenerational communication, a medium for the articulation of cultural identity vis-à-vis forms of nationalism and even homosexuality and homophobia in the Civil Rights and post-Civil Rights eras. These include: S. Frith, "Britbeat: Police and thieves (Hip-Hop culture blamed for U.K. crimes)" (1988); Doug Norman, *The Identity Politics of Queer Hip Hop* (2003); Toure', "Gay rappers: too real for Hip Hop?" (2003); Ryan Gierach, "Homosexual Hip-Hop rears it's [*sic*] friendly head" (2001); Matt Diehl, "Brash Hip Hop entrepreneurs" (1996); Mendl Lewis Obadike, "Hip Hop, queerness, and the faculty parking lot (or get used to it)" [n.d.]; Darryl Nelson, "Elitism in HipHop" (2001); Yvonne Bynoe, "The White Boy Shuffle" (2000); and David Kehr, "The Hip-Hop path across class borders" (2002); Todd Boyd, *Young, Black, Rich and Famous: The Rise of the NBA, the Hip-Hop Invasion and the Transformation of Hip Hop Culture* (2003). But, these still remain infant areas and warrant increased attention so as to round out the significant scholarly transformation of the freedom struggle of African Americans from that of selected individual leaders and major organizations to that of a true people's revolution.

BIBLIOGRAPHY

Works Cited

Aldridge, Delores and Young, Carlene (2002) *Out of the Revolution: The Development of Black Studies.* Baltimore, MD: Rowman & Littlefield.

Anderson, Elijah (1990) *Streetwise: Race, Class, and Change in an Urban Community.* Chicago: University of Chicago Press.

Anderson, Jack (2003) "Letting Hip-Hop convey humanity's struggle," *New York Times* (May 16).

Anonymous (1996) "Paid in full: Madison Avenue cashes in with Hip-Hop," *VIBE* 4: 7 (September).

Barksdale, Marcellus C. (1984) "Robert F. Williams and the indigenous civil rights movement in Monroe, North Carolina, 1961," *Journal of Negro History* 69 (2): 73–89.

Basu, Dipannita (1994) "Rap music, Hip-Hop culture, and the music industry in Los Angeles, in *CAAS* (Center for Afro-American Studies) *Report* 15 (1–2), 1992–1994. Los Angeles: UCLA.

Bates, Beth Tompkins (1997) "A new crowd challenges the agenda of the old guard in the NAACP, 1933–1941," *American Historical Review* 102 (2, April): 340–77.

Bayor, Ronald (1996) *Race and the Shaping of Twentieth-Century Atlanta*. Chapel Hill: University of North Carolina.

Bazin, Hugues (1995) *La culture hip-hop*. Paris: Desclée de Brouwer.

Bennett, Lerone (1969) *Before the Mayflower: A History of Black America*, 4th edn. Chicago: Johnson.

Berelsen, Bernard and Steiner, Gary A. (1967) *Human Behavior*. New York: Harcourt Brace.

Boyd, Todd (2003) *Young, Black, Rich and Famous: The Rise of the NBA, the Hip-Hop Invasion and the Transformation of Hip Hop Culture*. New York: Doubleday and Co.

Bracey, John H. and Rudwick, Elliott (1970) *Black Nationalism in America*. Indianapolis: Bobbs-Merrill.

Bradley, O. (1995) "Commentary: Hip Hop generation: American as apple pie," *Billboard* 107 (November 18).

Branch, Taylor (1988) *Parting the Waters: America in the King Years, 1954–1963*. New York: Simon & Schuster.

—— (1998) *Pillar of Fire: America in the King Years, 1963–1965*. New York: Simon & Schuster.

Brown, Elaine (1993) *Taste of Power: A Black Woman's Story*. New York: Doubleday.

Bynoe, Yvonne (2000) "The White Boy Shuffle," Urban Think Tank Institute. On line at: http://www.urbanthinktank.org/archives.cfm.

—— (2001) "New political thought in Hip Hop," Urban Think Tank Institute. On line at: http://www.urbanthinktank.org/archives.cfm.

Carmichael, Stokeley and Hamilton, Charles (1967) *Black Power: The Politics of Liberation in America*. New York: Random House.

Carmichael, Stokeley, with Thewell, Ekwuame Michael (2003) *Ready for the Revolution: The Life and Struggles of Stokeley Carmichael (Kwame Ture)*. New York: Scribners.

Carson, Clayborne (1981) *In Struggle: SNCC and the Black Awakening of the 1960s*. Cambridge, MA: Harvard University Press.

Chafe, William (1980) *Civilities and Civil Rights: Greensboro, North Carolina and the Black Struggle for Freedom*. New York: Oxford University Press.

Cheyney, Charise (2002) "Representing God: rap, religion and the politics of a culture." Urban Think Tank Institute. On line at: http://www.urbanthinktank.org.archives.

Clark, Kenneth (1965) *Dark Ghetto: Dilemmas of Social Power*. New York and London: Victor Gollancz.

Cleaver, Kathleen (2001) *Liberation and Imagination and the Black Panther Party: A New Look at the Panthers and Their Legacy*. New York: Routledge.

Conyers, James (ed.) (1997) *Africana Studies: A Disciplinary Quest for both Theory and Method*. New York: McFarland & Co.

Crawford, Vicki L., Rouse, Jacqueline Anne, and Woods, Barbara (eds.) (1990) *Women in the Civil Rights Movement: Trailblazers and Torchbearers, 1941–1965*. New York: Carlson.

Cruse, Harold (1967) *The Crisis of the Negro Intellectual*. New York: Quill.

Davis, Eisa (2000) "Hip-Hop theatre: the new underground," *The Source: The Magazine of Hip-Hop Music, Culture and Politics* (March).

Dent, Gina (ed.) (1992) *Black Popular Culture*. Seattle: Bay.

Diehl, Matt (1996) "Brash Hip-Hop entrepreneurs," *New York Times* 142: 50,635 (December 8).

Dillard, J. L. (1972) *Black English: Its History and Usage in the United States.* New York: Vintage Books.

Dittmer, John (1994) *Local People: The Struggle for Civil Rights in Mississippi.* Urbana: University of Illinois Press.

Eagles, Charles W. (2000) "Toward new histories of the civil rights era," *Journal of Southern History* 66.

Fairclough, Adam (1987) *To Redeem the Soul of America: The Southern Christian Leadership Conference and Martin Luther King, Jr.* Athens: University of Georgia Press.

Forman, Murray (2002) *The Hood Comes First: Race, Space, and Place in Rap and Hip Hop.* Middletown, CT: Wesleyan University Press.

Franklin, John Hope (1976) *Racial Equality in America.* Chicago: University of Chicago Press.

Franklin, John Hope and Moss, Alfred (1988) *From Slavery to Freedom: A History of Negro Americans,* 6th edn. New York: Alfred A. Knopf.

Frith, S. (1988) "Britbeat: police and thieves (Hip-Hop culture blamed for U.K. crimes)," *Village Voice* 33 (June 14).

Fuller, Hoyt (1996) *Journey to Africa.* New York: Third World Press.

Garrow, David J. (1986) *Bearing the Cross: Martin Luther King, Jr. and the Southern Christian Leadership Conference.* New York: Morrow.

Gayle, Addison (1972) *The Black Aesthetic.* New York: Doubleday.

Gierach, Ryan (2001) "Homosexual Hip-Hop rears it's *[sic]* friendly head," *Genre Magazine* (July).

Goings, Kenneth W. and Mohl, Raymond A. (1996) *The New African American Urban History.* Thousand Oaks, CA: Sage Publications, Inc.

Grant, Joanne (1999) *Ella Baker: Freedom Bound.* New York: John Wiley & Sons.

Green, Ben (1999) *Before His Time: The Untold Story of Harry T. Moore, America's First Civil Rights Martyr.* New York: Simon & Schuster.

Grier, William and Cobb, Price (1991) *Black Rage.* New York: Basic Books.

Guevara Rodriguez, Nancy (1985) "HIP-HOP: women in New York's street culture," MA thesis, Queens College.

Gutman, Herbert G. (1976) *The Black Family in Slavery and Freedom, 1750–1925.* New York: Pantheon Books.

Hall, Stuart (1996) *Critical Dialogues in Cultural Studies.* New York: Routledge.

Harrison, P. C. (1972) *The Drama of Nommo.* New York: Grove Press.

Henderson, Errol A. (1996) "Black nationalism and rap music," *Journal of Black Studies* 26 (January).

Herz, J. C. (1998) "The Japanese embrace Hip-Hop, and Parappa is born," *New York Times* (March 12).

Hine, Darlene Clark (1979) *Black Victory: The Rise and Fall of the White Primary in Texas.* New York: Kraus-Thomson.

—— (ed.) (1986) *The State of Afro-American History: Past, Present, and Future.* Baton Rouge: Louisiana State University Press.

Hine, Darlene Clark, Hine, William C., and Harrold, Stanley (2000) *The African American Odyssey.* New York: Prentice-Hall.

Holloway, Lynette (2002) "The angry appeal of Eminem is cutting across racial lines," *New York Times* (October 28).

Holt, Rackham (1964) *Mary McCleod Bethune, a Biography.* Garden City, NY: Doubleday.

Hornsby, Alton, Jr (2003) *A Short History of Black Atlanta.* Atlanta, GA: Apex Museum.

Hudson-Weems, Clenora (2000) *Emmett Till: The Sacrificial Lamb in the Modern Civil Rights Movement,* 3rd rev. edn. New York: Bedford.

Hunter, Tera (1996) *To Joy My Freedom: Southern Black Women's Lives and Labors after the Civil War.* Cambridge, MA: Harvard University Press.

Isaacs, Harold R. (1964) *New World of Negro Americans*. New York: Penguin.

Jackson, Walter A. (1990) *Gunnar Myrdal and America's Conscience: Social Engineering and Racial Liberalism, 1938–1987*. Chapel Hill: University of North Carolina Press.

Jones, Leroi (1963) *Blues People*. New York: Morrow Quill.

Karenga, M. R. (2002) *Introduction to Black Studies*. Long Beach: University of Sankore Press.

Kehr, David (2002) "The Hip-Hop path across class borders," *New York Times* (November 10).

Kelley, Robin D. G. (1990) *Hammer and Hoe: Alabama Communists during the Great Depression*. Chapel Hill: University of North Carolina Press.

—— (1994) *Race Rebels: Culture, Politics and the Black Working Class*. New York: Free Press.

—— (1997) "Identity politics and class struggle," *New Politics* VI (2) (Winter).

Kerner, Otto (1988) *The Kerner Report: The 1968 Report of the National Advisory Commission on Civil Disorders*. [Pantheon 1st edn.] New York: Knopf.

Klarman, Michael J. (1994) "How Brown changed race relations: the backlash theory" *Journal of American History* 81.

Kluger, Richard (1976) *Simple Justice: The History of Brown v. Board of Education, America's Struggle for Equality*. New York: Alfred A. Knopf.

Lee, Chana Kai (2000) *For Freedom's Sake: The Life of Fannie Lou Hamer*. Urbana: University of Illinois Press.

Levine, Lawrence W. (1977) *Black Culture and Black Consciousness: Afro-American Folk Thought from Slavery to Freedom*. New York: Oxford University Press.

Lewis, Earl (1991) *In Their Own Interests: Race, Class, and Power in Twentieth-Century Norfolk, Virginia*. Berkeley: University of California Press.

Livingston, S. T. (1998) "The ideological and philosophical influences on the Nation of Islam on hip-hop culture". Ph.D. dissertation, Temple University.

Lusane, Clarence (1993) "Rhapsodic aspirations: rap, race and power politics," *Black Scholar* 23.

McAdam, Doug (1988) *Freedom Summer*. New York: Oxford University Press.

McWhorter, Diane (2001) *Carry Me Home: Birmingham, Alabama. The Climactic Battle of the Civil Rights Revolution*. New York: Simon & Schuster.

Marable, Manning (1984) *Race, Reform and Rebellion: The Second Reconstruction in America, 1945–1982*. Jackson: University Press of Mississippi.

Mays, Benjamin Elijah (1961) *Born to Rebel: An Autobiography*. New York: Charles Scribner's Sons.

Meier, August and Rudwick, Elliott (1968) *CORE: A Study in the Civil Rights Movement*. New York: Oxford University Press.

Merritt, Carole (2002) *The Herndons: An Atlanta Family*. Athens: University of Georgia Press.

Miller, Allison E. (1990) "Hip-Hop in the 1990s: by any means necessary," MA thesis, University of North Carolina at Chapel Hill.

Moore, Jesse Thomas (1981) *A Search for Equality: The National Urban League, 1910–1961*. University Park: Pennsylvania State University.

Morris, Aldon D. (1984) *The Origins of the Civil Rights Movement. Black Communities Organizing for Change*. New York: Free Press.

Mufwene, Salikoko S. (ed.) (1993) *Africanisms in Afro-American Language Varieties*. Athens and London: The University of Georgia Press.

Myrdal, Gunnar, with Sterner, Richard and Rose, Arnold (1944) *An American Dilemma: The Negro Problem and Modern Democracy*. New York: Harper & Row.

Nelson, Darryl (2001) "Elitism in HipHop," Urban Think Tank Institute. On line at: http://www.urbanthinktank.org/archives.cfm.

Nelson, Havelock and Gomez, M. (ed.) (1992) *Bring the Noise: A Guide to Rap Music and Hip-Hop Culture*. New York: Harmony Books.

—— (1996) "Reggae and Hip-Hop come together," Billboard: The International Newsweekly of Music, Video and Home Entertainment 108 (36, September).

Nelson, H. and Gonzales, M. A. (1991) *Bring the Noise: A Guide to Rap Music and Hip Hop Culture*. New York: Harmony.

Norfleet, Dawn Michaelle (1997) "Hip-hop culture in New York City: the role of verbal musical performance in defining a community," PhD dissertation, Columbia University.

Norman, Doug (2003) *The Identity Politics of Queer Hip Hop*. University of Texas at Austin. On line at: http://www.cwrl.utexas.edu/normanpapers/QueerHipHop.pdf.

Norrell, Robert J. (1985) *Reaping the Whirlwind: The Civil Rights Movement in Tuskegee*. New York: Alfred A. Knopf.

Obadike, M. L. (no date) "Hip-Hop, Queerness, and the Faculty Parking Lot (or Get Used to It)." Available online at http://obadike.tripod.com/sweat/deepdic.html

Painter, Nell (1976) *Exodusters: Black Migration to Kansas after Reconstruction*. New York: Alfred A. Knopf.

—— (1979) *The Narrative of Hosea Hudson: His Life as a Negro Communist in the South*. Cambridge, MA: Harvard University Press.

Parsons, Talcott (1968) *Politics and Social Structure*. New York: Simon & Schuster.

Perkins, Margo (2000) *Autobiography as Activism: Three Black Women of the Sixties*. Jackson: University Press of Mississippi.

Phillips, Kimberley L. (1999) *Alabama North: African American Migrants, Community, and Working-Class Activism in Cleveland, 1915–45*. Champaign, IL: University of Illinois Press.

Potter, Russell A. (1995) *Spectacular Vernaculars: Hip Hop and the Politics of Postmodernism*. Albany: State University of New York Press.

Ransby, Barbara (2003) *Ella Baker and the Black Freedom Movement: A Radical Democratic Vision*. Chapel Hill: University of North Carolina Press.

Rhodes, Lodis (1972) "Black symbolism: a paradigm on the nature and development of black consciousness," PhD dissertation, University of Nebraska at Lincoln.

—— (1998) *Analysis of Contemporary Welfare Reform Issues*. Austin, TX: Lyndon B. Johnson School of Public Affairs.

Rodriguez, Cindy (1999) "Hip Hop at Harvard: rap music conference to feature artists, activists," *Boston Globe* (April 30).

Rose, Tricia (1994) *Black Noise*. Hanover, NH: Wesleyan University Press.

Rothschild, Mary Aickin (1982) *A Case of Black and White: Northern Volunteers and the Southern Freedom Summers, 1964–1965*. Westport, CT: Greenwood Press.

Sanders, Robert W., Sr (2000) *Bridging the Gap: Continuing the Florida NAACP Legacy of Harry T. Moore*. Tampa, FL: University of Tampa Press.

Sanneh, Kelefa (2001) "Hearing the voices of Hip-Hop," *New York Times* (February 9).

—— (2002) "Hip-hop divides: those who rap, those who don't," *New York Times* (December 22).

Sears, David O. (1981) *The Politics of Violence: The New Urban Blacks and the Watts Riots*. Washington, DC: University Press of America.

Sexton, Adam (ed.) (1995) *Rap on Rap: Straight Talk on Hip-Hop Culture*. New York: Delta.

Shabazz, Julian L. D. (1992) *The United States of America vs Hip Hop*. Hampton, VA: United Bros.

Shomari, Hashim A. (1995) *From the Underground: Hip-Hop Culture as an Agent of Social Change*. Fanwood, NJ: X-Factor Publications.

Silberman, Charles (1964) *Crisis in Black and White*. New York: Vintage.

Smith, D. (1994) "Dreaming America: hip hop culture," *Spin* 9 (March).

Stephens, Ronald Jemal (1996) "Keepin' it real: towards an Afrocentric aesthetic analysis of rap music and hip-hop subculture," PhD thesis, Temple University.

Thompson, R. F. (1983) *Flash of the Spirit*. New York: Vintage Books.

Toop, David (1994) *Rap Attack 2: African Rap to Global Hip Hop*. New York: Serpent's Tail.

Toure' (2003) "Gay rappers: too real for Hip Hop?" *New York Times* (April 20).

Trotter, Joe W. (ed.) (1991) *The Great Migration in Historical Perspective: New Dimensions of Race, Class and Gender*. Bloomington, IN: Indiana University Press.

Tyson, Timothy B. (1999) *Radio Free Dixie: Robert F. Williams and the Roots of Black Power*. Chapel Hill: University of North Carolina Press.

Urban Think Tank Institute (2004) On line at: http://www.urbanthinktank.org/archives.cfm.

Walker, Sheila (ed.) (2001) *African Roots/American Cultures: Africa in the Creation of the Americas*. New York: Rowman & Littlefield.

Ward, Brian (ed.) (1998) *Just My Soul Responding: Rhythm and Blues, Black Consciousness, and Race Relations*. Berkeley: University of California Press.

—— (ed.) (2001) *Media, Culture, and the Modern African American Freedom Struggle*. Gainesville, FL: University Press of Florida.

Weiss, Nancy J. (1989) *Whitney M. Young and the Struggle for Civil Rights*. Princeton, NJ: Princeton University Press.

Welsh-Asante, K. (ed.) (1994) *The African Aesthetic*. Westport, CT: Praeger.

West, Cornel (1993) *Race Matters*. Boston: Beacon Press.

Whitefield, Stephen J. (1988) *A Death in the Delta: The Story of Emmett Till*. New York: Free Press.

Williams, Erik J. (2001) "Only God can judge us, only God can save us: the Hip Hop soul of thugology" in Alvin H. Samy (ed.), *Hip Hop Culture: Language, Literature, Literacy and the Lives of Black Youth*, special issue of the *Black Arts Quarterly* (Summer).

Williams, Juan (1987) *Eyes on the Prize: America's Civil Rights Years, 1954–1965*. New York: Viking Press.

Williams, Robert F. (1962) *Negroes with Guns*. New York: Marzani & Munsell.

Wilson, Carol (1995) *Freedom at Risk: The Kidnapping of Free Blacks in America, 1780–1865*. Lexington: University Press of Kentucky.

Wilson, William Julius (1980) *The Declining Significance of Race: Blacks and Changing American Institutions*, 2nd edn. Chicago: University of Chicago Press.

Woodward, C. Vann (1974) *The Strange Career of Jim Crow*, 3rd rev. edn. New York: Oxford University Press.

Zinn, Howard (1964) *SNCC: The New Abolitionists*. Boston: Beacon Press.

CHAPTER THIRTY-ONE

Searching for Place: Nationalism, Separatism, and Pan-Africanism

AKINYELE UMOJA

Perhaps no concept in the history of American radicalism has been more maligned or misunderstood than the concept of the "black nation." The quest of Afro-American people for some form of territorial integrity and national self-determination has had a long and winding history . . . [T]he Afro-American people have given the concept of the "black nation" their own definition, utility, and both an organized and unorganized expression of its political intent.

. . . The idea of a "black nation" has not disappeared but has taken on an even newer expression. (William Eric Perkins, "Black Nation," in *Encyclopedia of the American Left*, 1992)

In March of 1968, 500 Black[1] Nationalists met in Detroit, Michigan, to discuss the direction of their movement at the Black Government Conference. The conference was convened by the Malcolm X Society, former associates of Malcolm Shabazz, continuing his work in Michigan. The roster of participants of this convention read like a who's who of Black Nationalists. Conference participants included the widow of Malcolm X, Betty Shabazz; former associates and confidants of Malcolm X, Imari Obadele, attorney Milton Henry, Hakim Jamal, Obaboa Owolo (Ed Bradley); the founder of the holiday Kwanzaa, Maulana Karenga; the poet and author Amiri Baraka; spiritual leader of the Yoruba Kingdom of the United States, Oserjiman Adefumi; and former Garveyite and Communist "Queen Mother" Audley Moore. At this conference, the participants declared their independence from the United States, demanded reparations as compensation for slavery and other violations of black human rights, identified South Carolina, Georgia, Alabama, Mississippi, and Louisiana as the national territory of the proposed Black nation, and established a provisional government for Blacks desiring to live outside the jurisdiction of the United States. The conference also voted to name the independent state the Republic of New Afrika.

The rejection of American national identity and the desire of Blacks to be independent from the jurisdiction from white society was nothing new. Over two centuries before George Washington, Thomas Jefferson, and other American patriots formed their American state, enslaved Africans in North America had rebelled to form independent African communities. Since the colonial period of United States history, the desire to have self-determination and sovereignty has been present among African descendants in America. The history of Black Nationalism, Separatism, and Pan-Africanism has reflected a search for home for enslaved Africans and their descendants in North America. In that searching for home, nationalism, separatism, and Pan-Africanism have competed with the liberal, integrationist ideological trends for the hearts and minds of Africans in North America. While expressions of nationalism have existed throughout the Black Experience in the United States, have even been a dominant trend in some periods, they have received marginal treatment from the academy. This chapter will explore the historical role of Black Nationalism, Separatism, and Pan-Africanism in the experience of African descendants in North America and their treatment in the historiography of the African Experience in the United States.

The nationalist/separatist tradition begins with the earliest presence of captive Africans in North America. This chapter sees Black nationalists as those persons of African descent in North America who seek a separate identity from American national identity and desire to "regain some form of separate existence as a free and distinct people" (Yaki Yakubu 1994: 1). Black nationalists/separatists do not view the United States as a multi-cultural, pluralist democracy. Nationalist identity is reflected in the chosen ethnic designation of nationalists (such as "New Afrikan," "African in America," "Asiatic," or "Black nation"). The USA is viewed by Black nationalists/separatists (called simply "nationalists" from here on) as a white supremacist settler colonial empire. Black nationalists believe Black people do not have the possibility of maintaining their collective integrity or humanity if they attempt to integrate into a white supremacist state. They seek some form of self-determination, up to and including independent statehood.

There are indications of Black advocacy and aspiration for political self-determination, independent statehood, and a developing national consciousness in every period of the Black Experience in the United States. Bracey, Meier, and Rudwick (1970) agree that nationalism has been the dominant ideological trend within the national Black community during certain periods in the history of African descendants in the United States. The turn of the eighteenth century (1790–1820), the late 1840s through the 1850s, the later decades of the nineteenth century through the 1920s, and the middle 1960s through the early 1970s are the moments in history when nationalism was in ascendancy or the dominant trend in Black communities throughout the United States. Without properly assessing the significance and nature of Black Nationalism, a limited and distorted picture of the historical reality of the Black Experience in the United States has been created.

Although Black aspirations to be part of the mainstream of US society have certainly been a significant part – even the dominant aspect – of Black protest, historically integration and assimilation have competed with nationalism for the hearts and minds of Black people. Some historians have argued that African descendants in the USA have exhibited an incipient and dynamic national consciousness. In a 1949 article, Herbert Aptheker addressed the issue of "Negro nationality." Aptheker showed the development of an incipient national consciousness among Black people from the late eighteenth century until the eve of the twentieth century. In a later work, he draws attention to

... the fact that the concept of Negro nationality, however rudimentary or distorted the forms, has been expressed by various sections of the Negro population for well over a hundred years. Of no other people within the United States is this true, and this fact constitutes a very significant feature of Negro history. (Aptheker 1956)

While the traditional historiography of the Black Experience has emphasized the struggle of Black people in each generation since enslavement to enter the American political, economic, and social mainstream, in reality people of African descent have also engaged in separatist movements ever since enslavement began. A persistent theme in the Black Experience is a historical interplay "between who 'want in' (of white America) and those of us (Black people) who 'want out' (of the United States to establish a new Black nation)" (Yaki Yakubu 1994: 1).

Liberal Interpretations of Black Nationalism

To reiterate, historically the Black struggle for liberation in the United States has revolved around three basic ideological trends – assimilation, pluralism, and nationalism. Advocates of assimilation seek to integrate Black people into the American mainstream politically, socially, and culturally. Assimilationists do not question the basic values of American society or the dominant paradigms. Pluralists believe ethnic and interest groups should be able to participate in the political and economic mainstream of American society, while maintaining their cultural identity. Some may seek to achieve pluralist goals through reformist or radical means. Nationalists seek a separate national identity from the dominant society and self-determination, up to an independent national state (Van Deburg 1992: 25–8). Within these trends fall a number of different viewpoints and expressions. Each of these trends has risen and declined in influence at different times in history. Individuals and organized groups have at different moments reflected aspects of more than one trend at the same time or changed from one position to another.

One of the issues in the historiography of Black Nationalism is the ongoing dialogue between scholars from the neo-liberal critics/interpreters and those sympathetic to Black Nationalism. Nationalism exists as a critique of the American liberal tradition. Political theorist Michael Dawson asserts that "black nationalism provided the most enduring challenge to both the black and white liberal traditions" (Dawson 2001: 85). Challenging pluralist conceptions, Black nationalists argue that – owing to racism and white supremacy – Blacks cannot achieve liberty, equality, and humanity within the context of American republican democracy. This has been a historic nationalist theme from Martin Delaney and Marcus Garvey through Queen Mother Audley Moore, Malcolm X, and Kwame Ture. In contrast, interpretations of Black Nationalism by scholars from the liberal tradition have initiated a lively debate with scholars who see nationalism as a viable and legitimate Black political expression and objective.

Liberal historians of Black protest have generally characterized Black liberation as a struggle to be included and accepted into US society. Viewing the United States as a plural democracy, liberal scholars see parallels between the ideologies of descendants of enslaved Africans and ethnic immigrants that came to the USA from Europe, Latin America, and Asia. For example, August Meier and Elliot Rudwick assert in the introduction to *Black Nationalism in America* (1970) that while a broad range of ideological viewpoints exists among ethnic immigrants, from assimilation to emigration (as in Jewish Zionism), the main thrust of ethnic ideologies is inclusion into US society. In particular, Meier and Rudwick suggest that ethnic immigrant efforts for solidarity and group power are just means to "secure integration into American society on an equal footing" (Bracey, Meier, and Rudwick 1970: liv).

While Meier and Rudwick represent a liberal interpretation in *Black Nationalism in America*, their co-editor John Bracey represents the voice of scholars sympathetic to the nationalist tradition. Offering a different conclusion in the introduction to the book, Bracey takes issue with his colleagues' thesis. Bracey contends that Black people's experience in the USA has been significantly different from that of ethnic immigrants because of the history of slavery and oppression. Bracey argues that Black people's status as an underdeveloped and colonized nation makes Black Nationalism similar to the anti-colonial nationalism of Third World national liberation movements. Bracey also asserts that Black Nationalism has been "persistent and intensifying" since the founding of the American republic (ibid: lvii). He argues that the "anti-nationalist bias of most historians" is a result of their lack of attention to the activity of the masses of Black people, which would indicate nationalist sentiments. Because of the "anti-nationalist bias," the trend toward Black autonomy and self-determination has been inadequately represented in the historiography (ibid: lix.).

The debate between Theodore Draper and Earl Ofari in *Black Scholar* also exemplifies the tension between liberal interpreters and nationalist sympathizers. Draper's book *Rediscovery of Black Nationalism* was motivated by his concern for the politics and perspectives of the Black Studies movement of the late 1960s and early 1970s. Draper links Black Studies to the 1960s Black Power movement and its nationalist antecedents in American history. He links the Black separatist tradition to the white-inspired colonization movements of the nineteenth century. The nineteenth-century desire to send "free" Blacks "back to Africa" is described by Draper as a "white fantasy to get rid of Blacks." On the other hand Black Nationalism is a "Black fantasy to get rid of whites." He argues that Black Nationalism, particularly as it was manifesting itself in the 1960s, was a divisive "fantasy" potentially leading to broader conflict in American society. He argued that through democratic processes Blacks could receive equality and inclusion into the mainstream of American society (Draper 1970: 176–81).

In the June 1971 issue of the *Black Scholar*, Black author Earl Ofari offered a critique of Draper's book. In response to *Rediscovery of Black Nationalism*, Ofari linked Draper with a tradition of liberal interpreters who have analyzed the Black Experience without consulting Black people. He characterized him as a "typical, know-it-all white liberal" and challenged not only Draper's interpretation but also his research. Ofari argued that Draper's lack of investigation and his liberal bias prevented him from understanding the nature of Black Culture and Black Nationalism. He also criticized Draper for not challenging the role of American capitalism and imperialism in the oppression of Africans globally, as well as inside the United States (Ofari 1970: 47–52). A response by Draper and a counter-response by Ofari appeared in the June 1971 issue of the *Black Scholar*. Draper, among other things, defended his characterization of Black culture as an ethnic, not a "national" culture, and his interpretation of Malcolm X's abandoning nationalism in the last year of his life (Draper 1971: 3–41). Ofari, reflecting a Black Marxian perspective, dismissed Draper and other white liberals and their Black counterparts, and argued for a scholarship that reflected the experiences of the "Black working class," calling for a "principled struggle for political control and self-determination" that is "Black working-class led" (Ofari 1971: 41–4).

Challenges of Contemporary Interpretation

One challenge for contemporary interpreters of the Black Experience is to accurately reflect nationalism – and aspirations for a separate existence – in previous generations, after uncovering evidence of it. One example of this is Russell Duncan's *Freedom's Shore: Tunis Campbell and the Georgia Freedmen*. Tunis Campbell, a nineteenth-century Black leader and activist, was born "free" in New Jersey. In 1865, at the close of the Civil War, Campbell was assigned by the Union Army to administer the Georgia Sea Islands. With a philosophy Duncan labeled "separatism for strength," Campbell swiftly redistributed the land to the freedmen on the islands. After observing white federal troops' abuse of freedpersons on Saint Helena Island in South Carolina, Campbell decided to organize autonomous Black communities on the Georgia Sea Islands. The Saint Catherine's community was organized for self-reliance and self-determination, with its own constitution, bi-cameral legislature, judiciary (including a supreme court), and a civilian militia.

Union General William Sherman's Field Order Number 15 redistributed land to Blacks in coastal South Carolina and Georgia, and prevented white planters who had abandoned the land during the Civil War from returning without federal approval. In the spirit of the order by Sherman, Saint Catherine's constitution ordered that whites not be allowed to come on the island without the permission of Campbell's government. As in other parts of "Sherman's Reservation," Saint Catherine's Blacks resisted when the Freedman's Bureau decided to pursue a policy of utilizing freed Blacks as contract laborers rather than promoting land redistribution. The Black Militia of Saint Catherine's would not allow former slavers to come back to the island to reclaim their former plantations. When federal officials were not permitted to enter the Island by militia forces, the US military was ordered to disarm the militia and expel it to the mainland (Duncan 1986: 23–32; Magdol 1977: 104; Harding 1983: 270–1).

Duncan believes that Campbell was not motivated by aspirations for sovereignty. He concludes "[W]hether Campbell ever seriously considered setting up a truly separate black nation on the Sea Islands is unknown . . . Surely he did not intend to establish a permanent black nation" (Duncan 1986: 21). Duncan cites Campbell's opposition to the white-controlled American Colonization Society in the 1840s as evidence that he was opposed to the establishment of a sovereign Black state. Duncan may not have been aware that in the late 1850s, up until the eve of the Civil War, Campbell was an officer in the emigrationist African Civilization Society. In a period when nationalism was a dominant ideological trend among "free" Blacks, Campbell was not alone – other Black leaders, including Martin Delaney, Daniel Payne, and Henry Highland Garnet, played significant roles in the African Civilization Society. Obviously, like other Black leaders, Campbell had developed nationalist sentiments in the face of the Dred Scott decision of 1857 and Fugitive Slave Law of 1850 (Brotz 1966: 191–6).

Another example of challenges in interpreting separatist aspirations and visions appears in *Slave Culture* by Sterling Stuckey, who has written extensively on nineteenth-century Black Nationalism. In *Slave Culture*, he quotes sections of a speech by Henry Highland Garnet to the New England Colored Citizens Convention in 1859. By that time Garnet had also moved to a more pronounced Black Nationalist position and was a leader in the emigrationist American Civilization Society. Garnet stated there was a need for a "grand center of Negro nationality, from which shall flow the streams of commerce, intellectual, and political power . . ." When asked where this "Negro nationality" would be located, he identified the southern states of the USA.

Because of the concentration and numbers of people of African descent in the South, Garnet saw the potential of self-determination there. Particularly if the transatlantic traffic in African labor were to be made legal again, Garnet believed African descendants in the South would have the necessary population to achieve independence. He compared the South to predominantly African descendant states and colonies in the Caribbean. Garnet continued "Hayti is ours . . . Cuba will be ours soon and we shall have every island in the Caribbean Sea." Given these developments, Garnet declared that if a "Negro nationality" did not emerge in the South "I am mistaken in the spirit of my people." However, Stuckey does not interpret Garnet's declarations as a desire for independent statehood, but rather a call for

> organized but dispersed political and economic power in the South, not a separate state, might have been what he had in mind as a nationalist objective . . . [a] black nation in America . . . would have been a last resort. (Stuckey 1987: 183–4)

The Dred Scott decision and the Fugitive Slave Act of 1850 were the last straw for many free Blacks in the USA in the 1850s. Any hope of American citizenship and equal rights was now very faint after the judicial and legislative branches of the US government abandoned any pretense of protecting or respecting Black human or civil rights. The objective of a Black state was common for the nationalists of the nineteenth century. Motivated by the American political climate in 1859, Garnet and several of his contemporaries had given up hope in the promise of American democracy.

Writing in a period when independent statehood for Blacks is not a popular demand, and when liberal and integrationist ideology are promoted by most Black public figures, recent scholars have found it difficult to properly evaluate nationalism in previous periods. Thus, it is necessary to interpret their statements in terms of the political consciousness and perceived possibilities of their time instead of current popular and dominant ideological viewpoints. Without this, historic Black Nationalism cannot be truly understood.

Classical Black Nationalism

Through his important scholarship, particularly in *The Golden Age of Black Nationalism* (1978) and an edited volume titled *Classical Black Nationalism* (1996), Wilson

Moses is responsible for the term "Classical Black Nationalism," which identifies nationalist ideology between the 1700s and the 1920s. In his edited volume of primary documents of nationalists during this period, Moses defines Classical Black Nationalism as "an ideology whose goal is the creation of an autonomous black nation-state, with definite geographical boundaries – usually in Africa" (Moses 1996: 1). Moses argues that nationalists of this period believed that "the hand of God directed their movement," in fact that the Divine had authored a specific purpose and destiny for all peoples, particularly Africans in the western hemisphere. He also proposes that classical nationalists be identified with the "cultural ideals" of Europeans and white Americans, as opposed to indigenous African or New World African cultural forms. In fact, these nationalists had come to identify with European and white American notions of "progress and civilization" (Moses 1978: 15–16).

Moses' notions of the nationalism of the eighteenth and nineteenth centuries are challenged by Sterling Stuckey's view of political and cultural development. In *Slave Culture* he approaches the development of Black identity and culture begun by enslaved Africans. Rather than African Americans being motivated by European cultural ideals and notions of Western Civilization, Stuckey argues that the "lingering memory of Africa" was a "principal avenue" for the development of Black solidarity in the eighteenth and nineteenth centuries (Stuckey 1987: 3). In an essay titled "Classical Black Nationalist thought," Stuckey suggests that "as formulated by African-American ideologists of the 1830s . . . this attitude (Black nationalism) probably owed more to African traditions of group hegemony (which persisted in some forms during slavery) than to any models of European thought or experience" (Stuckey 1994: 83). He argues that traditional African spirituality and Christianity were utilized as a cultural framework in the insurrections led by Denmark Vesey and Gabriel Prosser (ibid: 42–7). If we see these rebellions and other insurgent activity by enslaved Africans as having nationalist objectives, this gives us a very different ideological perspective from what is proposed by Moses. While older studies suggested they had certainly been influenced by, and had appropriated, the culture of their oppressors, the nationalism of enslaved Africans included root doctors and conjurers and their own Africanized forms of Christianity; and recent work on the Seminole Freedmen and other fugitive African rebels reveals the development of a culture of resistance, as opposed to the appropriation of European notions of "civilization" (Mulroy 1993: 1–5).

Scholarship on the Garvey Movement

The Universal Negro Improvement Association (UNIA) was the largest Black Nationalist and Pan-Africanist organization and movement in history. Under the leadership of its founder and spokesperson Marcus Garvey, the UNIA built an organization that in 1926 had over 814 branches in 38 states of the USA and 215 branches in the Caribbean, South and Central America, Europe, and Africa (Martin 1976: 14–17). As such, this movement is well represented in the historiography of nationalism. Those writing in the liberal tradition – including Gunnar Myrdal, Theodore Draper, and John Hope Franklin – have acknowledged the mass appeal that the UNIA had for common Black people in the United States, but characterize it as an unrealistic movement doomed to failure (Myrdal 1944: 749; Draper 1970:

51–6; Franklin and Moss 1988: 322). The first biography of Marcus Garvey was E. David Cronon's *Black Moses*. Consistent with the liberal interpretation of nationalism, he judged "there remains little of practical significance as a fitting monument to his labors" (Cronon 1955: 223–4). Displaying an anti-nationalist bias, Cronon often referred to Garvey as a racial chauvinist and offered "Garvey sought to raise high the walls of racial nationalism at a time when most thoughtful men were seeking to tear down those barriers" (ibid: 221).

The UNIA, often called the Garvey Movement, has had its defenders. Theodore Vincent challenged Cronon's assessment in *Black Power and the Garvey Movement* (1972). Vincent tied in the UNIA with the explosion of nationalism in the Black Power Movement of the 1960s. Then in 1974, John Henrik Clarke, with the assistance of UNIA leader (and Marcus Garvey's widow) Amy Jacques Garvey, edited *Marcus Garvey and the Vision of Africa*. Clarke, while acknowledging the shortcomings of the UNIA, credited the movement for creating a vision that would spark Black pride and consciousness in the United States and independence movements in Africa, through leaders like Ghana's Kwame Nkrumah (Clarke 1974: 325–9). These studies suggest that the legacy of the UNIA could be witnessed in the ascending nationalism and Pan-Africanism in the Black World during the 1960s and 1970s.

These themes were continued in the work of Robert Hill and Tony Martin. Hill edited seven volumes of Garvey and UNIA papers. In his general introduction to the papers, Hill argues that the UNIA was a forerunner to African independence movements and had significant political and cultural influence on the Civil Rights and Black Power movements in the United States (Hill 1983: xc, xxxv). Martin (1976) not only argues that the UNIA had an ideological influence that persisted in the Black community despite external attacks on the UNIA – by the American and European governments, and by integrationist and leftist political rivals – but that the movement actually expanded in the United States after the incarceration of Garvey in 1925.

It is also interesting to note the recent proliferation of research on the Garvey Movement as scholars recognize its significance as a social movement. As Vincent, Clarke, Hill, and Martin have noted, the triumph of Garveyism would not appear until the 1960s in nationalist and Pan-Africanist movements in the United States, the Caribbean, and Africa. Thus, even earlier critics had to reassess Garvey's significance. In the 1969 edition of *Black Moses*, Cronon offered, in the updated preface:

> With the advantage of today's perspective, I would no doubt have written a different book . . . modifying a few of my conclusions . . . Garvey's legacy of racial consciousness and pride impresses me today as more significant than it did in the mid 1950s, when I tended to underestimate the extent to which a younger generation could again be swayed by black chauvinist ideas. (Cronon 1955: xii–xiii)

The Nation of Islam and Malcolm X in the Historiography of Nationalism

After the decline of the UNIA, the Nation of Islam (NOI) became the largest nationalist organization and the movement with the most longevity. Starting in 1930, and still existing, it has been an important influence on Black life and culture in the United States. Early research on the Nation of Islam tended to be primarily religious or sociological. C. Eric Lincoln's *Black Muslims in America* was the first scholarly examination of the NOI. He praised the NOI's "insistence upon standards of personal and group morality," its ability to serve as a "'safe' outlet" from the hostility of white racism, and serving as a vehicle for Black pride and solidarity. On the other hand, he feared the possibility that the NOI's "virulent attacks on the white man" would lead to "a general increase in tension and mistrust" between Blacks and whites, and anti-Islamic sentiments in the United States (Lincoln 1961: 248–53). In the liberal, integrationist tradition, he labeled NOI calls for, and practices of, social separation from whites as dysfunctional behavior, and argued that

> a functional group is one that reinforces not the status quo . . . but the organic unity of society. Segregation is a dysfunctional part of America's status quo, though our irresistible trend is integration. In siding with the disease against the cure the Muslims are profoundly and decisively dysfunctional, both to the Negro community and the society as a whole. (ibid: 252)

While assailing the organization's separatism, Lincoln hoped that the NOI's stance would have a shock effect and would force a "white reappraisal" of the integrationist Civil Rights Movement, which was at that time viewed as "too pushy" or "radical" by many Americans of European descent (ibid: 251).

In 1962, Nigerian professor E. U. Essien-Udom's *Black Nationalism* took a slightly different view on the nationalism of the NOI. He saw nationalism playing a more prescriptive role as opposed to a problematic one. After interviewing and observing members of the Movement (including Elijah Muhammad and Malcolm X) for two years, he concluded that nationalism was a vehicle to challenge "white superiority" and Black "inferiority" in the minds of the Black masses, particularly among the poor and lower income (Essien-Udom 1962: 335–6). Essien-Udom argued that racism and lack of opportunity reinforced attitudes of Black inferiority, a sense of rejection on the part of Black people, and an "uneasy co-existence" between Blacks and whites. Black Nationalism, he asserted, is an effort to "'breakthrough' the vicious cycle which emerges from the relationship" (ibid: 326).

In recent years, scholars and journalists have produced biographic and historical studies on the Nation of Islam. Of these, *An Original Man: The Life and Times of Elijah Muhammad* by Claude Andrew Clegg and *In the Name of Elijah Muhammad: Louis Farrakhan and the Nation of Islam* by Mattias Gardnell stand out for their research and balance. Clegg's work is a critical examination of NOI leader Elijah Muhammad. The author acknowledges Muhammad's ideological and organizational contribution to Black life and culture in the United States. At the same time that Clegg recognizes Muhammad's positive contributions, he also raises contradictions in the NOI leader's personal life and his leadership of the movement (Clegg 1997: 282–4). Gardnell, a Swedish religious historian, examines the Nation of Islam from inception in the 1930s through the mid-1990s. As a student of Islam, he views the NOI as "a combination of the notion of militant Islam and the legacy of classical black nationalism" (Gardnell 1996: 8). Similarly to Essien-Udom, Gardnell responds to those who label the NOI as Black racists by saying "the black-man-is-God thesis of the Nation functions as a psychological lever, aiming to break through the mental chain of inferiority by which the African-American is said to be stuck at the bottom ladder of society" (ibid: 348).

One of the most renowned products of the NOI was Malcolm X. Various studies have attempted to document his life and interpret its meaning and message. The literature on the life and work of Malcolm X could be considered a part of NOI historiography, but – since Malcolm's activities in his last year went well beyond his work for NOI – they must be given a special focus.

As with his nationalist predecessors, Malcolm had his liberal critics. One example is Bruce Perry's *Malcolm: The Life and Legacy of a Man Who Changed Black America*. Perry proposes that Malcolm's radical nationalist politics were motivated by his psychic rebellion against his abusive father. Bruce Perry's Malcolm X is "a man in conflict," not with white supremacy or racial capitalism, but with his parent and ultimately also an adult father-figure, NOI leader Elijah Muhammad. According to Perry, "despite his efforts to attribute his unhappiness to white 'society,' they originated largely in his loveless, conflict ridden home" (Perry 1991: x).

As opposed to the tragic, conflicted figure that Perry presents, Marxist, radical multiculturalist,[2] Nationalist and Pan-Africanist scholars have presented Malcolm's nationalism as being a part of a tradition of resistance of people of African descent in the United States. The Marxist and nationalist/Pan-Africanists differ on interpreting Malcolm's ideological direction in the last year of his life. In 1967, Marxist author George Breitman argued in *The Last Year of Malcolm X* that "Malcolm was pro-socialist in the last year of his life, but not yet a Marxist." While pointing out that Malcolm X did not have confidence in white workers, Breitman asserted "if he lived long enough to witness such changes (the radicalizing of white workers), he would have welcomed an alliance with radicalized white workers and their organizations" (Breitman 1967: 50–1).

In his edited volume *Malcolm X: In Our Own Image*, radical multiculturalist Joe Wood argues that Malcolm X abandoned Black Nationalism in the last eleven months of his life. In his contribution, "Malcolm X and the new Blackness," Wood identifies two Malcolms: the nationalist of the NOI days and the post-nationalist Malcolm. Interpreting which Malcolm is more relevant for future generations, Wood offered:

> People interested in a more tolerant society have little use for Malcolm's narrow (and tattered) nationalism, his lack of political program, his sexism. His fixation on "race." The first mask (the nationalist Malcolm) simply needs to be changed. The second Malcolm, Malik, will speak for our new community. (Wood 1992: 16–17)

An associate of Malcolm in the Organization of Afro-American Unity, John Henrik Clarke gives an interpretation of Malcolm's transformation in the last year of his life that emphasizes his message of Black solidarity and Pan-Africanism. After leaving the Nation of Islam,

> he attempted to internationalize the civil rights struggle by taking it to the United Nations . . . His perennial call had always been for *black unity and self-defense* in opposition to the "integrationists'" program of nonviolence, passive resistance, and "Negro–white" unity. When he returned home from his trip (to Mecca and Africa) he was no longer

opposed to progressive whites uniting with revolutionary blacks ... But to Malcolm ... the role of the white progressive was not in black organizations but in white organizations in white communities, convincing and converting the unconverted to the black cause ... Malcolm had observed the perfidy of the white liberal and the American Left whenever Afro-Americans sought to be instruments of their own liberation. (Clarke 1990: xxi–xxii)

Illuminating the potential of Malcolm's Pan-Africanist vision, Clarke wrote:

Afro-Americans are not an isolated 25 million. There are over 100 million black people in the Western Hemisphere ... Malcolm knew if we unite these millions with the 300 million on the African continent the black man becomes a mighty force. (ibid: xxiii)

Most of his scholarly interpreters agree that he had a tremendous impact on the identity and awareness of a generation and a lasting effect on people of African descent in the United States, perhaps worldwide. Since he died as he was in ideological transition, Malcolm's legacy and direction will remain in debate by intellectuals.

Black Power Scholarship

The political environment gave momentum to a new development in the tradition of Black Nationalism. The nationalism of Malcolm X was certainly influential among a growing number of young activists and large sectors of the Black community. Many active in, or identifying with, the Civil Rights Movement became frustrated with the lack of effective intervention by the federal government to protect civil rights workers and local people involved in voter registration efforts. Also, many civil rights activists felt betrayed by the Democratic Party leadership seating a segregationist delegation at its 1964 Convention in Atlantic City. These events led elements of the Student Nonviolent Coordinating Committee and later the Congress of Racial Equality to shift from integrationist politics to the nationalistic slogan of "Black Power." As spontaneous rebellion spread through urban communities of the United States in the middle to late 1960s, "Black Power" also became a popular slogan for Black youth and urban nationalists. Finally, national liberation movements in Africa, Asia, and Latin America influenced the lexicon and vision of insurgency in the United States. Black Power became a political and cultural movement, with a variety of ideological expressions.

Compared to its predecessor the Civil Rights Movement, Black Power has not received much scholarly attention. In the Fall/Winter 2001 issue of the *Black Scholar*, Peniel Joseph addressed this matter. Joseph offered four reasons for lack of scholarly attention to Black Power: first, the retreat from insurgent politics in the United States since the early 1970s; second, the unwillingness of scholars to engage this period, viewed as "the 'evil twin' that wrecked civil rights"; third, the lack of archival material for this period; and, finally, the fact that "mainstream scholars" have not taken the topic seriously (Joseph 2001: 2).

While acknowledging Joseph's argument, significant interpretations of the Black Power Movement have been produced that have initiated interesting dialogues in the academic world. Theodore Draper's *Rediscovery of Black Nationalism* was motivated as a response and critique in the liberal tradition of the Black Nationalist legacy of Black Power. As with the scholarship on Malcolm X, more radical interpretations have analyzed Black Power. The fact that Marxists, radical multiculturalists, feminists, and nationalist sympathizers have made scholarly contributions interpreting nationalism fits Joseph's assertion that traditional scholars have not taken this subject seriously.

Black Awakening in Capitalist America by Robert Allen represents an early Black Marxist critique of Black Power. Recognizing the ideological diversity of the movement, Allen distinguished between insurgent (or revolutionary) nationalism and bourgeois nationalism (Allen 1998: 125–6). He also condemned the machinations of corporate capitalism to co-opt Black Power into a vehicle for the neo-colonial exploitation of poor and working Black people (ibid: 244–5). The 1970s and early 1980s brought a sharp feminist critique of patriarchy in the Black Experience, with a particular focus on Black Power and Black Nationalists. In 1979, Michelle Wallace's *Black Macho and the Myth of the Superwoman* sparked a vigorous national debate. Criticizing the male leadership of the Black Power Movement, Wallace stated:

> One could say, in fact, that the black man risked everything – All the traditional goals of revolution: money, security, the overthrow of the government – in pursuit of the immediate sense of his own power. *Also* [t]he black revolutionary of the sixties calls to mind nothing so much as a child who is acting for the simple pleasure of the reaction he will elicit from, the pain he will cause his father.

Reactions to Wallace's commentary exploded into the national Black dialogue. In its May/June issue, the *Black Scholar* was dedicated to "The Black sexism debate," which included such notable Black intellectuals as June Jordan, Robert Staples, Julianne Malveaux, Maulana Karenga, and Askia Toure. In 1981, *Ain't I A Woman? Black Women and Feminism* by bell hooks (a.k.a. Gloria Watkins) contributed to the feminist critique of Black Nationalism and the Black Power Movement; hooks identified the equating of Black Power with "a move for an emerging patriarchy" (hooks 1981: 97).

Building on the themes of Marxist and feminists, radical multiculturalists have offered serious critique of the Black Power Movement. *Is It Nation Time? Contemporary Essays on Black Power and Black Nationalism* represents a radical, pluralist assessment of the period. Edited by Eddie Glaude, Jr, *Is It Nation Time?* features articles by Gerald Horne, Robin D. G. Kelley, Cornel West, Adolph Reed, and Farah Jasmine Griffin. In the words of its editor, *Is It Nation Time?* attempts to engage Black nationalism, while offering critiques of shortcomings in the Black Power Movement. For example, Kelley's contribution on the Revolutionary Action Movement (RAM), titled "Stormy weather: reconstructing (inter)nationalism in the Cold War era," recognizes this often overlooked organization's ideological and activist contribution to the Black Liberation Movement, while criticizing "the politics of machismo and . . . romantic visions of revolution" within the organization (Glaude 2002: 13).

William Van Deburg's *New Day in Babylon* examines the cultural contribution of the Black Power Movement on people of African descent in the United States and American society in general. Van Deburg views Black Power through its "language, folk culture, religion, and the literary and performing arts" to assess how the movement "utilized available culture-based tools of persuasion." He argues the movement had a "lasting influence in American culture," which has outlived Black Power's political agenda (Van Deburg 1992: 9–10).

Studies of other Black Power organizations have provided a deeper look into the movement. Scholarship on the largest Black Nationalist movement of the period, the Black Panther Party (BPP), opened the door for new projects. Some have argued that the politics of the BPP did not reflect Black Nationalism, because of its Marxist-Leninist stand and alliance with white radicals. It must be remembered that, prior to 1971, the BPP demanded Black self-determination through a United Nations-supervised plebiscite and labeled itself a "revolutionary nationalist" organization (Umoja 2001: 14–15). However, as with other Black Power groups, with the exception of the Republic of New Afrika (later "New Afrika"), the BPP did not project a specific territory to form a nation state, but emphasized "highly localized, spatially defined demands for communal autonomy" (Pal Singh 1997: 66). Charles E. Jones' *The Black Panther Party Reconsidered* and Kathleen Cleaver and George Katsiaficus, *Liberation, Imagination and the Black Panther Party*, both include critical examinations by scholars and reflections by former BPP members.

Komozi Woodard's study *Nation Within A Nation: Amiri Baraka (Leroi Jones) and Black Power Politics* not only documents the political transformation of Baraka, the noted poet and political activist, but also explores the role of Black Nationalism in the United States. Reminiscent of the Meier/Rudwick *versus* Bracey debate, Woodard argues that Black people in the United States are not "an ethnic group along the same lines as Irish Americans, Jewish Americans, and German Americans, destined to be assimilated into American society." He asserts "African-Americans are an oppressed nationality subjugated by racial oppression in the United States." According to Woodard, Black Power and particularly Black Nationalism reflects a "distinct black national community" (Woodard 1999: 4–6).

The US Organization, founded in 1965 and headed by scholar-activist Maulana Karenga, was one of the most influential organizations of the Black Power Movement. The ideological and cultural contributions of US remain present in contemporary Black life. Scot Brown's *Fighting for US: Maulana Karenga, The US Organization and Black Cultural Nationalism* looks at the development of this organization, its leader, and its contribution to the Black Power movement, but critically assesses the internal dynamics and external factors for the decline of US (Brown 2003: 124). Black Power literature has often presented US as a collaborator with the enemies of the Black Power Movement, owing to its rivalry and conflict with the BPP, including the deaths of two BPP members on the campus of the University of California at Los Angeles. Brown presents US as victims of the federal government's COINTELPRO program, because FBI repression had a "deleterious impact on the internal stability" of the organization.

Yet, the study of the Black Power period of nationalism is still an emerging field. New organizational studies (of the League of Revolutionary Black Workers, RAM, Republic of New Afrika, Combahee River Collective, Black Power Conferences, and so on) as well as local studies are needed, from a variety of perspectives, to interpret this period of nationalism adequately for future generations. Within contemporary Hip-Hop, the group Dead Prez, for example, reminds us that nationalist consciousness is present in the twenty-first century. Paraphrasing Malcolm X, Dead Prez reiterates the continued embrace of a Black Nationalist identity with the rejection of an American one:

> I'm a African
> I'm a African, uhh
> And I know what's happenin
>
> . . . I'm not american, punk, democrat, or republican
> Remember that, most of the cats we know, be hustlin
> My momma work, all her life and still strugglin
> I blame it on the government and say it on the radio
> (what) and if you don't already know
> All these uncle tom ass kissin niggas gotta go. (Dead Prez)

While liberal politics dominate the discourse among and about Black people throughout the United States, Black Nationalism persists as an ideological trend. As long as racism exists in North America, and people of African descent find their status and humanity marginalized, African descendants will continue to search for place, and a variety of interpretations of the role of Black Nationalism will interact within the historiography of the Black Experience.

NOTES

1. This author spells "Black" with a capital "B." In the middle and late 1960s, millions of African descendants born in the United States embraced the term "Black" as their ethnic designation. Due to that choice of self-determination, I believe this term is used to identify for that a description of a color but to signify a culture, a political identity, and a consciousness.
2. I am using the term "radical multiculturalist" from Manning Marable's chapter "Black Studies, multiculturalism, and the future of education" in Floyd Hayes (ed.), *A Turbulent Voyage: Readings in African-American Studies* (San Diego, CA: Collegiate, 2000), 24–33. Marable defines "radical democratic multiculturalism" as "a transformationalist cultural critique." Intellectuals in this category seek the "radical democratic restructuring of the system of cultural and political power itself." I'm using this category to define post-Marxist radical scholars who often see "nationalism" as identity politics, which are undesirable in the construction in a democratic and plural society.

BIBLIOGRAPHY

Works Cited

Allen, Robert (1998) *Black Awakening in Capitalist America*. Oakland, CA: AKPress.
Aptheker, Herbert (1956) *Toward Negro Freedom*. New York: New Century.
Bracey, John, Meier, August and Rudwick, Elliot (1970) *Black Nationalism in America*. Indianapolis: Bobbs-Merrill.
Breitman, George (1967) *The Last Year of Malcolm X*. New York: Merit.
Brotz, Howard (ed.) (1966) *Negro Social and Political Thought, 1850–1920*. New York: Basic Books.

Brown, Scot (2003) *Fighting for US: Maulana Karenga, The US Organization and Black Cultural Nationalism*. New York: New York University Press.

Clarke, John Henrik (1974) *Marcus Garvey and the Vision of Africa*. New York: Vintage.

—— (1990) *Malcolm X: The Man and His Times*. New York: Africa World Press.

Clegg, Claude Andrew (1997) *An Original Man: The Life and Times of Elijah Muhammad*. New York: St. Martin's Press.

Cronon, E. David ([1955] 1969) *Black Moses: The Story of Marcus Garvey and the Universal Negro Improvement Association*. Madison, Wisc: University of Wisconsin Press.

Dawson, Michael (2001) *Black Visions: The Roots of Contemporary African-American Political Ideologies*. Chicago: University of Chicago Press.

Dead Prez (2004) "I'm an African," On line at: http://www.lyricsfreak.com/d/dead-prez/38332.html. Retrieved September 7, 2004.

Draper, Theodore (1970) *Rediscovery of Black Nationalism*. New York: Viking.

—— (1971) "A response to Earl Ofari," *Black Scholar* (June): 3–41.

Duncan, Russell (1986) *Freedom's Shore: Tunis Campbell and the Georgia Freedman*. Athens: University of Georgia Press.

Essien-Udom, E. U. (1962) *Black Nationalism: The Search for an Identity in America*. Chicago: University of Chicago Press.

Franklin, John Hope and Moss, Alfred (1988) *From Slavery to Freedom: A History of Negro Americans*. New York: McGraw-Hill.

Gardnell, Mattias (1996) *In the Name of Elijah Muhammad: Louis Farrakhan and the Nation of Islam*. Durham, NC: Duke University Press.

Glaude, Eddie, Jr (ed.) (2002) *Is It Nation Time? Contemporary Essays on Black Power and Black Nationalism*. Chicago: University of Chicago Press.

Harding, Vincent (1983) *There Is a River: The Black Struggle for Freedom in America*. New York: Vintage.

Hill, Robert (1983) *The Marcus Garvey and Universal Negro Improvement Association Papers*, vol. I. Berkeley: University of California Press.

hooks, bell (1981) *Ain't I A Woman? Black Women and Feminism*. Boston: South End Press.

Joseph, Peniel (2001) "Black liberation without apology: reconceptualizing the Black Power movement," *Black Scholar* 31 (3–4, Fall–Winter).

Karenga, Maulana (2002) *Introduction to Black Studies*, 3rd edn. Los Angeles: University of Sankore Press.

Lincoln, C. Eric (1961) *Black Muslims in America*. Boston: Beacon Press.

Livingston, Samuel Thomas (1998) "The ideological and philosophical influence of the Nation of Islam on Hip-Hop culture." PhD thesis, Temple University.

Magdol, Edward (1977) *A Right to Land: Essays on the Freedmen's Community*. Athens: University of Georgia Press.

Martin, Tony (1976) *Race First: The Ideological and Organizational Struggles of Marcus Garvey and the Universal Negro Improvement Association*. Dover, MA: Majority Press.

Moses, Wilson (1978) *The Golden Age of Black Nationalism, 1850–1925*. Oxford: Oxford University Press.

—— (1996) *Classical Black Nationalism: From the American Revolution to Marcus Garvey*. New York: New York University Press.

Mulroy, Kevin (1993) *Freedom on the Border: The Seminole Maroons in Florida, the Indian Territory, Coahuila, and Texas*. Lubbock, TX: Texas Tech University.

Myrdal, Gunnar, with the assistance of Sterner, Richard and Rose, Arnold (1944) *American Dilemma*. New York: Harper.

Ofari, Earl (1970) "The rediscovery of Black nationalism," *Black Scholar* (October): 47–52.

—— (1971) "A response to Theodore Draper," *Black Scholar* (June): 41–4.

Pal Singh, Nikil (1997) "The Black Panthers and the 'undeveloped country' of the Left" in Charles Jones (ed.), *The Black Panther Party Reconsidered*. Baltimore: Black Classics.

Perry, Bruce (1991) *Malcolm: The Life and Legacy of a Man Who Changed Black America*. Barrytown, NY: Station Hill.

Stuckey, Sterling (1987) *Slave Culture: Nationalist Theory and the Foundations of Black America*. New York: Oxford University Press.

—— (1994) *Going through the Storm*. Oxford: Oxford University Press.

Umoja, Akinyele Omowale (2001) "Repression breeds resistance: The Black Liberation Army and the radical legacy of the Black Panther Party" in Kathleen Cleaver and George Katsiaficus (eds.), *Liberation, Imagination, and the Black Panther Party*. New York: Routledge.

Van Deburg, William (1992) *New Day in Babylon: the Black Power Movement and American Culture, 1965–1975*. Chicago: University of Chicago.

Vincent, Theodore (1972) *Black Power and the Garvey Movement*. San Francisco: Ramparts.

Wallace, Michele (1979) *Black Macho and the Myth of the Superwoman*. London: Verso.

Wood, Joe (1992) *Malcolm X: In Our Own Image*. New York: St. Martin's Press.

Woodard, Komozi (1999) *Nation Within A Nation: Amiri Baraka (Leroi Jones) and Black Power Politics*. Chapel Hill: University of North Carolina Press.

Yaki Yakubu, Owusu (1994) *Who Are New Afrikan Political Prisoners and Prisoners of War?* Chicago: Crossroads Support Network.

Index